KT-445-026

THE ROUGH GUIDE TO

Vietnam

This eighth edition updated by

Ron Emmons and Martin Zatko

ROUGH
GUIDES

roughguides.com

Contents

Introduction to
Vietnam

Few countries have changed so much over such a short time as Vietnam. Since the savagery and slaughter of the American War, which ended in 1975, this resilient nation has undergone a total rejuvenation. It is a country on the move: access is now easier than ever, roads are being upgraded, hotels are springing up and Vietnam's raucous entrepreneurial spirit is once again alive and well since the old-style Communist system gave way to a socialist market economy. As the number of tourists visiting the country soars, their talk is not of bomb craters and army ordnance but of shimmering paddy fields and sugar-white beaches, full-tilt cities and venerable pagodas. Vietnam is a veritable phoenix arisen from the ashes.

The speed with which Vietnam's population has been able to put the bitter events of its recent past behind it, and focus its gaze so steadfastly on the future, often surprises visitors expecting to encounter ongoing resentment of the West. It wasn't always like this, however. The reunification of North and South Vietnam in 1975, ending twenty years of bloody civil war, was followed by a decade or so of hardline centralist economic rule from which only the shake-up of **doi moi** – Vietnam's equivalent of *perestroika*, beginning in 1986 – could awaken the country. This signalled a renaissance for Vietnam, and today a high fever of commerce grips the nation, from the flash new shopping malls and designer boutiques to the hustle and bustle of street markets and the booming cross-border trade with China. From a tourist's point of view, this is a great time to visit – not only to soak up the intoxicating sense of vitality and optimism, but also the chance to witness a country in profound flux. Inevitably, that's not the whole story. *Doi moi* is an economic policy, not a magic spell, and life, for much of the population, remains hard. Indeed, the move towards a market economy has predictably polarized the gap between rich and poor. Average monthly income for city-dwellers is around US$200, while in the poorest provinces workers may scrape by on as little as US$40 a month – a difference that amply illustrates the growing gulf between urban and rural Vietnam.

ABOVE CYCLOS IN THE OLD TOWN, HOI AN; **OPPOSITE** QUAN BA PASS (HEAVEN'S GATE), TAM SON

There is an equally marked difference between **north and south**, a deep psychological divide that was around long before the American War, and is engrained in Vietnamese culture. Northerners are considered reticent, thrifty, law-abiding and lacking the dynamism and entrepreneurial know-how of their more worldly wise southern compatriots. Not surprisingly, this is mirrored in the broader economy: the south is Vietnam's growth engine, it boasts lower unemployment and higher average wages, and increasingly glitzy Ho Chi Minh City looks more to Bangkok and Singapore than Hanoi.

Many visitors find more than enough to intrigue and excite them in Hanoi, Ho Chi Minh City and the other major centres, but despite the cities' allure, it's the country's striking **landscape** that most impresses. Vietnam occupies a narrow strip of land that hugs the eastern borders of Cambodia and Laos, hemmed in by rugged mountains to the west, and by the South China Sea – or the East Sea, as the Vietnamese call it. To the north and south of its narrow waist, it fantails out into the splendid deltas of the Red River and the Mekong, and it's in these regions that you'll encounter the paddy fields, dragonflies, buffaloes and conical-hatted farmers that constitute the classic image of Vietnam.

In stark contrast to the pancake-flat rice land of the deltas, Ha Long Bay's labyrinthine network of **limestone outcrops** loom dramatically out of the Gulf of Tonkin – a magical spectacle in the early morning mist. Any trip to the remote upland regions of central and northern Vietnam is likely to focus on the **ethnic minorities** who reside there.

Elaborate tribal costumes, age-old customs and communal longhouses await those visitors game enough to trek into the sticks. As for **wildlife**, the discovery in recent years of several previously unknown species of plants, birds and animals speaks volumes for the wealth of Vietnam's biodiversity and makes the improving access to the country's **national parks** all the more gratifying.

Where to go

The "Hanoi or bust" attitude, prompting new arrivals to doggedly labour between the country's two major cities, no matter how limited their time, blights many a trip to Vietnam. If you want to travel the length of the country at some leisure, see something of the highlands and the deltas and allow for a few rest days, you'll really need a month. With only two weeks at your disposal, the choice is either to hopscotch up the coast calling at only the most mainstream destinations or, perhaps better, to concentrate on one region and enjoy it at your own pace. However, if you do want to see both north and south in a fortnight, internal flights can speed up an itinerary substantially, and aren't too expensive.

For the majority of visitors, **Ho Chi Minh City** provides a head-spinning introduction to Vietnam. Set beside the broad swell of the Saigon River, the southern capital is rapidly being transformed into a Southeast Asian mover and shaker to compete with the best of them. The city's breakneck pace of life translates into a stew of bizarre characters and unlikely sights and sounds, and ensures that almost all who come here quickly fall for its singular charm. Furious commerce carries on cheek by jowl with age-old traditions; grandly indulgent colonial edifices peek out from under the shadows of looming office blocks and hotels; and cyclo drivers battle it out with late-model Japanese taxis in the chaotic boulevards.

FACT FILE

• The Socialist Republic of Vietnam, the **capital** of which is Hanoi, is one of the world's last surviving one-party **Communist states**. The others are China, Laos and Cuba.

• Vietnam has a **population** of 93 million, of which around seventy percent live in the countryside, giving Vietnam some of the highest rural population densities in Southeast Asia. Despite this, the country has a **literacy rate** of around 95 percent.

• **Tourist numbers** to Vietnam have risen from just two million in 2000 to a projected nine million in 2015, with a year-on-year increase of ten to thirty percent.

• The Vietnamese **language** is the only language in Indochina to use a Romanized script. However, its complex use of diacritical marks and six separate tones to indicate meaning make it very difficult for foreigners to learn.

• The war known to most Westerners as the Vietnam War is known to Vietnamese as the **American War** to distinguish it from other unwelcome incursions by the French, the Chinese and the Japanese.

• In 2013 Vietnam became the world's largest **exporter** of cashew nuts. It is also one of the world's biggest exporters of rice and coffee.

• The **motorbike** is the preferred form of transport for about ninety percent of Vietnamese; there are currently about forty million motorbikes on the road, and counting.

• Though the **ao dai** is universally recognized as Vietnam's national dress, it did not come into popular use until the 1930s.

• Vietnam is home to a tremendous diversity of **plant and animal life**, including some of the world's rarest species, such as the Asiatic black bear, Sarus crane and golden-headed langur.

Few tourists pass up the opportunity to take a day-trip out of the city to **Tay Ninh**, the nerve centre of the indigenous Cao Dai religion. The jury is still out on whether the Cao Dai Holy See constitutes high art or a dog's dinner, but either way it's one of Vietnam's most arresting sights, and is normally twinned with a stop-off at the **Cu Chi tunnels**, where Vietnamese villagers dug themselves a warren stretching over two hundred kilometres, out of reach of US bombing.

Another destination easily reached from Ho Chi Minh City is the **Mekong Delta**, where one of the world's truly mighty rivers finally offloads into the South China Sea; its skein of brimfull tributaries and waterways has endowed the delta with a lush quilt of rice paddies and abundant orchards. Tucked away to the west of the Delta, **Phu Quoc Island** is the perfect place to rest after the rigours of a road journey through Vietnam, or as a quick escape by plane from Ho Chi Minh City.

Da Lat, the gateway to the central highlands, is chalk to Ho Chi Minh City's cheese. Life passes by at a rather more dignified pace at an altitude of 1500m, and the fresh breezes that fan this oddly quaint hillside settlement provide the best air-conditioning in Vietnam. Minority people inhabit the countryside around Da Lat, but to sense the region's remoteness you'll need to push north to the modest towns of **Buon Ma Thuot**, **Pleiku** and **Kon Tum**, which are surrounded by E De, Jarai and Bahnar communities. Opt for Kon Tum, and you'll be able to visit minority villages independently or join treks that include river-rafting.

Northeast of Ho Chi Minh City, Highway 1, the country's jugular, carries the lion's share of traffic up to Hanoi and the north, though the recently completed Ho Chi Minh Highway offers drivers a tempting alternative route. For many people, the first stop along Highway 1 is at the delightful beach and sand dunes of **Mui Ne**, fast becoming one of Vietnam's top coastal resorts. Further north, **Nha Trang** offers the chance to party all night and sleep all day, or explore nearby hideaways such as Jungle Beach or Doc Let Beach. North of Nha Trang, **Quy Nhon** is one of the country's least touristed beach resorts, while the memorial at **Son My** village near Quang Ngai commemorates one of the ghastliest incidents in the American War.

Once a bustling seaport, the diminutive town of **Hoi An** perches beside an indolent backwater, its narrow streets of wooden-fronted shophouses and weathered roofs making it an enticing destination. Inland, the war-battered ruins of **My Son**, the greatest of the Cham temple sites, lie mouldering in a steamy, forest-filled valley. **Da Nang**, just up the coast, lacks Hoi An's charm, but good sleeping and eating options make it a convenient base for the area. From Da Nang a corkscrew ride over clifftop Hai Van Pass, or a straight run through the new 6km-long tunnel, brings you to the aristocratic city of **Hue**, where the Nguyen emperors established their capital in the nineteenth century on the banks of the languid Perfume River. The temples and palaces of this highly cultured city still testify to past splendours, while its Imperial mausoleums are masterpieces of architectural refinement, slumbering among pine-shrouded hills.

Only a hundred kilometres north of Hue, the tone changes as war sites litter the Demilitarized Zone (**DMZ**), which cleaved the country in two from 1954 to 1975. Over four decades of peace have done much to heal the scars, but the monuments that pepper these windswept hills bear eloquent witness to a generation of people who lost their lives in the tragic struggle. The DMZ is most easily tackled as a day-trip from Hue, after which most people hop straight up to Hanoi. And there's little to detain you on the northward trek, save the glittering limestone caverns of **Phong Nha**, the entrance to a massive underground river system tunnelling under the Truong Son Mountains, which includes Son Doong, discovered in 2009 and currently the largest known cave in the world. Then, on the very fringes of the northern Red River Delta, lie the ancient incense-steeped temples of **Hoa Lu** and, nearby, the mystical landscapes of **Tam Coc** and **Van Long**, where paddy fields lap at the feet of limestone hummocks.

Anchored firmly in the Red River Delta, **Hanoi** has served as Vietnam's capital for over a thousand years. It's a rapidly growing, decidedly proud city, a place of pagodas and dynastic temples, tamarisk-edged lakes and elegant boulevards of French-era villas, of seething commerce in the Old Quarter and stately government edifices. But Hanoi is also being swept along on a tide of change as Vietnam forges its own shiny, high-rise capital, throwing up new office blocks, hotels and restaurants.

From Hanoi most visitors strike out east to where northern Vietnam's premier natural attraction, **Ha Long Bay**, provides the perfect antidote to such urban exuberance,

rewarding the traveller with a leisurely day or two drifting among the thousands of whimsically sculpted islands anchored in its aquamarine waters. Ha Long City, on the northern coast, is the most popular embarkation point for Ha Long Bay, but a more appealing gateway is mountainous **Cat Ba Island**, which defines the bay's southwestern limits. The route to Cat Ba passes via the north's major port city, **Haiphong**, an unspectacular but genial place with an attractive core of faded colonial facades.

To the north and west of Hanoi mountain ranges rear up out of the Red River Delta. Vietnam's northern provinces aren't the

ABOVE BUN CA **OPPOSITE FROM TOP** RICE TERRACES, NINH BINH PROVINCE; FACE MASKS FOR TET CELEBRATIONS

WATER PUPPETS

Vietnam's unique contribution to the world of marionettes, **water puppetry** is a delightfully quirky form of theatre in which the action takes place on a stage of water. The tradition was spawned in the rice paddies of the northern Red River Delta where performances still take place after the spring planting. Obscured by a split-bamboo screen, puppeteers standing waist-deep in water manipulate the wooden puppets, some weighing over 10kg, which are attached to the end of long poles concealed beneath the surface. Dragons, ducks, lions, unicorns, phoenixes and frogs spout smoke, throw balls and generally cavort on the watery stage – miraculously avoiding tangled poles. Brief scenes of rural life, such as water-buffalo fights, fishing or rice planting, take place alongside the legendary exploits of Vietnam's military heroes or perhaps a promenade of fairy-like immortals. In the more sophisticated productions staged for tourists in Hanoi and Ho Chi Minh City, even fireworks emerge to dance on the water, which itself takes on different characters, from calm and placid to seething and furious, during naval battles.

easiest to get around, but these wild uplands are home to a patchwork of ethnic minorities and the country's most dramatic mountain landscapes. The bustling market town of **Sa Pa**, set in a spectacular location close to the Chinese border in the far northwest, makes a good base for exploring nearby minority villages, though a building boom has taken some of the shine off its laidback vibe. Southwest of Hanoi, the stilthouse-filled valley of **Mai Chau** offers an opportunity to stay in a minority village. Though few people venture further inland, backroads heading upcountry link isolated outposts and give access to the northwest's only specific sight, where the French colonial dream expired in the dead-end valley of **Dien Bien Phu**. East of the Red River Valley lies an even less-frequented region, whose prime attraction is its varied scenery, from the vertigo-inducing valleys of **Dong Van Karst Plateau Geopark** to the limestone crags and multi-layered rainforest of **Ba Be National Park**, and the remote valleys around **Cao Bang**, farmed by communities still practising their traditional ways of life.

OPPOSITE ETHNIC MINORITY WOMAN AT BAC HA MARKET

When to go

Vietnam has a tropical monsoon **climate**, dominated by the south or southwesterly monsoon from May to September and the northeast monsoon from October to April. The southern summer monsoon brings rain to the two deltas and west-facing slopes, while the cold winter monsoon picks up moisture over the Gulf of Tonkin and dumps it along the central coast and the eastern edge of the central highlands. Within this basic pattern there are marked differences according to altitude and latitude; temperatures in the south remain equable all year round, while the north experiences distinct seasonal variations.

In **southern Vietnam** the dry season lasts from December to late April or May, and the rains from May through to November. Since most rain falls in brief afternoon downpours, this need not be off-putting, though flooding at this time of year can cause problems in the Mekong Delta. Daytime temperatures in the region rarely drop below 20°C, occasionally hitting 40°C during the hottest months (March, April and May). The climate of the central highlands generally follows the same pattern, though temperatures are cooler, especially at night. Again, the monsoon rains of May to October can make transport more complicated, sometimes washing out roads and cutting off remoter villages.

Along the **central coast** the rainfall pattern reverses under the influence of the northeast monsoon. Around Nha Trang the wet season starts with a flourish in November and continues through December. Further north, around Hue and Da Nang, the rains last

AVERAGE TEMPERATURE AND RAINFALL

	Jan	Feb	Mar	Apr	May	Jun	Jul	Aug	Sep	Oct	Nov	Dec
HO CHI MINH CITY												
Temperature (°C)	27	28	29	30	29	29	28	28	27	27	27	27
Rainfall (mm)	15	3	13	43	221	330	315	269	335	269	114	56
DA NANG												
Temperature (°C)	22	23	24	27	29	30	30	30	28	26	25	23
Rainfall (mm)	102	31	12	18	47	42	99	117	447	530	221	209
HANOI												
Temperature (°C)	17	18	20	24	28	30	30	29	28	26	22	19
Rainfall (mm)	18	28	38	81	196	239	323	343	254	99	43	20

a bit longer, from September to February, so it pays to visit these two cities in the spring (Feb–May). Temperatures reach their maximum (often in the upper 30°C) from June to August, when it's pleasant to escape into the hills. The northern stretches of this coastal region experience a more extreme climate, with a shorter rainy season (peaking in September and October) and a hot dry summer. The coast of central Vietnam is the zone most likely to be hit by typhoons, bringing torrential rain and hurricane-force winds. Though notoriously difficult to predict, in general the typhoon season lasts from August to November.

Northern Vietnam is generally warm and sunny from October to December, after which cold winter weather sets in, accompanied by fine persistent mists which can last for several days. Temperatures begin to rise again in March, building to summer maximums that occasionally reach 40°C between May and August, though average temperatures in Hanoi hover around a more reasonable 30°C. However, summer is also the rainy season, when heavy downpours render the low-lying delta area almost unbearably hot and sticky, and flooding is a regular hazard. The northern mountains share the same basic climate, though temperatures are considerably cooler and higher regions see ground frosts, or even a rare snowfall, during the winter (Dec–Feb).

With such a complicated weather picture, there's no one particular season to recommend as the **best time** for visiting Vietnam. Overall, autumn (Sept–Dec) and spring (March and April) are probably the most favourable seasons if you're covering the whole country.

Author picks

From the breathtaking remoteness of the mountain communities in the north to the bustling floating markets of the Mekong, our authors trekked by bike, bus, boat and on foot to cover every corner of Vietnam for this new edition. Aside from the major sights, here are their personal picks.

Most spectacular view (p.423) Between Dong Van and Meo Vac in the country's extreme north, the mountain road snakes through the Ma Pi Leng Pass, where the views down to the Nho Quy River and across into China will make you gasp.

Most far-flung accommodation (p.313) A rare example of decent accommodation off the main tourist trail, *Phong Nha Farmstay* is situated close to the eponymous cave in a dreamy, field-filled setting. Their bike tours of the area are a delight, as are the delectable dishes (and cocktails) served up in the evening.

Best insight into minority lifestyle (p.316) The Pu Luong Nature Reserve is as yet comparatively unknown to outsiders, so you can trek through magnificent rice terraces, help prepare a tasty dinner and bed down in a stilthouse without swarms of foreigners spoiling the experience.

Tastiest meal (p.256) Little Hoi An has an almost bewildering selection of mouth-wateringly good restaurants, but *Morning Glory* just about takes the biscuit. For a reasonable price you can eat your fill of superbly prepared Hoi An specialities – only this time in an elegant restaurant, rather than a kindergarten-style plastic chair.

Most haunting musical performance (p.381) You will be mesmerized by Ca Tru, an ancient form of chamber music that is inscribed by UNESCO as an intangible heritage, at weekly performances in Hanoi.

Our author recommendations don't end here. We've flagged up our favourite places – a perfectly sited hotel, an atmospheric café, a special restaurant – throughout the guide, highlighted with the ★ symbol.

things not to miss

It's not possible to see everything that Vietnam has to offer in one trip – and we don't suggest you try. What follows, in no particular order, is a selective taste of the country's highlights: outstanding scenery, lively festivals, ancient sites and colonial architecture. Each one has a page reference to take you straight into the guide, where you can find out more. Coloured numbers refer to chapters in the Guide section.

1 ETHNIC MARKETS
Pages 406 & 407

Spectacular traditional dress and a lively atmosphere make the ethnic minority markets a must – especially those in Bac Ha and Can Cau.

2 THIEN MU PAGODA, HUE
Page 289

Vietnamese temples and pagodas reflect the country's diverse range of religions: Thien Mu Pagoda in Hue is a good example.

3 TET
Page 53

The most important festival in the Vietnamese calendar, Tet sees the New Year ushered in with colourful flower markets, spectacular fireworks and exuberant dragon dances.

4 CU CHI TUNNELS
Page 107

Look out for the spiked booby traps that Vietnamese guides reveal for visitors to the Cu Chi tunnels.

5 BIA HOI
Page 47

Bia hoi bars are fun, friendly, cheap and a great way to mingle with the locals. Order a bia hoi (lager-like draught) in any of the back lanes in the Old Quarter of Hanoi.

6 THE CITADEL, HUE
Page 278

The former capital's historic citadel, mausoleums and gardens are idiosyncratic enough to impress even the most jaded traveller.

7 WATER PUPPETS
Page 12

Enjoy a performance of *mua roi nuoc*, an art form developed in the Red River Delta around Hanoi.

8 EXPRESS SILK TAILORING
Page 258

Visit one of the many Hoi An tailors who can rustle up a made-to-measure silk dress or suit in just a few hours.

9 TREKKING AROUND SA PA
Page 397

Trek in the northern mountains around Sa Pa – a small market town perched on a plateau facing Fan Si Pan, Vietnam's highest peak.

10 LAK LAKE
Page 186

Paddle the serene waters of Lak Lake in a dug-out canoe, ride on an elephant or take a guided trek into the surrounding forests before a sunset feast overlooking the water.

11 PO KLONG GARAI
Page 222

These beautifully preserved brick towers are probably the finest example of Cham architecture in the country.

12 TAM COC
Page 321

Slow the pace down with a boat trip in the countryside among dramatic karst landscapes.

13 HOI AN
Page 247

With its rich cultural heritage, beautifully preserved merchants' houses and slow pace of life, Hoi An is a captivating place to spend a few days.

14 THE MEKONG DELTA
Page 112

Putter through this fertile farming region, surrounded by classic Vietnamese scenery.

15 TAKE A CYCLO RIDE
Page 37

The quintessential Vietnamese mode of transport gives you an up-close view of streetlife.

16 A BOAT TRIP IN HA LONG BAY
Page 338
The thousands of limestone islands jutting out of these silent waters have been dubbed the eighth natural wonder of the world.

17 CHILL OUT ON PHU QUOC
Page 161
Unspoilt beaches lined with coconut trees circle the island. You can also sail south to the unspoilt An Thoi islands for fine snorkelling.

18 RIDE THE REUNIFICATION EXPRESS
Page 33
Load your bike on, then sit back and relax as the train slowly chugs its way between Ho Chi Minh City and Hanoi.

19 COLONIAL ARCHITECTURE
Page 357
The legacy of French rule can be found in the impressive examples of colonial architecture, such as Hanoi's Opera House.

20 TRADITIONAL MUSIC
Page 480
Music is the most important of all Vietnam's performing arts and a traditional performance should feature on every itinerary.

21 BROWSE THE MARKETS
Page 86
Markets such as Binh Tay are good grazing grounds for snacks. Have a soup, spring roll, sticky rice cake – or even a baguette filled with pâté – to keep you going while you shop.

26

22 ADVENTURE SPORTS
Page 54

Rock-climbing, kitesurfing, kayaking and mountain biking are just a few of the heart-pumping activities awaiting thrill-seekers.

23 CAO DAI GREAT TEMPLE
Page 109

Vietnam's most charismatic indigenous religion goes in for exuberant architecture and ceremonies.

24 BAHNAR VILLAGES
Page 196

Spend the night in a communal house (*rong*) where timeless ceremonies are performed and village decisions made.

25 DONG VAN KARST PLATEAU GEOPARK
Page 421

Vietnam's most impressive mountainscapes are located in remote Ha Giang Province near the Chinese border.

26 STREET FOOD
Page 40

Soak up the atmosphere at a street kitchen and have your plate piled high with a selection of fresh food for next to nothing.

27 NHA TRANG
Page 225

Take a snorkelling trip in the emerald waters of the outlying islands around Nha Trang, or simply chill out on the beach.

Itineraries

The following itineraries will take you right around Vietnam, taking in the classic tourist sites and busy cities, as well as laidback beaches, quiet temples and remote mountain villages where you'd be hard-pushed to find another visitor. Don't worry about seeing everything – each of these routes will give you a good taste of the country.

THE GRAND TOUR

The classic tour for visitors to Vietnam, and with good reason – following this route gives you easy access to superb historical sights, high-octane nightlife, pristine beaches, mountain-dwelling minority groups and much more. It can easily eat up the full month of your visa.

❶ **Ho Chi Minh City** Although it's not the capital, most would agree that this buzzing, cosmopolitan city is the true hub of Vietnam – its range of bars, restaurants, shops and hotels is unsurpassed. **See p.66**

❷ **Da Lat** This mile-high mountain city is highly popular with travellers, and not just for its fresh air or cooler temperatures. Its relaxed atmosphere lends itself to a leisurely exploration of nearby sights, which include some wonderful minority villages. **See p.174**

❸ **Mui Ne** It's all about the beach at Mui Ne, a curl of sand now fringed with top-drawer resorts. However, there are still a few cheap places to stay and a couple of bars maintaining that old-fashioned backpacker vibe. **See p.215**

❹ **Nha Trang** Another place famed for its beach life, but with a totally different character to Mui Ne. This is one of Vietnam's party capitals, with bars galore attracting revellers with astonishingly long happy hours. Those who wake up before nightfall can hit the nearby Cham ruins, then sink into a mud bath. **See p.225**

❺ **Hoi An** This small city draws almost universally positive reactions from visitors. Its food is the best in the country, its lantern-lit buildings are truly spellbinding at night, the nearby sea is great for diving and the majestic Cham ruins of My Son are close by. **See p.247**

❻ **Hue** Notably relaxed for its size, Hue was capital of Vietnam's last dynasty, the Nguyen empire. Cross the Perfume River to the old Imperial City, a maze of opulent buildings that were home to emperors as recently as 1945. **See p.276**

❼ **Hanoi** The Vietnamese capital provides a truly startling contrast to Ho Chi Minh City – it has a far more traditional air and is home to some superb examples of colonial-era architecture. That said, its bars and restaurants are excellent too. **See p.342**

❽ **Ha Long Bay** There are few better ways to round off a Vietnamese tour than to take a trip to Ha Long Bay, a dizzying mass of limestone peaks jutting from the sea. Most visitors spend a night at sea on a wooden junk, after a feast of seafood and cocktails. **See p.338**

UNSEEN MEKONG DELTA

Eager to leave the tourist hordes behind? Our authors have never spotted another foreigner at the following locations.

ABOVE KHAI DINH MAUSOLEUM

❶ Sa Dec flower nurseries Apart from being the former home of French novelist Marguerite Dumas, Sa Dec is the base of over a hundred flower nurseries – a horticulturalist's dream. **See p.130**

❷ Hang Pagoda near Tra Vinh This Khmer-style pagoda painted in subtle pastel shades is home to many monks eager to practise their English, and also to hundreds of storks that roost in the treetops. **See p.126**

❸ Cape Ca Mau Take a speedboat from Ca Mau to Dat Mui, then hop on a xe om to Vietnam's southernmost point at Cape Ca Mau, where an observation tower offers views over mangrove swamps and the endless ocean. **See p.153**

❹ Highway 63 This narrow road from Ca Mau to Rach Gia passes classic delta scenes of commerce being conducted on canals and locals crossing precarious monkey bridges. **See p.153**

❺ Tra Su bird sanctuary Located near Chau Doc, this bird sanctuary is a wonderland of cajuput trees and waterways covered with lily pads that attract swarms of birds like egrets, cormorants and water cocks. **See p.138**

❻ Hon Chong Peninsula The beach doesn't compare with those on Phu Quoc, but it's extremely relaxing, especially on weekdays when you might be the only one swinging in a hammock beneath the casuarina trees. **See p.159**

ETHNIC CULTURE TOUR

Most of Vietnam's 54 ethnic minority groups live in the rugged hills of the north, and a circular journey from Hanoi passes several of the most interesting groups.

❶ White Thai in Mai Chau Girls with waist-length hair don traditional costumes and perform lively song and dance routines, then invite guests to share a huge jar of rice wine. **See p.416**

❷ Black Thai in Son La The most remarkable aspect of Black Thai clothing is the headdress, which features delicately embroidered panels. **See p.413**

❸ Red Dao near Sa Pa Easily spotted by their bright red headgear, the Red Dao are one of

the most colourful tribes in the north and cling fiercely to their traditional ways. **See p.399**

❹ Flower Hmong around Bac Ha These are hands down the north's most flamboyant dressers, and the women are constantly looking for new accoutrements at local markets. **See p.405**

❺ White Hmong near Dong Van Satins and sequins are highly favoured by this group who live in one of the north's most inhospitable, yet also stunningly scenic, settings. **See p.423**

❻ Tay near Ba Be Lake The Tay are the most numerous of all ethnic groups in Vietnam, and have a rich tradition of song and dance, which they occasionally perform for tourists. **See p.425**

CYCLIST IN HO CHI MINH CITY

Basics

Getting there

As one sign of Vietnam's burgeoning popularity as a tourist destination, the number of international flights hitting the country has been increasing steadily in recent years. The vast majority fly into Ho Chi Minh City and Hanoi, though there are also direct services to Da Nang from other Asian destinations, and several regional airports have been upgraded to international standard. However, a fair chunk of visitors still take the cheaper option of an indirect flight routed through Bangkok, Singapore or Hong Kong; a stay in one of these cities can be factored into your schedule, often at no extra cost.

You may well save even more by taking a bargain-basement flight to Bangkok, Kuala Lumpur or Singapore, and a separate ticket through one of the region's **low-cost carriers**, such as Jetstar, Tiger Airways and Air Asia, for the Vietnam leg.

Long-haul airlines that fly in and out of Hanoi and Ho Chi Minh City normally sell you an open-jaw ticket, which allows you to fly into one city and out of the other, leaving you to travel up or down the country under your own steam. **Vietnam Airlines** (Ⓦ vietnamairlines.com) is the national flag-carrier, and currently flies to over fifty destinations in seventeen countries; it's a quality operator, and part of the SkyTeam group.

Airfares always depend on the **season**, with the highest generally being July to August, during the Christmas and New Year holidays and around Tet, the Vietnamese New Year; fares drop during the "shoulder" season – September to mid-December – and you'll get the best prices during the low season, January to June.

You can often cut costs by going through a **specialist flight agent** – either a consolidator, who buys up blocks of tickets from the airlines and sells them at a discount, or a **discount agent**, who in addition to dealing with discounted flights

may also offer special student and youth fares and a range of other travel-related services such as travel insurance, rail passes, car rentals, tours and the like.

Lastly, combining Vietnam with other Southeast Asian countries is becoming increasingly popular – and a lot cheaper and easier – thanks to some good-value regional air deals (see p.30 for more information).

Flights from the UK and Ireland

Vietnam Airlines flies **from London Gatwick** to Ho Chi Minh City and Hanoi; there are no direct flights **from Ireland**. Note that you may save money by flying with a Southeast Asian carrier such as Singapore Airlines, Thai Airways, Malaysia Airlines or Cathay Pacific from London, via the airline's home city. In recent years the big Middle Eastern airlines, Qatar and Emirates, have also offered very competitive prices. Scheduled low-season **fares** from London start at around £450, rising to £600 or more at peak periods.

A good place to look for the best deals is the travel sections of the weekend newspapers and in regional listings magazines. Students and under-26s can often get **discounts** through specialist agents such as STA (Ⓦ sta.com) or USIT in Ireland (Ⓦ usit.ie). Whoever you buy your ticket through, check that the agency belongs to the travel industry bodies ABTA or IATA, so that you'll be covered if the agent goes bust before you get your ticket.

Flights from the US and Canada

In 2004 United Airlines became the first American carrier to resume direct flights to Vietnam since 1975. The airline operates a daily service **from San Francisco** to Ho Chi Minh City via Hong Kong. As yet, no other American or Canadian carriers offer direct services, which means you'll either have to get a flight to San Francisco or catch one of the many flights to a regional hub,

---

A BETTER KIND OF TRAVEL

At Rough Guides we are passionately committed to travel. We feel that travelling is the best way to understand the world we live in and the people we share it with – plus tourism has brought a great deal of benefit to developing economies around the world over the last few decades. But the growth in tourism has also damaged some places irreparably, and climate change is exacerbated by most forms of transport, especially flying. All Rough Guides' trips are carbon-offset, and every year we donate money to a variety of charities devoted to combating the effects of climate change.

such as Bangkok, Singapore or Hong Kong, and continue from there. Scheduled flights start at around US$1400 **from New York**, US$1200 **from Los Angeles**, CAN$2000 **from Vancouver** and CAN$2500 **from Toronto**.

Note that some routings require an **overnight stay** in another city such as Bangkok, Taipei, Hong Kong or Seoul, and often a hotel room will be included in your fare – ask the airline and shop around, since travel agents' policies on this vary. Even when an overnight stay is not required, going to Vietnam can be a great excuse for a stopover somewhere: most airlines will allow you one free stopover in either direction.

Flights from Australia and New Zealand

Direct flights between **Australia** and Vietnam are in surprisingly poor supply, with Vietnam Airlines operating routes from Ho Chi Minh City to Melbourne and Sydney (around AUS$1100). One reason for the dearth of direct services has been the profusion of far cheaper alternate routes, making use of the area's many budget airlines. You can make the journey with Jetstar via Singapore, to which there are direct services from Darwin, Melbourne and Perth, while Tigerair flies from Perth to Vietnam via Singapore; these can start at as little as AUS$250 one-way from Perth and Darwin, though you'll have to pay more from other Aussie cities. The alternative is to fly to another Asian gateway, such as Malaysia Airlines via Kuala Lumpur, Singapore Airlines via Singapore, or Thai Airways via Bangkok (all costing around AUS$1100 to AUS$1500), and then either get connecting flights or travel overland to Hanoi or Ho Chi Minh City; it often costs no more to stop off on the way.

From New Zealand, low-season fares with Malaysia Airlines, Thai, Qantas and Singapore Airlines are all around NZ$1500 to NZ$2200, with a change of plane in the carrier's home airport.

Flights from neighbouring countries

Regional air connections are becoming better and better – you can fly from many cities in **Cambodia**, **Laos**, **Malaysia**, **Thailand** and **southern China**, and budget options are increasing by the year. From **Singapore**, Jetstar flies to Ho Chi Minh City, Tiger Airways heads to both Hanoi and Ho Chi Minh City, and Silk Air does likewise to Ho Chi Minh

City and Da Nang. Air Asia offers daily services from Bangkok and Kuala Lumpur to both Hanoi and Ho Chi Minh City; VietJet Air does the same but only to Ho Chi Minh City. As with all discount airlines, prices depend on availability, so the earlier you book the better; prices can start as low as US$30. Otherwise, you're dependent on flag carriers such as Cambodia Angkor Air and Lao Airlines, though Vietnam Airlines occasionally offers some competitive deals.

Overland

It's increasingly popular to **enter Vietnam overland** from China, Laos or Cambodia, an option that means you can see more of the region than you would if you simply jetted in.

The **China border** is currently open to foreigners at Lao Cai (see p.401), Thanh Thuy near Ha Giang (see p.419), Ta Lung near Cao Bang (see p.425), Dong Dang/Huu Nghi Quan near Lang Son (see p.428) and Mong Cai (see p.427). Direct train services between Hanoi and Beijing via Dong Dang (42hr) leave Hanoi on Tuesdays and Fridays at 6.30pm; note that only soft-sleeper tickets are available and that in Vietnam you can board the train only in Hanoi. You'll need your passport with a valid Chinese visa when you buy the ticket.

From Laos, seven border crossings are currently open to foreigners: Lao Bao (see p.302), the easiest and most popular, some 80km west of Dong Ha; Cha Lo (see p.315); Cau Treo and Nam Can, to the north and northwest of Vinh (see p.315); Na Meo, northwest of Thanh Hoa; Bo Y, northwest of Kon Tum (see p.199); and Tay Trang, just west of Dien Bien Phu (see p.412). While it's perfectly possible – and cheaper – to use local buses to and from the borders, international bus services also run from Savannakhet and Vientiane to Hanoi, Dong Ha, Vinh, Da Nang and other destinations in Vietnam: these direct services are recommended, as regular reports of extortion or unnecessary difficulties continue to come in from those crossing independently.

From Cambodia you can travel by air-conditioned bus from Phnom Penh straight through to Ho Chi Minh City, via the Moc Bai crossing. Cheaper operators tend to use old buses and usually get you to switch at the border. Many tour companies in Phnom Penh will be able to organize boat-plus-bus services, which are a fun way to make the trip. There are two crossings in the Mekong Delta area – Vinh Xuong and Tinh Bien, which are respectively 30km north and 25km west of Chau Doc. There are also border crossings at Xa Xia, on the coast west of the delta, which is useful if you are coming from Kep or Sihanoukville on the Cambodian coast; and at Le Thanh in the central highlands, making it possible to go from Banlung in northeast Cambodia straight through to Pleiku.

As long as you have a **valid visa**, crossing these borders is generally not a problem, though you may still find the odd Vietnamese immigration official who tries to charge a "processing fee", typically one dollar. Most border gates are open from around 7am to 5pm and may close for an hour over lunch.

AIRLINES, AGENTS AND OPERATORS

Air Asia 🕸 airasia.com
Air France 🕸 airfrance.com
British Airways 🕸 britishairways.com
Cambodia Angkor Air 🕸 cambodiaangkorair.com
Cathay Pacific 🕸 cathaypacific.com
China Airlines 🕸 china-airlines.com
Emirates 🕸 emirates.com
Japan Air Lines 🕸 jal.com
Lao Airlines 🕸 laoairlines.com
Lufthansa 🕸 lufthansa.com
Jetstar 🕸 jetstar.com
Malaysia Airlines 🕸 malaysiaairlines.com
Qantas 🕸 qantas.com
Qatar 🕸 qatarairways.com
Silk Air 🕸 silkair.com
Singapore Airlines 🕸 singaporeair.com
Thai Airways 🕸 thaiair.com
Tiger Airways 🕸 tigerairways.com
United Airlines 🕸 united.com
VietJet Air 🕸 vietjetair.com
Vietnam Airlines 🕸 vietnamairlines.com

SPECIALIST TOUR OPERATORS ABROAD

WORLDWIDE

Abercrombie & Kent UK ☎ 0845 485 4723, US ☎ 1 800 554 7016, Australia ☎ 1300 797 010; 🕸 abercrombiekent.co.uk, 🕸 abercrombiekent.com, 🕸 abercrombiekent.com.au. Luxury tour specialist; trips featuring Vietnam come as part of a greater trip through Indochina.

Intrepid Travel UK ☎ 0808 274 5111, US ☎ 1 800 970 7299, Australia ☎ 1300 364 512, New Zealand ☎ 0800 600 610; 🕸 intrepidtravel.com. Affordable small-group trips, usually focusing on low-impact, cross-cultural contact. Tours can cover bits of Vietnam, the whole country or wider Indochina.

Peregrine Adventures UK ☎ 0845 004 0673, Australia ☎ 3 8601 4444; 🕸 peregrineadventures.com. Good local knowledge for an outfit that goes everywhere. Most tours are small-group and adventure-based, often with a focus on trekking, cycling or even food.

World Expeditions UK ☎ 020 8545 9030, US & Canada ☎ 1 800 567 2216, Australia ☎ 1300 720 000, New Zealand ☎ 0800 350 354; 🕸 worldexpeditions.com. Adventure company with a wide variety of programmes, including cycle tours and kayaking in Ha Long Bay. Also offers community project trips, where participants help renovate a local school, for example, and arrange charity challenges.

AUSTRALIA AND NEW ZEALAND

Active Travel Australia ☎ 02 6249 6122, 🕸 activetravel.com.au. Renowned outfit with a wide range of culture and adventure tours, plus customized itineraries.

Griswalds Vietnamese Vacations Australia ☎ 02 9430 6426, 🕸 vietnamvacations.com.au. Long-running Vietnam specialist offering small-group, tailor-made itineraries.

UK AND IRELAND

ebookers UK ☎ 020 3320 3320, Republic of Ireland ☎ 01 431 1311; 🕸 ebookers.com, 🕸 ebookers.ie. Low fares on an extensive selection of scheduled flights and package deals.

Exodus UK ☎ 0845 287 7644, 🕸 exodus.co.uk. Adventure-tour operator taking small groups on specialist programmes that take in trekking, biking, kayaking and cultural trips.

Imaginative Traveller UK ☎ 0845 287 2855, 🕸 imaginative-traveller.com. Affordable, small-group adventure tours from a responsible travel operator. The nine-day "Northern Vietnam Escape" tour is particularly popular.

Inside Vietnam UK ☎ 0117 244 3370, 🕸 insidevietnamtours.com. Well-run small-group or tailored individual packages from an operator now expending its scope across Asia. Its ten-night highlights tour is a popular option.

North South Travel UK ☎ 01245 608291, 🕸 northsouthtravel.co.uk. Friendly, competitive travel agency, offering discounted fares worldwide. Profits are used to support projects in the developing world, especially the promotion of sustainable tourism.

Regent Holidays UK ☎ 020 7666 1244, 🕸 regent-holidays.co.uk. Any operators that can organize good tours to North Korea will surely find Vietnam a piece of cake. Good-value, tailor-made tours available, as well as off-the-shelf itineraries a twelve-day "Highlights of Vietnam" trip.

responsibletravel.com UK ☎ 01273 823 700, 🕸 responsibletravel.com. UK-based online travel agent listing pre-screened holidays from responsible tourism operators.

STA Travel UK ☎ 0800 819 9339, US ☎ 1 800 781 4040, Australia ☎ 134 782, New Zealand ☎ 0800 474 400, South Africa ☎ 0861 781 781; 🕸 statravel.com. Worldwide specialists in independent travel; also student IDs, travel insurance, car rental, rail passes and more. Good discounts for students and under-26s.

Trailfinders UK ☎ 0845 054 6060, Republic of Ireland ☎ 01 677 7888; 🕸 trailfinders.com, 🕸 trailfinders.ie. One of the best informed and most efficient agents for independent travellers.

US AND CANADA

Artisans of Leisure ☎ 1 800 214 8144, 🕸 artisansofleisure.com. Luxury private and individually tailored tours, which often include cooking classes and spa therapy sessions.

Asian Pacific Adventures ☎ 1 800 825 1680, **ⓦ** asianpacific
adventures.com. Regional specialists offering tailor-made and
small-group tours, including trekking and hill-tribe markets.
Backroads ☎ 1 800 462 2848, **ⓦ** backroads.com. Cycling, hiking
and multi-sport tours, with the emphasis on going at your own pace.
Global Exchange ☎ 415 255 7296, **ⓦ** globalexchange.org.
A not-for-profit human rights organization that leads educational tours
of Vietnam.
Journeys International ☎ 1 800 255 8735, **ⓦ** journeysinternational
.com. Prestigious, award-winning operator focusing on eco-tourism and
small-group trips.
VeloAsia ☎ 1 888 681 0808, **ⓦ** veloasia.com. Indochina specialist
with a range of organized and tailor-made cycling adventure tours. Their
famed "Highlights of Vietnam" tour connects Hanoi and Ho Chi Minh City,
and lasts twelve days.

Getting around

**Though still a little rough around the
edges, Vietnam's transport network is
continuing to improve. Most travel takes
place on the roads, which are largely of
decent quality surface-wise, though it
must be said that almost every vehicle
on them is seemingly overtaking or
being overtaken at any given point in
time – accidents are common.**

The vehicles themselves are in pretty good
condition, however, with air-conditioned coaches
ferrying tourists (and an increasing number of
locals) up and down Highway 1, not really a
highway at all but a desperately narrow and shockingly busy thoroughfare that runs from Hanoi to
Ho Chi Minh City, passing through Hue, Da Nang
and Nha Trang en route. Trains run alongside
Highway 1, and their sleeper berths are far more
comfortable than buses for longer journeys. Lastly,
the domestic flight network continues to evolve,
and the cheap, comfortable services may save you
days' worth of travel by road or rail.

By plane

Flying comes into its own on longer hauls, and can
save precious hours or even days off journeys –
the two-hour journey **between Hanoi and Ho Chi
Minh City**, for instance, compares favourably with
the thirty to forty hours you would spend on the
train, and prices are often lower. Other **useful
services** from Hanoi and Ho Chi Minh City fly to
Hue, Da Nang, Nha Trang, and Phu Quoc Island.
Note that you'll need your passport with you when
taking internal flights.

The Vietnamese national carrier, Vietnam Airlines
(**ⓦ** vietnamairlines.com), operates a reasonably cheap,
efficient and comprehensive network of **domestic
flights**. The company maintains booking offices in
all towns and cities with an airport; addresses and
phone numbers are listed throughout the Guide.

Competition is keeping prices low on domestic
flights, with budget carriers having entered the
arena. Jetstar (**ⓦ** jetstar.com) now rivals Vietnam
Airlines for local coverage, as do VietJet Air
(**ⓦ** vietjetair.com). Lastly, Vasco (**ⓦ** vasco.com.vn)
also flies from Ho Chi Minh City to Con Dao and Ca
Mau, but it's better to book through its codeshare
partner Vietnam Airlines.

By rail

Given the amazing prices and regular services of
the open-tour buses, few travellers opt for the train.
However, **rail journeys** are well worth considering,
for several reasons. Firstly, major roads tend to be
lined in their entirety with ramshackle cafés, petrol
pumps, snack stands and mobile phone shops;
from the train, you'll actually see a bit of the countryside. Secondly, you'll be involved in far fewer near-
collisions with trucks, motorbikes or dogs. Thirdly,
you're almost guaranteed to get talking to a bunch
of friendly locals – and perhaps get to join in on the
feasts that some of them bring on board.

Vietnam Railways runs a single-track **train
network** comprising more than 2500km of line,
stretching from Ho Chi Minh City to the Chinese
border. Much of it dates back to the colonial period,
though it's gradually being upgraded. Most of the
services are still relatively slow, but travelling by
train can be far more pleasant than going by road –
though prices on the coastal route can't compare
with buses, you're away from the busy (and often
dangerous) Highway 1, and get to see far more of
the countryside. Keep a particularly close eye on
your belongings on the trains, and be especially
vigilant when the train stops at stations, ensure
your money belt is safely tucked under your clothes
before going to sleep and that your luggage is
safely stowed.

The most **popular routes** with tourists are the
shuttle from Da Nang to Hue (2–3hr), a picturesque
sampler of Vietnamese rail travel and the
overnighters from Hue to Hanoi (11–16hr) and from
Hanoi up to Lao Cai, for Sa Pa (8–9hr).

The railways' official **website** is in Vietnamese-
only (**ⓦ** vr.com.vn), so for up-to-date schedule and
price information, you're better off looking at
ⓦ seat61.com.

Services

The country's **main rail line** shadows Highway 1 on its way from Ho Chi Minh City to Hanoi, passing through Nha Trang, Da Nang and Hue en route. From Hanoi, three branch lines strike out towards the northern coast and Chinese border. One line traces the Red River northwest to **Lao Cai**, just an hour by bus from Sa Pa and also the site of a border crossing into **China**'s Yunnan Province; the rail on the Chinese side had been out of use at the time of writing, though it may well be up and running again by the time you read this. Another rail spur runs north to **Dong Dang**; this is the route taken by trains linking Hanoi and **Beijing**. The third branch, a shorter spur, links the capital with **Haiphong**.

Five **Reunification Express** services depart daily from Hanoi to Ho Chi Minh City and vice versa, a journey that takes somewhere between thirty and forty hours. The main services arrive between 3am and 5am in both Hanoi and Ho Chi Minh City.

On the **northern lines**, four trains per day make the run from Hanoi to Haiphong (2hr 30min) and two to Dong Dang (6hr). There are also four night trains (8–9hr) and a day service (10hr) to Lao Cai.

Trains usually leave on schedule from their departure points, and though delays can stack up further down the line, they're rarely too severe. Note that the only truly reliable way to learn the schedule is by checking those printed on the station wall.

Classes

When it comes to choosing which **class** to travel in, it's essential to aim high. At the bottom of the scale is a **hard seat**, which is just as it sounds, though bearable for shorter journeys; the carriages tend to be filthy, however, and since the windows are caged, views are poor and since one can actually feel like an animal. **Soft seats** offer more comfort, especially in the new air-conditioned carriages, some of which are double-decker; the newer berths, unfortunately, tend to have flatscreen TVs operating at an ear-splitting volume. On overnight journeys, you'd be well advised to invest in a berth of some description. The **hard-berth** compartments are quite comfortable and have six bunks, three either side – the cramped top ones are the cheapest, and the bottom ones the priciest – though some of the old hard-as-nails relics remain in service. Roomier **soft-berth** compartments, containing only four bunks, are always comfortable.

Note that luxury carriages are attached to regular services on a couple of routes from Hanoi. Those on trains to Hue and Da Nang are operated by Livitrans (ⓦlivitrans.com), and to Lao Cai by an assortment of companies.

Facilities

Reunification Express trains have **air-conditioning**, as do the overnight Lao Cai trains which have been upgraded with luxury soft-sleeper carriages. All trains are theoretically **non-smoking**; the rules are obeyed, by and large, in the sleeper rooms, though in hard-seat class, even the guards will be puffing away.

All train carriages have **toilets**, which are usually fine, if a little grubby; many are squat in nature, and these are far more likely to be dirty, and to be devoid of paper or running water. Those in the soft sleeper carriages are proper sit-down toilets, and are comparatively clean.

Simple **meals** are often included in the price of the ticket, but you might want to stock up with goodies of your own. You'll also have plenty of opportunities to buy snacks when the train pulls into stations – and from carts that ply the aisles.

Tickets

Booking ahead is wise, and the further ahead the better, especially if you intend travelling at the weekend or a holiday period (when the lower sleeper berths are often sold as six seats, resulting in chaos). Sleeping compartments should be booked at least a day or two before departure, and even further ahead for soft-sleeper berths on the Hanoi–Hue and Hanoi–Lao Cai routes. It's not possible to buy through tickets and break your journey en route; each journey requires you to buy a separate ticket from the point of departure. Getting tickets at the station is usually pretty painless, though hotels and travel agencies will be able to book for a fee – sometimes as low as 50,000đ, though often much more.

Fares vary according to the class of travel and the train you take; as a rule of thumb, the faster the train, the more expensive it is. Prices (which are always quoted in dong) change regularly, but as an indication of the fare range, on the most expensive services from Hanoi to Ho Chi Minh City you'll pay around 1,700,000đ for a soft-sleeper berth, and from around 1,250,000đ for a hard sleeper in the slowest trains; the equivalent fares for Hanoi to Hue are 800,000đ and 700,000đ respectively. Prices to Lao Cai vary from 140,000đ for a hard seat on the day train to 600,000đ for a soft sleeper.

By bus

Vietnam was once famed for bus drivers ripping off foreigners and cramming as many bodies as possible into their vehicles, but this is dying down; most routes now have tickets with fixed prices, and the advent of luxury "open-tour" buses on the main tourist trail saw comfort levels rocket. On the longer stretches, many buses are sleeper-berth for their whole length, though getting forty winks can be tough – the nature of local roads means that emergency stops are common, and Vietnamese drivers use their horn liberally, which can become grating very quickly on a long journey. **Security** remains an important consideration. Never fall asleep with your bag uncovered, and never leave belongings unattended.

Most travellers use buses to get around Vietnam – but never actually see a bus station. This is because the lion's share of tourist journeys are made on **privately operated** services, usually referred to as "open-tour" buses, which usually operate not from stations but the offices of the companies in question. The term comes from the fact that such companies typically sell through-tickets between Ho Chi Minh City and Hanoi, with customers free to stop off for as long as they like at the main points en route – Da Lat, Mui Ne, Nha Trang, Hoi An, Da Nang, Hue and Ninh Binh. There are drawbacks to doing this though (see box above).

Away from these private affairs, **national bus services** link all major cities in Vietnam, and most minor towns too, though travellers only tend to use them off the open-tour route.

Open-tour buses

On the whole, **open-tour buses** are a reasonably comfortable way to get around Vietnam: they have air-conditioning, limited seating and fixed timetables, which instantly gives them the edge over national services. In addition, the fact that they don't pick up as much on route makes them faster too, and competition is so fierce that prices are almost as low as those for the national bus network. Open-tour buses also call at the occasional tourist sight, such as the Marble Mountains and Lang Co, which can save considerable time and money when compared with doing the same thing independently. Buses are usually quite decent, but don't expect too much leg room, or any on-board toilets; some of the more expensive services have them, but the vast majority will pull in every few hours for a combined loo-and-snack break. This tends to be at mediocre and overpriced restaurants; it's a good idea to arm yourself with snacks before your journey. Another downside to open-tour buses is that you'll be encouraged to book into the company's own or affiliated hotels (usually right next to the drop-off point), though there's nothing to stop you staying elsewhere.

> ## THE DOWNSIDE OF OPEN-TOUR THROUGH TICKETS
>
> The majority of travellers opt for one-way through tickets with one of the open-tour companies, which enable you to traverse the whole country with just one ticket. However, this course of action is not without its drawbacks: if you lose your ticket, there's no refund; choose a bad company, you'll be saddled with them the whole way, and, in addition, you'll be obliged to stick to your company's daily schedule. Buying separate tickets en route will only cost a little more (if anything at all), yet give you far more freedom.

Services tend to run on time, and on longer trips, some take place overnight. Most of the overnight buses are filled with sleeper berths, which sounds nice and comfortable, but these are Vietnamese roads, and Vietnamese drivers – don't expect to get too much sleep. Also note that some **operators** are more reliable than others; Mai Linh and Hoang Long have good reputations; some other operators have very poor standards of service.

Ticket prices vary widely depending on which company you choose, and (if you're booking a through-ticket) how many stops you'd like to make en route; sample prices are US$35 and up from Ho Chi Minh City to Hanoi, US$25 from Ho Chi Minh City to Hue, and US$5 from Hue to Hoi An. You can either make firm bookings at the outset or opt for an open-dated ticket for greater flexibility, in which case you may need to book your onward travel one or two days in advance to be sure of a seat. Alternatively, you can buy separate tickets as you go along, which is recommended (see box above). Each main town on the itinerary has an agent (one for each operator) where you can buy tickets and make onward reservations. To avoid being sold a **fake ticket** or paying over the odds, it's best to buy direct from the relevant agent rather than from hotels, restaurants or unrelated tour companies.

Other buses

On the national bus network, the government is slowly upgrading **state buses**, replacing the rickety old vehicles with air-conditioned models, particularly on the more popular routes. It's not uncommon to find yourself crammed in among the luggage, which could be anything from live pigs in baskets to scores of sacks of rice. Progress can be agonizingly slow as buses stop frequently to pick up passengers or for meal breaks.

Tickets are best bought at bus stations, where **fares** are clearly indicated above the ticket windows. Prices are usually also marked on the tickets themselves, though there are still occasional cases of tourists being overcharged, particularly in more rural destinations, such as those from the Lao border. For long journeys, buy your ticket a day in advance since many routes are heavily oversubscribed.

Privately owned **minibuses** compete with public buses on most routes; they sometimes share the local bus station, or simply congregate on the roadside in the centre of a town. You can also flag them down on the road. If anything, they squeeze in even more people per square foot than ordinary buses, and often drive interminably around town, touting for passengers. On the other hand, they do at least run throughout the day, and serve some routes not covered by public services. Such services are ticketless, so try to find what the correct fare should be and agree a price before boarding – having the right change will also come in handy. You may also find yourself dumped at the side of the road before reaching your destination, and having to cram onto the next passing service.

Most major cities have their own local bus networks, though prices and standards vary. Try to ascertain the correct price and have the exact money ready before boarding as fare collectors will often take advantage of your captive position.

By ferry and boat

A boat-tour around Ha Long Bay is one of Vietnam's most enjoyable trips, while scheduled **ferries** sail year-round – weather permitting – to the major islands off Vietnam's coastline, including Phu Quoc, Cat Ba and Con Dao. In addition, ferry and **hydrofoil** services run from Haiphong to Cat Ba, and hydrofoils from Ho Chi Minh City to Vung Tau, and from Ha Long City to Mong Cai and Bai Tu Long. Though they are gradually being replaced by bridges, a few river ferries still haul themselves from bank to bank of the various strands of the Mekong from morning until night.

By car and jeep

Self-drive in Vietnam is not yet a viable option for tourists and other short-term visitors. However, it's easy to rent a car, jeep or minibus **with driver** from the same companies, agencies and tourist offices that arrange tours. This can be quite an economical means of transport if you are travelling in a group. Moreover, it means you can plan a trip to your own tastes, rather than having to follow a tour company's itinerary.

Prices vary wildly so it pays to shop around, but expect to pay in the region of US$70 per day for a car, and US$110 per day for a jeep or other 4WD, depending on the vehicle's size, age and level of comfort. When negotiating the price, it's important to clarify exactly who is liable for what. Things to check include who pays for the driver's accommodation and meals, fuel, road and ferry tolls, parking fees and repairs, and what happens in the case of a major breakdown. There should then be some sort of contract to sign showing all the details, including an agreed itinerary, especially if you are renting for more than a day; make sure the driver is given a copy in Vietnamese. In some cases you'll have to settle up in advance, though, if possible, it's best if you can arrange to pay roughly half before and the balance at the end.

By motorbike

Motorbike rental is possible in most towns and cities regularly frequented by tourists, and pottering around on one can be an enjoyable and time-efficient method of sightseeing. Lured by the prospect of independent travel at relatively low cost, some tourists cruise the countryside on motorbikes, but inexperienced bikers would do well to think very hard before undertaking any **long-distance biking**: the appalling road discipline of most Vietnamese drivers means that the risk of an accident is very real, with potentially dire consequences should it happen in a remote area. Well-equipped hospitals are few and far between outside the major centres, and there'll probably be no ambulance service.

On the other hand, many people ride around with no problems and thoroughly recommend it for both day-trips and touring. The best biking is to be found in the northern mountains, the central highlands and around the Mekong Delta, while the Ho Chi Minh Highway offers pristine tarmac plus wonderful scenery. Some also do the long haul up Highway 1 from Ho Chi Minh City to Hanoi (or vice versa), a journey of around two weeks, averaging a leisurely 150km per day.

There's no shortage of motorbikes **for rent** in Vietnam's major tourist centres; the average rate is around US$7 per day, with discounts for longer periods. You'll sometimes be asked to pay in advance, sign a rental contract and/or leave some form of ID (a photocopy of your passport should suffice). If you're renting for a week or so, you may be asked to leave a deposit, often the bike's value in dollars though it might also be your air ticket or departure card. In the vast majority of cases, this shouldn't be a problem.

Although it's technically illegal for non-residents to own a vehicle, there's a small trade in **second-hand motorbikes** in the two main cities – look at the noticeboards in hotels, travellers' cafés and tour agents for adverts. So far the police have ignored the practice, but check the latest situation before committing yourself. The bike of choice is usually a **Minsk 125cc**, particularly for the mountains; it's sturdy, not too expensive, and the easiest to get repaired outside the main cities.

Whether you're renting or buying, remember to check everything over carefully, especially brakes, lights and horn. Wearing a **helmet** is now a legal requirement, and most rental outlets have helmets you can borrow, sometimes for a small charge, though they may not be top-quality.

Note that international driving licences are not valid in Vietnam, but you will need your home **driving licence** and bike registration papers. You also need at least third-party **insurance**, which is available (with the aforementioned documentation) at Bao Viet insurance offices.

Though **road conditions** have improved remarkably in recent years, off the main highways they can still be highly erratic, with pristine asphalt followed by stretches of spine-jarring potholes, and plenty of loose gravel on the sides of the road. **Repair shops** are fairly ubiquitous – ask for *sua chua xe may* (motorbike repairs) – but you should still carry at least a puncture-repair kit, pump and spare spark plug. **Fuel** (*xang*) is cheap and widely available at the roadsides, often from bottles. Finally, try to travel in the company of one or more other bikes in case one of you gets into trouble. And if you want to get off the main highways, it really pays to take a guide.

By bicycle

Cycling is an excellent way of sightseeing around towns, and you shouldn't have to pay more than 50,000đ per day for the privilege, even outside the main tourist centres.

While you can now buy decent Japanese-made bikes in Vietnam, if you decide on a **long-distance cycling** holiday, you should really bring your own bike with you, not forgetting all the necessary spares and tools. Hardy **mountain bikes** cope best with the country's variable surfaces, though tourers and hybrids are fine on the main roads. Bring your own helmet and a good loud bell; a rear-view mirror also comes in handy.

When it all gets too much, or you want to skip between towns, you can always put your bike on the train (though not on all services; check when buying your ticket) for a small fee; take it to the station well ahead of time, where it will be packed and placed in the luggage van. Some open-tour buses will also take bikes – free if it goes in the luggage hold (packed up), otherwise you'll have to pay for an extra seat.

RULES OF THE ROAD

There's no discernible method to the madness that passes as a **traffic** system in Vietnam so it's extremely important that you don't stray out onto the roads unless you feel completely confident about doing so. The theory is that you **drive on the right**, though in practice motorists and cyclists swoop, swerve and dodge wherever they want, using their **horn** as a surrogate indicator and brake. Unless otherwise stated, the **speed limit** is 60kph on highways and 40kph or less in towns.

Right of way invariably goes to the biggest vehicle on the road, which means that motorbikes and bicycles are regularly forced off the highway by thundering trucks or buses; note that overtaking vehicles assume you'll pull over onto the hard shoulder to avoid them. It's wise to use your horn to its maximum and also to avoid being on the road after dark, since many vehicles either don't have functioning headlights or simply don't bother to turn them on.

On the whole the **police** seem to leave foreign riders well alone, and the best policy at roadside checkpoints is just to drive by slowly. However, if you are involved in an **accident** and it was deemed to be your fault, the penalties can involve fairly major fines.

When **parking** your bike, it's advisable to leave it in a parking compound (*gui xe*) – the going rate is from 5000đ for a motorbike and 2000đ for a bicycle – or paying someone to keep an eye on it. If not, you run the risk of it being tampered with.

If you want to see Vietnam from the saddle, note that there are several companies that offer specialist **cycling tours**. In addition to a few of the international tour operators (see p.31), there are local outfits such as Phat Tire (ⓦ phattireventures.com).

Organized tours

Ever-increasing numbers of tourists are seeing Vietnam through the window of a minibus, on **organized tours**. Ranging from one-day jaunts to two- or three-week trawls upcountry, tours are ideal if you want to acquaint yourself speedily with the highlights of Vietnam; they can also work out much cheaper than car rental. On the other hand, by relying on tours you'll have little chance to really get to grips with the country and its people, or to enjoy things at your leisure.

Hordes of state-owned and private **tour companies** compete for business – see our lists of well-established agents in Ho Chi Minh City (see p.91) and Hanoi (see p.370). While a few companies now put together more innovative itineraries, the vast majority offer similar tours. However, it pays to shop around since **prices** vary wildly depending, for example, on how many people there are in a group, the standard of transport, meals and accommodation, whether entry fees are included and so forth.

You'll also need to check carefully that the operator is financially sound, reliable and can deliver what is promised – *never* deal with a company that demands cash upfront or refuses to accept payment by credit card, and get references if you can. Check exactly what is included in the price, the maximum number of people on the trip and whether your group will be amalgamated with others if you don't want to be travelling round in a great horde. Bear in mind, as well, that you're far better off dealing directly with the company organizing the tour, rather than going through a hotel or other intermediary. Not only are you more likely to get accurate information about the details of the tour, but you'll also be in a much stronger position should you have cause for complaint.

The other alternative is to set up your own **custom-made tour** by gathering together a group and renting a car, jeep or minibus plus driver (see p.35).

Local transport

In a country with a population so adept at making do with limited resources, it isn't surprising to see the diverse types of **local transport**. While taxis are increasingly common and a number of cities now boast reasonable **bus services**, elsewhere you'll be reliant on a host of two- and three-wheeled vehicles for getting around.

Most common by far are motorbike taxis known as **xe om**. In the cities you'll rarely be able to walk twenty yards without being offered a ride; prices tend to start at around 10,000đ for very short runs, though this goes up after dark (as does the possibility of extortion). At all times the rules of bargaining apply: when haggling, ensure you know which currency you are dealing in (five fingers held up, for instance, could mean 5000đ, 50,000đ or US$5), and whether you're negotiating for a single or return trip, and for one passenger or two; it's always best to write the figures down. Should a difference of opinion emerge at the end of a ride, having the exact fare ready to press into an argumentative driver's hand can sometimes resolve matters.

Xe om have almost entirely replaced that quintessential Vietnamese mode of transport, the **cyclo**. These three-wheeled rickshaws comprising a "bucket" seat attached to the front of a bicycle can carry one person, or two people at a push, and are now only really found in tourist areas (though locals use them just as much as foreigners). Prices vary by area, and there are continuous stories of cyclo drivers charging outrageous sums for their services, so to avoid getting badly ripped off, find out first what a reasonable fare might be from your hotel; if the first driver won't agree to your offer, simply walk on and try another.

Taxis are now a common sight on the streets of all major cities. The vast majority are metered (with prices in dong) and fares are not expensive; a short ride within central Hanoi, for example, should cost around 30,000đ. Though standards have been improving with greater competition, some drivers need persuading to use their meters, while others dawdle along as the meter spins suspiciously fast, or take you on an unnecessarily long route. When arriving in a town, beware of drivers who insist the hotel you ask for is closed and want to take you elsewhere; this is usually a commission scam – be firm with your directions. In general, smarter-looking taxis and those waiting outside big hotels tend to be more reliable; the **Mai Linh** network has by far the best reputation, and you'll see their green cabs all across the land, while the white-coloured **Vinasun** armada are not far behind.

Accommodation

The standard of accommodation in Vietnam is, by and large, excellent. In the main tourist areas the range caters to all budgets, and though prices are a little expensive by Southeast Asian standards, the quality is generally good. Competition is fierce and with the construction boom still ongoing rooms are being added all the time – great for the traveller, as it keeps prices low and service standards high. There has been a massive increase in the number of luxury resorts along the coast (mainly aimed at the Asian package tour market), while backpackers and those travelling off the tourist trail will find good budget accommodation throughout the country.

Reservations

Another consequence of the number of new hotels springing up in recent years is that getting **a reservation** is no longer the nightmare it once was, and even among international-class hotels there are some bargains to be had, particularly at weekends; however, booking in advance is a must around the **Tet** festival in early spring (see p.53).

Tourist booth staff at the airports in Ho Chi Minh City and Hanoi will phone to reserve a room for you, and it's increasingly simple to book **online**. Be wary of asking advice from cyclo or taxi drivers, as travellers are often told that their hotel of choice is full or closed. It's also important to note that Vietnam is full of **copycat** businesses – to avoid being taken to a similarly named hotel, write down the street name and show it to your driver.

Once you've found a hotel, look at a range of rooms before opting for one, as standards can vary hugely within the same establishment. You'll also need to check the bed arrangement, since there are many permutations in Vietnam. A **"single"** room could have a single or twin beds in it, while a **"double"** room could have two, three or four single beds, a double, a single and a double, and so on.

Practicalities

When you **check in** at a Vietnamese hotel or guesthouse, you'll be asked for your **passport**, which is needed for registration with the local authorities. Depending on the establishment, these will be either returned to you the same night, or kept as security until you check out. If you're going to lose sleep over being separated from your passport, say you need it for the bank; many places will accept photocopies of your picture and visa pages. It's normally possible to pay your bill when you leave, although a few budget places ask for payment in advance.

Room rates fluctuate according to demand, so it's always worth bargaining – making sure, of course, that it's clear whether both parties are talking per person or per room. Your case will be that much stronger if you are staying several nights.

Bear in mind that hotel security can be a problem: never leave valuables lying about and keep documents with you at all times in a money pouch. High-end places might have safes; elsewhere you might be able to leave items in a locked drawer at reception (put everything in a sealed envelope and get a receipt). In the cheapest places, where the door might only be secured with a padlock, increase your security by using your own lock.

Hygiene can also be a problem at the budget end of things, with cockroaches and even rats roaming free; you can at least minimize health risks by not bringing foodstuffs or sugary drinks into your room.

Finally, **prostitution** is rife in Vietnam, and in less reputable hotels it's not unknown for Western men to be called on, or even phoned from other rooms, during the night.

ROOM RATES AND TAXES

Room rates are generally quoted in dong at hotel receptions, but we've converted them to US$ throughout the guide, based on those found at the time of writing for the cheapest double room. However, because of the extreme volatility of the exchange rate (which can change by hundreds or thousands of dong each week), these prices are subject to constant change.

All hotels charge ten percent **government tax**, while top-class establishments also add a **service charge** (typically five percent). These taxes may or may not be included in the room rate, so check to be sure. Increasingly, **breakfast** is included in the price of all but the cheapest rooms; in budget places it will consist of little more than bread with jam or cheese and a cup of tea or coffee, while those splashing out a little more may be greeted by a gigantic morning buffet.

Types of accommodation

Grading accommodation isn't a simple matter in Vietnam. The names used (guesthouse, mini-hotel, hotel and so on) can rarely be relied on to indicate what's on offer, and there are broad overlaps in standards. Vietnam's older hotels tend to be austere, state-owned edifices styled on unlovely Eastern European models, while many private mini-hotels make a real effort. Some hotels cover all bases by having a range of rooms, from simple fan-cooled rooms with cold water, right up to cheerful air-conditioned accommodation with satellite TV, fridge and mini-bar. As a rule of thumb, the newer a place is, the better value it's likely to represent in terms of comfort, hygiene and all-round appeal.

There are a burgeoning number of "**resorts**" appearing across the country. In contrast to the Western image of an all-inclusive complex, in Vietnam these are simply hotels, usually with pretty landscaped gardens, located on the beach or in the countryside. All that's included in the rate is breakfast, though it is possible to eat all your meals here.

Budget accommodation

The very cheapest form of accommodation in Vietnam is a bed in a **dormitory**, though as yet, very few cities have such facilities – there are dedicated hostels in Hanoi, Ho Chi Minh City, Hue and Nha Trang, where you can expect to pay US$6–10 for a bed, sometimes sharing common facilities. Do note that though most of these have private rooms, you'll pay less elsewhere. In the two main cities there are also a fair few budget guest-houses equipped with "backpacker" dorms – you'll generally find these around the De Tham enclave in Ho Chi Minh City, and the Old Quarter in Hanoi (see the respective chapters for more). In Hanoi there is also a small network of **youth hostels** fully accredited by Hostelling International (W hihostels .com); you'll need a current Youth Hostel card, which you can buy when checking in.

If you prefer your own privacy, you'll find simple fan rooms in either a guesthouse or **hotel** (*khach san*), with prices starting at around US$15; these are likely to be en suite, although you might not get hot water at this price level in the warmer south. Add air-conditioning, satellite TV and slightly better furnishings, maybe even a window, and you'll be paying up to US$25. Upgrading to US$25–35 will get you a larger room with better-standard fittings, usually including a fridge and bathtub, and possibly a balcony. Note that while many hotels advertise satellite TV, which channels you actually get varies wildly, let alone the quality of reception, so check first if it matters to you.

Mid- and upper-range accommodation

For upwards of US$35 per room per night, accommodation can begin to get quite rosy. Rooms at this level will be comfortable, reasonably spacious and well appointed with decent furniture, air-conditioning, hot water, fridge, phone and satellite TV in all but the most remote areas.

Paying US$35–80 will get you a room in a **mid-range hotel** of some repute, with in-house restaurant and bar, booking office, room service and so on. At the **top of the range** the sky's the limit. Most of the international-class hotels are located in the two major cities, which also have some reasonably charismatic places to stay, such as the *Metropole* in Hanoi (see p.374) and Ho Chi Minh's *Continental* (see p.93). However, in recent years developers have targeted Nha Trang, Hoi An, Da Nang and Ha Long City, all of which now boast upmarket resort hotels. Off the main trail, there are usually one or two upper-range hotels in each main city, though very few exist in the countryside.

Village accommodation and camping

As Vietnam's minority communities have become more exposed to tourism, staying in stilthouses or other **village accommodation** has become more feasible.

In the north of the country, notably around Sa Pa and in the Mai Chau Valley, you can either take one of the tours out of Hanoi which includes a home-stay in one of the **minority villages**, or make your own arrangements when you get there (see box, p.398). In the central highlands, the Pleiku and Kon Tum tourist offices can also arrange a stilthouse home-stay for you.

Accommodation usually consists of a mattress on the floor in a communal room. Those villages more used to tourists normally provide a blanket and mosquito net, but it's advisable to take your own net and sleeping bag to be on the safe side, particularly as nights get pretty cold in the mountains. Prices in the villages are US$5–15 per person per night, depending on the area and whether meals are included.

Where boat trips operate in the Mekong Delta, notably around Vinh Long, tour operators in Ho Chi Minh City or the local tourist board can arrange for visitors to stay with owners of **fruit orchards**, allowing a close-up view of rural life (see box, p.129).

Virtually no provisions exist in Vietnam for **camping** at the present time. The exceptions are at Nha Trang and Mui Ne, where some guesthouses offer tents for a few dollars a night when all rooms are full. Some tour companies also offer camping as an option when visiting Ha Long Bay (see box, p.339).

Food and drink

Light, subtle in flavour and astonishing in variety, Vietnamese food is generally boiled or steamed rather than stir-fried, as is more common elsewhere in Southeast Asia. In addition, rather than throwing in handfuls of spice, a huge emphasis is placed on fresh herbs and seasoning – no great surprise in this land of diverse climates.

In the south, **Indian** and **Thai** influences add curries and spices to the menu, while other regions have evolved their own array of specialities, most notably the foods of Hue and Hoi An. Buddhism introduced a **vegetarian** tradition to Vietnam, while much later the **French** brought with them bread, dairy products, pastries and the whole café culture (see p.46). The major tourist centres are now well provided with everything from street hawkers to hotel and Western-style restaurants, and even ice-cream parlours; in such places, you'll also find a few restaurants putting on **cooking classes**.

When it comes to the range of eating establishments, you'll find **hawkers** peddling their dish of the day from shoulder poles or handcarts, **street kitchens** – inexpensive joints aimed at locals – and

proper sit-down **restaurants** ranging from simple places serving unpretentious Vietnamese meals to top-class establishments offering high quality Vietnamese specialities and international cuisine. The quality and variety of food is generally better in the main towns than off the beaten track, where restaurants of any sort are few and far between. That said, you'll never go hungry; even in the back of beyond, there's always some stall selling a noodle soup or rice platter and plenty of fruit to fill up on.

Throughout the Guide we've given phone numbers and opening hours. While most eating establishments stay open throughout the year, some close over Tet (see p.53). Lastly, note that this guide includes a glossary of food and drink terms (see p.503).

Street kitchens

Eating on the street may not be to every visitor's taste, but those willing to take the plunge usually put it up among their favourite experiences in the country – the food is often better in quality to that found at restaurants, it's much cheaper, and a whole lot more fun. It's worth using a bit of judicious selection, however – look for places with a fast turnover, where the ingredients are obviously fresh. A bit of basic vocabulary will certainly help (see p.498).

Street kitchens range from makeshift food stalls, set up on the street round a cluster of pint-size stools, to eating houses where, as often as not, the cooking is still done on the street but you either sit in an open-fronted dining area or join the overspill outside. Both tend to have fixed locations, though

---

DINING PRACTICALITIES

Travellers to Vietnam will soon notice that the country runs to a somewhat different schedule – everything happens earlier here, and this goes for **mealtimes**, too. Outside the major cities and tourist areas, food stalls and street kitchens rarely stay open beyond 8pm, though they do stay open later in the south, especially in Ho Chi Minh City; restaurants, on the other hand, are usually open until fairly late.

You'll also get the chance to brush up your **chopstick-handling skills**, although other utensils are usually available, especially in Western-style restaurants or places frequented by tourists.

The use of **monosodium glutamate** (MSG) can be excessive, especially in northern cooking, and some people are known to react badly to the seasoning. A few restaurants in the main cities have cottoned on to the foibles of foreigners and advertise MSG-free food; elsewhere, try saying *khong co my chinh* (without MSG), and keep your fingers crossed. Note that what looks like salt on the table is sometimes MSG, so taste it first.

Lastly, when it comes to **paying**, the normal sign language will be readily understood in most restaurants. In street kitchens you pay as you leave – either proffer some dong to signal your intentions, or ask *bao nhieu tien?* ("how much is it?").

only the eating houses will have an address – which usually doubles as their name. Some places stay open all day (7am–8pm), while many close once they've run out of ingredients and others only open at lunchtime (10.30am–2pm). To be sure of the widest choice and freshest food, it pays to get there early (as early as 11.30am at lunchtime, and by 7pm in the evening), and note that the best places will be packed around noon.

Most specialize in one type of food, generally indicated (in Vietnamese only) on a signboard outside, or offer the ubiquitous **com** (rice dishes) and **pho** (noodle soups). **Com binh dan**, "people's meals", are also popular. Here you select from an array of prepared dishes displayed in a glass cabinet or on a buffet table, piling your plate with such things as stuffed tomatoes, fried fish, tofu, pickles or eggs, plus a helping of rice; expect to pay from around 25,000đ for a good plateful. Though it's not a major problem at these prices, some street kitchens overcharge, so double-check when ordering.

In a similar vein to street kitchens are **bia hoi outlets** (see box, p.45). Though these are primarily drinking establishments, many provide good-value snacks or even main meals.

Restaurants

If you're after more relaxed dining, where people aren't queuing for your seat, then head for a proper **restaurant** (*nha hang*), which will have chairs rather than stools, a name, a menu and will often be closed to the street. In general these places serve a more varied selection of Vietnamese dishes than the street kitchens, plus a smattering of inter-national – generally European – dishes. **Menus** at this level usually show prices, particularly in areas popular with tourists. If there are no prices on your menu, confirm them with staff before you start eating to avoid any potential overcharging issues.

In the main tourist haunts, you'll find cheap and cheerful **cafés** aimed at the backpacker market and serving often mediocre Western and Vietnamese dishes – from burgers and banana pancakes to spring rolls, noodles and other Vietnamese standards. Should you crave a reasonably priced Western-style breakfast, fresh fruit salad or a mango shake, these are the places to go.

As you move up the price scale, the decor and the cuisine become more sophisticated and the menu more varied. Some places have menus priced in dollars, and more and more accept credit cards. Usually menus indicate if there's a **service charge**, but watch out for an additional 3–4 percent on credit

---

BREAKFAST

Vietnamese traditionally breakfast on **pho** or some other noodle soup, reasoning that these provide enough energy to get through the day; many an expat has come around to this way of thinking. You may also find early-morning hawkers peddling *xoi*, a wholesome mix of steamed **sticky rice** with soya bean, sweet corn or peanuts. Simple **Western breakfasts** (such as bread with jam, cheese or eggs and coffee) are usually available in backpacker cafés or hotels. More upmarket places increasingly stretch to cereals and fresh milk, while some top-class hotels (and a whole bunch of cheaper ones) lay on the full works in their breakfast buffets. In towns, you could always buy jam and bread or croissants for a **do-it-yourself** breakfast.

---

card payments. These restaurants can be relatively fancy places, with at least a nod towards decor and ambience, and correspondingly higher prices.

The most popular **foreign cuisine** on offer is French, though larger cities boast some pretty good international restaurants, including Thai, Chinese, Tex Mex, Indian and Italian. You'll find these international cuisines, and upper-class Vietnamese restaurants, in Hanoi, Ho Chi Minh City, Hue, Da Nang, Hoi An and Nha Trang, though they're scarce in the rest of the country.

Vietnamese food

The staple of Vietnamese meals is **rice**, with noodles a popular alternative at breakfast or as a snack. Typically, rice will be accompanied by a fish or meat dish, a vegetable dish and soup, followed by a green tea digestive. The most commonly used **flavourings** are shallots, coriander and lemon grass. Ginger, saffron, mint, anise and a basil-type herb also feature strongly, and coconut milk gives some southern dishes a distinctive richness.

Even in the south, Vietnamese food tends not to be over-spicy; instead, chilli sauces or fresh chillies are served separately. Vietnam's most famous seasoning is the ubiquitous **nuoc mam**, a dark-brown, fermented, nutrient-packed fish sauce which is added during cooking or forms the base for various dipping sauces. Foreigners usually find the smell of the sauce pretty rank, but most soon acquire a taste for its distinctive salty-sweetness.

Soups and noodles

Though it originated in the north, one dish you'll find throughout Vietnam is **pho** (pronounced as the British say "fur"), a noodle soup eaten at any time of day but primarily at breakfast. The basic bowl of pho consists of a light beef broth, flavoured with ginger, coriander and sometimes cinnamon, to which are added broad, flat rice-noodles, spring onions and slivers of chicken, pork or beef. At the table you add a squeeze of lime and a sprinkling of chilli flakes or a spoonful of chilli sauce.

Countless other types of soup are dished up at street restaurants. **Bun bo** is another substantial beef and noodle soup eaten countrywide, though most famous in Hue; in the south, **hu tieu**, a soup of vermicelli, pork and seafood noodles, is best taken in My Tho. **Chao** (or *xhao*), on the other hand, is a thick rice gruel served piping hot, usually with shredded chicken or filleted fish, flavoured with dill and with perhaps a raw egg cooking at the bottom; it's often served with fried breadsticks (*quay*). Sour soups are a popular accompaniment for fish, while **lau**, a standard in local restaurants, is more of a main meal than a soup, where the vegetable broth arrives at the table in a steamboat (a ring-shaped metal dish on live coals or, nowadays, often electrically heated). You cook slivers of beef, prawns or similar in the simmering soup, and then drink the flavourful liquid that's left in the cooking pot.

Fish and meat

Among the highlights of Vietnamese cuisine are its succulent **seafood** and freshwater **fish**. Invented in Hanoi, *cha ca* is the most famous of these dishes: white fish sauteed in butter at the table with dill and spring onions, then served with rice noodles and a sprinkling of peanuts. Another dish found in more expensive restaurants is *chao tom* (or *tom bao mia*), consisting of savoury shrimp pate wrapped round sweet sugar cane and fried. *Ca kho to*, fish stew cooked in a clay pot, is a southern speciality.

Every conceivable type of meat and part of the animal anatomy finds itself on the Vietnamese dining table, though the staples are straightforward beef, chicken and pork. **Ground meat**, especially pork, is a common constituent of stuffings, for example in spring rolls or the similar *banh cuon*, a steamed, rice-flour "ravioli" filled with minced pork, black mushrooms and bean sprouts; a popular variation uses prawns instead of meat. Pork is also used, with plenty of herbs, to make Hanoi's *bun cha*, small **hamburgers** barbecued on an open charcoal brazier and served on a bed of cold rice-noodles with greens and a slightly sweetish sauce. One famous southern dish is *bo bay mon* (often written *bo 7 mon*), meaning literally **beef seven ways**, consisting of a platter of beef cooked in different styles.

Vegetables and vegetarian food

It is possible to find **vegetarian food** in Vietnam, though not always easy. Most restaurants offer a smattering of meat-free dishes, from stewed spinach or similar greens, to a more appetizing mix of onion, tomato, bean sprouts, various mushrooms, peppers and so on; places used to foreigners may be able to oblige with vegetarian spring rolls (*nem an chay* or *nem khong co thit*). At street kitchens you're likely to find tofu and one or two dishes of pickled vegetables, such as cabbage or cucumber, while

---

TEN VIETNAMESE FOODS TO TRY

Banh mi Baguette sandwich filled with greens and a choice of fillings including paté and freshly made omelette.

Banh xeo Fried pancake containing shrimp, pork, bean sprouts and egg.

Bun cha Seasoned, charcoal-grilled pork served with rice noodles and assorted foliage.

Ca kho to Caramelized fish in a clay pot.

Cha ca Butter-sautéed, dill-flavoured fish served with rice noodles.

Com tam Street-stand favourite consisting of barbecued beef served with rice and a fried egg.

Goi cuon Vietnam's most famous dish: translucent spring rolls packed with greens, coriander and various combinations of minced pork, shrimp or crab. In some places they're served with a bowl of lettuce and/or mint. A southern variation has barbecued strips of pork wrapped up with green banana and star fruit, and then dunked in a rich peanut sauce – every bit as tasty as it sounds.

Mi quang Unheralded noodle dish; ingredients vary by establishment, but expect shrimp, peanuts, mint and quail eggs.

Nom hua chuoi Banana-flower salad: a great veggie option.

Pho Noodles in broth: the national dish, though at its best in Hanoi.

VEGETABLE MARKET, HANOI >

JLINARY ADVENTURE TOURISM

Roving gourmets may want to try some of the more unusual meats on offer in Vietnam. **Dog meat** (*thit cay* or *thit cho*) is a particular delicacy in the north, where "yellow" dogs (sandy-haired varieties) are considered the tastiest. Winter is the season to eat dog meat – it's said to give extra body heat, and is also supposed to remove bad luck if consumed at the end of the lunar month. Worryingly, at some rural snack-shacks in the north you may get dog even if you've ordered something else. **Snake** (*thit con ran*), like dog, is supposed to improve male virility. Dining on snake is surrounded by a ritual, which, if you're guest of honour, requires you to swallow the still-beating heart. Another one strictly for the strong of stomach is *trung vit lon*, **embryo-containing duck eggs** boiled and eaten only five days before hatching – bill, webbed feet, feathers and all.

occasionally they may also have aubergine, bamboo shoots or avocado, depending on the season.

However, unless you go to a **specialist** vegetarian outlet, it can be a problem finding genuine veggie food: soups are usually made with beef stock, morsels of pork fat sneak into otherwise innocuous-looking dishes and animal fat tends to be used for frying.

The phrase to remember is *an chay* (vegetarian), or seek out a vegetarian rice shop (*tiem com chay*). Otherwise, make the most of the first and fifteenth days of the lunar month when many Vietnamese Buddhists spurn meat and you're more likely to find vegetarian dishes on offer.

Snacks

Vietnam has a wide range of **snacks and nibbles** to fill any yawning gaps, from huge rice-flour crackers sprinkled with sesame seeds to all sorts of dried fish, nuts and seeds. *Banh bao* are white, steamed dumplings filled with tasty titbits, such as pork, onions and tangy mushrooms or strands of sweet coconut. *Banh xeo*, meaning sizzling pancake, combines shrimp, pork, bean sprouts and egg, all fried and then wrapped in rice paper with a selection of greens before being dunked in a spicy sauce. A similar dish, originating from Hue – a city with a vast repertoire of snack foods (see box, p.286) – is *banh khoai*, in which the flat pancake is accompanied by a plate of star fruit, green banana and aromatic herbs, plus a rich peanut sauce.

Markets are often good snacking grounds, with stalls churning out soups and spring rolls or selling intriguing banana-leaf parcels of pate (a favourite accompaniment for bia hoi), pickled pork sausage or perhaps a cake of sticky rice.

A relative newcomer on the culinary scene is **French bread**, made with wheat flour in the north and rice flour in the south. Known as *banh mi*, baguettes – sometimes sold warm from streetside stoves – are sliced open and stuffed with pate, soft cheese or ham and pickled vegetables.

Fruit

With its diverse climate, Vietnam is blessed with both tropical and temperate **fruits**, including dozens of banana species. The richest orchards are in the south, where pineapple, coconut, papaya, mango, longan and mangosteen flourish. Da Lat is famous for its strawberries, while the region around Nha Trang produces the peculiar "dragon fruit" (*thanh long*). The size and shape of a small pineapple, the dragon fruit has skin of shocking pink, studded with small protuberances, and smooth, white flesh speckled with tiny black seeds. The slightly sweet, watery flesh is thirst-quenching, and so is often served as a drink, crushed with ice.

A fruit that is definitely an acquired taste is the durian, a spiky, yellow-green, football-sized fruit with an unmistakably pungent odour reminiscent of mature cheese and caramel, but tasting like an onion-laced custard. Jackfruit looks worryingly similar to durian but is larger and has smaller spikes. Its yellow segments of flesh are deliciously sweet.

Sweet things

Vietnam is not strong on desserts – restaurants usually stick to ice cream and fruit, although fancier international places might venture into tiramisu territory. Those with a sweet tooth are better off hunting down a bakery – there'll be one within walking distance in any urban area – or browsing around street stalls where there are usually candied fruits and other Vietnamese **sweetmeats** on offer, as well as sugary displays of French-inspired cakes and pastries in the main tourist centres.

Green-coloured *banh com* is an eye-catching local delicacy made by wrapping pounded glutinous rice around sugary, green-bean paste. A similar confection, found only during the mid-autumn festival, is the "earth cake", *banh deo*, which melds the contrasting flavours of candied fruits, sesame and lotus seeds with a dice of savoury pork fat. **Fritters** are popular among children and you'll find opportunistic hawkers outside schools, selling *banh chuoi* (banana fritters) and *banh chuoi khoai* (mixed slices of banana and sweet potato).

Most cities now have **ice-cream** parlours selling tubs or sticks of the local, hard ices in chocolate, vanilla or green-tea flavours, though it's prudent to buy only from the larger, busier outlets and not from street hawkers. More exotic tastes can be satisfied at the European- and American-style ice-cream parlours of Hanoi and Ho Chi Minh City, while excellent yoghurts are also increasingly available at ice-cream parlours, and even some restaurants.

Somewhere between a drink and a snack, **che** is made from taro flour and green bean, and served over ice with chunks of fruit, coloured jellies and even sweet corn or potato. In hot weather it provides a refreshing sugar-fix.

Drinks

Giai khat means "quench your thirst" and you'll see the signs everywhere, on stands selling fresh juices, bottled cold drinks or outside cafés and bia hoi (draught beer) outlets. Many drinks are served with ice, which is reliable in hotels, bars and restaurants, though less so from street-stands; if in doubt, saying *dung bo da, cam on* ("no ice, thanks") should do the trick.

BIA HOI KNOW-HOW

There are countless **bia hoi** (draught beer) outlets in most major cities in Vietnam, ranging from a few ankle-high stools gathered round a barrel on the pavement to beer gardens. Quality tends to be more consistent at the larger outlets supplied by major breweries such as Hanoi Beer and Halida (under the name Viet Ha), rather than the smaller places which usually buy their beer from microbreweries. On the whole, the more expensive – and colder – the beer, the better it is.

Bia hoi culture is about enjoying a few beers with a group of friends – usually all male, though in the cities you see a few women these days. People almost never drink alone and rarely drink without eating, so many places serve a range of snacks and more extensive dishes.

To **help you order** food in a bia hoi outlet, we've listed a few classic dishes below. Menus, if they exist, will be in Vietnamese. They normally give a price range for each dish, so you order a small, medium or large amount, for example, depending on the size of your group. To maximize the variety, it makes sense to order small quantities of several dishes and share. If no prices are indicated on the menu, be sure to ask when ordering. Usually a note with the running total is left on the table, so you can keep track of how much you're spending.

bo luc lac	cubed spicy beef and green pepper stir-fry
ca bo lo	oven-cooked fish
dau chien ron	fried tofu
dau tu xuyen	tofu in a Chinese pork and tomato sauce
de tai chanh	lightly cooked goat with green banana, pineapple and lemon
dua chuot che	sliced cucumber
ech chien bo	deep-fried battered frogs' legs
ech xao mang	frogs' legs with bamboo shoots
ga xe phay	shredded chicken salad with bean peanuts and basil
khoai tay ran	chips/French fries
lac	peanuts
muc chien bo	squid fried in butter
muc kho	dried squid
muc tam bot	battered squid
nem chua	minced spicy cured pork wrapped in banana leaf
nom du du	papaya salad
nom hoa chuoi	banana-flower salad
nom ngo sen	lotus-stem salad
oc xao xa ot	stir-fried snail, lemongrass and chilli
rau bi xaoi	leaf fried with garlic
bo/toi	beef/pumpkin
tho quay	roast rabbit
tom hap bia	shrimps steamed in beer
tom nuong	grilled shrimps

Water and soft drinks

Tap water is not safe to drink in Vietnam – since **bottled water** is both cheap and widely available, you shouldn't need to take the risk anyway. When buying bottled water check the seal is unbroken and the water is clear, as bottles are occasionally refilled from the tap. Tap water in Hanoi and Ho Chi Minh City is chlorinated and most travellers use it for brushing their teeth without problem, but this is not recommended in rural areas, where water is often untreated. Particular care should be taken anywhere where there is flooding as raw sewage may be washed into the water system. Avoid drinks with ice, or those that may have been diluted with suspect water.

On sale just about everywhere, locally made **soft drinks** are tooth-numbingly sweet, but cheap and safe – as long as the bottle or carton appears well sealed. The Coke, Sprite and Fanta hegemony also means you can find fizzy drinks in surprisingly remote areas. Oddly, canned drinks are usually more expensive than the equivalent-sized bottle, whether it's a soft drink or beer – apparently it's less chic to drink from the old-fashioned bottle.

A more effective thirst-quencher is fresh coconut juice, though this is difficult to find in the north. Fresh juices such as orange and lime are also delicious – just make sure they haven't been mixed with tap water. Sugar-cane juice (*mia da*) is safer, since it's pressed right in front of you, and quite delicious. Pasteurized milk, produced by Vinamilk, is now sold in the main towns and cities.

Tea and coffee

Tea-drinking is part of the social ritual in Vietnam. Small cups of refreshing, strong, green tea are presented to all guests or visitors: water is well boiled and safe to drink, as long as the cup itself is clean, and it's considered rude not to take at least a sip. Although your cup will be continually replenished to show hospitality, you don't have to carry on drinking; the polite way to decline a refill is to place your hand over the cup when your host is about to replenish it. Green tea is also served at the end of every restaurant meal, particularly in the south, and usually provided free.

Coffee production has boomed in recent years, largely for export, with serious environmental and social consequences. The Vietnamese drink coffee very strong and in small quantities, usually with a large dollop of condensed milk at the bottom of the cup. Traditionally, coffee is filtered at the table by means of a small dripper balanced over the cup or glass, which sometimes sits in a bowl of hot water to keep it warm. However, places accustomed to tourists increasingly run to fresh (pasteurized) milk, while in the main cities you'll now find fancy Western-style cafés turning out decent lattes and cappuccinos. Highland Coffee has become Vietnam's very own Starbucks-style chain, while out in the sticks you're best off going for cafés with a Trung Nguyen sign.

A TRADITIONAL TIPPLE

While beer and imported spirits are drunk throughout Vietnam, the traditional tipple is **ruou can**, or rice-distilled liquor. Until recently, *ruou can* was regarded as decidedly downmarket, the preserve of labourers, farmers and ethnic minorities. Nowadays, however, it's becoming popular among the middle class and especially young urban sophisticates – including a growing number of women – as city-centre bars and restaurants begin to offer better quality *ruou can*.

Recipes for *ruou can* are a closely guarded secret, but its basic constituents are regular or glutinous rice, the latter of which is said to be more aromatic and have a fuller, smoother taste. Selected herbs and fruits are sometimes steeped in the liquor to enhance its flavour and, supposedly, to add all sorts of medicinal and health benefits. You'll also see jars containing snakes, geckos and even whole crows. Traditionally, the basic ingredients are heated together and buried in the ground for a month or more to ferment. Nowadays, more modern – and hygienic – techniques are used to produce *ruou can* for general consumption. Look out for the high-quality rice-distilled liquors marketed under the Son Tinh brand (ⓦ sontinh.com).

The **ethnic minorities** of the northwest (Thai and Muong) concoct their own home-distilled *ruou can*, sometimes known as stem alcohol. Visitors are often invited to gather round the communal jar to drink the liquor through thin, bamboo straws. In more traditional villages it's regarded as a sacred ritual, which it would be an insult to refuse. You will hear the toast *Chuc suc khoe* (your health) and, for more serious drinking sessions, *Tram phan tram* (down in one)!

Alcoholic drinks

In Vietnam, drinking alcohol is a social activity to be shared with friends. You'll rarely see the Vietnamese drinking alone and never without eating. Be prepared for lots of toasts to health, wealth and happiness, and no doubt to international understanding, too. It's the custom to fill the glasses of your fellow guests; someone else will fill yours.

Canned and **bottled beers** brewed under licence in Vietnam include Tiger, Heineken, Carlsberg and San Miguel, but there are also plenty of very drinkable – and cheaper – local beers around, such as Halida, 333 (Ba Ba Ba) and Bivina. Some connoisseurs rate Bière la Rue from Da Nang tops, though Saigon Export, Hanoi Beer and BGI are also fine brews. Many other towns boast their own local beers; in many places, such as Haiphong and Thanh Hoa, it's simply named after the town, while Hue has a few brands including Huda and Hue Beer. They're all worth a try.

Roughly forty years ago technology for making **bia hoi** (draught beer) was introduced from Czechoslovakia and it is now quaffed in vast quantities, particularly in the north. Bia hoi may taste fairly weak, but it measures in at up to four percent alcohol. It's also ridiculously cheap – around 5000đ a glass – and supposedly unadulterated with chemicals, so in theory you're less likely to get a hangover. Bia hoi has a 24-hour shelf life, which means the better places sell out by early evening, and that you're unlikely to be drinking it into the wee hours. In the south, you're more likely to be drinking **bia tuoi** ("fresh" beer), a close relation of bia hoi but served from pressurized barrels. Outlets are usually open at lunchtime, and then again in the evening from 5pm to 9pm.

Rice wine, known as **ruou**, is the national spirit, and especially popular in rural areas, where it's often homemade – basically local moonshine, it's occasionally dangerous. The bottled versions are safer, though at 40 percent alcohol by volume they certainly pack a punch, which you'll most likely still be feeling the next morning.

Wine of the conventional kind is becoming increasingly popular in Vietnam – even in small towns, you'll easily track some down, and imported bottles continue to crop up in the most unexpected places. Local production dates from the French era, and is centred around Da Lat – the main producer is Vang Da Lat, bottles of which will cost from 50,000đ in a shop, and often double that at a restaurant. Only at top hotels, restaurants or specialist shops will you find decent imported bottles that have been properly stored; you'll be paying premium prices for these.

Health

Vietnam's health problems read like a dictionary of tropical medicine. Diseases that are under control elsewhere in Southeast Asia have been sustained here by poverty, dietary deficiencies, poor healthcare and the disruption caused by half a century of war. The situation is improving rapidly, however, and by coming prepared and taking a few simple precautions while in the country, you're unlikely to come down with anything worse than a cold or a dose of travellers' diarrhoea.

Before you go

When planning your trip it's wise to visit a **doctor** as early as possible, preferably at least two months before you leave, to allow time to complete any recommended courses of **vaccinations**. It's also advisable to have a troubleshooting **dental check-up** – and remember that you generally need to start taking **anti-malarial tablets** at least one week before your departure.

For up-to-the-minute information, contact a specialized **travel clinic**; most clinics also sell travel-associated accessories, including mosquito nets and first-aid kits.

Vaccinations

No **vaccinations** are required for Vietnam (except yellow fever if you're coming directly from an area where the disease is endemic), but typhoid and hepatitis A jabs are recommended; it's also worth ensuring you're up to date with boosters such as tetanus and polio. Additional injections to consider, depending on the season and risk of exposure, are hepatitis B, Japanese encephalitis, meningitis and rabies. All these immunizations can be obtained at international clinics in Hanoi, Ho Chi Minh City and Da Nang, but it's less hassle and usually cheaper to get them done at home. Get all your shots recorded on an **International Certificate of Vaccination** and carry this with your passport when travelling abroad.

For protection against **hepatitis A**, which is spread by contaminated food and water, the vaccine is expensive but extremely effective – an initial injection followed by a booster after six to twelve months provides immunity for up to ten years. **Hepatitis B**, like the HIV virus, can be passed on through unprotected sexual contact, blood transfusions and dirty needles. The very effective vaccine (three injections over six months) is recommended for anyone in a high-risk category, including those travelling extensively in rural areas for prolonged periods, with access to only basic medical care. It's also now possible – and cheaper – to have a combined vaccination against both hepatitis A and B; the course comprises three injections over six months.

The risk of contracting **Japanese encephalitis** is extremely small, but, as the disease is untreatable, those travelling for a month or more in the countryside, especially in the north during and soon after the summer rainy season (June–Oct), should consider immunization. The course consists of two or three injections over a month with the last dose administered at least ten days before departure. Note that it is not recommended for those with liver, heart or kidney disorders, or for multiple-allergy sufferers. If your plans include long stays in remote areas your doctor may also recommend vaccination against **meningitis** (a single shot) and **rabies**.

Mosquito-borne diseases

Both the Red River and Mekong deltas (including Hanoi and Ho Chi Minh City) have few incidences of mosquito-borne **malaria**. The coastal plain north of Nha Trang is also considered relatively safe. Malaria occurs frequently in the highlands and rural areas, notably the central highlands, as well as the southern provinces of Ca Mau, Bac Lieu and Tay Ninh. The majority of cases involve the most dangerous strain, *Plasmodium falciparum*, which can be fatal if not treated promptly. If you'll be spending time in the highlands, you should consider taking a course of anti-malarial drugs; check with your doctor before travelling to Vietnam.

Mosquitoes are also responsible for transmitting dengue fever and Japanese encephalitis. **Dengue** is carried by a variety of mosquitoes active in the daytime (particularly two hours after sunrise and several hours before sunset) and occurs mostly in the Mekong Delta, including Ho Chi Minh City, though the chances of being infected remain small. There is a more dangerous version called dengue haemorrhage fever, which primarily affects children but is extremely rare among foreign visitors to Vietnam. If you notice an unusual tendency to bleed or bruise, seek medical advice immediately.

The key **preventive** measure for all these considerations is to avoid getting bitten by mosquitoes in the first place. Mosquitoes are most active at dawn and dusk, so at these times wear long sleeves, trousers and socks, avoid dark colours and perfumes, which attract mosquitoes, and put repellent on all exposed skin. Sprays and lotions containing around thirty to forty percent DEET (diethyltoluamide) are effective and can also be used to treat clothes, but the chemical is toxic: keep it away from eyes and open wounds.

Many hotels and guesthouses provide mosquito nets over beds or meshing on windows and doors. Air-conditioning and fans also help keep mosquitoes at bay, as do mosquito coils and knockdown insecticide sprays (available locally), though none of these measures is as effective as a decent net.

AVIAN FLU

Avian flu or **bird flu** is a contagious disease normally limited to birds and, less commonly, pigs. However, the virus can spread to humans by direct contact with infected poultry or with contaminated surfaces. In the 2004–05 outbreak in Vietnam of the highly contagious **H5N1** strain of the disease, there were around sixty confirmed cases involving humans, of which some forty were fatal, according to the World Health Organization. The vast majority of people infected had direct contact with diseased birds. Since the initial outbreak, around 130 cases have been reported, the most recent in February 2014.

Evidence of human-to-human transmission has yet to be confirmed but the indications are that, if it is possible, it is extremely rare and has so far been limited to close family members. The main fear among health experts is that the virus will mutate into a form that is highly infectious to and easily spread among humans.

At present the risk to travellers visiting infected areas remains low. As a precaution, however, you are advised to avoid contact with live poultry and pigs, including live animal markets, and to eat only well-cooked poultry and eggs. Check the latest with your doctor or travel health specialist prior to travel. You'll also find up-to-date information on the following websets: Ⓦ avianinfluenza.org.vn and Ⓦ who.int/influenza/human_animal_interface/en.

Bites and creepy-crawlies

Bed bugs, fleas, lice or scabies can be picked up from dirty bedclothes, though this is relatively unusual in Vietnam. Try not to scratch bites, which easily become septic. Ticks picked up walking through scrub may carry a strain of typhus; carry out regular body inspections and remove ticks promptly.

Rabies is contracted by being bitten, or even licked on broken skin or the eyes, by an infected mammal. The best strategy is to give all animals, especially dogs, cats and monkeys, a wide berth.

Vietnam has several poisonous **snakes** but in general snakes steer clear of humans and it's very rare to get bitten. Avoid walking through long grass or undergrowth, and wear boots when walking off-road. If bitten, immobilize the limb (most snake bites occur on the lower leg) to slow down absorption of the venom and remove any tight-fitting socks or other clothing from around the wound. It's important to seek medical assistance as quickly as possible. It helps if you can take the (dead) snake to be identified, or at least remember what it looked like.

Leeches are more common and, though harmless, can be unpleasant. Long trousers, sleeves and socks help prevent them getting a grip. The best way to get rid of leeches is to burn them off with a lighted match or cigarette; alternatively rub alcohol or salt onto them.

Parasitic worms enter the body either via contaminated food, or through the skin, especially the soles of the feet. You may notice worms in your stools, or experience other indications such as mild abdominal pain leading, very rarely, to acute intestinal blockage (roundworm, the most common), an itchy anus (threadworm) or anaemia (hookworm). An infestation is easily treated with worming tablets from a pharmacy.

Heat trouble

Don't underestimate the strength of the tropical sun: **sunburn** can be avoided by restricting your exposure to the midday sun and liberal use of high-factor sunscreens. Drinking plenty of water will prevent **dehydration**, but if you do become dehydrated – the signs are infrequent or irregular urination – drink a salt and sugar solution.

Heatstroke is more serious and may require hospital treatment. Indications are a high temperature, lack of sweating, a fast pulse and red skin. Reducing your body temperature with a lukewarm shower will provide initial relief.

High humidity often causes **heat rashes**, **prickly heat** and **fungal infections**. Prevention and cure are the same: wear loose clothes made of natural fibres, wash frequently and dry off thoroughly afterwards. Talcum powder helps, particularly zinc oxidebased products (prickly heat powder), as does the use of mild antiseptic soap.

Sexually transmitted diseases

Until recently Vietnam carried out very little screening for sex workers, injecting drug users and other high-risk groups. As a result, **sexually transmitted diseases** such as gonorrhoea, syphilis and AIDS had been flourishing, though fortunately awareness is growing and the number of AIDS victims, at least, is levelling out. It is, therefore, extremely unwise to contemplate casual unprotected sex, and bear in mind that Vietnamese **condoms** (bao cao su) are often poor-quality (more reliable imported varieties are available in major cities).

Getting medical help

Pharmacies can generally help with minor injuries or ailments and in major towns you will usually find a pharmacist who speaks English. The selection of reliable Asian and Western products on the market is improving rapidly, and Ho Chi Minh City and Hanoi now have well-stocked pharmacies. That said, drugs past their shelf life and even counterfeit medicines are rife, so inspect packaging carefully, check use-by dates – and bring anything you know you're likely to need from home, including **oral contraceptives**. **Tampons** are sold in Hanoi and Ho Chi Minh City, but don't count on getting them easily elsewhere.

Local **hospitals** can also treat minor problems, but in a real emergency your best bet is to head for Hanoi or Ho Chi Minh City. Hospitals in both these cities can handle most eventualities and you also have the option of one of the excellent international medical centres. Addresses of clinics and hospitals can be found in our "Listings" sections for major towns throughout the book. Note that doctors and hospitals expect immediate cash payment for health services rendered; you will then have to seek reimbursement from your insurance company (make sure you get receipts for any payments you make).

The media

All media in Vietnam are under tight government control. There is, however, a slight glimmer of less draconian censorship, with an increasing number of stories covering corruption at even quite senior levels and more criticism of government policies and ministers, albeit very mild by Western standards.

Newspapers and magazines

Vietnam has several English-language **newspapers and magazines**, of which the daily *Viet Nam News* (Ⓦ vietnamnews.vn) has the widest distribution. It provides a brief – and very select – run-down of local, regional and international news, as well as snippets on art and culture. Though short on general news, both the weekly *Vietnam Investment Review* (Ⓦ vir.com.vn) and the monthly *Vietnam Economic Times* cover issues in greater depth and are worth looking at for an insight into what makes the Vietnamese economy tick.

Both also publish useful supplements (*Time Out* and *The Guide* respectively) with selective restaurant and nightlife **listings** mainly covering Hanoi and Ho Chi Minh City, plus feature articles on culture and tourist destinations. However, they have been superseded by the excellent free magazines *The Word* (Ⓦ wordvietnam.com) and *AsiaLife* (Ⓦ asialifemagazine.com/Vietnam), which both carry listings of bars and restaurants as well as articles on aspects of Vietnamese culture; look out for them in restaurants and bars that cater to foreigners.

Foreign publications such as the *International New York Times*, *Time*, *Newsweek*, *The Financial Times* and the *Bangkok Post* are sold by street vendors and at some of the larger bookshops and in the newsstands of more upmarket hotels in Ho Chi Minh City (see p.93) and Hanoi (see p.372).

Televison

Vietnamese **television** airs a mix of government-approved films, music shows, news programmes, soaps, sport and foreign (mostly American, Korean and Japanese) imports. VTV1, the main domestic channel, occasionally presents a news summary in English. However, most hotels provide satellite TV, offering BBC, CNN, MTV and HBO as standard.

Radio

The government **radio** station, Voice of Vietnam (Ⓦ english.vov.vn), began life in 1945 during the August Revolution. It became famous during the American War when "Hanoi Hannah" broadcast propaganda programmes to American GIs. Nowadays it maintains six channels, of which VOV5 broadcasts English-language programmes several times a day covering a whole range of subjects: news, weather, sport, entertainment and culture, even market prices. You can pick up the broadcasts on FM in and around Hanoi and Ho Chi Minh City.

To keep in touch with the full spectrum of international news, however, you'll need to go online or get a short-wave radio to pick up one of the world service channels, such as **BBC World Service** (Ⓦ bbc.co.uk/worldserviceradio) and **Voice of America** (Ⓦ voanews.com); local frequencies are listed on the relevant website.

Crime and personal safety

Vietnam is a relatively safe country for visitors, including women travelling alone. In fact, given the country's recent history, many tourists, particularly Americans, are pleasantly surprised at the warm reception that foreign travellers receive. That said, petty crime is on the rise – though it's still relatively small-scale and shouldn't be a problem if you take common-sense precautions. Generally, the hassles you'll encounter will be the milder sort of coping with pushy vendors and over-enthusiastic touts and beggars.

Petty crime

As a tourist, you're an obvious target for thieves (who may include your fellow travellers): carry your passport, traveller's cheques and other valuables in a concealed **money belt**. Don't leave anything important lying about in your room; use a safe, if you have one. A cable lock, or **padlock** and chain, comes in handy for doors and windows in cheap hotels, and is useful for securing your pack on trains and buses. It's not a bad idea to keep US$100 or so separate from the rest of your cash, along with insurance policy details and photocopies of important documents, such as the relevant pages of your passport including your visa stamp.

At street level it's best not to be ostentatious: forego eye-catching jewellery and flashy watches, try to be discreet when taking out your cash, and be particularly wary in **crowds** and on **public transport**. If your pack is on the top of the bus, make sure it's attached securely (usually everything is tied down with ropes) and keep an eye on it during the most vulnerable times – before departure, at meal stops and on arrival at your destination. On trains, either cable-lock your pack or put it under the bottom bench-seat, out of public view. The odd instance has been reported of travellers being drugged and then robbed, so it's best not to accept food or drink from anyone you don't know and trust. Bear in mind that when walking or riding in a cyclo you are vulnerable to moped-borne **snatch-thieves**; don't wear cameras or expensive sunglasses hanging round your neck and keep a firm grip on your bags. If you do become a target, however, it's best to let go rather than risk being pulled into the traffic and suffering serious injury.

The place you are most likely to encounter street crime is in **Ho Chi Minh City**, which has a fairly bad reputation for bag-snatchers, pickpockets and con artists. Be wary of innocent-looking kids and grannies who may be acting as decoys for thieves – especially in the bar districts and other popular tourist hangouts. It's best to avoid taking a cyclo at night, and you'd be unwise to walk alone at any time outside Districts One and Three.

Petty crime, much of it drug- and prostitution-related, is also a problem in **Nha Trang**, where you should watch your belongings at all times on the beach. Again, be wary of taking a cyclo after dark and women should avoid walking alone at night. Single males, on the other hand, are a particular target for "taxi girls", many of whom also double as thieves.

It's important not to get paranoid, however: crime levels in Vietnam are still a long way behind those of Western countries, and violent crime against tourists is extremely rare.

EMERGENCY PHONE NUMBERS

The following numbers apply throughout Vietnam. If possible, get a Vietnamese-speaker to call on your behalf.
Police ☎113
Fire ☎114
Ambulance ☎115

If you do have anything stolen, you'll need to go to the nearest **police** station to make a report in order to claim on your insurance. Try to recruit an English-speaker to come along with you – someone at your hotel should be able to help.

"Social evils" and serious crime

Since liberalization and *doi moi*, Vietnamese society has seen an increase in prostitution, drugs – including hard drugs – and more serious crimes. These so-called "**social evils**" are viewed as a direct consequence of reduced controls on society and ensuing Westernization. The police have imposed midnight closing on bars and clubs for several years now, mainly because of drugs, but also to curb general rowdiness, although you'll always find the occasional bar that somehow manages to keep serving, particularly around De Tham in Ho Chi Minh City. That apart, the campaign against social evils should have little effect on most foreign tourists.

Single Western males tend to get solicited by **prostitutes** in cheap provincial and seaside hotels, though more commonly by women cruising on motorbikes. Quite apart from any higher moral considerations, bear in mind that AIDS is a serious problem in Vietnam, though the epidemic has shown signs of stabilizing.

Finally, having anything to do with **drugs** in Vietnam is extremely unwise. At night there's a fair amount of drug selling on the streets of Ho Chi Minh City, Hanoi, Nha Trang and even Sa Pa, and it's not unknown for dealers to turn buyers in to the police. Fines and jail sentences are imposed for lesser offences, while the **death penalty** is regularly imposed for possessing, trading or smuggling larger quantities.

Military hazards and UXO

Not surprisingly, the Vietnamese authorities are sensitive about **military installations** and strategic areas – including border regions, military camps (of which there are many), bridges, airports, naval dockyards and even train stations. Anyone taking photographs in the vicinity of such sites risks having the memory card removed from their camera or being fined.

Unexploded ordnance from past conflicts still poses a threat in some areas; the problem is most acute in the Demilitarized Zone, where each year a number of local farmers, scrap-metal scavengers or children are killed or injured. Wherever you are, stick to well-trodden paths and never touch any shells or half-buried chunks of metal.

Beggars, hassle and scams

Given the number of disabled, war-wounded and unemployed in Vietnam, there are surprisingly few **beggars** around. Most people are actually trying hard to earn a living somehow, and many day-tours include a visit to a factory that employs disabled workers to produce handicrafts or local products.

At many tourist spots, you may well be swamped by a gaggle of children or teenagers selling cold drinks, fruit and chewing gum. Although they can sometimes be a bit overwhelming, as often as not they're just out to practise their English and be entertained for a while. They may even turn out to be excellent guides, in which case it's only fair that you buy something from them in return.

A common **scam** among taxi drivers is to tell new arrivals in a town that the hotel they ask for is closed or has moved or changed its name. Instead, they head for a hotel that pays them commission. This may work out fine (new hotels often use this method to become known), but more often than not it's a substandard hotel and you will in any case pay over the odds since the room rate will include the driver's commission. To avoid being ripped off, always insist on being taken to the exact address of your chosen hotel, at least just to check the story.

Another common complaint is that organized **tours** don't live up to what was promised. There are more people on the tour than stated, for example, or the room doesn't have air-conditioning, or the guide's English is limited. If it's a group tour and you've paid up front, unfortunately there's very little you can do beyond complaining to the agent on your return; you may be lucky and get some form of compensation, but it's very unlikely. As always, you tend to get what you pay for, so avoid signing up for dirt-cheap tours.

Women travellers

Vietnam is generally a safe country for women to travel around alone. Most Vietnamese will simply be curious as to why you are on your own and the chances of encountering any threatening behaviour are extremely rare. That said, it pays to take the normal precautions, especially **late at night** when there are few people on the streets and you should avoid taking a cyclo by yourself; use a taxi instead – metered taxis are generally considered safest.

Most Vietnamese women **dress** modestly, keeping covered from top to toe, unless their profession requires them to show off their assets. It helps to dress modestly too and to avoid wearing skimpy shorts and vests, which are considered by some men an invitation to paid sex. Topless sunbathing, even beside a hotel pool, is a complete no-no.

Festivals and religious events

The Vietnamese year follows a rhythm of festivals and religious observances, ranging from solemn family gatherings at the ancestral altar to national celebrations culminating in Tet, the Vietnamese New Year. In between are countless local festivals, most notably in the Red River Delta, honouring the tutelary spirit of the village or community temple.

The majority of festivals take place in spring, with a second flurry in the autumn months. One festival you might want to make a note of, however, is **Tet** (see box opposite); not only does most of Vietnam close down for the week, but either side of the holiday local transport services are stretched to the limit and international flights are filled by returning overseas Vietnamese.

Many Vietnamese festivals are **Chinese** in origin, imbued with a distinctive flavour over the centuries, but minority groups also hold their own specific celebrations. The ethnic **minorities** continue to punctuate the year with rituals that govern sowing, harvest or hunting, as well as elaborate rites of passage surrounding birth and death. The **Cao Dai** religion has its own array of festivals, while **Christian** communities throughout Vietnam observe the major ceremonies. Christmas is marked as a religious ceremony only by the faithful, though it's becoming a major event for all Vietnamese as an excuse to shop and party, with sax-playing santas greeting shoppers in front of malls.

The ceremonies you're most likely to see are **weddings and funerals**. The tenth lunar month is the most auspicious time for weddings, though at other times you'll also encounter plenty of wedding cavalcades on the road, their lead vehicle draped in colourful ribbons. Funeral processions are recognizable from the white headbands worn by mourners, while close family members dress completely in white. Both weddings and funerals are characterized by streetside parties under makeshift marquees, and since both tend to be joyous occasions, it's often difficult to know what you're witnessing, unless you spot a bridal gown or portrait of the deceased on display.

TET: THE VIETNAMESE NEW YEAR

"Tet", simply meaning festival, is the accepted name for Vietnam's most important annual event, properly known as **Tet Nguyen Dan**, or festival of the first day. Tet lasts for seven days and falls sometime between the last week of January and the third week of February, on the night of the new moon. This is a time when families get together to celebrate renewal and hope for the new year, when ancestral spirits are welcomed back to the household and when everyone in Vietnam becomes a year older – age is reckoned by the new year and not by individual birthdays.

There's an almost tangible sense of excitement leading up to midnight on the eve of Tet, though the welcoming of the new year is now a much more subdued – and less dangerous – affair since firecrackers were banned in 1995. Instead, all the major cities hold fireworks displays.

PREPARATIONS

Tet is all about **starting the year afresh**, with a clean slate and good intentions. Not only is the house scrubbed, but all debts are paid off and those who can afford it have a haircut and buy new clothes. To attract favourable spirits, good-luck charms are put in the house, most commonly cockerels or the trinity of male figures representing prosperity, happiness and longevity. The crucial moments are the first minutes and hours of the new year as these set the pattern for the whole of the following year. People strive to avoid arguments, swearing or breaking anything – at least during the first three days when a single ill word could tempt bad luck into the house for the whole year ahead. The first visitor on the morning of Tet is also vitally significant: the ideal is someone respected, wealthy and happily married who will bring good fortune to the family; the bereaved, unemployed, accident-prone and even pregnant, on the other hand, are considered ill-favoured. This honour carries with it an onerous responsibility, however: if the family has a bad year, it will be the first-footer's fault.

ONG TAU

Tet kicks off seven days before the new moon with the festival of **Ong Tau**, the god of the hearth (23rd day of the twelfth month). Ong Tau keeps watch over the household throughout the year, wards off evil spirits and makes an annual report of family events, good or bad, to the Jade Emperor. In order to send Ong Tau off to heaven in a benevolent mood, the family cleans its house from top to bottom, and makes offerings to him, including pocket money and a new set of clothes. Ong Tau returns home at midnight on the first chime of the new year and it's this, together with welcoming the ancestral spirits back to share in the party, that warrants such a massive celebration.

FEASTS AND GOOD FORTUNE

The week-long festival is marked by **feasting**: special foods are eaten at Tet, such as pickled vegetables, candied lotus seeds and sugared fruits, all of which are first offered at the family altar. The most famous delicacy is *banh chung* (*banh tet* in the south), a thick square or cylinder of sweet, sticky rice that is prepared only for Tet. The rice is wrapped round a mixture of green-bean paste, pork fat and meat marinated in *nuoc mam*, and then boiled in banana leaves, which impart a pale green colour. According to legend, an impoverished prince of the Hung dynasty invented the cakes over two thousand years ago; his father was so impressed by the simplicity of his son's gift that he named the prince as his heir.

Tet is an expensive time for Vietnamese families, many of whom save for months to get the new year off to a good start. Apart from special foods and new clothes, it's traditional to give children red envelopes containing *li xi*, or lucky money, and to decorate homes with spring blossoms. In the week before Tet, flower markets grace the larger cities: peach blossoms in the north, apricot in Hue and mandarin in the south. Plum and kumquat (symbolizing gold coins) are also popular, alongside the more showy, modern blooms of roses, dahlias or gladioli.

Most festivals take place according to the **lunar calendar**, which is also closely linked to the Chinese system with a zodiac of twelve animal signs. The most important times during the lunar month (which lasts 29 or 30 days) are the full moon (day one) and the new moon (day fourteen or fifteen). Festivals are often held at these times, which also hold a special significance for Buddhists, who are supposed to pray at the pagoda and avoid eating meat during the two days. On the eve of each full moon, Hoi An now celebrates a **Full-Moon Festival**: traffic is barred from the town centre, where traditional games, dance and music performances take place under the light of silk lanterns.

All Vietnamese calendars show both the lunar and solar (Gregorian) months and dates, but to be sure of a festival date it's best to check locally.

A FESTIVAL CALENDAR

Tet Late Jan to mid-February. The most important date in the Vietnamese festival calendar is New Year (see box, p.53).

Tay Son Festival Late Jan to mid-February. Martial arts demonstrations in Tay Son District (near Quy Nhon) plus garlanded elephants on parade.

Water-Puppet Festival February. As part of the Tet celebrations a festival of puppetry is held at Thay Pagoda, west of Hanoi.

Lim Singing Festival February–March. Two weeks after Tet, Lim village near Bac Ninh, in the Red River Delta, resounds to the harmonies of "alternate singing" (*quan ho*) as men and women fling improvised lyrics back and forth.

Hai Ba Trung Festival March. The two Trung sisters are honoured with a parade and dancing at Hanoi's Hai Ba Trung temple.

Perfume Pagoda March–April. Vietnam's most famous pilgrimage site is Chua Huong, west of Hanoi. Thousands of Buddhist pilgrims flock to the pagoda for the festival, which climaxes on the full moon (fourteenth or fifteenth day) of the second month, though the pilgrimage continues for a month either side.

Den Ba Chua Kho March–April. The full moon of the second month sees Hanoians congregating at this temple near Bac Ninh, to petition the goddess for success in business.

Thanh Minh April. Ancestral graves are cleaned and offerings of food, flowers and paper votive objects made at the beginning of the third lunar month.

Phat Dan May. Lanterns are hung outside the pagodas and Buddhist homes to commemorate Buddha's birth, enlightenment and the attainment of Nirvana.

Chua Xu Festival May. The stone statue of Chua Xu at Sam Mountain, Chau Doc, is bathed, and thousands flock to honour her.

Tet Doan Ngo Late May to early June. The summer solstice (fifth day of the fifth moon) is marked by festivities aimed at warding off epidemics brought on by the summer heat. This is also the time of dragon-boat races.

Trang Nguyen (or Vu Lan) August. The day of wandering souls is the second most important festival after Tet. Offerings of food and clothes are made to comfort and nourish the unfortunate souls without a home, and all graves are cleaned. This is also time for the forgiveness of faults, when the King of Hell judges everyone's spirits and metes out reward or punishment as appropriate. Until the fifteenth century prisoners were allowed to go home on this day.

Do Son Buffalo-fighting Festival August. Held in Do Son village, near Haiphong.

Kate Festival September–October. The Cham New Year is celebrated in high style at Po Klong Garai and Po Re Me, both near Phan Rang.

Trung Thu September–October. The mid-autumn festival, also known as Children's Day, is when dragon dances take place and children are given lanterns in the shape of stars, carp or dragons. Special cakes, *banh trung thu*, are eaten at this time of year. These are sticky rice cakes filled with lotus seeds, nuts and candied fruits and are either square like the earth (*banh deo*), or round like the moon (*banh nuong*) and containing the yolk of an egg.

Whale Festival September–October. Crowds gather at Lang Ca Ong, Vung Tau, to make offerings to the whales.

Oc Bom Boc Festival November–December. Boat-racing festival in Soc Trang.

Da Lat Flower Festival late December/New Year. An annual extravaganza in which the city shows off the abundance of blooms grown locally.

Christmas December 24. Midnight services at the cathedrals in Hanoi and Ho Chi Minh City and much revelry in the streets.

Sports and outdoor activities

Though Vietnam was slow to develop its huge potential as an outdoor adventure destination, things have really changed in the last few years. Apart from trekking in the mountainous north, visitors can now also go rock-climbing, canyoning, sea kayaking or kitesurfing, among other activities. Da Lat has emerged as Vietnam's adventure sports capital and Mui Ne its surf city, though some sports like mountain biking can be done throughout the country.

Trekking

The easiest and most popular areas for **trekking** are in the northwest mountains around Sa Pa (see p.397) and Mai Chau (see p.416). Sa Pa is also the starting point for ascents of the country's highest peak, Fan Si Pan, though this is likely to become less popular with the opening of a cable car to the summit in 2015. Other options include hiking around Kon Tum (see p.196) or Da Lat (see p.174) in the central highlands or in one of Vietnam's many national parks, including Phong Nha-Ke Bang, Cat Ba, Cuc Phuong, Bach Ma, Cat Tien and Yok Don. In Yok Don you can even go elephant trekking, though prices are rather steep. If you'd like to steer clear of the tourist hordes, a trek in the Pu Luong Nature Reserve (see p.316) is a good way to go.

There's no problem about striking out on your own for a day's hiking. However, for anything more adventurous, particularly if you want to overnight in villages, you'll need to **make arrangements in advance**. This is easily done either before you arrive in Vietnam or through local tour agents, most of which offer organized tours and home-stay accommodation. In most cases you can also make arrangements through guesthouses and guides on the spot. Note that it's essential to take a guide if you are keen to get off the beaten track: many areas are still sensitive about the presence of foreigners.

Cycling and motorbiking

Mountain biking is becoming increasingly popular in Vietnam. The classic ride is from Hanoi to Ho Chi Minh City, a journey of between two and three weeks. Previously, this would have taken you along Highway 1, battling with trucks and buses, but now the more switched-on tour companies are offering excursions down the Ho Chi Minh Highway which runs along the western Truong Son mountain chain, and is so far thankfully free of heavy traffic. This route is also becoming popular among motorbike enthusiasts.

The area around Sa Pa is a focus for biking activity, with tour operators offering excursions to suit all levels of experience and fitness. You can choose from half-day excursions to multi-day outings including overnighting in minority villages. Other good areas for exploring by bike include Mai Chau, Bac Ha, Da Lat and the Mekong Delta. If you prefer to ride mostly on the flat, note that Mai Chau and the Delta are the best places.

North Vietnam is also popular among the **motorbiking** fraternity. Specialist outfits in Hanoi (see p.370) organize tailor-made itineraries taking you way off the beaten track. Two of the most popular motorbike adventures in the country are the northwest loop (from Hanoi to Sa Pa and back) and the Dong Van Karst Plateau Geopark (from Hanoi to Ha Giang Province and back). If you enjoy motorbike trips but don't fancy riding yourself, hook up with the Easy Riders in Da Lat (see p.180), who can arrange short or long itineraries anywhere in the country for reasonable prices.

Watersports

With its 3000km coastline, Vietnam should be a paradise for watersports, but the options remain fairly limited at present, for a variety of reasons. One is simply a matter of access: the infrastructure is not yet in place (though this is changing fast). More crucial is the presence of potentially dangerous **undercurrents** along much of the coast, accompanied by strong winds at certain times of year. Many

of the big beach resorts have guards or put out flags in season indicating where it's safe to swim. Elsewhere, check carefully before taking the plunge.

While many of the beaches along the coast are great for **swimming**, the best are those around Mui Ne and Nha Trang, with Hoi An and Da Nang close behind. There are also some delightfully quiet beaches around Ca Na (see p.221) and to the south of Quy Nhon (see p.236). Mui Ne is the country's top venue for **windsurfing** and **kitesurfing**, both of which are now hugely popular; in fact, Mui Ne hosts an international kitesurfing competition each spring (usually Feb).

Phu Quoc Island (see p.160), off Vietnam's southern coast, is also famed not only for its fabulous beaches but also as the country's top spot for **snorkelling** and **scuba-diving**. The Con Dao Islands and Nha Trang are other popular places to don a snorkel or wet suit, but wherever you dive, it's worth noting that standards of maintenance aren't always great, so check equipment carefully and only go out with a properly qualified and registered operator that you trust.

Heading inland, the rivers and waterfalls around Da Lat provide good possibilities for **canyoning** and **rock-climbing**, though Cat Ba Island is a good alternative if you'd like to combine rock-climbing with sightseeing in Ha Long Bay.

In north Vietnam Ha Long Bay is the watersports centre, while rock-climbing here is becoming big as well, organized from Cat Ba. Most boat tours of the bay allow time for swimming and kayaking – weather permitting – while there are decent beaches on Cat Ba and better still on remote Quan Lan Island. A few tour agents offer **sea-kayaking** trips on the bay, sometimes overnighting in a basic hut or tent on a deserted beach (see p.339).

Other activities

Vietnam has over 850 species of birds, including several that have only been identified in the past few years. The best places for **birdwatching** are the national parks, including Cuc Phuong (famous also for its springtime butterfly displays), Bach Ma and Cat Tien. The rare Sarus crane, among many other species, spends the dry season in and around the Tram Chim National Park in the Mekong Delta. For more information check out ⓦ vietnambirding.com or ⓦ birdwatchingvietnam.net.

Finally, there are now dozens of excellent **golf** courses in Vietnam – around Ho Chi Minh City, Hanoi, Phan Thiet, Da Nang and Da Lat among others – all with much cheaper green fees than in the West.

Shopping

Souvenir-hunters will find rich pickings in Vietnam, whose eye-catching handicrafts and mementos range from colonial currency and stamps to fabrics and basketware crafted by the country's ethnic minorities, and from limpet-like conical hats to fake US Army-issue Zippo lighters. Throughout the Guide, we've highlighted places to shop, but in general you'll find the best quality, choice and prices in Ho Chi Minh City, Hanoi and Hoi An. Though you'll find more shops now have fixed prices, particularly those catering to tourists, in markets and rural areas prices are almost always open to negotiation (see box below).

Clothing, arts and crafts

Few Western tourists leave Vietnam without the obligatory **conical hat**, or *non la*, sewn from rain- and sun-proof palm fronds; at around 30,000đ for a basic version, they're definitely an affordable keepsake. From the city of Hue comes a more elaborate version, the **poem hat**, or *non bai tho*, in whose brim are inlays which, when held up to the light, reveal lines of poetry or scenes from Vietnamese legend. Vietnamese women traditionally wear the **ao dai** – baggy silk trousers under a knee-length silk tunic slit up both sides. Extraordinarily elegant, *ao dai* can be bought off the peg anywhere in the country for around US$30; or, if you can spare a few days for fitting, you can have one tailor-made for US$50–100, depending on the material.

Local **silk** is sold by the metre in Vietnam's more sizeable markets and in countless outlets in Hoi An, along Dong Khoi in Ho Chi Minh City and on Hanoi's Hang Gai. These same shops also sell ready-made clothes and accessories, including embroidered silk handbags and shoes, and most also offer tailoring. In general, Hoi An's tailors have the best reputation, either working from a pattern book or copying an item you take along. Just make sure you allow plenty of time for fittings.

Embroidered **cotton**, in the form of tablecloths, sheets and pillowcases, also makes a popular souvenir. Meanwhile, the sartorial needs of backpackers are well catered for in major tourist destinations, where **T-shirt** sellers do brisk business. Predictably popular designs include a portrait of Uncle Ho, and the yellow Communist star on a red background.

Traditional handicrafts

Of the many types of traditional handicrafts on offer in Vietnam, **lacquerware** (*son mai*) is among the most beautiful. It is also incredibly light, so won't add significantly to your baggage weight. Made by applying multiple layers of resin onto an article and then polishing vigorously to achieve a deep, lustrous sheen, lacquer is used to decorate furniture, boxes, chopsticks and bangles and is sometimes embellished with eggshell or inlays of **mother-of-pearl** (which is also used in its own right, on screens and pictures) – common motifs are animals, fish and elaborate scrolling. More recently, the lacquerware tradition has been hijacked by more contemporary icons, and it's now possible to buy colourful lacquerware paintings of Mickey Mouse, Tin Tin and Batman. Imported synthetic lacquer has also made an appearance. These brightly coloured, almost

---

THE ART OF BARGAINING

The Vietnamese, not unreasonably, see tourists as wildly rich – how else could they afford to stop working and travel the world – and a **first quoted price** is usually pitched accordingly. It makes sense, therefore, to be prepared.

First of all, do your homework. Find out the approximate going rate for the item that interests you, either from your hotel or fellow travellers, or from one of the increasing number of fixed-price shops – remembering to take into account the difference in quality, for example, between mass-produced and hand-crafted goods.

The trick then is to remain **friendly** and amused, but also to be realistic: traders will quickly lose interest in a sale if they think you aren't playing the game fairly. Any show of aggression, and you've lost it in more ways than one. If you feel you're on the verge of agreement, **moving away** often pays dividends – it's amazing how often you'll be called back.

Keep a sense of **perspective**. If a session of bargaining is becoming very protracted, step back and remind yourself that you're often arguing the toss over mere pennies – nothing to you, but a lot to the average Vietnamese.

metallic, finishes may not be for the purist, but they make for eye-catching bowls, vases and all sorts of household items.

Bronze, **brass** and **jade** are also put to good use, appearing in various forms such as carvings, figurines and jewellery. In Hue, brass and copper **teapots** are popular. Of the porcelain and ceramics available across the country, thigh-high **ceramic elephants** and other animal figurines are the quirkiest buys – though decidedly tricky to carry home. Look out, too, for boxes and other knick-knacks made from wonderfully aromatic **cinnamon** and **camphor wood**. For something a little more culturally elevated, you could invest in a **water puppet** or a traditional **musical instrument** (see p.483).

Vietnam's **ethnic minorities** are producing increasingly sophisticated fare for the tourist market. Fabrics – sometimes shot through with shimmering gold braid – are their main asset, sold in lengths and also made into **purses, shoulder bags** and other accoutrements. The minorities of the central highlands are adept at **basketwork**, fashioning backpacks, baskets and mats, and **bamboo pipes**. Hanoi probably has the greatest variety of **minority handicrafts** on sale, though you'll also find plenty available in Ho Chi Minh City. In the far north, Sa Pa is a popular place to buy Hmong clothes, bags and **skull-caps**, and you'll find lengths of woven fabrics or embroidery in markets throughout the northern mountains.

Paintings

A healthy fine arts scene exists in Vietnam, and **painting** in particular is thriving. In the galleries of Hanoi, Ho Chi Minh City and Hoi An you'll find exquisite works in oil, watercolour, lacquer, charcoal and silk weaving by the country's leading artists. Hanoi is the best single place to look for contemporary art.

For the top names you can expect to pay hundreds or even thousands of dollars. Buyer beware, however: many artists find it lucrative to knock out multiple copies of their own or other people's work. You'll need to know what you're doing, or to buy from a reputable gallery.

A cheap alternative is to snap up a reproduction of a famous image by Dali or Van Gogh, while something essentially Vietnamese are reproductions of Communist **propaganda posters**, which are on sale everywhere.

Books, stamps and coins

You can buy photocopied editions of almost all the **books** ever published on Vietnam from strolling vendors in Hanoi and Ho Chi Minh City. However, because of the success of these pirated books, bookstores rarely stock the originals. There is a limited range of locally published coffee-table books, histories and guides available from bona-fide bookshops and the more upmarket hotels. Both Hanoi and Ho Chi Minh City have secondhand bookshops where you can exchange or buy used books, but the choice is limited, so if you're a fussy reader, stock up before your journey (or buy ebooks online).

Philatelists meanwhile will enjoy browsing through the old Indochinese **stamps** sold in the souvenir shops of Hanoi and Ho Chi Minh City. Similarly, old **notes** and **coins**, including French-issue piastres and US Army credits, are available.

Memorabilia, trinkets and food

Army surplus gear is still a money-spinner, though fatigues, belts, canteens and dog tags purportedly stolen from a dead or wounded GI are bound to be fakes. The green **pith helmets** with a red star on the front, worn first by the NVA during the American War and now by the regular Vietnamese Army, find more takers. Other items that sell like hot cakes, especially in the south, are fake **Zippo lighters** bearing such pithy adages as "When I die bury me face down, so the whole damn army can kiss my ass" and "We are the unwilling, led by the unqualified, doin' the unnecessary for the ungrateful", though they're not at all authentic GI issue. In Ho Chi Minh City, extravagant wooden **model ships** are sold in a string of shops on Hai Ba Trung, at the east side of Lam Son Square.

Finally, **foodstuffs** that may tempt you include coffee from the central highlands, candied strawberries and artichoke tea from Da Lat, coconut candies from the Mekong Delta, preserved miniature tangerines from Hoi An and packets of tea and dried herbs and spices from the northern highlands. As for **drinks**, most of the concoctions itemized on p.502 are securely bottled. The Soc Tinh range of rice-distilled liquor makes an attractively packaged souvenir.

Travelling with children

Travelling through Vietnam with children can be challenging and fun. The Vietnamese adore kids and make a huge fuss of them, with fair-haired kids coming in for even more manhandling than usual.

The main concern will probably be **hygiene**: Vietnam can be distinctly unsanitary, and children's stomachs tend to be especially sensitive to bacteria. Avoiding spicy foods will help while their stomachs adjust, but if children do become sick it's crucial to keep up their fluid intake, so as to avoid dehydration. Bear in mind, too, that **healthcare facilities** are fairly basic outside Hanoi and Ho Chi Minh City, so make sure your travel insurance includes full medical evacuation.

Long bus journeys are tough on young children, so wherever possible, take the train or plane – at least the kids can get up and move about in safety. There are reduced fares for children on domestic flights, trains and open-tour buses. On trains, for example, it's free for under-5s (as long as they sit on your lap) and half-price for children aged 5 to 10. Open-tour buses follow roughly the same policy, though children paying a reduced fare are not entitled to a seat; if you don't want them on your lap you'll have to pay full fare. Tours are usually either free or half-price for children.

Many budget **hotels** have family rooms with one double and two single beds, which are generally good value. At more expensive hotels under-12s can normally stay free of charge in their parents' rooms and baby cots are becoming more widely available.

Activities

One activity that kids love as much as adults is playing on the beach, and Vietnam has some superb **beaches** with affordable resorts in places like Phu Quoc Island (see p.160), Nha Trang (see p.225) and Hoi An (see p.258). Many beach resorts offer boat rides or water sports such as kayaking, but make sure the kids put on plenty of sunscreen. Some resorts, such as the *Anantara Hoi An* (see p.255), also provide hands-on activities such as lantern making.

Some of the better organized **national parks**, like Cuc Phuong (see p.317) and Cat Tien (see p.174), have well-marked trails and offer the possibility of spotting rare animals as well as a host of unusual tropical plants.

Vietnam has some of the world's most impressive **cable cars** taking visitors to fun destinations. Take the kids to check out a long one (over 3km) to Vinpearl Land Amusement Park on Hon Tre near Nha Trang (see p.228), or a high one (over 1300 metres altitude gain) to Ba Na Hill Station (see p.272) on a day-trip from Da Nang.

All big cities have **amusement parks** and **water parks**, which are a great way to beat the heat. In Ho Chi Minh City, head for Dam Sen Water Park (see p.106), or in Buon Ma Thuot there's the Dak Lak Water Park (see p.189). While on the topic of water, the one unmissable activity for kids in Vietnam is a performance of **water puppets**, either in Hanoi (see p.381) or Ho Chi Minh City (see p.103).

Travel essentials

Addresses

Locating an **address** is rarely a problem in Vietnam, but there are a couple of conventions it helps to know about. Where two numbers are separated by a slash, such as 110/5, you simply make for no. 110, where an alley will lead off to a further batch of buildings – you want the fifth one. Where a number is followed by a letter, as in 117a, you're looking for a single block encompassing several addresses, of which one will be 117a. Vietnamese cite addresses without the words for street, avenue and so on; we've followed this practice throughout the Guide except where ambiguity would result.

Costs

With the average Vietnamese annual income hovering around £900–1200/US$1500–2000/€1140–1500, daily expenses are low, and if you come prepared to do as the locals do, then food and drink can be incredibly cheap – and even accommodation needn't be too great an expense. However, constantly rising petrol prices mean that transport costs are creeping up all the time. **Bargaining** is very much a part of everyday life, and almost everything is negotiable, from fruit in the market to a room for the night (see box opposite).

By eating at simple com (rice) and pho (noodle soup) stalls, picking up local buses and opting for the simplest accommodation there's no reason why you shouldn't be able to adhere to a **daily budget** in the region of £12–15/US$20–25/€15–19. Upgrading to more salubrious lodgings with a few mod cons, eating good food followed by a couple of beers in a bar and signing up for the odd minibus tour and visiting a few sights could bounce your expenditure up to a more realistic £24–30/US$40–50/€30–38. A fair mid-level budget, treating yourself to three-star hotels and more upmarket restaurants, would lie in the £30–60/US$50–100/€38–76 range, depending on the number and type of tours you took. And if you stay at the ritziest city hotels, dine at the swankiest restaurants and rent cars with drivers wherever you go, then the sky's the limit.

Admission charges

Admission charges are usually levied at museums, historic sights, national parks and any place that attracts tourists – sometimes even beaches. Charges at some **major sights** range from a dollar or two up to around £3–4/US$5–6/€4–5 for the Cham ruins at My Son or Hue's citadel and royal mausoleums. Elsewhere, however, the amount is usually just a few thousand dong. Note that there's often a hefty additional fee for **cameras** and **videos** at major sights.

Apart from those with some historical significance, **pagodas and temples** are usually free, though it's customary to leave a donation of a few thousand dong in the collecting box or on one of the altar plates.

Culture and etiquette

With its blend of Confucianism and Buddhism, Vietnamese society tends to be both conservative and, at the same time, fairly tolerant. This means you will rarely be remonstrated with for your **dress** or behaviour, even if your hosts disapprove of it. By following a few simple rules, you can minimize the risk of causing offence. This is particularly important in rural areas and small towns where people are less used to the eccentric habits of foreigners.

As a visitor, it's recommended that you err on the side of caution. Shorts and sleeveless shirts are fine for the beach, but are not welcome in pagodas, temples and other religious sites. When dealing with officialdom, it also pays to look as neat and tidy as possible. Anything else may be taken as a mark of disrespect.

Women in particular should dress modestly, especially in the countryside and ethnic minority areas, where revealing too much flesh is regarded as offensive.

It's also worth noting that **nudity**, either male or female, on the beach is absolutely beyond the pale.

When entering a Cao Dai temple, the main building of a pagoda or a private home it's the custom to remove your **shoes**. In some pagodas nowadays this may only be required when stepping onto the prayer mats – ask or watch what other people do. In a pagoda or temple you are also expected to leave a small donation.

Officially, **homosexuality** is regarded as a "social evil", alongside drugs and prostitution. However, there is no law explicitly banning homosexual activity and, as long as it is not practised openly, it is largely ignored. Indeed, the number of openly gay men has increased noticeably in recent years, particularly in Ho Chi Minh City and Hanoi, and homosexuality is discussed more frequently in the media, although the lesbian scene remains very low-key. Although outward discrimination is rare, this is still a very traditional society and it pays to be discreet in Vietnam. For more information, consult the excellent Utopia Asia website, ⓦutopia -asia.com.

As in most Asian countries, it's not done to get angry, and it certainly won't get things moving any quicker. Passing round cigarettes (to men only) is always appreciated and is widely used as a social gambit aimed at progressing tricky negotiations, bargaining and so forth.

Tipping, while not expected, is always appreciated. In general, a few thousand dong should suffice. Smart restaurants and hotels normally add a service charge, but if not ten percent is the norm in a restaurant, while the amount in a hotel will depend on the grade of hotel and what services they've provided. If you're pleased with the service, you should also tip the guide, and the driver where appropriate, at the end of a tour.

PRICING POLICY

Although Vietnamese law requires that all **prices** are quoted in dong, you'll find many hotels, the more upmarket restaurants, tour agents and so forth still use US dollars and, occasionally, euros. To reflect this and to avoid exchange-rate fluctuations, throughout the Guide we quote prices in the currency used on the spot.

Incidentally, don't be alarmed if you notice that Vietnamese pay less than you for plane tickets, at some hotels and at certain sights: Vietnam maintains a **two-tier pricing system**, with foreigners sometimes paying many times more than locals. The good news for tourists is that the system is being phased out, with prices for foreigners being adjusted downwards while those for Vietnamese rise to meet them. A single price system now applies on the trains, for example, while the gap has gradually been narrowing for air travel. It will take several more years before the practice disappears completely, however, and for the moment it remains something of a grey area, particularly as regards hotels and bus tickets, where the amount you pay may well depend on the person you happen to be dealing with.

Other social conventions worth noting are that you shouldn't touch **children** on the head and, unlike in the West, it's best to ignore a young baby rather than praise it, since it's believed that this attracts the attention of jealous spirits who will cause the baby to fall ill.

Electricity

The **electricity** supply in Vietnam is 220 volts. Plugs generally have two round pins, though you may come across sockets requiring two flat pins and even some requiring three pins. Adaptors can be found in any electrical shop. Power supplies can be erratic, so be prepared for cuts and surges.

Entry requirements

All foreign nationals need a **visa** to enter Vietnam, with certain exceptions: citizens of Sweden, Denmark, Norway, Finland, Japan and South Korea do not need a visa if they are travelling to Vietnam for less than fifteen days, have a passport valid for three months following the date of entry and hold a return air ticket. Citizens of certain ASEAN-member countries, including Thailand, Malaysia and Singapore are also exempt for stays of up to thirty days. Tourist visas are generally valid for thirty days and for a single entry, though three-month multiple-entry visas are also available. A standard thirty-day visa costs the local equivalent of US$60–80, depending on how quickly you want it processed.

Applying for a visa

Though visitors can **apply for a visa** in their country of residence, either from the embassy direct, or through a specialist visa agent or tour agent, it's more convenient for most people to get their visa online. If you apply in person at the embassy, processing normally takes around a week, though many embassies also offer a more expensive "express" service. By contrast, the normal service for an online visa is just two days, and frequently you'll receive your approval letter within just one day. There are several websites that offer a **Vietnamese visa online** service, and most, including ⓦ vietnamvisa.com, are reliable. **Prices** range from US$17–20 processing fee plus US$45 "stamping fee" (for a one-month, single-entry visa), to US$35 plus US$95 "stamping fee" (for a three-month, multiple-entry visa). On receipt of your fee (usually within 24hr), you'll be sent an **approval letter** to print out and present to immigration on arrival, along with an application form (available at the desk), photographs and the stamping fee. The process is very efficient and currently only requires a short wait on arrival, though this wait could get longer if the system becomes more popular. If you follow this route, look out for the **Visa on Arrival desk** at the airport before you pass through immigration.

To apply for a **tourist visa**, you have to submit an **application form** with one or two passport-sized photographs (procedures vary) and the fee. The visa shows specific start and end **dates** indicating the period of validity within which you can enter and leave the country. The visa is valid for entry via Hanoi, Ho Chi Minh City and Da Nang international airports and any of Vietnam's land borders open to foreigners (see p.30).

Business visas are valid for one month upwards and can be issued for multiple entry, though you'll need a sponsoring office in Vietnam to underwrite your application.

One-year **student visas** are relatively easy to get hold of, for example, if you enrol on a Vietnamese language course at one of the universities; you'll be required to attend a minimum number of classes per week to qualify. It's easiest to arrange it in advance, but you can enter Vietnam on a tourist visa and apply for student status later – the only downside is that you may have to leave the country in order to get the visa stamp.

Special circumstances affect **overseas Vietnamese** holding a foreign passport: check with the Vietnamese embassy in your country of residence for details.

Visa extensions

Thirty-day extensions are issued in Hanoi, Ho Chi Minh City, Nha Trang, Da Nang, Hue and Hoi An. Applications have to be made via a tour agent. In general they take three days to process and cost around US$25 for the first one-month extension. However, since it's now easy to apply for a three-month visa in the first place, few visitors require this service.

Holders of **business visas** can apply for an extension only through the office that sponsored their original visa, backed up with reasons as to why an extension is necessary.

Incidentally, **overstaying** your visa will result in a fine of US$10–25 a day, depending on the mood of the immigration official, and is not recommended.

Vietnamese embassies and consulates

A full list of Vietnamese embassies and consulates is available at ⓦ vietnamtourism.com.

Australia Embassy: 6 Timbarra Crescent, O'Malley, Canberra, ACT 2606 ☎ 02 6286 6059, ✉ vnemb.au@mofa.gov.vn. Consulate: Suite 205, Level 2 Edgecliff Centre, 202–233 New South Head Rd, Edgecliff, NSW 2027 ☎ 02 9327 2539.

Cambodia Embassy 440a Monivong Blvd, Phnom Penh ☎ 023 726 274, ⓦ vietnamembassy-cambodia.org. Consulates: Sihanoukville ☎ 034 934 039, ✉ tlsqsiha@camintel.com; Road No.3, Battambang ☎ 053 952 894, ✉ lsqvnbat@camintel.com.

Canada Embassy 55 Mackay St, Ottowa K1M 2B2 ☎ 613 236 0772, ⓦ vietnameseembassy.org/canada-ottowa.

China Embassy: 32 Guang Hua Lu, Jian Guo Men Wai, PO Box 00600, Beijing ☎ 10 6532 1155, ✉ vnemb.cn@mofa.gov.vn. Consulates: 2nd floor, B Building North, *Landmark Hotel*, Qiaoguang Rd (Haizhu Square), Guangzhou ☎ 20 8330 5916; 15f Great Smart Tower, 230 Wanchai Rd, Hong Kong ☎ 852 2591 4510; 507 Hong Ta Mansion, 155 Beijing Rd, Kunming 65001 ☎ 871 351 5889, ✉ tlsqcm@yahoo.com.

Ireland 2nd Floor, Sentinel Place, 41a Ly Thai To, Hanoi; ☎ 04 3974 3291 ext 610.

Lao PDR Embassy: 1 That Luang Rd, Vientiane ☎ 021 413 409, ✉ vnemb.lao@mofa.gov.vn. Consulates: 31 Ban Pha Bat, Pakse ☎ 031 212 827, ✉ vnemb.la@mofa.gov,vn; 118 Sisavangvong Rd, Savannakhet ☎ 06 212418, ✉ lanhsusavan@mofa.gov.vn.

Malaysia 4 Persiaran Stonor, 50450 Kuala Lumpur ☎ 03 2148 4534, ⓦ mofa.gov.vn/vnemb.my.

New Zealand Level 21, Grand Plimmer Tower, 2 Gilmer Terrace, PO Box 8042, Wellington ☎ 04 473 5912, ⓦ vietnamembassy -newzealand.org.

Singapore 10 Leedon Park, Singapore 267887 ☎ 06 462 5938.

Thailand Embassy: 83/1 Wireless Rd, Bangkok 10330 ☎ 02 2515 836, ✉ vnemb.th@mofa.gov.vn. Consulate: 65/6 Chatapadung, Khonkaen 40000 ☎ 043 242 190, ✉ konkaen.th@mofa.gov.vn.

UK Embassy: 12–14 Victoria Rd, London W8 5RD ☎ 020 7937 1912, ✉ vnemb.uk@mofa.gov.vn.

US Embassy: 1233 20th St NW, Suite 400, Washington DC 20036 ☎ 202 861 0737, ⓦ vietnamembassy-usa.org. Consulate: 1700 California St, Suite 430, San Francisco, CA 94109 ☎ 415 922 1707, ⓦ vietnamconsulate-sf.org.

Insurance

It is essential to have a good **travel insurance policy** to cover against theft, loss and illness or injury. It's also advisable to have medical cover that includes evacuation in the event of serious illness, as the local hospitals aren't that great. Most policies exclude so-called dangerous sports unless an extra premium is paid: in Vietnam this can include scuba diving, whitewater rafting, kitesurfing, rock-climbing and trekking. If you're doing any motor-bike touring, you are strongly advised to take out full medical insurance including emergency evacu-ation; make sure the policy specifically covers you for biking in Vietnam, and ascertain whether

ROUGH GUIDES TRAVEL INSURANCE

Rough Guides has teamed up with **WorldNomads.com** to offer great travel insurance deals. Policies are available to residents of over 150 countries, with cover for a wide range of adventure sports, 24hr emergency assistance, high levels of medical and evacuation cover and a stream of travel safety information. Roughguides.com users can take advantage of their policies online 24/7, from anywhere in the world – even if you're already travelling. And since plans often change when you're on the road, you can extend your policy and even claim online. Roughguides.com users who buy travel insurance with WorldNomads. com can also leave a positive footprint and donate to a community development project. For more information, go to ⓦ roughguides.com/travel-insurance.

benefits will be paid as treatment proceeds or only after you return home, and whether there is a 24-hour medical emergency number. If you need to make a claim, you should keep receipts for medicines and medical treatment, and in the event that you have anything stolen, you must obtain an official statement from the police.

Internet

Accessing the **internet** in Vietnam has become a great deal easier, though it is still monitored and controlled by a government fearful of this potentially subversive means of communication. Occasionally social networking sites like Facebook have been blocked.

There's no problem about logging on in the major cities and tourist centres in Vietnam, where most cafés provide **wi-fi**, while many hotels also offer in-room computers. Most upmarket and budget hotels offer wi-fi broadband access in your room – usually free, though top-end hotels often charge a hefty fee for the privilege. Even remote regions are wired to the web these days, though the service may be slower.

Laundry

Most top- and mid-range hotels provide a **laundry service**, and many budget hotels too, but rates can vary wildly, so it's worth checking first. In the bigger cities, especially in tourist areas, you'll find laundry shops on the street, where the rate is usually around 20,000đ per kilo. Washing is often given a rigorous scrubbing by hand, so don't submit anything delicate.

Mail

Mail can take anything from four days to four weeks in or out of Vietnam, depending largely where you are. Services are quickest and most reliable from the major towns, where eight to ten days is the norm. **Overseas postal rates** are reasonable: a postcard costs around 10,000đ, while the price of a letter is in the region of 18,000đ for the minimum weight. **Express Mail Service** (EMS) operates to most countries and certain destinations within Vietnam; the service cuts down delivery times substantially and the letter or parcel is automatically registered. For a minimum-weight dispatch by EMS (under 500g), you'll pay around US$30 to the UK or the US, and US$21 to Australia.

When **sending parcels** out of Vietnam, take everything to the post office unwrapped since it will be inspected for any customs liability and wrapped for you, and the whole process, including wrapping and customs inspection, will cost you upwards of 30,000đ. Pirated CDs and DVDs and any other suspect items will be seized. It's advisable to register any package containing valuable items.

Maps

Decent maps of the country include the *Travel Map of Vietnam* (1:1,250,000), published by the Vietnam Publishing House of Natural Resources, Environment and Cartography (NARENCA), which is updated annually, or Nelles' (1:1,500,000) map of Vietnam, Laos and Cambodia: both feature plans of Ho Chi Minh City and Hanoi. Alternatively, the locally produced maps you'll find on sale in all the major towns and tourist destinations in Vietnam aren't bad.

As with elsewhere in the world, Google Maps can be very useful, though they are sometimes prone to wild errors, so cross-check with other online maps where possible.

Money

Vietnam's unit of currency is the **dong**, which you'll see abbreviated as "đ", "d" or "VND" after an amount. Notes come in denominations of 500đ, 1000đ, 2000đ, 5000đ, 10,000đ, 20,000đ, 50,000đ, 100,000đ,

EXCHANGE RATES

At the time of writing, the **exchange rate** was around 33,000đ to £1; 20,000đ to US$1; 29,000đ to €1; 19,000đ to CAN$1; 19,000đ to AUS$1; and 17,000đ to NZ$1. Recently the country has been plagued by high inflation rates, so these exchange rates are liable to fluctuate. For the latest exchange rates go to ⓦ xe.com.

200,000đ and 500,000đ, coins in 200đ, 500đ, 1000đ, 2000đ and 5000đ (though coins are rarely seen). In addition to the dong, the **American dollar** operates as a parallel, unofficial currency and it's a good idea to carry some dollars as a back-up to pay large bills. On the whole, though, it's more convenient to operate in dong, and you'll often find dong prices are slightly lower than the equivalent in dollars.

Dong are not available outside Vietnam at present, but there are ATMs in all international airports. Most **banks** and **exchange bureaux** don't charge for changing foreign currency into dong; banks in major cities will accept euros and other major currencies, but elsewhere may only accept dollars. Some tour agents and hotels will also change money, though at a less attractive rate than the banks, and some jewellery shops in Vietnam will exchange dollars at a slightly better rate than the banks, but this practice has now been outlawed. Wherever you change money, ask for a mix of denominations (in remote places, bigger bills can be hard to split), and refuse really tatty banknotes, as you'll have difficulty getting anyone else to accept them.

There's also a comprehensive network of **ATMs**, many open 24 hours: most accept Visa, MasterCard and American Express cards issued abroad. The maximum withdrawal is between two and five million dong at a time (depending on the bank), with a charge of 20,000–30,000đ per transaction (in addition to whatever surcharges your own bank levies). In Hanoi and Ho Chi Minh City you'll also find ATMs operated by ANZ and HSBC. These accept a wider range of cards, including those in the Cirrus and Plus networks.

Major **credit cards** – Visa, MasterCard and, to a lesser extent, American Express – are accepted in Vietnam's main cities and major tourist spots. All top-level and many mid-level hotels will accept them, as will a growing number of restaurants, though some places levy surcharges of three to four percent.

Traveller's cheques are less common now that ATMs are so widespread, but can be cashed at major banks (you need your passport as ID), for a commission of up to two percent. Vietinbank generally charges the lowest rates: at the time of writing these were 0.50 percent (minimum US$2) when changing into dong and 1.25 percent (minimum US$2) into dollars or other foreign currencies. Vietcombank waives commission on American Express travellers' cheques.

Having **money wired** from home via MoneyGram (UK ☎0800 026 0535, US ☎1 800 666 3947; ⓦmoneygram.com) or Western Union (US ☎1 800 325 6000, ⓦwesternunion.com) is never cheap, and should be considered a last resort. It's also possible to have money wired directly from a bank or post office in your home country to a bank in Vietnam, although this has the added complication of involving two separate institutions; money wired this way normally takes two working days to arrive, and charges vary according to the amount sent.

Opening hours

Basic hours of business are 7.30–11.30am and 1.30–4.30pm, though after lunch nothing really gets going again before 2pm. The standard closing day for **offices** is Sunday, and many now also close on Saturdays, including most government offices.

Most **banks** tend to work Monday to Friday 8–11.30am and 1–4pm, though some stay open later in the afternoon or may forego a lunch break. In tourist centres you'll even find branches open evenings and weekends. **Post offices** keep much longer hours, in general staying open from 6.30am through to 9pm with no closing day. Some sub-post offices work shorter hours and close at weekends.

Shops and **markets** open seven days a week and in theory keep going all day, though in practice most stallholders and many private shopkeepers

---

PUBLIC HOLIDAYS

January 1 New Year's Day
Late January/mid-February (dates vary each year): Tet, Vietnamese New Year (four days, though increasingly offices tend to close down for a full week)
10th day of 3rd lunar month (usually April): Vietnamese Kings Commemoration Day (aka Hung Kings Festival)
April 30 Liberation of Saigon, 1975
May 1 International Labour Day
September 2 National Day

---

will take a siesta. Shops mostly stay open late into the evenings, perhaps until 8pm or beyond in the big cities.

Museums tend to close one day a week, generally on Mondays, and their core opening hours are 8–11am and 2–4pm. **Temples** and **pagodas** occasionally close for lunch but are otherwise open all week and don't close until late evening.

Telephones

Mobile phones are ubiquitous in Vietnam – there's now more than one phone per user. However, transport centres like airports and bus stations still maintain a few functioning land line booths, which accept only pre-paid phone cards, not coins. All post offices also operate a public phone service, where the cost is displayed as you speak and you pay the cashier afterwards. Local calls are easy to make and are often free, though you may be charged a small fee of a few thousand dong for the service.

Nearly all post offices also offer IDD (international direct dialling) services. Rates cost around 5000đ per minute (depending where you are calling). Using the prefix 171 reduces rates by a further 10–20 percent. The 171 service can be used from any phone, except for operator-assisted calls or faxes: post offices will charge a small fee for using it.

Mobile phones

If you want to use your own **mobile phone** in Vietnam, the simplest – and cheapest – thing to do is to buy a SIM card and a prepaid phone card locally. Both the big phone companies, Vinaphone (ⓦvinaphone.com.vn) and Mobifone (ⓦmobifone .com.vn), offer English-language support and similar prices, though Vinaphone perhaps has the edge for geographical coverage (which extends pretty much nationwide). At the time of writing, Vinaphone starter kits including a SIM card cost 100,000đ (with 50,000đ worth of calls credited to your account). Further prepaid cards are available in various sizes from 100,000đ to 500,000đ. Phone calls cost slightly more than from a land line, while sending an SMS message costs 250–500đ in Vietnam and about 2500đ internationally. However, rates are falling rapidly as more competitors enter the increasingly deregulated market. All major phone companies also offer competitively priced packages that include 3G.

The other, far more expensive, option is to stick with your home service-provider – though you'll need to check beforehand whether it offers international roaming services. In many cases it

---

DIALLING CODES

All phone numbers in Vietnam consist of nine to eleven digits, with the first two to four digits representing the area code and the remaining digits the specific number. The complete number must be dialled whether you are phoning locally or long distance.

To **call Vietnam from abroad**, dial your international access code, then ☎84 + number minus the first 0.

To **call abroad from Vietnam**, dial either ☎171 00 or just ☎00 followed by the country code (see below) + area code minus first 0 + number.

Australia ☎61	**New Zealand** ☎64
Canada ☎1	**UK** ☎44
Ireland ☎353	**US** ☎1

---

could work out cheaper to just buy a simple mobile phone in Vietnam for around US$20 and give everyone your new number.

Time

Vietnam is seven hours ahead of London, twelve hours ahead of New York, fifteen hours ahead of Los Angeles, one hour behind Perth and three hours behind Sydney – give or take an hour or two when summer time is in operation.

Tourist information

Tourist information on Vietnam is at a premium. The Vietnamese government maintains a handful of **tourist promotion offices** and a smattering of accredited travel agencies around the globe, most of which can supply you with only the most general information. A better source of information, much of it based on firsthand experiences, is the internet, with numerous **websites** around to help you plan your visit. Some of the more useful and interesting sites are ⓦtravelfish.org, a regularly updated online guide to Southeast Asia; ⓦactivetravelvietnam .com, with helpful information about national parks and beaches; and ⓦrustycompass.com, candid reviews of attractions, hotels and restaurants by an expat resident.

In Vietnam itself there's a frustrating dearth of free and impartial advice. The **state-run tourist offices** – under the auspices of either the Vietnam National Administration of Tourism (ⓦvietnamtourism.com) or the local provincial organization – are thinly disguised tour agents, profit-making concerns which don't take kindly to being treated as information bureaux, though the official website has a lot of useful information about destinations and practicalities such as visas. In any case, Western concepts of information don't necessarily apply here – bus timetables, for example, simply don't exist. The most

you're likely to get is a glossy brochure detailing agents' tours and affiliated hotels.

You'll generally have more luck approaching hotel staff or one of the many **private tour agencies** operating in all the major tourist spots, where staff have become accustomed to Westerners' demands for advice.

Another useful source of information, including restaurant and hotel listings as well as feature articles, is the growing number of **English-language magazines**, such as *Asialife*, *The Word* and *The Guide* (see p.50). There's also a government-run **telephone information service** (☎1080) with some English-speaking staff who will answer all manner of questions – if you can get through, since the lines are often busy.

Travellers with special needs

Although Vietnam is home to so many war-wounded, few provisions are made for the disabled, so you'll have to be pretty self-reliant. It's important to contact airlines, hotels and tour companies as far in advance as possible to make sure they can accommodate your requirements.

Getting about can be made a little easier by taking internal flights, or by renting a private car or minibus with a driver. Taxis are widely available in Hanoi, Ho Chi Minh City and other major cities. Even so, trying to cross roads with speeding traffic and negotiating the cluttered and uneven pavements – where pavements exist – pose real problems. Furthermore, few buildings are equipped with ramps and lifts.

When it comes to **accommodation**, Vietnam's new luxury hotels usually offer one or two specially adapted rooms. Elsewhere, the best you can hope for is a ground-floor room, or a hotel with a lift.

One, albeit expensive, option is to ask a tour agent to arrange a **customized tour**. Contact one of the recommended agents in Ho Chi Minh City (see p.91) or Hanoi (see p.370) for more information.

Working and studying in Vietnam

Without a prearranged job and work permit, don't bank on finding work in Vietnam. With specific skills to offer, you could try approaching some of the Western companies operating in Hanoi and Ho Chi Minh City.

Otherwise, **English-language teaching** is probably the easiest job to land, especially if you have a TEFL (Teaching English as a Foreign Language), TESOL (Teacher of English to Speakers of Other Languages) or CELTA (Certificate in English Language Teaching to Adults) qualification. Universities are worth approaching, though pay is better at private schools, where qualified teachers earn upwards of US$20 an hour. In either case, you'll need to apply for a work permit, sponsored by your employer, and then a working visa. Private tutoring is an unwieldy way of earning a crust, as you'll have to pop out of the country every few months to procure a new visa. Furthermore, the authorities are clamping down on people working without the proper authorizations.

The main English-language teaching operations recruiting in Vietnam include the British Council (Ⓦbritishcouncil.vn), ILA Vietnam (Ⓦilavietnam.com), Language Link Vietnam (Ⓦlanguagelink.edu.vn) and RMIT International University (Ⓦrmit.edu.vn). The TEFL website (Ⓦtefl.com) and Dave's ESL Café (Ⓦeslcafe.com) also have lists of English-teaching vacancies in addition to lots of other useful information.

There are also opportunities for **volunteer work**. Try contacting the organizations listed below, or look on the websites of the NGO Resource Centre Vietnam (Ⓦngocentre.org.vn) and Volunteer Abroad (Ⓦvolunteerabroad.com).

STUDY, WORK AND VOLUNTEER PROGRAMMES

Australian Volunteers International Australia ☎ 03 9279 1788, Ⓦaustralianvolunteers.com. Postings for up to two years, focusing on rural development, vocational education and capacity building.

British Council UK ☎ 0161 957 7755, Ⓦbritishcouncil.org. TEFL vacancies are posted at Ⓦbritishcouncil.org/jobs/careers, or call ☎ 020 7389 4385.

Brockport Vietnam Project US ☎ 1 800 298 7869, Ⓦbrockportabroad.com. Opportunities for American undergraduates and graduates to study in Da Nang, and to participate in community service activities.

Council on International Educational Exchange (CIEE) US ☎ 1 207 553 4000, Ⓦciee.org. This non-profit organization runs semester and academic-year programmes in Vietnam.

Earthwatch Institute UK ☎ 01865 318838, US and Canada ☎ 1 978 461 0081, Australia ☎ 03 9016 7590; Ⓦearthwatch.org. Long-established international charity with environmental and archeological research projects worldwide, including Vietnam. Participation mainly as a paying volunteer but fellowships for teachers and students are available.

Global Volunteer Network UK ☎ 0800 032 5035, US ☎ 1 800 963 1198, Australia ☎ 1800 203 012; Ⓦglobalvolunteernetwork.org. Non-governmental organization that supports the work of local communities through the placement of international volunteers.

Voluntary Service Overseas (VSO) UK ☎ 020 8780 7500, Ⓦvso.org.uk. A British government-funded organization that places volunteers in various projects around the world.

Volunteers for Peace US ☎ 802 540 3060, Ⓦvfp.org. Non-profit organization with links to a huge international network of "workcamps", two- to four-week programmes that bring volunteers together from many countries to carry out needed community projects. Most workcamps are in summer, with registration by April or May.

Ho Chi Minh City and around

HO CHI MINH CITY

1

Ho Chi Minh City and around

Reverberating to the whirr of a million motorbikes, Ho Chi Minh City – or Thanh Pho Ho Chi Minh, to give it its full Vietnamese title – is a metropolis on the move. By turns chaotic, elegant, exotic and zestful, this has long been one of Asia's more interesting cities; more than eight million souls live here, making it more populous than the national capital, Hanoi. As a result of the sweeping economic changes wrought by *doi moi* in 1986, this effervescent city has changed its image from that of a war-torn wreck to one of a thriving metropolis, challenging Singapore, Bangkok and the other Southeast Asian powerhouses. All the accoutrements of economic success are here – fine restaurants, flashy hotels, glitzy bars and clubs, and shops selling imported luxury goods – adding a glossy veneer to the city's hotchpotch landscape of French colonial architecture, venerable pagodas and austere, Soviet-style housing blocks.

Sadly, however, Ho Chi Minh City (often abbreviated to **HCMC**) is still full of people for whom economic progress has not yet translated into food, housing and jobs. Vendors roam the tourist enclaves hawking books, postcards, lottery tickets and cigarette lighters; limbless mendicants haul themselves about on crude trolleys; and watchful pickpockets prowl crowded streets on the lookout for unguarded wallets. Though the number of beggars is gradually declining, tourists must quickly come to accept them as a hassle that goes with the territory. In addition, the arrival, en masse, of wealthy Westerners has lured many women into prostitution, for which the go-go bars of Dong Khoi became famous during the American War.

If Hanoi is a city of romance and mellow charms, then Ho Chi Minh City is its antithesis, a fury of sights and sounds, and the crucible in which Vietnam's rallying fortunes are boiling. Few corners of the city afford respite from the cacophony of **construction work** casting up new office blocks and hotels with logic-defying speed. An increasing number of cars and minibuses jostle with an organic mass of state-of-the-art Honda SUVs, choking the tree-lined streets and boulevards. Amid this melee, the local people go about their daily life: smartly dressed schoolkids wander past streetside baguette-sellers; women shoppers ride motorbikes clad in gangster-style bandanas to protect their skin from the sun and dust; while teenagers in designer jeans chirrup into mobile phones. Much of the fun of being in Ho Chi Minh City derives from the

BURNING INCENSE, JADE EMPEROR PAGODA

Highlights

❶ Bitexco Tower Enjoy the superlative views from the upper levels of the city's tallest building, and newest icon. **See p.78**

❷ Ben Thanh Market A teeming Vietnamese market *par excellence*… check the city's pulse here on an early morning stroll. **See p.79**

❸ War Remnants Museum The city's most moving museum, a stark reminder of man's inhumanity to man. **See p.81**

❹ Jade Emperor Pagoda Beautifully carved woodwork, an eclectic collection of deities and a constant fog of incense, all combine to make this the city's most fascinating temple. **See p.84**

❺ Cho Lon Take an improvised wander around the streets of "big market" – the city's occasionally manic Chinatown. **See p.85**

❻ HCMC cafés Linger over a latte and watch the world roll by at one of the city's hip cafés, such as the *Napoli* or *La Fenetre Soleil*. **See p.100**

❼ Dong Khoi shops The boutiques on and around this famous street specialize in silks and paintings. **See p.104**

❽ A day-trip north Two of the biggest draws for travellers to HCMC – the Cu Chi tunnels and Cao Dai temple – are actually outside the city itself, and best tackled on a day-tour. **See p.107**

HIGHLIGHTS ARE MARKED ON THE MAPS ON P.70, P.72 & P.85

1

simple pleasure of absorbing its flurry of activity – something best done from the seat of a cyclo or a roadside café. To blink is to miss some new and singular sight, be it a motorbike stacked high with piglets bound for the market, or a boy on a bicycle rapping out a staccato tattoo on pieces of bamboo to advertise noodles for sale.

For some visitors, the American war is their primary frame of reference and such historical hot spots as the **Reunification Palace** rank highly on their itineraries. In addition, ostentatious reminders of French rule abound, among them such memorable buildings as **Notre Dame Cathedral** and the grandiose **Hotel de Ville** – but even these look spanking-new when compared to gloriously musty edifices like **Quan Am Pagoda** and the **Jade Emperor Pagoda**, just a couple of the many captivating places of worship across the city. And if the chaos becomes too much, you can escape to the relative calm of the **Botanical Gardens** – also home to the city's **History Museum** and **zoo**.

It's one of Ho Chi Minh City's many charms that once you've exhausted, or been exhausted by, all it has to offer, paddy fields, beaches and wide-open countryside are not far away. The most popular trip **out of the city** is to the **Cu Chi tunnels**, where villagers dug themselves out of the range of American shelling. The tunnels are often

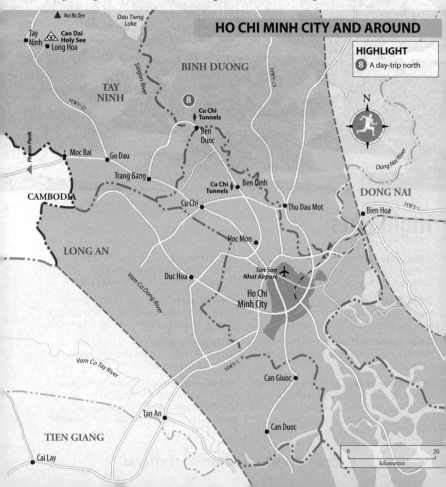

HO CHI MINH CITY AND AROUND

HIGHLIGHT

8 A day-trip north

1

THE STREET OF MANY NAMES

Slender **Dong Khoi**, running for just over 1km from Le Duan to the Saigon River, has long mirrored Ho Chi Minh City's changing fortunes. The French knew the road as **Rue Catinat**, a tamarind-shaded thoroughfare that constituted the heart of French colonial life. Here the *colons* would promenade, stopping at chic boutiques and perfumeries, and gathering at noon and dusk at cafés such as the *Rotonde* and *Taverne Alsacienne* for a Vermouth or Dubonnet, before hailing a *pousse-pousse* (a hand-pulled variation on the cyclo) to run them home. With the departure of the French in 1954, President Diem saw fit to change the street's name to **Tu Do**, "Freedom", and it was under this guise that a generation of young American GIs came to know it, as they toured the glut of bars – *Wild West*, *Uncle Sam's*, *Playboy* – that sprang up to pander to their more lascivious needs. After Saigon fell in 1975, the more politically correct monicker of **Dong Khoi**, or "Uprising", was adopted, but the street quickly went to seed in the dark, pre-*doi moi* years, and by the Seventies had gone, in the words of Le Ly Hayslip, from "bejewelled, jaded dowager to shabby, grasping bag lady".

twinned with a tour around the fanciful Great Temple of the indigenous Cao Dai religion at **Tay Ninh**. A brief taster of the Mekong Delta at **My Tho** (see p.118) or a dip in the South China Sea at **Ho Coc** are also eminently possible in a long day's excursion.

The **best time to visit** tropical Ho Chi Minh City is in the dry season, which runs from December through to April. During the wet season, May to November, there are frequent tropical storms, though these won't disrupt your travels too much. Average temperatures, year-round, hover between 26°C and 29°C, though March, April and May are the hottest months.

Brief history

Knowledge of Ho Chi Minh City's early history is sketchy at best. Between the first and sixth centuries, the territory on which it lies fell under the nominal rule of the **Funan Empire** to the west. Funan was subsequently absorbed by the Kambuja peoples of the pre-Angkor **Chen La Empire**, but it is unlikely that these Imperial machinations had much bearing on the sleepy fishing backwater that would later develop into Ho Chi Minh City.

Khmer fishermen eked out a living here, building their huts on the stable ground just north of the delta wetlands, which made it ideal for human settlement. Originally named **Prei Nokor**, it flourished as an entrepôt for Cambodian boats pushing down the Mekong River, and by the seventeenth century it boasted a garrison and a mercantile community that embraced Malay, Indian and Chinese traders.

Such a dynamic settlement was bound to draw attention from the north. By the eighteenth century, the **Viets** had subdued the kingdom of Champa, and this area was swallowed up by Hue's **Nguyen Dynasty**. With new ownership came a new name, **Saigon**, thought to be derived from the Vietnamese word for the kapok tree. On the outbreak of the **Tay Son Rebellion**, in 1772, Nguyen Anh bricked the whole settlement into a walled fortress, the eight-sided **Gia Dinh Citadel**. The army that put down the Tay Son brothers included an assisting **French** military force, who grappled for several decades to undermine Vietnamese control in the region and develop a trading post in Asia. Finally, in 1861, they seized Saigon, using Emperor Tu Duc's persecution of French missionaries as a pretext. The 1862 **Treaty of Saigon** declared the city the capital of French Cochinchina.

Colonial-era Saigon

Ho Chi Minh City owes much of its form and character to the French colonists: channels were filled in, marshlands drained and steam tramways set to work along its regimental grid of tamarind-shaded boulevards, which by the 1930s sported names like Boulevard de la Somme and Rue Rousseau. Flashy examples of European

1

architecture were erected, cafés and boutiques sprang up to cater for its new Vermouth-sipping, baguette-munching citizens and the city was imbued with such an all-round Gallic air that Somerset Maugham, visiting in the 1930s, found it reminiscent of "a little provincial town in the south of France, a blithe and smiling little place". The French colonials bankrolled improvements to Saigon with the vast profits they were able to cream from exporting Vietnam's **rubber** and **rice** out of the city's rapidly expanding seaport.

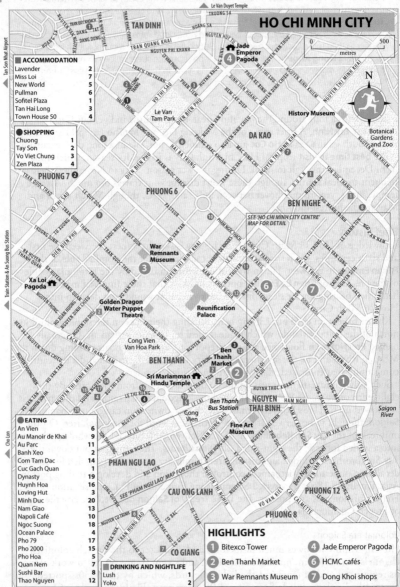

HO CHI MINH CITY

0 — 500
metres

N

ACCOMMODATION
Lavender	2
Miss Loi	7
New World	5
Pullman	6
Sofitel Plaza	1
Tan Hai Long	3
Town House 50	4

SHOPPING
Chuong	1
Tay Son	2
Vo Viet Chung	3
Zen Plaza	4

EATING
An Vien	6
Au Manoir de Khai	9
Au Parc	11
Banh Xeo	2
Com Tam Dac	14
Cuc Gach Quan	1
Dynasty	19
Huynh Hoa	16
Loving Hut	3
Minh Duc	20
Nam Giao	13
Napoli Café	10
Ngoc Suong	18
Ocean Palace	4
Pho 79	17
Pho 2000	15
Pho Hoa	5
Quan Nem	7
Sushi Bar	8
Thao Nguyen	12

DRINKING AND NIGHTLIFE
| Lush | 1 |
| Yoko | 2 |

HIGHLIGHTS
1 Bitexco Tower	4 Jade Emperor Pagoda
2 Ben Thanh Market	6 HCMC cafés
3 War Remnants Museum	7 Dong Khoi shops

SEE 'HO CHI MINH CITY CENTRE' MAP FOR DETAIL

SEE 'PHAM NGU LAO' MAP FOR DETAIL

HO CHI MINH CITY ORIENTATION

HCMC is divided into **24 districts**, though tourists rarely travel beyond districts One, Three and Five. The **city centre** – which makes up much of District One – hugs the west bank of the Saigon River; traditionally the French Quarter of the city, this area is still widely known as Saigon. It's filled to near bursting point with hotels (mostly mid- to upper-range), shops and restaurants, and boasts a fair few sights, including some delectable examples of colonial architecture.

Just to the southwest is an area variously referred to by the names of its **three main roads**. Facing a pleasant stretch of quasi-parkland, **Pham Ngu Lao** is the largest of the three; **Bui Vien** is a small street which fills up with beer-guzzling backpackers and locals each evening; while connecting the two is **De Tham**, the drop-off point for most of those arriving in HCMC on an open-tour bus.

North of the backpacker zone is the **Reunification Palace**, one of the city's best sights and surrounded by other appealing places to visit. **North of the centre** you'll find some great Buddhist monuments, as well as a good museum and zoo.

Lastly, way out west across an uninspiring stretch of no-man's-land is the district of **Cho Lon**, famed for its large Chinese population and the many colourful temples and shrines built by their ancestors.

On a human level, however, French rule was invariably harsh; dissent crystallized in the form of strikes through the 1920s and 1930s, but the nationalist movement hadn't gathered any real head of steam before **World War II**'s tendrils spread to Southeast Asia. At its close, the **Potsdam Conference** of 1945 set the British Army the task of disarming Japanese troops in southern Vietnam. Arriving in Saigon two months later, they promptly returned power to the French; so began thirty years of war, though Saigon itself saw little action during this conflict.

Saigon in the American War

Following the partition of Vietnam in 1954 (see p.442), Saigon was designated the capital of the **Republic of South Vietnam** by President Diem. In the mid-1960s, the city became the nerve centre of the American war effort – as well as its R&R capital, with a slough of sleazy bars along Dong Khoi (known then as Tu Do) catering to GIs on leave from duty. Despite the Communist bomb attacks and demonstrations by students and monks that periodically disturbed the peace, local entrepreneurs prospered on the back of the tens of thousands of Americans posted here. The gravy train ran out of steam with the withdrawal of American troops in 1973, and two years later the **Ho Chi Minh Campaign** rolled into the city and through the gates of the presidential palace and the Communists were in control. Within a year, Saigon had been renamed **Ho Chi Minh City**.

Post-reunification

The **war years** extracted a heavy toll: American carpet-bombing of the Vietnamese countryside forced millions of refugees into the relative safety of the city, and ill-advised, post-reunification policies triggered a social and economic stagnation whose ramifications still echo like ripples on a lake. Persecution of southerners with links to the Americans saw many thousands sent to re-education camps. Millions more fled the country by boat.

Only in 1986, when the **economic liberalization**, *doi moi*, was established, and a market economy reintroduced, did the fortunes of the city show signs of taking an upturn. Today the city's resurgence is well advanced, and its inhabitants are eyeing the future with unprecedented optimism – legions of new high-rise buildings sprouting up in the city centre, and other parts of town, hint at the size of a burgeoning middle class, while the culinary options, and the cultural make-up of the city itself, grow ever more cosmopolitan.

1

The city centre

Ho Chi Minh City's de facto city centre is **Lam Son Square**, a road crossing flanked by prime specimens of **colonial-era architecture**. The square sits on **Dong Khoi**, one of the city's main streets, which runs through the centre of District One. Though currently undergoing massive changes, with entire blocks being razed and towering monoliths transforming its image further still, the street still has some character in the form of chic boutiques with eye-catching window displays, and cute cafés in which to pause between shopping or sightseeing.

One block west of Dong Khoi is **Nguyen Hue**, created when Saigon's French administrators laid Charner Boulevard over a filled-in canal and down to the Saigon River. Their brief was to replicate the elegance of a tree-lined Parisian boulevard, and in its day this broad avenue was known as the Champs Elysées of the East; its contemporary incarnation, however, has little character except on Sundays and at festival time (see box, p.77).

The sights listed below follow a general route southwest from the cathedral at the top of Dong Khoi. From here, you can spend half a day mopping up sights – and the odd coffee or snack – on your way south to **Me Linh Square**, where a statue of Tran Hung Dao points across the river.

Notre Dame Cathedral

Off top end of Dong Khoi • Sunrise to sunset • Free

Up at Dong Khoi's northern end, the twin compass-point spires of **Notre Dame Cathedral** have, for decades, been one of Saigon's handiest landmarks. An attractive redbrick building of late nineteenth-century vintage, its interior boasts only scant decoration bar the few stained-glass windows above and behind its altar, and its marble relief *Stations of the Cross*. There's plenty of scope for people-watching, however, as a steady trickle of Catholics pass through in their best silk tunics and black pants, fingering rosary beads, their whispered prayers merging with the insistent murmur of the traffic outside. A statue of the **Virgin Mary** provides the centrepiece to the small **park** fronting the cathedral, where cyclo drivers loiter and kids hawk postcards and maps. Take a close look at Mary's face, as on occasion locals swear they have seen her shed tears.

The General Post Office

Off top end of Dong Khoi • Daily 6am–10pm • Free

Just off the cathedral's southeastern corner is the **General Post Office**, a classic colonial edifice unchanged since its completion in the 1880s; it's worth a peek inside for the nave-like foyer, lent character by two huge map-murals, one charting Saigon and its environs in 1892, the other the telegraphic lines of southern Vietnam and Cambodia in 1936. Further in, a huge portrait of Uncle Ho sporting a healthy tan and warm smile gazes down at the aged wooden benches and tables of the cavernous main hall.

Hotel de Ville

Le Thanh Ton

The stately edifice that stands at Nguyen Hue's northern extent is the former **Hotel de Ville**, the city's most photographed icon and an ostentatious reminder of colonial Europe's stubborn resolve to stamp its imprint on the countries it subjugated, no matter how incongruous. Built between 1902 and 1908 as the city's administrative hub, this wedding cake of a building today houses the People's Committee behind its showy jumble of Corinthian columns, classical figures and shuttered windows, and is not open to the public. A **statue of Uncle Ho** cradling a small child watches over the tiny park fronting the building, where flowerbeds add a splash of colour.

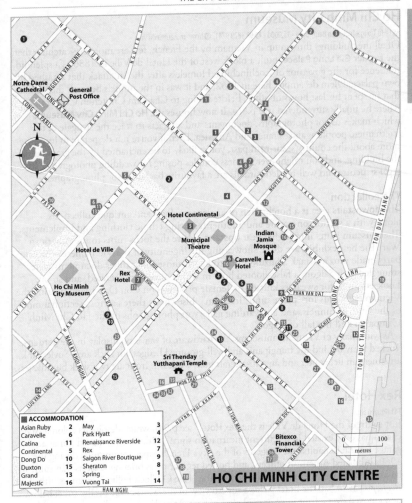

HO CHI MINH CITY CENTRE

■ ACCOMMODATION

Asian Ruby	2	May	3
Caravelle	6	Park Hyatt	4
Catina	11	Renaissance Riverside	12
Continental	5	Rex	7
Dong Do	10	Saigon River Boutique	9
Duxton	15	Sheraton	8
Grand	13	Spring	1
Majestic	16	Vuong Tai	14

● EATING

3T Quan Nuong	33	Lemongrass	21
Augustin's	20	Mai Thai	29
Camargue	8	Maxim's	31
Cha Ca La Vong	28	Matsuzakaya	4
Café Eon	36	Mogambo	38
Elbow Room	37	Modern Meets Culture	13
Fanny's	32	Mon Hue	2
Ganesh	15	Ngon	10
Gartenstadt	25	Pho 24	19
Hoa Tuc	7	Quan Bui	3
Hoi An	1	Refinery	9
Highlands Coffee	14	Sense	24
Jaspa's	27	Skewers	6
Kem Bach Dang	23	Temple Club	34
Kia Coffee	17	Vuon Kieng	18
La Fenetre Soleil	11	Vietnam House	22
La Fourchette	26	Wrap & Roll	12
La Perle de l'Orient	35	Xu	16
Le Jardin	5	ZanZBar	30

■ DRINKING AND NIGHTLIFE

Apocalypse Now	9
Bernie's	3
Blanchy's Tash	8
Blue Gecko	1
Chu	5
Drunken Duck	16
Eon Heli Bar	17
Ice Blue	13
La Fenetre Soleil	6
Level 23	12
Number 5 Bar	18
Pacharan	7
Phatty's	15
Rooftop Garden	11
Saigon Saigon	10
Sax n' Art	14
Vasco's	4
Wild Horse	2

● SHOPPING

Apricot Gallery	11
Art Arcade	4
Artbook	14
Diamond Plaza	1
Fahasa	13
Ipa-nima	12
Khai Silk	6
Lotus Gallery	10
Nagu	3
Nga	8
Saigon Centre	15
T&V	7
Viet Thanh	5
Vincom Centre	2
Zakka	9

Ho Chi Minh City Museum

65 Ly Tu Trong • Tues–Sun 8am–5pm • 15,000đ • ☎ 08 3829 9741, ⊛ hcmc-museum.edu.vn

Of all the buildings thrown up in Vietnam by the French, few are more eye-catching than the former **Gia Long Palace**, built a block west of the Hotel de Ville in 1886 as a splendid residence for the governor of Cochinchina. Homeless after the air attack that smashed his own palace, Diem decamped here in 1962, and it was in the tunnels beneath the building that he spent his last hours of office, before fleeing to Cha Tam Church in Cho Lon where he finally surrendered (see p.86). It now houses the **Ho Chi Minh City Museum**, which makes use of photographs, documents and artefacts to trace the struggle of the Vietnamese people against France and America. Even if you're not desperate to learn more about the country's war-torn past, you're likely to be enchanted by the grandeur of the building, and you might even witness couples posing for wedding photographs, as the regal structure and well-tended gardens are a favourite backdrop for photographers.

The collection

The **downstairs** area is a hotchpotch of ancient artefacts and antique collections, along with a section on nature and another featuring ethnic clothing and implements. The museum shifts into higher gear **upstairs**, where the focus turns to the American War. The best exhibits are those showcasing the ingenuity of the Vietnamese – bicycle parts made into mortars, a Suzuki motorbike in whose inner tubes documents were smuggled into Saigon, a false-floored boat in which guns were secreted, and so on. Look out, too, for sweaters knitted by female prisoners on Con Dao Island bearing the Vietnamese words for "peace" and "freedom". Elsewhere, there's a cross-sectional model of the Cu Chi tunnels, and a rewarding gallery of photographs of the Ho Chi Minh Campaign and the fall of Saigon.

As with many of Vietnam's museums, the hardware of war is on display in the **gardens**. Tucked away behind the frangipanis and well-groomed hedges out back are a Soviet tank, an American helicopter and an anti-aircraft gun, while out front are two sleek but idle jets.

Rex Hotel

141 Nguyen Hue

Just south of the Hotel de Ville is the **Rex Hotel** (see p.94), which despite its colonial-style charm has only existed in its current incarnation since 1976. Having started out as a garage for the Renaults and Peugeots of the city's French expat community, during the 1960s it billeted American officers, and hosted regular press briefing sessions that came to be known by jaded members of the press as the "Five O'Clock Follies". From its fifth-floor *Rooftop Garden* bar, the hotel yields a superb view of the whirl of life on the street below, best enjoyed over a fruit juice or cool glass of beer. At night, the hotel's emblem, a giant crown, lights up on the terrace, providing the city with one of its best-known landmarks.

The Hotel Continental

132–134 Dong Khoi

Dong Khoi briefly widens where the smart, white walls of the **Hotel Continental** announce your arrival in **Lam Son Square**. Once a bastion of French high society, and still one of the city's premier addresses, the hotel's front terrace was the place to see and be seen earlier last century. Little wonder, then, that **Somerset Maugham**'s nose for a story led him here in the mid-1920s: "Outside the hotels are terraces," he recounted, "and at the hour of the aperitif, they are crowded with bearded, gesticulating Frenchmen drinking the sweet and sickly beverages… which they drink in France and they talk nineteen to the dozen in the rolling accent of the Midi… It is very agreeable to sit under the awning on the terrace of the Hotel Continental, with an innocent drink before you, [and] read in the local newspaper heated controversies upon the affairs of the colony." Sadly the terrace no longer exists; if you want to tap into the history of the place, the best you can do is to ensconce yourself in the hotel's café.

The Municipal Theatre

Lam Son Square

On the eastern side of Lam Son Square you'll find the cyclopean, domed entrance of the century-old **Municipal Theatre**. The National Assembly was temporarily housed here in 1955, but today, lovingly restored to its former glory, it once again presents fashion shows, drama and dance, though only occasionally.

The Caravelle Hotel

19–23 Lam Son Square

Facing the theatre is the 1958-built, and now grandiosely revamped, **Caravelle Hotel**, which in a former incarnation found favour with Western journalists assigned to cover the war – its terrace bar saw many a report drafted over a stiff drink. A stroll to the river from here will take you past two of the city's more venerable hotels, the lovingly restored **Grand** (see p.93) on the left, followed thirty metres later on the right by the lavish, riverfront **Majestic** (see p.94).

The Saigon River

Both Dong Khoi and Nguyen Hue end at the Saigon River. In colonial times, the **quay** hugging its confluence with the Ben Nghe Channel provided new arrivals with their first real glimpse of Indochina – scores of coolie-hatted dock-workers lugging sacks of rice off ships, shrimp farmers dredging the oozy shallows, and junks and sampans bobbing on the tide under the vigilant gaze of *colons* imbibing at nearby cafés. Arriving by steamer in 1910, Gabrielle Vassal felt as if "all Saigon had turned out" to welcome her ship, adding that "some expected friends, while others came in the hope of meeting acquaintances, or as mere spectators. One was reminded of a fashionable garden party, for the dresses and equipages were worthy of Paris itself." These days the only river traffic consists of hydrofoils bound for Vung Tau, a few tourist boats and the odd barge.

Sri Thenday Yutthapani Temple

66 Ton That Thiep • Daily sunrise to sunset • Free

With its colourful sculpted gate tower (known as a *gopuram*), the peaceful **Sri Thenday Yutthapani Temple** looks out of place on Ton That Thiep, a trendy strip of boutiques

---

HAVING FUN THE NGUYEN HUE WAY

Nguyen Hue isn't the most beautiful thoroughfare in town, but each Sunday evening the city's trendsetting youth converge here on their motorbikes to circle round and round, girlfriends riding pillion, in a strange ritual that recreates the traffic jams that they suffer through on weekdays. During **Tet** the street also bursts into life, hosting a vast, riotously colourful flower market which draws Vietnamese belles in their thousands to pose in their best *ao dai* among the roses, sunflowers, chrysanthemums and conical orange trees. Much the same thing happens at **Christmas**, albeit with flashy LEDs in place of most flowers, and festive costumes in place of the *ao dai* – the clement temperatures at this time mean that many girls choose to wear Santa hats, red tops and red miniskirts. The Vietnamese have newly discovered the pleasures of picture-taking, and during the evenings the perpetual necessity of avoiding camera sight-lines means that it takes ages to get around at this time.

and bars. The place manages a certain rag-tag charisma, the lavish murals normally associated with Hindu temples replaced by faded paintings of Jawaharlal Nehru, Mahatma Gandhi and various deities from the Hindu pantheon, plus a ceiling gaily studded with coloured baubles and lamps. Steps beyond the topiary to the right of the main sanctuary lead to a roof terrace that's dominated by a weather-beaten tower of deities, whose ranks have been infiltrated by two incongruous characters dressed like public schoolboys in braces, shorts and striped ties.

Indian Jamia Mosque

66 Dong Du • Daily sunrise to sunset • Free

Though glitzy boutiques predominate along Dong Khoi below the *Caravelle*, they haven't yet managed entirely to eradicate the past and it's still possible to winkle out relics of old Saigon. South of Lam Son and just off Dong Du lie the white and blue-washed walls of the 1930s **Indian Jamia Mosque**, now towered over by the *Sheraton* (see p.94). The rounded curves of its arches and its slender minarets make a stark contrast to the utilitarian design of the hotel next door and there's a reassuring sense of peace that's enhanced by the slumbering worshippers lazing around the complex. If you're feeling peckish, check out the simple **restaurant** that is tucked round the back of the mosque, serving cheap and tasty dishes, many of which are vegetarian.

Bitexco Financial Tower

2 Hai Trieu • Daily 9.30am–9.30pm (Fri & Sat 9.30am–10pm); last ticket 45min before closing • 200,000đ • Saigon Skydeck ☎ 083 915 6868, ⓦ saigonskydeck.com

With its tapered shape and distinctive helipad protruding like a tongue near the top, the sleek, glass **Bitexco Financial Tower** is already one of Saigon's most memorable icons, despite only having being completed in 2010. Its base is an uninteresting mix of mall space and offices, but visitors flock to take in the sweeping views from the **Saigon Skydeck** on the 49th floor, 178m above the ground. Look upwards and you'll see the lip of the helipad on the floor above; look down and you should spot a few familiar sights, such as Ben Thanh market, the Hotel de Ville, the Opera House and the tips of the spires of Notre Dame Cathedral far below you.

A little money-saving tip for you: there's a decent **café** on the floor above the Skydeck, where the coffee, drinks and ice cream are overpriced, but still cost less than tickets for the deck itself – it's free to take the lift to this level, where you'll essentially get the same view with a free latte, and some change to boot.

Around Pham Ngu Lao

Referred to by most backpackers as "the backpacker area", the jumble of streets around **Pham Ngu Lao** do, indeed, contain the overwhelming majority of the city's budget accommodation options. There are pricier places here, too, and the same goes for the area's many places to eat – everything from trendy restaurants serving foreign nosh to streetside shacks serving exactly what you see in and on their various tubs and shelves. If you've been to Bangkok's Khaosan Road, you may remark on a certain similarity – it's most evident during the evening, when Bui Vien finds itself crammed with locals and not-so-locals drinking **cheap beer** on tiny chairs. During the daytime, it's one of the city's more pleasant places to **shop**; a little further afield you can visit some great **markets**, including hugely popular Ben Thanh and the lesser-visited Dan Sinh (see box, p.105).

PHAM NGU LAO

0   100
metres

■ ACCOMMODATION					● EATING		■ DRINKING AND NIGHTLIFE		● SHOPPING	
An An	15	Lac Vien	10		Asian Kitchen	2	Allez-Boo	1	Blue Dragon	4
Beautiful Saigon	16	Liberty Parkview	2		Bamboo Garden	4	Cyclo Bar	6	Bookworm	2
Bich Duyen	4	Long Hostel	5		Bobby Brewers	7	Go 2	5	Ginkgo	3
Cat Huy	12	Madam Cuc	13		Café Zoom	9	Le Pub	3	Nam Phuong	5
Eco Backpackers	7	Ngoc Minh	9		Dinh Y	3	Spotted Cow	7	Nhut Van	6
Elios	1	Ngoc Thao	6		La Cantina	1	Thi Café & Lounge	4	Sapa	1
Gia Vien	3	Pink Tulip	14		Pepperoni's	8	Tunnel Bar	2		
Hello	11	Saigon			Pho Quynh	5				
Hong Han	17	Backpackers	8		Sozo	6				

Fine Art Museum

97a Pho Duc Chinh • Tues–Sun 9am–5pm • 10,000đ • ☎ 08 3829 4441

Set in a grand colonial mansion, Ho Chi Minh City's **Fine Art Museum** is worth a visit to view some of the country's best Cham and Oc Eo relics (see p.432). The first floor hosts temporary exhibitions, while the courtyard out back is given over to commerce in the form of artworks on sale by various city galleries. If you're in the market for a piece of Vietnamese art, it's worth checking these places out as standards are high and some prices are affordable. Revolutionary art dominates the second floor, relying heavily on hackneyed images of soldiers, war zones and Uncle Ho, though a few offerings capture the anguish and turmoil of the conflicts. Things get better on the third floor where there's an impressive collection of Oc Eo and Cham statues, gilt Buddhas and other antiquities.

Ben Thanh Market

Junction of Le Loi and Le Lai • Sunrise to sunset • Free

There's much more beneath the pillbox-style clock tower of **Ben Thanh Market** than just the cattle and seafood pictured on its front wall. The city's busiest market for almost a century, and known to the French as the Halles Centrales, Ben Thanh's dense knot of trade has caused it to burst at the seams, disgorging stalls onto the surrounding pavements. Inside the main body of the market, a tight grid of aisles, demarcated according to produce, teems with shoppers; if it's souvenirs you're after, a reconnaissance here will reveal conical hats, basketware, bags, shoes, lacquerware, Da Lat coffee and Good Morning Vietnam T-shirts. Sadly, all stalls are now designated "fixed price", so there's no more good-natured bargaining, and prices are generally a bit higher than elsewhere.

Walk through to the wet market along the back of the complex, and you'll find buckets of eels, clutches of live frogs tied together at the legs, heaps of pigs' ears and snouts and baskets wedged full of hens, among other gruesome sights. If you can countenance the thought of eating after seeing – and smelling – this patch of the market, com, pho and baguette stalls proliferate towards the back of the main hall. In the evenings, foodstalls specializing in seafood set up along the sides of the market, attracting a mixed crowd of locals and tourists.

1

Sri Mariamman Hindu Temple

45 Truong Dinh • Sunrise to sunset • Free

A block northwest of Ben Thanh, the aroma of jasmine and incense replaces the stench of butchery at Truong Dinh's **Sri Mariamman Hindu Temple**. Less engaging than Sri Thendayyutthapani (see p.77), Sri Mariamman's imposing walls are sometimes lined with vendors selling oil, incense and jasmine petals. The walls are topped by a colourful *gopuram*, or bank of sculpted gods. Inside, the gods Mariamman, Maduraiveeran and Pechiamman reside in stone sanctuaries reminiscent of the Cham towers upcountry, and there are more deities set into the walls around the courtyard.

The Reunification Palace and around

One of Ho Chi Minh City's most popular, and important, sights is the **Reunification Palace**, set in a patch of parkland just to the west of the city centre, and within walking distance. The area has enough to keep you occupied for at least half a day: poke east and you'll find yourself at the hulking, red-brick **Notre Dame Cathedral**, head northwest and you'll soon hit the **War Remnants Museum**, while a walk west will take you through **Cong Vien Van Hoa Park** towards **Xa Loi Pagoda**.

The Reunification Palace

135 Nam Ky Khoi Nghia • Daily 7.30–11am & 1–4pm • 30,000đ, tours 200,000đ per group

Five minutes' stroll north up Nam Ky Khoi Nghia from the Ho Chi Minh City Museum, a red flag billows proudly above the **Reunification Palace**. A whitewashed concrete edifice with all the charm of a municipal library, the complex occupies the site of the former Norodom Palace, a colonial mansion erected in 1871 to house the governor-general of Indochina. After the French departure in 1954, Ngo Dinh Diem commandeered this extravagant monument as his presidential residence, but after sustaining extensive damage in a February 1962 assassination attempt by two disaffected Southern pilots, the place was condemned and pulled down. The present building was named the Independence Palace on its completion in 1966, only to be retitled the Reunification Hall when the South fell in 1975 (see box below). The reversion to the label "Palace" was doubtless made for its tourist appeal.

THE TAKING OF THE PRESIDENTIAL PALACE

The **Reunification Palace** is of enormous significance to the Vietnamese – on April 30, 1975, the storming of its gates by a tank belonging to the Northern Army became the defining moment of the **fall of Saigon** and the South. These days, two tanks stand in the grounds as a reminder of the incident.

Of the many Western journalists on hand to witness the spectacle, none was better placed than English journalist and poet **James Fenton**, who conspired to hitch a ride on the tank that first crashed through the gates:

"The tank speeded up, and rammed the left side of the palace gate. Wrought iron flew into the air, but the whole structure refused to give. I nearly fell off. The tank backed again, and I observed a man with a nervous smile opening the centre portion of the gate. We drove into the grounds of the palace, and fired a salute. An NLF soldier took the flag and, waving it above his head, ran into the palace. A few moments later, he emerged on the terrace, waving the flag round and round. Later still, there he was on the roof. The red and yellow stripes of the Saigon regime were lowered at last."

Inside the palace, **Duong Van Minh** ("Big Minh"), sworn in as president only two days before, readied to perform his last presidential duty. "I have been waiting since early this morning to transfer power to you," he said to General Bui Tin, to which the general replied: "Your power has crumbled. You cannot give up what you do not have."

The palace

Spookily unchanged from its working days, much of the building's **interior** is a time capsule of Sixties and Seventies kitsch: pacing its airy banqueting rooms, conference halls and reception areas, it's hard not to think you've strayed into the arch-criminal's lair in a James Bond movie. Most interesting is the **third floor**, where, as well as the presidential library (with works by Laurens van der Post and Graham Greene alongside heavyweight political tomes), there's a curtained projection room, and an entertainment lounge complete with tacky circular sofa and barrel-shaped bar. Nearby, a set of sawn-off elephant's feet add an eerie touch to the decor. Perhaps the most atmospheric part of the building is the **basement** and former command centre, where wood-panelled combat staff quarters yield archaic radio equipment and vast wall maps.

The War Remnants Museum

28 Vo Van Tan • Daily 7.30am–noon & 1.30–5pm • 15,000đ • ☎ 08 3930 6664

A block north of Cong Vien Van Hoa Park, the **War Remnants Museum** is a highly popular attraction, though not one for the faint-hearted. Unlike at the Ho Chi Minh City Museum, you are unlikely to be distracted here by the building that houses the heart-rending exhibits – a distressing compendium of the horrors of modern warfare. Some of the instruments of destruction are on display in the courtyard outside, including a 28-tonne howitzer and a ghoulish collection of bomb parts. There's also a guillotine that harvested heads at the Central Prison on Ly Tu Trong, first for the French and later for Diem.

The collection

Inside, a series of halls present a grisly portfolio of **photographs** of mutilation, napalm burns and torture. Most shocking is the gallery detailing the effects of the 75 million litres of defoliant sprays dumped across the country: beside the expected images of bald terrain, hideously malformed foetuses are preserved in pickling jars. A gallery that looks at international opposition to the war as well as the American peace movement adds a sense of balance, and makes a change from the self-glorifying tone of most Vietnamese museums. Accounts of servicemen – such as veteran B52 pilot Michael Heck – who attempted to discharge themselves from the war on ethical grounds are also featured. Artefacts donated to the museum by returned US servicemen add to the reconciliatory tone.

At the back of the museum is a grisly mock-up of the **tiger cages**, the godless prison cells of Con Son Island (see p.207), which could have been borrowed from the movie set of *Papillon*.

Cong Vien Van Hoa Park

Adjoining the western edge of the Reunification Palace's grounds, **Cong Vien Van Hoa Park**, also known as Tau Dan Park, is a municipal space whose tree-shaded lawns are pleasant for a stroll and heave with life each Sunday. During the colonial era, the park's northernmost corner was home to one of the lynchpins of French expat society, the **Cercle Sportif**, a Westerners-only sports club where the *colons* gathered to swim and play tennis before sinking an aperitif and discussing the day's events. Today it functions as the Workers' Sports Club and also houses the Golden Dragon Water Puppet Theatre.

Golden Dragon Water Puppet Theatre

55b Nguyen Thi Minh Khai • 50min shows daily at 5pm, 6.30pm and sometimes 7.45pm • 240,000đ • Tickets on the door or book through ☎ 08 3840 4027

If you sink into the depths of depression on leaving the War Remnants' Museum, cheer yourself up at this **water puppet theatre**; few people fail to be enchanted at their first

1

THE SELF-IMMOLATION OF THICH QUANG DUC

In the early morning of June 11, 1963, a column of Buddhist monks left the **Xa Loi Pagoda** and processed to the intersection of Cach Mang Thang Tam and Nguyen Dinh Chieu. There, **Thich Quang Duc**, a 66-year-old monk from Hue, sat down in the lotus position and meditated as fellow monks doused him in petrol, and then set light to him in protest at the repression of Buddhists by President Diem, who was a Catholic. As flames engulfed the impassive monk and passers-by prostrated themselves before him, the cameras of the Western press corps rolled, and by the next morning the grisly event had grabbed the world's headlines. More self-immolations followed, and Diem's heavy-handed responses at Xa Loi – some four hundred monks and nuns were arrested and others cast from the top of the tower – led to massed popular demonstrations against the government. Diem, it was clear, had become a liability. On November 2, he and his brother were assassinated after taking refuge in Cho Lon's Cha Tam Church (see p.86), the victims of a military coup.

encounter with these waterborne buffoons. The tradition of water puppetry is much stronger in the north (see p.12), but it's such an appealing aspect of Vietnamese culture that there's plenty of demand for shows in the south as well. The early evening timing of the shows make them a fun activity with the kids before bed or dinner; they consist of a dozen or so sketches on themes like rearing ducks and catching foxes, boat racing and unicorns playing with a ball.

Xa Loi Pagoda

89 Ba Huyen Thanh Quan • Daily 6–11.30am & 2–9pm • Free

Vapid **Xa Loi Pagoda**, a short walk west of the War Remnants Museum, became a hotbed of Buddhist opposition to Diem in 1963. The austere, 1956-built complex is unspectacular, its most striking component a tall **tower** whose unlovely beige blocks lend it a drabness that even six tiers of Oriental roofs can't quite dispel. The main **sanctuary**, accessed by a dual staircase (men scale the left-hand flight, women the right), is similarly dull: beyond a vast joss-stick urn inventively decorated with marbles and shards of broken china, it's a lofty hall featuring a huge gilt Buddha and fourteen murals that narrate his life. Turn left and around the back of the Buddha, and you'll come across a shrine commemorating **Thich Quang Duc** and the other monks who set fire to themselves in Saigon in 1963 (see box above). Quang Duc's is the ghostly figure holding a set of beads, to the left of the shrine.

North of the centre

North of Notre Dame Cathedral, **Le Duan Boulevard** runs between the Botanical Gardens and the grounds of the Reunification Palace. Known as Norodom Boulevard to the French, who lined it with tamarind trees to imitate a Gallic thoroughfare, it soon became a residential and diplomatic enclave with a crop of fine pastel-hued colonial villas to boot. Its present name doffs a cap to Le Duan, the secretary-general of the Lao Dong, or Workers Party, from 1959 until his death in 1986. Turn northeast from the top of Dong Khoi and the sense of harmony created by Le Duan's graceful colonial piles ends abruptly with a number of brand-new edifices. There's ample sightseeing potential here, however: the **Jade Emperor Pagoda** and **Le Van Duyet Temple** are undervisited, if anything, while closer to the centre, the city's **Botanical Garden**, **zoo** and **History Museum** all sit in the same swathe of land.

The Botanical Gardens

Junction of Le Duan and Nguyen Binh Khiem • Daily 7am–6pm • 12,000đ

The pace of life slows down considerably – and the odours of cut grass and frangipani blooms replace the smell of exhaust fumes – when you duck into the city's **Botanical Gardens**, accessed by a gate at the far eastern end of Le Duan, and bounded to the east by the Thi Nghe Channel. Established in 1864 by the Frenchmen Germain and Pierre (respectively a vet and a botanist), the gardens' social function has remained unchanged in decades, and their tree-shaded paths still attract as many courting couples and promenaders as when Norman Lewis followed the "clusters of Vietnamese beauties on bicycles" and headed there one Sunday morning in 1950 to find the gardens "full of these ethereal creatures, gliding in decorous groups, sometimes accompanied by gallants". In its day, the gardens harboured an impressive collection of tropical flora, including many species of orchid. Post-liberation, the place went to seed but nowadays a bevy of gardeners keep it reasonably well tended, and portrait photographers lurk to take snaps of you framed by flowers.

The zoo

Forming part of the gardens is the city **zoo**, home to camels, elephants, crocodiles and big cats, and also komodo dragons – the latter a gift from the government of Indonesia. Unfortunately, conditions are rather poor and some animals look half-crazed, so it could be a harrowing experience if you're an animal lover. There's also an **amusement park** that is sometimes open, and you can get an ice cream or a coconut from one of the several **cafés** sprinkled around the grounds.

The History Museum

2 Nguyen Binh Khiem • Tues–Sun 8–11am & 1.30–4.30pm • 15,000đ • ☎ 08 3829 8146 • Water puppetry shows on the hour from 10am–4pm, except 1pm; 40,000đ

A pleasing, pagoda-style roof crowns the city's **History Museum**, next to the Botanical Gardens. It houses fifteen galleries illuminating Vietnam's past from primitive times to the end of French rule by means of a decent if unastonishing

---

OPERATION FREQUENT WIND

Located at 4 Le Duan, the current nondescript building that houses the US Consulate was built right on top of the site of the infamous **former American Embassy**, where a commemorative plaque is now the only reminder of its existence and significance in the American War. Two events immortalized the former building on this site, in operation from 1967 to 1975 and left standing half-derelict until 1999 as a sobering legacy. The first came in the pre-dawn hours of January 31, 1968, when a small band of **Viet Cong commandos** breached the embassy compound during the nationwide Tet Offensive. That the North could mount such an effective attack on the hub of US power in Vietnam was shocking to the American public. In the six hours of close-range fire that followed, five US guards died, and with them the popular misconception that the US Army had the Vietnam conflict under control.

Worse followed seven years later, during "**Operation Frequent Wind**", the chaotic helicopter evacuation that marked the US' final undignified withdrawal from Vietnam. The embassy building was one of thirteen designated landing zones where all foreigners were to gather upon hearing the words, "It is 112 degrees and rising" on the radio followed by Bing Crosby singing *White Christmas*. At noon on April 29, 1975, the signal was broadcast, and for the next eighteen hours scores of helicopters shuttled passengers out to the US Navy's Seventh Fleet off Vung Tau. Around two thousand evacuees were lifted from the roof of the embassy alone, before Ambassador Graham Martin finally left with the Stars and Stripes in the early hours of the following morning. In a tragic postscript to US involvement, as the last helicopter lifted off, many of the Vietnamese civilians who for hours had been clamouring at the gates were left to suffer the Communists' reprisals.

1

array of artefacts and pictures. Dioramas of defining moments in Vietnamese military history – including Ngo Quyen's 938 AD victory at Bach Dang (see p.328) – lend the collection some cohesion.

Should you tire of Vietnamese history, try exploring other halls, focusing on such disparate subjects as Buddha images from around Asia; seventh- and eighth-century Champa art; and the customs and crafts of the ethnic minorities of Vietnam. There's also a room jam-packed with exquisite ceramics from Japan, Thailand and Vietnam, and you could round off your visit at the **water-puppetry theatre**.

Jade Emperor Pagoda

73 Mai Thi Luu • Daily 5am–7pm • Free

A few blocks northwest of the Botanical Gardens, the **Jade Emperor Pagoda**, or Chua Phuoc Hai, was built by the city's Cantonese community at the beginning of the twentieth century. If you visit just one temple in town, make it this one, with its exquisite panels of carved gilt woodwork, and its panoply of weird and wonderful deities, both Taoist and Buddhist, beneath a roof that groans under the weight of dragons, birds and animals.

The main buildings

To the right of the temple's tree-lined front **courtyard** is a grubby pond whose occupants have earned the temple its alternative moniker of Tortoise Pagoda. Once over the threshold, look up and you'll see Chinese characters announcing: "The Only Enlightenment is in Heaven" – though only after your eyes have adjusted to the fug of joss-stick smoke. A statue of the **Jade Emperor** lords it over the main hall's central altar, sporting an impressive moustache, and he's surrounded by a retinue of similarly moustached followers.

A rickety flight of steps in the chamber to the right of the main hall runs up to a **balcony** looking out over the pagoda's elaborate **roof**. Set behind the balcony, a neon-haloed statue of Quan Am (see p.454) stands on an altar. Left out of the main hall, meanwhile, you're confronted by Kim Hua, to whom women pray for fertility; judging by the number of babies weighing down the female statues around her, her success rate is high. The Chief of Hell resides in the larger chamber behind Kim Hua's niche. Given his job description, he doesn't look particularly demonic, though his attendants, in sinister black garb, are certainly equipped to administer the sorts of punishments depicted in the ten dark-wood reliefs on the walls before them.

Le Van Duyet Temple

Dinh Tien Hoang • Sunrise to sunset • Free

A national hero is commemorated at the **Temple of Marshal Le Van Duyet**, known locally as Lang Ong and sited at the top of Dinh Tien Hoang, in the region of the city where the **Gia Dinh Citadel** once stood. A military mandarin and eunuch, Le Van Duyet (1764–1832) succeeded in putting down the Tay Son Rebellion, and later became military governor of Gia Dinh.

The temple itself, which underwent extensive renovations in 2008, stretches through three halls behind a facade decorated with unicorns assembled from shards of chinaware. Inside, a bronze statue of the marshal sits in front of an altar, flanked by an ancient pair of tusks. A steady stream of visitors pay their respects by burning incense, while the ringing of a brass bell adds to the pious mood. On the first day of the eighth lunar month, to coincide with the marshal's birthday, a **theatre** troupe dramatizes his life; and there's more activity around Tet, when crowds of pilgrims gather to ask for safekeeping in the forthcoming year. Strolling around the grounds reveals the **tombs** in which the marshal and his wife are buried.

Cho Lon

The dense cluster of streets comprising the Chinese ghetto of **Cho Lon** was once distinct from Saigon, though it blends seamlessly into present-day HCMC and is linked to the centre by the five-kilometre-long umbilical cord of Tran Hung Dao. The distinction was already somewhat blurred by 1950, when Norman Lewis found the city's Chinatown "swollen so enormously as to become its grotesque Siamese twin", and the steady influx of refugees into the city during the war years saw to it that the two districts eventually became joined by a swathe of urban development.

A short stroll around Cho Lon (whose name, meaning "**big market**", couldn't be more apposite) will make clear that, even by this city's standards, the mercantile mania here is breathtaking. The largest of Cho Lon's many covered markets are Tran Phu's An Dong, built in 1991, and the more recent but equally vast An Dong II. If you're looking to sightsee rather than shop, then historic **Binh Tay** is of far more interest. You'll get most out of Cho Lon simply by losing yourself in its amorphous mass of life: amid

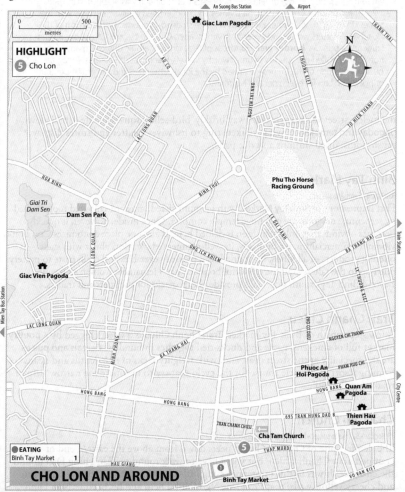

CHO LON AND AROUND

1

THE HISTORY OF CHO LON

The **ethnic Chinese**, or **Hoa**, first began to settle at Cho Lon around 1900; many came from existing enclaves in My Tho and Bien Hoa. The area soon became the largest Hoa community in the country, a title it still holds, with a population of over half a million. Residents gravitated towards others from their region of China, with each congregation commissioning its own places of worship and clawing out its own commercial niche – thus the Cantonese handled retailing and groceries, the Teochew dealt in tea and fish, the Fukien were in charge of rice, and so on.

The great wealth that Cho Lon generated had to be spent somewhere. By the early twentieth century, sassy restaurants, casinos and brothels existed to facilitate this. Also prevalent were **fumeries**, where nuggets of opium were quietly smoked from the cool comfort of a wooden opium bed. Among the expats and wealthy Asians who frequented them was Graham Greene, and he recorded his experiences in *Ways of Escape*. By the 1950s, Cho Lon was a potentially dangerous place to be, its vice industries controlled by the **Binh Xuyen** gang. First the French and then the Americans trod carefully here, while Viet Minh and Viet Cong **activists** hid out in its cramped backstreets – as Frank Palmos found to his cost, when the jeep he and four other correspondents were riding in was ambushed in 1968.

Post-reunification, Cho Lon saw hard times. As Hanoi aligned itself increasingly with the Soviet Union, Sino–Vietnamese tensions became strained. Economic **persecution** of the Hoa made matters worse, and, when Vietnam invaded Chinese-backed Cambodia, Beijing launched a punitive **border war**. Hundreds of thousands of ethnic Chinese, many of them from Cho Lon, fled the country in unseaworthy vessels, fearing recriminations. Today, the business acumen of the Chinese is valued by the local authorities, and the distemper that gripped Cho Lon for over a decade is a memory.

the melee, streetside barbers clip away briskly, bird-sellers squat outside tumbledown **pagodas and temples**, heaving markets ring to fishwives' chatter and stores display mushrooms, dried shrimps and rice paper.

Binh Tay Market

Hau Giang • Sunrise to sunset

First impressions of **Binh Tay Market**, with its multi-tiered, mustard-coloured roofs stalked by serpentine dragons, are of a huge temple complex. Once inside, however, it quickly becomes obvious that only mammon is deified here. If any one place epitomizes Cho Lon's vibrant commercialism, it's Binh Tay, its well-regimented corridors abuzz with stalls offering products of all kinds, from dried fish, pickled vegetables and chilli paste to pottery piled up to the rafters, and the colourful bonnets that Vietnamese women so favour. Beyond Binh Tay's south side, stalls provide cheap snacks for shoppers and traders.

Tran Chanh Chieu

A few steps north of Binh Tay market, **Tran Chanh Chieu** is a street clogged by a **poultry market** full of chickens, geese and ducks tied together in bundles. **Cereals and pulses** are the speciality at the street's east end, with weighty sacks of rice, lentils and beans forming a sort of obstacle course for the cyclo that try to negotiate the narrow strip of roadway still visible.

Cha Tam Church

25 Hoc Lac • Sunrise to sunset • Free, but small tip expected

The slender spire of **Cha Tam Church** peers down from above the eastern end of cramped Tran Chanh Chieu, but you'll have to walk round to Tran Hung Dao to find the entrance. It was in this unprepossessing little church, with its Oriental outer gate and cheery yellow walls, that President Ngo Dinh Diem and his brother Ngo Dinh

1

Nhu holed up on November 1, 1963, during the coup that saw them chased out of the Gia Long Palace (see p.76). Early the next morning, Diem phoned the leaders of the coup and surrendered. An M-113 armoured car duly picked them up, but they were shot dead by ARVN soldiers before the vehicle reached central Saigon.

With clearance from the janitor (who's usually somewhere around hoping for a tip) you can clamber up into the **belfry** and under the bells, Quasimodo-style, to join the statue of St Francis Xavier for the fine views he enjoys of Cho Lon. The janitor can also point out the pew where Diem and his brother sat praying as they awaited their fate.

Nguyen Trai

Cho Lon's greatest architectural treasures are its temples and pagodas, many of which stand on or around **Nguyen Trai**, whose four-kilometre sweep northeast to Pham Ngu Lao starts just north of Cha Tam Church.

Quan Am Pagoda

12 Lao Tu • Sunrise to sunset • Free

North of Nguyen Trai's junction with Chau Van Liem, on tiny Lao Tu, **Quan Am Pagoda** is the pick of the bunch in this part of town. Set back from the bustle of Cho Lon, it has an almost tangible air of antiquity, enhanced by the film of dust left by the incense spirals hanging from its rafters. Don't be too quick to dive inside, though: the pagoda's ridged roofs are impressive enough from the outside, their colourful crust of "glove-puppet" figurines, teetering houses and temples from a distance creating the illusion of a gingerbread house. Framing the two door gods and the pair of stone lions assigned to keeping out evil spirits are gilt panels depicting petrified scenes from traditional Chinese court life – dancers, musicians, noblemen in sedan chairs, a game of chequers being played.

When Cho Lon's Fukien congregation established this pagoda well over a century ago, they dedicated it to the Goddess of Mercy, but it's **A Pho**, the Queen of Heaven, who stands in the centre of the main hall, beyond an altar tiled like a mortuary slab. A pantheon of deities throngs the open courtyard behind her, decked out in sumptuous apparel and attracting a steady traffic of worshippers. Twin ovens, flanking the main chamber, burn a steady supply of fake money offerings and incense sticks.

Phuoc An Hoi Pagoda

Hung Vuong • Sunrise to sunset • Free

Three minutes' walk north of the Quan Am Pagoda, **Phuoc An Hoi Quan Pagoda** (aka Minh Huong Pagoda) is a disarming place. Beyond the menacing dragons and sea monsters patrolling its roof, and the superb wood carving depicting a king being entertained by jousters and minstrels hanging over the entrance, is the temple's

---

SHOPS ON HAI THUONG LAN ONG

Five minutes' walk towards the river from the Cha Tam Church, along Tran Hung Dao, through the cloth market, brings you out at the eastern end of the street. **Shops** specializing in Chinese and Vietnamese **traditional medicine** have long proliferated here, identifiable by the sickly sweet aroma that hangs over them. Named after a famous herbalist who practised and studied in Hanoi two centuries ago, the street is lined by dingy shophouses banked with cabinets whose wooden drawers are crammed full of herbs. Step over the sliced roots laid out to dry along the pavement and peer inside any one of the shops, and you'll see rheumy men and women weighing out prescriptions on ancient balances. Steepled around them are boxes, jars and paper bags containing anything from dried bark to antler fur and tortoise glue. Predictably popular is **ginseng**, the Oriental cure-all said to combat everything from heart disease to acne. Also available are monkey-, tiger- and rhino-based medicines – despite a government ban on these products.

1

sanctuary, in which stately Quan Cong sits, instantly recognizable by his blood-red face, and fronted by two storks standing on top of turtles fashioned from countless plectrum-shaped ceramic shards.

Thien Hau Pagoda

Nguyen Trai • Sunrise to sunset • Free

Thien Hua Pagoda is popular with women making offerings to Me Sanh, Goddess of Fertility, and to Long Mau, Goddess of Mothers and Newborn Babies. When Cantonese immigrants established the temple towards the middle of the nineteenth century, they named it after Thien Hau, Goddess of Seafarers. New arrivals from China would have hastened here to express their gratitude for a safe passage across the South China Sea. Three statues of her stand on the altar, one behind the other, while a large mural on the inside of the front wall depicts her guiding wildly pitching ships across a storm-tossed sea. The temple's most attractive aspect is its roof, bristling with so many figurines you wonder how those at the edge can keep their balance.

North of Cho Lon

Two of Ho Chi Minh City's oldest and most atmospheric places of worship, the **Giac Lam** and **Giac Vien Pagodas**, are tucked away in the hinterland to the north of Cho. Also nearby is **Dam Sen leisure park**. The best way to get to these destinations is by xe om or cyclo, as they are hidden away in the backstreets.

Giac Lam Pagoda

118 Lac Long Quan • Sunrise to sunset • Free

You'll see the gate leading up to **Giac Lam Pagoda** on Lac Long Quan, a couple of hundred metres northeast of its intersection with Le Dai Hanh. From the gate, a short track passes a newish tower (its seven levels are scaleable and afford good city views) and a cluster of monks' tombs on its way to the actual pagoda. Built in 1744, rambling Giac Lam is draped over 98 hardwood pillars, each inscribed with traditional *chu nom* characters (Vietnamese script, based on Chinese ideograms). From its terracotta floor-tiles and extravagant chandeliers to the antique tables at which monks sit to take tea, Giac Lam is characterized by a clutter that imbues it with an appealingly fusty feel, and a reassuring sense of age.

The funerary chamber

The entrance to the temple is at the back right of the building, which takes you through to the funerary chamber, flanked by row upon row of gilt tablets above photos of the deceased. The many-armed goddess that stands in the centre of the chamber is **Chuan De**, a manifestation of Quan Am. A right turn leads to a **courtyard-garden** around which runs a roof studded with blue and white porcelain saucers.

The classroom

Monks occasionally sit studying on the huge wooden benches in the peaceful old **classroom** at the back of the complex. The panels in this chamber depict the ten Buddhist hells; study them carefully, and you'll see sinners being variously minced, fed to dogs, dismembered and disembowelled by fanged demons.

The main sanctuary

To the left of the funerary chamber as you enter the pagoda is the **main sanctuary**, whose multi-tiered altar dais groans under the weight of the many Buddhist and Taoist

1

statues it supports (remember to take off your shoes before entering). Elsewhere in this chamber you'll spot an ensemble of oil lamps balanced on a Christmas-tree-shaped wooden frame. Worshippers pen prayers on pieces of paper, which they affix to the tree and then feed the lamps with an offering of oil. A similar ritual is attached to the bell across the chamber, though in this case people believe that their prayers are hastened to the gods by the ringing of the bell.

Giac Vien Pagoda

Lac Long Quan • Sunrise to sunset • Free

Hidden away in a maze of backstreets, **Giac Vien Pagoda** was founded in the late eighteenth century, and is said to have been frequented by Emperor Gia Long. On entering its red doors daubed with yellow *chu nom* characters, visitors are confronted by banks of old photos and funerary tablets flanking long refectory-style tables. The two rows of black pillars lend an arresting sense of depth to this first chamber, which is dominated by a panel depicting a ferocious-looking red lion. Continue around the stone walls (crafted, incongruously, in classical Greek style) and into the **main sanctuary**, and you'll find a sizeable congregation of deities, as well as a tree of lamps similar to the one at Giac Lam. The monks residing in Giac Vien are hospitable to a fault, and you'll probably be invited for a cup of tea before you leave.

ARRIVAL AND DEPARTURE

HO CHI MINH CITY

The lion's share of new **arrivals** to Vietnam fly into Ho Chi Minh City's Tan Son Nhat Airport, which is also, of course, a major hub for internal flights. Arriving overland, you'll end up either at the train station, a short distance north of the downtown area, at one of a handful of bus terminals inconveniently scattered across the city, or right in the centre on De Tham at the end of an open-tour bus ride.

BY PLANE

Tan Son Nhat Airport is 7km northwest of the city centre. Facilities include duty-free; foreign exchange and plenty of ATMs; taxi, limo and hotel booking desks; a post office (daily 9am–10pm); and left-luggage facilities (daily 7.30am–10pm; 60,000đ per bag per day, 100,000đ for larger items).

Taxi The journey downtown takes about 30–45min. The easiest way into the city centre is by metered taxi (140,000–210,000đ) from outside the terminal. Make sure the driver switches on the meter, since many still ask for $25, claiming it'll be the same in the end; as ever, Mai Linh and Vinasun are the best companies to go with. Note that most drivers insist on your paying the 10,000đ entrance fee both on their way in and out of the airport, even though they only have to stump up the cash once, on exit. If you're set on a particular hotel, ensure that your driver knows exactly where you want to go (show him in writing if possible). Alternatively, many hotels offer a pick-up service for advance bookings, typically in the 420,000đ range.

Bus If you don't have much baggage, you can get the #152 a/c bus (every 15min; 5000đ) from the domestic terminal, 200m to the right of the international terminal, to Dong Khoi and Pham Ngu Lao. A xe om will run you into town for about 100,000đ, but you'll have to bargain hard: to find one, walk outside the airport gates (only a hundred metres or so).

Domestic flights Vietnam's constantly growing network of domestic flights connects Ho Chi Minh City with every other major town in the country, which is good news for visitors with limited time. Fares are very reasonable, and flying to places like Hanoi, Hue, Nha Trang and Da Lat can save both bags of time and a very sore backside.

Airlines Air France, 130 Dong Khoi ☎ 08 3829 0981; British Airways, 114 Nguyen Hue ☎ 08 3930 2933; Cathay Pacific, 5f Centec Tower 72–74 Nguyen Thi Minh Khai ☎ 08 3822 3203; China Airlines, 37 Ton Duc Thang ☎ 08 3911 1591; Emirates, 115 Nguyen Hue ☎ 08 3911 3099; Japan Airlines, 4f Hotel Nikko, 235 Nguyen Van Cu ☎ 08 3925 7808; Jetstar Pacific, 117 Vo Thi Sau ☎ 08 6290 7349; Lufthansa Airport, T2 ☎ 09 0661 6102; Malaysia Airlines, 37 Ton Duc Thang ☎ 08 3829 2529; Singapore Airlines, 29 Le Duan ☎ 08 3823 1588; Thai Airways, 29 Le Duan ☎ 08 3822 3365; United Airlines, 115 Nguyen Hue ☎ 08 3823 4755; VietJet Air, 35 Nguyen Kiem ☎ 08 3551 6220; Vietnam Airlines, 126 Hung Vuong ☎ 08 3844 6667.

Destinations Buon Ma Thuot (5–6 daily; 1hr); Ca Mau (1–2 daily; 1hr); Can Tho (1–2 daily; 1hr); Con Dao (5–6 daily; 1hr); Da Lat (3 daily; 50min); Da Nang (10–16 daily; 1hr 10min); Haiphong (5–7 daily; 2hr); Hanoi (1–2 hourly; 2hr); Hue (4–5 daily; 1hr 20min); Nha Trang (8 daily; 1hr 10min); Phu Quoc (7–18 daily; 1hr); Pleiku (4–5 daily; 1hr 15min); Quy Nhon (2–3 daily; 1hr 10min).

BY TRAIN

Train station Trains from the north pull in at the Ga Saigon (☎08 3843 6528), 3km northwest of town, on Nguyen Thong. Since it's a few kilometres from the centre, it's best to take a taxi (about 60,000–70,000đ), though you might save a dollar if you bargain furiously with a xe om driver.

Tickets Vietnamese trains are oversubscribed, so book as far ahead as possible – particularly for a sleeping berth (see p.33). Most tour operators, as well as some guest-houses and hotels, can reserve tickets for a small fee. The official agent for the railways is Saigon Railways Tourist Service Company, 275c Pham Ngu Lao (☎08 3836 7640), which has computerized reservations and doesn't charge any extra commission.

Destinations Da Nang (5 daily; 15–20hr); Dieu Tri (6 daily; 11–13hr); Hanoi (5 daily; 30–41hr); Hue (5 daily; 21–23hr); Muong Man (5 daily; 3–4hr); Nha Trang (6 daily; 6–7hr); Ninh Binh (4 daily; 34–37hr); Quang Ngai (5 daily; 13–16hr); Thap Cham (6 daily; 5–6hr); Vinh (5 daily; 29–33hr).

BY BUS

Regular buses stop at a clutch of different terminals, while most arrivals from Phnom Penh in Cambodia usually terminate on De Tham, in the heart of the budget accommodation area (see map, p.79).

Mien Dong bus station Buses to and from the north arrive at this sprawling station 5km northeast of the city on Xo Viet Nghe Tinh; the #26 bus shuttles between here and Ben Thanh bus station.

Ben Thanh bus station Centrally located, the bus station is a five-minute walk from the budget hotel district.

Mien Tay bus station Buses to and from the southwest terminate here, 10km west of the city centre in An Lac District; take a taxi or a #2 bus to Ben Thanh bus station.

Shuttle buses Well-signposted shuttle buses between Mien Tay (#2) and Mien Dong (#26) terminals make it possible to bypass central Ho Chi Minh City altogether in the event that you want to travel direct from the Mekong Delta to the north, or vice versa.

Destinations Buon Ma Thuot (7hr); Ca Mau (8hr 30min); Can Tho (4hr); Chau Doc (6hr); Da Lat (7hr); Da Nang (21hr); Hanoi

---

TOUR AGENTS

Tour agencies abound in Ho Chi Minh City and offer a range of itineraries, from one-day whistle-stop tours around the region to lengthy trips upcountry including accommodation. Most of the recommended operators below can lay on **tailor-made itineraries**, **private cars** and personal **guides** for you, but be aware that we receive numerous reports of inefficient and **unscrupulous companies**, so it's worth choosing your agent carefully. Provisos and tips on signing up for a tour in Vietnam are listed in Basics (see p.37).

Ann Tours 58 Ton That Tung ☎08 3925 3636, ⓦann tours.com. Highly recommended, it offers good-value, tailor-made tours.

Buffalo Tours 81 Mac Thi Buoi ☎08 3827 9170, ⓦbuffalotours.com. This Western-managed set-up specializes in customized tours throughout Indochina.

Delta Adventure Tours 267 De Tham ☎08 3920 2112, ⓦdeltaadventuretours.com. Highly recommended for its boat tours to the Cu Chi tunnels, the Mekong Delta or all the way to Phnom Penh.

Exotissimo Travel 80–82 Phan Xich Long ☎08 3995 9898, ⓦexotissimo.com. Has an extensive tour programme that includes special interests, Laos and Cambodia add-ons.

Grandeur Journeys 225 Hai Ba Trung ☎08 3823 5331, ⓦgrandeurjourneys.com. Organizes custom itineraries throughout Indochina and can deal with requests for specialized tours.

Innoviet 158 Bui Ven ☎08 2216 5303, ⓦinnoviet .com. This company runs eco-friendly, small-group bike and boat tours of the Delta as well as half-day city tours.

Kim Travel 189 De Tham ☎08 3920 5552, ⓦkimtravel.com. A veteran of the independent travel scene, it offers open-tour buses, flight and rail bookings, car and minibus rental and guides.

The Sinh Tourist 246–248 De Tham ☎08 3838 9597, ⓦthesinhtourist.com. Offers cut-price organized tours of Vietnam, open-bus tours, guides, visa services, buses and boats to Cambodia and vehicle rental. Beware of copycat operators with similar names.

Sinhbalo Adventure Travel 283/20 Pham Ngu Lao ☎08 3837 6766, ⓦsinhbalo.com. A super-efficient set-up that specializes in customized tours such as bicycle expeditions along the Ho Chi Minh trail (see ⓦcyclingvietnam.net), motorbike tours, long-distance boat cruises and kayaking in the Mekong Delta. It also has a wealth of reliable travel info.

TNK Travel 216 De Tham ☎08 3920 4766, ⓦtnk travelvietnam.com. Cheap tours to destinations country-wide from this operator, which gets good feedback from those who sign up for them.

XO Tours ☎09 3308 3727, ⓦxotours.vn. Xe om rides with a difference – this company uses *ao dai*-wearing girls for its interesting range of city tours, which include food, shopping and Saigon-by-night options.

1

(41hr); Ha Tien (9hr); Hue (25hr); My Tho (2hr); Nha Trang (10hr); Phan Thiet (4–5hr); Qui Nhon (13hr); Vung Tau (2hr).

BY TOUR BUS

Many of the tour operators concentrated around De Tham sell tickets for open-tour buses that crisscross the country. Tickets, information and departing buses, which leave daily in the early morning or evening, can be found at the various companies' offices around De Tham and Pham Ngu Lao. Sample fares from Ho Chi Minh City are as follows, often including stops in intervening destinations: Da Lat $13, Hanoi $39–50, Hoi An $23, Hue $30, Mui Ne $8, Nha Trang $10 and Phnom Penh $11.

BY BOAT

Boat trips One of the most popular boat trips from Ho Chi Minh City is to Phnom Penh, with a stopover in Chau Doc in the delta. Visas can be organized by tour agents, and if you book with a company like Delta Adventure Travel (see p.91), you won't have to change boats halfway. Prices start at around $30 per person. It's also possible to take a boat trip to the Cu Chi tunnels (see box, p.107) or the Mekong Delta (see p.112). These trips leave from various docks along the river, but your fee will include transport to and from the hotel or booking office.

Hydrofoils to and from Vung Tau make approximately hourly departures from the Passenger Quay of Ho Chi Minh City (Bach Dang Wharf), opposite the end of Ham Nghi at 2 Ton Duc Thang. For tickets (200,000đ, or 250,000đ on weekends) and further information, contact the Vina Express booth at the jetty (daily 6.30–11am & 1.30–4.30pm; ☎08 3829 7892); services often sell out on weekends.

Destinations Vung Tau (about 8 daily; 1hr 15min).

GETTING AROUND

Faint-hearted visitors to Ho Chi Minh City will blanch on first encountering the chaos that passes for its **traffic system**. Thousands of motorcycles, bicycles and cyclo fill the city's streets and boulevards in an insectile swarm that is now supplemented by a burgeoning number of cars and minibuses, most with their horns constantly blaring. A new metro system is set to be up and running by 2018, though the initial line will not be of much use to travellers.

By cyclo For many visitors a leisurely cyclo ride around HCMC adds a uniquely Vietnamese touch to the experience. They are a dying breed here, since the local government is in the process of phasing them out – they are already forbidden to enter many key streets in the city centre, so if your rider seems to be taking a circuitous route, he may not be doing so to bump up the fare. Scams, however, are commonplace. Agree on a rate of 70,000–100,000đ an hour (showing notes if possible, to avoid any zero-related misunderstandings); you'll likely have to haggle. Though it's feasible to ride two (very small) passengers to a cyclo, the corresponding rise in cost and lessening of comfort make this a false economy.

By taxi Taxis are inexpensive and worth considering if only to avoid interminable haggling over fares. They're easy to flag down on the street, though it's just as easy to call for a pick-up wherever you are. The flag fare is 12,000đ but you can still traverse a decent chunk of the city for 40,000đ, so they are well worth considering, especially given the horrifying pollution levels of the city's streets. Stick with reliable companies like Mai Linh (☎08 3838 3838) and Vinasun (☎08 3827 2727), as many other drivers rig their meters to ratchet up the dong.

By xe om Expect to pay 25,000–30,000đ for a short ride around town.

On foot Despite the city's massive sprawl, the majority of its attractions are conveniently clustered so that it is quite feasible to explore many of them on foot. But first you have to learn to cross the streets where the traffic never stops. There's an art to crossing the street in Vietnam: besides nerves of steel, a steady pace is required – motorbike riders are used to dodging pedestrians, but you'll confuse them if you stop in your tracks. Also note that during rush hour, motorbikes use certain pavements as temporary roads.

By bus Few visitors ever take a public bus, though it's relatively easy to hop on one to Cho Lon from the backpacker district. When leaving the city, Ben Thanh bus station is a useful point of departure, linking other long-distance bus stations in Ho Chi Minh City, as well as offering direct services to Vung Tau and other places. It'll cost 5,000đ per ride.

Motorbike and bicycle rental This is the cheapest way to get around HCMC – 130,000đ and 40,000đ per day respectively, though you'll need bravery far beyond that necessary to cross the street to survive in the traffic. Most hotels and guesthouses can arrange a motorbike for you, though bicycles are a bit more difficult to track down. One place they have both is at 185b Pham Ngu Lao, a few steps east of the junction with De Tham.

By rental car Many tour operators and hotels offer car rental plus driver for $70–100 per day, depending on the vehicle and driver's proficiency in English.

INFORMATION

Tourist information For practical information with no strings attached, enquire at your guesthouse or hotel. Your hosts should also be able to provide you with a basic map of the city centre, while a more detailed map is available from bookshops and street hawkers.

Listings For information about what's on in Ho Chi Minh

City, you'll find in many hotels and restaurants the free magazines *The Word* (wordhcmc.com) or *Asia Life* (asialifemagazine.com), which are aimed at expats. Both are published monthly.

ACCOMMODATION

There are thousands of **hotel** rooms in Ho Chi Minh City, ranging from windowless cupboards to sumptuous suites, yet the city is so popular that rooms can be difficult to find, especially in December and January. The best hotels are located around Dong Khoi in the city centre, and there are some smart mini-hotels on nearby Mac Thi Buoi. Ho Chi Minh City's budget enclave centres around Pham Ngu Lao, De Tham and Bui Vien, though there are some smarter options here too. The area sits roughly 1km west of the city centre but is still convenient for visiting most city attractions; in addition, restaurants, bars and shops are significantly cheaper out here. If the De Tham region is too crowded for you, note that there's a smaller clutch of budget hotels in an alley a few blocks south off Co Giang.

ESSENTIALS

Advance bookings will save you hauling your bags round the streets, and might even secure you a pick-up from the airport or station.

Breakfast Bar the budget flophouses, most hotels include breakfast in the price; exceptions, which are typically higher-end establishments, have been noted here. Note that if breakfast is included in the price, you may be able to lop a chunk from the rates if you choose to forgo it. You can also expect bread, spreads and juice at the city's hostels.

Hostels Until recently, there were very few dorm beds to be found in Ho Chi Minh City, but a recent glut of guesthouses featuring such facilities has popped up in the De Tham area. Few of them exude a truly hostel-like vibe; also note that many are unofficial operations which do not pay tax, and therefore risk being closed down at any moment.

Prices are usually quoted in dollars, which is just as well since the dong equivalents can stretch into the tens of millions. You'll be able to pay in either currency. Note that places at the upper end of the scale routinely quote without the 10% tax and 5% service which will be added on; prices listed here are all-inclusive rates for the cheapest double in high season.

Traffic noise This is a big issue in Ho Chi Minh City, and many hotels are fitting double glazing in an attempt to block it out; keep this in mind when choosing a room if you're a light sleeper.

THE CITY CENTRE

Asian Ruby 26 Thi Sach 08 3827 2839, asianruby hotel.com; map p.75. This centrally located mid-range hotel is the first of a growing chain with a winning combination of convenient locations, comfy rooms and helpful staff. Rooms are welcoming, with bedside control panels, thick mattresses and bright artwork. **$70**

★**Caravelle** 19 Lam Son Square 08 3823 4999, caravellehotel.com; map p.75. The city's most prestigious hotel is steeped in history, and since its opening in 1959 its fortunes have echoed those of the country. A new 24-storey wing was opened in 1998, since when it has led the pack with its luxurious rooms and suites, impeccable service and fine dining options. Complimentary wi-fi in rooms is a real bonus, and a sundowner at the *Saigon Saigon* bar on the rooftop of the old building (see p.77) is an essential experience. Breakfast is not included in the rates; also note that prices go down a bit on weekends. **$210**

Catina 109 Dong Khoi 08 3829 6296, hotelcatina .com.vn; map p.75. A nice little option, right at the heart of Dong Khoi, though there's nothing special about the decor, which is smart yet a little soulless – this place is all about location. Superior rooms are rather cramped and usually windowless, so it's worth paying the $15 extra for a deluxe room. **$85**

Continental 132–134 Dong Khoi 08 3829 9201, continentalvietnam.com; map p.75. The grandly carpeted staircases, marbled floors and dark-wood doors of this venerable address's halls and corridors convey a colonial splendour that doesn't quite extend to its rooms, though some boast commanding views down Dong Khoi. The rack rates are also ridiculous – expect to lop almost half off. **$195**

Dong Do 35 Mac Thi Buoi 08 3827 3637, dongdo hotelvn.com; map p.75. Nicely furnished mini-hotel bookended at the bottom by an extremely brown lobby, and at the top by a restaurant with a view of the bustle around Dong Khoi. Staff are friendly and helpful, and discounts are available for longer stays. **$30**

Duxton 63 Nguyen Hue 08 3822 2999, saigon .duxtonhotels.com; map p.75. There are nearly two hundred spacious, coffee-colour-carpeted rooms in this classy hotel. Each is equipped with a big desk and a tub in the bathroom, and the hotel also boasts a restaurant and a great outdoor pool. You'll save around $20 if you forgo breakfast. **$125**

Grand 8 Dong Khoi 08 3823 0163, grandhotel.vn; map p.75. This restored 1930s hotel boasts over two hundred rooms; the large, comfortable suites in the old wing are best, with comfortable furnishings and polished wooden floors. Modern facilities include a swimming pool and jacuzzi. Expect to take a nice big slice from the over-high rack rates. **$220**

1

★**Lavender** 208–210 Le Thanh Ton ☎08 2222 8888, ⓦlavenderhotel.com.vn; map p.72. Situated in a prime shopping spot, just along the road from the Ben Thanh market, this friendly, professionally run hotel features smallish but cosy, carpeted rooms with full facilities, and purpley trims all over the place. Book online for the best prices. $65

★**Majestic** 1 Dong Khoi ☎08 3829 5517, ⓦmajestic saigon.com.vn; map p.75. A historic 1920s riverfront hotel that oozes character. All the rooms are charming, especially those with a river view, and the staff fall over themselves to be helpful. There's a first-floor pool and rooftop bar too. $250

May 28–30 Thi Sach ☎08 3823 4501, ⓦmayhotel .vn; map p.75. With a good downtown location, this new place features a pool, spa and fitness centre. Rooms are bright with solid furnishings and ADSL connections. $80

★**Park Hyatt** 2 Lam Son ☎08 3824 1234, ⓦsaigon .park.hyatt.com; map p.75. Enjoying a prime spot on Lam Son Square, and staring down over the Municipal Theatre, this simply oozes class, with over 250 classically elegant rooms, two stylish restaurants, and a pool and spa. $275

Renaissance Riverside 8–15 Ton Duc Thang ☎08 3822 0033, ⓦmarriott.com; map p.75. This smart hotel in a modern building down by the river offers a challenge to other top-line hotels in the vicinity with its immaculate rooms and personalized, friendly service. It has a neat rooftop pool where barbecues are held at the weekend, as well as the relaxing *Atrium Lounge* with refreshments and free internet. Rates do not include breakfast. $225

Rex 141 Nguyen Hue ☎08 3829 2185, ⓦrexhotel vietnam.com; map p.75. A series of recent makeovers have re-established this as one of the the city's most appealing options, though the plush rooms and central location don't quite justify the price-tag. A sundowner on the fifth-floor terrace is a memorable treat whether you're staying here or not (see p.76). $185

Saigon River Boutique 58 Mac Thi Buoi ☎08 3822 8558, ⓦsaigonriverhotel.com; map p.75. This mini-hotel has been through several recent incarnations; the present one is quite pleasing, with budget-boutiquey flourishes from top to toe. The rooms are large for the price, and some have balconies; also note that there's a wonderful rooftop bar-restaurant area. $38

Sheraton 88 Dong Khoi ☎08 3827 2828, ⓦsheraton grandtower.com; map p.75. A towering monolith on Dong Khoi, ideally located for shopping and sights. Sumptuous rooms, but whether they justify the high prices is open to question. $230

★**Sofitel Plaza** 17 Le Duan ☎08 3824 1555, ⓦsofitel .com; map p.72. One of the jewels in Ho Chi Minh City's crown, firmly established as a favourite with business travellers. The hi-tech, open-plan lobby is a masterpiece,

the rooftop pool is simply stunning, and its rooms and facilities boast luxurious elegance with the most modern trimmings. $170

★**Spring** 44–46 Le Thanh Ton ☎08 3829 7362, ⓦspringhotelvietnam.com; map p.75. From the moment you step into the lobby, you can tell there's something special about this place. With its spiral staircase, and Roman-style statuary and columns, it's the epitome of budget-chic; throw in top-quality services, a convenient location, and carpeted rooms with cable TV and bathtubs. Rates are way below what you'd pay for comparable places elsewhere in town. $45

Tan Hai Long 14–16 Le Lai ☎08 3827 2738, ⓦtanhai longhotel.com.vn; map p.72. One of a chain of mini-hotels offering comfortable, if cramped, mid-range rooms. This one is right next to the Ben Thanh market, ideal for shopping and well positioned to get to most sights; some rooms have great views, thanks to the wide open area in front of the hotel. $60

Vuong Tai 20 Luu Van Lang ☎08 3521 8597, ⓦvuong taihotel.com; map p.75. Small hotel set on a shoe-shop-lined street east of the market; you can't miss its gleaming, gold-coloured lobby. Rooms are pretty, if simple, with nice bathrooms; some of the cheaper ones have smaller windows, but better views. $40

PHAM NGU LAO AND AROUND

An An 40 Bui Vien ☎08 3837 8087, ⓦanan.vn; map p.79. Though it doesn't look like much from the lobby, rooms are bright and airy at this welcoming mini-hotel; all come with a/c, bathtubs and internet connections, though light sleepers should opt for one away from the front side. $40

Beautiful Saigon 62 Bui Vien & 40/19 Bui Vien ☎08 3836 4852, ⓦbeautifulsaigonhotel.com; map p.79. These two mini-hotels in the heart of the budget district offer some of the best value around. Well-equipped rooms (most with computers), smartly dressed staff and free breakfasts come at budget prices. Number 2, tucked down an alley, is a bit quieter and has a good restaurant too. $30

Bich Duyen 283/4 Pham Ngu Lao ☎08 3837 4588, ⓔbichduyenhotel@yahoo.com; map p.79. Great-value rooms on a quiet sidestreet, with friendly, English-speaking staff – what more could you possibly need? Perhaps a window, for rooms with which you'll have to pay a little more. $17

Cat Huy 353/28 Pham Ngu Lao ☎08 3920 8716, ⓦcathuyhotelvn.com; map p.79. One has to admire the chutzpah of a place billing itself "maybe the best one-star hotel you've ever stayed in". And it really is good for the price, with nice rooms and attentive service. It's signed off Pham Ngu Lao, down an alley that initially looks forbidding, but gets better as you go along. $30

Eco Backpackers 264 De Tham ☎08 3836 5836, ✉ecobackpackershostel@gmail.com; map p.79. New operation with capsule-style dorm beds – a little more privacy for a lower price – and a convenient location right next to the open-tour bus stops. Private rooms all feature double bunk beds, and so can sleep up to four. Dorm beds $6, room $16

Elios 231–235 Pham Ngu Lao ☎08 3838 5584, ⓦelioshotel.vn; map p.79. This swish place, with over ninety compact and snug rooms, is a good example of how things are changing in the city's main budget district. Efficient, helpful staff, a rooftop restaurant and wi-fi in all rooms; the main drawback is the busy road outside. $65

Gia Vien 174/4 Pham Ngu Lao ☎08 3920 9988, ⓦgiavienhotel.com; map p.79. The best venue on one of De Tham's more gentrified streets – restaurants, bars and moto-pests galore, but it's actually quite nice. Rooms here are comfy and fair value for the price; their bathrooms have been decorated with rare attention. $37

Hello 373/49 Pham Ngu Lao ☎08 3920 9049, ✉hello_hotel_vn@yahoo.com; map p.79. Tucked away at the corner of a side-alley, this has some of the quietest rooms in the De Tham area. The pretty breakfast area by the lobby is another plus, and functions as a pleasant place to start your day. $65

Hong Han 238 Bui Vien ☎08 3836 1927, ✉hotel honghan@yahoo.com; map p.79. Agreeable place on De Tham's main nightlife thoroughfare; rooms at the front can be a bit noisy, but they're all nicely decorated with artwork and the like. The balcony-style breakfast area is a nice bonus. $60

Lac Vien 28/12–14 Bui Vien ☎08 3920 4899, ⓦlacvienhotel.com; map p.79. Enjoying a quiet location in the middle of an alley, the superior and VIP rooms at *Lac Vien* are some of the best choices in the budget district. Standard rooms are not such a good deal as they lack windows, but the superior upgrade is just $4 more. $32

Liberty Parkview 265 Pham Ngu Lao ☎08 3836 4556, ⓦlibertyhotels.com.vn; map p.79. One of the nicer venues on Pham Ngu Lao itself, this place offers stylish rooms with wi-fi, satellite TV and tea- and coffee-making facilities, plus a decent buffet breakfast served in its ninth-floor restaurant. Rooms with park view cost a bit more, but it's certainly worth considering the splurge. $60

Long Hostel 373/10 Pham Ngu Lao ☎08 3836 0184, ✉longhomestay@yahoo.com; map p.79. Friendly, family-style operation with a few slightly musty dorm rooms, good private rooms, and a lovely back-alley location. Dorm beds $8, rooms $20

★**Madam Cuc** 127 Cong Quynh ☎08 3836 8761, ⓦmadamcuchotels.com; map p.79. The genial Madam Cuc pays more attention to detail than most, resulting in a range of wholesome rooms, some sleeping up to four. Staff

are well informed and helpful and breakfast, fruit, tea and coffee are included in the price of the room. They will also collect from the airport. If this place is full, note they have three more branches where you'll find a similarly warm welcome, efficient staff and good-value rooms. $25

Miss Loi 178/20 Co Giang ☎08 3837 9589, ✉missloi @hcm.fpt.vn; map p.72. Located out of sight of the De Tham activity, this spotlessly clean and cosy guesthouse has a range of rooms in a quiet backstreet community. $16

New World 76 Le Lai ☎08 3822 8888, ⓦsaigon.newworldhotels.com; map p.72. A benchmark on the Ho Chi Minh City hotel scene since its opening in 1993 – over five hundred luxurious rooms complemented by impressive sports and leisure facilities, cutting edge restaurants and a business centre. $250

Ngoc Minh 283/11–13 Pham Ngu Lao ☎08 3837 6407, ⓦngocminh-hotel.net; map p.79. Located in a narrow alley and tucked away from the honking horns on Pham Ngu Lao, this place has a range of competitively priced rooms, all with a/c, cable TV and wi-fi. $25

Ngoc Thao 241/4 Pham Ngu Lao ☎08 3837 0273, ✉ngocthaohotel@yahoo.com; map p.79. Super-friendly guesthouse with comfortable dorm rooms, all en suite, and a lovely location on one of the area's most charming back-alleys. Dorm beds $7, rooms $18

★**Pink Tulip** 40/11 Bui Vien ☎08 3837 3567, ⓦpinktuliphotel.com; map p.79. This family-run establishment is almost certainly the cheapest place in town to feature a functional lift – a nice little surprise, as are the pleasantly decorated rooms, the amiable staff, and the wonderful breakfasts. A real find. $25

★**Pullman** 148 Tran Hung Dao ☎08 3838 8686, ⓦpullmanhotels.com; map p.72. Visible from much of the Pham Ngu Lao area, this is a relatively new stab at luxury, and one that has really come off – the rooms have been lovingly designed with pleasing artwork and docks for audio devices, there's an excellent on-site spa, and the views from the rooftop restaurant are quite superb. Very fair value for what you get. $90

Saigon Backpackers 373/27 Pham Ngu Lao ☎08 3837 0230, ⓦsaigonbackpackershostel.com; map p.79. No relation to the more professionally run *Backpackers* operations in Hanoi and Hue, this is nonetheless a decent enough place, with a pool table down below and rooms that are comfy, if a little musty. Staff run free city tours twice a week. Dorm beds $8, doubles $22

★**Town House 50** 50e Bui Thi Xuan ☎08 3925 0210, ⓦtownhousesaigon.com; map p.72. Fantastic, secluded little venue at the end of a tiny sidestreet, a short walk north of the backpacker zone. Rooms don't quite live up to the promise of the charming lobby and friendly staff, but they're still good value; note that in some of the private rooms there's only a curtain, rather than a door, to the toilets. Dorm beds $12, doubles $35

1

EATING

Ho Chi Minh City has more culinary sophistication than anywhere else in Vietnam, including Hanoi. A mouthwatering array of international cuisine awaits: the regular French, Italian and Indian options, mixed up with Korean, Japanese, German and far more. Most importantly, of course, there's a gut-busting gamut of good local food, from budget to fine dining. Aside from lower-end street stalls (see Basics, p.40, for tips on how to spot a good one), recent years have seen a crop of gentrified places selling similar food in greater comfort: some are cheap chain operations, others offer a more sophisticated experience. At the other end of the scale, some of the swankier restaurants lay on reasonably priced **set menus**, and also live **traditional music**, in order to lure diners. Finally, **café culture**, introduced by the French, is still very much alive in Ho Chi Minh City, and there are numerous places at which to round dinner off with an ice cream, crêpe or sundae. Earlier in the day, the same venues offer the chance to linger over a coffee and watch the world go by.

ESSENTIALS

Where to eat The bulk of travellers eat in two main areas: the city centre, with its profusion of quality establishments; and the budget area, concentrated around De Tham, Pham Ngu Lao and Bui Vien, where many establishments cater exclusively to tourists.

Prices By Vietnamese standards, many of the restaurants listed here are incredibly expensive – eat at one and you'll probably spend enough to feed a local family for a week or two. However, by Western standards many of them are low-priced, and the quality of cooking is consistently high. Tipping is not expected, though some restaurants do not quote tax or service charges on their price lists; the admission is usually made at the bottom of each menu page. These days you're far more likely to see prices quoted in dong than dollars, though at some venues you can pay with either.

Information There are several sites and blogs on hand to guide you through Saigon's maze of eating options, though being expat-focused, they tend to highlight places away from the main tourist areas. One of the better ones is ⓦ eatingsaigon.com, while pan-Southeast Asian site ⓦ travelfish.org also has decent restaurant lists.

Vegetarians As well as dedicated vegetarian establishments like *Loving Hut* (see opposite) and *Dinh Y* (see opposite), places such as *Com Tam Tac* (see opposite) and *Asian Kitchen* (see p.98) have veggie components to their menus, as do Indian restaurants such as *Ganesh* (see p.98).

VIETNAMESE BUDGET AND MID-RANGE

3T Quan Nuong 29–31 Ton That Tiep ☎ 09 0835 7530; map p.75. This hugely popular rooftop spot serving Vietnamese barbecue is located right above *Fanny's* (see p.100). Order your choice of meat, seafood and veg, and cook it to your taste at the table. Best to go with a group, and best to book ahead at weekends (do it through a Vietnamese friend as little English is spoken). Most dishes 70,000–150,000đ. Daily 5–11pm.

Bamboo Garden 40/15 Bui Vien ☎ 08 3837 2677; map p.79. It's worth tracking down this place, which is hidden in a narrow alley east of De Tham, for Vietnamese staples including tasty *banh xeo* (40,000đ), and more adventurous meals such as tilapia in ginger (120,000đ). Daily 7am–11pm.

★**Banh Xeo** 46a Dinh Cong Trang ☎ 08 3824 1110; map p.72. The eponymous Vietnamese pancakes (70,000đ), stuffed with a mixture of shrimps, pork, beans, bean sprouts and egg, are the speciality at this streetside eatery off Hai Ba Trung. They're so tasty that the place has become a must-visit spot for many travellers. Daily 10am–9pm.

★**Binh Tay Market** off Thap Moi; map p.85. The city's most characterful market makes a great place to eat – head to the line of stalls at the back. It's terribly unfair to single out any particular purveyor for praise, but when you're done with the savoury component, head to the *che* girls at #23 to sample Vietnam's tastiest dessert – incredibly cheap at 7,000đ a bowl. Daily 10am–11pm.

★**Cha Ca La Vong** 36 Ton That Thiep ☎ 08 3915 3343; map p.75. Love at first smell in a restaurant whose Hanoi counterpart is one of the oldest in the country. Take a step inside and you'll instantly be hit by the dill-heavy aroma of a secret combination of herbs and spices used with their signature (ie, only) dish: *cha ca la vong*, or fried fish, cooked at the table for 170,000đ a portion and served with noodles and other sides. Daily 11am–2pm & 3–10pm.

COOKING CLASSES AND TOURS

Why leave the food in Vietnam when you can take some cooking skills home with you? Try the **classes** at *Hoa Tuc* restaurant (see opposite; ⓦ saigoncookingclass.com), which cost $45 including a market visit, and allow you to whip up three dishes and a dessert (Tue–Sun, 10am–1pm or 2–5pm); or Mai Home (ⓦ vietnamsaigoncookingclass.com), which runs half-day courses for $33, and eight-day marathons for $160. It's also possible to go on **culinary tours** of the city: Saigon Streeteats (ⓦ saigonstreeteats.com) does half-day trips from $35 per person; and the all-female XO team (ⓦ xotours.vn) offers evening motorbike tours, focusing on rare culinary treats, from $68.

Com Tam Dac 73 Suong Nguyet Anh ☎ 08 3926 0333; map p.72. Cosy venue decorated with a lime green-and-brown pallette. Simple Vietnamese dishes cost around 50,000đ, and include a fair few veggie choices. Daily 7am–11pm.

★**Cuc Gach Quan** 9 & 10 Dang Tat ☎ 08 3848 0144; map p.72. Facing off across a quiet road, these twin venues have exploded in popularity since a certain Brangelina popped by on their visit to 'Nam. The two-headed publicity-hound chose well, for what's on offer is a splendidly simple take on local cuisine (most dishes 90,000–140,000đ), served in a tranquil, down-to-earth environment. Daily 10am–11pm.

Dinh Y 171b Cong Quynh; map p.79. Cheap but tasty vegetarian food prepared by Cao Dai adherents in a convenient location by Thai Binh market. Dishes start at 22,000đ, and there's little over 50,000đ. Daily 6.30am–9pm.

Hoa Tuc 74 Hai Ba Trung ☎ 08 3825 1677, ⓦ hoatuc .com; map p.75. Wedged into a lovely, expat-heavy enclave of expensive eateries, this is the best looking of the bunch yet surprisingly cheap; check out starters like tofu with mint, pepper and lime (55,000đ) or cheap rice or noodle mains, or splash out on something like battered squid in tamarind sauce (175,000đ). They also run excellent cooking classes (see p.96). Daily 11am– 11pm.

Huynh Hoa 26 Le Thi Rieng ☎ 08 3925 0885; map p.72. Semi-official holder of the best *banh-mi*-in-town award, with reams of travellers popping by every day to sample the Vietnamese sandwich (28,000đ). The secret? Fresh ingredients, and a far greater attention to hygiene than normal – this is one place in which you won't find hairs in your bun. Daily 2.30pm–midnight.

★**Loving Hut** 38 Huynh Khuang Ninh ☎ 08 3820 9702, ⓦ hoadanghut.com; map p.72. On a sidestreet near the Jade Emperor Pagoda (see p.84), this is a great find for veggies and vegans; the bulk of dishes on the menu are in the 45,000–70,000đ range, and they're all absolutely delicious. Even carnivores would enjoy their fabulous pho, and the smart, a/c environment is pretty cool too; the photo-roster of well-known dishes on the wall is a nice touch, and just about the only place you'll see Pamela Anderson flanked by Socrates and Gandhi. Daily 9.30am–2pm & 4.30–9pm.

Minh Duc 35 Ton That Tung ☎ 08 3839 2240; map p.72. It's worth escaping the tourist enclave around De Tham at lunchtime to join the scrum of locals at this point-and-eat place, where a wide range of well-prepared local dishes is on display (around 35,000đ a dish). Daily 10am–10pm.

Mon Hue 11 Le Thanh Ton ☎ 08 6272 4761; map p.75. In keeping with the boutique-budget trend, this chain serves good Hue food in a bright, cheerful atmosphere. Most are here for the *bun bo hue* noodle soup (53,000đ),

though the menu's full of tasty ideas, and there's cheap fruit juice (from 18,000đ). Daily 6am–11pm.

★**Nam Giao** 136/15 Le Thanh Ton ☎ 08 3825 0261; map p.72. Excellent Hue food served in this atmospheric yet simple place, tucked away down a manicure-heavy alley behind Ben Thanh market. Join the throng of locals and a smattering of tourists to sample the famous *bun bo hue* (50,000đ) or a tasty *banh khoai* (38,000đ). Daily 7.45am–10pm.

★**Ngon** 160 Pasteur ☎ 08 3827 7131; map p.75. Be sure to take at least one meal in this wonderful venue, spectacularly set in a yellow-and-white cream-cake of a colonial building – take your seat inside by the pool, or outside amid palm leaves and chunky yellow pillars. Two lines of chefs whip up all sorts of Vietnamese specialities in no time at all; the only surprise is that they're incredibly cheap, with most dishes weighing in at 50,000–80,000đ. It's very popular, so be prepared to wait for a table at peak eating times. Daily 7am–midnight.

Pho 24 5 Nguyen Thiep ☎ 08 3822 8260; map p.75. If the thought of eating from a street stall makes you shudder, sample your first bowl of pho (from 49,000đ), the nation's signature dish, in this spotless diner. The chain boasts over a dozen branches in District One alone; this one's pretty central. Daily 6.30am–10pm.

Pho 2000 2f 1–3 Phan Chu Trinh ☎ 08 3822 2788; map p.72. A great value spot, located above a café next to Ben Thanh market, and boasting good views of the Bitexco tower (see p.78). Clean surroundings and big bowls of delicious noodle soup (65,000đ) and other Vietnamese staples. Daily 6.30am–11pm.

★**Pho Hoa** 260c Pasteur ☎ 08 3829 7943; map p.72. High-quality pho shops proliferate along Pasteur; none are better than this one, which many connoisseurs rate the best in the city. Their huge bowlfuls of soup (50,000đ) are complemented with chunks of chicken or beef, while there's plenty of fresh greens on the tables to add yourself. Daily 6am–midnight.

Pho Quynh 323 Pham Ngu Lao; map p.79. For a backpacker-zone eatery, this gets a lot of local custom, and is the place to head if you feel the need to slurp down a bowl of beef noodle soup (50,000đ), which is up there with the best in town. Daily 24hr.

★**Quan Bui** 17a Ngo Van Nam ☎ 08 3829 1515; map p.75. What a pleasant place – the pretty floor-tiling and gentrified atmosphere contrast nicely with the noise from the bikes racing past. For somewhere as pretty as this, the food's cheap, and the menu varied; try the chicken sautéed in tamarind (89,000đ), or flash-fried tofu in a passion-fruit dressing (59,000đ). Daily 7am–midnight.

Quan Nem 15e Nguyen Thi Minh Khai ☎ 08 6299 1478; map p.72. Though a bit far from the centre, it's worth the trip north to this popular place. There are only two things on the menu: *nem cua ben* (fried, fist-sized crab spring rolls;

1

39,000đ) and *bun cha hanoi* (barbecued beef; 57,000đ), served with dipping sauce and a miniature forest of leaves. Daily 10am–10pm.

Sense 48 Nguyen Hue ☎ 08 3824 5519; map p.75. Hue specialities occupy most of the menu at this gorgeous little eatery, whose tables feature jade-effect plates and shocking pink tablemats – fancy, but the food's nice and cheap. Try the *cao lau* (65,000đ), *bun cha* (55,000đ) or *banh beo* (39,000đ). Daily 10.30am–10.30pm.

Wrap & Roll 62 Hai Ba Trung ☎ 08 3822 2166; map p.75. Handy outlet of a specialist spring roll chain, serving street food (most dishes 35,000–78,000đ) in a sanitized, a/c environment. Choose from a host of ingredients, peel off a rice wrapper and get rolling. Daily 10am–11pm.

VIETNAMESE HIGHER-END

An Vien 178a Hai Ba Trung ☎ 08 3824 3877; map p.72. Tucked away from the main road, this place is extremely intimate, with many different alcoves and corners on three floors, all sumptuously decorated, and with high-quality Vietnamese food to match; there's a fragrant park just around the corner if you want to walk those calories off. Main courses 140,000–200,000đ. Daily 9am–1pm.

Hoi An 11 Le Thanh Ton ☎ 08 3823 7694; map p.75. Refined, traditional Vietnamese food is served in a sumptuous wooden house. It's not cheap, with spring rolls going for 200,000đ and seafood mains from 250,000đ; if you're in a real dong-splashing mood, opt for one of the huge sets (from 740,000đ). It's wise to book ahead. Daily 11am–2pm & 5.30–11.30pm.

La Perle de l'Orient off Ton Duc Thang ☎ 08 3827 5050; map p.75. The best-looking of the flotilla of ship-restaurants which set sail every evening. Set courses only available (from 319,000đ), but it's more about the experience than the food. Daily 7–9.15pm.

Lemongrass 4 Nguyen Thiep ☎ 08 3822 4005; map p.75. A decent, upmarket establishment where the highly rated Vietnamese food is eaten under what look like illuminated parasols; you should be able to fill up for around 200,000đ. Come at 7pm, and you'll be able to listen to traditional live music. Main courses 105,000–315,000đ. Daily 11am–2pm & 5–10pm.

Maxim's 17 Dong Khoi ☎ 08 8829 6676; map p.75. Dangling lanterns announce your arrival at this, one of the few venues in HCMC where you can enjoy traditional Vietnamese dishes in a plush environment, with a performance of classical local music and dance to accompany it. Try their clay pot dishes, especially the stewed fish and pork (240,000đ) or red snapper (320,000đ). Daily 10am–10pm.

Ngoc Suong 106 Suong Nguyet Anh ☎ 08 3925 6939; map p.72. This giant, mansion-like place is the most atmospheric branch of this hugely popular chain of seafood restaurants, and draws big crowds every evening. Figure

on around 300,000đ per head, before drinks; reservations recommended. Daily 10am–10.30pm.

Pho 79 79 Syong Nguyet Anh ☎ 08 3926 2929; map p.72. Housed in a lovely old 1930s colonial house and its garden, this restaurant is now going for the sex-sells approach, with its waitresses wearing rather revealing attire. However, the food's good and not too expensive; it's essentially a compendium of Vietnamese staples (100,000đ and up), though with interesting additions such as frog and crocodile. Daily 10am–10pm.

Temple Club 29–31 Ton That Thiep ☎ 08 3829 9244, ⊛ templeclub.com.vn; map p.75. Excellent Vietnamese food at around 250,000đ a dish is served in a wonderful, relaxed atmosphere with tasteful decor. There's also a comfy lounge bar out back. Daily 11.30am–midnight.

Vietnam House 93–95 Dong Khoi ☎ 08 3829 1623, ⊛ vietnamhousesaigon.com; map p.75. Occupying a splendid, louvred colonial building, this offers a cracking introduction to Vietnamese food, featuring a wide à la carte menu as well as set lunches and dinners; try the calamari fried spring rolls (115,000đ) or *banh xeo* (125,000đ). There's a pianist on the ground floor and traditional folk music upstairs at 7–9pm. Daily 10am–11pm.

Xu 71–75 Hai Ba Trung ☎ 08 3824 8468, ⊛ xusaigon .com; map p.75. This super-cool, minimalist venue is revered as one of the city's most innovative fusion restaurants – think coconut-braised pork belly (250,000đ) and lotus seed felafel (120,000đ). Most dishes are prepared to be shared; it's best to go with a small group. The main restaurant is upstairs, while downstairs is more a lounge bar, where a DJ spins tunes on weekends. Daily 11am–midnight.

OTHER ASIAN CUISINE

★**Asian Kitchen** 185/22 Pham Ngu Lao ☎ 08 3836 7397; map p.79. Tucked away down the pleasant narrow alley east of De Tham, this is most likely the friendliest restaurant in the whole area. Their menu is surprisingly wide, with Western dishes such as the large English breakfast (80,000đ) augmented by tasty Vietnamese and Japanese ones. For a fusion of the latter two, try the delectable crocodile sashimi (89,000đ). Daily 7am–midnight.

Dynasty New World Hotel, 76 Le Lai ☎ 08 3822 8888; map p.72. The porcelain-and-bonsai decor is elegant at this classy restaurant, and the food just as splendid, featuring delicious *dim sum* at lunchtime (from 55,000đ per plate). Set menus start at around 600,000đ, but the sky's the limit if you plump for delicacies like bird's-nest soup or shark's fin. Mon–Sat 11.30am–2.30pm & 6–10pm; Sun 11.30am–2.30pm.

Ganesh 38 Hai Ba Trung ☎ 08 3823 4785; map p.75. The best value of the area's several Indian restaurants, with curry plus rice or naan clocking in around the

150,000đ mark. Their veggie dishes are particularly good, spanning a range of Indian cooking from north to south. Daily 11.30am–2.30pm & 5.30–10.30pm.

Mai Thai 13 Ton That Thiep ☎ 08 3821 2920; map p.75. Most central of the Thai restaurants in town, an attractive place with spicy curries and *tom yam* soup that are sure to bring tears to your eyes. Good set lunches go for around 90,000đ. Daily 11am–10pm.

Matsuzakaya 17/34a Le Thanh Ton; map p.75. Tucked into a wonderfully calm residential enclave which many an expat calls home, this pair of restaurants sell cheap, passable Japanese food – one corner does good ramen, the other curry rice, with both going from just 80,000đ. Daily 11am–10pm.

Ocean Palace 2 Le Duan ☎ 08 3911 8833; map p.72. This elegant, high-ceilinged Chinese restaurant just opposite the History Museum (see p.83) is a great place to relax after filling your mind with Vietnam's complex past. Order up a few *dim sum* baskets (some of the best in Saigon, around 50,000đ each), or go for the roasted suckling pig or crispy duck, both of which are excellent. Wash it down with a beer or glass or two of wine, then walk it off in the zoo, just across the road. Main courses 100,000–200,000đ. Daily 10am–2.30pm & 6–10.30pm.

Sushi Bar 2 Le Thanh Ton ☎ 08 3823 8024, ⓦ sushibar .com.vn; map p.72. Highly rated sushi or sashimi mix in the heart of HCMC's Japantown; dishes go from 18,000–100,000đ (you'll need a fair few to fill up, of course), and there's also Japanese beer and sake on offer. Daily 10am–11.30pm.

WESTERN CUISINE

Augustin's 10 Nguyen Thiep ☎ 08 3829 2941; map p.75. Hidden down a pleasant, narrow lane linking Dong Khoi and Nguyen Hue, this intimate bistro serves well-cooked but pricey French dishes. Mains 60,000đ and up. Mon–Sat 11.30am–2pm & 6–10.30pm.

★**Au Manoir de Khai** 251 Dien Bien Phu ☎ 08 3930 3394; map p.72. This is the nearest you're likely to get to feeling like a colonial of consequence, as the staff treat all guests with great deference. Stunning surroundings, tranquil atmosphere, sensational French food, such as grilled lamb tenderloin with Dijon mustard sauce (350,000đ), and an extensive wine list. Daily 11am–2pm & 6–9.30pm.

★**Au Parc** 23 Han Thuyen ☎ 08 3829 2772; map p.72. Stylish place, conveniently located between Notre Dame Cathedral and Reunification Palace, serving great breakfasts (150,000đ and up) and salads (120,000đ or so), with a good deli counter and a few nice Turkish options. Gets a bit busy downstairs, so head upstairs for a more relaxed environment. Mon–Sat 7.30am–10.30pm, Sun 8am–5pm.

Camargue 191 Hai Ba Trung ☎ 08 3824 3148; map p.75. A colonial-style modern villa with rattan furniture and wooden ceiling fans sets the scene of a bygone era for this expensive French restaurant. The menu is constantly changing, but features dishes like beef carpaccio and lamb tenderloin with couscous. It's set back from the main road down a narrow lane. Main courses 255,000–508,000đ. Daily 6–11pm.

Elbow Room 52 Pasteur ☎ 08 3821 4327; map p.75. This cosy diner specializes in comfort food such as eggs Benedict (140,000đ) or Philly cheese steak (175,000đ) – just open the door, and see if you can resist the delicious smells emanating from the kitchen. There's also a well-stocked bar and live music on Friday evening. Daily 8am–11pm.

Gartenstadt 34 Dong Khoi ☎ 08 3822 3623; map p.75. German bar-restaurant that's smaller, more atmospheric and more authentic than other similar options around town. Schnitzels start at 220,000đ, though their sausage, sauerkraut, bread and mustard deals are a bargain at 120,000đ. There's also a good selection of German beers, some on draught. Daily 10.30am–midnight.

Jaspa's 33 Dong Khoi ☎ 08 3822 9925; map p.75. Classy venue, whose menu features international fusion cuisine such as salt and pepper steak with wasabi mash (475,000đ); cheaper mains are available from 185,000đ and up. They've another branch serving similar meals at 74/7 Hai Ba Trung. Daily 8.30am–midnight.

La Cantina 175/3 Pham Ngu Lao ☎ 09 0279 9962; map p.79. One of the best and most hassle-free options on this foreigner-friendly road, and it's pretty swish-looking for the price; try nachos with the works for 79,000đ, a large Irish breakfast for 110,000đ, or any number of other tasty dishes. Daily 6.30am–2am.

La Fourchette 11 Ngo Duc Ke ☎ 08 3829 8143, ⓦ lafourchette.com.vn; map p.75. Ho Chi Minh City's oldest French restaurant boasts an intimate atmosphere at this two-floor restaurant (non-smoking upstairs). The short menu features imported steaks and set lunches; as a base, figure on 100,000đ for a starter, and 250,000đ for a main. Daily 11.30am–2.30pm & 6.30–10pm.

Le Jardin 31 Thai Van Lung ☎ 08 3825 8465; map p.75. Excellent French food at reasonable prices (from 60,000đ) served in a pleasant garden setting. Very popular, and not very big, so advance booking is advisable. Daily 11am–2pm & 6–9pm.

Mogambo 50 Pasteur ☎ 08 3825 1311; map p.75. Home-made pies (205,000đ), bangers and mash (150,000đ) and big burgers attract a steady stream of resident expats and tourists to this small but cosy place – it's friendly, and staff are well drilled as regards serving curious foreigners. Daily 10am–10.30pm.

Pepperoni's 111 Bui Vien ☎ 08 3920 4989; map p.79. Above the *Spotted Cow* bar, this place serves pizzas, pasta, steaks and daily specials (80,000–120,000đ), with

1

frequent offers such as two pizzas for the price of one. Daily 8.30am–11pm.

Refinery 74/7c Hai Ba Trung ☎08 3823 0509, ⓦtherefinerysaigon.com; map p.75. Set back from busy Hai Ba Trung, this cute little bistro has a relaxed, almost colonial-era air, and is extremely popular with local expats. It serves an appealing range of dishes, many homemade – they include gazpacho (60,000đ) and swordfish with lime and parsley mash (225,000đ). To round things off, choose from beers, cocktails and a good selection of wines. Daily 11am–late.

Skewers 9a Thai Van Lung ☎08 3822 4798, ⓦskewers -restaurant.com; map p.75. Superlative Mediterranean cuisine – everything from French to Levantine – made using simple and healthy ingredients. Try the pan-fried salmon with nicoise salad (300,000đ), or all manner of yummy dips; be sure to check the blackboard for daily specials. Mon–Fri 11.30am–2pm & 6–10pm, Sat & Sun 6–10pm.

ZanZBar 19–21 Dong Khoi ☎08 6291 3686; map p.75. Not your typical HCMC restaurant by any means – it looks more like a swanky bar, and doubles as such in the evenings. They're proud of their salmon (250,000đ) and other seafood, as well as the sumptuous Angus steaks. Daily 7am–1am.

CAFES AND ICE-CREAM PARLOURS

Bobby Brewer's 45 Bui Vien ☎08 3920 4090, ⓦbobby brewers.com; map p.79. If you're having a coffee break, then why not take in a film too? All-day movies (many Vietnam-related) show at this lounge – check out the website for what's on now. Daily 8am–11pm.

Café Eon 50f Bitexco Tower, 2 Hai Trieu ☎08 6291 8750; map p.75. The highest café in the city boasts accordingly lofty prices – 120,000đ for a coffee may seem ridiculous, as may 169,000đ for a fruit juice, though notably they're still both lower than the ticket price to the observation deck one level down (see p.78). Daily 8am–late.

Café Zoom 169a De Tham ☎09 3850 0997; map p.79. The place for Vespa and Lambretta fanatics to hang out, with a close-up view of the action at one of the city's busiest junctions. Coffee only comes Vietnamese-style (25,000đ), while there's all sorts of snacks to munch on, including German sausage, sourdough toast and Tex-Mex options. Daily 7am–2am.

★**Fanny's** 29–31 Ton Thap Thiep; map p.75. Ice-cream specialist serving up little scoops of heaven from 34,000đ, served with tiny Vietnamese hats. In addition to the regular flavours, have a crack at ginger, passion fruit, cinnamon or soursop. With its wrought-iron chairs and magazines to

---

BUYING YOUR OWN FOOD: MARKETS AND SUPERMARKETS

With baguettes, cheese and fruit in such abundant supply in Vietnam, making up a picnic is easy. All the basics can be found at any of the city's **markets**, though if you're homesick for peanut butter, Vegemite or other such exotica, you'll need to head for a specialist **supermarket** or **provisions store**.

MARKETS

A stroll through a wet or fresh market in Vietnam, gazing at all the familiar and unfamiliar items on sale, is an essential activity for every visitor to the country. Don't be surprised if you get dragged into a conversation either, as Vietnamese do much of their socializing in the markets.

The handiest market for De Tham is **Thai Binh market**, down at the southwestern end of Pham Ngu Lao. Just about as near, and larger, is **Ben Thanh market** (see p.79), the central market in the city centre. Cho Lon is served by **Binh Tay market** (see p.86) on its southwestern border and by **An Dong market**, northeast of it at the junction of Tran Phu and An Duong Vuong.

SUPERMARKETS AND PROVISIONS STORES

Annam Gourmet Shop 16–18 Hai Ba Trung. Huge downtown deli, pandering to the whims of expats and visitors alike.

Co-op Mart 189c Cong Quynh. Large, Western-style supermarket within easy walking distance of De Tham, selling clothes, toys, household goods, cosmetics and a good selection of Western foods. There's also a large branch at 168 Nguyen Dinh Chieu.

Minimart 250 De Tham. Snacks, drinks and basic toiletries on sale in the budget district.

Nhu Lan Bakery 66–68 Ham Nghi. Famed bakery

selling bread, croissants and cakes.

Parkson Plaza 39–45 Le Thanh Ton. On the fourth floor of this shopping mall is a supermarket selling a good range of imported goods.

Thuong Xa Supermarket 135 Nguyen Hue. On the first floor of this centrally located shopping plaza, this large supermarket sells, among other things, Western tinned and dairy products.

Veggy's 29a Le Thanh Ton. Well stocked with imported meats, cheeses and cereals, this place is a popular shopping spot for local expats.

read, it's a great place to kick back and cool off for an hour or two. Daily 8am–11pm.

Highlands Coffee 7 Con Truong Lam Son; map p.75. Vietnam's answer to *Starbucks* has branches all over the city, but this is the best-located, snuggling into the back of the opera house. The coffee's passable; have it Viet-style for 29,000đ, or with an Italian name from 44,000đ. Daily 7.30am–11pm.

Kem Bach Dang 26 & 28 Le Loi; map p.75. Twin open-fronted ice-cream parlours, revered for extravagant creations (70,000đ or so), some of which feature fruits from Da Lat. The one that's open to the road is a magnet for beggars, who periodically stray inside; the other is sealed off and occasionally stinks of durian, but has good evening views from its upper floors. Daily 9am–11.30pm.

★**La Fenetre Soleil** 1st floor, 44 Ly Tu Trong ☎08 3824 5994; map p.75. This quirky café has an offbeat feel, with a mismatch of furniture and bare brick walls – not to mention using a French name to denote Japanese cuisine. Apart from good coffee and shakes, they serve good set lunches and cocktails, with shisha pipes too; try the *karaage* (fried chicken; 90,000đ). It's just next to the Ho Chi Minh City Museum, in case you need a rest after that. Daily 10am–midnight.

Modern Meets Culture 44b Ly Tu Trong ☎08 3822 2495; map p.75. You'll see haircuts galore at this hipster hangout – it's a good (not to mention smoke-free) place to meet some of Saigon's more characterful youngsters.

Coffees are fine (35,000đ and up), though their smoothies are even better (from 55,000đ). Daily 7am–11pm.

Napoli Café 7 Pham Ngoc Thach ☎08 3829 0583; map p.72. This place, a short stroll northwest of the cathedral, is hugely popular among locals for a short break in the day or to listen to the band in the evening – the latter sees fancy lanterns lit up among the palm trees. Choose from a modest selection of main dishes, cakes, pastries and sundaes or indulge in the *mangia e bevi* – a sensational blend of ice cream, orange juice and fresh fruit (68,000đ). Daily 7.30am–11pm.

Sozo 176 Bui Vien ☎09 0930 6971, ⓦsozocentre.com; map p.79. A great place for a slow and relaxing breakfast or a midday break, this café serves excellent cakes and cookies; its passion fruit cheesecake is a great choice (60,000đ). Under-privileged kids are employed; all profits go into staff training. Head upstairs to escape the street noise. Daily 6.30am–10.30pm.

Thao Nguyen 7f 138 Nam Ky Khoi Nghia; map p.72. On the other side of the road from the Reunification Palace, this top-floor cafe-bar sees surprisingly little custom; come here for a coffee (50,000đ) or Orange Julius (55,000đ) over a great view. Daily 8am–10pm.

Vuon Kieng off Ton Duc Thang; map p.75. Saigon's prime water-watching coffee spot, though the view is ugly in a rather beautiful way: huge communist billboards, hulking tower-blocks, heavily laden barges and floating branches. Coffee from 45,000đ. Daily 7am–11pm.

DRINKING AND NIGHTLIFE

Ho Chi Minh City boasts a good range of **nightlife**, although an ongoing **crackdown** on late opening means you'll probably be tucked up in bed by midnight unless you're in the De Tham area. Many of the bars listed below feature **live music** either every night or at the weekend. In most places, such as *17 Saloon*, you'll find Filipino bands performing well-rehearsed covers of current hits and old favourites, though there's also a growing base of local musicians who are making a name for themselves in venues like *Thi Café* and *Yoko*. It isn't unheard of for big showbiz names from the West to make appearances in HCMC, so check out the local press for details. The **free monthly magazines**, *The Word* and *Asia Life*, carry up-to-the-minute listings of the city's latest bars, plus the hottest new clubs and any more highbrow entertainment on offer.

ESSENTIALS

Bars and pubs in Ho Chi Minh City range from hole-in-the-wall dives to elegant cocktail lounges that would not be out of place in a European capital. The area around Dong Khoi is predictably well endowed, and another boozy enclave exists around Le Thanh Ton, Hai Ba Trung and Thi Sach, where a glut of places, ranging from slick yuppie haunts to watering holes that hark back to the raunchy GI bars of the 1960s, has developed to cater for expats renting apartments nearby. At the other end of the scale, all the cheap restaurants and cafés around De Tham turn their hand to drink at night – fine if you're willing to forego atmosphere in order to save a dollar or two on a beer, and great for meeting like-minded tourists.

Prices vary wildly: a Saigon beer at a streetside café in De Tham will cost you around 15,000đ, but you can multiply that by four or five in a more upmarket bar on Dong Khoi. One way to economize while downtown is to take advantage of early-evening happy hours, or check out the surprisingly cheap and tasty bia hoi (see box, p.103).

CENTRAL HO CHI MINH CITY

Apocalypse Now 2c Thi Sach ☎08 3824 1463; map p.75. Dark and cavernous, with two dancefloors and a compact garden, "Apoc Lip" (as it's known to locals) is a real pioneer of the city's nightlife scene. It's always rowdy and sweaty at weekends with an eclectic crowd, though it can be rather dull during the week. There's a 150,000đ cover charge on weekends, which includes one free drink. Daily 7pm–late.

1

★**Bernie's** 74a 19 Thai Van Lung ☎08 3822 1720; map p.75. Just about the most authentic-looking of the city's several Irish and English pubs, and very popular with expats for its good atmosphere, well-stocked bar (including draught Guinness and Sapporo) and comforting Western menu. Try the full Irish breakfast (170,000đ). Daily 7am–midnight.

Blanchy's Tash 95 Hai Ba Trung ☎09 0902 8293, ⓦblanchystash.com; map p.75. Super-cool cocktail lounge that's currently one of the most popular places in the area, especially on the occasions when international DJs drop by for a spin (think Danny Rampling and Grand Master Flash). Wednesdays are ladies' night. Daily 6pm–late.

Blue Gecko 31 Ly Tu Trong ☎08 3824 3483; map p.75. Expat hangout offering pub atmosphere with pool, darts and sports on TV. Happy hour is 5–7.30pm; at other times the drinks are still affordable, with beers costing around 25,000đ. Daily 5pm–late.

Chu 158 Dong Khoi ☎08 3842 8831; map p.75. This oval-shaped bar is a convenient and inexpensive venue for evening entertainment, with live music (mostly Sixties and Seventies songs) from 9pm–1am, plus an eclectic menu that includes beef pie, spaghetti, Asian dishes and ice creams. Beer from 55,000đ. Daily 8am–1am.

★**Drunken Duck** 58 Ton That Thiep ☎08 3915 2853; map p.75. On trendy Ton That Thiep, this is pretty decent for a "girlie" bar – female travellers and expats regularly visit, and feel no discomfort. They offer a huge range of shooters, cocktails with aptly themed names ("Aquackalypse Now" being one example) and a full range of beers. Daily 6pm–late.

Eon Heli Bar Bitexco Tower, 2 Hai Trieu ☎08 6291 8752, ⓦeon51.com; map p.75. By far the loftiest bar in the city, peering out from the Floor 52 – that's the helipad level – of the Bitexco Tower (see p.78). Views are predictably good, though prices aren't as high as you might expect; cocktails are 290,000đ and beers go from 150,000đ, though do remember that entry is free – a visit to the observation deck two floors down would cost you 200,000đ anyway. Daily 11.30am–2am.

Ice Blue 54 Dong Khoi ☎08 3822 2264; map p.75. Traditional English pub-style bar, with a dartboard, a friendly atmosphere and a range of international beers; 4–8pm is happy hour. Daily 4pm–late.

La Fenetre Soleil 1st floor, 44 Ly Tu Trong ☎08 3824 5994; map p.75. Functioning as a chill-out café during the day, this little gem turns its hand to mixing cocktails and filling shisha pipes in the evenings. Daily 11.30am–midnight.

Level 23 Sheraton Hotel, 88 Dong Khoi ☎08 3827 2828, ⓦlevel23saigon.com; map p.75. This is a great spot for after-dinner cocktails (185,000đ) while enjoying panoramic views of the city, and if you're in the mood, the band might get you dancing too. 7pm–midnight.

Lush 2 Ly Tu Trong ☎08 3824 2496, ⓦlush.vn; map p.72. This elegant club is one of the top places for the city's movers and shakers, both expats and locals, to let their hair down at the weekend, when it gets packed – hip-hop night on Friday is particularly well attended. Weekdays it can be pretty dead, though Ladies' Night on Tuesdays and "Thirsty Thursdays" (two-for-one specials) usually draw a crowd. Daily 6pm–late.

Number 5 Bar 44 Pasteur ☎09 0380 1676; map p.75. This place has a similar formula to *Phatty's* round the corner – a big bar area with plenty of bar stools, pretty waitresses, comfort food and sports on TV. Daily 3pm–1am.

Pacharan 97 Hai Ba Trung ☎08 3825 6024, ⓦpacharan saigon.com; map p.75. Smart, three-floored Spanish place just behind the Municipal Theatre, serving tapas and a wide range of drinks – it has an admirable range of wines and sherries by the glass, starting at 75,000đ and ending just shy of the stratosphere. Live Spanish music some nights. Daily 10am–late.

Phatty's 46–48 Ton That Tiep ☎08 3821 0796, ⓦphattysbar.com; map p.75. This sports bar and grill is regularly packed with punters watching rugby or Aussie Rules. There are enough screens, it seems, for every customer to be watching a different channel, even if the result is a bit cacophonous. Spirits from 85,000đ, beers from 40,000đ, and huge cocktail jugs 240,000đ. Daily 9am–11pm.

Rooftop Garden Rex Hotel, 141 Nguyen Hue ☎08 3829 2185; map p.75. A drink amid the fairy-lit topiary and clumsy model animals of the *Rex* fifth-floor terrace is still *de rigueur* on a trip to the city – at least for those who can afford it, for drinks here do not come cheap. Daily 7am–late.

Saigon Saigon Caravelle Hotel, 19 Lam Son Square ☎08 3823 4999; map p.75. Located on the tenth floor of the *Caravelle*, this bar is one of the city's best sunset spots, with dreamily romantic views if the weather is deciding to co-operate; there are two-for-one drinks specials around this time, though it's still fairly pricey. There's also live music each evening. Daily 9am–midnight.

Sax n' Art 28 Le Loi ☎08 3822 8472; map p.75. Slick, atmospheric jazz club with mellow sounds from the house band, led by saxophonist Tran Manh Tuan, starting at 9pm, and sometimes featuring good vocalists. Cover charge 90,000đ. Daily 5pm–midnight.

Vasco's 74/7d Hai Ba Trung ☎08 3824 3149; map p.75. Live bands on Fri and DJs on Thurs and Sat, plus a good range of food (French, Italian and Asian) at this hip bar with a casual/smart ambience in a former

BIA HOI

If you can't afford the price of a bottle of Saigon beer, you might try a **bia hoi**, where locals glug cheap local draught beer at around 7000đ a glass. These spit-and-sawdust bars tend to open in the afternoon and close around 8–9pm, though some stay open later. They crop up all over the city, but by far the most popular place is De Tham, a road which essentially becomes a huge, open-air bar in the evening. Do note, however, that the quality of the beer can vary tremendously – several foreigners died after drinking contaminated bia hoi in 2013.

opium refinery set back from the main road. Daily 11am–midnight.

Wild Horse 8a1/d1 Thai Van Lung ☎08 3825 1901, ⓦwildhorsesteakhouse.com; map p.75. You can't miss the giant barrel front of this saloon-type place, complete with swinging doors and trophy heads, and specializing in imported steaks and international dishes. Live music too – mostly covers of Western pop hits. Daily 10am–2pm & 4–midnight.

★**Yoko** 22a Nguyen Thi Dieu ☎08 3933 0577; map p.72. If you get fed up with the lack of variety in music bars, head on round to *Yoko*, named after John Lennon's missus, where you'll catch talented bands pumping out blues/rock, reggae and jazz, etc 9.30–11.30pm every night of the week. Add to this the warm atmosphere of the place and decent drinks (cocktails 120,000đ), and you've got one of HCMC's best live music venues. Daily 6pm–late.

PHAM NGU LAO AND AROUND

Allez-Boo 187 Pham Ngu Lao ☎08 3837 2505; map p.79. One of the biggest foreigner magnets in town, this attractive venue doesn't quite live up to its reputation and pleasing bamboo and thatch decor; the quality of their food has gone down of late, but it remains a good drinking hole, with the upper floors turning into dancefloors of a sort if there's a big crowd in. Daily 24hr.

Cyclo Bar 163 Pham Ngu Lao ☎08 3920 1567; map p.79. This congenial place with dartboard and pool table offers draught beer and cocktails as well as comfort food such as bangers and mash. Three floors and sports on TV. Daily 9am–late.

Go 2 187 De Tham ☎08 3836 9575; map p.79. This large, four-storey bar and restaurant on the corner of Bui Vien is packing them in, with a little help from a small army of barkers who steer passers-by inside. The outdoor seats are popular with people-watchers, while on some evenings the rooftop space turns into a grill area. Daily 24hr.

★**Le Pub** 175/22 Pham Ngu Lao ☎08 3837 7679; map p.79. The clue's in the name here – a winning mix of French bar and English pub, tucked away down a charming lane off Pham Ngu Lao. Moodily attractive it may be, but there's often some serious drinking going on, perhaps best evidenced by nightly promotions and large cocktail jugs (220,000đ). Daily 9am–late.

Spotted Cow 111 Bui Vien ☎08 3920 7670; map p.79. Smart, amiable sports bar, located in the heart of the budget district. It's a good place to meet up with other travellers or expat residents while enjoying a glass of grog, or a game of footy. Their food is pretty decent, too. Daily 9am–midnight.

★**Thi Café & Lounge** 224 De Tham ☎08 2210 2929; map p.79. In the daytime this place functions as a chill-out café, a good place to check email or have a chat. However, around 9pm on most nights it morphs into one of the city's most interesting bars for live acoustic music, performed by locals and itinerant musicians. Well worth checking out. Daily 7.30am–late.

Tunnel Bar 111 De Tham ☎09 3322 1190; map p.79. Set up like a military bunker and decorated with camouflage gear, gas masks and the like, this is by far the quirkiest place to drink on De Tham. Despite the bombastic pretensions, it's an amiable place, and beer is super-cheap at just 15,000đ. Daily 10am–2am.

ENTERTAINMENT

Cinemas If you feel like a movie, head to Diamond Cinema complex on the thirteenth floor of Diamond Plaza (see p.104; ☎08 3822 7897); Galaxy Cinema, 116 Nguyen Du (☎08 3822 8533); or Bobby Brewer's Movie Lounge, 45 Bui Vien (see p.100).

Conservatory of Music 112 Nguyen Du ☎08 3824 3774. Western and Vietnamese classical music, performed by the HCMC Youth Chamber Music Club, which can be scheduled on demand.

Municipal Theatre Lam Son Square ☎08 3829 9976. Hosting all sorts including ballet, opera and classical music, shows at this delightful venue (see p.77) rotate every few months, and can often be very entertaining; tickets tend to start at 630,000đ, and you'll usually get 10% off by booking at the theatre itself.

Water puppetry can be seen at the Golden Dragon Theatre (see p.81) or at the History Museum (hourly 10am–4pm, except 1pm; 40,000đ).

1

SHOPPING

Ho Chi Minh City can be a dangerous place to go **shopping**, as you'll likely buy more than you intended once you see the prices. For cheap and cheerful **souvenirs** (see box below), head for Ben Thanh market, Le Loi or De Tham; for something precious and pricey, browse the upmarket boutiques along Dong Khoi and its tentacles, such as Dong Du and Mac Thi Buoi. **Bargaining** is an essential skill to cultivate if you're going to be doing much shopping in these areas. Lastly, **shopping malls** attract curious crowds with their glitz and glamour; some offer distractions in the form of cinemas and bowling alleys, and they can provide air-conditioned respite from the heat or simple retail therapy for those who've been travelling too hard.

DEPARTMENT STORES AND SHOPPING MALLS

Diamond Plaza 34 Le Duan; map p.75. Probably the city's most diverse mall, featuring a department store, supermarket, fitness centre, hospital, swimming pool, bowling alley, cinemas and serviced apartments. Daily 10am–9.30pm.

Saigon Centre 65 Le Loi; map p.75. You'll find cafés, souvenir shops, clothing boutiques, Western-brand stores, a small department store and a supermarket in this highly convenient location between downtown and the budget area. Popular with youngsters on photo-frenzy dates and group meets. Daily 9am–9pm.

Vincom Centre 70–72 Le Thanh Ton; map p.75. One of HCMC's newer malls, containing a selection of Western and Vietnamese designer labels, and housing a few cafés and restaurants. Daily 9.30am–10pm.

Zen Plaza 54–56 Nguyen Trai; map p.72. Black and white eight-storey shopping complex, packed with cosmetics, toys, electrical and household goods and video games. A cafeteria on the top floor has stunning views of the city. Daily 9am–10pm.

BOOKS, NEWSPAPERS AND MAGAZINES

Artbook 43 Dong Khoi ☎08 3822 0838; map p.75. While most books here are art- or architecture-related, there's lots more as well and titles are well displayed in this attractive store. Daily 9am–9pm.

Bookworm 4 Do Quang Dao ☎08 3838 9487; map p.79. There are plenty of secondhand books to choose from at this small café, which has board games for you to play while making your choice or drinking your drink. Daily 7am–midnight.

Fahasa 40 Nguyen Hue ☎08 3775 2987; map p.75. Large bookstore with a wide selection of English-language

titles, including guidebooks, maps, some novels and magazines. However, being government-run, you won't find anything deemed even slightly subversive (including this guidebook). Daily 9am–8pm.

CLOTHING AND BAGS

★**Blue Dragon** 1b Bui Vien ☎08 2210 2084; map p.79. In Vietnam, you know that your business idea has traction when all and sundry start to ape it. That's happening with goods sold at this wonderful little store, which specializes in bags made from material culled from old advertising hoardings; they come in all sizes from fanny-pack to backpack, via laptop, and some of the results are undeniably artistic. Prices are all marked; you'll pay 100,000đ for a small satchel that will allow you to tote your guidebook around in comfort. Daily 9am–10.30pm.

Ginkgo 54–56 Bui Vien ☎08 6270 5928; map p.79. The Bui Vien area is chock-full of places selling T-shirts, but this store is a cut above the rest, with a wide range of colourful, Vietnam-centric designs – occasionally humourous or artistic. They also claim to be eco-friendly. Daily 9am–9pm.

★**Ipa-nima** 77–79 Dong Khoi ☎08 3822 3277, ⌨ipa -nima.com; map p.75. With branches in Singapore, Berlin, Tokyo and Kuala Lumpur, this is perhaps the best-known Vietnamese fashion brand overseas, even if the designer herself is from Hong Kong. She specializes in fabulous handbags, which range from subtle chic to exaggeratedly ostentatious; they're actually pretty affordable, at least in relation to the handbag price tags of the West. Daily 10am–8pm.

Khai Silk 107 Dong Khoi ☎08 3829 1146; map p.75. One of several downtown outlets for the creations of one

SAIGON SOUVENIRS

Saigon is one of Asia's great souvenir-hunting destinations. Paintings on rice paper, silk *ao dai*, lacquerware, embroidered cloth, musical instruments and ethnic garments are all popular choices, as are **curios** such as opium pipes, antique watches, French colonial stamps and banknotes, while the cheapest items are the ubiquitous T-shirts and conical hats. Visitors interested in Vietnam's history will find a wealth of copied **books** on the subject, sold in tourist areas by wandering vendors with a metre-high stack near their hip. For something different, intriguing **model ships** are sold on Cao Ba Quat, north of the Municipal Theatre, just east of the *Caravelle Hotel* facing the *Highland Coffee*.

MARKET SHOPPING

Ho Chi Minh City's biggest market is **Ben Thanh** (see p.79), which has a huge variety of cheap clothes (*ao dai* under $30) and all kinds of souvenirs like chopstick sets and carved seals, though unfortunately all stalls there are now fixed price.

Dan Sinh market, behind the Phung Son Tu Pagoda at 104 Yersin, has a section specializing in army surplus, both American and Vietnamese. Here you can pick up khaki gear, Viet Cong pith helmets, old compasses and Zippo lighters embossed with pearls of wisdom coined by GIs, such as "We are the unwilling, led by the unqualified, doing the unnecessary for the ungrateful." Keep in mind that none of this equipment is likely to be original, even if it looks a bit battered.

Across the road from the Fine Art Museum (see p.79), the small **Le Cong Kieu market** is lined with "antique" shops selling Oriental and colonial bric-a-brac such as opium weights and vases, though your chances of finding genuine antiques are slim. Keep in mind when shopping here that the Vietnamese are very good at making new things look old.

For other smaller souvenirs, check out the shops along **Le Loi** and **Dong Khoi** for old **coins**, **stamps**, notes and **greetings cards** featuring typical Vietnamese scenes hand-painted onto silk.

of the city's top designers, selling exclusive outfits at high prices; the designs are a tasteful fusion of Western and Vietnamese motifs, and even a shawl is likely to set you back a couple of million đong. You'll find smaller (and usually pricier) stores from the same chain in some of the city's top hotels. Daily 9.30am–10pm.

★**Vo Viet Chung** 115 Ly Tu Trong ☎08 3914 2008, ⓦvovietchung.com; map p.72. VOV, as he's often referred to, is one of Vietnam's top designers, and the man most responsible for bringing the *ao dai* into the international fashion realm. There are more "regular" items on sale in his Saigon showroom, though each and every item here is an innovative little work of art. Bring money. Daily 10am–8pm.

HANDICRAFTS, FABRICS AND ANTIQUES

Art Arcade 151 Dong Khoi; map p.75. A number of stands selling paintings, lacquerware and ceramics, plus Buddha statues, old watches and trinkets. In addition, there are usually a few quirky goods being sold outside by vendors who disappear whenever the police are around. Daily about 8am–8pm.

★**Nagu** 155 Dong Khoi ☎08 3936 9379, ⓦzantoc .com; map p.75. Twee it may be, but this great shop contains some perfect present material – teddy bears made from Vietnamese-style patterned fabric, wearing tiny conical hats (from 330,000đ). Some of them wear *ao dai* too, and you can have names sewn into the feet. Daily 9am–10pm.

★**Nga** 41 Mac Thi Buoi ☎08 3823 8356, ⓦhuongnga finearts.com; map p.75. Itself designed something like a giant lacquered box, this shop contains some stunningly decorated lacquerware furniture that would certainly become conversation pieces back home. If chairs are too big for your backpack, there are other items of home decor too. Daily 8am–10pm.

Sapa 209 De Tham ☎08 3836 5163; map p.79. Attractive garments and artefacts, some genuinely designed along the lines of Vietnamese ethnic minority group costumes and trinkets, others mere facsimiles of "ethnic"-style fashion. Daily 7am–10pm.

Tay Son 198 Vo Thi Sau ☎08 3932 5708, ⓦtayson.vn; map p.72. Frequented by tourist groups, who arrive to watch processes such as making lacquerware, and browse their large warehouse of furniture, wooden carvings and lacquered art. It's a bit out of the way, but prices are usually far lower than you'd pay for the same things on Bui Vien or Dong Khoi. Daily 8am–6pm.

Viet Thanh 137 Dong Khoi ☎08 3824 2735; map p.75. Shop with a delightful selections of belts, handbags, picture frames, pendants and purses, mostly made with crocodile skin, but sometimes also ostrich or python. Daily 8am–9.30pm.

Zakka 73 Pasteur ☎08 3829 1516; map p.75. High-quality tailor selling divine ready-to-wear silk creations, but perhaps more notable for lovely trinkets, including fabric pins (23,000đ) and hand-stamped floral-print bags (415,000đ). Daily 10am–8pm.

PAINTINGS

Apricot Gallery 50–52 Mac Thi Buoi ☎08 3822 7962, ⓦapricotgallery.com.vn; map p.75. One of the city's most exclusive galleries, with intriguing, original oils by local artists from $650 upwards. Daily 9am–6pm.

Lotus Gallery 67 Pasteur ☎08 3829 2695; map p.75. If you're in the market for original Vietnamese art, be it traditional or contemporary, there's a good range on show here over two floors. Daily 9am–6pm.

Nam Phuong 105 Bui Vien ☎08 3837 1281; map p.79. One of many artists making a living by reproducing classic images in the travellers' quarter; good work and reasonable prices. Daily 8am–9pm.

1

TAILORS

Chuong 270 Hai Ba Trung ☎ 08 3823 0484; map p.72. A long-established and reliable tailor located a few blocks north of downtown; figure on $250 for a suit and $60 for a shirt. One slight problem is that suits can take up to a month to make; you'd have to order soon after touchdown in Vietnam and pick up just before maxing out your visa. Another slight problem is that there's little English spoken. Daily 8am–8.30pm.

Nhut Van 107 Bui Vien; map p.79. Long-standing tailor in the budget district with many satisfied customers. Shirts can go for as little as $15. Daily 8am–9pm.

★ T&V 39 Dong Du ☎ 08 3824 4556, ⓦ triciaandverona .com; map p.75. Slightly more expensive than the bulk of the city's tailors, but worth it for the fresh and original designs. Some staff speak English, which makes everything easier; shirts are around $50, suits more like $180–250, and there are plenty of ladieswear choices. Daily 9am–7pm.

SPORTS AND ACTIVITIES

If you're done with HCMC's sights, there are plenty of ways in which to up (or lower) your pulse across the city. Most of the upmarket hotels have gym facilities, some of which can be used by non-guests for a fee, while for unbridled pampering, check out ⓦ spasvietnam.com for a complete listing of the many spas and treatments on offer here.

GOLF

Vietnam Golf and Country Club Long Thanh My Village, District Nine ☎ 08 6280 0124, ⓦ vietnamgolfcc .com. High-quality venue with two 18-hole courses (one designed by Lee Trevino) and a driving range; membership isn't required, and Mondays are the cheapest days on which to play a round. You can even spend the night in their on-site villas, if you so desire.

MASSAGE AND SPAS

Traditional Vietnamese Massage Institute 185 Cong Quynh ☎ 08 3839 6697. If you'd like to ease your aches and pains, head for this simple venue, where blind masseurs and masseuses will smoothen your kinks for 60,000đ/hr. Daily 9am–9pm.

RUNNING

Hash House Harriers ⓦ saigonh3.com. For runners and walkers, the Hash House Harriers meet at the *Caravelle Hotel* every Sunday at 1.30pm. There's a hash fee of 220,000đ.

SWIMMING AND LEISURE FACILITIES

Dai The Gioi Water Park 600 Ham Tu in Cho Lon. This attractive park has pools (50,000đ) and slides (55,000đ). Combined entry 80,000đ, children 60,000đ. Mon–Fri 8am–9pm, Sat & Sun 10am–6pm.

Hotel Pools Park Hyatt, Renaissance and Sofitel. For a daily fee of 100,000–200,000đ you can use the facilities at these pools if you are not a guest. Some include use of sauna and steam bath. Diamond Plaza shopping centre (see p.104) also has a pool.

Lam Son 242 Tran Binh Trong. Located on a rooftop above an all-night karaoke bar, this is an inexpensive but busy pool favoured by locals – as well as backpackers who like the sound of the modest 18,000đ entry fee. Tue–Sun 5.30am–noon & 1–6.30pm.

Lan Anh Country Club 291 Cach Mang Thang ☎ 08 3862 7144. Favoured by expats, try the relatively cheap pool (30,000đ) and international-standard tennis courts, squash courts and gym here (from 50,000đ). Daily 6am–9pm.

DIRECTORY

Banks and exchange There are ATMs all over the city, while most banks can exchange cash. Sacombank at 211–213 Pham Ngu Lao (Mon–Fri 7.30–11.30am & 1–4.30pm, Sat 7.30–11am) is convenient for those staying around Pham Ngu Lao. Otherwise, foreign exchange kiosks on Nguyen Hue and Le Loi have extended daily opening times.

Consulates Australia, Landmark Building, 5b Ton Duc Thanh ☎ 08 3821 8100; Cambodia, 41 Phung Khac Khoan ☎ 08 3829 2751; Canada, 10f Metropolitan Building, 235 Dong Khoi ☎ 08 3827 9899; China, 39 Nguyen Thi Minh Khai ☎ 08 3825 2459; Indonesia, 18 Phung Khac Khoan ☎ 08 3825 1888; Laos, 93 Pasteur ☎ 08 3829 7667; Malaysia, 2 Ngo Duc Ke ☎ 08 3829 9023; New Zealand, Suite 804, 8f Metropolitan Building, 235 Dong Khoi ☎ 08 3822 6907; Singapore, Saigon Centre, 65 Le Loi ☎ 08 3822 5174; Thailand, 77 Tran Quoc Thao ☎ 08 3932 7637; UK, 25 Le Duan ☎ 08 3825 1380; US, 4 Le Duan ☎ 08 3820 4200.

Courier services DHL, 4 Phan Thuc Duyen, Tan Binh District ☎ 08 3844 6203; FedEx, 146 Pasteur, close to the *Rex Hotel* ☎ 08 3829 0995.

Dentists Starlight Dental Clinic, 2 Bis Cong Truong Quoc Te (☎ 08 3822 6222), is an international-standard dental clinic. The International SOS Dental Clinic (☎ 08 3829 8424) at 163a Nam Ky Khoi Nghia has a 24hr emergency centre.

Emergencies Dial ☎ 113 for the police, ☎ 114 in case of fire or ☎ 115 for an ambulance; if possible, get a Vietnamese speaker to call on your behalf.

Hospitals and clinics International SOS Clinic, 167a Nam Ky Khoi Nghia (☎ 08 3829 8424), has international doctors, can arrange emergency evacuation and has a 24hr emergency service (☎ 08 3829 8520). Columbia Saigon, 8 Alexandre De Rhodes (☎ 08 3823 8888) has multinational doctors with 24hr emergency cover and evacuation. HCM City Family Medical Practice, Diamond Plaza, 34 Le Duan

(☎08 3822 7848) is an international clinic with multi-national doctors and specialist knowledge of vaccinations, as well as 24hr emergency cover and evacuation. The International Medical Centre, 1 Han Thuyen (☎08 3827 2366) is a French-run, non-profit, 24hr hospitalization centre with in-patient wards, intensive care and emergency surgery.

Laundry Most hotels and guesthouses will wash clothes for you, and some higher-end venues dry-clean too, but rates vary wildly so check first. There are also a number of laundry and dry-clean operators around Pham Ngu Lao, where rates are from 10,000đ per kilo.

Pharmacies There are several pharmacies in and around the De Tham area, such as 65 Bui Vien, while the one at 389 Hai Ba Trung is reputed to be the best stocked in the city.

Police Main police station is at 73 Yersin ☎08 3829 7073. You must first go to the police station in the ward where the crime took place to obtain an initial report before coming here; try to avoid lunchtime visits, as there's likely to be nobody on duty.

Post offices The GPO (daily 6am–10pm) is beside the cathedral at the head of Dong Khoi; poste restante is kept here.

Visas Visa extensions and re-entry visas must be organized through an agent or tour operator; the process takes about four days and usually costs $25.

Around Ho Chi Minh City

When Ho Chi Minh City's blaring horns and pushy vendors become too much for you, you'll find you can get quite a long way **out of the city** in a day. With public transport slow and erratic, day-trips are best arranged through a tour operator (see box below). The single most popular trip out of the city takes in one or both of Vietnam's most memorable sights: the **Cu Chi tunnels**, for twenty years a bolt hole, first for Viet Minh agents, and later for Viet Cong cadres; and the weird and wonderful **Cao Dai Holy See** at Tay Ninh, the fulcrum of the country's most charismatic indigenous religion. While it's possible to see both places in a day (indeed, most people do), be prepared to spend most of the day on the road.

The Cu Chi tunnels

Both sites daily 7am–5pm • 90,000đ each • Shooting range about 300,000đ per clip or 20,000đ per bullet, depending on which rifle you choose

During the American War, the villages around the district of **Cu Chi** supported a substantial **Viet Cong** (VC) presence. Faced with American attempts to neutralize them, they quite literally dug themselves out of harm's way, and the legendary **Cu Chi tunnels** were the result. Today, tourists can visit a short stretch of the tunnels, drop to their

---

VISITING THE CU CHI TUNNELS AND THE CAO DAI TEMPLE

By far the easiest way of reaching the Cu Chi tunnels and the Cao Dai temple is to take a **guided bus tour** from one of the innumerable **travel agencies** operating around the Pham Ngu Lao area. In fact, it's often possible to book such a trip without leaving the comfort of your accommodation – most guesthouses team up with a particular agency, and though they'll want their own piece of the pie, the extra fee paid by the traveller is usually small, if it exists at all. Hotels are a different matter; many run their own tours, and the prices are usually a fair bit higher than those given here. In general, signing up through your hotel will please them and give you some kind of come-back should things go wrong.

Most agencies will **charge** in the region of 130,000đ per person for a half-day trip to the tunnels, and 180,000đ for a full-day sojourn to the tunnels and temple; this will include an English-speaking guide, though it'll cost extra for lunch, and admission fees to the tunnels. Tours usually leave at 8am, with half-dayers returning at 3pm or so, and full-day trips finishing around 6pm.

Another interesting option is to take a **boat tour** to the tunnels (☎08 6290 9410) from Bach Dang pier (see p.75); it'll cost 1,870,000đ per person all in (including lunch and hotel pick-up), or 1,100,000đ if you're prepared to go by bus at least some of the way.

Lastly, some people prefer to go by **taxi**, which will set you back around $60 including both sights and waiting time. It's also possible to hit the temple by **public transport**; see the individual account for details.

1

CU CHI: A HISTORY

When the first spades sank into the earth around Cu Chi, the region was covered by a rubber plantation tied to a French tyre company. Anti-colonial **Viet Minh** dug the first tunnels here in the late 1940s; intended primarily for storing arms, they soon became valuable hiding places for the resistance fighters themselves. Over a decade later, VC activists controlling this staunchly anti-government area, many of them local villagers, followed suit and went to ground. By 1965, 250km of tunnels crisscrossed Cu Chi and surrounding areas – just across the Saigon River was the notorious guerrilla power base known as the **Iron Triangle** – making it possible for the VC guerrilla cells in the area to link up with each other and to infiltrate Saigon at will. One section daringly ran underneath the Americans' Cu Chi Army Base.

Though the region's compacted red clay was perfectly suited to tunnelling, and lay above the water level of the Saigon River, the **digging parties** faced a multitude of problems. Apart from the snakes and scorpions they encountered as they laboured, there was the problem of inconspicuously disposing of the soil by spreading it in bomb craters or scattering it in the river under cover of darkness. American bombing made timber scarce, so the tunnellers had to resort to stealing iron fence posts from enemy bases. Tunnels could be as small as 80cm wide and 80cm high, and were sometimes four levels deep; **vent shafts** (to disperse smoke and aromas from underground ovens) were camouflaged by thick grass and termites' nests. In order to throw the Americans' dogs off the scent, pepper was sprinkled around vents, and sometimes the VC even washed with the same scented soap used by GIs.

TUNNEL LIFE

Living conditions below ground were appalling for these "human moles". Tunnels were foul-smelling, and became so hot by the afternoon that inhabitants had to lie on the floor in order to get enough oxygen to breathe. The darkness was absolute, and some long-term dwellers suffered temporary blindness when they emerged into the light. At times it was necessary to stay below ground for weeks on end, alongside bats, rats, snakes, scorpions, centipedes and fire ants. Some of these unwelcome guests were co-opted to the cause: boxes full of scorpions and hollow bamboo sticks containing vipers were secreted in tunnels, where GIs might unwittingly knock them over.

Within the multi-level tunnel complexes, there were latrines, wells, meeting rooms and dorms. Rudimentary **hospitals** were also scratched out of the soil. Operations were carried out by torchlight using instruments fashioned from shards of ordnance, and a patient's own blood was caught in bottles and then pumped straight back using a bicycle pump and a length of rubber hosing. Such medical supplies as existed were secured by bribing ARVN soldiers in Saigon. Doctors also administered herbs and acupuncture – even honey was used for its antiseptic properties. **Kitchens** cooked whatever the tunnellers could get their hands on. With rice and fruit crops destroyed, the diet consisted largely of tapioca, leaves and roots, at least until enough bomb fragments could be transported to Saigon and sold as scrap to buy food.

THE END OF THE LINE

American attempts to **flush out** or destroy the tunnels proved ineffective – one frustrated soldier compared the task to filling "the Grand Canyon with a pitchfork". GIs would lob down gas or grenades or else go down themselves, armed only with a torch, a knife and a pistol. Booby-traps made of sharpened bamboo stakes awaited them in the dark, as well as "bombs" made from Coke cans and dud bullets found on the surface. Tunnels were low and narrow, and entrances so small that GIs often couldn't get down them, even if they could locate them.

Another American tactic aimed at weakening the resolve of the VC guerrillas involved dropping leaflets and broadcasting bulletins that played on the fighters' fears and loneliness. Although this prompted numerous desertions, the tunnellers were still able to mastermind the **Tet Offensive** of 1968. Ultimately, the Americans resorted to more strong-arm tactics to neutralize the tunnels, sending in the B52s freed by the cessation of bombing of the North in 1968 to level the district with **carpet bombing**. The VC's infrastructure was decimated by Tet, and further weakened by the **Phoenix Programme**. By this time, though, the tunnels had played their part in proving to America that the war was unwinnable. At least twelve thousand Vietnamese guerrillas and sympathizers are thought to have perished here during the American War, and the terrain was laid waste – pockmarked by bomb craters, devoid of vegetation, the air poisoned by lingering fumes.

PHAN THI KIM PHUC

Several kilometres northwest of Cu Chi, Highway 22 slices through idyllic paddy flatlands before reaching **Trang Bang**, where the photographer Nick Ut captured one of the war's most horrific and enduring images – that of a naked girl, severely burnt, running along the highway, fleeing a napalm attack. Now married and living in Canada, **Phan Thi Kim Phuc** was named a goodwill ambassador for UNESCO in 1997. Despite third-degree burns covering half of her body, she remains remarkably unembittered, stating "I am happy because I am living without hatred."

hands and knees and squeeze underground for an insight into life as a tunnel-dwelling resistance fighter. Some sections of the tunnels have been widened to allow passage for the fuller frame of Westerners but it's still a dark, sweaty, claustrophobic experience, and not one you should rush into unless you're confident you won't suffer a subterranean freak-out.

There are two sites where the tunnels can be seen – **Ben Dinh** and, 15km beyond, **Ben Duoc**, though most foreigners get taken to Ben Dinh.

Ben Dinh

Guided tours of Ben Dinh kick off in a thatched hut, where a map of the region, a cross-section of the tunnels and a black and white movie bristling with national pride fill you in on the background. From there, you head out into the bush, where your guide will point out lethal booby-traps, concealed trap doors and an abandoned tank. There are several models showing how unexploded ordnance was ingeniously converted into lethal mines and traps, and a demonstration of how smoke from underground fires was cleverly dispersed far from its source.

When you reach the shooting range, you have the chance to shoulder an M16 or AK47 and shoot off a few rounds, or stop at the adjacent souvenir and snack stalls. Finally, you get the chance to stoop, crawl and drag yourself through a section of the tunnels about 140m long (with frequent escape routes for anyone who can't hack it). It only takes 10–15min to scramble through, but the pitch blackness and intense humidity can be discomforting, so when you emerge, you'll be glad you don't have to live down there for weeks on end as the VC did.

Ben Duoc

The tunnel experience at **Ben Duoc** is similar to that at Ben Dinh, but with fewer foreign tourists and a cheesier atmosphere – better if you're claustrophobic, though scoring few points for authenticity. The original tunnels have been expanded, and for an extra fee you'll be able to don soldier gear to crawl through them. Afterwards, you'll be able to fire off a few rifle rounds. These tunnels are further from HCMC and often best attacked by taxi (figure on around $50 for this alone, and add another $20 if you'd like to see the Cao Dai temple too).

Cao Dai Great Temple

Daily sunrise to sunset • Free • Most visit on a tour (see box, p.107) but if you'd rather go it alone, take one of the infrequent buses to Tay Ninh which depart from Ho Chi Minh City's An Suong station; ask the driver to drop you off at the front gates of the temple

A few kilometres off the highway Highway 22, in the town of Long Hoa, sits the enigmatic **Cao Dai Great Temple**, or Cathedral, of the Holy See of Tay Ninh District. A grand gateway marks the entrance to the grounds of the 1927-built structure. At first sight, the temple seems to be subsiding (an optical illusion created by the rising steps inside it), but your initial impressions are more likely to be dominated by what Graham Greene described as a "Walt Disney fantasia of the East, dragons and snakes in Technicolor".

1

CAO DAI

The basic tenets of **Cao Dai** were first revealed to **Ngo Van Chieu**, a civil servant working in the criminal investigation department of the French administration on Phu Quoc Island, at the beginning of the 1920s. A spiritualist, Ngo was contacted during a seance by a superior spirit calling itself Cao Dai, or "high place". This spirit communicated to him the basics of the Cao Dai creed, and instructed him to adopt the Divine Eye as a tangible representation of its existence. Posted back to Saigon soon afterwards, Ngo set about evangelizing, though according to French convert and chronicler Gabriel Gobron the religion didn't gather steam until late in 1925, when Ngo was contacted by a group of mediums sent his way by the Cao Dai.

At this stage, **revelations** from the Cao Dai began to add further meat to the bones of the religion. Twice already, it informed its mediums, it had revealed itself to mankind, using such vehicles as Lao-tzu, Christ, Mohammed, Moses, Sakyamuni and Confucius to propagate systems of belief tailored to suit localized cultures. Such religious intolerance had resulted from this multiplicity, that for the **third alliance** it would do away with earthly messengers and convey a universal religion via spirit intermediaries, including Louis Pasteur, William Shakespeare, Joan of Arc, Sir Winston Churchill and Napoleon Bonaparte. The revelations of these "saints" were received using a *planchette* (a pencil secured to a wooden board on castors, on which the medium rests his hand, sometimes known as a *corbeille-à-bec*).

Though a fusion of Oriental and Occidental religions, propounding the concept of a **universal god**, Cao Dai is primarily entrenched in Buddhism, Taoism and Confucianism, to which cause-and-effect creeds, elements of Christianity, Islam and spirituality are added. By following its five commandments – Cao Dai followers must avoid killing living beings, high living, covetousness, verbal deceit and the temptations of the flesh – adherents look to hasten the evolution of the soul through reincarnation.

The religion was effectively **founded** in October 1926, when it was also officially recognized by the French colonial administration. Borrowing the structure and terminology of the Catholic Church, Cao Dai began to grow rapidly, its emphasis on simplicity appealing to disaffected peasants, and by 1930 there were five hundred thousand followers. In 1927, Tay Ninh became the religion's Holy See; Ngo opted out of the papacy, and the first pope was **Le Van Trung**, a decadent mandarin from Cho Lon who saw the error of his ways after being visited by the Cao Dai during a seance.

Inevitably in such uncertain times, Cao Dai developed a **political agenda**. Strongly anti-French during World War II, subsequently the Cao Dai militia turned against the Viet Minh, with whom they fought, using French arms, in the French War. By the mid-Fifties, the area around Tay Ninh was a virtual fiefdom of Cao Dai followers. In *The Quiet American*, Graham Greene describes the Cao Dai militia as a "private army of 25,000 men, armed with mortars made out of the exhaust-pipes of old cars, allies of the French who turned neutral at the moment of danger". Even then, however, they were feuding with the rival Hoa Hao sect, and in a few years their power had waned.

Post-liberation, the Communist government confiscated all Cao Dai land, though it was returned ten years later. Today, the religion continues to thrive in its twin power bases of Tay Ninh District and the Mekong Delta.

CAO DAI SERVICES

A major attraction is attending one of the daily **services** at the temple (daily 6am, noon and 6pm), and most tours usually arrange their visit to coincide with the midday one. Though other times are inconvenient, they do offer the opportunity to concentrate on what's happening without the accompanying roadshow of hundreds of flashing cameras. Before services, visitors are shepherded upstairs and past the traditional **band** that plays behind the front balcony, and on into the gods, from where they can look down on proceedings and take photographs. Most worshippers dress in white robes, though some dress in yellow, blue and red, to signify the Buddhist, Taoist and Confucian elements of Cao Dai. Priests don square hats emblazoned with the Divine Eye. At the start of a service, worshippers' heads nod, like a field of corn in the breeze, in time to the clanging of a gong. Then a haunting, measured **chanting** begins, against the insect whine of the string band playing its own time. As prayers and hymns continue, incense, flowers, alcohol and tea are offered up to the Supreme Being.

Despite its Day-Glo hues and rococo clutter, this gaudy construction somehow manages to bypass tackiness. Two square, pagoda-style **towers** bookend the front facade, whose central portico is topped by a bowed, first-floor balcony and a **Divine Eye**. The most recurrent motif in the temple, the eye, is surrounded by a triangle, as it is on the American one-dollar bill. A figure in semi-relief emerges from each tower: on the left is Cao Dai's first female cardinal, Lam Huong Thanh, and on the right, Le Van Trung, its first pope.

The interior

The eclectic ideology of Cao Dai is mirrored in the **interior**. Part cathedral and part pagoda, it draws together a potpourri of icons and elements under a vaulted ceiling, and daubs them all with the primary colours of a Hindu temple. Men enter the cathedral through an entrance in the right wall, women by a door to the left, and all must take off their shoes. Inside the lobby, a **mural** shows the three "signatories of the 3rd Alliance between God and Mankind": French poet Victor Hugo and the fifteenth-century Vietnamese poet, Nguyen Binh Khiem, are writing the Cao Dai principles of "God and humanity, love and justice" in French and Chinese onto a shining celestial tablet. Beside them, the Chinese nationalist leader Sun Yat Sen holds an inkstone, a symbol of "Chinese civilization allied to Christian civilization giving birth to Cao Dai doctrine", according to a nearby sign.

The nave

Apart from service times (see box opposite) tourists are welcome to wander through the **nave** of the cathedral, as long as they remain in the aisles, and don't stray between the rows of **pink pillars**, entwined by green dragons, that march up the chamber. Cut-away windows punctuate the outer walls, their grillework consisting of the Divine Eye, surrounded by bright pink lotus blooms. Walk up the shallow steps that lend the nave its litheness, and you'll reach an **altar** that groans under the weight of assorted vases, fruit, paintings and slender statues of storks.

The **papal chair** stands at the head of the chamber, its arms carved into dragons. Below it are six more chairs, three with eagle arms, and three with lion arms, for the cardinals. Dominating the chamber, though, and guarded by eight scary silver dragons, a vast, duck-egg-blue **sphere**, speckled with stars, rests on a polished, eight-sided dais. The ubiquitous Divine Eye peers through clouds painted on the front. You'll see more spangly stars and fluffy clouds if you look up at the sky-blue **ceiling**, with mouldings of lions and turtles.

The Mekong Delta

FLOATING MARKET, CAN THO

2

The Mekong Delta

From its lofty source in the Tibetan Himalayas, the mighty Mekong River tumbles down through China's Yunnan province, squeezes between Thailand and Laos, then slides through Cambodia before hitting Vietnam. Here, in a flat, comma-shaped delta protruding from the south of the country, the river fragments and spreads out into innumerable tributaries and rivulets, all meandering slowly seawards. It's in and around the delta's myriad waterways that you'll find some of Vietnam's most iconic images: paddy fields of shimmering emerald, endless horizons punctuated by coconut trees, cone-hatted farmers hauling fruit and sugar cane from the ground, and markets to which all goods are sold from colourfully painted boats. Keep an eye out and you'll also see children riding on the backs of water buffalo, bright yellow incense sticks drying at the roadside, and locals scampering over monkey bridges or rowing boats on the delta's maze of channels.

To the Vietnamese, the region is known as Cuu Long, or "**Nine Dragons**", a reference to the nine tributaries of the Mekong River which dovetail across plains fashioned by millennia of flood-borne alluvial sediment. These rich soils have turned the delta into Vietnam's rice bowl, an agricultural miracle that pumps out more than a third of the country's annual food crop – not just rice, but also sugar cane, coconut and fruit – from just ten percent of its total land mass. Such bounty has come at a cost, since this is now also one of Vietnam's most densely populated areas: you may notice, when travelling between the various settlements by road, that the traffic is almost city-like in nature, and that the surrounding countryside is rarely visible behind twin ranks of housing, shops, cafés and more. Another negative point is a relative dearth of actual tourist sights – not really a problem, since you'll be visiting for the area's unique culture and topography in any case.

Southwest of Ho Chi Minh City, buses emerge from the city's unkempt urban sprawl and into the pastoral surrounds of the Mekong Delta's **upper plains**. The delta is too modest to flaunt its full beauty so soon, but glimpses of rice fields hint at things to come, their burnished golds and brilliant greens interspersed with the occasional white ancestral grave. There are over a dozen towns in the delta with facilities for tourists, though some are rarely visited as they are not on the way to anywhere.

Closest to HCMC is the town of **My Tho**. This is well geared up for boat trips, and near enough to Ho Chi Minh City to be seen on a day-trip: it affords an appetizing glimpse of the delta's northernmost tributary, the Tien Giang. From My Tho, laidback

PHU QUOC ISLAND

Highlights

❶ Khmer pagodas Marvel over the rich colours and fancy script of Cambodian-style temples around Tra Vinh. **See p.126**

❷ An Binh Island Take a super-cheap ferry ride from Vinh Long to this delightfully untouristed island, whose mazy waterways and low-rise housing are the delta area in miniature. **See p.128**

❸ Home-stays Spend the night in rural communities, observing daily aspects of Vietnamese culture, and getting to know your hosts. **See box, p.129**

❹ Chau Doc Visit a Cham village and fish farms on the river, and explore nearby Sam Mountain. See p.134

❺ Boat trips Drift along a series of narrow canals, visiting floating markets and fruit orchards around Can Tho. **See p.147**

❻ Hillside rail-ride Unleash your inner child on an odd rail-car system, which runs up a hillside near the charming coastal town of Ha Tien. **See p.158**

❼ Phu Quoc Island Sprawl on its gorgeous beaches, ride a motorbike through its mountainous interior and dive or snorkel around the coastline. **See p.160**

HIGHLIGHTS ARE MARKED ON THE MAP ON P.116

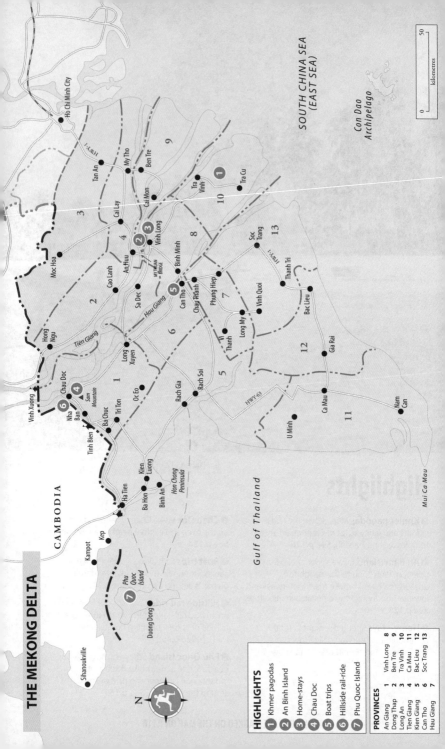

THE MEKONG DELTA

CAMBODIA

Sihanoukville

Kampot

Kep

Phu Quoc Island

Duong Dong

7

Gulf of Thailand

Ho Chi Minh City

Tan An

My Tho

Ben Tre

Cai Lay

Cai Mon

Moc Hoa

Cao Lanh

An Huu

Vinh Long

2 **3**

MY THO — Bloc

Binh Minh

Sa Dec

Hau Giang

Can Tho

5

Chau Thanh

Phung Hiep

Soc Trang

Thanh Tri

Hong Ngu

Tien Giang

Long Xuyen

Vi Thanh

Long My

Vinh Quoi

Bac Lieu

Chau Doc

4

Sam Mountain

Vinh Xuong

Nha Ban

6

Tinh Bien

Ba Chuc

Tri Ton

Oc Eo

Rach Gia

Rach Soi

HWY 63

Gia Rai

Ca Mau

Nam Can

Ha Tien

Ba Hon

Binh An

Kien Luong

Hon Chong Peninsula

U Minh

Mui Ca Mau

Tra Vinh

Tra Cu

1

SOUTH CHINA SEA
(EAST SEA)

Con Dao
Archipelago

10

8

9

13

12

11

HIGHLIGHTS

1 Khmer pagodas
2 An Binh Island
3 Home-stays
4 Chau Doc
5 Boat trips
6 Hillside rail-ride
7 Phu Quoc Island

PROVINCES

An Giang	1	Vinh Long	8
Dong Thap	2	Ben Tre	9
Long An	3	Tra Vinh	10
Tien Giang	4	Ca Mau	11
Kien Giang	5	Bac Lieu	12
Can Tho	6	Soc Trang	13
Hau Giang	7		

N

0   50

kilometres

THE MEKONG RIVER

By the time it reaches Vietnam, the **Mekong River** has already covered more than 4000km from its source high on the Tibetan Plateau; en route it traverses southern China, skirts Burma (Myanmar), then hugs the Laos–Thailand border before cutting down through Cambodia and into Vietnam – a journey that makes this Asia's third-longest waterway, after the Yangtze and Yellow rivers. **Flooding** has always blighted the delta; ever since Indian traders imported their advanced methods of irrigation more than eighteen centuries ago, networks of canals have been used to channel the excess water, but the rainy season still claims lives from time to time.

It's difficult to overstate the influence of the river: the lifeblood of the rice and fruit crops grown in the delta, it also teems with craft that range in size from delicate rowing boats to hulking sampans, all painted with distinctive eyes on the prow. These continue an ancient tradition and were originally intended to scare off "river monsters", probably crocodiles.

2

Ben Tre and the bounteous fruit orchards besieging it are only a hop and a skip away. Further south, across a major arm of the Mekong, is modest **Tra Vinh**, whose surrounds are dotted with spectacular Cambodian temples. To the west is **Vinh Long**, another jumping-off point for boat trips and a pleasant town to boot. Heading west again, there's little of interest until you hit the ebullient town of **Chau Doc**, near the Cambodian border; nearby **Sam Mountain** provides a welcome undulation in the surrounding plains, while the opening of the border here has brought a steady stream of travellers going on to Phnom Penh by boat, and several of them rest up a few days here before leaving the country.

Southeast of Chau Doc is **Can Tho**, the delta's largest city and yet another popular base for boat-trips and visits to **floating markets**. From here it's possible to take a loop-trip around the southern half of the delta area; first up is the Khmer stronghold of **Soc Trang**, a visit to which is especially rewarding if your journey coincides with the colourful Oc Om Bok festival (Nov or Dec), during which the local Khmer community takes to the river to stage spectacular longboat races. Further on, at the foot of the delta, the swampland that surrounds **Ca Mau** can be explored by boat. A boat-ride north is the charming, unassuming town of **Rach Gia**, while pressing on northwest to the border will bring you to **Ha Tien**, a remote frontier town surrounded by Khmer villages, which is the best place to hop on a boat to Phu Quoc. The town has also become popular for its **international border crossing**, which allows beach bums to slide along the coast to Sihanoukville in Cambodia or vice versa. Last, but not least, is **Phu Quoc Island** itself – though developing at speed and growing more popular with each passing year, it remains one of the best beach destinations in the land.

Given its seasonal flooding, **the best time to visit** the delta is, predictably enough, in the dry season, which runs from December to May.

Brief history

It may come as a surprise to learn that agriculture gripped the Mekong Delta area relatively recently. Under **Cambodian** sway until the close of the seventeenth century, the region was sparsely inhabited by the *Khmer krom*, or "downstream Khmer", whose settlements were framed by swathes of marshland. The eighteenth century saw the Viet **Nguyen** lords steadily broaden their sphere of influence to encompass the delta, though by the 1860s **France** had taken over the reins of government. Sensing the huge profits to be gleaned from such fertile land, French *colons* spurred Vietnamese peasants to tame and till tracts of the boggy delta; the peasants, realizing their colonial governors would pay well for rice harvests, were quick to comply. Ironically, the same landscape that had served the French so well also provided valuable cover for the Viet Minh resistance fighters who sought to overthrow them; later it did the same for the Viet Cong, who had well-hidden cells here – inciting the Americans to strafe the area with bombs and defoliants.

2

GETTING AROUND THE RIVER AND DELTA

Inevitably the best way to experience river life is on a **boat trip**. Day-trips can be organized in Ho Chi Minh City, My Tho, Cai Be, Vinh Long, Can Tho or Chau Doc, while some tour operators offer two- or three day live-aboard trips (see box, p.129). Since most day tours follow a similar itinerary (a visit to a floating market and stops at cottage industries on the shore), you'll probably want to choose just one. Though Can Tho is most popular for its good range of hotels and restaurants, you're likely to see more tourists than locals in the nearby floating markets. A good alternative is Vinh Long, from where boats head out in many different directions through the canals of An Binh Island to the floating market at Cai Be.

Most visitors hurtle around the delta on a **tour bus** out of Ho Chi Minh City, denying themselves the chance to sink into the languid life of the region. With time in hand, it's far more satisfying to **hire a vehicle** or take **local transport** – not nearly as daunting a prospect as it is up the coast, since the number of settlements with hotels means journeys can be kept relatively short. Traffic has to stop occasionally at the **ferries** that make road travel in the delta possible, though completion of some long-awaited bridges is speeding up travel times. The enforced halts at the ferries are at least enlivened by strolling hawkers. Locals used to do much of their travelling on the **passenger and cargo boats** that crawl around the delta's waterways, but the increased prevalence of motorbikes has led to many routes being cut, so this is no longer a viable way of getting around for visitors.

If you really want to do the delta in style, sign up for an overnight trip on one of the *Bassac* boats (☎0710 3829540, ⓦtransmekong.com; around $250 per person). These are former rice barges converted into floating hotels, offering a cosy cabin and gourmet meals to accompany the classic delta sights. The most popular trip is from Cai Be to Can Tho, stopping off at a few rural villages along the way and joining the throng at Cai Rang floating market in the morning.

Another luxury option, with similar itinerary and rates, is the Song Xanh **sampan** cruise (☎09 1227 0058, ⓦvietnamluxurytravel.com). If these rates sound a bit steep, Saigon-based Delta Adventure Tours (☎08 920 2112, ⓦdeltaadventuretours.com) offers a more basic three-day, two-night Mekong cruise, taking in Cai Be, Sa Dec, Long Xuyen and Chau Doc for just $55 per person.

My Tho

Seventy kilometres out of Ho Chi Minh City lies **MY THO**, an amiable market town that nestles on the north bank of the Mekong River's northernmost strand, the Tien Giang, or Upper River. My Tho's proximity to Ho Chi Minh City means that it receives the lion's share of day-trippers to the delta, resulting in a scrum of pushy vendors crowding round each tour bus that arrives. Nevertheless, the town can come as a great relief after the onslaught of manic HCMC, its uncrowded boulevards belying a population of around 220,000, and you can easily escape the melee by hopping onto a boat, wandering into the backstreets, or merely staying the night – the vast majority of visitors to the town sleep elsewhere, lending the place a pleasingly local evening atmosphere.

The river's **traffic** – which ranges from elegant sampans to vast, lumbering cargo boats, unpainted and crude – is best viewed from Lac Hong Park at the eastern end of 30 Thang 4 street, where you're sure to catch sight of the most characteristic feature of the boats in the delta – staring eyes painted onto their prows. In the evenings, especially at weekends, this corner of town is packed as families stroll up and down, interspersed with sellers of balloons, popcorn and even tropical fish. At night, young lovers huddle on their motor-bikes, while men play shuttlecock football on the street under the intent gaze of a statue of nineteenth-century anti-French hero Nguyen Huu Huan, who studied in My Tho.

Brief history

My Tho's daily influx of visitors seems rather appropriate, given the town's history. Following the collapse of the Ming dynasty in the late seventeenth century, Chinese immigrants fleeing Taiwan (then known as Formosa) established the town, along with a Vietnamese population keen to make inroads into a traditionally Khmer-dominated region. Two centuries later the French, wooed by the district's abundant rice and fruit crops, rated it highly enough to post a garrison here and to lay a (now-defunct) rail line to Saigon; while the American War saw a consistent military presence in town. Today My Tho's commercial importance is as pronounced as ever, something a walk through the town's busy market amply illustrates.

The market

Beside Bao Dinh canal, between Le Dai Hanh and Thu Khoa Huan streets • Sunrise to sunset • Free

Follow the direction of the canal up along Trung Trac and you'll soon be gobbled up by My Tho's vast **market**, which is at its busiest early in the morning. As well as the usual piles of fruit, cereals and tobacco, several stalls sell ships' chandlery, their heaped fishing nets almost indistinguishable from the fresh noodles on sale nearby.

Cao Dai Temple

Ly Thuong Kiet • Sunrise to sunset • Free

Head west of the town centre on Ly Thuong Kiet for the **Cao Dai Temple**, which is worth a look for its colourful architecture. It is, in effect, a small-scale replica of the Holy See in Tay Ninh (see p.109), with an all-seeing Divine Eye above the entrance,

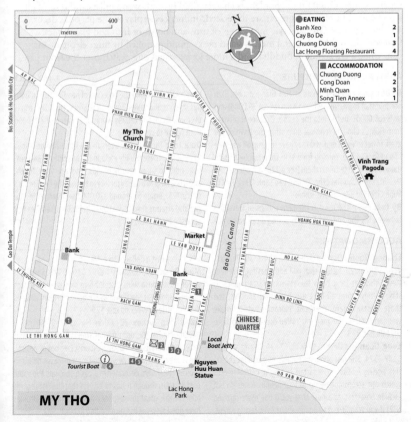

MY THO

dragons writhing up columns and images of the odd mix of characters – such as Victor Hugo and Sun Yat Sen – that comprise the religion's saints. Note also the herb garden to the right of the temple, which is used to concoct remedies for ailments of the poor.

The Chinese Quarter

To the east of the Bao Dinh Canal, the region just south of Dinh Bo Linh Street is home to My Tho's modest **Chinese Quarter**, though there's little to betray its existence other than a feverish sense of commerce. Shopfronts here are piled to the rafters with sugar-cane poles, watermelons and fish awaiting transportation to Ho Chi Minh City, as well as half-hatched eggs (containing chick embryos), prized as the perfect complement to a bia hoi.

Vinh Trang Pagoda

60a Nguyen Trung Truc • Sunrise to sunset • Free • Xe om from centre about 20,000đ

A worthwhile side-trip if you're in town is to make the short journey on foot or cyclo up Nguyen Trung Truc to the attractive **Vinh Trang Pagoda**, with its rajah's palace-style front facade. Since its construction in 1849 it has been renovated several times, most recently in 2002. The entrance, round to the right, leads into the heart of the temple, where a tiny courtyard is flanked by the cubicles where the monks sleep. The main chamber, beyond the miniature mountain to your left, is characterized by dark-wood pillars and tons of gilt woodwork, but of more interest are the eclectic influences at play in the pagoda's decor – classical pillars, Grecian-style mouldings of urns and bowls of fruit and glazed tiles. Outside, the tombs of several monks stand near a pond patrolled by huge elephant-ear fish, while a tall standing Buddha, and a more jovial seated one, watch over the front gate.

ARRIVAL AND DEPARTURE MY THO

By bus Most buses terminate at Tien Giang station, 3km northwest of town, from where xe om (about 30,000đ) and taxis (65,000đ) shuttle into the centre. Occasional services from HCMC's Cho Lon terminal drop off in the town centre itself. To get to Vinh Long, you may have to jump off a service bound for Can Tho; coming from Vinh Long can be trickier, though the main terminal there (see p.128) can advise.
Destinations Can Tho (2hr 30min); Cao Lanh (2hr); Ho Chi Minh City (1hr 30min–2hr 30min).

By taxi By far the most convenient means of travelling between My Tho and Ben Tre is by taking a cab across the

river bridge; negating the necessity of heading to and from bus stations and taking super-slow buses, the 15km trip is over in a flash, and usually works out at around 240,000đ from centre to centre.

On a tour The bulk of visitors to My Tho arrive on a tour from HCMC. These usually include the bus rides in and out, boat rides to some nearby islands, a village walk, lunch, and a boat trip to a candy factory in the nearby Ben Tre area (see p.123); figure on around 220,000đ per head, all in. You can also arrange similar boat tours in My Tho itself (see box opposite for details).

ACCOMMODATION

Chuong Duong Opposite the GPO at 10, 30 Thang 4 ☎07 3387 0875. Sitting riverside and boasting excellent views, this has long been the town's smartest place to stay; its tidy rooms all have a/c, hot water and TVs, and those upstairs have riverfront balconies which make wonderful places for morning coffee or a nightcap from the minibar. $25

Cong Doan Beside the GPO at 61, 30 Thang 4 ☎07 3387 4324. Still just about acceptable as a budget choice, this ageing edifice has spartan but light double rooms which can accommodate up to four people. Rates do not include breakfast, and note that you'll pay more (around $12) if you want a/c; do enquire about river-facing rooms,

which only cost a dollar or so extra. $8

Minh Quan 69, 30 Thang 4 ☎07 3397 9979. Small but sweet guesthouse with tasteful furnishings and modern fittings. Rooms at the front have good river views, as does the nice little café/bar up top. $20

Song Tien Annex 33 Thien Ho ☎07 3397 7883. Nestling within the tight grid of streets in from the boat jetty, and operated by Tien Giang Tourist (see box opposite), this is one of the town's newest and most professionally run choices. Rooms are decorated in pleasing browns and some contain tubs, though it has to be said that the floorboards aren't always great so ask to see a few. Communal balconies have good views of the surrounding hubbub. $22

BOAT TRIPS

Several companies offer boat trips from the tourist boat centre (6–8, 30 Thang 4) to the islands in the Mekong; most tours head for Thoi Son, Phung and Qui islands. **Tien Giang Tourist Company** (❶07 3387 3184, ⓦtiengiangtourist.com) and **Ben Tre Tourist Company** (❶07 3387 9103, ⓦbentretourist.vn) are the most reliable; both charge $20–35 per person for a tour of just over three hours, depending how many people are in the group. You may be interested in their two-day options, which are more or less the same but including one night's home-stay, and an extra $10 per head. Local boats, which you can find at the small jetty on Trung Trac, are much cheaper, and $25 should get you an entire boat for a two- to three-hour trip. However, bear in mind that the owners of these boats are not licensed or insured to carry tourists, so it's a bit of a risky business – you're far more liable to get ripped off.

2

EATING

Though there's nowhere to get very excited about in town, tour groups will get taken to one of a couple of **places to eat** just outside My Tho; if you've any leeway over what's served, ask for the locally famous elephant-ear fish. If you're staying on in town, stroll round the **night market** that opens up each evening beside the tour boat offices on 30 Thang 4.

Banh Xeo 46 70, 30 Thang 4 ❶07 3387 4696. Down by the riverside, this simple eatery serves up filling *banh xeo*: pancakes stuffed with shrimp, beansprouts, shredded chicken and pork. Expect to pay around 50,000đ per dish; one may be large enough to feed two, if you're not too hungry. Daily 8am–10.30pm.

★**Cay Bo De** 22 Nam Ky Khoi Nghia ❶07 3388 3528. Nam Ky Khoi Nghia has three eponymous restaurants located almost side by side, serving filling and nutritious bowls of *hu tieu* (noodles with seafood and meat); there's also a vegetarian version. This is usually eaten as a breakfast meal by locals, though the restaurant's popularity has resulted in its opening hours being extended into the evening. You'll fill up for 60,000đ per head. Daily 6am–7.30pm.

Chuong Duong 10, 30 Thang 4 ❶07 3387 0875. This hotel restaurant, which specializes in seafood, is the best dining option in the town centre, with large, reasonably priced portions served on a breezy terrace overlooking the Mekong. It's very popular among locals and domestic visitors, and can be crowded at times. Mains 60,000đ–140,000đ; shellfish buffets from 300,000đ. Daily 6am–11pm.

Lac Hong Floating Restaurant 30 Thang 4 ❶07 3625 0130. Over on the far side of the tour boat jetty, and more or less right in front of the tour boat offices, this floating restaurant is quite classy, and offers a good range of dishes (50,000–180,000đ) accompanied by occasional breezes off the river. Daily 10am–10pm.

DIRECTORY

Banks There's an ATM next to the *Cong Doan* hotel, 61, 30 Thang 4, and another at Vietinbank, at the western end of Thu Khoa Huan. The Agribank at the opposite end of Thu Khoa Huan on the corner of Le Loi will change dollars for dong.

Post office The post office is conveniently located opposite the boat jetties on Le Thi Hong Gam, where you can also find internet access.

Around My Tho

Day-trippers tend to see little of My Tho as they disgorge from tour buses and embark on a **boat trip** (see above) round two or three of the **islands** in the Tien Giang branch of the Mekong River. Arranging trips locally tends to lead to a more relaxed and enjoyable experience, but you'd probably need to sleep over at least one night. Note that some tours also include a visit to the floating market at **Cai Be**, which is far closer to Vinh Long (see p.126).

Tan Long

Beyond its chaotic shoreline of stilthouses and boatyards, **Tan Long** ("Dragon Island"), the least frequently visited island, boasts bounteous sapodilla, coconut and banana plantations, as well as highly regarded longan orchards. As with the other islands, Tan Long is sparsely inhabited, by small communities of farmers and boat-builders.

2

Thoi Son

Thoi Son ("Unicorn Island") is the largest of the four islands and many of the organized tours out of Ho Chi Minh City stop here for lunch and fruit sampling. Narrow canals allow boats to weave through its interior. Gliding along these slender waterways, overhung by handsome water-palm fronds that interlock to form a cathedral-like roof, it's easy to feel you're charting new territory. Swooping, electric-blue kingfishers and sumptuously coloured butterflies add to the romance. Local tours do not always include **lunch** in the price, but all tours will stop somewhere you can get refreshment.

Qui Island

Qui ("Turtle") **Island** is the newest of the group, having been formed by sediment in the river then stabilized by planting mangroves, and is overflowing with longans, dragon fruit, mango, papaya, pineapple and jackfruit. There is a small, family-run **coconut candy factory**, just opposite here along the Ben Tre coastline, where you can watch the coconut being pressed and the extracted juice being mixed with sugar and heated, then dried and cut into bite-size pieces. You can buy a box to take home.

Phung Island

Phung ("Phoenix") Island is famed as the home of an offbeat religious sect set up three decades ago by the eccentric **Coconut Monk**, Ong Dao Dua (see box below), although there's not much left to see from his era, and only the skeleton of the open-air **complex** he established remains. Among its mesh of rusting staircases and platforms, you'll spot the rocket-shaped elevator the monk had built to whisk him up to his private meditation platform. Elsewhere are nine dragon-entwined pillars, said to symbolize the Mekong's nine tributaries and betraying a Cao Dai influence. The Coconut Monk's story is told (in Vietnamese) on a magnificent **urn**, which he is said to have crafted himself out of shards of porcelain from France, Japan and China.

Dong Tam Snake Farm

10km west of My Tho • Daily 7am–5.30pm • 20,000đ • Xe om to farm around 50,000đ

Run by the military, the **Dong Tam Snake Farm** breeds snakes for their meat and skins. Watching the sluggish pythons and cobras sleeping in cages is not a particularly pretty sight, though there are several other animals on display in a small zoo, including porcupines, monitor lizards, otters, monkeys, eagles, peacocks and an enormous albino

---

ONG DAO DUA, THE COCONUT MONK

Ong Dao Dua, the **Coconut Monk**, was born Nguyen Thanh Nam in the Mekong Delta, in 1909. Aged 19, he travelled to France where he studied chemistry until 1935, when he returned home, married and fathered a child. During a lengthy period of meditation at Chau Doc's Sam Mountain (see p.138) he devised a new religion, a fusion of Buddhism and Christianity known as **Tinh Do Cu Si**. By the 1960s, this new sect had established a community on Phung Island, where the monk lorded it over his followers from a throne set into a man-made grotto modelled on Sam Mountain. The monk became as famous for his idiosyncrasies as for his doctrine: his name, for instance, was coined after it was alleged he spent three years meditating and eating nothing but coconuts.

Unfortunately, the Coconut Monk never got to enjoy his "kingdom" for long: his belief in a peaceful reunification of North and South Vietnam (symbolized by the map of the country behind his grotto, on which pillars representing Hanoi and Saigon are joined by a bridge) landed him in the jails of successive South Vietnamese governments, and the Communists were no more sympathetic to his beliefs after 1975. Ong Dao Dua died in 1990.

turtle. One of the farm's most popular products is Cobratox – a cream that includes cobra venom and stings on application, but is rated by many as an effective cure for rheumatism.

Ben Tre

The few travellers who push on beyond My Tho into Ben Tre province are rewarded with some of the Mekong Delta's most breathtaking scenery. **BEN TRE** itself is a pleasant and industrious town displaying none of the wounds of its past (apart from a heavily populated cemetery and proud war memorial), and makes an agreeable contrast to the tourist bustle of nearby My Tho. Though short on specific sights, the surrounding countryside is lush and photogenic. It's a relaxing and friendly place to hole up for a couple of days, with a

buzzing **market** and a new **riverside promenade**, which makes a pleasant place to stroll in the morning or evening. With a bicycle or motorbike, you can explore the maze of trails on both sides of the river. For more of an adventure, head out of town on a boat trip along the **Ben Tre coastline**, where labyrinthine creeks afford marvellous scope for exploring, and sometimes include stops at apiaries, rice-wine and sugar-processing workshops.

Brief history

Famed for its fruit orchards and coconut groves (Vietnamese call it the "coconut island"), Ben Tre province has proved just as fertile a breeding ground for revolutionaries, first plotting against the French, and later against the Americans, and was one of the areas seized by the Viet Cong during the Tet Offensive of 1968. Of the US bombing campaign against the provincial capital itself, a US major was quoted as saying, "It became necessary to destroy the town in order to save it" – a classic wartime analysis. Until recently the province was isolated by the Mekong's wide arms, but the Rach Mieu Bridge from My Tho, opened in 2009, is starting to bring a rush of visitors; this increase in popularity has, as yet, had little effect on scruffy Ben Tre town, though change cannot be far away.

ARRIVAL AND DEPARTURE

BEN TRE

By bus The opening of the new bridge to Ben Tre means that almost all visitors now arrive by road: buses terminate at the new bus station on Highway 60, about 2km northwest of the town centre (a 35,000đ cab ride). Most buses head to and from HCMC (1hr 45min–2hr 30min); city buses to My Tho leave from the road outside, though these stop everywhere and can take up to 45min for the 15km journey.

By taxi Cabs are the fastest way to travel between My Tho and Ben Tre; it'll be around 240,000đ from centre to centre.

By boat It was once possible to ride cargo boats all around the delta, though those connecting Ben Tre and Tra Vinh are some of the last survivors. You'll have to sequester the help of your accommodation for ticket purchase and advice on the latest pick-up points; the boats leave Ben Tre daily at 9am (120,000đ; 6hr). In addition, Mango Cruises, the travel arm of *Mango Home* (see p.124), runs costly a/c overnight cruises (2–5 people) to Can Tho and Chau Doc; mainly using canals instead of big rivers, these trips feature a few fun activities, and average out at around $380 per person per night.

GETTING AROUND AND TOURS

Car and bicycle rental Located at 65 Dong Khoi to the north of the centre, Ben Tre Tourist Company (daily 7–11am & 1–5pm; ☎07 5382 9618) can organize car rental, bicycles and some tours, including boat trips.

Tours *Mango Home* (see below) runs good half-day trips from the riverbank it calls home; a nice mix of cycling and rowing, these cost around $75 per person (plus $15 for lunch), with most of the proceeds directed to local businesses.

ACCOMMODATION

TOWN CENTRE

Ham Luong 200c Hung Vuong ☎07 5356 0560, ⓦham luongtourist.com.vn. One of Ben Tre's smarter hotels, located in a relatively pleasant area along the riverfront. Rooms have traditional furnishings with smart fixtures and fittings, while the fourth floor café/bar overlooking the river is a great spot to relax. The place is particularly good value for single travellers, with tiny rooms going from just $12. $25

Phuong Hoang 16 Hai Ba Trung ☎07 5357 5377. Ben Tre has precious good value at the budget end of the scale, though there are a few cheapies on the north bank of Truc Giang Lake. This is the pick of a sorry bunch; the management are hardly switched on, while rooms are bare and you may end up sharing them with a cockroach or two. $7

Viet Uc 144 Hung Vuong ☎07 5251 1888. This riverside alternative to the *Ham Luong* is the newest hotel in town, and already boasts its best location and facilities. The rooms aren't exactly huge, but they're well equipped; all have a/c and TVs, while some have bathtubs and river views (the latter for a slightly higher price). There's also a smart café abutting the lobby. $25

OUT OF TOWN

★**Mango Home** My Thanh village ☎07 5351 1958, ⓔnhung@mangocruises.com. A great little addition to the Ben Tre scene, this family-run, community-focused place is located around 6km from town in the middle of semi-rural nowhere – you'll have to take a cab, following the hotel's instructions, then either walk or call for a pick-up. Its collection of sweet rooms is arrayed around a charming stretch of riverbank, and they also run tours (see p.123). Given the dearth of anywhere else to eat in the nearby area, it's a nice surprise that the food served here is both tasty and fairly priced. $45

★**Thao Nhi Guest House** Hamlet 1, Tan Thach village ☎09 0812 3488, ⓔthaonhitours@yahoo.com. A cheap and adventurous option, set in the grounds of a longan orchard 12km from town. It has a range of rooms, including wooden cabins with fan and shared bathroom, and larger ones with a/c. The boss organizes enjoyable boat trips to watch a sunrise or sunset over the Mekong River; be sure to agree on prices beforehand. Bicycles are available for free to guests, though again do double-check that this is the case. The atmosphere is very relaxing – the kind of place to settle in for a few days – and its restaurant has a good menu that features elephant-ear fish and huge prawns. It's about 6km from the new bus station, but if you call ahead they'll arrange a pick-up. $6

EATING

Ben Tre's dismal culinary scene certainly won't be featuring on any of your Facebook posts or postcards home. Dong-pinchers should make a bee-line for the grimy **market** area, inside which you'll find a range of cheap noodles and other simple fare.

Ben Tre Floating Restaurant 60 Hung Vuong, about 3km west of the centre ☎07 5382 2492. A fine venue for a sunset drink, though worse for food – the menu of Vietnamese dishes (mains around 90,000đ) is rather limited, and nothing's that tasty. Don't forget your mosquito repellent. Daily 10am–10pm.

Ham Luong 200c Hung Vuong ☎07 5356 0560. The ground-floor restaurant here is a reliable stand-by, serving up a good range of Vietnamese stir-fries and soups (80,000đ and up) as well as steak and chips (160,000đ),

though it's sometimes booked by wedding parties. Way up above, the rooftop café-bar is a decent place to kick back with a coffee, fruit concoction or cocktail, while enjoying great views over the river. Daily 6am–10pm.

Quan 160 160c Hung Vuong. Just east of the *Ham Luong*, this cute, neighbourly little place specializes in *hu tieu* (noodles with seafood and meat) for just 25,000đ, and *banh canh* (noodles with veggies and all-sorts) for 35,000đ. Wash it down with some sugar cane juice (8000đ). Daily 7am–7pm; often closes early.

Tra Vinh

TRA VINH is an outback market town whose 800-metre-square grid of broad, tree-lined streets and smattering of colonial piles have yet to see tourists in any numbers. Most visitors come here to watch the **storks** at nearby **Hang Pagoda** (see p.126), although the town's low-key charm makes it a pleasant place to spend a day or two. At the very least,

Tra Vinh is worth a half-day detour from Vinh Long, especially since the area between the two towns is a real delta rarity – devoid of roadside clutter or heavy traffic (for the road beyond Tra Vinh basically goes nowhere), you can actually see plenty of countryside from the bus here: vivid green rice paddies, fringed by coconut and water palms. This is Khmer country; as you get nearer to Tra Vinh, distinctive pagodas begin to appear beside the road, painted in rich pastel shades of lilac, orange and turquoise, their steep horned roofs puncturing the sky. Altogether there are over **140 Khmer pagodas** scattered around the province.

2

The pagodas and church

Just south of the market, at the junction of Pham Thai Buong and Tran Quoc Tuan, the Chinese **Ong Pagoda** is well worth a visit, as it's a very active place of worship and there's always something interesting going on. North of the town centre up Le Loi, the **Ong Met Pagoda** is very different, sporting a distinctive Khmer-style roof above colonial arches and shutters: you're assured of a friendly reception here from the monks studying at its English school. Immediately north is the pretty **Tra Vinh Church**, an imposing buttressed construction; it's fronted by a statue of Christ above the entrance, while waves of stonework ripple up its spire.

The river

Unusually, Tra Vinh isn't ostensibly dominated by a branch of the Mekong – you'll have to journey a couple of hundred metres east the town centre to find the river, and a hike through the **market** to riverside Bach Dang makes the most engaging approach. The bridge 100m north of the fish market commands great views of the **Tra Vinh River**, whose eddying waters run canal-straight to the north. In places the river is almost corked by boats moored seven or eight deep.

ARRIVAL AND DEPARTURE   TRA VINH

By bus and minibus Buses from the west hit the southwest corner of Tra Vinh, terminating about 800m from the centre of town at the bus station on Nguyen Dang, off Dien Bien Phu. Ask staff at the tourist office to point you towards the various operators in central Tra Vinh, who usually provide shuttle services to the actual start point. Regular buses bypass Vinh Long (see p.128 for details), though you can get there direct aboard minibuses which run to no set schedule, and no set price – figure on 30,000–75,000đ, depending on how many other passengers there are, and how fast you'd like to get there. Destinations Can Tho (2hr); Ho Chih Minh City (5hr); Vinh Long (1hr 30min).

By boat One of the delta's last cargo-boat services connects (for now) Ben Tre and Tra Vinh; ask at the town's tourist office (see below) for tickets and advice. The boats leave from a jetty north of Tra Vinh daily at 9am (120,000đ; 6hr).

INFORMATION

Tourist information The extremely helpful Tra Vinh Tourist Company at 64–66 Le Loi (☎07 4385 8556, ☎07 4385 8768) can provide local information, as well as book – or at least advise on – bus and ferry tickets.

There's usually some English spoken here.
Services The Agribank, one block west of the market at 70–72 Le Loi, will change US dollars, and has an ATM. The post office is on Hung Vuong, just opposite *Thanh Tra Hotel*.

ACCOMMODATION

Hoan My 105a Nguyen Thi Minh Khai ☎07 4386 2211. Set on the main road just west of town (you may spot it on the bus-ride in), this mini-hotel looks very ordinary from the outside, but inside it has tastefully furnished rooms, some with massage showers. The most expensive rooms are huge and have private balconies. If it's full, note there are similar options in the nearby area. **$15**

Palace 3 Le Thanh Ton ☎07 4386 4999. One of the smartest places in the town centre, and located just off the corner of a pleasant park, this seems to have been transported from a bygone era with its chunky traditional furniture, high ceilings and all-round mock-colonial air. Even the polite welcome from the staff harks back to a time when courtesy counted above all. **$16**

2

Thanh Tra 1 Pham Thai Buong ☎ 07 4385 3626. Large hotel with a central location and reasonable restaurant, factors which make it the most popular choice for a wide range of travellers. Rooms are smart but lack character; in addition, some are rather dingy, so take a look first. $18

EATING

Thanh Tra Hotel 1 Pham Thai Buong. The top-floor restaurant of the *Thanh Tra* hotel serves an unexciting but reliable range of Vietnamese staples (35,000đ for simple rice or noodle dishes; 100,000–200,000đ for meats), and boasts modest views from the windowside tables. It may not be gourmet food, but it's one of the few places in town with an English menu, and it's in a very convenient location in the town centre. Daily 6am–9pm.

Tuy Huong 8 Dien Bien Phu. Opposite the front of the market, *Tuy Huong* offers a range of Chinese and Vietnamese dishes (25,000–100,000đ), such as sweet and sour prawns or fresh spring rolls, in a no-frills, open-air café environment. Good spot for people watching. Daily 7am–8pm.

Ba Om Pond

Daily 24hr • Free • 5km southwest of town, a signposted road on the left runs down to the pond; buses to and from Vinh Long pass the short approach road here, minibuses can usually drop you off directly, while a xe om from the centre of Tra Vinh costs around 40,000đ

Ba Om Pond is beloved of Tra Vinh picnickers and courting couples. Around the pond, drinks and snack vendors lie in wait for visitors, but although it can get crowded at weekends, on weekdays it is usually restful. Bordered by grassy banks, and shaded by towering, aged trees whose roots clutch at the ground, Ba Om is cloaked with plants that attract flocks of birds in the late afternoon.

Ang Pagoda

Behind Ba Om Pond • Sunrise to sunset • Free

The area across the far side of the pond has been a Khmer place of worship since the eleventh century, and today it's occupied by **Ang Pagoda**. Steep roofed and stained with age, the pagoda makes an affecting sight, especially when it echoes with the chants of its resident monks. Fronting it is a nest of stupas guarded by stone lions, while murals inside depict scenes from the Buddha's life. In season, rice from the pagoda's paddy fields is heaped next to the altar, where it's watched over by an impressive golden Sakyamuni image and a host of smaller ones. Several Cambodian monks are resident here, and you'll find them eager to practise their English with visitors.

Hang Pagoda

Hang Pagoda is around 6km south of town along Dien Bien Phu • Daily 24hr • Free • No public transport to the pagoda; xe om about 65,000đ for the return trip

The sight of the hundreds of **storks** that nest in the grounds of this Khmer pagoda is one that will linger in the memory. Timing, however, is all-important, and you should aim to catch these magnificent creatures before dusk, when they wheel and hover over the treetops, their snowy wings catching the evening's sunlight. It's a stirring sight, though you might find yourself distracted by the saffron-robed monks who clamour to practise their English. They may also show you their wood-carving workshop, where there's usually someone at work on a wooden rat or tiger. Hang Pagoda itself – an arched stone gate to the left of the main road betrays the entrance to the compound – is nothing to write home about. Dominating it is a **Sakyamuni statue**, hooped by a halo of fairy lights and flanked by murals depicting scenes from his life.

Vinh Long

Ringed by water and besieged by boats and tumbledown stilthouses, the island that forms the heart of **VINH LONG** town has the feel of a medieval fortress. However, if you

find yourself yearning for a peaceful backwater, first impressions will be a let-down; central Vinh Long is hectic and noisy, its streets a blur of buses and motorbikes. Make for the waterfront, though, and it's a different story, with hotels, restaurants and cafés conjuring up something of a riviera atmosphere. From here you can watch the **Co Chien River** roll by, dotted with sampans, houseboats and the odd raft of river-weed. Though there's little to see or do in town, Vinh Long offers some of the most interesting **boat trips** in the delta – to the Cai Be floating market, coconut candy workshops, fruit orchards or even overnighting in home-stays.

Vinh Long Museum

Phan Boi Chau • Tues–Thurs 8–11am & 1.30–4.30pm, Fri & Sat 6–9pm • Free

Of Vinh Long's few specific sights, the **Vinh Long Museum**, facing the waterfront, is worth a look if you haven't already visited war museums elsewhere. Displays in various buildings include historical finds from the region, farming implements and musical instruments, as well as a gruesome photographic catalogue of the province's pummelling during the American War. In the gardens are tanks, a helicopter and planes from the war, as well as a guillotine from French colonial times.

Cau Lac Bo Huu Tri

Le Van Tam

West of the Vinh Long Museum, look out for the impressive French colonial building, **Cau Lac Bo Huu Tri**. This oddly shaped mansion, with its red-tiled roof and shuttered windows topped by mouldings of garlands, recalls the ghosts of French *colons* and rice merchants. The place is now run by the government as a social club for retirees, and if

2

> ## PHAN THANH GIAN
>
> Born in Vinh Long Province in 1796, the mandarin diplomat **Phan Thanh Gian** was destined to be involved in a chain of events that shaped over a century of Vietnamese history.
>
> On August 31, 1858, French naval forces attacked Da Nang, citing persecution of Catholic missionaries as their justification. The French colonial land-grab, that would culminate in 1885 in the total conquest of Vietnam, had begun. By 1861, the three eastern provinces of Cochinchina had been conquered by the **French Expeditionary Corps**, and although there were popular anti-French uprisings Emperor Tu Duc sold out the following year, when the three provinces were formally ceded to the French by the **Treaty of Saigon**, which was signed by Phan Thanh Gian. A year later he had the opportunity to redress the situation, when he journeyed to Paris as ambassador to Emperor Napoleon III, to thrash out a long-term peace – the first Vietnamese ambassador ever to be despatched to Europe.
>
> However, efforts to reclaim territory given up under the terms of the treaty failed, and by 1867 France moved to take over the rest of Cochinchina. Unable to persuade the spineless Tu Duc to sanction popular uprisings, Phan Thanh Gian embarked on a hunger strike in protest at French incursions and Hue's ineffectuality. When, after fifteen days, he had still not died, he swallowed **poison**, and his place among the massed ranks of Vietnamese heroes was assured.

anyone is around, they probably won't mind you peeking in the front door at the fancy furnishings with mother-of-pearl inlay, a bust of Uncle Ho and a few meeting rooms.

Van Thanh Mieu Temple

Off Tran Phu • Daily 5–11am & 1–7pm • Free

The **Van Thanh Mieu Temple** sits 2km down the road that runs parallel to the Rach Long Canal to the southeast of town. If you wander into the tiny lanes that back onto the river along the way, you can watch tiles and coffins being made in the simplest of surroundings, and you might even be invited to take a tea with the friendly locals.

The temple itself, located at the end of an avenue of tall trees, is dedicated to Confucius – unusually for southern Vietnam – and a heavily bearded portrait of him watches over proceedings, while a wooden statue of Chu Van An (1292–1370), one of his disciples, stands in front of the altar. Another temple at the front of the compound honours local mandarin Phan Thanh Gian (see box above), who is pictured in red robes, flanked by slender storks. Fronting the temple are two cannons that rained fire on the French in 1860. Unfortunately, both temples are often kept locked, though the gardener or caretaker may be able to open them for you (for which a small donation would be appreciated).

An Binh Island

Ferry from centre 5min • 5000đ

Sometimes called Minh Island, **An Binh Island** is a jigsaw of bite-sized pockets of land, skeined by a fine web of channels and gullies which eventually merge, to the east, with the province of Ben Tre. This idyllic landscape is crisscrossed by a network of dirt paths, making it ideal for a morning's rambling or cycling, though you'll need to take your own refreshments. You're best advised to take the minor road heading west just as you hit **Chua Tien Chau**, the first temple from the jetty; this is a pleasingly calm stretch with very little traffic, and plenty of curious locals. Note that there's also simple accommodation here (see opposite).

ARRIVAL AND DEPARTURE   **VINH LONG**

By bus State-run buses, including jalopies to Sa Dec, pull into the bus station on 3 Thang 2 in the centre of town, which is also used as a base for private minibuses to Tra Vinh (see p.124). Private buses use the main bus station, a couple of kilometres west of town on Nguyen Hue; from here take a xe om (about 30,000đ) or taxi (50,000đ or so) into the centre. Also note that from HCMC or elsewhere around the delta, you may end up buying tickets for buses that merely pass by, rather than stop in, Vinh Long; in this case, you'll likely be dumped unceremoniously at a roundabout near to the main bus station.

Destinations HCMC (3hr); Sa Dec (50min); Tra Vinh (1hr 30min).

By taxi The only place within affordable taxi range is Sa Dec (see p.130); it'll cost around 400,000đ from centre to centre.

INFORMATION

Tourist information For information about boat trips or home-stays, check the state-run Cuu Long Tourist (☎07 0382 3616), whose main office is in the *Cuu Long* hotel: they charge $25 to send two people on a three-hour tour of Cai Be floating market, fruit orchards and the narrow waterways of An Binh Island; shell out another $10 and you'll get yourself an English-speaking guide, a dance-and-music performance and another hour in the boat.

Services Vietinbank at 143 Le Thai To exchanges cash and has an ATM. The post office is in the middle of town at 12c Hoang Thai Hieu, where there's also internet access.

ACCOMMODATION

Most of Vinh Long's accommodation options are located near the boat jetty on the northern edge of town. The local tourist board can also arrange for visitors to stay with the owners of fruit orchards, allowing a close-up view of rural life (see box below).

TOWN CENTRE

Cuu Long Phan Boi Chau ☎07 0382 3656. This government-run place is looking rather faded now, though while details like polyester sheets and thin aluminium doors don't impress, it's still decent value for money. The location is ideal, while some rooms have fine views of the Vinh Long riviera; all include satellite TV, a/c, hot water and breakfast across the road. **$18**

Phung Hoang 2h Hung Vuong ☎07 0382 5185. This mini-hotel represents some of the best value in town. It has a dozen or so rooms with varying sizes and facilities, all with chintzy furnishings, and the staff are very friendly. **$7**

Van Tram Boarding House 4, 1 Thang 5 ☎07 0382 3820. Just five rooms here, but all are a good size and well equipped with TVs, fridges, hot water and a/c. Add in its prime location and the result is great value. **$15**

AN BINH ISLAND

Nam Thanh 172/9 Binh Luong ☎07 0385 8883. If you want that DIY feeling, head to this simple, homely guesthouse on An Binh island (see opposite). It sits in a gorgeous location, a short, signed short walk from the ferry jetty. Prices include free bike rental and two meals. Per person **$12**

EATING AND DRINKING

★**Café Them Sua** 87 Trung Nu Vuong ☎09 1389 9904. A pleasing little café that wouldn't look out of place in HCMC – the downstairs level is surprisingly smart, while its tree-surrounded rooftop vies with the riverfront for Vinh Long's best views. It'll set you back 18,000đ for most juices, and 25,000đ for shakes or something resembling an Orange Julius. It's located on an alley just off the main road. Daily 10am–10pm.

★**Com Tam He Pho** 14 Phan Thai Buong ☎09 1389 9904. Buzzing with locals every night, this is the friendliest

---

HOME-STAYS IN THE DELTA

While the Vietnamese are generally gregarious people, it's unusual for foreigners to be invited into their homes. However, most visitors are curious about local culture, so it's not surprising that **home-stays** are becoming ever more popular, and those located on tranquil islands of the delta, surrounded by acres of orchards, are particularly attractive.

For around $15 a head, plus $10 for the boat, you'll be transported to your host's (usually isolated) abode, shown around the gardens, given a tasty dinner – most likely including the delicious elephant-ear fish, a delta speciality – and lodgings for the night, either in a bed or hammock in a spare room. Bathroom facilities are basic, sometimes with squat toilets and bucket baths, but generally clean. If you book your home-stay with a tour operator like Sinhbalo Adventures (see p.91), you can also spend the day kayaking between water palms along narrow canals, or cycling along narrow lanes between coconut, mango and papaya trees.

2

> ## BOAT TRIPS FROM VINH LONG
>
> The cheapest and simplest way to cruise the river is to hop on the An Binh Ferry on Phan Boi Chau, and cross the Co Chien River (5min; 5000đ) to reach **An Binh Island** (see p.128). However, most people fork out for a day or half-day **boat trip** to take in the colourful tapestry of everyday delta life, organized either through Cuu Long Tourist or Mekong Travel (see p.129), or through local boatmen always on the look-out for customers near the tourist jetty. These tours often include the option of overnighting in a **home-stay** (see box, p.129) in a totally rural environment; though as they increase in popularity, some start to resemble guesthouses rather than home-stays, with visitors put up in custom-built bamboo huts separated from the family home.
>
> Most tour itineraries also head upriver to the floating market at **Cai Be** (see below), stopping to visit fruit orchards, and rice-paper and candy factories en route; some tours add a fish lunch at a rural outpost. Watching the river traffic, from the tiny rowing boats to huge sampans loaded with rice husks (fuel for the nearby brick kilns), is fascinating, and stepping ashore from time to time reveals insights into the lifestyles of the locals – a simple, unhurried existence quite at odds with the bustle of the Delta towns.

of several cheap *com tam* places abutting the road just over the bridge from the police station. Plates of their delicious grilled pork-on-rice go from just 15,000đ; a 50,000đ note will get you two, plus a few bangers and a can of pop. Daily 3–10pm.

Hoa Nang Café 1 Thang 5. With a long river frontage, this is a perfect place to sip a cool drink while watching the sun sink into the Mekong. Occasionally plays host to screaming karaoke soon afterwards. Coffees from 8000đ. Daily 7am–11pm.

Pho 91 91, 2 Thang 9. Slurp-worthy pho in the town's best noodle joint; the greens are nice and fresh, the broth both sweet and meaty, and the atmosphere typically Vietnamese. Bowls go from just 20,000đ. Daily 6am–9pm.

Phuong Thuy Phan Boi Chau, opposite the Cuu Long hotel ☎ 07 0382 3656. Operated by the *Cuu Long* (see p.129) and built out over the river, this boasts the best location of the town's restaurants, though the Vietnamese food is only average and service is indifferent. It's far better in the evening, when locals gather on the tables outside to eat tasty shellfish and drain a few beers. Mains 40,000–100,000đ. Daily 6am–10pm.

Cai Be Floating Market

Cai Be's floating market is one of the most popular in the delta, and also the most distinctive because of its backdrop of a slender cathedral spire. Throughout the day boats of all sizes throng in the waters of the Tien Giang, with fruit vendors displaying a sample of their produce suspended from a stick. The market reaches its busiest at around midday when busloads of visitors roll in to Cai Be village on organized tours from Ho Chi Minh City, 110km away. They are shepherded on to boats for a few hours to explore the market and fruit orchards on nearby islands before zipping back to the city. While this may be convenient for those who are short of time, it's all a bit rushed and the midday heat can be oppressive. If you have a more relaxed schedule, meandering through the picturesque channels of An Binh Island between Vinh Long and Cai Be market, or overnighting in a home-stay (see box, p.129) before visiting the market in the morning, offers a more rewarding experience.

Sa Dec

A cluster of brick and tile kilns on the riverbank announces your arrival in the dusty town of **SA DEC**, a little over 20km upriver of Vinh Long. French novelist Marguerite Duras lived here as a child (see box opposite), and decades later the town's stuccoed shophouse terraces, riverside mansions and remarkably busy stretch of the rumbling Mekong provided the backdrop for the movie adaptation of her novel *The Lover*.

The home of Huynh Thuy Le
255a Nguyen Hue • Open daily 8am–5pm • 30,000đ • ☎ 06 7377 3937

Sa Dec's best place for a wander is **Nguyen Hue**, whose umbrella-choked lanes hide an extensive riverside market. Waterfront comings and goings are observed by rheumy old men playing chequers, and women squat on their haunches, selling fruit from wicker baskets.

Nestled among the tumbledown riverside houses stands the former home of **Huynh Thuy Le**, who became the lover of Marguerite Duras in the 1930s (see box below). The old family home, now administered by Dong Thap Tourism, features some elaborate carved panels and lashings of gold lacquer work, as well as some photos of the couple in question, though interestingly none of them together.

Tu Ton Rose Garden
Off Le Loi • Daily 8–11am & 1–5pm • Free • Xe om about 40,000đ

A few kilometres north of town by the river, Sa Dec's famed **flower nurseries** consist of more than a hundred farms cultivating a host of ferns, fruit trees, shrubs and flowers. The expansive grounds of **Tu Ton Rose Garden** get the lion's share of tourists visiting the area. In addition to the varieties of roses cultivated here (among them the Brigitte Bardot, the Jolie Madame and the Marseille), over 580 species of plants are grown, ranging from orchids, carnations and chrysanthemums, through to medicinal herbs and pines grown for export around Asia. Bear in mind that the nurseries are overrun on Sundays by tourists from Ho Chi Minh City, who come to pose for photos among the blooms; and that things get particularly busy and colourful in the run-up to Tet, as farms prepare to transport their stocks to the city's flower markets.

ARRIVAL AND DEPARTURE   SA DEC

By bus Buses terminate 300m southeast of the town centre. It's quite walkable, and just after you cross the bridge the town's three main arteries – riverside Nguyen Hue, then busier Tran Hung Dao and Hung Vuong – branch off one after another to your right. Note that to get to or from Chau Doc or HCMC by sleeper bus, you'll likely need to pay the full fare between the two cities.

Destinations Chau Doc (3hr 30min, including ferry); HCMC (3hr 30min); Long Xuyen (2hr, including ferry); Vinh Long (50min).
By taxi The only place within affordable taxi range is Vinh Long (see p.126); it'll cost around 400,000đ from centre to centre.

MARGUERITE DURAS
Marguerite Duras (1914–96) was born to French parents in a suburb of Saigon, and lived in various locations in Vietnam and Cambodia before going, aged 18, to study at the Sorbonne in France. She wrote many novels, plays and film scripts including the autobiographical novel *The Lover* (1984), which sold over three million copies and was translated into forty languages. Its subject is an interracial affair between a 15-year-old French girl and her middle-aged Chinese lover, set in 1930s Indochina. Duras had little sympathy for her peers, of whom she wrote, "I look at the (French) women in the streets of Saigon. They don't do anything, just save themselves up… Some of them go mad…some are deserted for a young maid." Duras clearly had no intention of letting life pass her by in this way, even if it meant becoming the subject of the town's gossip.

Though her novels are principally about the inner thoughts of her characters, she also describes the landscape around Sa Dec as it still appears today: "In the surrounding flatness, stretching as far as the eye can see, the rivers flow as if the earth slopes downward."

If you visit Sa Dec with a tour guide, they will almost inevitably take you to look at her former house beside the river – an old colonial villa that now belongs to the People's Committee.

2

ACCOMMODATION AND EATING

Com Thuy 439 Hung Vuong ✆ 06 7386 1644. A popular lunch spot serving Vietnamese staples; there are no prices on its English menu, so ask when ordering. Try some spring rolls, a steamy soup or a stir-fry; it's 50,000đ or under for most dishes. Daily 7am–9pm.

★**My Ngoc** 150 Hung Vuong ✆ 06 7386 2379. Friendly clutch of ladies serving up delectable *banh*

canh, a hearty noodle soup featuring meat, quail eggs, bamboo shoots and much more. It's just 50,000đ per bowl. Daily 5am–9pm.

Thao Ngan 2 An Duong Vuong ✆ 06 7377 4255. More or less the only decent place to stay in town, with a friendly owner, and an elevator to hoist you up to plain, but clean, rooms that are fair value for the price. $12

Cao Lanh and around

West of My Tho, and Cai Be, Highway 1 crosses the My Thuan Bridge on its way to Vinh Long and Can Tho. Just before the bridge, however, at An Huu, Highway 30 branches north, rolling into modest **CAO LANH** 34km later. The town is no oil painting and offers little unless you're charmed by **wading birds**; its location beside the western edge of the **Plain of Reeds** makes Cao Lanh an ideal launching pad for trips out to the storks and cranes that nest in the nearby swamplands. Coming from Ho Chi Minh City, you'll pass the two great concrete tusks (intended to resemble lotus petals) of the **war memorial** as you veer onto the main drag, Nguyen Hue. One tusk bears a hammer and sickle, the other a Vietnamese red star.

The burial place of Nguyen Sinh Sac

Pham Huu Lau, about 1km west of the town centre • Daily 24hr • Free

On the southwestern outskirts of town, a landscaped park contains a monument, shaped like an open clam, which marks the burial place of Ho Chi Minh's father, **Nguyen Sinh Sac**. The park's area has recently been expanded to include several examples of stilted houses typical of the south, as well as a replica of Ho Chi Minh's

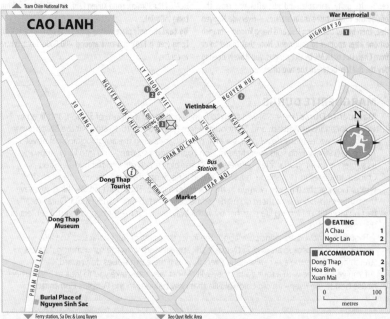

CAO LANH

EATING
A Chau 1
Ngoc Lan 2

ACCOMMODATION
Dong Thap 2
Hoa Binh 1
Xuan Mai 3

house in Hanoi. With a lake and benches in shady areas, it's a pleasant place to pass an hour or so.

Dong Thap Museum

Just off Pham Huu Lau, to the left beyond the first bridge • Mon 7–11.30am, Tues–Sun 7–11.30am & 1.30–5pm • Free

While in town, it's worth having a look around the **Dong Thap Museum**. Though there are no English signs, there is a well-organized display of fossils, skulls, farming tools, fishtraps, basketware and textiles, as well as the inevitable paintings of heroic Vietnamese forces repelling French and American troops.

Tram Chim National Park

45km northwest of Cao Lanh

Of the 220 species of birds nesting at **Tram Chim National Park** (previously called the Tam Nong Bird Sanctuary), it's the sarus cranes, with their distinctive red heads, that most visitors come to see, though numbers have sadly declined drastically in recent years, and there's not much to be seen outside the months of December to May. In flight above the marshland of the sanctuary, the slender grey birds reveal spectacular black-tipped wings. **Cranes** feed not from the water but from the land, so when the spate season (July–Nov) waterlogs the delta, they migrate to Cambodia. Visiting the park, however, can be very expensive (over $100 per day for a small group), so this is a trip for committed bird enthusiasts only: if you're keen, ask at the office of Dong Thap Tourist in Cao Lanh for details (see below).

Xeo Quyt Relic Area

You'll need to approach the tourist office (see below) if you want to take a trip out to **Xeo Quyt Relic Area**, deep in the cajeput forest 30km southeast of Cao Lanh. Day tours here used to go by boat but now it's a road trip. The district's dense cover provided the perfect bolthole for Viet Cong guerrillas during the American War, and from 1960 to 1975 the struggle against America and the ARVN was masterminded from here. The boggy nature of the terrain made a tunnel system similar to that of Cu Chi (see p.107) unfeasible, so they made do with six submerged metal chambers sealed with tar and resin. Suspecting the base's existence, Americans bombed the area regularly, and even broadcast propaganda from the air to demoralize its occupants, but by developing a policy of "going without trace, cooking without smoke, speaking without noise", the cadres residing here escaped discovery throughout the war.

ARRIVAL AND DEPARTURE   CAO LANH AND AROUND

By bus Buses to and from Cao Lanh stop at the bus station, right in the town centre. From destinations south, buses cross the Tien Giang via the Cao Lanh ferry, around 4km southwest of town.

Destinations HCMC (3hr 30min); Sa Dec (50min); Vinh Long (1hr 20min).

INFORMATION

Tourist information Dong Thap Tourist (daily 7–11.30am & 1.30–5pm; ☎ 06 7385 5637), whose office is at 2 Doc Binh Kieu, just off the main road, Nguyen Hue, is the place for information about visits to the nearby bird sanctuaries. Very little English is spoken, so dedicated twitchers might be better off approaching tour operators in Ho Chi Minh City.

ACCOMMODATION

Dong Thap 48 Ly Thuong Kiet ☎ 06 7387 2669. This place is run by the army and when they aren't chanting in the yard next door it's one of the quietest spots in town. Basic rooms are small but well equipped, while the biggest is a huge suite with cosy armchairs and balcony. $16

Hoa Binh 1km east of the town centre on Highway 30

☎ 06 7385 1469. Slightly industrial-looking from the outside, the "Peace Hotel" is actually one of the smartest choices in town, with bright, tiled floors and modern furnishings. It's situated, rather symbolically, across from the war memorial. $\overline{\$20}$

Xuan Mai Just west of the post office at 33 Le Qui Don ☎ 06 7385 2852. This place has been subject to a half-hearted make-over, but make sure you check the room first, as some are very dingy. Its larger rooms have bathtubs and breakfast is included in the price. $\overline{\$13}$

EATING

A Chau 42 Ly Thuong Kiet ☎ 06 7385 2202. Almost next door to *Dong Thap*, this is popular for parties, and features a good range of dishes such as rice with fried pork and vegetables for around 50,000đ. Daily 7am–9pm.

Ngoc Lan 210 Nguyen Hue ☎ 06 7385 1498. If you walk down Cao Lanh's main street at lunchtime, this simple place is likely to be the most crowded. Plenty of rice and noodle dishes from 25,000đ. Daily 7am–10pm.

Chau Doc

Sitting merrily on the languid banks of the Hau Giang, **CHAU DOC** is the only delta town bar Can Tho in which you are likely to see foreigners in any significant numbers. Since the opening of the border to Cambodia a few kilometres north of town, the place has boomed in popularity, and it makes a decent book-end to a stay in Vietnam. The town came under Cambodian rule until it was awarded to the Nguyen lords in the mid-eighteenth century for their help in putting down a localized rebellion. The area still sustains a large Khmer community, which combines with local Cham and Chinese to form a diverse social melting pot. Just as diverse is Chau Doc's religious make-up: as well as Buddhists, Catholics and Muslims, the region supports an estimated 1.5 million devotees of the indigenous Hoa Hao religion (see box, p.136). Forays by Pol Pot's genocidal Khmer Rouge into this corner of the delta led to the Vietnamese invasion of Cambodia in 1978.

As with many delta towns, there's little of sightseeing interest here bar a market and a couple of temples. However, there are several places of interest to visit in the surrounding area, including a **Cham community** and brooding **Sam Mountain** with its kitsch pagodas. Further afield are a bird sanctuary, a battlefield from the American War and the scene of a Khmer Rouge massacre.

The covered market

Main entrance on Quang Trung • Daily 7am–6pm • Free

The obvious place to begin an exploration of Chau Doc is at its **covered market**, where the overspill of stalls and street vendors spreads from Quang Trung to Tran Hung Dao, and from Dong Du to Nguyen Van Thoai. This is one of the delta's biggest markets and is packed with a phenomenal range of produce, much of which is unfamiliar to Western eyes. Even if you have explored other markets in the region, it's well worth picking your way through the rows of neatly stacked stalls of fresh produce, household goods, fish and flowers.

Along the river

To the east of the covered market, stalls are crammed into narrow alleyways that run towards the river, where you're greeted by a multitude of bobbing boats and waterside activities. If you wander south by the river from here, you'll find a narrow park bordering the river that features a tall statue celebrating the local catfish and makes a pleasant place for a breezy stroll in the morning or evening.

Quan Cong Temple

Tran Hung Dao • Daily sunrise–sunset • Free

A four-tiered gateway deep in the belly of the open market announces **Quan Cong Temple**. Beyond the courtyard, two rooftop dragons oversee its entrance and the outer

2

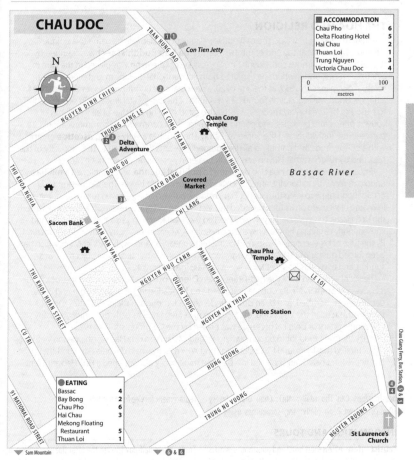

CHAU DOC

N

Con Tien Jetty

TRAN HUNG DAO

NGUYEN DINH CHIEU

THUONG DANG LE

LE CONG THANH

Quan Cong
Temple

Delta
Adventure

DONG DU

BACH DANG

Covered
Market

TRAN HUNG DAO

Bassac River

THU KHOA NGHIA

CHI LANG

Sacom Bank

PHAN VAN VANG

NGUYEN HUU CANH

PHAN DINH PHUNG

Chau Phu
Temple

LE LOI

THU KHOA HUAN STREET

QUANG TRUNG

NGUYEN VAN THOAI

Police Station

CU TRI

HUNG VUONG

91 NATIONAL ROAD STREET

TRUNG NU VUONG

NGUYEN TRUONG TO

St Laurence's
Church

Sam Mountain

■ ACCOMMODATION	
Chau Pho	6
Delta Floating Hotel	5
Hai Chau	2
Thuan Loi	1
Trung Nguyen	3
Victoria Chau Doc	4

0 —————————— 100
metres

● EATING	
Bassac	4
Bay Bong	2
Chau Pho	6
Hai Chau	3
Mekong Floating Restaurant	5
Thuan Loi	1

Chau Giang Ferry, Bus Station, ⑤ & ⑤

walls' vivid murals. Inside the temple is the red visage of Quan Cong, sporting green robe and bejewelled crown, and surrounded by a sequin-studded red velvet canopy.

Chau Phu Temple

Main entrance on corner of Tran Hung Dao and Nguyen Van Thoai • Daily sunrise–sunset • Free

A few steps southeast through the covered market stalls along Tran Hung Dao, the lofty chambers of **Chau Phu Temple** offer a cool respite from the heat outside, and fans of gilt woodwork will find much to divert them. It was built in 1926 to honour Thoai Ngoc Hau (1761–1829), a local hero whose elaborate tomb is located at the base of Sam Mountain (see p.138).

ARRIVAL AND DEPARTURE   **CHAU DOC**

By bus The bus station comes as a nice surprise – a large, neat place with free wi-fi. It's roughly 3km southeast of town on Le Loi: around 20,000đ by xe om, or 55,000đ by cab. Destinations Ca Mau (7hr); Can Tho (3hr); Ha Tien (3hr); Ho Chi Minh City (6hr); Long Xuyen (1hr 30min).

By ferry The tourist jetty where most boat tours leave from is south of town on Le Loi, connected to *Delta Floating Hotel*; buy your tickets here or at the Delta agency in town. Chau Giang is reached by a car ferry (10min; 1000đ), which departs from the jetty a little further down Le Loi.

THE HOA HAO RELIGION

Sited 20km east of Chau Doc, the diminutive village of Hoa Hao lent its name to a unique religious movement at the end of the 1930s. The **Hoa Hao Buddhist sect** was founded by the village's most famous son, Huynh Phu So. A sickly child, Huynh was placed in the care of a hermitic monk under whom he explored both conventional Buddhism and more arcane spiritual disciplines. In 1939, at the age of 20, a new brand of Buddhism was revealed to him in a trance. Upon waking, Huynh found he was cured of his congenital illness, and began publicly to expound his breakaway theories, which advocated purging worship of all the clutter of votives, priests and pagodas, and paring it down to simple unmediated communication between the individual and the Supreme Being. The faith has a fairly strong **ascetic** element, with alcohol, drugs and gambling all discouraged. Peasants were drawn to the simplicity of the sect, and by rumours that Huynh was a faith healer in possession of prophetic powers.

Almost immediately, the Hoa Hao developed a **political agenda**, and established a **militia** to uphold its fervently nationalist, anti-French and anti-Communist beliefs. The Japanese army of occupation, happy to keep the puppet French administration it had allowed to remain nominally in charge of Vietnam on its toes, provided the sect with arms. For themselves, the French regarded the Hoa Hao with suspicion: Huynh they labelled the "Mad Monk", imprisoning him in 1941 and subsequently confining him to a psychiatric hospital – where he promptly converted his doctor. By the time of his eventual release in 1945, the sect's uneasy alliance with the Viet Minh, which had been forged during World War II in recognition of their common anti-colonial objectives, was souring, and two years later Viet Minh agents **assassinated** Huynh.

The sect battled on until the mid-Fifties when **Diem's purge** of dissident groups took hold; its guerrilla commander, Ba Cut, was captured and beheaded in 1956, and by the end of the decade most members had been driven underground. Though in the early Sixties some of these resurfaced in the Viet Cong, the Hoa Hao never regained its early dynamism, and any lingering military or political presence was erased by the Communists after 1975.

Today there are thought to be somewhere around two million Hoa Hao worshippers in Vietnam, concentrated mostly around Chau Doc and Long Xuyen. Some male devotees still sport the distinctive long beards and hair tied in a bun that traditionally distinguished a Hoa Hao adherent.

Destinations Can Tho (daily; 4hr); Chau Giang (every 10min); Phnom Penh (daily; 4hr; sometimes using bus replacement service from border).

INFORMATION AND TOURS

Tourist information Most hotel and guesthouse owners can help out with local information, as well as arrange local excursions and onward travel, including boat services to and from Phnom Penh.

Tours Both Delta Adventure (☎07 6358 4222, ⓦdelta adventuretours.com), which has offices at *Delta Floating Hotel* (see below) and *Vinh Phuoc* hotel, 12–14 Quang Trung, offers half-day trips to the local floating market, a fish farm and Cham village (about $12/person), and day-trips to Tup Duc (about $25/person). To get to Tra Su, Tup Duc and Ba Chuc, either join a tour with one of the companies mentioned above, or rent a motorbike and be prepared to get lost a few times before arriving at your destination, as road signs are few and far between.

ACCOMMODATION

★**Chau Pho** 88 Trung Nu Vuong ☎07 6356 4139, ⓦchauphohotel.com. Spacious, well maintained rooms with expansive views from the upper floors make this the best mid-range option in town, though it is several blocks from the riverside action. It also has tennis courts and a classy restaurant (see opposite). $35

Delta Floating Hotel Just south of the tourist jetty, ☎07 6356 3810, ⓦdeltaadventuretours.com. Basic rooms over the river (fixed, in fact, not floating), all with en-suite bathrooms and a ringside view of the action on the water. Check the room first as some are a bit musty;

those in the "luxury" wing ($24) are nicer, though the noise from the restaurant upstairs can filter down. $15

★**Hai Chau** 61 Thuong Dang Le ☎07 6626 0066, ⓦhaichauhotel.com. A wonderful recent addition to the Chau Doc accommodation scene: cheap, well-appointed rooms; amiable, English-speaking staff; and a lobby-restaurant that's worth a visit even if you're not staying here (see opposite). You'll pay around $4 more for a room with a window – well worth it. $20

Thuan Loi 275 Tran Hung Dao ☎07 6386 6134. This riverside mini-hotel offers some of the best value in town, plus a truly authentic delta-like atmosphere. Both fan and a/c rooms (the latter $4 extra) are clean and comfortable; try to get one overlooking the river. Also has a restaurant affording a great front-seat view of the Mekong. $10

Trung Nguyen 86 Bach Dang ☎ 07 6356 1561, ⓦ trungnguyenhotel.com.vn. Very smart mini-hotel, right in the town centre, with fifteen smallish but well-furnished rooms, all with small balconies. Staff are very helpful and efficient, and they rent out bicycles and motorbikes ($2 and $8 per day respectively) too. $16

Victoria Chau Doc 1 Le Loi ☎ 07 6386 5010, ⓦ victoria hotels-asia.com. Just 300m southeast of the town centre, this colonial-style hotel lords it over the river. The rooms are tastefully furnished with *Indochine* elegance and some have glorious river views, though one has to say that they represent poor value for the sky-high prices. They've a lovely restaurant and bar on site (the *Bassac*), as well as a small swimming pool with river view. $185

EATING

Chau Doc has more places to eat than most Mekong Delta towns, catering to diners looking for something tasty and cheap as well as those looking for some ambience. A snack at one of the **food stalls** around the market, particularly on Tran Hung Dao, Chi Lang and Le Cong Thanh, is a good option if you're feeling adventurous.

Bassac Victoria Chau Doc, 1 Le Loi ☎ 07 6386 5010. Imaginative iterations of Western and Asian dishes, such as roast loin of lamb (375,000đ), roasted duck breast (300,000đ) or simple pho (75,000đ), served in a romantic riverside dining terrace overlooking the Mekong and the hotel pool. There's also an attractive adjoining bar with pool table and backgammon, ideal for a sundowner (85,000đ). Daily 11am–2pm & 6–10pm.

★ **Bay Bong** 22 Thuong Dang Le ☎ 07 6386 7271. A visit here is a treat after a long day on the move. With its plastic stools and tables, it may look like any other hole-in-the-wall eatery, but the food is wonderfully prepared – go for their speciality, catfish in clay pot (55,000đ). Daily 7am–9pm.

Chau Pho 88 Trung Nu Vuong ☎ 07 6356 4139. The smart, ground-floor dining area of this hotel may lack riverside views, but the food, mostly Vietnamese with a few Western options, is excellent and the service is very attentive. Try the grilled chicken satay (130,000đ), or the basa fish in banana leaf (110,000đ). Daily 7am–9pm.

Hai Chau 61 Thuong Dang Le ☎ 07 6626 0066. This new hotel also makes a great place to eat. Their colourful picture menu highlights the highlights: try seafood soup (80,000đ), chicken in orange (80,000đ), or even a slice of banana bread (20,000đ). Daily 5.30am–8.30pm.

Mekong Floating Restaurant Just south of the tourist jetty on Le Loi ☎ 07 6356 3810. Located on the riverbank above the *Delta Floating Hotel*, this place is popular among backpackers – more for its cheap beer and river views than the motley selection of meals (most around 85,000đ). Daily 7am–10pm.

★ **Thuan Loi** 275 Tran Hung Dao ☎ 07 6356 1561. Enjoy the riverside action at this rustic guesthouse restaurant: check out the chickens stored in the labyrinth of bamboo poles underneath the main building. The menu features simple Vietnamese staples but is surprisingly extensive; figure on 15,000–20,000đ for veggies or spring rolls, 30,000–40,000đ for meat mains, and 40,000–70,000đ for seafood dishes. Daily 7am–10pm.

DIRECTORY

Banks Sacombank, 88 Dong Du, can exchange foreign currency, and also has an ATM.

Bicycle and motorbike rental Available at *Trung Nguyen* hotel ($2 & $8 per day respectively).

Hospital Opposite the *Victoria Chau Doc* on Le Loi.

Pharmacy 14 Nguyen Huu Canh.

Post office On the corner of Le Loi and Nguyen Van Thoai (daily 6am–10pm); it also has internet access.

Chau Doc Floating Market

Opposite tourist jetty on Bassac River • Daily 5–9am • Boatman will row you there for a small fee

Since this floating market was only established recently, you have to wonder whether it's more for the benefit of tourists than locals. Nevertheless, if you've managed to get this far through the delta without visiting any of the other floating markets along the way, it's certainly worth a look. As usual, boats advertise their products by hanging a sample from a stick on the deck.

Con Tien Island and Chau Giang District

Two settlements just a stone's throw from Chau Doc across the Hau Giang river are worth venturing out to, and most people visit both on a half-day tour (see opposite).

One is the cluster of **fish-farm houses** floating on the river next to **Con Tien Island**, above cages of catfish that are fed through a hatch in the floor. Fish farming is big business in the delta, and some of these cages can be over 1000 cubic metres in size.

The other settlement is a **Cham community** in Chau Giang District, which you can visit independently via a ferry from a jetty south of the tourist jetty on Le Loi. Admid the traditional wooden houses, you'll discover the sarongs and white prayer caps that betray the influence of Islam, as do the twin domes and pretty white minaret of the **Mubarak Mosque**.

Sam Mountain

Free • Around 40,000đ from Chau Doc by xe om to base, or 70,000đ to summit

Arid, brooding **Sam Mountain** rises dramatically from an ocean of paddy fields just west of Chau Doc. It's known as Nui Sam to Vietnamese tourists, who flock here in their thousands to worship at its clutch of pagodas and shrines. Even if the temples don't appeal, the journey up the hill is good fun. As you climb, you'll pass massive boulders that seem embedded in the hillside, as well as some plaster statues of rhinos, elephants, zebras and a Tyrannosaurus rex near the top. From the top, the **view** of the surrounding, pancake-flat terrain is breathtaking, though the hill is, in fact, only 230m high. In the rainy season, the view is particularly spectacular, with lush paddy fields scored by hundreds of waterways, though in the dry season the barren landscape is hazy and less inspiring. There's a tiny military outpost at the summit, from which you can gaze into Cambodia on one side, Chau Doc on the other.

Tay An Pagoda

At the foot of Sam Mountain, the first temple you'll see is kitsch **Tay An Pagoda**, built in 1847. It's the pick of the bunch, its frontage awash with portrait photographers, beggars, incense-stick vendors and bird-sellers (releasing one from captivity accrues merit, though some clever vendors train the birds to fly back later). The number of gaudy statues inside exceeds two hundred: most are of deities and Buddhas, but an alarmingly lifelike rendering of an honoured monk sits at one of the highly varnished tables in the rear chamber. To the right of this room an annexe houses a goddess with a thousand eyes and a thousand hands, on whose mound of heads teeters a tiny Quan Am.

Chua Xu Temple

Fifty metres west of Tay An, **Chua Xu Temple** honours Her Holiness Lady of the Country, a stone statue said to have been found on Sam's slopes in the early nineteenth century, though the present building, with its four-tiered, glazed green-tile roof, dates only from 1972. Inside, the Lady sits in state in a marbled chamber, resplendent in colourful gown and headdress. Glass cases in corridors either side of her are crammed to bursting with splendid garb and other offerings from worshippers, who flood here between the 23rd and 25th of the fourth lunar month, to see her ceremonially bathed and dressed. Shops in front of the temple sell colourful baskets of fruit that locals buy to offer to Her Holiness.

Tra Su Bird Sanctuary

23km from Chau Doc, just north of Chi Lang on Highway 948 • 120,000đ entry • 75,000đ per person for a 90min boat ride; 150,000đ for the boat if there are too few people • Around $20 to rent a car for the return trip from Chau Doc

Tra Su consists of a protected forest of cajuput trees and wetlands that attract a great variety of birds including storks, egrets, cormorants, peafowl and water cocks. Once here, you'll be able to take a boat ride around the sanctuary, combined with a walk to a viewing tower. Even if you're not a dedicated birder, you'd probably enjoy floating around this watery wonderland with its huge lily pads and moss-shrouded trees.

Ba Chuc

40km southwest of Chau Doc • Daily 9am–6pm • Free • Take Highway 91 and then Highway N1 along the border towards Ha Tien and turn south on to Highway 3T for the last few kilometres • Around $35 to rent a car for the return trip from Chau Doc

A sweep of staggeringly beautiful countryside southwest of Chau Doc conceals a far from peaceful history. Refugees fleeing Pol Pot's Cambodia boosted the Khmer population here in the late 1970s, and pursuit by the Khmer Rouge ended in numerous indiscriminate massacres; a grisly memorial to the worst of these, at the village of **BA CHUC**, stands as testament to that horrific era.

Memorials

The **memorial** in the centre of the village pays homage to the 3157 villagers massacred, most of them clubbed to death, in two weeks during April 1978. Only two villagers survived the tragedy. An unattractive concrete canopy fails to lessen the impact of the eight-sided memorial: behind its glass enclosure, the bleached skulls of the dead of Vietnam's own "killing fields" are piled in ghoulish heaps, grouped according to age to highlight the youth and innocence of many of the dead.

Many of the victims were killed in the adjacent **Phi Lai Pagoda**, where bloodstains on the walls and floor can still be easily seen. A signboard in Vietnamese beside a tiny door below the altar notes that forty villagers perished here when a grenade was thrown into the cramped space.

Between the memorial and the pagoda is a small room, where a horrific set of black-and-white photos taken just after the massacre shows buckled, abused corpses scattered around the countryside. Some of the images on display are extremely disturbing and you should not enter if you are a sensitive type. There are also a few cafés and food stalls set up to cater to visitors to the site.

Long Xuyen

The large, spread-out town of **LONG XUYEN** attracts few foreign visitors, though the unusual cathedral, the well-organized **museum**, **Tiger Island** and the nearby **stork garden** are all worth a look if you're passing through – with Chau Doc and Can Tho so close, there's precious little reason to stay here. You'll be able to get your bearings from the cathedral, whose spire is shaped in the form of two upstretched arms whose hands clasp a cross.

My Phuoc Communal Hall

Nguyen Hue • Daily sunrise to sunset • Free

Near the eastern end of Nguyen Hue, the dragon-stalked roofs of the grandest building in town, the **My Phuoc Communal Hall**, shelter carved pillars and embroidered banners in the temple-like interior. Nearby is a very large statue of a meek-looking **Ton Duc Thang**: born locally, he was successor to Ho Chi Minh as president of the Democratic Republic of Vietnam, giving the town its main claim to fame.

Tiger Island

Ton Duc Thang Exhibition House • Daily 7–11am & 1–5pm • Free • Access to Tiger Island by ferry from the eastern end of Nguyen Hue; 1000d, 2000d with bike

You can visit Ton Duc Thang's birthplace and childhood home at **My Hoa Hung Village** on **Tiger Island**. Here you will find the **Ton Duc Thang Exhibition House**, which displays well-presented photos and memorabilia such as the leg irons he wore in Con Dao prison, the prime-ministerial bicycle and the plane that took him from Hanoi to Saigon in 1975 to celebrate victory. The island is very tranquil and unspoilt, and home-stays here can be arranged (see p.142).

An Giang Museum

11 Ton Duc Thang on the corner of Ly Thuong Kiet • Tue–Sun 7.30–11am & 1.30–5pm • 15,000₫

Also worth a look, particularly for its display of Oc Eo relics (see box, p.142), is the **An Giang Museum**, housed in a grand edifice in the northern part of town. On the first floor the focus is on the different religions practised in the region – Catholicism, Buddhism and Hoa Hao. On the second floor is a treasure trove of remnants of Oc Eo culture. Among the exhibits are a large lingam and a wooden Buddha that is so decayed it is now almost unrecognizable, as well as delicate items of gold jewellery. Other displays focus on minority culture, particularly the Cham, and the inevitable documenting of the local revolutionary movement and battles against the French and Americans. Unfortunately, there are no signs in English.

Bang Lang Stork Garden

About 15km south of Long Xuyen on Highway 9 • Daily 6am–6pm • 20,000₫ • Xe om from Long Xuyen will cost around 180,000₫ round-trip

South of Long Xuyen is one of the Mekong Delta's best stork sanctuaries, the **Bang Lang Stork Garden**, with thousands of birds wheeling, swooping and squabbling over nesting places at dusk. The most obvious birds here are, in fact, egrets, but there are indeed plenty of Asian openbill storks, along with a few adjutants and black-necked storks; you'll also likely see herons and pelicans. Turn up an hour before sunset to witness the memorable sight. Wearing a hat might help, since the site is smothered with their droppings.

2

Oc Eo

40km west of Long Xuyen on Highway 943 • As it's difficult to find, you're best off arranging a trip through An Giang Tourist (see below)

Excavations at the site of the vanished port of **Oc Eo** during the late 1990s uncovered gold jewellery, bowls and skeletons in vases, all dating back over a thousand years to the Funan Empire (see box below) – though, as these precious objects have now been shifted to museums around the country, you'd need to be pretty keen about history to get much from the modest building foundations that remain on-site. The ride here is an enjoyable diversion into the back lanes of the delta, however, passing rice fields, lotus ponds and fruit orchards along the way. It's also possible to continue on Highway 943 to Chau Doc, though it's a bumpy road and progress is slow.

ARRIVAL AND DEPARTURE — LONG XUYEN

By bus Most buses stop on Pham Cu Luong, off Tran Hung Dao a couple of kilometres south of town, though local buses, including some from Chau Doc, pull up at the bus station about 2km to the north of town, also on Tran Hung Dao. Note that arrivals from Sa Dec and destinations north often make use of a ferry to cross the Hau Giang.
Destinations Ca Mau (6hr); Chau Doc (1hr 30min); Ha Tien (5hr); Ho Chi Minh City (5hr); Sa Dec (2hr).

INFORMATION

Tourist information The main office of An Giang Tourism is at 80e Tran Hung Dao (daily 7–11am & 1–5pm; ☎07 6384 1036); the staff are helpful with local information and can arrange home-stays on Tiger Island.

ACCOMMODATION

Dong Xuyen 9a Luong Van Cu ☎07 6394 2260, ✉dongxuyenag@hcm.vnn.vn. The fanciest-looking place in town occupies almost an entire block and boasts sauna, jacuzzi and carpeted rooms with all facilities, though the service is rather sloppy. $26
Kim Anh 5–9 Thi Sach ☎07 6394 2551, ✉kimanh -hotel@hcm.vnn.vn. An eight-storey block in a central location, boasting comfy rooms and a palatial suite on the top floor. Rooms are equipped with a/c, satellite TV, minibar and hair dryers. Surprisingly, rates do not include breakfast. $17
Thai Binh 2 4–8 Nguyen Hue ☎07 6384 1859, ✉07 6384 6451. You'll find some of the cheapest rooms in town here (those with a/c cost around double), but don't expect much in the way of service and try to avoid proximity to the karaoke rooms. Rates do not include breakfast. $6

EATING

As a change from local food, or if you just need a/c and a chocolate sundae, note that the area around the cathedral has a few international fast-food chain outlets, including *KFC*, *Jollibee* and *Lotteria*.

OC EO AND THE FUNAN EMPIRE

Between the first and sixth centuries AD, the western side of the Mekong Delta, southern Cambodia and much of the Gulf of Siam's seaboard came under the sway of the Indianized **Funan Empire**, an early forerunner of the great Angkor civilization. The heavily romanticized annals of contemporary Chinese diplomats describe how the Funan Empire was forged when an Indian Brahmin visiting the region married the daughter of a local serpent-god, and how the serpent rendered the region suitable for cultivation by drinking down the waters of the flood plains. Such fables are grounded in truth: Indian traders would have halted here to pick up victuals en route from India to China, and would have disseminated not only their Hindu beliefs, but also their advanced irrigation and wet-rice cultivation methods.

One of Funan's major trading ports, **Oc Eo**, was located between Long Xuyen and Rach Gia. In common with other Funan cities, Oc Eo was ringed by a moat and consisted of wooden dwellings raised off the ground on piles. Given the discovery of Persian, Egyptian, Indian and Chinese artefacts (and even a gold coin depicting the Roman Emperor Marcus Aurelius) at Oc Eo sites, the port must have played host to a fair number of traders from around the world. To view **artefacts** from the site, visit the museums at Long Xuyen and Rach Gia, or the Fine Arts Museum in Ho Chi Minh City (see p.79).

The Funan Empire finally disappeared in the seventh century, when it was absorbed into the adjacent **Chen La** Empire.

Hong Phat 242/4 Luong Van Cu ☏ 07 6384 2359. Smart place with tasty Chinese and Vietnamese fish and meat dishes in a clean, brightly lit dining room. Try the ribs stewed with pepper (45,000đ). Daily 9am–9pm.
Long Xuyen 19 Nguyen Van Cung ☏ 07 6384 1927.

The most reliable restaurant in town is at this otherwise disappointing hotel, whose ground-floor restaurant serves tasty dishes such as shrimp fried with cauliflower (80,000đ) and steak and chips for just 50,000đ. Daily 6am–10pm.

DIRECTORY

Airlines Vietnam Airlines' office (☏ 07 684 3248) is located in the *Dong Xuyen* hotel, which also has an ATM.
Banks Vietinbank, just north of the *Long Xuyen* hotel on Luong Van Cu, can exchange money and also has an ATM.

Hospital The town's hospital is north of the centre on Le Loi.
Post office Long Xuyen's post office (daily 6am–10pm) is at 106 Tran Hung Dao, to the north of the centre.

Can Tho

At the confluence of the Can Tho and Hau Giang rivers, there's a lot to like about **CAN THO**. Though the delta's largest city by some way, with a population of just over one million, its riverside centre is refreshingly urbane – not to mention something of a surprise, after you've navigated your way through the urban sprawl encasing the town – and the city is a major mercantile centre and transport interchange. Can Tho was the last city to succumb to the North Vietnamese Army, a day after the fall of Saigon, on May 1, 1975 – the date that has come to represent the reunification of the country. The recent re-opening of the former US air base for commercial flights, as well as the enormous effort of completing the biggest bridge in the delta, shows that this city features large in government plans for future development.

As with so many settlements in the area, Can Tho is a little short on actual sights. However, some of the best restaurants in the delta are located here; what's more, the abundant **rice fields** of Can Tho Province are never far away, and at the intersections of the canals and rivers that thread between them are some of the delta's best-known **floating markets**. All in all, it's perhaps the delta's best place in which to take a **boat trip**.

Can Tho Museum

1 Hoa Binh • Tue–Thurs 8–11am & 2–5pm, Sat & Sun 8–11am & 6.30–9pm • Free

Broad Hoa Binh is the city's backbone, and the site of the impressive **Can Tho Museum**, which presents "the history of the resistance against foreign aggression of Can Tho people" as well as local economic and social achievements. Despite the enormity of the place and the extensive signs in English, it's all a bit drab apart from a few highlights like models of a teahouse and a herbalist treating patients.

Munirangsyaram Pagoda

36 Hoa Binh • Sunrise to sunset • Free

Two hundred and fifty metres southwest of the Can Tho Museum, the 1946-built **Munirangsyaram Pagoda** warrants examination only if the more impressive Khmer pagodas around Tra Vinh or Soc Trang aren't on your itinerary. Entrance into the pagoda compound is through a top-heavy stone gate weighed down with masonry reminiscent of Angkor Wat, but there is little to see inside apart from a few plaster Buddha images.

The waterfront

Walking east along Nguyen Thai Hoc deposits you bang in the middle of the city's **riverside promenade**, which extends along Hai Ba Trung; keep an eye out for an

2

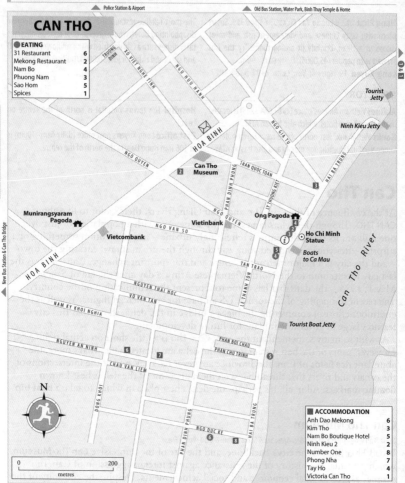

CAN THO

● **EATING**

31 Restaurant	6
Mekong Restaurant	2
Nam Bo	4
Phuong Nam	3
Sao Hom	5
Spices	1

Tourist Jetty

Ninh Kieu Jetty

TRUONG DINH

XO VIET NGHE TINH

NGU HUU HANH

NGO GIA TU

HOA BINH

NGO QUYEN

TRAN QUOC TOAN

PHAN DINH PHUNG

Can Tho Museum ②

LI THUONG KIET

HAI BA TRUNG

③

Munirangsyaram Pagoda 🏠

NGO VAN SO

NGO QUYEN

Vietinbank

Ong Pagoda 🏠 ④

Vietcombank

(i) ③ Ho Chi Minh Statue ⊙

⑤

TAN TRAO

LE THANH TON

④ *Boats to Ca Mau*

HOA BINH

Can Tho River

NGUYEN THAI HOC

VO VAN TAN

NAM KY KHOI NGHIA

Tourist Boat Jetty

NGUYEN AN NINH

⑥ ⑦

PHAN BOI CHAU

PHAN CHU TRINH

⑤

CHAU VAN LIEM

DONG KHOI

PHAN DINH PHUNG

NGO DUC KE

⑥ ⑧

HAI BA TRUNG

N

New Bus Station & Can Tho Bridge

0 _____ 200
metres

■ **ACCOMMODATION**

Anh Dao Mekong	6
Kim Tho	3
Nam Bo Boutique Hotel	5
Ninh Kieu 2	2
Number One	8
Phong Nha	7
Tay Ho	4
Victoria Can Tho	1

imposing silver **statue** of a waving Uncle Ho. The whole riverfront is now lined by beds of plants and stone seats: the old market has also been replaced by a covered area with souvenir stalls and an excellent restaurant. As with most delta towns, this riverside area gets crowded in the evenings as locals come out for a stroll in the cooler air. Waterfront **cafés** will rustle up a fresh coconut or a pot of green tea and from your seat you can watch the relentless sampan traffic of the Can Tho River.

Ong Pagoda

Just north of the Uncle Ho statue, **Ong Pagoda** is a colourful place built in the late nineteenth century by wealthy Chinese townsman Huynh An Thai. Inside, a ruddy-faced Quan Cong presides, flaunting Rio Carnival-style headgear. On his left is Than Tai, to whom a string of families come on the first day of every month, asking for money and good fortune. On his right is Thien Hau, the protector of sailors. There's also a small chamber dedicated to Quan Am to the left of the main hall.

ARRIVAL AND DEPARTURE

CAN THO

By plane Formerly Binh Tuy US military airbase, Can Tho's aiport is at Tra Noc, about 6km northwest of the city centre. Inside the airport are a cafeteria, souvenir shops, currency exchange, hotel booking and tourist information desks. Taxis (around 100,000đ) and xe om (more like 50,000đ) await arriving planes. Services are slowly being added; in addition to the following destinations, and occasional charters from Taiwan, flights from Nha Trang, Da Lat, Da Nang and possibly China are expected to follow soon. Vietnam Airlines' main office is at 66 Nguyen An Ninh (☎ 0710 384 4320).

Destinations Con Dao (4 weekly; 1hr); Hanoi (2 daily; 2hr); Ho Chi Minh City (1–2 daily; 1hr); Phu Quoc (1 daily; 45min).

By bus In 2010 the much-touted bridge across the Hau Giang River to Can Tho (see box below) was finally completed, making the archaic ferry service redundant and cutting travel time to and from Ho Chi Minh City. The bridge brings traffic to the south side of the city, where a new bus station on 3 Thang 2 (to the southwest of the city centre) accommodates most long-distance buses. However, the old bus station on Nguyen Trai (to the northwest of the city centre) is still functioning, so you might find yourself dropped here. Both are just a short xe om ride (10,000–20,000đ) from the centre.

Destinations Bac Lieu (3hr); Ca Mau (5hr); Chau Doc (2hr 30min); Ha Tien (5hr); Ho Chi Minh City (4hr); Long Xuyen (1hr 30min); My Tho (2hr 30min).

ACCOMMODATION

Hai Ba Trung and Chau Van Liem together form the axis of Can Tho's healthy **hotel** scene, with the more expensive and mid-range properties clustered around the northern end of Hai Ba Trung, and budget places located around Chau Van Liem and streets further south.

Anh Dao Mekong 70 Nguyen An Ninh ☎ 0710 381 9502, ⊚ khachsananhdaomekong.com. This relatively new venue is the city's best "flashpacker" option, with a range of spotless, stylishly designed rooms. $30

★ **Kim Tho** 1a Ngo Gia Tu ☎ 0710 222 2228, ⊚ kimtho .com. Squeezing in beside the established hotels along the riverfront, this twelve-storey place is giving stiff competition with its state-of-the-art fixtures and fittings, plus sweeping river views. There's a nice little café on the ground level. $45

Nam Bo Boutique Hotel 1 Ngo Quyen ☎ 0710 381 9138, ⊚ nambocantho.com. Renovated colonial building which accommodates not only the new *Nam Bo* restaurant, but also a boutique hotel with just seven rooms. They are not particularly spacious, but all are well equipped with the latest gadgetry; head on up to the rooftop bar for some lovely river views. $140

Ninh Kieu 2 3 Hoa Binh ☎ 0710 625 2335, ⊚ ninhkieu hotel.com. One of the newest hotels in town, and

proximate to international three-star norms, this has rooms that are good value for the price – bar the standard ones, which are a wee bit poky. Try for one at the front of the building, since the sparkly night-time view is rather nice. $48

Number One 1b Ngo Duc Ke ☎ 0710 382 9444. The best place in town at the super-budget price level, with rooms that are kept clean, hot water that works, and staff that happily dodge linguistic problems to arrange tours or tickets. $8

Phong Nha 70 Nguyen An Ninh ☎ 0710 382 1615. Located in a smart new building, this is the best of three hotels of the same name in town, and is one of Can Tho's best budget options. All rooms have a/c and bathrooms are spotless. $15

★ **Tay Ho** 42 Hai Ba Trung ☎ 0710 382 3392. After a thorough renovation, this cheap and cheerful place right on the riverfront stands out as the best budget deal in town, especially if you can get one of the two rooms with

---

BRIDGING THE DELTA

The **Mekong River** deposits tons of fertile earth on the delta each year, making the region's produce so abundant, but it also provides a barrier to swift travel, forcing drivers to queue for hours to cross its countless channels by slow, lumbering ferries. In the late 1990s a plan was hatched to build huge **bridges** at three key points in the delta – My Thuan, My Tho and Can Tho – in order to cut down journey times. The first of these, at My Thuan, crossing the Tien Giang, opened in 2000 and immediately slashed hours off journey times. The second, linking My Tho and Ben Tre, suffered delays but finally opened in early 2009. The third and biggest project, crossing the widest of the Mekong's nine arms (the Hau Giang) at Can Tho, was the scene of a tragic accident in September 2007 when a 90-metre section of an approach ramp collapsed, killing more than fifty workers. Construction was delayed for a while but was finally completed in 2010, and now visitors arriving by land pass over the longest cable-stayed bridge in Southeast Asia as they approach Can Tho.

riverfront views for around $15. Staff are adept at organizing boat tours, right down to the hand-drawn explanatory maps. $10

Victoria Can Tho Cai Khe Ward ☎0710 3810111, ⓦ victoriahotels-asia.com. Built and furnished in classic French-colonial style, but with all the modern facilities you'd expect from the delta's first international standard hotel. It's set in a grand riverside location across a bridge to the north of the town centre and surrounded by lush tropical growth. $220

EATING

Can Tho is well endowed with good, affordable **restaurants**, most serving Vietnamese food, though there are plenty that also offer international dishes. Those along Hai Ba Trung target a primarily foreign market, while locals tend to patronize places around the **market** and along Nam Ky Khoi Nghia.

31 Restaurant 31 Ngo Duc Ke ☎0710 382 5287. Simple café serving up tasty and cheap Vietnamese dishes enjoyed by all in a no-frills environment. However, it's not a place to relax as there's a bustle of tour groups constantly coming and going from the attached hotel. Mains from 35,000đ. Daily 6am–11pm.

★**Mekong Restaurant** 38 Hai Ba Trung ☎0710 382 1646. This long-established favourite is still hard to top for its cheap, flavoursome Vietnamese and Chinese meals, as well as succulent chateaubriand steaks for 115,000đ. There is also a good vegetarian selection, and another room out back if it's packed out front. Daily 8am–2pm & 4–10pm.

Nam Bo 1 Ngo Quyen ☎0710 381 9138. French café-inspired place with attractive furnishings, swirling fans, and an intimate atmosphere throughout the day. Innovative dishes like prawn with mango sauce, tempting salads, sandwiches and desserts cost less than you may think; mains start at 100,000đ, though do think about taking advantage of the good-value special sets. There's also a neat bar area on the roof that's ideal for a pre- or post-dinner drink. Daily 6am–11pm.

Phuong Nam 48 Hai Ba Trung ☎0710 381 2077. This place enjoys a great riverfront location right next to the Mekong, and benefits from occasional overspill from that popular venue. Like the competition, it serves a good range of cheap and tasty Western and Vietnamese dishes; their sets (from 110,000đ) are particularly good value, and often feature fish or pork in clay pot, catfish soup, or calamari in satay sauce. Daily 10am–2pm & 5–10pm.

★**Sao Hom** Hai Ba Trung ☎0710 381 5616. Most of Can Tho's riverfront restaurants are actually separated from the water by Hai Ba Trung, but this wonderful place, housed under an almost market-like roof, is bang on the ripples – right next to where hungry tourists disembark from boat trips. Despite this, prices are low and quality very high; the pumpkin flower fritters (55,000đ) and fish fried in tamarind sauce (120,000đ) are recommended, though there are Western items such as quiche, spaghetti and duck à l'orange here too. Daily 6am–11pm.

Spices Victoria Can Tho hotel, Cai Khe Ward ☎0710 381 0111. Fine dining in a tasteful ethnic interior, or outside on the romantic riverside terrace, and the extensive menu, with appetizers such as *banh cuon* (rice pancakes stuffed with pork, shrimp and salmon eggs; 135,000đ) and main courses from 180,000đ, makes the detour to this hotel restaurant worth the effort. Daily 6am–10pm.

DIRECTORY

Banks Vietcombank, 7 Hoa Binh (Mon–Fri 7–11am & 1–5pm), changes cash and has an ATM. Vietinbank at 9 Phan Dinh Phung (Mon–Fri 7.30am–noon & 1–6pm) charges similar rates.

Bicycle and motorbike rental Enquire at the *Huy Hoang* hotel, 35 Ngo Duc Ke. Rates are around 50,000đ a day for a bicycle, and 130,000đ a day for a motorbike.

Hospital The general hospital is located 3km west of the centre on Highway 91B.

Pharmacy 31b Chau Van Liem and 78 Hai Ba Trung.

Police 67–69 Hung Vuong, northwest of the city centre.

Post office 2 Hoa Binh (daily 6am–9pm). IDD, internet and express mail service.

Sports Non-residents can use the swimming pool and tennis courts at *Victoria Can Tho* hotel (floodlit in the evening) for a few dollars.

Supermarket There is a huge Co-op Mart at the junction of Hoa Binh and Ngo Quyen.

Waterpark Can Tho Water Park (☎0710 376 3343; Mon–Fri 8.45am–5.30pm, Sat & Sun 7.45am–5.30pm; 40,000đ), in Cai Khe Ward to the north of town, has several pools, water chutes and slides in a large, landscaped area.

Binh Thuy Temple

Le Hong Phong • Daily 7.30–10.30am & 1.30–5.30pm • Free • From 80,000đ return by xe om

Six kilometres north of Can Tho along the road to Long Xuyen, the **Binh Thuy Temple** began life in the nineteenth century as a *dinh*, or communal house for travellers to rest in. The present building dates back to 1909, and immediately catches the eye with its

2

BOAT TRIPS AND FLOATING MARKETS

Every morning an armada of boats takes to the web of waterways spun across Can Tho Province and makes for one of its **floating markets**. Everything your average villager could ever need is on sale, from haircuts to coffins, though predictably fruit and vegetables make up most of what's on offer. Each boat's produce is identifiable by a sample hanging off a bamboo mast in its bow, but it's difficult to get colourful pictures, as the produce is stored below.

CAI RANG

7km out of Can Tho is **Cai Rang**, the most commonly visited of the two major nearby markets. You'll have to be prepared to queue up with all the other tourist boats before you can weave among the fervent waterborne activity, with drinks vendors clamouring to make a sale. Nevertheless, it's a fun experience, especially if you can get there between 7am and 8am. This market is particularly active on Sundays.

PHONG DIEN

Another 10km west from Cai Rang and you're at modest **Phong Dien**, whose appeal is that it sees relatively few tourists and correspondingly friendly locals. If you wish to stay longer here, try the purpose-built *My Khanh Village* (☎0710 3846260, ⓦmykhanh.com; from $20), nearby at 335 Lo Vong Cung, with wooden bungalows in a shady setting and a good-sized pool. Its attractions (geared mostly to domestic visitors) include an ancient house, a pond full of crocodiles, caged monkeys and a pig-racing track, plus a pony and trap to take visitors round the site. Animal-rights activists might not enjoy it, but conditions here are better than at most such places in Vietnam. There are also demonstrations on making rice cakes and brewing wine, and traditional musicians perform in the evenings. Few Western visitors stay here, so it's a good way to meet some Vietnamese.

VISITING THE MARKETS

Most organized tours take you to Cai Rang or Phong Dien early in the morning, then make a leisurely return to the city, via the maze of picturesque canals and orchards that surround it, usually stopping to sample star fruit and sapodilla, longan and rambutan along the way. Agencies charge between 200,000đ and 250,000đ per person for such a tour, depending on the itinerary and type of boat. As usual, unofficial boat operators are cheaper, charging about 100,000đ per hour for a simple sampan: women prowl for customers along Hai Ba Trung, and some can be friendly and informative, but be on the lookout for scams. Do note that most boats have no shelter from sun or rain; bring a hat, sun-block and water. Phong Dien is more easily reached by **hiring a xe om** (about 90,000đ), then renting a sampan (about 80,000đ) for an hour's rowing among the buyers and sellers.

green-tiled eaves framed by frangipani trees. Though it appears small from outside, the cool interior runs very deep, and the walls are decorated with images of Chinese gods and Vietnamese heroes. Between the sturdy wooden pillars are several altars, with some ghoulish characters guarding one of them with axes raised.

The Duong Home

144 Bui Huu Nghia • Daily 8am–noon & 2–5pm • Small donation expected

Down a sidestreet opposite Binh Tuy Temple is the beautiful **Duong Home**, which was used in the 1992 filming of *The Lover* (see p.497). A classic example of French colonial architecture, its shuttered windows and elaborate stucco decorations conceal a spacious living room featuring period furnishings with mother-of-pearl inlay. Note the intricately carved panels beside the pillars, where a bat sits at the summit of a menagerie of animals; unlike in the West, where bats symbolize vampires, in the East they are seen as a portent of good luck. The current residents are often on hand to show visitors round, and the adjacent orchid garden contains what is thought to be the tallest cactus in the country.

Soc Trang

Straddled across an oily branch of the Mekong, **SOC TRANG** lacks the panache of other delta towns, though on the fifteenth day of the tenth lunar month (Nov–Dec) it springs to life as thousands converge to see traditional Khmer boats (*thuyen dua*) racing each other during the **Oc Om Boc festival**.

Khleang Pagoda

In the middle of town on Nguyen Chi Thanh • Sunrise to sunset • Free

Khmer pagodas are ten-a-penny in this region, but the **Khleang Pagoda**, located in the heart of Soc Trang, is one of the most impressive. It is surrounded by a two-tiered terrace and the doors and windows are adorned with traditional Khmer motifs in greens, reds and golds. Inside is a wonderful golden Sakyamuni statue, though unfortunately the doors are often locked.

Khmer Museum

23 Nguyen Chi Thanh • Mon–Sat 7.30–11.30am & 1.30–4.30pm • Free

Directly opposite the Khleang Pagoda, the **Khmer Museum** houses some low-key exhibits including stringed instruments made of snakeskin and coconut husks, and some wonderfully colourful food covers, shaped like conical hats, but with a stippled surface.

Dat Set Pagoda

163 Mau Than 68 • Sunrise to sunset • Free

Head north from the Khleang Pagoda along Mau Than 68 for a few minutes, and you'll see the **Dat Set pagoda** on the right. Also known as the Buu Son Tu Pagoda, it is constructed almost entirely from clay, with a smart sheet-metal roof to keep the rain off. Dat Set makes a welcome change from the more numerous Khmer pagodas in this region of the delta. Chinese visitors flock here to see the pagoda's impressive and highly colourful collection of clay statues; many are life-size, with animals and figures from Chinese mythology being the most popular subjects. The pagoda is also home to some truly gargantuan candles that look like pillars, weigh around 200kg each and are said to last for seventy years of continuous burning.

Mahatup Pagoda

2km south of town off Le Hong Phong • Sunrise to sunset • Free • Around 50,000d by xe om (taxis cannot proceed directly to the pagoda), including waiting time

Mahatup Pagoda, aka the Bat Pagoda, is famed for its vast community of golden-bodied **fruit bats**, which spectacularly take to the skies at dusk. A fire in 2007 destroyed much of the main building, but reconstruction is now complete, and a large pond has also been added behind the temple. Plan to get here around 5.30pm – as the drop in temperature wakes them, you'll see the bats spinning, preening and flapping their matt-black wings, some spanning 1.5m.

Khmer monks have worshipped at this site for four hundred years, and it is often busy with Vietnamese visitors. Inside, bright murals bearing the names of the Khmer communities around the world that financed them recount the life of the Buddha. Outside, look out for the graves of four pigs behind the large hall to the right opposite the pagoda, each of which had five toenails (pigs usually have four). Since such animals are believed to bring bad luck, they are honoured with well-tended resting places to ward off any evil tendencies. The tombstones are painted with their likenesses and the dates of their passing on.

ARRIVAL AND DEPARTURE   SOC TRANG

The waterway running roughly west to east splits Soc Trang in two, with most of the town nestling on its south bank. The town's spine is Hai Ba Trung, which runs across the water, before becoming Tran Hung Dao on the southern outskirts.

By bus The bus station is at the northern end of town on Nguyen Chi Thanh. Buses to Ho Chi Minh City leave every half hour; services are less frequent to other destinations in the delta, though for Can Tho, Vinh Long and My Tho you can opt pay the full price to HCMC and travel in comfort before being turfed off en route.

Destinations Bac Lieu (1hr 30min); Ca Mau (3hr); Can Tho (1hr 30min); Ho Chi Minh City (5hr); My Tho (3hr 30min); Vinh Long (2hr).

INFORMATION

Tourist information Staff at Soc Trang Tourist, at 104 Le Loi (daily 7–11am & 1.30–5pm; ☎079 382 2024), can usually help with local information.

Services The post office in the centre of town at 1 Tran Hung Dao, with internet access. There's an ATM in front of the *Khanh Hung* hotel.

ACCOMMODATION AND EATING

Khanh Hung 17 Tran Hung Dao ☎079 382 1026. Located in the centre of town, this place has 53 rooms ranging from basic and cheap to carpeted suites that have seen better days. Its central location and friendly staff make it the most convenient base in town, but check a few different rooms before deciding. The handy, on-site restaurant won't win any prizes, but it's the only place in town with an English menu. $10

★ **Ngoc Thu** 3km out of town at km 2127 on Highway 1 ☎079 361 3108, ⓦngocsuonghotel.com. If you have your own transport, or don't mind a few xe om or taxi rides, this is the best place to stay in Soc Trang. It has a range of comfortable rooms, with two pools and a tennis court; the cheaper rooms at the back are particularly good value. $14

Que Huong 128 Nguyen Trung Truc ☎079 361 6122. This is a newish place set on a quiet backstreet with spacious, well-equipped rooms that include ADSL cables, while there's also wi-fi in the lobby. $14

Bac Lieu

Beyond Soc Trang the landscape becomes progressively more waterlogged and water palms hug the banks of the waterways that crisscross it. A little over 40km southwest of Soc Trang, Highway 1 dips south towards the town of **BAC LIEU**, before veering off west to Ca Mau. It may be the back end of nowhere, but Bac Lieu's prosperity is evident in new shopping complexes and upmarket homes around the centre. The source of this prosperity is overseas Vietnamese, many of whom hail from this region. Although there are few sights to set the pulse racing, the town has the only accommodation between Soc Trang and Ca Mau and is in good proximity to the nearby **Bac Lieu Bird Sanctuary**.

Bac Lieu Bird Sanctuary

Daily 7.30am–5pm • 15,000đ • Arrange transport through Bac Lieu Tourist Company (see p.150)

Well worth the visit, the **Bac Lieu Bird Sanctuary** is 6km southwest of Bac Lieu town towards the coast. There is an observation tower and paths among the cajeput forest, along which local guides can lead you. Lots of birds can be seen here from July to December, including herons, egrets and, just possibly, endangered painted storks, but there is little to see from January to June. Guides are necessary and will appreciate a tip, even though their English skills are limited.

ARRIVAL AND DEPARTURE   BAC LIEU

By bus The bus station is 1.5km west of town. There are frequent departures to Ho Chi Minh City, and less regular departures to other destinations in the delta; if you'd like to hit Can Tho, My Tho or certain other destinations north, HCMC-bound buses will take you, though you may have to pay the full route fare. Some buses also head west to Ca Mau.

Destinations Ca Mau (2hr); Can Tho (3hr); HCMC (6hr); My Tho (4hr 30min).

INFORMATION

Tourist information The Bac Lieu Tourist Company, at 2 Hoang Van Thu (daily 7–11am & 1–5pm; ☎0781 382 4272), is conveniently situated next to the *Bac Lieu* hotel, though the staff are not terribly helpful.

Services Sacombank is at no. 82 Tran Phu where you can exchange money. There's an ATM conveniently located in front of the *Bac Lieu*, while the post office is in the centre of town at 20 Tran Phu.

ACCOMMODATION

Bac Lieu 4–6 Hoang Van Thu ☎0781 395 9697. The town's main hotel was undergoing major renovation at the time of writing. Rooms are a decent size, complete with a/c, cable TV and hot water, but only some have a view, so ask to take a look first; in addition, a few are downright filthy. $\overline{\underline{18}}$

★**Cong Tu** 13 Dien Bien Phu ☎0781 395 3304. For a bit of character, head to this palatial colonial villa, sitting pretty on the riverside. It boasts just ten rooms with fancy furnishings and high ceilings, so finds itself quite popular – best to book ahead. $\overline{\underline{15}}$

EATING AND DRINKING

Bac Lieu 4–6 Hoang Van Thu. The *Bac Lieu's* ground-floor restaurant offers set menus of Vietnamese cuisine starting at 100,000đ, as well as à la carte dishes such as fish prepared with various sauces at around 60,000đ. Service is reasonably efficient, but the atmosphere is somewhat sterile. Daily 6am–10pm.

Cong Tu 13 Dien Bien Phu. The café at this hotel is highly atmospheric, with tables ranged around a covered courtyard, and its wide-ranging menu includes lots of fish dishes, making this the favourite dining venue in town. Mains from 55,000đ. Daily 7am–10pm.

Kitty On the corner of Ba Trieu and Tran Phu. Your best option for nightlife in Bac Lieu is to join the overseas Vietnamese at this first-floor bar, which wouldn't look out of place in Ho Chi Minh City. They serve cocktails, beers and coffee, as well as a reasonable range of Vietnamese dishes. Daily 10am–11pm.

Ca Mau

A pancake-flat region composed of silt deposited by the Mekong, the **Ca Mau Peninsula** constitutes not only the end of mainland Vietnam, but of former Indochina as well. **CA MAU** itself, Vietnam's southernmost town of any size, has a frontier feel to it, though rapid development has brought many changes since 1989, when travel writer Justin Wintle described it as a "scrappy clutter…a backyard town in a backyard province", though there are still pockets of squalor here and there. Ca Mau sprawls across a vast area, with broad boulevards connected by potholed lanes and a couple of busy bridges spanning the Phung Hiep Canal that splits the town in two. To the west, the town is bordered by the Ganh Hao River, which snakes past as though trying to wriggle free before the encroaching stilthouses squeeze the life from it.

Although few Western travellers currently visit Ca Mau, there are speedboats that cover the journey to and from Rach Gia in less than three hours, while improvements to Highway 63 have made the journey by road less arduous. Incorporating Ca Mau in a circular tour of the area is now a tempting possibility, as it takes you off the tourist trail and through some classic delta scenes.

The market

Le Loi • Sunrise to sunset

Along the north bank of the Phung Hiep Canal, which divides the town, is the rag-tag squall of the **market** that lurks on the banks of the canal. A shantytown of corrugated iron, canvas and sacking, it is a bustling centre for packing fish for sale and shipment. As such, it doesn't have the photogenic appeal of most delta markets.

Cao Dai Temple

Phan Ngoc Hien • Sunrise to sunset • Free

Worth a look for its ornate towers, Ca Mau's Cao Dai temple is evidence of how deeply rooted the religion is in the Mekong Delta; these temples are a distinctive feature of

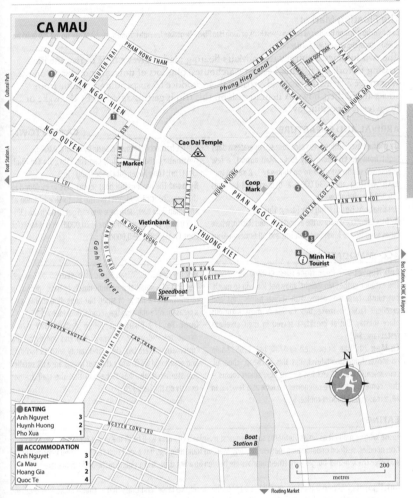

CA MAU

2

EATING
Anh Nguyet	3
Huynh Huong	2
Pho Xua	1

ACCOMMODATION
Anh Nguyet	3
Ca Mau	1
Hoang Gia	2
Quoc Te	4

▼ Floating Market

many delta towns and add a playful splash of colour with their Disneyesque decorations. This particular one isn't great, to be honest – it scores high for concrete and low for atmosphere, and if you've made it as far as Ca Mau you'll doubtless have seen better examples. However, a couple of parks opposite the temple offer shady areas to escape the bustle of town near the canal.

Cultural Park

2km west of Ca Mau • Daily 8am–5.30pm • 10,000đ • About 30,000đ by xe om

This is one of the town's most intriguing attractions, at least during the rainy season (July–Nov), though its name is something of a misnomer. It is, in fact, a **bird sanctuary** teeming with storks and many other birds that nest in the trees in easily observed fenced-off areas. The huge park also has a mini zoo featuring elephants, monkeys, deer and other animals, as well as lots of pavilions and picnic spots. Arrive about 4pm to explore the park then watch the birds arriving to roost.

The Floating Market

Boat from boat station B, south of town on west bank of Ganh Hao River • Negotiate fee with boatmen; expect to pay around 200,000đ for the 30–40min trip downstream and back

The two-kilometre journey to Ca Mau's floating market gives a taste of riverine life, passing factories, a fish market and warehouses, plus lots of flotsam and jetsam, on the way to see a string of boats advertising their produce by suspending a sample from sticks above their bows. A definite risk on this trip is getting splashed by the wake of huge ferries speeding by.

ARRIVAL AND DEPARTURE   CA MAU TOWN

By plane Vasco Airlines (ⓦ vasco.com.vn) operates a daily flight from Ho Chi Minh City to Ca Mau airport, a few kilometres southeast of town on Highway 1. A xe om into town will cost about 30,000đ, and there will be taxis (55,000đ) waiting too.
Destinations Ho Chi Minh City (daily; 1hr).
By bus Almost next door to the airport is the bus station, where buses from Ho Chi Minh City, Can Tho and other destinations

pull up. Transport into town is again by xe om (30,000đ).
Destinations Bac Lieu (2hr); Can Tho (5hr); Ho Chi Minh City (7hr); Long Xuyen (6hr); Soc Trang (3hr).
By boat The most useful boat services are to be found at the speedboat pier, located on the south side of town at 162 Phan Boi Chau; from here you can get to Rach Gia (3hr; 125,000đ); Nam Can (1hr 15min; 70,000đ) or Dat Mui (for Cape Ca Mau; 3hr; 150,000đ).

ACCOMMODATION

Anh Nguyet 207 Phan Ngoc Hien ☎ 0780 356 7666. The exterior of the "Moonlight" may not look up to much, but plush, carpeted rooms with stylish furnishings and excellent facilities make this Ca Mau's most luxurious place to stay. Buffet breakfast served in their excellent restaurant. $49
Ca Mau 20 Phan Ngoc Hien ☎ 0780 383 1165. Again no looker from street level, but this is cheap, cheerful, conveniently located and has surprisingly smart rooms – they come in a full five categories, so look at a few. All in all, a reasonable budget choice. $10

Hoang Gia 27–29 Tran Hung Dao ☎ 0780 381 9999. The best of a small glut of mini-hotels to have sprung up recently, with a range of small but appealing rooms, and a pleasant café abutting the second-floor lobby. $15
Quoc Te 179 Phan Ngoc Hien ☎ 0780 382 6745, ✉ quoctehotel@yahoo.com.vn. Top-end rooms at the "International" are big, clean and comfy with all facilities and occasional wi-fi, while cheaper rooms are a bit smaller and stuffier. It also has to be said that the staff are not exactly on the ball. $20

EATING

Those who've made it as far as Vietnam's southernmost mainland city may well be in the mood for something that's not rice, noodles, seafood or barbecued matter. The Coop Mart on Tran Hung Dao has a food court on its second floor, featuring a *Jollibee* chicken-and-burger joint (their sundaes are heaven on a hot day), and a simple pizza-and-pasta place.

Anh Nguyet 207 Phan Ngoc Hien ☎ 0780 356 7666. The restaurant at this hotel has tasty food and a relaxing ambience, though staff seem permanently flummoxed. There are a few Western dishes as well as a comprehensive range of Vietnamese cuisine; seafood is their speciality, and you'd be best off going for something like their sumptuous mudfish clay pot (80,000đ). Daily 6am–9pm.
★**Huynh Huong** Bui Thi Truong ☎ 0780 357 5566. This café comes as a lovely surprise in remote Ca Mau. There are a variety of sitting areas, the most interesting one resembling an English garden with its white-painted metal chairs, leafy canopies, dangling flowerpots, roses

on the table, and grass that – though fake – is pleasant to bare feet. Coffees from 12,000đ, fruit juices 20,000–25,000đ. Daily 6am–10pm.
★**Pho Xua** 239 Phan Ngoc Hien ☎ 0780 356 6666. Set in traditional pavilions with wooden pillars around a shady garden, this is the best spot in town for a meal. It has a fairly extensive menu of Vietnamese dishes in English and plenty of appealing seafood options, many of which are priced by the kilo; try the shrimp stir-fry (80,000đ) or sautéed squid (125,000đ). This said, there's nothing wrong with their starters (55,000đ), soups (30,000đ) or rice dishes (from 95,000đ). Daily 8am–midnight.

DIRECTORY

Bank To exchange cash or use an ATM, head to Vietinbank at 94 Ly Thuong Kiet (Mon–Fri 7.30–11am & 1.30–4.30pm), or any number of other banks.

Post office The main post office (daily 6am–10pm) is opposite Vietinbank, on Luu Tan Tai; internet is available here.

GET YOUR KICKS ON HIGHWAY 63

Of all the roads that crisscross the Mekong Delta, few have such a strong sense of what this watery world is all about as **Highway 63**, which zigzags north from Ca Mau to Minh Luong, just south of Rach Gia – a distance of a little over 100 kilometres. The road is sealed all the way, though it's often no wider than a single track road, and for most of its journey it follows narrow canals that carry a real hotchpotch of vessels going about their business. If you don't have your own transport, take a **bus** from Ca Mau to Rach Gia to follow this highway.

At **Vinh Tuan** it crosses a wide canal, allowing great views of river life, though parking on the bridge is illegal, so park near and walk on to it. There are also several **monkey bridges** across the canals – fragile structures consisting of narrow tree trunks, which require the assured balance of a monkey to cross them (hence the name). Like many other aspects of local culture, monkey bridges are disappearing fast, but Highway 63 still offers a fascinating glimpse of traditional life in the delta. Near the end of the highway, you need to cross a wide river by ferry at Tac Cau, where you'll see huge fishing ships loading ice to freeze their catch.

Around Ca Mau

The **marshes** circling Ca Mau form one of the largest areas of swampland in the world, covering about 150,000 hectares and home to a variety of wading birds. As you might expect, **waterways** are the most efficient means of travel in this part of the country – a point pressed home by the slender ferries moored in all the villages the road passes. The Ca Mau Peninsula was a stronghold of resistance against France and America, and for this it paid a heavy price, as US planes dumped millions of gallons of Agent Orange over it to rob guerrillas of jungle cover. Further damage has been done by the shrimp-farm industry, but pockets of mangrove and cajeput forests remain, inhabited by sea birds, wading birds, waterfowl and also honey bees, attracted by the mangrove blossoms.

Mui Ca Mau National Park

About 100km south of Ca Mau • 10,000d • Speedboat to Dat Mui (see below), then either rent a local boat or hop on a xe om (about 60,000d return) to Mui Ca Mau (Cape Ca Mau)

This voyage to the end of the earth may not quite be a Jules Verne epic, but it's a fun and satisfying way to pass a day, as you get to visit not only the **southernmost point of Vietnam** but also the end of mainland Southeast Asia. The speedboats that take you through the throng of life in the delta can get pretty crowded, but if you're lucky you might get a window seat to look out on the houses, shacks and boats that line the river.

A road runs to the national park from the isolated hamlet of **Dat Mui**, though to get further into the spirit of things, you may prefer to negotiate a fare with a local boatman. The latter is also the best way of navigating the national park itself, though most visitors content themselves with a wander around the paths surrounding the main visitor centre – from these you'll make out wooden houses, shrimping ponds, and the odd "monkey bridge". You can take a photo of yourself standing beside a boat-shaped monument marking the latitude (8 degrees north) and longitude (104 degrees east) of this remote location, then gaze out over the endless ocean and the mountainous Khoai Island just off the coast. There's even a **look-out tower** from where you can get good views over the mangrove forests, and a restaurant on stilts over the water.

Rach Gia

There's something a little special about **RACH GIA**, a thriving port community of around two hundred thousand people, teetering precariously over the Gulf of Thailand. For most foreign visitors it is simply a place to overnight en route to

2

Phu Quoc Island, but stay on for the night and escape from the incessant motorbike buzz of the main streets, and you'll be able to bask in a languid, easygoing air stemming from the town's seaside location.

A small islet in the mouth of the Cai Lon River forms the hub of the town, but the urban sprawl spills over bridges to the north and south of it and onto the mainland. It's worth taking a walk along **Bach Dang** or **Tran Hung Dao** to watch the activity on the boats of all sizes that clutter the port. Men and women darn and fold nets, charcoal-sellers hawk their wares to ships' captains and roadside cafés heave with fishermen – many of whom have seen the bottoms of a few beer bottles – awaiting the next tide.

The museum

27 Nguyen Van Troi • Mon–Fri 7.30–11am & 1.30–5pm • Free

Rach Gia's **museum** is the single worthwhile sight in the town centre, and even that probably won't distract you for more than half an hour. It's housed in a recently renovated colonial house that displays wartime photos and souvenirs, along with relics from nearby Oc Eo – shards of pottery, coins and bones, and the skeleton of a whale in a mesh-fronted shed to the right of the main building.

RACH GIA

EATING	
Hai Au	2
Hoa Binh-Rach Gia	3
Ni Ken	4
Tay Do	1

ACCOMMODATION	
Hoa Binh-Rach Gia	5
Hong Yen	1
Kim Co	3
Sealight	4
Tam Xuan	2

THE HEROICS OF NGUYEN TRUNG TRUC

From 1861 to 1868, **Nguyen Trung Truc** spearheaded anti-French guerrilla activities in the western region of the delta: statues in the centre of Rach Gia and at the temple dedicated to him depict him preparing to unsheathe his sword and harvest a French head. In 1861, he masterminded the attack that culminated in the firing of the French warship *Esperance* – an event which, in the minds of many Vietnamese, signified that the tide of the conflict was about to change. As a wanted man, Truc was forced to retreat to Phu Quoc, from where he continued to oversee the campaign. Only after the French took his mother hostage in 1868 did he turn himself in and in October of the same year he was executed by a firing squad in the centre of Rach Gia. Defiant to the last, his final words could have been lifted from a Ho Chi Minh speech: "So long as grass still grows on the soil of this land, people will continue to resist the invaders."

Nguyen Trung Truc Temple

18 Nguyen Cong Tru • Sunrise–sunset • Free

Of Rach Gia's handful of pagodas, only the **Nguyen Trung Truc Temple** is really worth making an effort to see. It's also conveniently located right next to the jetty from which hydrofoils leave for Phu Quoc, so if you enter or leave Rach Gia in this manner, it's quite possible to take a quick look on your way.

Inside, a portrait of Nguyen in black robe and hat provides the main chamber with its centrepiece. Up at the main altar, a brass urn flanked by slender storks standing on turtles is said to hold the ashes of local hero **Nguyen Trung Truc** (see box above). In front of the temple is a statue of Trung Truc drawing his sword; there's a similar one in the very centre of town (see map opposite).

ARRIVAL AND DEPARTURE

RACH GIA

By plane Arriving at the airport, it's a 7km taxi ride into town (about 100,000đ). For tickets or information, contact Vietnam Airlines at 16 Nguyen Trung Truc (☎0773 924320). Destinations Ho Chi Minh City (daily; 45min); Phu Cuoc (daily in season; 30min).

By bus Buses to and from points north (such as Ha Tien and Hon Chong) pull up at Rach Gia's local bus station on Nguyen Binh Kiem, 500m north of the town centre. Arrivals and departures from other destinations use the bigger bus terminal at Rach Soi, 7km southeast of Rach Gia; a taxi will cost around 100,000đ.
Destinations Can Tho (3hr); Ha Tien (2hr 30min); Ho Chi

Minh City (6–7hr); Long Xuyen (2hr).

By boat Arriving and departing boats use one of two piers. Daily services to and from Phu Quoc Island depart from the small quay 200m west of the Nguyen Trung Truc Temple; at the time of writing, they left Rach Gia at 8am, 9am & 1pm (320,000đ; 2hr 30min). Buy your ticket the day before, if possible, from the Superdong office at the pier (☎0773 877742, ☎0773 877741); staff at your accommodation may also be able to help. From Rach Meo quay, 5km south of town on Ngo Quyen, express boats and regular boats leave for and arrive from Ca Mau (3hr; 125,000đ) and other destinations in the delta.

INFORMATION

Tourist information Kien Giang Tourist at 11 Ly Tu Trong (Daily 7.30–11.30am & 1–5pm; ☎0773 962024) is perhaps the least helpful of all provincial tourist offices in the delta, so you'll need to rely on your hotel for local information.

Services Vietcombank, which offers currency exchange and an ATM, is north of the river on Mac Cuu. The hospital is at 46 Le Loi, and there's a pharmacy north of the centre at 14a Tran Phu. The post office (daily 6.30am–10pm), with internet access, is on Mau Than.

ACCOMMODATION

★**Hoa Binh-Rach Gia** 3–7 Co Bac ☎0773 553355, ⓦhoabinhrachgiaresort.com.vn. Part of the Hoa Binh chain, this new hotel is by far Rach Gia's most appealing accommodation option. Within walking distance of the seafront promenade, it's a relaxed venue with a charming, foliage-surrounded pool, a decent café (see p.156), and

friendly, English-speaking staff. $40
Hong Yen 259–261 Mac Cuu ☎0773 879095. A kilometre north of the centre, this hotel has an inconvenient location but it makes up for it with spacious rooms equipped with desks and bathtubs, free wi-fi and friendly staff. $8

Kim Co 141 Nguyen Hung Son ☎0773 879610. Centrally located, and emblazoned with aquamarine go-faster stripes, this is probably the most convenient budget option in town; brightly painted, good-sized rooms come with cable TV and wi-fi. $15

Sealight A11, 3 Thang 2 ☎0776 255777, ⓦsealight hotel.vn. A weird place: towering nineteen storeys over the Rach Gia coastline, it stands out like a sore thumb, and rather bizarrely most windows in its rooms face the city, rather than the sea. There are never anywhere near enough guests, and its echoey lobby seems rather forlorn. However, such bad planning makes for good-value rooms, which are comfy enough, especially at deluxe level ($30) and above. $20

Tam Xuan 19 Tran Quang Dieu ☎0773 920325. Overlooking the northern branch of the Cai Lon River, the "Wild Rose" is worth considering for its well-equipped and attractively furnished rooms. You could even splash out $24 for the enormous 3-bed room and have enough space to throw a party. $14

EATING

Hai Au 2 Nguyen Trung Truc ☎0773 863740. Watch an arm of the Mekong sliding languidly into the sea from the open terrace of the town's best seafood reastaurant. They specialize in steamboat and fish (from 85,000đ per dish), though there are plenty of meat and veg options too, often steamed in beer or coconut juice. Daily 6am–10pm.

Hoa Binh-Rach Gia 3–7 Co Bac ☎0773 553355. The grassy, outdoor seating area of this charming hotel (see p.155) is certainly the most urbane place to eat or drink in Rach Gia. There's not much on the menu, with *com tam* as the pick (from 33,000đ), though it's a wonderful place to relax with a fresh carrot juice (23,000đ) or something similar. Daily 10am–10pm.

★**Ni Ken** 35–36 Co Bac ☎0773 813399. This simple barbecue joint, just back towards town from the *Hoa Binh-Rach Gia*, is just about the town's most popular place with locals, who crowd around every night for some meat, seafood or veggie skewers (from 15,000đ each) and a few beers. Daily 10am–11pm.

Tay Do 6 Nguyen Du ☎0773 915211. This no-frills eatery has an English menu and is popular with locals, serving a variety of traditional Vietnamese dishes. It's down a little side-street east of the park, and makes a good lunch stop if you're exploring the town. Mains from 80,000đ. Daily 10am–9pm.

Ha Tien

Small, breezy and extremely likeable, **HA TIEN** is not your typical delta town. Here it's the sea, rather than an assortment of rivers and rivulets, which shape a place now buzzing with Western travellers. Visitor numbers have been rocketing in recent years thanks to the **opening of the border** to foreigners at Xa Xia, just north of Ha Tien, and it's now possible to head directly to Cambodia's coastal towns of Kep and Sihanoukville without passing through Phnom Penh; in addition, **hydrofoil services to Phu Quoc** now offer a shorter and cheaper route to the island than from Rach Gia. Thus this town, which until recently had an end-of-the-line feel, is bristling with commerce, and coming to terms with its newfound popularity.

Brief history

Founded by Chinese immigrant **Mac Cuu** in 1674, with the permission of the local Cambodian lords, **Ha Tien** thrived thanks to its position facing the Gulf of Thailand and astride the trade route between India and China. By the close of the seventeenth century, Siam (later Thailand) had begun to eye the settlement covetously, and Mac Cuu was forced to petition Hue for support. The resulting alliance, forged with Emperor Minh Vuong in 1708, ensured Vietnamese military protection, and the town continued to prosper. Mac Cuu died in 1735, but the familial fiefdom continued for seven generations, until the French took over in 1867. Subsequently, Ha Tien became a resistance flash-point, with Viet Minh holing up in the surrounding hills, and even sniping at French troops from the **To Chau Mountain**, to the south.

The riverside

Central Ha Tien still has a few quaint, shuttered, colonial buildings in its backstreets, though the original **market**, now relocated west along the riverbank, has been razed to

2

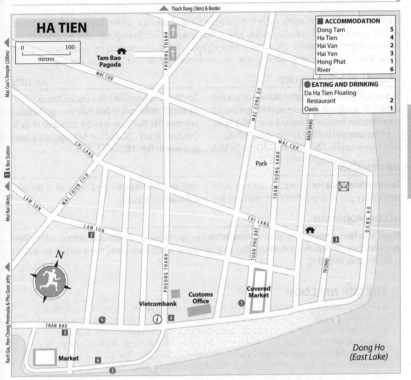

HA TIEN

0 ——— 100
metres

Mac Cuu's Temple (200m) ◄

Tam Bao
Pagoda

PHUONG THANH

MAC CUU

MAC CONG DU

CHI LANG

🚉 & Bus Station ◄

MAC THIEN TICH

LAM SON

Mui Na (4km) ◄

LAM SON
2

PHUONG THANH

Park

MAC CUU

BACH DANG

THAM TUONG XANH

CHI LANG

TUAN PHU DAT

TO CHAU

DONG HO

Covered
Market

Customs
Office
1

Vietcombank

@

ⓘ **4**

TRAN HAU
5

Market
6

2

N

Rach Gia, Hon Chong Peninsula & Phu Quoc Jetty ◄

Dong Ho
(East Lake)

■ ACCOMMODATION
Dong Tam 5
Ha Tien 4
Hai Van 2
Hai Yen 3
Hong Phat 1
River 6

● EATING AND DRINKING
Da Ha Tien Floating
Restaurant 2
Oasis 1

make way for a new **riverside park**. The former pontoon bridge that made the corner of Tran Hau and Dong Ho a busy area has also been removed, leaving the only access to town via the huge **bridge** to the southwest of town. The riverside is now an enjoyable place to stroll, watching fishing boats unloading on the opposite bank, and by following Tran Hau eastwards and then continuing north on Dong Ho, you can enjoy pleasant views and often an agreeable breeze blowing off the so-called East Lake (Dong Ho). In fact, it is not a lake, rather a large inlet where the To Chau River flows out to the sea.

Tam Bao Pagoda

At junction of Mac Thien Tich and Phuong Thanh • Sunrise–sunset • Free

The colourful **Tam Bao Pagoda** is set in tree-lined grounds dominated by an attractive lotus pond, a huge statue of Quan Am and a large reclining Buddha. Out the back of the pagoda, said to have been founded by Mac Cuu himself, is a pretty garden tended by the resident nuns, its colourful flowers interspersed with tombs. In the rear chamber of the pagoda, a statue of the goddess with a thousand hands and a thousand eyes sits on a lurid pink lotus, while behind her are photos and funerary tablets remembering the local dead.

Mac Cuu temple and burial place

Off Mac Cuu • Sunrise to sunset • Free

Mac Cuu lies buried on a hillside rising from a road named after him, just east of the centre. Before ascending the hill, check out his temple at the base; here, electric "incense" sticks glow constantly before Mac Cuu's funerary tablet, keeping the memory of Ha Tien's founding father alive. His actual **grave** is further up the hill, guarded by two swordsmen, a white tiger and a blue dragon. From this vantage point, there are good views over the mop-tops of the coconut trees below and down to the sea.

ARRIVAL AND DEPARTURE HA TIEN

By bus Buses terminate at the rather desolate bus station off Highway 80, a couple of kilometres north of town and just a few kilometres from the Cambodian border post at Xa Xia. To get into town from here take a xe om (about 15,000đ). Destinations Can Tho (5hr); Chau Doc (4hr); Ho Chi Minh City (8hr); Long Xuyen (6hr); Rach Gia (2hr 30min).

By boat Hydrofoils to and from Ham Ninh, on Phu Quoc's east coast (1hr 30min), dock on the south bank of the To Chau River. Tickets (230,000đ) can be bought at any hotel; they leave Ha Tien at 8am and 1.15pm.

INFORMATION

Tourist information The town's tourist office was out of service at the time of writing. Even if it re-opens, the best place to ask for basically anything at all is the *Oasis* restaurant (see opposite).

ACCOMMODATION

As part of Ha Tien's construction boom, several **new hotels** have opened recently, giving visitors plenty of options. Many are clustered around the market, and although they are mostly geared to Vietnamese guests, they drop their rates radically in the off-season (May–Oct).

THE MUI NAI LOOP

A pleasant half or full day can be spent exploring the countryside around Ha Tien, with a convenient circular loop northwest of town meaning you won't need to backtrack. This makes an ideal bike ride – and an even better motorbike route – when the weather is good.

Strike off west along Lam Son. At the end of the road, turn left and continue straight at a small roundabout. A **war cemetery** serves as a landmark on the right 2.5km from town, and where the road forks, branch left, signposted Nui Den (lighthouse). Follow this road to the coast and along a winding stretch of road with some beautiful views until you reach the entrance to Mui Nai beach (10,000đ per bike).

A pleasant – if not idyllic – 400m-long curve of sand, shaded by coconut palms and backed by lush green hills, **Mui Nai beach** offers reasonable swimming in clean, shallow waters. The beach is very popular among Vietnamese, and there are several resorts here, though they're all overpriced and poorly maintained; the *Hong Phat* (see opposite) is a good cheaper option. There are a few other restaurants and beachside cafés, so you can kick back and crack open a few crabs while enjoying a fresh coconut juice or a refreshing slice of watermelon.

Leave the beach at the far end and turn immediately to your left, and you'll soon find yourself at the base of a highly enjoyable **rail ride** (20,000đ). Pulleys tug your go-kart-like vehicle (sits one or two) up the hillside, and you're ushered off at the top to take in some superlative views into Cambodia; the way back down is even more fun, since you can control the braking with odd hand-levers (build up some space between yourself and the kart in front, and you can really let yourself fly).

Back on the coast road, you'll weave your way between rice fields, shrimp farms, water buffalo wallowing in ponds and signs reading "Frontier Area". You'll see the 48m-high granite outcrop housing Thach Dong, or Stone Cave, long before you reach it; 3–4km past Mui Nai the road reaches a junction, where a left turn leads to the Cambodian border.

Turn right at this junction and very shortly the road passes a cluster of food stalls that mark the entrance to **Thach Dong** (daily 6.30am–6pm; 10,000đ per bike). A monument shaped like a defiant clenched fist stands as a memorial to 130 people killed by Khmer Rouge forces near here in 1978. Beyond this, steps lead up to a **cave pagoda** that's home to a colony of bats. Its shrines to Quan Am and Buddha are unremarkable, but balconies hewn from the side of the rock afford great views over the hills, paddy fields and sea below. Look to your right and you're peering into Cambodia.

From here, continue along the circular road that will bring you, after a few kilometres, back into Ha Tien.

Dong Tam 83 Tran Hau ☎0773 950555. This smart place, also known as *Du Hung 2*, has a variety of rooms, all with a/c, cable TV and wi-fi, and the enthusiastic staff can help with travel plans. Bikes and motorbikes for rent too. **$15**

Ha Tien 36 Tran Hau ☎0773 851563. For some time this was the town's most luxuriant accommodation, and though now upstaged by the *River* it's pretty decent value. Rooms here have surprisingly good carpetting and the place is tastefully designed, but ask to see a room first as some are a bit dingy. **$20**

Hai Van 55 Lam Son ☎0773 852872. This long-established hotel has simple but clean rooms in the old wing, as well as smart a/c rooms in a new wing. They also have some large suites that are a steal at $13. **$8**

Hai Yen 15 To Chau ☎0773 851580. An efficiently run place with helpful and informative staff. The bright,

decent-sized rooms are good value and those on the upper floors have good views of Dong Ho. **$12**

Hong Phat Mui Nai beach ☎0773 951661. The best option on Mui Nai beach (see opposite); track it down if you feel like staying out of town. It features reasonable air-conditioned rooms, and also boasts a restaurant – quite useful, given its distance from anything similar. **$20**

River Dang Thuy Tram ☎0773 955888. The town's first upper-end hotel is a mixed bag. Staff are helpful and rooms plushly appointed, some boasting superlative river views. Eccentricities include being pointed to a different place for breakfast every day, while to access their small swimming pool you have to exit the hotel and walk down the road (then usually back again, to ask for the key). As it's rarely even quarter-full, expect to halve the rack rates. **$90**

EATING AND DRINKING

In the evening, a **night market** sets up along Tran Hau, some stalls selling souvenirs and others selling seafood, attracting crowds of locals and the odd foreigner.

Da Ha Tien Floating Restaurant Dang Thuy Tram ☎0773 955888. Operated by the *River* hotel, this characterful wooden vessel makes a pretty fun place to eat or drink a cocktail (65,000đ) of an evening, taking in the wind and the rippling waves. The menu seems to change every day, but there's usually a choice between Western and Vietnamese dishes; prices can be cheap, too, with some mains starting at just 35,000đ. Daily 7am–10pm.

★**Oasis** 42 Tuan Phu Dat ☎0773 701553. This English-run venue is by far the western delta's best place for Western grub. Dishes don't always *quite* live up to their tantalizing promise, such as hummus, guacamole and Greek salads (all around 60,000đ), and full English breakfasts (80,000đ). However, it's an amiable place, and a good spot in which to socialize over a beer (from 10,000đ); there are some imported brands available, too. Daily 9am–10pm.

DIRECTORY

Banks The Vietcombank at 4 Phuong Thanh can exchange cash, and also has an ATM.

Post office The post office (daily 6.30am–9pm) is on To Chau, a short walk north of the river.

Vehicle rental Though nowhere officially rents vehicles, most hotels can help out; ask staff at the *River* hotel or

Oasis restaurant, who will get you a motorbike for the day for around 200,000đ.

Visas Cambodian visas are available at the border at Xa Xia ($25), but it's better to get one in Ho Chi Minh City to avoid any overcharging, which happens a little too often.

Hon Chong Peninsula

Just 30km south of Ha Tien lies the **Hon Chong Peninsula**. A string of offshore isles has earned this region the moniker "mini-Ha Long", but it's as a coastal resort that it draws throngs of Vietnamese and a smattering of foreigners. The approach to the peninsula is blighted by unsightly cement factories belching out clouds of smoke, but head further along and you'll find calm beaches fringed with palms and casuarinas, which remain among the most attractive in the delta. Right at the southern tip of the peninsula, the main area of note is fairly compact (a bay-like stretch of around 6km); with your own wheels it's easy to scoot between the various sights and beaches.

Bai Duong

Admission 5000đ when staff are on duty; free otherwise

The most picturesque beach on the peninsula is right at the end of the road – **Bai Duong**, named after the casuarina trees that line its sands. After passing pandanus, tamarind and

2

sugar-palm trees, the coastal track ends at a towering cliff, in front of which stands **Sea and Mountain Pagoda** ("Chua Hai Son") and a cluster of souvenir and food stalls. Go into the temple grounds, and look for an opening in the rock that leads into **Cave Pagoda** ("Chua Hong"). A low doorway leads from its outer chamber to a grotto in the cliff's belly, where statues of Quan Am and several Buddhas are lit by coloured lights. The cramped stone corridor that runs on from here makes as romantic an approach to a beach as you could imagine, though the stench of the resident bats somewhat spoils the atmosphere.

The beach

As you hit Bai Duong's stretch of sand, the rugged rocks out to sea in front of you constitute **Father and Son Isle** ("Hon Phu Tu"), though it is now rather a misnomer as "Father", the bigger of the two pillars of rock, fell crashing in to the sea in 2006. The beach here is reasonably attractive, though still too shallow for swimming.

ARRIVAL AND DEPARTURE   **HON CHONG PENINSULA**

By bus Irregular buses ply the route between Hon Chong and Rach Gia (about 2hr). Coming from Ha Tien, you'll have to take a Rach Gia-bound bus and get off at Ba Hon, then take a xe om (about 60,000đ) the last few kilometres to Bai Duong. Alternatively, you can ride here from Ha Tien on a motorbike in around an hour.

ACCOMMODATION AND EATING

All of the options listed here are located on the road running along the south of the peninsula, one which finishes at Bai Duong beach.

An Hai Son ☎0773 759226. Located in the centre of the bay, facing the sea (but with no sea views), this place is well managed and has smart rooms with a/c, TVs and fridges, as well as decent restaurants. There are also tennis courts and free bicycles for guests' use. **$17**

Green Hill Guesthouse ☎0773 854369. Perched on the hillside at the western end of the bay, this family-run hotel lives up to its billing, its handful of beautifully furnished rooms all commanding sweeping views of the bay and representing a good deal. **$17**

★**Hon Trem Resort** ☎0773 854331. Boasts a prime location on a small isthmus poking out from the middle of the bay. All of its compact villas ($60–70) enjoy great views from a steep hillside, as well as spacious rooms in a new block that are extremely comfortable and well equipped. Add a gorgeous swimming pool and great beach views, and you've got the best spot to lay your head. Their restaurant is also the best place to eat in the area, with a wide range of Vietnamese dishes at 95,000–250,000đ. **$40**

Phu Quoc Island

One of Vietnam's most popular holiday destinations, **PHU QUOC ISLAND** rises from the country's slender southern tip like a genie released from a bottle. Virtually unknown by outsiders a decade ago, its soft-sand beaches, swaying palms and limpid waters have been casting spells on visitors ever since its tourism potential was finally unlocked in the late 1990s. Progress was initially slow – electricity from the mainland only arrived in 2013, and even today some resorts subsist on generator power alone – but a recent glut of construction means that Phu Quoc is now challenging Nha Trang as Vietnam's top beach destination.

Phu Quoc is located in the Gulf of Thailand just 15km off the coast of Cambodia, a country that still has territorial claims on the island (which they refer to as Ko Tral). Phu Quoc's isolation made it an attractive hiding place for two of the more famous figures from Vietnam's past. **Nguyen Anh** holed up here while on the run from the Tay Son brothers in the late eighteenth century, and so too, in the 1860s, did **Nguyen Trung Truc** (see box, p.155). Today, over eighty thousand people – and a sizeable population of indigenous dogs (recognizable by a line of hair running up the spine instead of down) – dwell on the island, famous throughout Vietnam for its black pepper and its fish sauce (*nuoc mam*), which is graded like olive oil.

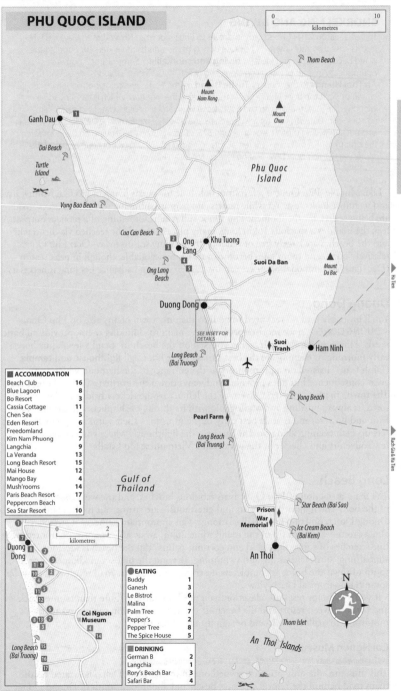

PHU QUOC ISLAND

2

0 ——————— 10
kilometres

Thom Beach

▲ *Mount Ham Rong*

▲ *Mount Chua*

Ganh Dau ● **1**

Dai Beach

Turtle Island

Phu Quoc Island

Vung Bao Beach

Cua Can Beach

2
3
Ong Lang ● Khu Tuong
4
5

Ong Lang Beach

Suoi Da Ban

▲ *Mount Da Bac*

Duong Dong ●

SEE INSET FOR DETAILS

Suoi Tranh ● Ham Ninh

Long Beach (Bai Truong)

6

Vong Beach

Pearl Farm

Long Beach (Bai Truong)

Gulf of Thailand

Star Beach (Bai Sao)

Prison War Memorial

Ice Cream Beach (Bai Kem)

An Thoi ●

N

Thom Islet

An Thoi Islands

ACCOMMODATION

Beach Club	16
Blue Lagoon	8
Bo Resort	3
Cassia Cottage	11
Chen Sea	5
Eden Resort	6
Freedomland	2
Kim Nam Phuong	7
Langchia	9
La Veranda	13
Long Beach Resort	15
Mai House	12
Mango Bay	4
Mush'rooms	14
Paris Beach Resort	17
Peppercorn Beach	1
Sea Star Resort	10

Ha Tien ►

Rach Gia & Ha Tien ►

0 ——— 2
kilometres

Duong Dong
7
8
2
1 9
3
10
2
4
5
11
12
6
8 13 7
3

Coi Nguon Museum

14

Long Beach (Bai Truong)
15
16
17

● EATING

Buddy	1
Ganesh	3
Le Bistrot	6
Malina	4
Palm Tree	7
Pepper's	2
Pepper Tree	8
The Spice House	5

■ DRINKING

German B	2
Langchia	1
Rory's Beach Bar	3
Safari Bar	4

2

> ### SNORKELLING AND DIVING
>
> There's a reason why visitors come in droves to Phu Quoc from November to May, and why resorts raise their rates then. It's because during those months the waters surrounding the island become limpid and ideal for **diving and snorkelling**. Some visitors snorkel optimistically in front of resorts on Ong Lang Beach, but the best locations are around the **An Thoi Islands** to the south or **Turtle Island** off the northwest coast, both of which can be visited by boat trip from Phu Quoc. At these reefs – the former of which is rated by some as the best dive site in Vietnam – you can float above brain and fan corals, watching parrot fish, scorpion fish, butterfly fish, huge sea urchins and a host of other marine life. Most resorts can sort out snorkelling trips, charging around $15–20 per person (depending on the number in the group), which includes gear rental, fishing and lunch. Diving will, of course, cost a little more; see the Rainbow Divers listing (see p.165) for an idea of prices.

Like Mui Ne, Phu Quoc is a favourite bolt-hole for expats living in Ho Chi Minh City, and its future looks rosy. Yet while resorts and bars are springing up fast and access roads are being sealed, for the moment Phu Quoc still retains something of a pioneer outpost feel; the island is a spacious 46km long, many places can only be reached via dirt tracks and the beaches are largely free of vendors. In the rainy season (May–Oct) Phu Quoc is relatively quiet, and room rates become more easily negotiable, though in peak season (Dec–Jan), accommodation prices can increase sharply and advance booking is necessary.

Duong Dong

You'll probably find no real need to go into the only town of any size on Phu Quoc – **DUONG DONG** – since most resorts, and the main road linking them, provide all basic needs. However, it's worth dragging yourself off the beach to spend a few hours here; early morning or evening are the best times. There is a small **lighthouse** and **temple** (Dinh Cau) situated on a promontory at the entrance to the harbour, which is of no great consequence but does provide good **views** down the northern part of Long Beach. The town's **market**, on Ngo Quyen, to the left across the rickety bridge in the centre of town, is always bustling and photogenic with its throng of shoppers and displays of fruit and flowers, and is at its best early in the morning. There's also a **night market** that sets up each evening along Vo Thi Sau near the lighthouse, where you can pick up a few souvenirs and check out the good-value Vietnamese food stalls.

Long Beach

The main attraction of Phu Quoc is its fabulous beaches, and the **west coast** has some of the best. The majority of resorts and guesthouses are strung out to the south of Duong Dong, on **Long Beach** (Bai Truong) – an appropriate name, as it stretches almost to the southern tip of the island some 20km away. Most resorts are fronted by fine stretches of soft yellow sand and coconut palms, and the beach is ideal for sunbathing, sunset watching and swimming. Beyond the first seven kilometres or so south of town the beach is completely deserted, and the coast road southward provides some classic tropical beach views.

If you're here for rest and relaxation, you need do nothing more than saunter back and forth between resort and the beach. If you get restless, you can always rent a motorbike to explore the island or sign up for a boat trip.

Coi Nguon Museum

149 Tran Hung Dao • Daily 7am–5pm • 20,000đ • ☎ 0773 980206, ⓦ coinguonmuseum.com

This museum, the only privately owned one in the Mekong Delta, is located on the main road behind the resorts on Long Beach and about 5km south of Duong Dong;

it is well worth a visit to get an overview of Phu Quoc's natural and political history. The carefully arranged exhibits include whale, dugong and swordfish skeletons, samples of sand and petrified wood, a fantastic variety of shells, a potted history of the island's past, ceramics from shipwrecks and, if you make it up to the fifth floor, sweeping views along the coast. There are also handicrafts made of local materials on sale, though a shell-encrusted chair might be a bit big for the backpack.

Phu Quoc Pearl Farm

Daily 8am–5pm • ⓦ treasuresfromthedeep.com

2

About halfway down Long Beach, the **Phu Quoc Pearl Farm** is worth a look to see how pearls are cultured or to pick up a souvenir. There's an interesting display on the complex process, and some stunning (and pricey) jewellery on sale. Look out for the Kiwi flag on the sign out front, as some of owner Grant's ex-employees have set up rival farms nearby and pay taxi drivers to lead visitors their way.

Northern Phu Quoc

The west coast north of Duong Dong is a bit more rugged, but the beautiful bays tucked along **Ong Lang Beach** (Bai Ong Lang) are certainly worth visiting, and a few cosy resorts, separated from each other by rocky headlands, offer the chance to really get away from it all. Ong Lang Beach is much quieter than Long Beach, and has a few coral reefs just off the coast, though for really good snorkelling you'd need to join a boat trip to the north or south end of the island. North of Ong Lang, there are a few more attractive beaches called **Cua Can**, **Vung Bao** and **Dai**. Resorts are beginning to spring up here too, though the region still has a feel of splendid isolation (see box below).

Southern Phu Quoc

The **east coast** is, so far, largely undeveloped, though it does have a good surfaced road running halfway up it (from An Thoi to Ham Ninh and Duong Dong) that

---

EXPLORING THE INTERIOR BY BIKE

Phu Quoc is the kind of island that is ideal for exploration, and there is little traffic, making it easy to ride a **motorbike** around. Over seventy percent of the island is forested at present, and the hills of the north are particularly verdant. If you do this, be aware that few roads are surfaced, so you are likely to return to your resort at the end of the day covered in a film of red dust – wearing a helmet is compulsory and a face-mask is a good idea too.

All over the island, and especially in the north, you will pass by **pepper plantations**, the plants easily identifiable as climbers on three-metre-high poles; at places like **Khu Tuong**, a few kilometres inland from Ong Lang Beach (see map, p.161), they welcome visitors to look around. There are also two cleansing **streams** in the centre of Phu Quoc: **Suoi Da Ban** and **Suoi Tranh**. A walk beside them reveals moss-covered boulders, tangled vines and small cascades, though they tend to dry up between January and May.

One highly recommended route to follow heads north out of Duong Dong; turn right when you hit the end of Tran Hung Dao, left across the bridge, then right again in the direction of Thom Beach. This is a fast, easy road, though things get rather more wild if you turn left at the first main junction you hit (after 12km or so). The red-earth road heading from here to Ganh Dau is absolutely splendid: no traffic, corners and bumps that can cope with a bit of speed, and an ever-present forest aroma. When hitting the end of the road in Ganh Dau, you could turn right and have a meal or fruit juice at the *Peppercorn Beach Resort* (follow the signs). Turning left instead will take you onto a road running along the coast; this area is becoming more developed, but there are plenty of tranquil spots before you rejoin the main road back to Duong Dong.

2

offers some respite from the constant dust kicked up off the dirt roads throughout the rest of the island.

Star Beach

Signposted just north of the T-junction where the road from Long Beach meets the road up the east coast, **Star Beach** (Bai Sao) is a hot contender for best beach on the island. Its dazzling white sand and pale blue water are mesmerizing and while the waves crash on Long Beach during the monsoons, Star Beach is often calm. A few **beach restaurants** do a healthy trade, particularly at weekends when the beach gets overrun with locals, and there are even a couple of places offering lodgings (see opposite). In season there are kayaks for rent and half-day snorkelling trips by boat.

Other beaches

A little south of Bai Sao, **Ice Cream Beach** (Bai Kem) is also a blinding white colour, but the military generally prohibit entry to foreigners not arriving on a boat tour.

In the middle of the east coast, **Vong Beach** and Ham Ninh provide jetties for hydrofoils arriving from Rach Gia and Ha Tien. There's no beach to speak of at Vong Beach – just mud flats. The only other beach on the east coast is **Thom Beach**, in the extreme northwest of the island, which is only reached after a wearing, 35 kilometre-long motorbike ride over rough roads from Duong Dong, and has virtually nothing in the way of facilities.

The war memorial and former prison

Prison Tue–Sun 7.30–11am & 1.30–5pm • Both free

In the south of the island, two unusual attractions are located almost opposite each other: the **war memorial** and the former **prison** (Nha Tu Phu Quoc). The war memorial, perched on a slight rise beside the main road about a kilometre south of the junction of the roads down the west and east coasts, marked on the map (see p.161), consists of three abstract forms, in one of which is cut the shape of a human, while the prison's small museum chronicles its use to detain enemies of the state, though there is no English signage.

ARRIVAL AND DEPARTURE   **PHU QUOC ISLAND**

Whether you arrive by air or by sea, you will likely be besieged by **touts** trying to drag you off to their favoured hotel or guesthouse, so it's a good idea to have somewhere in mind before arrival. If you have made a prior booking, most resorts provide a **free airport transfer**, saving you a lot of hassle and expense.

By plane Flights land at the sparkly, new Phu Quoc Airport, around 9km south of Duong Dong town, and less from many of the resorts lying in between the two. Reservations are best made online, though staff at your accommodation may be able to help out too. Taxis will be able to take you into town from the airport, though many resorts arrange free pick-ups and drop-offs as a matter of course.
Destinations Can Tho (daily; 45min); Hanoi (1–2 daily; 2hr); Ho Chi Minh City (4–7 daily; 1hr); Rach Gia (daily in season; 30min).

By boat Speedboats run between Rach Gia and Vong Beach, while those from Ha Tien can arrive there or at Ham Ninh. It's best to buy your ticket in advance; ask your hotel or guesthouse to help you, or visit the offices at the top of Tran Hung Dao, just behind the northern end of Long Beach (some offer through-tickets to Cambodian destinations, via Ha Tien). To get to the Long Beach resorts or Duong Dong from the piers, make use of the taxis (up to 230,000đ), or minibuses (from 30,000đ, though you may have to haggle).
Destinations Ha Tien (1 daily; 230,000đ; 1hr 30min); Rach Gia (4 daily; 320,000đ; 2hr 30min).

GETTING AROUND

By xe om or taxi There is currently no organized bus service so – unless you hire a motorbike – you'll have to take a taxi or xe om to get around the island.
By motorbike Prices are 150,000–250,000đ a day depending on the type of motorbike you rent. This is an exciting option, and even first-time riders should be okay

as long as they can avoid torrential downpours or the hugest potholes. Most resorts and guesthouses rent motorbikes, or will know where to point you – check yours over carefully, as many of these machines are falling apart. Wear a helmet, face-mask (for the dust) and plenty of sunscreen.

TOURS

There are numerous operators strung along the road linking the resorts. Most resorts and guesthouses can also arrange boat tours, including visits to the local pearl farm on Long Beach, or an evening's squid fishing, using coloured plastic shrimps as bait.

John's Tours 143 Tran Hung Dao ☎0919 107086, ⓦjohnsislandtours.com. Long-established operator with a wide range of tours, many of which run daily (in season, at least): try snorkelling and fishing ($17 per person), a full-day cruise including the same ($30), or night-fishing for squid and barbecuing up the results ($15).

Rainbow Divers 11 Tran Hung Dao ☎0913 400964, ⓦdivevietnam.com. Well-organized operator running diving trips with hotel pick-up on most days during the diving season (early Nov–late May). It'll be around $30 for snorkelling or $85 for two dives, including all equipment and lunch or fruit. They also offer PADI courses in open-sea (3-day; $255) and advanced diving (2-day; $375).

ACCOMMODATION

Accommodation options are expanding fast and many new places were under construction at the time of writing. Not all mid-range places include air conditioning, TV and fridge, so check before booking if these are important (the first one certainly can be). While resorts on **Ong Lang Beach** are quieter, they are separated from each other by headlands, so there's no choice when it comes to eating, as there is on **Long Beach**. Bear in mind that during the rainy season (May–Oct), many small places close for several months and those that are open reduce their prices. By contrast, it can be difficult to find a room in the high season, so advance booking is advised for more upmarket places.

LONG BEACH

★**Beach Club** ☎0773 980998, ⓦbeachclubvietnam .com. Under English management, this small, well-run place offers simple, pleasant rooms and bungalows in one of the most tranquil spots on Long Beach. There's a low-key, friendly vibe to the place and the kitchen turns out some excellent food, both Vietnamese and Western. Rooms $35, bungalows $45

Blue Lagoon ☎0773 994499, ⓦsasco-bluelagoon -resort.com. More of a hotel than a resort, this may appeal to those who favour comfort over the semi-rustic beachside lifestyle. It is on the beach, however, and features a splendid pool, a great restaurant, and well-appointed rooms with quality bedding. $85

★**Cassia Cottage** ☎0773 848395, ⓦcassiacottage .com. An absolutely beautiful mini-resort, whose airy rooms exude cinnamon, nutmeg and other pleasing aromas – their restaurant (see p.167) isn't called *The Spice House* for nothing. Even the smallest rooms are nice and large, while the swimming pools are a delight. $35

Eden Resort ☎0773 985598, ⓦedenresort.com.vn. This stylish resort features well-equipped, spacious rooms in the main building and bungalows set in beautifully landscaped gardens, as well as a spa and good-sized pool. The resort fronts a wild stretch of beach, and the capable staff can help make travel and tour arrangements. $140

Kim Nam Phuong ☎0773 846319. One of the few remaining budget resorts on Phu Quoc, this place is located near the top end of Long Beach; some bungalows come with a/c and hot water, while cheaper rooms are smaller with fans and cold water. $15

Langchia ☎0939 132613, ⓦlangchia-hostel.com. The best backpacker place on Phu Quoc. Though their single, 16-bed dorm room can get a wee bit crowded, few guests seem to mind, especially after a drink from the bar (see p.167). Staff are courteous and willing to please, and there's breakfast included in the price. Dorm beds $10

★**La Veranda** ☎0773 982988, ⓦlaverandaresort .com. The presence of this Accor property on Long Beach is a clear sign of developers' confidence in the island's appeal. It occupies a lovely, French-colonial-style building with luxurious rooms, a small pool, spa, a delightful restaurant, and super-efficient staff. Ask about discounts from the rack rates. $205

Long Beach Resort ☎0773 981818, ⓦlongbeach -phuquoc.com. This top-end resort takes ancient architecture as its theme, and indeed the entrance looks like the gateway to Hue's Imperial City. Rooms continue the theme with traditional furnishings, long drapes and simple tiled floors. At the back of the resort is a pool and bridge leading over a lotus pond to the beach. $185

Mai House ☎0773 847003, ⓦmaihousephuquoc.com. *Mai House* consists of attractive thatched bungalows set far apart from each other in a lush garden under towering palms. Rooms are stylishly furnished and feel very cosy, with thick mattresses on the canopied beds and bamboo chairs on a secluded veranda. Add at least $20 for a/c rooms. $75

Mush'rooms ☎0126 471 4279. Phu Quoc's de facto backpacker choice until the *Langchia* opened its doors, this is still going strong. It's about as simple as you can imagine, and a fair walk from most of the main road's culinary options, but the price is right. Dorm beds $6

Paris Beach Resort ☎0773 994548, ⓦphuquocparis beach.com. Snuggled up to the *Beach Club*, this place offers clean bright rooms or bungalows, some with beach views, though some are very cramped together. The restaurant here with its huge and varied menu is a definite bonus. Rooms $35, bungalows $60

2

Sea Star Resort ☎0773 982161, ⊛seastarresort.com. This attractive and well-managed place has a nice shady patch of beach in front and is excellent value, as the decent-sized rooms have all facilities. $55

ONG LANG BEACH

Bo Resort ☎0773 986142, ⊛boresort.com. Pleasant, tastefully furnished bungalows made of wood and thatch on a steep hill overlooking a gorgeous stretch of beach, with a well-appointed restaurant too. The bungalows enjoy some privacy, so it's ideal for an escape, but it's a bit of a clamber to those at the top of the hill. $65

Chen Sea ☎0773 995895, ⊛centararesorts.com. The southernmost and most expensive resort on Ong Lang Beach features luxurious rooms in a mixed traditional and modern style, some with private pool. There's also a large, beachfront, communal pool, a diving and watersports centre, a solarium deck, a spa, a mini library and a recreational activities programme. Expect generous discounts from the stratospheric rack rates. $500

★Freedomland ☎0226 586802, ⊛freedomland phuquoc.com. One of the newer places on Ong Lang, this has instantly become the most popular, thanks to charming rooms and common areas that make the place feel more like a Thai-island hipster hangout than something in Vietnam – treehouses, outdoor showers, eco-friendliness and a bar selling "secret" alcohol. No a/c, no TV, nobody cares. $30

★Mango Bay ☎0903 382207, ⊛mangobayphuquoc .com. This place enjoys a lovely, tranquil location and offers spacious, stylish bungalows, made with local soil using eco-friendly techniques, with fans and large verandas (no a/c or TV). The coast is rocky in front but there are deserted sandy bays on each side. $145

OTHER BEACHES

Peppercorn Beach ☎0773 989567, ⊛peppercorn beach.com. Snuggled in solitude off the island's north-western flank, this is a grand choice for those wishing to get away from it all. There are only eight rooms here, and they're often taken up for weeks at a time – in season, you'll be lucky to get a booking at less than a month's notice. Mercifully, given its somewhat remote setting, meals at the restaurant are both affordable and of good quality. $160

EATING

Duong Dong's night market (see p.162) is a great place to sample authentic **Vietnamese dishes** at very cheap prices. Not surprisingly, every beach resort, apart from the cheapest guesthouses, has its own restaurant; most have reasonable menus and some have sea views, but the quality is erratic and prices are often inflated. Bear in mind if you stay anywhere but **Long Beach**, you'll be more or less limited to your resort's restaurant unless you have a rented motorbike. Long Beach may be busier, but you do get several dining choices in a small area.

Buddy 26 Nguyen Trai, Duong Dong ☎0773 994181. Good place for a cooling ice cream (40,000đ) or a nice, thick shake (70,000đ) if you make a trip to town. Sandwiches (about 65,000đ), all-day breakfasts (135,000đ), as well as reliable local info if the Kiwi owner happens to be there. Daily 8am–10pm.

Ganesh 97 Tran Hung Dao ☎0773 994917. All the quality you'd expect of the pan-Vietnamese Indian chain, with images of Gandhi and colourful Indian architecture peering down at you as you wolf down your meal – most mains cost around 100,000đ (a little more for chicken or lamb), and filling thali sets start at 170,000đ. Wash it all down with a lassi (40,000đ). Daily 10am–11pm.

Le Bistrot On the lane leading to La Veranda resort, Long Beach ☎0773 982200. Relaxing place with pool table offering French and international dishes (from 75,000đ), and with a children's playground in the garden. Popular for dining in the day, or choosing a drink from the well-stocked bar in the evening. Daily 10am–midnight.

Malina La On the land leading to Mai Resort ☎0166 7284602. Unfortunately, many Western tourists sneer at Vietnam's ever-increasing contingent of Russian travellers. Here's a great place to put lazy stereotypes to rest – a small restaurant serving excellent Russian staples, including tasty *pilmeny* dumplings (70,000đ), and what is without doubt the best borshch in Vietnam (110,000đ). Daily 8am–10pm.

Palm Tree On the lane leading to La Veranda, Long Beach ☎0913 722642. Great traditional Vietnamese dishes plus a seafood barbecue every evening in the high season. It's just opposite the entrance to *La Veranda* and doesn't enjoy beach views, but this place is all about taste, not ambience, and prices seem just a bit cheaper here than anywhere else (from 60,000đ for main courses). Daily 7am–11pm.

Pepper's 89 Tran Hung Dao, on the main road near the north end of Long Beach, ☎0773 848773. The place to go for pizzas (from 85,000đ for a medium), grills and jumbo salads; somewhat oddly, there are also a couple of German dishes on the menu. Though it doesn't have beach views, it's a pleasant, breezy spot and staff are very welcoming. They do hotel deliveries too – there's something special about having pizza on your balcony or veranda. Daily 10am–11pm.

Pepper Tree La Veranda resort, Long Beach ☎0773 982988. This classy, first-floor restaurant in a colonial-style building makes an ideal place for a splurge. Plenty of seafood on offer, such as steamed sea bass with artichokes in clam butter (400,000đ), in a refined atmosphere. Daily 11.30am–2pm & 6.30–10.30pm.

★**The Spice House** Cassia Cottage ☎0773 848395. Set in what seems for all the world a large, beachside garden, this top-notch hotel restaurant is rarely too busy outside breakfast time. Check the blackboard for daily specials; on offer most days are caramelized shrimps and rice (150,000đ), or regular Vietnamese veggie staples (85,000đ); alternatively, come here for a juice (45,000–60,000đ), or an evening cocktail (115,000đ, including the "Spice House", made with cinnamon, apple and coconut). Daily 10am–10pm.

DRINKING

German B Tran Hung Dao ☎0166 40538380. Not exactly the friendliest place in town, this main-road joint is nevertheless a fine place for beer (20,000đ for a big bottle of Saigon) and pool. It's super cheap, and great German bar food sweetens the deal – you'll soon be slavering over one of their tasty wursts (60,000đ). Daily 9am–10pm.

Langchia Long Beach ☎0939 132613. This hostel is fronted by a small bar, which is a cheap and pleasant place to make new travel friends whether you're staying here or not. Closes a bit early, but the beach is just a short walk away, so buy a couple of bottles and sit out watching the stars. Daily 7am–9pm.

★**Rory's Beach Bar** Next to La Veranda resort, Long Beach ☎0125 7499749. Aussie-owned beach venue that's without doubt the best nightlife option in Phu Quoc – indeed, sometimes it feels like the only "proper" one. Chairs on the beach, campfires, a pool table and decent beer (draught from 40,000đ)… what more could you want? Daily 9am–midnight, often later.

Safari Bar Tran Hung Dao ☎0905 224600. "Where you can party like animals"… the slogan should say it all. With cheap beer (always ice-cold), good music and a pool table, this place is lots of fun, especially when full of guests from the neighbouring *Mush'rooms* hostel (see p.165). Daily noon–midnight, often later.

DIRECTORY

Bank The Vietcombank at 20, 30 Thang 4 in Duong Dong will exchange money and has an ATM.

Hospital and pharmacies There is a hospital towards the eastern end of 30 Thang 4, and there are pharmacies along Ngo Quyen beside the market.

Post office The post office (7am–8pm) is also on 30 Thang 4, where internet access is available.

The central highlands

MARKET, KON TUM

The central highlands

Fragrant with flowers for much of the year, and home to thundering waterfalls, immense longhouses and umpteen minority cultures, it's something of a surprise that Vietnam's central highlands are among the least-visited parts of the country. The bulk of travellers shoot along the coast to the east, and even those who prefer mountains to beaches usually head to the larger, more spectacular ranges in northern Vietnam. True, the central highlands score lower for scenic beauty, and the area's minority groups may be less colourful, but there's still a lot to see here. With the exceptions of majestic Da Lat and enjoyably intimate Kon Tum, the appeal of the area lies outside its urban pockets: there are two national parks to choose from, and a wealth of minority home-stay options – and barely a tourist in sight.

Bounded to the west by the Cambodian and Lao borders, the central highlands' fertile red soils yield considerable **natural resources**, among them coffee, tea, rubber, silk and hardwood. Not all of the highlands, though, have been sacrificed to plantation-style economies of scale – pockets of **primeval forest** still thrive, where wildlife including elephants, bears and gibbons somehow survived the days when the region was a hunting ground for Saigon's idle rich and Hue's idle royalty.

For most visitors who ascend to these altitudes, the main target is **Da Lat**, an erstwhile French mountain retreat that appears very romantic from afar, when the mists roll over its pine-crested hilltops, though some find it disappointing close-up, with its dreary architecture and tacky tourist trappings. The city itself is not without its charms, among them a bracing climate, some beguiling colonial buildings, picturesque bike rides and a market overflowing with delectable fruits and vegetables.

Heading northwest from Da Lat, you'll pass pretty **Lak Lake**, an attractive body of water surrounded by minority villages. Then comes a series of gritty highland towns whose reputations rest less on tourist sights than on the villages and open terrain that ring them. First comes **Buon Ma Thuot**, a surprisingly busy place considering its far-flung location. While the city itself has little to detain the visitor, the surrounding waterfalls and E De minority villages certainly do; it's also the gateway for treks into **Yok Don National Park**.

Pleiku to the north is another less-than-lovely city, though again encircled with a ring of delightful minority villages – this time Jarai and Bahnar. Further north again is **Kon Tum**, by far the most attractive and relaxing of these three provincial capitals; you'll be able to take in three **Bahnar villages** on an afternoon's walk from the city centre, and mop up a few other minority groups farther afield.

Your highland experience will vary enormously depending on **when you visit**. The dry season runs from November through to April. To see the region at its atmospheric best, it's better to go in the wet season, May to October, although at this time the rain can make some outlying villages inaccessible.

COFFEE GROWING

Highlights

❶ Dambri Waterfalls The most impressive waterfalls in the highlands – stand right below them and feel the spray on your face. **See p.173**

❷ Da Lat Abseil down a waterfall or pose for pictures on a pony in the capital of adventure sports and kitsch. **See p.174**

❸ Ride the rails Chug your way through highland scenery on the short train ride to Trai Mat village, 7km east of Da Lat. **See p.185**

❹ Lak Lake Paddle around Lak Lake in a dug-out canoe at dawn and watch the sunrise shimmer across its surface. **See p.186**

❺ Coffee country Enjoy a cup of fresh coffee in Vietnam's capital of caffeine, Buon Ma Thuot. **See p.187**

❻ Kon Tum Kick back for a few days in tourist-lite Kon Tum, a small, agreeable city that simply deserves more tourists. **See p.196**

❼ Bahnar villages Overnight in a dramatically tall communal *rong* in a Bahnar village near Kon Tum. **See p.196**

HIGHLIGHTS ARE MARKED ON THE MAP ON P.172

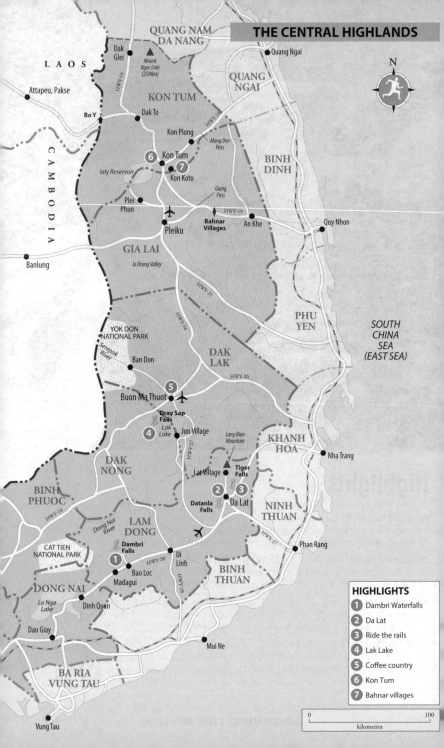

THE CENTRAL HIGHLANDS

N

LAOS

CAMBODIA

QUANG NAM DA NANG

Dak Glei

Mount Ngoc Linh (2598m)

Attapeu, Pakse

Bo Y

Dak To

KON TUM

Dak To

Kon Plong

Mang Den Pass

6 Kon Tum

7 Kon Kotu

Ialy Reservoir

Plei Phun

Pleiku

Giang Pass

Bahnar Villages

An Khe

HWY-19

GIA LAI

Ia Drang Valley

Banlung

HWY-25

YOK DON NATIONAL PARK

Serepok River

Ban Don

DAK LAK

HWY-26

5 Buon Ma Thuot

Dray Sap Falls

4 Lak Lake

Jun Village

HWY-27

Lang Bian Mountain

DAK NONG

Lat Village

Tiger Falls

2 Datanla Falls

3 Da Lat

KHANH HOA

Nha Trang

BINH PHUOC

HWY-14

Dong Nai River

LAM DONG

CAT TIEN NATIONAL PARK

1 **Dambri Falls**

HWY-20

Di Linh

Bao Loc

Madagui

BINH THUAN

HWY-28

NINH THUAN

HWY-27

Phan Rang

DONG NAI

La Nga Lake

Dinh Quan

Dau Giay

Mui Ne

BA RIA VUNG TAU

Vung Tau

QUANG NGAI

Quang Ngai

QUANG NGAI

HWY-

BINH DINH

Quy Nhon

PHU YEN

SOUTH CHINA SEA (EAST SEA)

HIGHLIGHTS

1 Dambri Waterfalls
2 Da Lat
3 Ride the rails
4 Lak Lake
5 Coffee country
6 Kon Tum
7 Bahnar villages

0   100
kilometres

MINORITY ISSUES IN THE CENTRAL HIGHLANDS

The Jarai and Bahnar are merely the major chunks of the highlands' patchwork of **ethnic minorities**. Cocooned in woolly jumpers, scarves and bobble hats, the highlanders are the undoubted highlight of a trip through the area, but many groups are struggling to maintain their identities in the face of persistent pressure from Hanoi to assimilate – a number of rather large protests have taken place in the highlands since the turn of the century, with the central government's reactions widely criticized by international governments and human rights groups (see p.452). Sensitive to the minority rights issue, the Vietnamese authorities only opened this region to foreigners in 1993, and while you're free to travel independently between the major cities, visiting one of the highlands' many minority villages independently can be difficult: in most cases you'll need to go through a local tourist office (and pay handsomely for the privilege). In each area, it's best to double-check the current regulations, especially concerning **overnight stays** in villages.

Bao Loc and around

3

The vast majority of travellers pass straight from Ho Chi Minh City to Da Lat, but buses sometimes screech to a brief halt on the causeway traversing **La Nga Lake**, from where the **houseboats** cast adrift on its waters are only a zoom lens away; locals use foot-powered rowing boats to access their homes, which double as fish farms. In time the hills yield to the tea, coffee and mulberry plantations of the **Bao Loc Plateau**. Here, the town of **BAO LOC** is the best place for a pit stop between Ho Chi Minh City and Da Lat, and it's also a jumping-off point for visits to nearby **Cat Tien National Park** and **Dambri Waterfalls**. Though there are no sights of interest in the town itself, the undulating hills nearby provide fertile soil for the cultivation of **tea** and **coffee**, while locals also cultivate the mulberry bushes of whose leaves **silkworms** are so fond. Those with their own transport will be able to scoot around this highly attractive area; alternatively, rent a taxi or xe om for a half-day.

Dambri Waterfalls

18km north of Bao Loc • Daily 7am–5pm • 10,000đ, lift costs 5000đ • Xe om from Bao Loc around 250,000đ return • From Da Lat, take a tour or "Easy Rider" xe om (see box, p.180)

Surrounded as they are by dense forest, the **Dambri Falls** are much more attractive than any of those in the vicinity of Da Lat, and the only ones worth visiting in the dry season. The road to the falls, which branches north from Highway 20 just east of Bao Loc, bisects rolling countryside carpeted by coffee, tea and pineapple plantations.

Once you arrive, there are **two paths** leading to the falls. The main one to the right leads to the top of the falls, where some ugly fencing stands between you and a precipice over which a torrent of white water tumbles over the 80m drop. From here, you can descend to the base of the falls by steep steps, or those feeling lazy can take a **lift**. A second path, to the left by a restaurant, leads down a steep stairway among towering trees to a superb view of the falls from in front. The two paths are linked by a bridge over the river, where you're likely to get drenched in spray, even during the dry season. The path continues downstream to a smaller cascade, **Dasara Falls**, but the trail can be slippery after rain.

ACCOMMODATION

BAO LOC AND AROUND

Memories 193 Tran Phu ☎0633 864129. Providing superb value for the price, this modest hotel just south of central Bao Loc now constitutes the town's default budget accommodation – especially important for the many bikers and Easy Rider riders who pass through this neck of the woods. Rooms are large, hot water reliable, and service friendly, but note that you'll pay a bit more for a/c. **$10**

Seri Bank 5 Road 28/3 ☎0633 864150. The smartest and most comfortable hotel in town, set back from the main highway behind a small lake. It's a far larger place than you'd expect in this neck of the woods, and has a good range of facilities, including a small sauna. **$30**

Cat Tien National Park

Entry 50,000đ, payable at park office about 100m before ferry crossing to park headquarters; park limits visitor numbers, so book ahead • ⓣ 0613 669228, ⓦ namcattien.vn

The area's outstanding attraction is **Cat Tien National Park**, a protected area situated 150km north of Ho Chi Minh City and about 50km west of Bao Loc. The park covers the largest lowland tropical rainforest in south Vietnam, and hosts nearly 350 species of birds, over 450 species of butterflies and over one hundred mammals, including wild cats, elephants, monkeys and the rare Javan rhinoceros. Don't bank on seeing a rhino, as the few residing here are in a secluded reserve closed to visitors. Crocs are a different story, since a clutch reside in an area around 12km from the park entrance (8km by boat, 4km on foot).

ARRIVAL AND DEPARTURE
CAT TIEN NATIONAL PARK

By bus If you're coming from Ho Chi Minh City by public transport, take a bus for Da Lat from Mien Dong station; tell the driver you want "Vuon Quoc Gia Cat Tien" (Cat Tien National Park), and you'll be dropped at the km125 junction at Tan Phu town. From here, xe om (about 170,000đ) cover the final 24km to the park along a narrow surfaced road; the park can organize a car for 400,000đ. If you're arriving from the north (including Da Lat and Bao

Loc), a signposted road (also surfaced) to the park branches right just before the small town of Madagui; from here it's also about 170,000đ by xe om.

By tour Some tour operators, such as Sinhbalo tours in Ho Chi Minh City (see p.91) and Phat Tire Ventures in Da Lat (see box, p.184), can organize tours, some of them day-trips, which include a visit to the park.

GETTING AROUND

By jeep or pick-up Though a dozen walking trails exist, the catch is that you need to hire a jeep or pick-up from the park HQ to get to the start of most of them (at least $15), plus a guide to go with you ($20–25), so a day out

can easily cost over $50. There's also a night safari ($10), though few people spot more than a flash of deer eyes before the panicked creatures flee.

ACCOMMODATION

Forest Floor Lodge 2km from park HQ ⓣ 0613 669890, ⓦ vietnamforesthotel.com. A spectacular, resort-style affair, with rooms either in well-appointed wooden lodges, or "deluxe tents" that are more like treehouse dwellings. Their Hornbill Bar offers tasty meals and cold beers, while staff can also organize a range of park activities, even if

you're not staying here. $140
Park accommodation ⓣ 0613 669228, ⓦ namcattien .vn. The park HQ has a few simple rooms with a/c, as well as a campsite with two-person tents. Basic meals available. Camping $8, double $15

Da Lat and around

Vietnam's premier hill station, **DA LAT**, sits tucked into the mountain folds of the **Lang Bian Plateau** at an altitude of around 1500m. A beguiling amalgam of winding streets, picturesque churches, bounteous vegetable gardens and crashing waterfalls, this quaint colonial curio is a great place to chill out, literally and metaphorically; if its cool air gets you in the mood for action, you could try trekking to minority villages, mountain-biking and rock-climbing (see box, p.184).

By tacit agreement during the American War, both Hanoi and Saigon refrained from bombing the city and it remains much as it was half a century ago. However, it's important to come to Da Lat with no illusions. With a population of around 200,000, the city is anything but an idyllic backwater: sighting its forlorn architecture for the first time in the 1950s, Norman Lewis found the place "a drab little resort", and today its colonial relics and pagodas stand cheek by jowl with some of the dingiest examples of East European construction anywhere in Vietnam. Moreover, attractions here pander to the domestic tourist's predilection for swan-shaped pedal-boats and

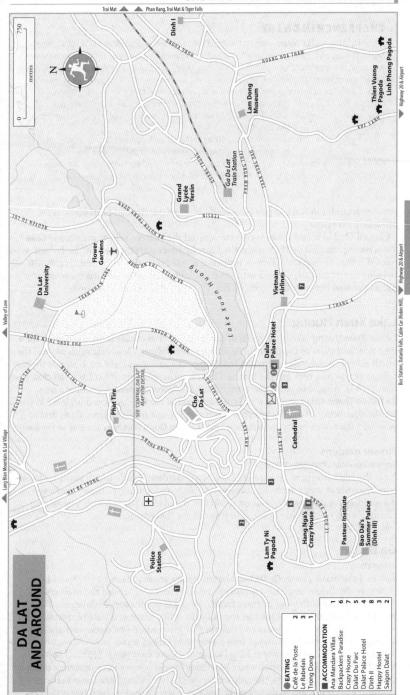

DA LAT
AND AROUND

Trai Mat ▲▲   ▲ Phan Rang, Trai Mat & Tiger Falls

Dinh I

HOANG HOA THAM

Lam Dong
Museum

Thien Vuong
Pagoda

Linh Phong Pagoda

Highway 20 & Airport

N

0   750
metres

3

Grand
Lycée
Yersin

Ga Da Lat
Train Station

Flower
Gardens

Da Lat
University

Lake Xuan Huong

Vietnam
Airlines

Dalat
Palace Hotel

Valley of Love

Bus Station, Datanla Falls, Cable Car (Robin Hill)

Highway 20 & Airport

Cho
Da Lat

SEE CENTRAL DA LAT
MAP FOR DETAIL

Phat Tire

Cathedral

Lang Bian Mountain & Lat Village

Hang Nga's
Crazy House

Pasteur Institute

Bao Dai's
Summer Palace
(Dinh III)

Lam Ty Ni
Pagoda

Police
Station

Dinh II

● EATING

Café de la Poste	2
Le Rabelais	3
Trong Dong	1

■ ACCOMMODATION

Ana Mandara Villas	1
Backpackers Paradise	6
Crazy House	7
Dalat Du Parc	5
Dalat Palace Hotel	4
Dinh II	8
Happy Hostel	3
Saigon Dalat	2

THE FRENCH IN DA LAT

It was **Dr Alexander Yersin** who first divined the therapeutic properties of Da Lat's temperate climate on an exploratory mission into Vietnam's southern highlands, in 1893. His subsequent report on the area must have struck a chord: four years later Governor-General Paul Doumer of Indochina ordered the founding of a convalescent hill station, where Saigon's hot-under-the-collar *colons* could recharge their batteries, and perhaps even take part in a day's game-hunting. The city's Gallic contingent had to pack up their winter coats after 1954's Treaty of Geneva, but by then the cathedral, train station, villas and hotels had been erected, and the French connection well and truly forged.

The French elite who once maintained **villas** in Da Lat preferred to site their homes on a hill to the southeast of the city centre, rather than in the maw of its central area. The villas that they built along Tran Hung Dao survive today, some renovated and others in a sad state of disrepair, but they evoke the feel of the colonial era more than anywhere else in Da Lat.

pony-trek guides in full cowboy gear, while at night the city can be as bleak as an off-season ski resort.

Central Da Lat forms a rough crescent around the western side of man-made **Lake Xuan Huong**, created in 1919 when the Cam Ly River was dammed by the French, who named it the "Grand Lac". French influence is still evident in its central area, whose twisting streets and steps, lined with stone buildings rising to red-tiled roofs, cover a hillock located between the streets of Bui Thi Xuan and Phan Dinh Phung.

Lake Xuan Huong

Glassy **Xuan Huong** lake is the focus of the town; its 7km circumference is perfect for a bike ride, and parts of the promenade are great for walkers. Head eastwards around the north side of the lake along **Nguyen Thai Hoc**, and you'll soon leave the bustle of the city behind as you pass between the lake and the extensive grounds of Da Lat's **golf club** (see box, p.184). After this, you'll soon reach Da Lat's **flower gardens**. Continue along **Ba Huyen Thanh Quan** and trace its broad arc around the lake. As you double back, you'll see the slate belfry of the **Grand Lycée Yersin** peeping out from the trees above and to your left; the town's pretty **train station** and the **Lam Dong Museum** are just to the east.

Flower gardens

Tran Nhan Tong • Daily 7.30am–5pm • 15,000đ

Near the lake's northern end are Da Lat's **flower gardens**, inside which paths lead you past hydrangeas, roses, orchids, poinsettia, topiary and a nursery. There's nothing outstanding on display here, but on weekends the place is packed with Vietnamese taking photos of each other posing in front of the flowerbeds.

Ga Da Lat

Off Quang Trung

East of Lake Xuan Hong, **Ga Da Lat**, the city's train station, dates to 1938 and is a real time capsule. Below its gently contoured red-tiled roof and behind the multicoloured Art Deco windows striping its front facade, its ticket booths are reminiscent of a provincial French station. Outside, the rail yard is in a charming state of dilapidation, with cattle grazing on the grass and flowers that grow among its tracks and ancient locomotives; one has been turned into a neat little café of sorts.

Trains ran on the rack railway linking Da Lat to Thap Cham (see p.215) and beyond from 1933 until the mid-Sixties, when Viet Cong attacks became too persistent a threat for them to continue. Nowadays, the only services are those heading 7km across horticultural land and market gardens to the village of **Trai Mat**, a few kilometres away (see p.185).

Lam Dong Museum

4 Hung Vuong • Mon–Sat 7.30–11.30am & 1.30–4.30pm • 4000đ

Set on a hill beyond the eastern end of Tran Hung Dao, the **Lam Dong Museum** is the best in the central highlands; the displays are thoughtfully laid out and provide a tantalizing taste of the region's rich history. Exhibits include Cham artefacts from recent archeological digs as well as a collection of rice jars, ceramics and jewellery found in tombs, and some vicious-looking spears. The museum also gives a thorough introduction to the lifestyles of the local minority groups such as the Ma, Koho and Churu, along with a map showing their distribution in the province and many of their handicrafts and household implements. There's also a display covering the French and American Wars, though it is little different to similar displays around the rest of the country.

Dalat Palace Hotel

12 Tran Phu • ☎ 0633 825444 • ⓦ dalatpalace.vn

Running west to east just south of the city centre, **Tran Phu** cradles two of the city's most memorable French-era buildings. One is the splendidly restored 1920s **Dalat Palace Hotel**, the social heart of colonial-era Da Lat. Still a great place to stay (see p.181), it has

3

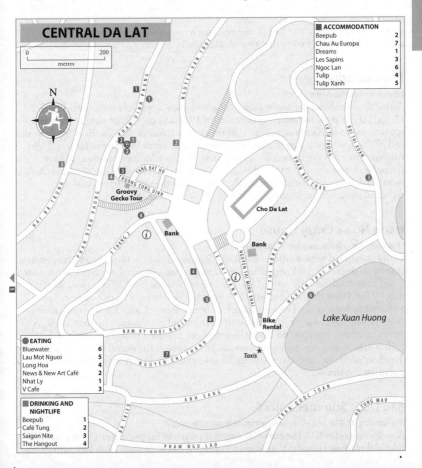

CENTRAL DA LAT

0   200
metres

N

▮ ACCOMMODATION	
Beepub	2
Chau Au Europa	7
Dreams	1
Les Sapins	3
Ngoc Lan	6
Tulip	4
Tulip Xanh	5

Groovy
Gecko Tour

Cho Da Lat

ⓘ Bank

Bank

Bike
Rental

Lake Xuan Huong

Taxis

● EATING	
Bluewater	6
Lau Mot Nguoi	5
Long Hoa	4
News & New Art Café	2
Nhat Ly	1
V Cafe	3

▮ DRINKING AND NIGHTLIFE	
Beepub	1
Café Tung	2
Saigon Nite	3
The Hangout	4

COUNTRYSIDE DETOURS

From central Da Lat, two roads wiggle south, offering pleasant detours out into the countryside – taking one, or both, of the bike rides outlined below will put a little definition on your calves.

The larger of the two roads is **Khe Sanh**, which branches south off Tran Hung Dao opposite Pham Hong Thai, and further south leads back to Highway 20. The first thing of note you'll come to is **Thien Vuong Pagoda**, remarkable for its trio of four-metre-tall sandalwood statues (Sakyamuni, in the centre, rubs shoulders with the Goddess of Mercy and the God of Power), imported from Hong Kong in 1958, and for the huge **statue of Buddha** seated on a lotus, 100m up the hill above the pagoda. Stalls in front of Thien Vuong hawk the usual candied strawberries, artichoke tea and *cu ly* to the Vietnamese tourists who flock here, many of whom are young girls who come from all over Vietnam to pray for good fortune and a successful marriage.

Running parallel to Khe Sanh to the east, though sadly not linked in any easily navigable way, **Hoang Hoa Tham** leads to colourful **Linh Phong Pagoda**, which is fronted by a gateway bearing a fierce, panting dragon face with protruding eyes. Behind its gaudy yellow doors, the pagoda exudes a peaceful aura. Its resident nuns are very friendly and the remote location affords peerless views of the cultivated and wooded valley below.

great views of Lake Xuan Huong, and enjoying a long, cool drink overlooking its manicured lawns is a luxury that's worth the expense.

The cathedral

Tran Phu • Sunrise to sunset • Free

Across the road from the *Dalat Palace Hotel* and a few steps west along Tran Phu, Da Lat's dusty pink **cathedral**, consecrated in 1931 and completed eleven years later, is dedicated to St Nicholas, protector of the poor; a statue of him stands at the opposite end of the nave to the simple altar, with three tiny children loitering at his feet. Light streaming in from the cathedral's seventy stained-glass windows, mostly crafted in Grenoble, teases a warm, sunny glow from the mellow pink of the interior walls. A tiny metal cockerel perched almost invisibly at the top of the steeple has earned the cathedral its rather unglamorous moniker, "Chicken Church".

Hang Nga's Crazy House

3 Huynh Thuc Khang • Daily 8.30am–7pm • 40,000đ • ☎ 0633 822070

Easily combined with a visit to Bao Dai's Summer Palace is **Hang Nga's Crazy House**, shaped to resemble the knotted trunks of huge trees and another place that visitors – not to mention the citizens of Da Lat – either love or hate. While most merely pop by for a visit, it also functions as a guesthouse (see p.181); day-visitors are welcome to look around any unoccupied rooms, most of which have entertaining *Alice in Wonderland*-style interiors with mirrors and mushrooms in abundance. A selection of photographs on the walls inside the entrance provide clues as to how such a bizarre construction got planning permission – its owner, Hang Nga, is the daughter of former president Truong Chinh, and therefore is above the usual planning constraints.

Bao Dai's Summer Palace

Daily 7am–5pm • 15,000đ • Bear left onto Le Hong Phong 500m west of the cathedral

Also known as **Dinh III**, the erstwhile summer palace of Emperor Bao Dai is a suitably splendid place to visit. Built between 1933 and 1938, it provided Bao Dai with a bolt hole between elephant-slaughtering sessions. The building is palatial, though not in a traditional style – Art Deco would be a better description. Etched with stark white grouting, its mustard-coloured bulk is set amid rose and pine **gardens**. Nautical portholes punched into its walls give it the distinct look of a ship's bridge, as does the mast-like pole sprouting from its roof. The place is surrounded by the usual attractions – pony rides and dressing up in minority costume – and the exit forces you to pass through a gauntlet of souvenir stalls.

Downstairs

Past the two large blue metal lanterns flanking the front entrance (where you'll have to don shoe covers which make it quite tempting to skate your way around the building's polished floors), the first room to your right is Bao Dai's **working room**, dominated by a bust of the man himself, and home both to the Imperial motorbike helmet, and to a small book collection. Buffalo horns in the **reception room** come from animals bagged by Bao Dai himself on one of his hunting forays into the forests around Da Lat. His queen preferred more sedate pastimes, and would have tinkled on the piano here. The palace's most elegant common room is its **festivities room** or dining room, though catching a whiff of furniture polish in this dark, echoing chamber, it's hard to imagine the royal revelries that once went on here.

Upstairs

Royal ghosts are far easier to summon upstairs, where the musty **Imperial bedrooms** seem just to have had the dustsheets whipped back for another royal season. Princes and princesses all had their quarters, as did the queen, whose chamber features a chaise longue that looks unnervingly like a dentist's chair. But the finest room, predictably enough, went to Bao Dai, who enjoyed the luxury of a balcony for his "breeze-getting and his moon-watching". Out on the landing, look out for a bizarre mini-sauna, labelled a *Rouathermique*.

| ARRIVAL AND DEPARTURE | DA LAT AND AROUND |

By plane Lien Khuong Airport (❶0633 843373) is 29km from town south of the city, off the road to Ho Chi Minh City. Vietnam Airlines buses meet each flight (40,000đ), or you can hop in a taxi for 450,000đ or so. If you'd like to use the buses to head back to the airport, ask at your accommodation – staff may be able to organize a free pick-up. Otherwise, buses depart 2hr before flights from outside the *Ngoc Phat* hotel, south of the lake. The main Vietnam Airlines Booking Office is at 2 Ho Tung Mau (daily 7.30–11.30am & 1–4.30pm; ❶0633 833499).
Destinations Da Nang (1 daily; 1hr 20min); Hanoi (2–3 daily; 1hr 40min); Ho Chi Minh City (3 daily; 50min).
By train The only services from Da Lat station, which

constitutes a sight in itself (see p.176), are the irregular ones to Trai Mat village (5 daily; 40min). Although there is a schedule in place, in practice trains are very unlikely to run with fewer than fifteen passengers.
By bus Buses from Ho Chi Minh City, Nha Trang and elsewhere arrive at Da Lat bus station, located about 1km south of the city centre on 3 Thang 4. Most of the reliable open-tour operators run shuttle services into town; failing that, it's a short xe om or taxi ride, and also within walking distance. Regular travellers rate *Sinh Café* buses the best to and from Ho Chi Minh City, and Orange Bus to and from Nha Trang.
Destinations Buon Ma Thuot (4hr); Da Nang (16hr); Ho Chi Minh City (7hr); Nha Trang (4hr); Phan Rang (3hr).

GETTING AROUND

Da Lat is too hilly for cyclo, and the horse-drawn carts that were once one of the city's more attractive features are pretty much a thing of the past (apart from trots around the lake in high season), so for journeys of any distance you'll have to rely on xe om and taxis.

By bicycle or motorbike If you're fit, you might consider renting a bicycle or tandem (about 60,000đ a day), though with all the steep hills, a motorbike makes more sense (from 120,000đ a day); both are available

from hotels and tour operators.
By car Renting a car and driver for the day (also easily arranged through hotels or tour operators) costs around $50.

3

EASY RIDERS

Those travelling through central Vietnam will surely, at some stage, hear references to the famed **Easy Riders**. Though the term is now used to describe pretty much any motorbike driver willing to go beyond day-trip distance, the concept started life in Da Lat; the success of the initial Easy Riders group (ⓦ vietnam-motorcycle-easyriders.com) spawned a glut of copycat operators (this is Vietnam, after all), many of which now go under totally different names. The "real" ones rarely disappoint, though some copycat operators are just as good – ask travellers for untainted on-the-ground advice.

The machinations of Vietnamese tour operations mean that it's hard to give any cast-iron recommendations. However, the best place to go shopping for a budding Vietnamese Dennis Hopper is the bottom end of **Truong Cong Dinh**, where several competing outfits vie for your affections. Most are able to produce telephone directory-size books filled with glowing recommendations, but copying is rife and these are to be taken with a pinch of salt.

Prices range from around $15 a day for a tour of the main sights in the city to around $75 a day for a longer trip, usually including accommodation and entrance fees to sights; feel free to suggest your own itinerary. The standards and prices of local operators change like the wind; however, there is a simple trick for those planning to go on a long tour – go on a short one first. Spending a day, or even a half-day, with your prospective driver will give you a good indication of what they'll be like on a week-long trip.

INFORMATION

Tourist information The handful of tourist offices in Da Lat can all arrange guides, bus tickets, car hire and tours; the main one is Da Lat Travel Services, though *Sinh Café*; TM Brothers has offices here too. If you plan to go trekking to minority villages, you may need to get a permit from the police and be accompanied by a certified guide. You can skirt around the red tape by signing up for a tour of one or several days with one of Da Lat's adventure sports operators which also offer mountain-biking, rock-climbing and abseiling outings. Phat Tire Ventures is a reliable outfit (see box, p.184).

ACCOMMODATION

Enduringly popular with both Western and domestic tourists, Da Lat has a wide range of **places to stay**, from cheap, windowless rooms to luxury, international-standard hotels. However, if your visit coincides with a **public holiday**, especially Tet, be warned that prices increase by up to fifty percent, and you'll need either to arrive early or **book ahead**. The densest concentrations of budget hotels lie on Phan Dinh Phung; ask for a room at the back, as the main road can be noisy. Several upmarket hotels operate downtown, but there are many more out in the open spaces south and west of the city centre. Check that prices include hot water – a luxury in much of southern Vietnam, but a necessity in Da Lat. Air-conditioning is neither necessary nor usually provided.

CENTRAL DA LAT

Beepub 74 Truong Cong Dinh ☎ 0633 825576, ⓔ quang_vohoang@yahoo.com; map p.177. Staying at a bar may not seem like such a great idea, but the rooms are upstairs away from the noise, and they're surprisingly attractive. Rooms $15, dorms $5

Chau Au Europa 76 Nguyen Chi Thanh ☎ 0633 822870, ⓔ europa@hcm.vnn.vn; map p.177. Professionally run place with a range of rooms. All are dazzlingly clean with homely touches – an extra $5 secures a front room with view. Staff are extremely helpful and there's free internet and wi-fi. $15

★ **Dreams** 151 Phan Dinh Phung ☎ 0633 833748, ⓦ dreamshoteldalat.com; map p.177. The default accommodation setting for Da Lat's budget travellers – you're advised to book at least a couple of days ahead. Its good reputation is well deserved, with helpful and highly friendly staff, clean rooms with modern bathrooms,

free use of the jacuzzi and sauna upstairs and unbeatable fresh passion fruit juice at breakfast. They have two similar locations on the same road; the newest one is a little pricier, but features splendid rooms. $25

Les Sapins 60 Truong Cong Dinh ☎ 0633 830839, ⓦ lessapins60dalathotel.com; map p.177. Accessed through an attached ground-floor café, this is a small and relatively new place with English-speaking staff and cute rooms, some of which have little balconies. A good option if you want to be close to the action, but far away from it at the same time. $12

Ngoc Lan 42 Nguyen Chi Thanh ☎ 0633 822136, ⓦ ngoclanhotel.vn; map p.177. Spacious, well-equipped rooms with good views over the lake at this four-star hotel, where rooms and common areas alike have been plastered with pleasant purples and mauves. It's a bit overpriced, but facilities are excellent; in addition, the ground-floor restaurant is a good place to eat whether you're staying here or not. $85

★**Tulip** 14 Nguyen Chi Thanh ☎ 0633 510991, ⊛ tulip hoteldalat.com; map p.177. A nice new option with partial lake views and well-appointed rooms that provide excellent value for money. Staff speak little English but are willing to please and keep the place spick and span. $\overline{\$28}$

★**Tulip Xanh** 80–81 Hai Thuong ☎ 0633 903815, ✉ tulipxanhdalat.hotel@gmail.com; map p.177. Not to be confused with its near namesake, this has become hugely popular with the city's backpackers. Some rooms have been very nicely decorated for the price; one slight negative is that it's a bit of an uphill slog from the centre. Rooms $\overline{\$14}$, dorms $\overline{\$5}$

OUTER DA LAT

Ana Mandara Villas Le Lai ☎ 0633 555888, ⊛ anamandara-resort.com; map p.175. This new complex of luxury villas is located in spacious grounds just outside the city centre. While boasting every conceivable comfort inside, the complex is in a humble village area, offering a good opportunity to connect with local society. $\overline{\$240}$

Backpackers Paradise 58 Hoang Van Thu ☎ 0633 556179, ✉ backpackersdalat@gmail.com; map p.175. Though a little hard to find, it's worth hunting down this hostel south of the centre; dorms are slightly cramped, but the private rooms are a steal, many of them coming with little tellies. Rooms $\overline{\$10}$, dorms $\overline{\$5}$

Crazy House 3 Huynh Thuc Khang ☎ 0633 822070; map p.175. Da Lat's quirkiest sight is also its quirkiest place to stay. Rooms are small for the price, and it's worth noting that you'll have tourists crawling around from 7am to 7pm, but it's not too much of a problem if you plan the day accordingly. $\overline{\$25}$

★**Dalat Du Parc** 7 Tran Phu ☎ 063? duparc.vn; map p.175. A sympathetica edifice that makes the ideal place to stay stretch to a room at the nearby Dalat creaks up to pleasant, well-ventilated rooms with elega... interiors and polished wooden floors. Outside peak season it's possible to get some superb deals via their website. $\overline{\$57}$

★**Dalat Palace Hotel** 12 Tran Phu ☎ 0633 825444, ⊛ dalatpalace.vn; map p.175. Da Lat's most magnificent colonial pile sits in manicured grounds, still radiating its 1920s splendour. All rooms are lavishly appointed and decked out with period furnishings, including clunky telephones and massive bathtubs. Gorgeous, but it often feels a little empty. Book online for the best deals. $\overline{\$210}$

Dinh II 12 Tran Hung Dao ☎ 0633 822092; map p.175. If you fancy living like a colonial but can't afford the rates at the Dalat Palace or Ana Mandara, then this place, also known as the Palace 2, is your spot. The huge rooms in the main house, once home to the French governor, are beautifully furnished and the complex is surrounded by pines. $\overline{\$35}$

★**Happy Hostel** 5/3 Ba Trieu ☎ 0987 639053, ✉ happyhosteldalat@gmail.com; map p.175. Hostel which functions almost like a family home; it's certainly friendly enough to be one. Many of the dorm rooms feature double beds, and some only have room for three guests – plenty of room, in other words. Also very good at arranging tours and giving general travel advice. Rooms $\overline{\$10}$, dorms $\overline{\$5}$

Saigon Dalat 2 Hoang Van Thu ☎ 0633 556789, ⊛ saigondalathotel.com; map p.175. This new four-star hotel makes a reasonable attempt at capturing a bygone era with its traditional furnishings, though it includes modern touches like flat-screen TVs. You're likely to pay just over half the advertised rates. $\overline{\$125}$

EATING

Da Lat has abundant food stalls and a broad range of restaurants serving Vietnamese, Chinese and international cuisines. Head to the **central market** for pho, com and the like, as well as one or two vegetarian stalls, signed as com chay; you can even buy picnic provisions of bread, cheese and cake at the market too, complemented by fresh local berries. Note that you'll also see a fair few places serving bun bo and other types of Hue cuisine – apparently, sixty percent of Da Lat's current population can trace their origins back to Hue.

Bluewater 2 Nguyen Thai Hoc ☎ 0633 531668; map p.177. Also known as Thanh Thuy, this is an attractive restaurant perched over the lake; considering the location, the food is pretty fair on the wallet. The best and most authentic items on the menu are the soups (from 50,000đ), large affairs which are made for sharing; try the chrysanthemum and minced pork one, or the sour and spicy Sichuanese option. Daily 6am–11pm.

★**Café de la Poste** 12 Tran Phu ☎ 0633 825777; map p.175. Modern, French-style café opposite the Dalat Du Parc hotel. Grand colonial in style, it's a tad pricey (buffet breakfast 160,000đ, set lunch or dinner 330,000đ), yet just about worth the splurge for the good croques monsieurs,

pasta and pizza, and Vietnamese fusion dishes (try the trout in ginger and chive sauce, 240,000đ). If your budget allows, it's also a good place for cocktails, and there's a decent wine selection. Daily 5.30am–10pm.

Lau Mot Nguoi 16b Nguyen Chi Thanh ☎ 0633 515989; map p.177. You'll see "Single Hot Pot" on the sign, and that's just what you get (59,000đ) – a real treat if you've turned up in Da Lat of a chilly evening, and especially convenient for solo travellers. They also sell good squid kebabs (25,000đ each) and a small range of other comestibles. Daily 8am–10pm.

Le Rabelais The Dalat Palace Hotel, 7 Tran Phu ☎ 0633 825777, ⊛ dalatpalace.vn; map p.175. This place can be quite a treat, since for much of the day, you'll have it almost

3

rely to yourself. Given the palatial setting, replete with waitresses clad in beautiful *ao dai*, this gives one licence to play emperor or empress over High Tea, served 3–5.30pm (330,000đ). In the evening, mains from the largely French menu usually go for around double that; you could always just pop in for a coffee (80,000đ). Daily 5.30am–9.30pm.

★**Long Hoa** 6, 3 Thang 2 ☎ 0633 822934; map p.177. Great place with French-café ambience, attentive staff, and superbly made Vietnamese dishes. Kick off with a strawberry wine aperitif, while for dessert the home-made yoghurt takes some beating. As for the mains, figure on 80,000đ for veggies or rice dishes, or 120,000đ for meatier options. Daily 11.30am–2.30pm & 5.30–9pm.

News & New Art Café 70 Truong Cong Dinh ☎ 0633 510089; map p.177. Located in the heart of the budget hotel district, this is the better of two similarly named places sitting almost side by side, selling a range of Vietnamese staples (from 75,000đ) and passable coffee (20,000đ); in the evening, order some Dalat wine (20,000đ per glass), or a cocktail (80,000đ). Daily 10am–midnight.

Nhat Ly 88 Phan Dinh Phung ☎ 0633 822773; map p.177. Hugely popular with Vietnamese and foreigners alike for its wide menu of dishes at very reasonable prices (from 50,000đ). Often packed to the gills at mealtimes, but do note that there's an overflow room out back. Daily 9am–9pm.

★**Trong Dong** 220 Phan Dinh Phung ☎ 0633 821889; map p.175. Now under new management, this old favourite has ditched its formerly homely atmosphere for something more polished (bar the tartan-effect tablecloths, which remain in situ). The food's still fantastic, though – try the fried lotus root with minced shrimp and pork (58,000đ), the superb pho (65,000đ), or the more adventurous eel, frog or rabbit highland specialities. Daily 11am–3pm & 5–9pm.

★**V Cafe** 1/1 Bui Thi Xuan ☎ 0633 520215, ☎ vcafe dalatvietnam.com; map p.177. A bit removed from the budget hotel district, but worth tracking down for its cosy atmosphere and good cooking, including some great home-made pies and cakes, at affordable prices. Check out the daily specials, or the spinach cannelloni (115,000đ), breakfast burritos (105,000đ) and green curries (99,000đ) always go down well. There are some good veggie dishes too. Daily 8am–10pm.

DRINKING AND NIGHTLIFE

Da Lat's take on **nightlife** generally means a cup of coffee in one of the city's atmospheric **cafés**; there's not much more to it unless you fancy a game of pool or a dance at one of the hotel discos.

★**Beepub** 74 Truong Cong Dinh ☎ 0633 825576; map p.177. The most happening place in town at the time of writing, regularly packed to the rafters with travellers and young Vietnamese. There's often live music, or the DJs and cheapish beer (30,000đ) will keep people entertained – as might the sign to the toilet (known here as the "beep room"). Daily 6.30am–9.30pm.

Café Tung 6 Khu Hoa Binh ☎ 0633 821390; map p.177. Leather upholstery, dark varnished wood, lemon walls and tabletops, amber lampshades, 1950s French crooners on the sound system and a smiling Mona Lisa on the wall… this is truly a café lost in time. It's perhaps at its most atmospheric in the evening, over a bottle of beer; the only surprise is how few

people seem to have discovered it. Daily 6.30am–9.30pm.

The Hangout 71 Truong Cong Dinh ☎ 099 333 3664; map p.177. Easy Rider-affiliated place aimed at travellers, with a pool table, cheap beer and motorbikes for rent. A good place to take the pulse of Da Lat and make some local friends, though it has to be said that their beer can taste somewhat dodgy. Daily 9am–midnight.

Saigon Nite 11a/1 Hai Ba Trung ☎ 0633 820007; map p.177. Small, homely place that's Da Lat's longest-standing Western-style bar, with pool table, darts and a reasonable selection of CDs. The guest books chronicle a stream of drunk but contented customers; most go for the cheap beer (20,000đ). Daily 3pm–midnight.

SHOPPING

The market, **Cho Da Lat**, stands on top of a hill in the city centre. A charmless reinforced-concrete structure, it nevertheless houses a staggering range of fruit and vegetables. Strawberries, beetroot, fennel, artichokes, avocados, blackberries and cherries grown in the market gardens surrounding the city are all sold here, along with a riot of flowers. Artichoke teabags, with their diuretic properties, make quirky **souvenirs**, and candied Da Lat strawberries are also sold at many stalls. **Montagnards** carrying their chattels in backpacks are a fairly common sight too, especially early in the morning when they come to trade with stallholders.

DIRECTORY

Banks Vietcombank, 6 Nguyen Thi Minh Khai, and Sacom-bank on Hoa Binh Square change cash, and have ATMs.
Hospital Lam Dong Hospital, 4 Pham Ngoc Thach ☎ 0633 834158.

Police 9 Tran Binh Trong ☎ 0633 822032.
Post office 14 Tran Phu (daily 7.30am–5.30pm), with poste restante, IDD, fax and DHL courier services.

3

ACTIVITIES IN AND AROUND DA LAT

There is some spectacular scenery in the vicinity of Da Lat, which lends itself to challenging treks, bike rides and other **adventure activities**.

TOUR OPERATORS

A number of local tour operators can help to organize most of the following activities. Hotel pick-up usually comes as part of the package.

Groovy Gecko 65 Truong Cong Dinh ☎ 0633 836521, ⓦ groovygeckotours.net.

★**Phat Tire Ventures** 109 Nguyen Van Troi ☎ 0633 829422, ⓦ ptv-vietnam.com.

ACTIVITIES

Bike riding There are a number of excellent day- and half-day bike routes around Da Lat. Many head north to Lat Village (see p.186), or south into the countryside (see box, p.178), but it's also possible to organize trips to further-flung locations such as Buon Ma Thuot, Nha Trang or even Hoi An.

Canyoning There's a beautiful canyon fifteen minutes from Da Lat by car; the adventurous climbing course requires ropes and a bit of bravery. Half-day trips are $30-45 per person.

Golf The eighteen-hole course just off central Da Lat (see map, p.175) boasts inspiring views from some tees. Fees start at around $95 per person, including caddy.

Hiking Most local tour operators will be able to organize a guided hike, with everything from half-day to week-long walks and treks; figure on around $30 per person per day. Again, Lat Village and the surrounding area is a popular destination, while the above operators will be able to take you into more uncharted territory.

Tennis Both the *Dalat Palace* and *Dalat Du Parc* have tennis courts, available to guests for free, and non-guests for a small fee.

Whitewater rafting Phat Tire Ventures runs rafting and kayaking trips on routes including rapids of class 2, 3 and 4. Kayaking from $39 per person including hike, rafting from $72 per person.

East of Da Lat

The wide area to the east of Da Lat conceals some appealing sights, including **Dinh I**, one of several Bao Dai palaces in the area; **Tiger Falls**, one of the best of the many cascades surrounding Da Lat; and **Trai Mat Village**, a super little place connected to Da Lat by **vintage trains**. These run both infrequently and irregularly; if you'd like to see all three sights it pays to take the train out to Trai Mat first, then return by xe om or taxi, seeing the falls and palace on the way.

Dinh I

1 Tran Quang Dieu • Daily 7.30–11.30am & 1.30–4.30pm • 5000đ

About 3km east of the train station, a small lane leads south off Hung Vuong to **Dinh I**. A number of its features and 1930s furnishings are very similar to Bao Dai's Summer Palace, Dinh III (see p.178), but if you're prepared to trek out to Dinh I, you'll find better views over the city, a more peaceful setting and fewer visitors. The building was used as Bao Dai's workplace, and the conference room upstairs, with its large map of the country, has a business-like air to it. There are several evocative photos on the walls of the other rooms, including one of Bao Dai in a racing car and another of his concubines. Other points of interest include a doorway to a secret tunnel and an archaic phone switchboard at the entrance to the building.

Tiger Falls

On Trai Mat road • Daily 7.30am–5pm • 10,000đ

Some 4km east of the train station, and located at the end of a precarious switchback road, are the **Tiger Falls**, the most popular cascades in the wider Da Lat area. A steep concrete stairway leads down to the base of the falls, which tumble from a great height and offer good photo opportunities – this makes them a very popular destination for Vietnamese, so you're unlikely to be able to enjoy the place alone. Surrounding the base of the falls is a series of pools and boulders; this makes for an ideal picnicking spot for those who have prepared food in advance, but there's also a simple restaurant catering to those who haven't.

Trai Mat

Train services daily at 7.45am, 9.50am, 11.55am, 2pm, 4.05pm • 45min journey • 124,000đ

The village of **Trai Mat** is just 7km from Da Lat, and ideally placed for a short excursion. Most head there by **train** (see p.179), the line taking you east past some interesting, if not particularly beautiful, countryside. The village itself rewards exploration – Linh Phuoc Pagoda is the main draw, but if you have more time (or are willing to get a xe om back), grab a bite to eat or hunt down the beautiful Cao Dai temple on a rise just east of the village.

Linh Phuoc Pagoda

The highlight of Trai Mat is **Linh Phuoc Pagoda**, an incredibly ornate building which showcases the art of tessellation, whereby small pieces of broken china or glass are painstakingly arranged in cement. The first thing to catch the eye is the huge dragon in the courtyard to the right of the main building, constructed from over twelve thousand carefully broken beer bottles. Artwork inside the pagoda is even more intricate, with mosaic dragons entwined around the main hall's pillars, while stairs lead up on the left to colourfully inlaid galleries, shrines and good views. The deep sound of resonating bells, rung by devotees, makes the main hall very atmospheric.

3

South of Da Lat

There are a few great sights in the area just south of Da Lat, all concentrated around the modest rise of **Robin Hill**. Near the summit you'll find a lake and temple, with the **Datanla Falls** thundering (or trickling, in drier months) off its eastern flank.

Robin Hill and Lake Tuyen Lam

Cable-car rides daily 7.30–11.30am & 1.30–5pm, 70,000đ return • Boat trips 250,000đ for up to five people • Xe om to base of cable car around 25,000đ; also within easy cycling range

As you leave Da Lat to the south on Highway 20, a slip road to the right leads to the top of **Robin Hill**, crowned by a huge **cable-car** terminus and the appealing **Truc Lam Pagoda**. Rides in the cable car offer decent views over the slopes around the city; the twelve-minute trip deposits you near **Lake Tuyen Lam**, a placid and attractive expanse of water on which you can take a boat trip or relax over a coffee.

Datanla Falls

200m east of Lake Tuyen Lam, signposted on the right of the road as "Thac Datanla" • Daily 7am–5pm

The **Datanla Falls** can easily be combined with a visit to nearby Lake Tuyen Tam. In Koho, *datanla* means "water under leaves", and that pretty much sums up the place: from the car park, it's a steep fifteen-minute clamber down to the falls, probing some splendidly lush forest. The falls themselves are not terribly thrilling, their muddy waters cascading onto a plateau spanned by a wooden footbridge that provides a hackneyed photo opportunity.

North of Da Lat

The sights clustered to the north of Da Lat are rather more far-flung than those to the east and south, though it's still quite possible to tackle them all in a half-day – or a full one if you choose to ascend **Lang Bian Mountain**. This rises just beyond **Lat Village**, an appealing place in which to experience a little Montagnard culture; taking a different road north out of Da Lat will soon bring you to the **Valley of Love**, a beautiful, if somewhat schmaltzy, place popular with local tourists.

The Valley of Love

5km north of Da Lat • Daily 7am–5pm • 20,000đ

Thung Lung Tinh Yeu, or the **Valley of Love**, was a hunting spot for Bao Dai and his courtiers in the 1950s, before a dam project in 1972 flooded part of the valley and created **Lake Da Thien**. The valley's still waters and wooded hills are actually quite enticing, though the music blasting from souvenir stalls and the buzzing of rented motorboats do not enhance the aura of romance. Kitsch diversions such as pony rides round the lake escorted by a cowboy are also on offer, while just outside the complex there's a small crazy golf course – pretty awful, but an amusing diversion.

Lat Village

14km north of Da Lat along Xo Viet Nghe Tinh • Cycle, or take one of the hourly green buses heading up Phan Dinh Phung in Da Lat (2000đ)

Until recently, a trip up to **Lat Village** was almost de rigeur with backpacker visitors to Da Lat, but it now receives plenty of small tour groups and has been slightly over-gentrified. Still, it remains a worthwhile excursion for those interesting in seeing minority life. The village's thatch-roofed bamboo stilthouses are occupied by Chill and Ma, but mostly Lat, groups of Koho peoples eking out a living growing rice, pulses and vegetables. The various paths running through the village are easy to follow so a guide is not essential, though one can be easily arranged through any of Da Lat's tour operators.

Lang Bian Mountain

From Lat Village, you'll see the peak (2169m) of **Lang Bian Mountain** looming above you to the north. It's a 4hr ascent on foot, though by car you can drive up to the canopy of pines on the lower peak. Inevitably, a corny legend has been concocted to explain the mountain's formation. The story tells of two ill-starred lovers, a Lat man called Lang and a Chill girl named Bian, who were unable to marry because of tribal enmity. Broken-hearted, Bian passed away, and the peaks of Lang Bian are said to represent her breast heaving its dying breath. Bian's death seems not to have been wholly in vain: so racked with guilt was her father, that he called a halt to tribal unrest by unifying all of the local factions into the Koho.

Lak Lake

Gong performances $100 per group • Canoe rides $20

A hundred and fifty kilometres northwest of Da Lat and 40km south of Buon Ma Thuot, Highway 27 passes serene **LAK LAKE**, a charming spot that has become very popular with tourists. Five thousand people, mostly from the Mnong community, once lived on the lake itself, but have since moved into distinctive longhouses in shoreside villages. There are a number of (slightly cheesy) activities available here, including musical gong performances and elephant rides; note that the latter are not recommended, since you'll be sitting atop a metal cage that's doubtless extremely painful for the poor pachyderm. Still, the lake itself is a glorious place, as once attested by Emperor Bao Dai himself – he grabbed some of the best sites in southern Vietnam for his many palaces, so it comes as no surprise to learn that he had one here, in a prime spot on a small hill overlooking the lake. The palace is long gone, but the site is now home to a small hotel (see opposite).

Jun Village

Southern side of lake, just off main road

If you're intent on getting the whole minority village experience, complete with grunting pigs and squawking chickens waking you in the morning, head on round to **Jun Village**, a thriving Mnong community on the west side of the hill, whose longhouses crowd together near the shore – to say hello in their local tongue, use

kuro-me to men and *kuro-e* to women. Dak Lak Tourist (see below) has a
here, and a longhouse where it's possible to stay overnight.

ARRIVAL AND INFORMATION

By bus Although Lak Lake is mostly geared towards organized tour groups, it's possible to arrive here independently on the local buses heading between Da Lat (3hr 30min–4hr) and Buon Ma Thuot (1hr 30min–2hr). Unfortunately, it's not easy to arrange onward transport to Da Lat from Lak Lake – or even to pick it up, if you've purchased a ticket in advance. To B different story, for there are local buses linking it with the lake approximately once per hour (see p.189). All buses set down and pick up at Jun Village, to the south of the lake.
Information For bookings and enquiries, contact Dak Lak Tourist Office (☎ 0500 3852246, ⊚ daklaktourist.com.vn).

ACCOMMODATION

Staff at the following will likely speak little English, but you'll be able to book through Dak Lak tourist office (see above), which operates both of the following establishments and organizes the village stays too.

★**Bao Dai Residence** On a rise off the southeastern shore of the lake ☎ 0500 358 6184. The walls of Bao Dai's old palace boasts some intriguing snaps of Vietnam's last emperor and a few well-appointed rooms whose large windows afford fabulous views over the lake. With a decent restaurant too, it's far and away the best place to stay hereabouts. $35
Jun Village To the south of the lake ☎ 0500 385 2246. Accommodation is available at just over a dozen long-houses in Jun Village itself; arrange things through Dak Lak Tourist Office (see above). Mosquito nets and mattresses are provided in the longhouses themselves, and there are outside toilet facilities. Note that you're likely to be woken up early by village activity. $9
Lak Resort To the east of the lake ☎ 0500 358 6184. Snuggled into a protected bay to the east of the hill, this resort consists of both smart, brick bungalows with a/c, TV and fridge in the rooms, and two longhouses beneath a grove of trees. Staff in traditional Mnong dress dish up reasonable food at the floating restaurant. Rooms $35, longhouse bed $5

Buon Ma Thuot and around

To a Vietnamese, **BUON MA THUOT** means only one thing: **coffee**. Vietnam is the world's second-largest producer of the bean, and this is where most of its best stuff is grown. Such is the profusion of cafés here that the place simply has to be near the top of the world's caffeine-consumed-per-person charts; though no venues are particularly memorable, it would be a pity to leave town without sampling some of its most famous product for yourself.

All this said, and despite the highland location, first impressions of Buon Ma Thuot are unlikely to be all that favourable – its sprawl of modern buildings are splayed across a grid of grubby, characterless streets, and there's little to keep you occupied in the way of attractions. However, a range of good accommodation means that, if you're on your way through the highlands, this is a logical place to hunker down for a day or two; some end up developing an affinity for the place, and staying longer than they'd intended.

However, the main draw of Buon Ma Thuot is what can be found in its environs: nearby minority villages with **longhouses**; traditional minority communities (mostly E De people) at **Ako Dhong** on the northern outskirts of town and in the surrounding countryside at **Ban Don** near **Yok Don National Park**; and some wonderful waterfalls. Between April and July you'll see the city surrounded by millions of lemon-coloured butterflies, wafting through the air like yellow petals.

Brief history

During French colonial times, Buon Ma Thuot developed on the back of the coffee, tea, rubber and hardwood crops that grew in its fertile red soil, and was the focal point for the **plantations** that smothered the surrounding countryside: plantation owners and other *colons* would amuse themselves by picking off the elephants, leopards and tigers once prevalent in the area. In later years Americans superseded the French, but they were long e by the time the North Vietnamese Army (NVA) swept through in March 1975, making Buon Ma Thuot the first "domino" to fall in the Ho Chi Minh Campaign. These days, the town is surprisingly affluent with a spate of buildings under construction and flash cars buzzing around its streets. In a neat reversal of the norm, urban renewal is occurring from the outside in, and the centre is still appealingly grubby.

Khai Doan Pagoda

89a Phan Boi Chau • Sunrise to sunset • Free

One of central Buon Ma Thuot's few sights is the **Khai Doan Pagoda**, built in 1951 to honour Emperor Khai Dinh's wife, Hoang Thi Cuc, who was also mother of the last emperor, Bao Dai. Unfortunately, the complex was undergoing substantial renovation at the time of writing, and even local monks were unsure of what would remain of its interesting fusion of E De longhouse and Hue Imperial architecture – early indications were that brick and cement would prevail.

3

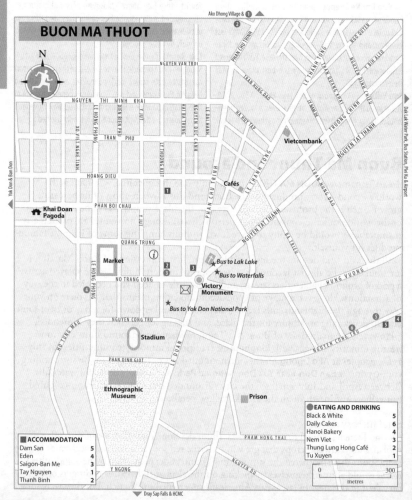

BUON MA THUOT

ACCOMMODATION
Dam San	5
Eden	4
Saigon-Ban Me	3
Tay Nguyen	1
Thanh Binh	2

EATING AND DRINKING
Black & White	5
Daily Cakes	6
Hanoi Bakery	4
Nem Viet	3
Thung Lung Hong Café	2
Tu Xuyen	1

Ethnographic Museum

Le Duan • Daily 8am–4pm • 20,000đ

To find out more about the cultures of the local minority groups, head to the **Ethnographic Museum**, set in a large and intriguingly designed building to the south of the centre – a bizarre fusion of tribal and contemporary styles, though one that looks more and more sloppy and concrete-rich the closer you approach.

The interior is split into three sections – people, biodiversity and history. The latter focuses more on modern times, its main angle being the local people's (apparent) dedication to the cause. The biodiversity section features a miniature zoo's worth of stuffed animals, the regular run-down of local wood and rock samples, and a rather pathetic coffee display. The ethnographic section is far more diverting, with mock-up miniature longhouses, and examples of tribal baskets, clothing and ornaments. Keep your eyes peeled for a waistcoat made of bark, funerary statues of peacocks and tusks, and vicious mahouts' spikes and thorny harnesses – both instruments for taming elephants.

Ako Dhong

About 2km from the city centre, and best approached by xe om. Otherwise, follow Phan Chu Trinh towards the northeast, then turn left on Tran Nhat Duat

On the town's northern fringes is the tidy E De weaving village of **Ako Dhong**. Don't come expecting any real insights into tribal culture – the sturdy longhouses have clean-swept yards and trim hedges, giving the feel of an affluent suburb. However, it's an absorbing place in its own way – the tantalizing aroma of roasting coffee beans often fills the air, and the gentle clack-clack emanating from the buildings signals the weavers at work. It's quite alright to poke your head into a couple of the buildings hereabouts, though since they're people's homes, do so with care.

Dak Lak Water Park

Nguyen Chi Thanh, 4km northeast of centre • Daily 8am–5.30pm • 40,000đ • ☎ 0500 3950381

If you're in need of cooling down, head for the pools and water flumes of **Dak Lak Water Park**, which can come as a blessed relief on one of Buon Ma Thuot's many scorching summer days. The complex is rather smaller than similar facilities in other countries, and centred on an artificial mountain, from which the slides race down: it is best to come during the week when it is less busy.

ARRIVAL AND DEPARTURE   BUON MA THUOT AND AROUND

By plane The airport is 8km east of town on the road towards Da Lat; a taxi into town costs around 120,000đ. Vietnam Airlines (☎ 0500 3954442) is at 19 Ama Thanh Long.
Destinations Da Nang (1 daily; 1hr 10min); Hanoi (2 daily; 1hr 40min); Ho Chi Minh City (5–6 daily; 1hr).
By bus The bus station (☎ 0500 387 6833) is 3km northeast of town on Nguyen Tat Thanh; several a/c express services

arrive daily from Nha Trang and Ho Chi Minh City, but in the direction of Pleiku there's little bar crowded minibuses. Some companies offer free hotel pick-up; it's certainly worth enquiring about this at your accommodation, since it would save you the long trek out to the station.
Destinations Da Nang (12hr); Ho Chi Minh City (7–8hr); Nha Trang (4hr); Pleiku (5hr).

INFORMATION

Tourist information The Dak Lak Tourist Office is at 53 Ly Thuong Kiet (☎ 0500 385 2246, ⌨ daklaktourist.com.vn), and staff can arrange car rental, guides, visa extensions and tours. You'll also need to check here before visiting surrounding

villages: although the situation in Dak Lak Province is fairly relaxed, some villages – particularly those near the Cambodian border – are still theoretically off limits, while others are not permitted to house foreign guests overnight.

ACCOMMODATION

There are plenty of places to **stay** in Buon Ma Thuot, catering for most budgets, though few of them have much character. Most of the cheaper options are clustered along Ly Thuong Kiet, while mid-range hotels are scattered around town.

3

★**Dam San** 212–214 Nguyen Cong Tru ☎0500 385 1234, ⊛www.damsanhotel.com.vn. A good-value place to stay, about 1km from the centre, which is no bad thing. Its smart rooms are furnished with tasteful local textiles and most have lovely views across a lush hillside. There's also a pool and tennis courts. **$38**

Eden 228 Nguyen Cong Tru ☎0500 384 0055, ⊛eden hotelbmt.com.vn. The default Easy Rider base at the time of writing (see box, p.180), and as such quite a hub of activity when there are a few such travellers in town – the small table outside often finds itself groaning under the weight of umpteen bottles of Saigon. Rooms are merely okay, but the good service, quiet location and friend-making potential are plus points. **$17**

Saigon-Ban Me 30 Nguyen Chi Thanh ☎0500 368 5666, ⊛saigonbanmehotel.com.vn. The most salub-rious place to stay in the city, and with a wonderfully central location to boot. Lifts whisk guests up from the neat lobby to even neater rooms, while elsewhere on the complex you'll find a decent restaurant, a fitness centre and a sauna. **$85**

Tay Nguyen 110 Ly Thuong Kiet ☎0500 385 1009. Located near the town centre, this place has a range of ageing but functional rooms; mercifully, this L-shaped building is set back from the road and therefore quieter than much of the competition. **$20**

Thanh Binh 24 Ly Thuong Kiet ☎0500 385 3812. Pretty much the only hostel in the Central Highlands, with extremely cheap dorm rooms that, incredibly, aren't all that bad. The private rooms are more or less the same thing (spartan, acceptably clean) with fewer beds, though do try to nab one with a window if at all possible. Dorms **$3**, private rooms **$11**

EATING AND DRINKING

Dining in Buon Ma Thuot is unlikely to get the pulse racing, though there are a few quirky options here and there. For budget evening fare, try the stalls on Y Jut and surrounding roads. More importantly, it would also be a crime to visit the heart of Vietnam's **coffee industry** without tasting the product itself, and there are plenty of opportunities in the city's cafés; they're scattered all over town, but there's a particular concentration along the south end of Le Thanh Tong, known to locals as "Coffee Street".

Black & White 171 Nguyen Cong Tru ☎0500 385 6275. One of the sharpest-looking cafés in town, its interior decorated along the monochrome lines hinted at by the name. However, the prices are pleasingly normal consider-ing the arty ambience – a coffee should set you back around 12,000đ. The fact that the art on display is local, yet almost entirely devoid of predictable "ethnic" motifs, is another plus. Daily 8am–9pm.

Daily Cakes 137 Nguyen Cong Tru ☎0500 629 1959. There's no shame in admitting that the words "pizza" and "pasta" carry more resonance in a place as remote as Buon Ma Thuot – all the more reason to head to this little hole-in-the-wall restaurant, which doles out pizzas ranging in size from tiny (25,000đ) to fairly large (90,000đ), as well as simple spaghetti meals (30,000đ or so). Daily 8am–10pm.

Hanoi Bakery 123–127 Le Hong Phong ☎0913 436277. Large, well-stocked bakery, which can provide all your picnic, or ad-hoc breakfasting, needs. Daily 6.30am–8pm.

Nem Viet 14–16 Ly Thuong Kiet ☎0500 381 8464. The best of the many *nem* (spring roll) joints lined up along this road – or at least the most hygienic. Their tasty *nem* go for around 35,000đ a portion; you'll get cuts of meat, tons of greens, plenty of sauce and circles of rice paper to roll the lot up in, and the end result is absolutely delicious. Daily 8am–10pm.

★**Thung Lung Hong Café** 153 Phan Chu Trinh ☎0500 386 5221. Snuggled at the base of a steep valley at the end of a sidestreet off Phan Chu Trinh, this oddball café is hugely popular among locals and, given the dearth of nightlife in Buon Ma Thuot, a godsend for visitors too – come for a drink under a constellation of neon and twinkly LED lights. Daily 8am–9.30pm.

★**Tu Xuyen** 245 Phan Chu Trinh, just off junction with Nguyen Dinh Chieu ☎0500 395 3799. Locals love this modest-looking goat hotpot venue, and though a little far from the centre, it's well worth the walk or a short xe om ride. Try the curried variety – a little boiling bowl of goodness for just 110,000đ. Daily 8am–10pm.

ELEPHANT RACE FESTIVAL

If you're in Buon ma Thuot in spring, don't miss the **Elephant Race Festival**, which takes place on the banks of the Serepok River near Ban Don. It's usually held in the third lunar month but preparations take place for weeks beforehand – those who own elephants in the area spend time fattening up their beasts on local fruit and crops. The race itself is usually brief but blazing, the elephants encouraged (or distracted) by the loud drumming of gongs. Ask at Dak Lak Tourist for dates and details.

DIRECTORY

Banks Vietcombank, 6 Tran Hung Dao, changes foreign currency and has an ATM – there are many more around the town centre.

Post office The post office (daily 7am–8.30pm) is on Le Duan, just south of Victory Monument; it also offers Internet access.

Waterfalls around Buon Ma Thuot

Several **waterfalls** near Buon Ma Thuot Thuot are worth visiting, especially in the wet season, though unless you're a real falls fan you can be selective. **Dray Sap** and **Dray Nur**, situated side by side, are the most impressive and most popular.

Trinh Nu Falls

Daily 8am–6pm • 30,000đ

Comprising a narrow chute of water approached by a steep path, these small falls are the first you'll come to when approaching from the city – watch out for a signed left-turn. The boulders lining the river here are highly picturesque, though the area is in the process of turning into a resort of sorts – in fact, it may soon make a more appealing place to stay than central Buon Ma Thuot. At the top of the falls is a restaurant with small, inviting pavilions overlooking the river – a good spot to rest up for refreshment or lunch.

Dray Sap and Dray Nur Falls

8am–6pm • 30,000đ ticket gives access to both falls

The crescent-shaped **Dray Sap** and neighbouring **Dray Nur Falls** are among the most spectacular waterfalls in the central highlands. After a short descent down steps from the car park, a wooden **suspension bridge** to the left leads to Dray Nur, which, though not as wide as Dray Sap, carry more water in the dry season; even at such times, it's quite a spectacle to watch the mist swirling around and beneath the ledge-like crag that the water topples over. On the other hand, at the end of the wet season, in September, water levels are usually too high for the short walk to the falls to be accessible. Almost 15m high and over 100m wide, Dray Sap doesn't mean "waterfall of smoke" for nothing: a fug of invigorating spray sags the air around. The area round the falls can get very crowded at weekends and on public holidays, but midweek a trip here makes a pleasant outing for a half or full day.

ARRIVAL AND DEPARTURE   WATERFALLS AROUND BUON MA THUOT

The falls are around 25km southwest of Buon Ma Thuot; follow Highway 14 for 20km southwest of town, then turn left at the village of Ea Ting. Just 1km down this road, a left turn leads to Trinh Nu Falls; Dray Sap and Dray Nur are a further 9km along.

By bus The falls are accessible on the hourly bus #13 (20,000đ), which you can pick up on Phan Chu Trinh (see map, p.188).
By tour Most people go as part of a tour, which is certainly the easiest option; Dak Lak Tourism (see p.189) offers good

day-long packages including the falls, Yok Don National Park (see below) and Lak Lake (see p.186) for 580,000đ per person.
By bike You can rent a motorbike from most hotels; figure on around 200,000-250,000đ for a half-day.

Yok Don National Park

Vietnam's largest wildlife preserve, **Yok Don National Park**, covers over a thousand square kilometres of land between the hinge of the Cambodian border and the **Serepok River**, about 45km from Buon Ma Thuot. Much of it is comprised of deciduous forest land, though the place can seem surprisingly dry for most of the year. If you start off early in the morning you might see E De and other minority peoples leaving their split-bamboo thatch houses for work in the fields, carrying their tools in raffia backpacks. In addition, over sixty species of animals, including tigers, leopards and bears, and more than 450 types of birds, populate the park; most, however, reside deep in the interior. Of all its wildlife, **elephants** are what Yok Don is best known for;

PARK ACTIVITIES

There are a number of **activities** on offer in Yok Don, an increasingly switched-on national park. Basic **hiking** is the most popular, though you'll need a guide ($40 full-day, $20 half-day); the area in the vicinity of the park office is not terribly interesting, though heading further afield increases the chance of animal sightings considerably. One interesting variation is a night hike ($10; seven-person minimum); at certain times of year, shine a torch into the darkness and you'll see the eyes of thousands and thousands of frogs staring back at you. Crocodile sightings are another exciting possibility. During daylight hours, it's also possible to take a short **boat-ride** along the Serepok ($20 per boat), or have an **elephant trekking tour**; the latter are not recommended owing to the unfriendly metal cages plonked atop the beasts.

the tomb of the greatest elephant hunter of them all – Y Thu Knu (1850–1924), who had a lifetime tally of 244 – is located beyond the final hamlet from the park entrance.

Ban Don

The three sub-hamlets that comprise the village of **BAN DON** lie a few kilometres beyond Yok Don's park HQ, on the bank of the crocodile-infested Serepok River. Khmer, Thai, Lao, Jarai and Mnong live in the vicinity, though it's the **E De** that make up the majority. They adhere to a matriarchal social system, whereby a groom takes his bride's name, lives with her family and, should his wife die subsequently, marries one of her sisters so that her family retains a male workforce. Houses around the village, a few of which are longhouses, are built on stilts, and some are decorated with ornate woodwork.

However, village life in Ban Don has become overwhelmingly commercial as the Ban Don Tourist Centre has organized its residents into a tourist-welcoming taskforce. It's possible to spend the night here, though you'll only truly appreciate Yok Don by heading further into the park; one exception is during March, when the **annual elephant festival** is held (see box, p.190).

ARRIVAL AND DEPARTURE   YOK DON NATIONAL PARK

On a tour Most people visit the park on an organized tour. These can be arranged at Dak Lak Tourism (see p.189), which runs tours from around 320,000đ per person, or more popular ones including the falls near Buon Ma Thuot and Lak Lake (580,000đ).

By bus The hourly public bus #15 (25,000đ) runs from Nguyen Tat Thanh in Buon Ma Thuot (see map, p.188); these usually terminate a few hundred metres from the park entrance. On the occasions that they stop further away, the remaining distance will easily be covered by xe om.

By taxi A taxi from Buon Ma Thuot costs around $60, including 2hr waiting time – this is what drivers expect of local tourists, but negotiate for longer if you'd like to truly make use of the park.

ACCOMMODATION

Park accommodation Overnight accommodation in the park includes the twin-bedded cabin-style rooms in the guesthouse by the park office, a campground, and forest stations in the park. While it's possible to just turn up at the park office, you'll certainly save time by booking through Dak Lak Tourist office (see p.189). Twins **$15**

Pleiku

It has to be said that **PLEIKU**, the capital of Gia Lai province, is the runt of the Central Highland litter. It lacks the majesty of Da Lat, the coffee of Buon Ma Thuot and both the beauty and unhindered minority-visiting of Kon Tum, so only crops up on visitors' agendas if they're heading to or from Laos or Cambodia, or merely in need of a rest in between long bus-rides. The city is not terribly easy on the eye either, having been wrecked during the war (see box opposite); so little was left standing that a near-total reconstruction was required when hostilities ceased – in other words, in the very height of 1980s Soviet design. However, many come to enjoy the city's relatively carefree air, as well as the chance to visit a range of fascinating minority villages in the nearby area. The town itself is slowly being polished too, with the visually pleasing **Minh Thanh Pagoda** a neat recent addition to the city's modest roster of sights.

Ho Chi Minh Museum

1 Phan Dinh Phuong • Mon–Fri 7.30–11am & 1–5pm • Free

The **Ho Chi Minh Museum**, to the north of the town centre, features swords, crossbows, bamboo xylophones, a weaving loom and a pair of Uncle Ho's sandals, but no English signs. Unfortunately, of all the similar museums dotted around the land, few score more highly on the glorifying scale – there's a rather distasteful focus on the local ethnic communities' apparently uncompromising adoration for Uncle Ho.

Gia Lai Museum

Tran Hung Dao • Mon–Fri 7.30–11am & 1–5pm • Free

The **Gia Lai Museum** is, mercifully, a little better than its Ho Chi Minh counterpart. Most of the sparse exhibitions on display in this giant building follow the regular proforma for the museums of Vietnamese provincial capitals – a run-down of local rocks, wood and animals (badly stuffed to an almost comical degree, especially the angry dog), together with some clay and metal fragments. Far more interesting are the Cham reliefs, replicas of a Bahnar grave and longhouse, and displays of minority-group weaving. At the time of writing, the whole complex and its surrounds were being readied for beautification – grass, ponds and the like.

Minh Thanh Temple

Off Nguyen Viet Xuan • Daily sunrise to sunset • Free

The newest attraction in town is probably its best – the surprisingly spectacular **Minh Thanh Temple**, recently erected a couple of kilometres south of the city centre. Though devoid of any real history, and largely made of concrete rather than wood, it may just tempt you into taking a few pictures – try the sinuous dragons growling from each corner of the main hall's roof. From within, sonorous bells and gongs chime a lovely, almost musical sound if there's a slight breeze. The star of show, however, was still under construction at the time of writing – a **nine-tiered pagoda**, resplendent in vermillion and gold. Further down the gentle hillside that the complex calls home, you'll find a few cheery statues, ponds and bridges.

ARRIVAL AND DEPARTURE   **PLEIKU**

By plane The airport (☎0593 825097) lies 7km northeast of the city, from where taxis (about 130,000đ) and xe om (try for 60,000đ) make the journey to the centre; Vietnam Airlines, at 18 Le Lai (Mon–Sat; ☎0593 823058), can

THE ROLLING THUNDER CAMPAIGN

The band of peaks to the west of Highway 14 en route to Pleiku, and the rugged terrain buttressing them, constituted one of the American War's major combat theatres. It was an NVA (North Vietnamese Army) attack on Pleiku, in February 1965, that elicited the "Rolling Thunder" campaign (see p.445); the war's first conventional battle of any size was fought in the **Ia Drang Valley**, southwest of Pleiku, eight months later. Hundreds of Americans died at Ia Drang, but many times more Communists perished, spurring America to claim victory by dint of a higher body count. A decade later, in March 1975, Pleiku was abandoned when NVA troops overran Buon Ma Thuot. As the South's commanding officers flew by helicopter to safety, two hundred thousand Southern soldiers and civilians were left to make their own way down to the coast, hounded at every step by NVA shells.

arrange onward flight reservations.

Destinations Da Nang (daily; 50min); Hanoi (2 daily; 1hr 25min); Ho Chi Minh City (4 daily; 1hr 25min).

By bus The bus station is off Ly Nam De, a short way east of the centre; taxis (55,000đ) and xe om (25,000đ) wait to take

passengers into town. Note that there are daily international services (departing at 7am or 8am) to Attapeu and Pakse in Laos, and Banlung in Cambodia's Rattanakiri province.

Destinations Buon Ma Thuot (4–5hr); Da Nang (10hr); Kon Tum (1hr 30min); Quy Nhon (4hr).

INFORMATION

Tourist office Gia Lai Eco-Tourist (☏0593 760898, ⍟gialaiecotourist.com) has a branch at 82 Hung Vuong, and can provide information as well as arrange expensive, tailor-made trekking, battlefield tours and overnight stays

in minority villages (see below).

Services Vietcombank at 62 Phan Boi Chau can exchange cash, and has an ATM.

ACCOMMODATION

Accommodation in Pleiku is decidedly uninspiring; there's a smattering of near-identical cheap options in the city centre, though almost nothing at the middle or higher end.

★**Duc Long** 117–119 Tran Phu ☏0593 748777. You can't miss the bank-owned tower housing this hotel – it's one of the tallest buildings in Pleiku, or indeed the entire Central Highlands. The rooms, mostly located on the high-teen floors, are both large and of fair quality, and some have good views over the market area. **$20**

★**HAGL Hotel** 1 Phu Dong ☏0593 718450, ⍟hagl .com.vn. By far the most comfortable option around: its rooms are spacious and well equipped with desks and bathtubs, and those on the upper floors have good views across the countryside. Good value, and a nice place to treat yourself if you've been on a central highland slog.

It's about 1km east of the town centre. **$50**

Hung Vuong 2 Le Loi ☏0593 824270. This cheapie is well located in the centre, on the way to the bus station and airport, and isn't such a terrible place to stay either – decent, simple rooms, and a surprisingly attractive on-site branch of *Highland Coffee*. **$10**

Tre Xanh 18 Le Lai ☏0593 715787. A decent choice bordering the mucky grid of streets facing the city market. Rooms are large enough and service attentive, and you can use the on-site travel agency to organize a tour of local minority villages. **$15**

EATING

Acacia Restaurant at the HAGL Hotel ☏0593 718450. A good range of Vietnamese dishes, as well as a few Western ones – spaghetti Bolognese may suddenly seem very tempting to those who've made it as far as Pleiku. Considering the fact that it's in the city's poshest hotel, prices are surprisingly reasonable (you can eat for under 100,000đ), and the service fast. One major downside is that it's a fair walk from the centre. Daily 9am–9pm.

Café Tennis 61 Quang Trang. Reasonable place for a decent coffee. It is, in fact, located next to a tennis court – come at the right time and you may even be able to see a few games. Daily 8am–10pm.

Hu Tieu Nam Vang 69 Tran Phu, ☏0593 822811. Occupying a lime-green, Soviet-style building near the market, this is up there with the best cheap eats in town – it'll set you back just 25,000đ for a delicious plate of *com tam*. Daily 10am–8pm.

Villages around Pleiku

This far north in the highlands, the **Jarai** (see p.470) and, to a lesser extent, the **Bahnar** (see p.469) outnumber the E De, though many of them have been assimilated into mainstream Vietnamese culture. You'll need a **guide** to tour any of these villages.

Plei Phun Jarai village

Around 34km northwest of Pleiku, **PLEI PHUN** is by far the most commonly visited of the local Jarai villages. Your guide will show you around the headman's house, the local graveyard and village spring. As is common with this particular tribe, the incredibly ornate graveyards are the main focus of interest, and you'll see roughly hewn **hardwood statues** depicting figures in a range of moods placed around each family grave. In the past the Jarai would stick bamboo poles through the earth and into a fresh grave,

through which to "feed" the dead, though now they tend to leave fruit and bowls of rice on the top.

Bahnar villages

A group of four secluded but easily accessible **Bahnar villages** lie 38km east of Pleiku, en route to Quy Nhon, where **Dek Tu**, **De Cop**, **De Doa** and **Dek Rol** rub shoulders with one another across a small area of forests and streams. Small split-bamboo and straw houses on stilts proliferate through these orderly communities, and each one boasts an impressive, steeply thatched *rong*, or communal house, where ceremonies are performed, local disputes are resolved and decisions taken. As at Plei Phun, the **graveyards** are particularly interesting, particularly that of Dek Tu, where the practice of feeding the dead is prevalent; unlike the Jarai, however, each of the deceased here has his own individual grave complete with a small sloping roof. Ladders made out of bamboo poles are leant against the graves to aid the journey to a new life; some are adorned with surprising ornaments, including wooden American fighter jets.

3

INFORMATION

VILLAGES AROUND PLEIKU

Tourist information Gia Lai province is notoriously defensive of its few remaining traditional settlements – authorities don't approve of individuals making forays into the wilds, insisting that you should always be with a licensed guide. If you try to bypass this regulation and just turn up in villages, you'll get little cooperation from the locals, who receive a cut from visitor fees – and face potential punishment from the authorities for your unauthorized intrusion.

Guides To visit the Jarai or Bahnar villages, you'll need to be with an official guide from Gia Lai Eco-Tourist (see p.194) or another agency; these cost from $15 for a half-day and $25 for a whole one, and you'll have to fund their transportation.

ACCOMMODATION

Home-stays It's possible to arrange a home-stay in the largest Bahnar village, De Cop. Gia Lai Tourist has commandeered a house on stilts here, from where you can visit each village on a one-day hike. A two-day programme visiting both Plei Phun and these villages works out about $35 a head for a group of five people.

Kon Tum

The sleepy, friendly town of **KON TUM** sits on the edge of the Dakbla River, and makes one of the best bases in the central highlands – unlike busy Buon Ma Thuot and concrete-heavy Pleiku, this provincial capital makes a highly pleasant place to stay. It also has a few sights of its own, including some sterling colonial-era architecture – some of the most beautiful buildings in the country. However, most are here to use Kon Tum as a springboard for jaunts to outlying villages of the **Bahnar** and other minorities such as the **Sedang** (see p.471), **Gieh Trieng** and **Rongao**. There are about 650 minority villages in the province, of which only a few have been visited by foreigners, so the scope for adventure here is broad.

Kon Tum's riverside promenade along the Dakbla River is a fine place for a stroll – especially on fair-weather evenings, when it seems as if half the town stops by. It would also be the perfect place for a beer, but only the bars on the other side of the road seem to sell bottles – and even then, they're usually warm and only for on-site drinking. You may spot the town's museum near the river, sitting incongruously near the bridge, but it's really not worth visiting.

Tan Huong Church

92 Nguyen Hue • Sunrise to sunset • Free

You can't miss the grand bulk of **Tan Huong Church**, which sports colourful, pastel-shaded bas-reliefs (look out for George slaying a dragon) on its Peach Melba-coloured facade. Considering Kon Tum's remote location, the church is a surprisingly elegant building; the original structure was completed in the 1850s but the place has been

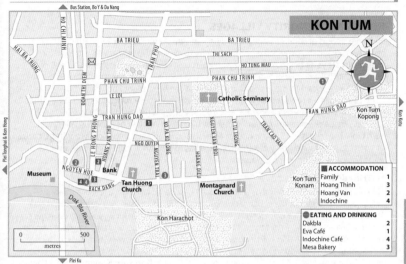

restored several times since. Be sure to peek inside the interior, a charming place with dark wooden columns and a couple of stained-glass windows.

Montagnard Church

Nguyen Hue • Sunrise to sunset • Free

Also known as the "Wooden Church", this stunning edifice was built by the French in 1913, and has been frequently restored since then. A statue of Christ stands over the front entrance; below him, a stained-glass window neatly fuses the classic Christian symbol of the dove with images of local resonance – a Bahnar village and an elephant. In the grounds is a statue of nineteenth-century French bishop Stephen Theodore Cuenot, who established the diocese of Kon Tum. Mass is held in the Bahnar language – they don't mind curious foreigners popping their heads in, but be respectful if taking any pictures. Try to arrive at around 4.30pm.

Catholic seminary

56 Tran Hung Dao • Sunrise to sunset • Free

Kon Tum's **Catholic seminary** is certainly worth a look for its impressive architecture. Set in the middle of garden-filled grounds, its appearance is far more European than Vietnamese. The soft cream colour of the seminary walls is offset by dark wood, and though few of the rooms are open to visitors, the gardens are a great place to relax for half an hour.

ARRIVAL AND DEPARTURE	**KON TUM**

By plane The nearest airport is less than an hour down the road in Pleiku (see p.193), though you'll need to use your initiative to get to Kon Tum without hitting Pleiku first. Highway 14 is around 1km west of the terminal; either wait for one of the irregular Kon Tum-bound buses, or prepare to haggle with a xe om driver.

By bus The bus station is to the northwest of town on Phan Dinh Phung. From here, it's best to take a xe om (30,000đ)

to the town centre, which is about 3km away. Also note that Kon Tum is a port of call for buses heading between Pleiku or Quy Nhon and the Lao towns of Attapeu and Pakse; the exact stopping points have been in a state of flux for some time, so try asking at your accommodation if you'd like to buy a ticket.

Destinations Da Nang (5hr); Pleiku (1hr); Quang Ngai (5hr); Quy Nhon (5hr).

3

KON TUM'S MINORITY VILLAGES

There are dozens of Bahnar villages encircling Kon Tum. As most are free from the official restrictions that hang over Pleiku, you're at liberty to explore this area at will, although for **overnight stays** it's best to check first with the tourist office (see opposite); if you opt for its guided tours it'll work out at around $25 per person per day. Prices are often a little lower at *Eva Café* (see opposite), whose knowledgeable staff speak excellent English.

All Bahnar villages have at their centre a longhouse known as a **rong**. Built on sturdy **stilts** with a platform and entrance at either end (or sometimes in the middle), the interior is generally made of split bamboo and protected by a towering thatched roof, usually about 15m high. The *rong* is used as a venue for festivals and village meetings, and as a **village court** at which anyone found guilty of a tribal offence has to ritually kill a pig and a chicken, and must apologize in front of the village.

WITHIN KON TUM

One good thing about Kon Tum is that you don't have to go far to get a feel of a minority village, as there are a couple of Bahnar villages within the town itself. First comes **Kon Harachot**, whose immaculate *rong* faces a football field – if you're lucky, you may even get to see an all-Bahnar game. To get there, head east along Nguyen Hue, and take any right turn up until Hoang Dieu; Ly Thai To will bring you straight to the *rong*. The walk from here to the river is delightful, especially during or after sunset; take any road heading west. Heading the other way, following Nguyen Hue to its eastern end brings you to **Kon Tum Konam**, while following Tran Hung Dao to the east takes you directly to **Kon Tum Kopong**, where there is another wonderful example of a *rong*. Villagers at Kon Tum Kopong are big on **basket-weaving**, and you might chance upon locals cutting bamboo into thin strips and crafting them into sturdy baskets, which they sell very cheaply in the local market.

PLEI THONGHIA AND KON HONGO

The villages of **Plei Thongia** and **Kon Hongo**, respectively 1km and 4km west of Kon Tum, are inhabited by members of the Rongao, one of the smaller minority groups in the region. Women are often busy weaving in the shade of their simple, wooden huts, **ox carts** trundle along the dusty road and children splash about in the Dakbla River down below. It's possible to walk to Plei Tonghia – heading north from the Dakbla bridge, turn left at Ba Trieu and just keep going (don't be tempted to walk or cycle along the river bank, since it's a hard slog, mostly the wrong way). Kon Hongo is within cycling distance but a little tricky to find – it's easier to take a xe om there (30,000đ) and work your way back on foot.

KON KOTU

About 5km to the east of Kon Tum is the most frequently visited of Bahnar villages, **Kon Kotu**. Though now linked to Kon Tum by a surfaced road, it makes a pleasant walk to go there by **country paths** (contact the local tourist office for details) and it's possible to overnight in the village *rong*. To get there **by road**, follow Tran Hung Dao east out of town until you reach a suspension bridge over the river at **Kon Klor**. Turn left 200m beyond the bridge and follow the road to Kon Kotu. Though the village church is absolutely huge, and fairly pretty to boot, it's still the immaculate *rong* that commands the most attention. No nails were used in the construction of the bamboo walls, floor and the impossibly tall thatch roof of this lofty communal hall. It also doubles as an occasional **overnight stop** for local trekking tours organized by Kon Tum Tourist (see opposite), in either a simple guesthouse ($12 per person), or the longhouse itself ($10).

YA CHIM

About 17km southwest of Kon Tum is the village of **Ya Chim**, where there are a few Jarai cemeteries that can be visited, though it's best to go with a guide from Kon Tum Tourist as they are tricky to find. Wooden posts, some of them carved in the form of mourning figures, surround the graves, and personal possessions such as a bicycle or TV are placed inside. The graves are carefully tended for a period of three to five years after death and offerings are brought to the site daily. At the end of this period a buffalo is sacrificed to make a feast for the villagers and the grave is abandoned in the belief that the spirit of the deceased has now departed.

INFORMATION

Tourist office Kon Tum Tourist (☎0603 863334, ✉ktourist@dng.vnn.vn) is open daily 7–11am & 1–5pm, on the ground floor of the *Dakbla* hotel. It rents out bikes and can, in theory, organize a wide range of tours, including trekking, river trips and traditional dance performances. In practice, there is not always an English-speaker present, on which occasions you'll be lucky to get more than a shrug and a smile.

ACCOMMODATION

★Family 235 Tran Hung Dao ☎0603 862448, ✉familyhotelkt@yahoo.com. A fantastic option which is lassoing in more and more of Kon Tum's budget travellers. The friendly staff speak English and advise on trips in and around town, while the garden area is a marvellously pleasant place in which to relax. $20

Hoang Thinh 117 Nguyen Hue ☎0603 958958. Far prettier than you'd expect for the price, rooms are a steal at this friendly little guesthouse, whose rooms is arrayed off a spiral staircase (you can also use the lift). They've a wide variety of rooms for such a small place; try for the ones with little balconies. $10

Hoang Van 1a Hoang Van Thu ☎0603 917555. Even more of a bargain than *Hoang Thinh* just down the road, this is a fantastic guesthouse whose well-designed lobby looks, if not always functions, like that of a "real" hotel. The rooms are no different, even though the very cheapest have no windows; all have small tubs and TV. $12

Indochine 30 Bach Dang ☎0603 863335, ⓦindochine hotel.vn. Enjoying a prime riverside location, the town's fanciest hotel is perhaps not as grand as its wistful name may lead you to believe, but it's still decent value. Rooms are cosy and carpetted, and those facing the river have great views. $40

EATING AND DRINKING

★Dakbla 168 Nguyen Hue ☎0602 210584. This simple restaurant seems to lure in every one of Kon Tum's independent travellers. The menu is full of cheap and tasty dishes: try the bitter melon and egg (50,000đ), hotpots to be cooked at the table (80,000–180,000đ), or wild boar dishes (110,000đ and up; like pork, but tougher). Staff also sell a selection of ethnic souvenirs. Daily 6.30am–8.30pm.

★Eva Café 1 Phan Chu Trinh ☎0603 862448, ✉family hotelkt@yahoo.com. An excellent place in which to savour some Kom Tum coffee is this quirky café, run by a local sculptor, whose work is also displayed here. Built to vaguely resemble a stilthouse, its surrounding garden yields fountains, wooden sculptures of distorted faces and a waterfall trickling down the back wall. The friendly, English-speaking staff also put on excellent tours to surrounding villages (see box opposite). Coffees and juices for 25,000đ or so. Daily 6am–10pm.

Indochine Café 30 Bach Dang ☎0603 863335. Your eyebrows are likely to go a bit Roger Moore the first time you see this hotel's new café – with river views, fish ponds and curved columns of bamboo giving off a neo-forest feel, it would still count as attractive in Hanoi or HCMC. The service doesn't live up to the appearance, but it's still a grand place for coffee (12,000đ), juices (20,000–30,000đ) or cute bowls of ice cream (23,000đ). They even have some breakfast staples, while in the evening you can make use of the super-cheap beer prices (from 13,000đ). Daily 6.30am–10pm.

Mesa Bakery 80 Nguyen Hue ☎0603 913200. Just the ticket if you're looking for a few provisions to pop in your bag on a village hike, this bakery produces mountains of decent bread, mini-pizzas, cookies and the like. Daily 7am–10pm.

DIRECTORY

Banks It's possible to change money at the BIDV Bank at 1 Tran Phu, where there's also an ATM; there's another at the Agribank at 88 Tran Phu.

Post office 205 Le Hong Phong.

MOVING ON TO LAOS

The **international border crossing** from the central highlands to Laos, open at Bo Y 80km northwest of Kon Tum, provides access to the rarely visited region of southern Laos; heading on west it takes you to Isaan, in the forgotten northeast of Thailand – three off-the-beaten track Southeast Asian destinations in one. Though in theory you can obtain a thirty-day Lao visa at the border ($30–45; two passport photos required), it's best to get your visa in advance at the Lao consulate in either Ho Chi Minh City (see p.106) or Da Nang (see p.270) or their Hanoi embassy (see p.384), as border officials are notorious for extorting unscheduled payments from travellers in order to prevent administrative delays (especially on weekends, or "after hours"). There are daily bus departures from Pleiku and Quy Nhon, both via Kon Tum, to Attapeu and Pakse in Laos.

The southern coast

RED SAND DUNES NEAR MUI NE

The southern coast

Beaches are, for many travellers, the prime reason for a visit to South East Asia; in Vietnam, they're most prevalent along the country's convex southern coastline. A recent deluge of Russian tourists has added to the slow but steady increase in visitors that has taken place over recent decades – Cyrillic-text signs are now ubiquitous in the main resort areas of Nha Trang and Mui Ne, which have both seen their popularity go through the roof and are now adding culinary sophistication and top-drawer accommodation to their coastal charms. There are also a number of less-heralded beaches to track down, and even a few islands, but the region has ample historical significance too – this was once the domain of the kingdom of Champa, whose magnificent ruins still dot the coast. An Indianized trading empire, Champa was courted in its prime by seafaring merchants from around the globe, but became steadily marginalized from the tenth century onwards by the march south of the Vietnamese.

4

These days a few enclaves around Phan Thiet and Phan Rang are all that remain of the **Cham people**, but the remnants of the towers that punctuate the countryside – many of which have recently been restored – recall Champa's former glory (see p.432).

Despite the influx of tourism, **sea fishing** is the region's lifeblood and provides a living for a considerable percentage of the population. Fleets of fishing boats jostle for space in the cramped ports and estuaries of the coastal towns, awaiting the turn of the tide; and fish and seafood drying along the road are a common sight. The fertile soil blesses the coastal plains with coconut palms, rice paddies, cashew orchards, sugar cane fields, vineyards and shrimp farms. One of the most commonly seen fruits here, especially around Phan Thiet, is the dragon fruit, which grows on plants with distinctive, octopus-like tentacles.

Vietnam's southernmost beaches are not on the southern coast at all, but on the former French prison islands of **Con Dao**. While many beaches elsewhere are now experiencing high-octane development, Con Dao retains a laidback, unhurried air that tempts many to stay far longer than they'd planned. Back on the mainland, the first town of note is **Vung Tau**, once a French seaside resort, and now a smart, oil-rich town with passable beaches; much better ones can be found further up the coast. In reality, few travellers have the time or inclination to meander along the beaches between Vung Tau and Mui Ne, but with your own transport and an adventurous spirit you'll find somewhere to pace out a solitary set of footprints in the pristine sand.

Just a short way up the coast, you'll never be alone at **Mui Ne** itself. Almost unheard of until very recently, its transition from being the country's best-kept secret to one of its most high-profile resorts happened almost overnight. It's perhaps a sign of things to come for Vietnamese tourism – slick resorts rubbing shoulders

BEACH AT NHA TRANG

Highlights

❶ Con Dao Archipelago Discover the site of Vietnam's most feared prison, which now welcomes divers, trekkers and beach bums. **See p.205**

❷ Mui Ne Stay in a fancy resort at Mui Ne and go kitesurfing in the breezy bay. **See p.215**

❸ Ca Na beach Everyone knows about Nha Trang and Mui Ne, but the southern coast still has a few virtually deserted beaches – this pristine stretch being one such example. **See p.221**

❹ Cham architecture Get up close to the impressive Po Klong Garai towers, just outside

Phan Rang, and other Cham towers in the region. **See box, p.222**

❺ Underwater activities Snorkel or dive in the clear waters off the islands near Nha Trang. **See box, p.229**

❻ Mud baths Wallow in a mud bath at the Thap Ba Hot Springs near Nha Trang. **See p.233**

❼ Quy Nhon Spend a couple of days meandering around this relatively unsung beach city with a pleasant chilled-out vibe, great seafood and some of the coast's best Cham ruins. **See p.236**

HIGHLIGHTS ARE MARKED ON THE MAP ON P.204

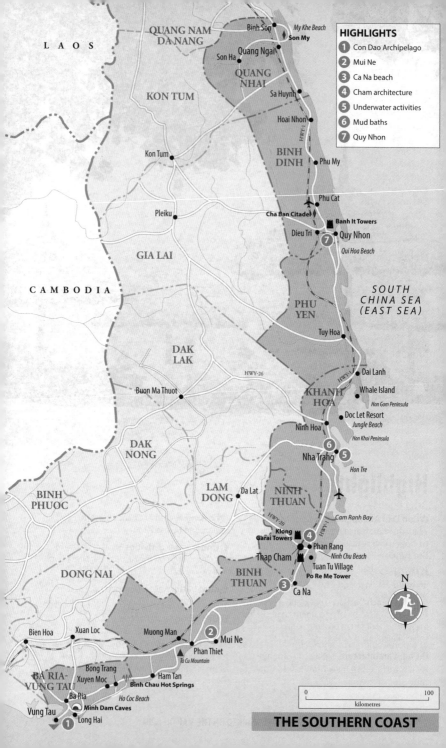

THE SOUTHERN COAST

HIGHLIGHTS

1 Con Dao Archipelago
2 Mui Ne
3 Ca Na beach
4 Cham architecture
5 Underwater activities
6 Mud baths
7 Quy Nhon

LAOS

QUANG NAM
DA NANG

Binh Son
My Khe Beach
Son My
Quang Ngai
Son Ha
QUANG
NHAI
Sa Huynh

KON TUM

Hoai Nhon

Kon Tum

BINH
DINH

Phu My

Pleiku

Phu Cat

Cha Ban Citadel
Banh It Towers
Dieu Tri
7 Quy Nhon
Qui Hoa Beach

GIA LAI

CAMBODIA

PHU
YEN

DAK
LAK

Tuy Hoa

Buon Ma Thuot

HWY-26

Dai Lanh

KHANH
HOA

Whale Island
Hon Gom Peninsula

Doc Let Resort
Jungle Beach

DAK
NONG

Ninh Hoa
Hon Khoi Peninsula

6 5
Nha Trang
Hon Tre

BINH
PHUOC

LAM
DONG
Da Lat

NINH
THUAN

Cam Ranh Bay

HWY-20

Klong
Garai Towers
4
Thap Cham
Phan Rang
Ninh Chu Beach
Tuan Tu Village
Po Re Me Tower

DONG NAI

BINH
THUAN

3
Ca Na

Bien Hoa
Xuan Loc

Muong Man
2
Mui Ne

Phan Thiet
Ta Cu Mountain

BA RIA-
VUNG TAU

Bong Trang
Xuyen Moc
Ham Tan
Binh Chau Hot Springs

Ba Ria
Ho Coc Beach
Minh Dam Caves

Vung Tau
1
Long Hai

SOUTH
CHINA SEA
(EAST SEA)

N

0   100
kilometres

along a fine sweep of soft sand, looking out over aquamarine waters. This tourist enclave attracts a steady stream of overseas visitors, as well as providing an idyllic short break for Ho Chi Minh City's expats and growing middle-class. Those who feel that a day sunbathing is a day wasted will prefer to rest up around **Phan Rang**, site of **Po Klong Garai**, the most impressive of the many **tower complexes** erected by the once-mighty Champa empire.

North of Phan Rang, Highway 1 ploughs through sugar-cane plantations, blinding white salt flats and shrimp farms on its way into **Nha Trang**. Here travellers can enjoy the best of both worlds – a combination of Cham towers and beach activities, the latter including diving and snorkelling trips. Nha Trang also has the southern coast's greatest range of accommodation and restaurants, and is a deservedly popular place. Other more secluded beaches that warrant an expedition further north include **Doc Let** and **Sa Huynh**, while for a little more civilization, **Quy Nhon** makes a useful halt above Nha Trang. The scars of war tend not to intrude too much along this stretch of the country, though many visitors make time to visit **Quang Ngai**, where Vietnam's south-central arc of coastline culminates, and view the sombre site of the notorious **My Lai** massacre perpetrated by US forces in 1968.

The Con Dao Archipelago

Vietnam is book-ended to the south by the admirably unspoilt **Con Dao Archipelago**, a confetti-like spray of sixteen emerald-green islands, cast adrift in the South China Sea some 185km south of Vung Tau. The sleepy nature of the archipelago belies some tumultuous history – under French occupation, Con Dao was home to the most feared prison in the country, and haunting remnants of that time are still visible. However, most come here to get away from such negative thoughts, and since regular flights began recently, the archipelago has taken its first steps to welcoming tourists.

The biggest island in the archipelago, **Con Son** is its undisputed hub of activity, and the only place with any tourist facilities. Bar diving and perhaps a short trip to a neighbouring island, for now this is the only accessible part of Con Dao – no bad thing, since Con Son itself is an arrestingly beautiful place with some striking colonial buildings. While you're based here, try **trekking** in the national park, **diving** off the surrounding islands, watching **sea turtles** laying eggs, or lounging on various uncrowded **beaches**.

Brief history

The British East India Company established a **fortified outpost** on Con Son in 1703. Had this flourished, the island may by now have been a more diminutive Hong Kong or Singapore, given its strategic position on the route to China. But within three years, the Bugis mercenaries drafted in to construct and garrison the base from Sulawesi – in Indonesia – had murdered their British commanders, putting paid to this early experiment in colonization. Known then as Poulo Condore, Con Son was still treading water when the American sailor John White spied its "lofty summits" a little over a century later, in 1819. White deemed it a decent natural harbour, though blighted by "noxious reptiles, and affording no good fresh water".

The island finally found its calling when decades later the French chose it as the site of a **penal colony** for anti-colonial activists, and Con Son's savage regime soon earned it the nickname **Devil's Island**. Prisoners languished in squalid pits called "tiger cages", which featured metal grilles instead of roofs, from which guards sprinkled powdered lime and dirty water on the inmates. As the twentieth century progressed the colony developed into a sort of unofficial "revolutionary university". Older hands instructed their greener cell-mates in the finer points of Marxist–Leninist theory, while the dire conditions they endured helped reinforce the lessons.

4

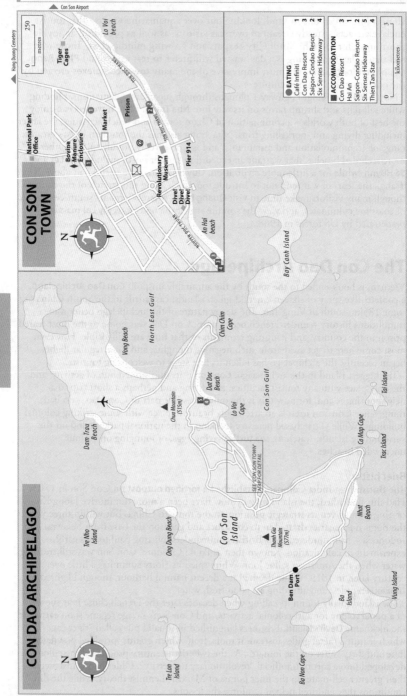

CON DAO ARCHIPELAGO

CON SON TOWN

Con Son Airport

Hang Duong Cemetery

Lo Voi beach

Tiger Cages

Prison

National Park Office

Bovine Manure Enclosure

Market

Revolutionary Museum

Pier 914

Dive! Dive! Dive!

An Hai beach

Bay Canh Island

0 — 250 metres

North East Gulf

Vong Beach

Chua Mountain (515m)

Chim Chim Cape

Dat Doc Beach

La Voi Cape

Con Son Gulf

Tai Island

Ca Map Cape

Trac Island

SEE CON SON TOWN MAP FOR DETAIL

Dam Trau Beach

Ong Dung Beach

Con Son Island

Thanh Gia Mountain (577m)

Nhat Beach

Nho Island

Ben Dam Port

Vung Island

Ba Island

Tre Lon Island

Ba Non Cape

0 — 3 kilometres

● EATING
Café Infiniti 1
Con Dao Resort 3
Saigon-Condao Resort .. 2
Six Senses Hideaway .. 4

■ ACCOMMODATION
Con Dao Resort 3
Hai An 1
Saigon-Condao Resort .. 5
Six Senses Hideaway ... 2
Thien Tan Star 4

Con Son Town

Village-like **CON SON TOWN** is the largest settlement, and home to almost all of the island's accommodation and restaurants. Its peaceful promenade makes a beautiful place for a walk, past the huge gnarled trunks of the malabar almond trees as colourful fishing boats bob in the bay. The promenade is punctuated by **Pier 914**, whose curious name derives from one estimate of the number of prisoners who died during its construction; nowadays it's a great place to listen to the sea at night, perhaps with a beer in hand.

Few come to Con Dao for its sightseeing potential, but in and around the town centre are a few historical sights should you ever tire of diving, eating and lazing around.

The Revolutionary Museum

Directly behind Pier 914 • Mon–Sat 7.30–11.30am & 1.30–5pm • Free

The island's museum is rarely visited, and staff are likely to be surprised when you turn up – if they're awake. The pictures of old Con Dao are unlikely to detain you for too long; also look out for the poorly stuffed black squirrel, the island's most distinctive animal, in the first hall.

The prison

Daily 7.30–11.30am & 1.30–5pm • 20,000đ

The many cells in the now-defunct **prison** remain littered with shackles, placed painfully close together. In a couple of exhibition cells, emaciated statues show how the Vietnamese inmates spent their days crowded together, unless they were selected for the "tiger cages" or the "solariums", where they were exposed to the elements in roofless rooms. There are more tiger cages just to the east in a separate former-museum complex, accessible by path from the main road.

Hang Duong Cemetery

About 1km northeast of town on Nguyen An Ninh • Daily 24hr • Free • No shorts or sleeveless tops

The graves in the **Hang Duong Cemetery** add a tangible layer to the island's tragic past. All are unmarked, but one stands out – bright-coloured combs lie deposited on the grave of Vo Thi Sau, who in 1952 became the first woman to be executed here, at the age of 19. If you're game, try swinging by around midnight, when locals usually gather to burn offerings to the revolutionary heroine – quite a spectacle.

Bovine manure enclosure

Just off Vo Thi Sau • Daily 24hr • Free

If the morbid mood gets you, you could even visit the **bovine manure enclosure**, located on the way to the national park headquarters. The prison warders used to march prisoners into this windowless room, then pump it full of manure as a form of torture or execution, depending on their whim.

Beaches

After visiting the historic monuments and trekking across the island you may want to focus on some serious relaxation. **Lo Voi** and **An Hai** beaches, which front the town, are not bad, though the bay is often cluttered with fishing boats. Other good beaches around the island are **Dam Trau** and **Bai Ong Dung** in the north and **Bai Dat Doc** to the east of town, but you'll likely need to **rent a motorbike** (see box, p.208) to get there.

ACTIVITIES ON CON SON

HIKING

A hike along one of the island's many trails in the national park may be more appealing than a tour of the prison. Some trails, such as one heading straight north to **Ong Dung Beach**, are well marked and can be followed independently, while others, such as to **Thanh Gia Mountain**, the island's highest peak at 577m, require the services of a guide. Birdwatchers might be lucky enough to spot rare species such as the red-billed tropicbird or the pied Imperial pigeon. Make sure to take plenty of water and food, as there is nothing available outside the town. The **Con Dao National Park headquarters** are located north of the town centre at 29 Vo Thi Sau (☎0643 830669), and have information about hiking trails – it's also possible to hire a guide here.

BIKING

Renting a bike is a piece of cake; most hotels charge from 150,000đ per day, though do note that there are almost no petrol stations on the island – one has been marked on the map (see p.206). The roads are virtually empty, even in the middle of the village, for most of the day. You basically have two options: heading north from Con Son Town, you'll pass the *Six Senses* resort and the airport before reaching **Dam Trau beach**, located down a side-trail branching off to the west. Alternatively, it's an easy journey south to Ca Map Cape, at which point you'll swing northwest towards the small settlement of **Ben Dam** where most of the fishing boats dock. Its population is mostly an interesting mix of sailors and prostitutes.

DIVING

The best diving months are April and May, when visibility can be over 20m. One interesting new option is the **wreck** of a 65m-long Thai freighter – usually home to schools, perhaps even universities, of fish. There are two good operators on the island, both of which have a full range of services from snorkelling trips to full PADI courses (see opposite).

Other islands

Renting a boat to explore other islands can be incredibly tricky, not to mention expensive if you're not travelling in a group. Contact Dive! Dive! Dive! (see opposite) or *Con Dao Resort* (see opposite) for advice

You'll find plenty of deserted beaches and healthy coral reefs on some of the outlying islands. From June to October it is possible to watch sea turtles laying eggs at night on nearby **Bay Canh Island**; less predictable are occasional sightings of dugongs, which are endearing mammals (also known as sea cows) that feed only on seagrass, grow up to three metres long and weigh up to 400kg.

ARRIVAL AND DEPARTURE   THE CON DAO ARCHIPELAGO

By plane The Vietnam Air Services Company (VASCO; ☎083 8422790; best booked through the Vietnam Airlines website, ⓦvietnamairlines.com.vn) operates a few small, propeller-driven planes to Con Son airport, which is around 15km northeast of town. Most of the major hotels run shuttle services, which meet the planes and drop back off before flights; wherever you're staying, you can catch a ride with one for 50,000đ. The journey into town gives a tantalizing glimpse of the island's rugged beauty and windswept, deserted beaches.

Destinations Can Tho (4 weekly; 1hr); Ho Chi Minh City (3–5 daily; 1hr).

By boat The only services from mainland Vietnam leave from Vung Tau (daily Apr–June, in theory; 12hr), and arrive at Ben Tam Port on the west of the island. This can't be recommended, though – schedules are next to useless since the boats leave when they want, and you won't save all that much money when transport to Vung Tau and lost time are factored in. If you're still keen, contact Vung Tau Tourist (see p.212).

ACCOMMODATION

Be warned that you'll pay far more here than you would for similar facilities on the mainland. This is not a great place for budget travellers – there are a few family guesthouses, but none can be wholeheartedly recommended.

Con Dao Resort 8 Nguyen Duc Thuan ☎0643 830939, ⓦ condaoresort.vn. Probably the best beach location on Con Son, this hotel has a good swimming pool, comfortable rooms and large buffet breakfasts. Staff can also arrange boat trips. $70

Hai An Ho Thanh Tong ☎0169 682 0563. The most reliable of the several guesthouses in the centre – not saying much, but rooms are comfortable enough and the service friendly. $25

Saigon-Condao Resort 18–24 Ton Duc Thang ☎0643 830336, ⓦ saigoncondao.com. Not a bad choice at all for those on a moderate budget, with a small pool and most rooms offering good views of the beach. They have a few cheaper (slightly stuffy) villas set apart from the main building, and boast one of the town's best restaurants. $85

Six Senses Hideaway Dat Doc Beach ☎0643 831222, ⓦ sixsenses.com. One of Vietnam's most exclusive resorts, a few minutes' drive up the coast from Con Son Town. The modern, timber-framed villas are rather gorgeous – the bamboo-covered outdoor showers are a particularly nice touch, as is the fact that islanders form a healthy chunk of the staff. There's also a pristine stretch of private beach, and a butler to take care of guests' every need. $610

Thien Tan Star 4 Nguyen Duc Thuan ☎0643 630123, ⓦ thientanstarhotel.com. One of the newest, and best, budget choices in town. Rooms are nicely decorated for the price, and though service can be lacking (as it is across the island), the location is good. Pay a little extra and you'll get a room with a modest sea view. $35

EATING

Café Infiniti Corner of Pham Van Dong and Tran Huy Lieu. Newish place that's popular with visitors and the island's few expats, largely on account of the fact that it's the only place around with Western food on the menu – it's 100,000đ for sandwiches, 150,000đ or so for pizzas, and there's ice cream to enjoy it all with. The friendly local owner is also a good source of Con Dao advice. Daily 7am–11pm.

Con Dao Resort 8 Nguyen Duc Thuan ☎0643 830939, ⓦ condaoresort.vn. The outdoor bar/restaurant at this hotel is the best place on the beach for an evening drink. The food's good too, and prices are reasonable – simple dishes go from 70,000đ. Daily 8am–11pm.

★**Saigon-Condao Resort** 18–24 Ton Duc Thang ☎0643 830336, ⓦ saigoncondao.com. This hotel's open-air restaurant is by far the best in Con Dao Town, and prices are surprisingly fair – by way of example, 100,000đ will get you a coral fish steak with chilli and lemongrass, a plate of sliced bitter melon and a glass of fresh lemonade. Daily 8am–10pm.

Six Senses Hideaway Dat Doc Beach ⓦ sixsenses.com. So secluded that if you're staying here, you'll be eating here anyway. The restaurant and juice/cocktail bar are superb and also open to non-guests, but bring money – you'll have to add a zero to prices that you'd expect to pay elsewhere. Daily 8am–10pm.

DIRECTORY

Bank There are now several ATMs dotted around town (including one outside the Vietinbank, at the junction of Le Duan and Le Van Viet), as well as an Agribank just outside the main market. However, these do still occasionally go down – consider bringing enough money to cover your stay.

In an emergency, you could try asking the hotels.

Diving ★Dive! Dive! Dive! Nguyen Hue (☎0643 830701, ⓦ dive-condao.com); Rainbow Divers (at *Six Senses* resort, ☎0905 577671, ⓦ divevietnam.com).

Post office Nguyen Thi Minh Khai.

Vung Tau

VUNG TAU is one of those places that divides opinion – it's deemed scruffy by some and agreeable by others, and in fact you may well leave town with your foot in both camps. Its popularity stems from the hydrofoil connection to Ho Chi Minh City – the promise of beaches and a seaside atmosphere just a quick river ride away makes Vung Tau a default weekend bolt hole for stressed-out Saigonese. Located on a hammer-headed spit of land jutting into the mouth of the Saigon River, it was once a thriving riviera-style beach resort; the city's **offshore oil** industry and steadily growing port have transformed it into a more business-oriented conurbation. Locals are fond of swimming on the town's **beaches**, but they're all second-rate despite recent attempts to clean them up. However, the boardwalk along **Bai Sau**, known to seasoned expats as "Back Beach", remains a pleasant place for an evening stroll, and perhaps a light seafood meal; "Front Beach", where the ferries arrive, has more traffic and less appeal.

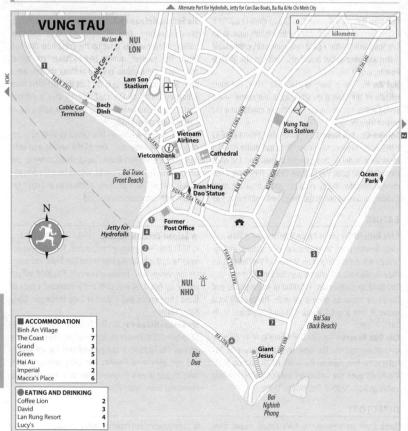

Alternate Port for Hydrofoils, Jetty for Con Dao Boats, Ba Ria & Ho Chi Minh City

VUNG TAU

0   1
kilometre

ACCOMMODATION

Binh An Village	1
The Coast	7
Grand	3
Green	5
Hai Au	4
Imperial	2
Macca's Place	6

EATING AND DRINKING

Coffee Lion	2
David	3
Lan Rung Resort	4
Lucy's	1

Brief history

Portuguese ships are thought to have exploited the city's deep anchorage as early as the fifteenth century. By the turn of the twentieth, French expats, who knew the place as "Cap Saint-Jacques", had adopted it as a retreat from the daily rigmarole of Saigon, and set to work carving colonial villas into the sides of **Nui Lon** and **Nui Nho**, two low hills near the coast. Shifts in Vietnam's political sands duly replaced French visitors with American GIs; with them gone, and the Communist government in power, the city became a favoured launch pad for the vessels that spirited away the **boat people** in the late 1970s (see box, pp.450–451).

Nui Lon

Cable car station on Tran Phu • Daily 7.30am–6pm • 100,000đ return

Just north of the city centre, **Nui Lon** is the highest peak in Vung Tau, and commands predictably sweeping views from its 201m-high summit. While it's possible to walk to the top, or take a xe om, most choose to make the ascent by **cable car**. At the top you'll find a small park, which is particularly good for families; known officially as the Ho May Tourism Resort, it includes a cherry blossom orchard and a peacock garden. There are also a couple of small lakes here – all very cheery.

Bach Dinh

12 Tran Phu • Daily 7am–5pm • Small admission fee

One of the few remaining colonial structures worth a look is the imposing **Bach Dinh**, a mansion peeping out from behind a vanguard of frangipani and bougainvillea. Built at the end of the nineteenth century, the "White Palace" served as a holiday home to Vietnam's political players, hosting such luminaries as Paul Doumer, governor-general of Indochina (for whom it was originally erected), emperors Thanh Thai and Bao Dai and President Thieu.

Inside you can see the building's collection of "valuable antique items", excavated from a seventeenth-century shipwreck off Con Dao; among the exhibits are such unmissables as "dry burned fruits", "beard-tweezers" and "pieces of stone in the ship". Upstairs is a display of Cambodian Buddhist statuary and shards of old pottery, but they are eclipsed by the commanding views of the bay.

Nui Nho

Accessible via Hai Dang, a small lane starting just north of the hydrofoil jetty

On Nui Nho hill stands the town's **lighthouse**. Built in 1910, it seems to have been based on a child's sketch of a space-rocket, and is a popular place for locals to walk or jog to in the morning and evening. The views from here out to sea and across town make for good photos. Note that the foothills in these parts are studded with almost a dozen pagodas, all accessible to the public.

Giant Jesus

Approach via a stairway from the southern end of Ha Long • Daily 7.30–11.30am & 1.30–5pm • Free

Vung Tau's own little touch of Rio, the 28m-high **Giant Jesus** sits on a low peak a few hundred metres further south of Nui Nho. Cherubs wielding harps and trumpets herald your approach to the outstretched arms of the city's most famous landmark. Climb the steps inside the wind-buffeted statue and you can perch, parrot-like, on Jesus's shoulder, from where you'll enjoy giddying views of the surrounding seascape.

Bai Sau

If swimming and sun-seeking brought you to Vung Tau, your best bet is to head for the sands of **Bai Sau** ("Back Beach"), far and away Vung Tau's widest, longest (5km) and best, which is still not saying much. Backed by hotels, it's not exactly a tropical paradise, though on weekends, when it's cluttered with kids, deckchairs and umbrellas, and the fruit- and seafood-vendors are out in force, it's pleasant enough. At the time of writing, a boardwalk of sorts was being constructed along the length of the beach – probably a good thing, and a sign that the city plans to treat the beach with respect.

ACTIVITIES IN VUNG TAU

Other than hiking on top of the hills of Nui Lon or Nui Nho, there are a couple of interesting ways to while away the time in Vung Tau.

Ocean Park (daily 6.30am–5.30pm; free), which occupies a 700m beach frontage on Bai Sau, rents out watersports equipment, and offers beach games, lifeguards, showers and a smart restaurant.

If you enjoy a flutter and are in town on a Saturday or Sunday night (7.30–10pm; 50,000đ) head for the Lam Son Stadium at 15 Le Loi, Vietnam's only venue for **greyhound racing** – in fact, it's one of the few such places in South East Asia.

The **Paradise golf course** (☎0643 823366) is a decent eighteen-hole range off Bai San; a round will cost about $95, including caddy.

4

ARRIVAL AND DEPARTURE VUNG TAU

There's no airport in town, though you can book domestic or international **flights** at Vietnam Airlines (21 Tran Hung Dao, ☎ 0643 856099), a few doors along from the tourist office.

By bus All buses terminate at the bus station at 192 Nam Ky Khoi Nghia, where xe om and taxis will be on hand to ferry you to a hotel.

Destinations Da Lat (6hr); Ho Chi Minh City (2hr).

By boat and hydrofoil Hydrofoils from Ho Chi Minh City dock at a large terminal at the south end of Bai Truoc (also known as "Front Beach"). It's within walking distance of a number of hotels, and a lot of restaurants, though seemingly half the town will be waiting to take you away in a taxi. Several boat companies offer services; Greenlines is most frequent. Note that tickets (200,000đ) often sell out at weekends, when they also cost more (250,000đ). In bad weather, the hydrofoils occasionally have to use a more sheltered location 12km away; free shuttle buses will be provided. This second location is also the departure point for ferries to Con Dao, though these services have been becoming less and less reliable.

Destinations Con Dao (1 daily, in theory; 12hr); Ho Chi Minh City (every 30min; 1hr 15min).

GETTING AROUND

By xe om, cyclo and taxi Once in Vung Tau, you can get around by cyclo, xe om or taxi. Given the city's sprawling layout, it's hard to give specific prices, though such is the level of competition that you'll be able to ascertain the right amount by simply asking a few drivers.

By bike For more independence, you can pay slightly more than the average in the rest of Vietnam to rent a bicycle (up to 75,000đ per day) or motorbike (from 150,000đ per day) through most hotels.

INFORMATION

Tourist information For local maps and information, go to Vung Tau Tourist (☎ 0643 856445, ⓦ vungtautourist.com.vn) at 29 Tran Hung Dao, whose staff can help book ferry tickets to Con Dao.

ACCOMMODATION

Most of Vung Tau's classier (and more expensive) places tend to be clustered around **Front Beach** (Bai Truoc), with a wider range of options on **Back Beach** (Bai Sau); both are appealing places in their own right, though in general Front Beach is better for those here to relax and see the sights, and Back Beach for those with sandy pleasures in mind. Weekend rates are higher than weekdays, as the town is invaded by swarms of escapees from Ho Chi Minh City.

FRONT BEACH

Binh An Village 1 Tran Phu ☎ 0643 510016, ⓦ binhanvillage.com. Although it's a stretch from town, this is the most appealing place in the area. The ten individually furnished and decorated rooms enjoy fabulous sea views, and some have private gardens as well. However, many feel that it's horrendously overpriced, and that standards fall some way short of expectations. $100

Grand 2 Nguyen Du ☎ 0643 856888, ⓦ grandhotel.com.vn. Swanky place with smart, though slightly old-fashioned, rooms, as well as attentive staff and good facilities for business travellers. The hotel is right on the front and many of its rooms boast delightful sea views. $90

Hai Au 124 Ha Long ☎ 0643 856178, ⓔ haiauhotel@hcm.vnn.vn. Right opposite the ferry terminal, this aging beast was Vung Tau's first proper hotel, and it shows in its faded decor, empty banqueting halls and minimal staff. However, the rooms aren't too bad at all, and rates have dropped to the degree that it's now one of the best-value places in town. $20

BAI SAU (BACK BEACH)

The Coast 300a Phan Chu Trinh ☎ 0643 627778, ⓦ thecoasthotel.com.vn. One of the few good upper-to-mid-range places in town, with a secluded location, though very near the beach. Rooms are every bit as good as at more expensive competitors, and there's a decent restaurant. $40

Green 147c Thuy Van ☎ 0646 251003, ⓦ greenhotel.vn. This mid-range, smart hotel provides excellent bang for your buck, with splendidly appointed rooms, most of which offer sea views. There's no swimming pool, but you do get to use the one at Ocean Park (see box, p.211) for half-price. $50

Imperial 159–163 Thuy Van ☎ 0643 628888, ⓦ imperialhotel.vn. One of the most attractive hotels on the Back Beach strip, with Roman stylings in the lobby and smart, modern-looking rooms; the ones on upper floors have good sea views. $150

★**Macca's Place** 31 Lac Long Quan ☎ 0643 527042. The best of the budget pack, with an Aussie owner who knows just what travellers expect. Two of those things are food and beer, and the on-site restaurant and bar cater to both of those needs; the rooms themselves are nicely decorated and often surprisingly large. The only problem: it's some way from the beach. $20

EATING AND DRINKING

With a large number of resident expats, Vung Tau supports a more cosmopolitan span of restaurants than your average Vietnamese town; French cuisine weighs in heavily, but it's also possible to find spaghetti and burgers as well as delicious Vietnamese seafood – Bai Sau beach is a good place to head for the latter. In addition, there are a number of expat bars in the centre – many are open until the last customers leave.

Coffee Lion 96 Ha Long. This is a great local pick, with cheap noodle dishes (25,000đ), banh mi (15,000đ) and tasty coffee. Their seats face the sea, and most of them fill up in the evenings – a pleasantly local atmosphere. Daily 8am–10pm.

★**David** 92 Ha Long. ☎0643 521012. The best Western-food option in town, selling a pleasing range of meals – they're justly proud of their home-made pasta and wood-fired pizzas, while sea bass (225,000đ) and oysters (133,000đ) are tasty alternatives. Daily 8am–10pm.

Lan Rung Resort 3–6 Ha Long. ☎0643 526010. This hotel may be aimed more at honeymooning locals than foreign tourists, and it may look like a giant wedding cake, but its seafront seafood restaurant is a quality affair – try the oysters (32,000đ each), tilapia (240,000đ) or sea bass (460,000đ). You'll also be tempted to guzzle down a microbrewed beer. Daily 6am–10pm.

Lucy's 138 Ha Long. ☎0643 858896. A great place for western breakfast (120,000đ), burgers (85,000đ) or shepherd's pie (155,000đ), not to mention a beer in the evening. One other plus point is the location, raised slightly from street level – it's far harder for touts to try to sell you sunglasses. Daily 7am–11pm.

DIRECTORY

Banks Vietcombank, 27 Tran Hung Dao (Mon–Fri 7–11.30am & 1.30–4pm) has a 24hr ATM.

Post office The post office (7am–8.30pm) is at 408 Le Hong Phong.

The Ba Ria coast

4

As you move up the coast of Ba Ria province from Vung Tau, the **beaches** gradually get more enticing. Since the region is near to Ho Chi Minh City, you have to go quite a way before you escape the hordes of domestic tourists who head for the area at weekends and on public holidays, though weekdays can be blissfully quiet. **Public transport** is scarce on this stretch, and you really need a rental vehicle to explore the road that hugs the coast much of the way from Vung Tau to Mui Ne – one which provides glimpses of rural life as well as the salty tang of the nearby sea.

Long Hai

LONG HAI sits below a wall of impressive mountains some 25km from Vung Tau. It's very popular with Vietnamese, not least because the beach here is wider and far, far more appealing than those in Vung Tau. A string of recently built resorts bookend the town to the east; to the west, and sheltered from the sea thanks to its location on the north side of a small peninsula, is the dock area, complete with a huge flotilla of fishing boats and assorted coracles sporting brightly coloured flags.

Minh Dam caves

To get to the caves, take the coastal road east from Long Hai, then a signed left turn just beyond *Thuy Duong Resort*

The **Minh Dam caves**, just around the cape from Long Hai, were a Communist bolt hole from 1948, from where you can enjoy prodigious views of the rice fields that quilt the coastal plain stretching to the horizon to the northeast, and of the boulder-strewn coastline below. The caves are not much more than gaps between piled boulders, yet with a little imagination it's still possible to picture Viet Minh and Viet Cong soldiers lounging, cooking and sleeping here. Bullets have left pockmarks on some of the rocks, and joss sticks are still lodged in crevices in memory of those who fell here. Since there are many forks in the path, however, you really need a guide to find your way around – they're best organized through one of the nearby resorts.

ARRIVAL AND DEPARTURE

By bus Long Hai is served by buses from Ho Chi Minh City's Mien Dong station (2hr); coming from Vung Tau, you'll need to take a bus to Ba Ria and then change, or take a xe om direct for about 200,000đ.

ACCOMMODATION AND EATING

Few foreigners stay at Long Hai, and those that do so tend to bypass the town altogether and head straight to the **resort area** just east; there are also a fair fancy places northeast up the coast. Note that all places listed here see prices rocket at weekends. Most people eat where they stay, but there are a few **food stalls** by the road leading up to the *Military Guest House*. All the hotels listed below are on Road 44.

CENTRAL LONG HAI

★ **Alma Long Hai** ☎ 0643 868227. This lovingly restored former residence of Emperor Bao Dai overlooks a stretch of deserted coastline. Its thatch-roofed bungalows are discreetly set among pine-studded hills, and sport gorgeous bamboo furnishings and fittings, and huge bathtubs. Facilities also run to a business centre, swimming pool and charming open-air terraced restaurant. $175

Military Guest House 298 Doan An Dieu ☎ 0643 868316. The pick of Long Hai's smattering of budget guesthouses, located at the end of the road that runs into the village. It has basic rooms with a choice of fan or a/c, and looks out over a wide expanse of beach shaded by casuarinas. Doubles $20, suites $30

Thuy Duong Resort ☎ 0643 886215, ⓦ thuyduong resort.com.vn. A good mid-range option, standing behind a fine beach lined with casuarinas: its accommodation ranges from pleasant beach huts to luxurious suites in the main hotel, with leisure facilities including a pool and tennis courts. $75

ALONG THE COAST

★ **Ho Tram Beach Resort** ☎ 0643 781525, ⓦ hotramresort.com. A thoroughly classy resort whose characterful rooms boast elegant furnishings and fittings; these are augmented by luxurious spa facilities, including a superb restaurant. It's a full 22km northeast of Long Hai, though the hotel does operate (costly) shuttle buses. $150

Loc An Resort ☎ 0643 886377, ⓦ locanresort.com. Budget resort nestled 14km northeast of Long Hai, beside a lagoon cut off from the sea by a line of sand dunes: it has cosy rooms with all facilities, and bicycles and tandems are available for guests' use. Unless you have your own wheels, you'll need to take a taxi or xe om to get here. $55

Binh Chau Hot Springs

20km northeast of Long Hai • Entry 20,000đ; communal pool 30,000đ; private mini-pools 50,000đ per person per hour • ☎ 0643 791036, ⓦ saigonbinhchau.com

The **Binh Chau Hot Springs** have been developed into a kind of theme park with the addition of a golf-driving range, tennis courts, sand volleyball court, billiards and ox-cart rides around the site. The sulphurous waters bubbling hellishly in the streams and wells here all vary greatly in temperature; old people soothe their aching limbs in the foot-soaking stream, while elsewhere visitors boil eggs sold on site to make up ad hoc picnics. You can bathe in the mineral waters of the "Dreaming Lake", a communal **swimming pool**, but renting your own **mini-pool** is a more tempting option. There are also a sauna, massage and mud baths in the main complex.

ARRIVAL AND DEPARTURE

There's no public transport to the springs; guests tend to arrive on package tour buses or with their own vehicle. However, it's only 6km from Binh Chau village, accessible on the highly irregular coastal buses linking Mui Ne and Vung Tau. From here you can pick up a xe om for the final stretch.

ACCOMMODATION

Binh Chau Hot Springs ☎ 0643 871131, ⓦ saigon binhchau.com. Part of the eponymous operation on Ho Coc Beach, this is an equally good place to stay – it's a question of whether you'd like to be closer to the springs or the beach. Rooms vary considerably in style – try to see a couple before choosing, and try to grab one with mountain views. There's no public transport here – call ahead to arrange pick-up. $60

Phan Thiet

The unassuming capital of Binh Thuan Province, **PHAN THIET** has little of interest for foreigners, who prefer the sands of Mui Ne just along the coast (see below). However, the very absence of tourists is, for some, a draw in itself and the town is likeable enough, particularly where Highway 1 crosses the Tran Hung Dao bridge, beside which lies a picture-perfect fleet of fishing boats. In addition, Phan Thiet has **Doi Duong**, its own perfectly acceptable stretch of beach, and one very popular with the Vietnamese – to get to the best bit, head around 700m northeast from the main entrance point on Nguyen That Thanh.

Ho Chi Minh Museum

Museum and school Tues–Sun 7.30–11.30am & 1.30–4.30pm • 10,000đ

Trung Trac skirts the city centre en route to the sedate riverside **Ho Chi Minh Museum**. As with other such museums around the country, its exhibits include memorabilia of Ho's life from his early days abroad up to his death in 1969, such as his white tunic, walking stick, sandals and metal helmet. Next door is a school where Ho once taught; its rooms have remained unchanged since his brief spell here, and effortlessly conjure up another age.

ARRIVAL AND DEPARTURE

PHAN THIET

By train Phan Thiet station – the closest one to Mui Ne (see below) – is served by a small branch line, with two direct connections daily to and from Ho Chi Minh City. Otherwise, the nearest main line station to Phan Thiet is at Muong Man, 15km to the west, a 200,000đ ride away by xe om, and near double that by taxi.

Destinations from Phan Thiet Ho Chi Minh City (2 daily; 3hr 10min–4hr).

Destinations from Muong Man Da Nang (5 daily; 12–17hr); Ho Chi Minh City (5 daily; 3–5hr); Hue (5 daily; 14–18hr); Nha Trang (5 daily; 4–6hr).

By bus The bus station is 2km north of the centre on Tu Van Tu. If you're really set on staying here, you should be able to get Mui Ne-bound open-tour buses to drop you off, rather than taking local services. Note that there's also a shuttle bus linking Phan Thiet and Mui Ne (every 15min; 13,000đ).

Destinations Ho Chi Minh City (4hr); Nha Trang (5hr).

ACCOMMODATION AND EATING

There are many places to stay in Phan Thiet, though the **culinary scene** isn't terribly exciting. As you'd expect, there's plenty of seafood on offer, but no specific establishments stand out from the crowd – most travellers end up eating at their hotel.

DuParc Ocean Dunes ☎0623 822393, ⓦphanthiet resorts.com. A mammoth, but attractive, resort with two swimming pools and free use of bicycles, as well as the wonderful *Sea Horse* restaurant. However, its main draw is a superb eighteen-hole golf course. Note that you should be able to lop a fair bit from the over-high rack rates. **$185**

The Palms ☎0623 810226, ⓦthepalmsvietnam.com. Swish mid-ranger overlooking the *Novotel* golf course. The design of both the rooms and the complex in general is a cut above what you'd expect at this price range, and the restaurant is excellent – they're proud of their steaks, but also serve good Vietnamese food. **$55**

Mui Ne

If you want evidence of how quickly things can change in Vietnam, take a trip to the beach strip of **MUI NE**. Until recently, this was a sleepy, yet pristine, backwater ignored by domestic and international tourists alike – partly down to the fact that Highway 1 juts inland along this section of coast. However, the secret was unveiled during an eclipse of the sun in the mid-1990s, which had its optimum viewing spot here; it took a little while for big business to arrive, but what you'll see here now is 10km of resorts, sitting almost wall to wall and essentially blocking any view of the beach from the coastal road. More are being built all the time, thanks to a second surge in Mui Ne's

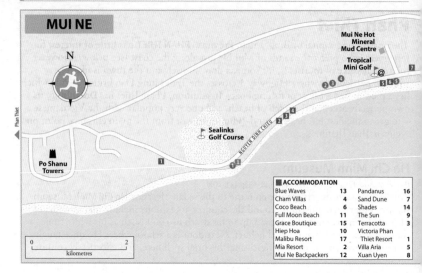

◼ ACCOMMODATION			
Blue Waves	13	Pandanus	16
Cham Villas	4	Sand Dune	7
Coco Beach	6	Shades	14
Full Moon Beach	11	The Sun	9
Grace Boutique	15	Terracotta	3
Hiep Hoa	10	Victoria Phan	
Malibu Resort	17	Thiet Resort	1
Mia Resort	2	Villa Aria	5
Mui Ne Backpackers	12	Xuan Uyen	8

popularity – as with Nha Trang up the coast, Russian tourists are now arriving en masse, and this is one of the few places in Southeast Asia in which Cyrillic text vies for supremacy with Roman.

There's no doubt that its laidback atmosphere is one of its best features, but Mui Ne is also something of a tourist enclave, separated as it is from any Vietnamese community. This probably won't bother you if you're looking for unadulterated beachside relaxation, but if you crave interaction with locals or a higher-octane nightlife scene, you'd be better off heading on up to Nha Trang. Another potential problem at Mui Ne is that the strong winds and surf tend to erode parts of the beach between August and December, so you might just find the waves lapping onto the garden of your chosen resort. However, good stretches of soft sand can always be found with a little exploration.

Sights, as such, are thin on the ground, bar some **Cham towers** and the almost otherworldly **Fairy Springs**. Instead, this is a place of action and inaction – when you're done lounging around by the hotel pool, go for a spot of crazy golf, head uphill for a mud-bath, then drink the night away.

Po Shanu Towers

Off coastal road • Daily 7am–5pm • 10,000đ • Accessible on buses linking Mui Ne and Phan Thiet (see opposite)

On the western fringe of Mui Ne are the **Po Shanu Towers**, Cham ruins which date from the eighth century. While they can't compare with monuments like Po Klong Garai near Phan Rang (see p.222), they are worth a look as the towers – two big, one small – are in reasonable repair, and the site occupies a pretty hilltop location with good views.

MUI NE ORIENTATION

Mui Ne stretches for over 10km along one main road – resorts make up most of the seaward side, especially to the west of the curl; these peter out further east, where budget hotels start to pop up. All along, the non-seaward side of the road is made up of restaurants and cheap hotels. Heading further east, the beach finally disappears too, before the road reaches the actual **village and harbour of Mui Ne**, where fishing boats cluster together in their hundreds.

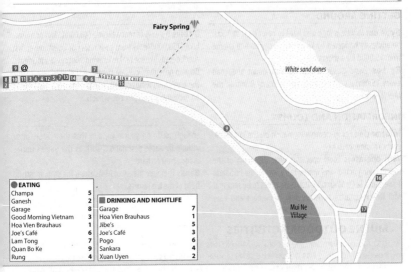

EATING

Champa	5
Ganesh	2
Garage	8
Good Morning Vietnam	3
Hoa Vien Brauhaus	1
Joe's Café	6
Lam Tong	7
Quan Bo Ke	9
Rung	4

DRINKING AND NIGHTLIFE

Garage	7
Hoa Vien Brauhaus	1
Jibe's	5
Joe's Café	3
Pogo	6
Sankara	4
Xuan Uyen	2

Fairy Spring

North of Mui Ne, signed from the main road • Daily 24hr • Free

Mui Ne's famed **Fairy Spring** is in fact a narrow stream running through a psychedelic landscape of red **sand dunes**, which are accessible via an uphill, inland turn just west of Mui Ne village. You're best advised to kick off your shoes and pad your way along the course of the stream itself – a highly pleasurable, not to mention stunningly beautiful, experience. You'll be able to follow the stream for a couple of kilometres, though most find themselves hiking up the adjacent dunes at some point; the softness of the sand makes them a little tricky to climb (you'll need three steps to travel the distance of two), but the resulting views are ample reward. The sand can also get very **hot**, so it makes sense to go early or late in the day, when the colours are also at their most spectacular.

White dunes

Northeast of Mui Ne, signed from the main road • Daily 24hr • Free • Quad-biking and dune-buggying best organized through one of the many agencies in town

In Mui Ne, sand-based fun is not confined to the beach – just north of Mui Ne village, in an area known as the **white dunes**, you'll be able to get your fix of **quad-biking** and **dune-buggying**. You'll likely run into local kids offering **plastic sledges** for hire – great fun in theory, though in practice it's hard to slide for more than a few metres.

ARRIVAL AND DEPARTURE   MUI NE

By bus The majority of travellers arrive in Mui Ne on open-tour buses, which drop off outside the relevant company offices. Most hotels will be able to book an onward ticket, often for buses that pick up right outside the front door. Local buses are few and far between, bar the shuttle buses linking Phan Thiet and Mui Ne (every 15min; 13,000đ); there's also a single, juddering, daily service down to Vung Tau.

Destinations Ho Chi Minh City (4hr); Nha Trang (5hr).

By train Many expats go by train from Ho Chi Minh City to Phan Thiet (see p.215), which cuts out the stress of traffic jams and delays on the buses. Getting back this way can be hard, since tickets often sell out and the station is some distance from the beach – buy your return ticket in Ho Chi Minh City, if you're sure about your dates. If you're heading to or from the north, the nearest station is in remote Muong Man (see p.215), a tiny village that's a minimum 200,000đ from Mui Ne on a xe om.

GETTING AROUND

By xe om Mui Ne is long and hard to cover on foot. You'll be endlessly badgered by xe om drivers, who will charge from 15,000đ for a short ride.

By bus Basic buses bump up and down the road every 15min; it's 9000đ from any A to any B within the Mui Ne area.

By bike It's easy to rent a bicycle (40,000đ/day) or motorbike (150,000đ/day) from your resort or guesthouse; first check details like the brakes to avoid unnecessary incidents. Do also note that, outside the more sheltered resort strip, the area's high winds can often make it tricky to get around on something with just two wheels.

INFORMATION AND TOURS

Information For in-depth information on the local area, visit ⓦ muinebeach.net.

Tour operators Local operators offer day tours of the region taking in the sand dunes, Fairy Spring, the Po Shanu Towers and Ta Cu Mountain. However, it has to be said that Mui Ne's local attractions are few in number and easy enough to do on your own, and that these tours often include missable destinations such as the guide's uncle's dragon fruit orchard.

Banks There are plenty of ATMs along the strip, mostly in front of the big resorts.

MUI NE OUTDOOR ACTIVITIES

Though the number one activity at Mui Ne is relaxing on the beach, there's a lot more to do besides. The place has become hugely popular with **windsurfers** and **kitesurfers**; there are also a couple of good **golf courses** (plus a crazy one) in the area; and, though not an activity as such, you may find it hard to pass up the chance to **wallow in mud** at a local hot springs.

WATERSPORTS

Mui Ne is heaving with **wind- and kitesurfers** when the wind is up between August and April; the strip even hosts an event in the Asian Windsurf Tour each February. There are a number of establishments that offer equipment rental; the following also give lessons in windsurfing ($55 per hour) and kitesurfing ($60). It costs about the same if you'd simply like to rent the equipment, and Mui Ne is the perfect place to hone your skills – the winds here can be gusty and aggressive, so anywhere else will seem easy by comparison.

★**Jibes** 90 Nguyen Dinh Chieu ⓣ0623 847008, ⓦwindsurf-vietnam.com. Quality operator with savvy instructors, excellent equipment and the best surfing bonhomie in town.

Mr. Lee's Kite School 78 Nguyen Dinh Chieu ⓣ 0974 804695. Based at *Xuan Uyen* hotel (see p.220), this is about the cheapest reliable operator in town.

They have only a few instructors, so it's best to contact them well in advance.

Sailing Club 24 Nguyen Dinh Chieu ⓣ0623 847440, ⓦsailingclubkiteschool.com. A little pricier than the rest, but then again, expert instructors and top-end equipment don't usually come cheap.

GOLF

There are two decent golf courses in the Mui Ne area. First is the **Ocean Dunes Golf Club**, on the grounds of the *DuParc Ocean Dunes* in Phan Thiet (see p.215). Larger and newer is the **Sealinks Golf and Country Club** (ⓣ0623 741666, ⓦsealinkscity.com), which sprawls across the hills at the entrance to Mui Ne. Both boast fabulous ocean views, and cost a shade under $100 per round, including caddy.

Less refined, though a lot of fun, is the crazy golf "course" at **Tropical Minigolf** (9.30am–midnight); it's 100,000đ per person, though (somewhat amazingly) for 120,000đ they'll give you a beer to waltz around the course with, while 150,000đ can upgrade you to a cocktail.

MUD BATHS

Mui Ne may only have one mud-bath centre compared with Nha Trang's three, but it's a real winner. The **Mui Ne Hot Mineral Mud Centre** (ⓣ0623 743482; 6am–9pm) moved to a gleaming new location uphill from the coastal road in 2012 – all very fancy, right the way down to the underwater seats encircling the pool's cocktail bar. The rates vary depending on what kind of service you'd like; the regular mud bath will set you back 570,000đ for a couple, or 390,000đ for just the one, and you'll get a free swimsuit (if you need one), towel and bottle of water. If you're not into mud and would simply like to use the pool, jacuzzis and sunbeds, it's just 80,000đ per person.

ACCOMMODATION

Since the main activity in Mui Ne is lazing on the beach, choosing where to stay is the biggest decision to make while here. Budget options are limited, as the resort's upmarket image means that many places that previously offered cheap rooms have now upgraded their facilities and prices – though of course this means there is more choice in the moderate and expensive categories. Bear in mind that many places bump their prices up at weekends. Not everywhere along the beach has street numbers; places are often identified by kilometre distance along the road from Phan Thiet.

Blue Waves 94a Nguyen Dinh Chieu ☎0623 847989, ⓦtiendatresort.com.vn. Also known as the "Tien Dat", this is about as cheap a resort as you'll find along the strip. Rooms aren't super-swish but they're comfortable and fairly priced; you'll pay about twenty percent more for those facing the sea. $50

★**Cham Villas** 32 Nguyen Dinh Chieu ☎0623 741234, ⓦchamvillas.com. Mini-resort with only a handful of luxurious, well-appointed villas – just about representing value for money. A good place to go if you're seeking some peace and quiet; spa treatments are also available. $145

Coco Beach 58 Nguyen Dinh Chieu ☎0623 847111, ⓦcocobeach.net. This French-run resort has 28 tasteful, thatched wooden bungalows and some family-size villas, complete with verandas, Cham-style fabrics, a/c and all modern comforts, set among tropical gardens off the beach. The relaxed style and friendly staff have made this an established favourite. $170

Full Moon Beach 84–90 Nguyen Dinh Chieu ☎0623 847008, ⓦfullmoonbeach.com.vn. Attractive and sturdy beachfront establishment, featuring thatched bamboo huts with verandas and spacious rooms, some on stilts and with attached bathrooms; rates include breakfast. Also note that this is the location of *Jibe's*, one of Mui Ne's best bars (see p.221). $70

Grace Boutique 144a Nguyen Dinh Chieu ☎0623 743357, ⓦgraceboutiqueresort.com. One of Mui Ne's friendliest resorts, which is one reason why it has become a real favourite with Ho Chi Minh City-fleeing expats, many of whom return again and again (there are only fourteen rooms, so it helps to book ahead). Almost uniquely in Vietnam, smoking is prohibited across the resort, which also features a small infinity pool and an equally minuscule restaurant. $120

Hiep Hoa 80 Nguyen Dinh Chieu ☎0623 847262, ⓔhiephoatourism@yahoo.com. Just eight smart but basic rooms and a handful of bungalows, some with fans and others a/c, in this tiny, friendly compound facing a fine stretch of beach. $20

Malibu Resort Ward 5 ☎0623 849669, ⓦmalibu resortmuine.com. Located to the east of the main bay, this place feels extremely secluded – come here if you want to relax. Rooms are spacious and smartly furnished, and in addition to the modest swimming pool there's a small bar-restaurant – a good thing, given the location. $65

★**Mia Resort** 24 Nguyen Dinh Chieu ☎0623 847440, ⓦmiamuine.com. Delightfully landscaped resort featuring rooms and bungalows with thatched roofs and mustard-coloured walls, plus imaginative interiors with good use of local textiles. Swimming pool, popular bar and restaurant too. $115

★**Mui Ne Backpackers** 88 Nguyen Dinh Chieu ☎0623 847047, ⓦmuinebackpackers.com. Extremely well-run hostel, good for both dorm accommodation and private rooms, plus a few bungalows at the back, with all guests free to use the small pool and join in the inevitable night-time bar-crawl. Note that the increased popularity of the place should have resulted in a second venue by the time you read this – a good thing, as the first one is often fuly booked. Dorm $8, double $30

Pandanus Km 5 ☎0623 849849, ⓦpandanusresort .com. Sitting in near-solitude east of the strip, and indeed east of Mui Ne village itself, this is a smart resort with staff who genuinely seem eager to please. It boasts elegant rooms and a landscaped garden, plus pool, spa and restaurant overlooking the beach; the breakfasts here are excellent. $135

Sand Dune 117 Nguyen Dinh Chieu ☎0623 741168. At the upper end of budget, this is a neat (and fairly large) place with small but cheery rooms, and a good tour information desk in the lobby. The hotel reception is actually hidden away upstairs – you'll have to ask, and perhaps wait until someone arrives to serve you. $20

★**Shades** 98a Nguyen Dinh Chieu ☎0623 743237, ⓦshadesmuine.com. You'll have to book early to stay at this fantastic boutique hotel. There are just eleven individual apartments here, all super-hip in design; rooms include neat touches like double-glazing, flat-screen TVs and kitchen facilities. $60

The Sun 117c Nguyen Dinh Chieu ☎0623 741737. One of the few budget options in the centre of the strip, this chilled-out venue is particularly popular with wind-surfers, some of whom end up staying for weeks. Rooms are arrayed across cheery, lemon-coloured buildings. $15

★**Terracotta** 28 Nguyen Dinh Chieu ☎0623 847610, ⓦterracottaresort.com. Boasting one of the best reputations on the strip, this immaculate resort as gardens that could double as golf lawns, as well as elegant rooms and amiable staff – it's a great pick and competitively priced. $100

Victoria Phan Thiet Resort Km 9 ☎0623 813000, ⓦvictoriahotels-asia.com. The cottages set among tropical gardens feature spacious interiors with tasteful European decor and all mod cons. The management can arrange excursions and guests have free use of mountain bikes. $190

★**Villa Aria** 60a Nguyen Dinh Chieu ☎0623 741660, ⓦ villaariamuine.com. This place certainly has a bit of wow factor. The large, bright, airy rooms have been decorated with rare attention; there's a massage pavilion looking onto the swimming pool, which itself looks onto the sea; and the restaurant prides itself on fresh fruits,

veggies and seafood. $\overline{5}$**140**

Xuan Uyen 78 Nguyen Dinh Chieu ☎0623 847476. A range of simple but incredibly cheap bungalow rooms, some with sea view. One of Mui Ne's few real backpacker hang-outs, it also serves reasonably priced food and drinks in the beachside chill-out area. $\overline{5}$**10**

EATING

What Mui Ne lacks in cultural attractions, it makes up for with gastronomic diversity. As well as the resorts and hotels, all of which have their own restaurants, there's no shortage of independent eating joints and bars along the strip. All of the following restaurants are open through the day, though note that you'll struggle to find anywhere to eat after 10pm.

★**Champa** 58 Nguyen Dinh Chieu ☎0623 847111. On a delightful terrace at *Coco Beach Resort*, this serves top-class French cuisine (dinner only) with impeccable service and prices from about 240,000đ for a main dish. Daily 3–10pm.

Ganesh 57 Nguyen Dinh Chieu ☎0623 741330. This small but attractive restaurant is Mui Ne's only Indian option, and is just as authentic as its sister restaurants elsewhere in Vietnam. Thali platters are a good choice, and start at 160,000đ; alternatively, try the *malai kofta* (minced cottage cheese balls with spices; 89,000đ) or fish masala (99,000đ), and wash the lot down with a very tall mango lassi (49,000đ). Daily 11am–10pm.

Garage 259 Nguyen Dinh Chieu. Like a little piece of Russia exiled to the Vietnamese coast, it's well worth the small journey from the centre of the strip to this fun bar/restaurant. As well as providing an opportunity to bond with some of the many Russian travellers visiting Mui Ne, the food here is pretty darn good – borshch (40,000đ), beetroot salad (50,000đ) and blini pancakes (from 30,000đ) are good choices. Pool competitions on Saturday nights, and drinks every night (see below). Daily 9am–2am.

Good Morning Vietnam 57 Nguyen Dinh Chieu ☎0623 847585. As elsewhere in Vietnam, this is a safe option for those with a hankering for pizza (from 97,000đ), of which they have around twenty varieties. Gnocchi, ravioli and pasta dishes are great too, and cost around 120,000đ; they've also a modest wine list. Daily 8am–11pm.

Hoa Vien Brauhaus 2a Nguyen Dinh Chieu ☎0623 741383. Way out on the western edge of the strip, this serves a tasty mix of Asian dishes and local seafood, though

it's the few Czech ones that stand out – try the sausages (110,000đ), schnitzel-style pork (180,000đ) or Slovakia's current number one dish, fried cheese (180,000đ). Oh, and then there's the beer (see below). Daily 8am–10pm.

★**Joe's Café** 86 Nguyen Dinh Chieu ☎0623 847177. The best Western food on the strip, with a range of great burgers – have them stuffed with mushroom and mozzarella (149,000đ) or beetroot, egg, cheese and spice (139,000đ). The ice cream is awfully tempting on a hot day, especially the passion fruit sorbet (30,000đ). Also a great bar (see opposite). Daily 7am–midnight.

Lam Tong 92 Nguyen Dinh Chieu ☎0623 847598. This breezy, no-frills place is right on the beach and has some of the lowest prices on the strip (around 59,000đ for squid, shrimp or fish mains). They turn the grills on in the evening, when you'll also likely be enquiring about the cheap beer (12,000đ for a bottle of Saigon). Daily 8am–9.30pm.

★**Quan Bo Ke** 146 Nguyen Dinh Chieu ☎0937 239915. Pleasingly local in nature, this is the best of several similar ventures packed into the same tight area on the way to Mui Ne Village. You can sit right above the waves from which your meal was plucked – a tray of grilled shellfish can be yours from 50,000đ (make sure they're not undercooked), two large seafood kebabs cost 100,000đ, and there are plenty more point-to-order possibilities. Daily 10am–11pm.

Rung 65b Nguyen Dinh Chieu ☎0623 847589. The name of this restaurant means "forest" in Vietnamese, and thanks to tree-trunk seating, a treehouse atmosphere and other quirky decor, that's exactly what it feels like here. The menu is, suitably, full of animals to eat; try something normal, or go for frog, eel, snake, ostrich or crocodile (most mains 120,000–200,000đ). Daily 2–10pm.

DRINKING AND NIGHTLIFE

Mui Ne's nightlife is improving in direct proportion to the number of visitors looking for action. Most staying at the resorts tend to drink there too. Bars often close at dawn in peak season, while at quieter times you may find many of them closed.

★**Garage** 259 Nguyen Dinh Chieu. This Russian restaurant is worth mentioning for its fun atmosphere and good vodka selection. If you feel like something different, try the "Russian Flag" – a shot tricolored white,

blue and red in honour of the motherland (70,000đ). Daily 9am–2am.

Hoa Vien Brauhaus 2a Nguyen Dinh Chieu ☎0623 741383. The microbrewed beer at this restaurant is probably the tastiest alcohol available in Mui Ne. Glasses of the good stuff cost from 40,000đ; dark and red beers are available too. Daily 8am–10pm.

Jibe's 90 Nguyen Dinh Chieu ☎ 0623 847008. The main base of the local kitesurfing community, and for good reason – the drinks are good and cheap (cocktails 80,000đ), the comfy seating encourages chatting with friends old or new, and the atmosphere is uber chilled. The sea views help, too. Daily 7am–late.

Joe's Café 86 Nguyen Dinh Chieu ☎ 0623 847177. This restaurant also makes a fine place to drink, especially in the evening when there's usually live music. Beers from 25,000đ. Daily 7am–midnight.

Pogo 138 Nguyen Dinh Chieu ☎ 0907 387600. Sometimes hectic and sometimes chilled, this is one of the best bars in the area. Suck on a beer (25,000đ), cocktail (80,000đ) or shisha (150,000đ), while squashing sand in

between your toes. Good burgers, too, and 100,000đ will get you a free flow of rum and coke from 10pm to 1am. Daily 8pm–2am.

★**Sankara** 90 Nguyen Dinh Chieu ☎ 0623 7411122. This rather pricey bar is by far the trendiest in Mui Ne; its various nooks and crannies surround an open-air pool, and the whole joint is illuminated with gentle lighting in the evening. Beers are cheap at 20,000đ; cocktails will set you back more like 110,000đ. Also note that they often host yoga classes in the morning and/or early evening. Daily 10am–midnight, often later.

Xuan Uyen 78 Nguyen Dinh Chieu ☎ 0623 847476. The tiny beachside terrace at the back of this hotel makes cheap cocktails (from 25,000đ) and is about as close in feel to "old" Mui Ne as you're going to get – rickety chairs, hole-dotted umbrellas and a wonderful beach view. Daily early morning to late.

Ca Na

Given its proximity to the highway, the small town of **CA NA** is a more relaxing place than you would think – it might even tempt you into staying overnight. Beyond the coracles parked along the beach, the water is invitingly clear and snorkelling is a possibility, though you'd be wise to ask locals where to wade in as the coral here is razor sharp. If you crave a little more solitude, a spine of decent dunes back up another good stretch of sand 2km south; a fifteen-minute walk east of the resort area is the **main village** itself, characterized by the blue fishing boats typical of coastal Vietnam.

ARRIVAL AND DEPARTURE   CA NA

By train Ca Na's station is on the main line, 2km north of the beach and village – around 20,000đ by xe om.
By bus Buses stop right next to the beach resort. You

should be able to get open-tour buses to drop you off, though arranging a pick-up can be troublesome. The only regular services are to Phan Rang (1hr).

ACCOMMODATION AND EATING

Ca Na has a few cheap places to stay, and that's about that; both establishments listed here have attached restaurants, which are your best bet for food. Both lie in between highway and beach, a short walk east of the bus stop, and about 1.7km south of the train station.

Ca Na ☎ 0683 761320. Cheap and a little scruffy, this guesthouse has rooms set in distinctive, high-roofed bungalows – a nice idea, though sloping walls mean that parts of the room are next to inaccessible. $15
Hon Co ☎ 0683 760999. A budget resort, at least in

layout, this is a surprisingly nice place for somewhere as remote as Ca Na. You can opt to stay in the regular hotel section, rather than the bungalows; the whole place is aimed at domestic tourists, and the karaoke room can get rather noisy. $20

Phan Rang and around

Although **PHAN RANG** is an unlovely place, whose western limits have fused with the neighbouring town of **Thap Cham**, the area is rich in historical attractions. The name of the latter, meaning "Cham Towers", gives a clue to the primary reason for stopping here. This region of Vietnam once comprised the Cham **kingdom of Panduranga** (see box, p.222), and the nearby remnants of **Po Klong Garai** are some of the best preserved in the country. The excellent **Po Re Me** towers – nearly as good – are also in the area.

CHAM ARCHITECTURE

The weathered but beguiling **towers** that punctuate the scenery upcountry from Phan Thiet to Da Nang are the only remaining legacy of **Champa**, an Indianized kingdom that ruled parts of central and southern Vietnam for over fourteen centuries (see p.432). From murky beginnings in the late second century, Champa rose to unify an elongated strip from Phan Thiet to Dong Hoi, and by the end of the fourth century Champa comprised four provinces: **Amaravati**, around Hue and Da Nang; **Vijaya**, centred around Quy Nhon; **Kauthara**, in the Nha Trang region; and **Panduranga**, which corresponds to present-day Phan Thiet and up to Phan Rang. The unified kingdom's first capital, established in the fourth century in Amaravati, was **Simhapura** ("Lion City"); nearby, just outside present-day Hoi An, **My Son**, Champa's holiest site and spiritual heartland, was established (see p.261).

To honour their gods, Cham kings sponsored the construction of the **religious edifices** that still stand today; the red-brick ruins of their towers and temples can be seen all along the coast of south-central Vietnam. While they never attained the magnificence of Angkor, their greatest legacy was a striking architectural style characterized by a wealth of exuberant sculpture. The typical Cham **temple complex** is centred around the **kalan**, or sanctuary, normally pyramidal inside, and containing a *lingam*, or phallic representation of Shiva, set on a dais that was grooved to channel off water used in purification rituals. Having first cleansed themselves and prayed in the **mandapa**, or meditation hall, worshippers would then have proceeded under a **gate tower** and below the *kalan*'s (normally) east-facing vestibule into the sanctuary. Any ritual objects pertaining to worship were kept in a nearby repository room, which normally sported a boat-shaped roof.

Cham towers crop up at regular intervals all the way up the coast from Phan Thiet to Da Nang, and many of them have been restored in recent years. A handful of sites representing the **highlights** of what remains of Champa civilization would include: Po Klong Garai towers (see below); Thap Doi towers (see p.237); Po Re Me Tower (see p.224); My Son (see p.261); and Po Nagar towers (see p.228).

4

Tuan Tu, one of Vietnam's most appealing Cham villages, lies near Phan Rang, as does **Ninh Chu Beach**, a glorious sweep of wide sand that is sometimes deliciously quiet on weekdays, but often overrun with Vietnamese at weekends.

If you'd just like to see Po Klong Garai, you won't need to visit Phan Rang at all – the towers will eat up an hour, at the most, and it's a long day-trip from Mui Ne or Nha Trang. With some clever scheduling, you can merely get on the next train – there are places to eat around the station.

Quan Cong Temple

In the centre of Phan Rang on Thong Nhat • Daily sunrise to sunset • Free

The only thing to see in Phan Rang itself is the **Quan Cong Temple**, dedicated to Chinese deity, Guan Yu, and dating from the 1860s. It has faded, pink-wash walls that rise to three consecutive roofs, each draped on huge red wooden piles imported from China, and laden with fanciful figurines and dragons. Quan Cong himself is at the head of the third and final chamber, framed by ornate gilt woodwork and rows of pikes. There's a decent **market** just south of the temple, one popular with local Cham people.

Po Klong Garai

Daily 7am–5pm • 15,000đ • Complex visible from Thap Cham station (20,000đ by xe om); to walk, head south and take the road under the tracks • 50,000đ from Phan Rang by xe om

Elevated with fitting grandeur on a granite mound known as Trau Hill, the **Po Klong Garai Cham towers** are among the most spectacular sights on the southern Vietnamese coast. Dating back to around 1400 and the rule of King Jaya Simharvarman III, the

complex comprises a *kalan*, or sanctuary, a smaller gate tower and a repository, under whose boat-shaped roof offerings would have been placed. It's the 25m-high *kalan*, though, that's of most interest. From a distance its stippled body impresses; up close, you see a bas-relief of six-armed Shiva cavorting above doorposts etched with Cham inscriptions and ringed by arches crackling with stonework flames, while other gods sit cross-legged in niches elsewhere around the exterior walls.

Inside the complex

Push deeper into the *kalan*'s belly and there's a *mukha* lingam fashioned in a likeness of the Cham king, Po Klong Garai, after whom the complex is named. In days gone by, the statue of Shiva's bull (Nandi) that stands in the vestibule would have been "fed" by farmers wishing for good harvests; nowadays it gets a feed only at the annual **Kate Festival** (the Cham New Year), a great spectacle if you're here around October. On the eve of the festival, there's traditional Cham music and dance at the complex, followed, the next morning, by a lively procession bearing the king's raiment to the tower.

Po Re Me Tower

8km south of Phan Rang and Thap Cham on Highway 1 • Daily 7.30am–6pm • Free • Track hard to find, so take a xe om (about 100,000đ return from Phan Rang)

If Po Klong Garai inspires further interest in Cham towers, you could make the trickier journey out to **Po Re Me Tower**. Like its near-neighbour, the tower (which draws its name from the last Cham king) enjoys a fine hilltop location, though its four storeys tapering to a lingam are sturdier and less finished than Po Klong Garai. Its high point is the splendid bas-relief at the *kalan*'s entrance, depicting Shiva manifest in the image of mustachioed King Po Re Me waggling his arms, and watched over by two Nandis. Po Re Me is also a focus of Cham festivities during the Kate Festival (see p.54).

Tuan Tu Village

3–4km from central Phan Rang, though unsigned and hard to track down by yourself • Xe om around 100,000đ for the round-trip

There's still a Cham presence around Phan Rang. **Tuan Tu Village** is home to more than a thousand Cham people – who are largely **Muslim** today, as you'll soon divine from the headcloths that they favour over conical hats. They maintain an unpretentious, 1966-built **mosque** free of any trappings, not even a minaret; it's located behind a well, to the right of the settlement's only road. Also keep any eye out for the distinctive **Cham text**, dotted liberally about the place and, with its Southeast Asian swirls, rather more beautiful than Vietnam's somewhat messy Roman writing. Locals are friendly and not used to seeing visitors – don't be surprised to find yourself invited for tea or coffee.

Ninh Chu Beach

Some 5km northest of Phan Rang is Ninh Chu beach, a more indolent alternative to trekking around Phan Rang's Cham towers. The beach is a reasonably clean and wide crescent of sand – soft, if not exactly golden. Ninh Chu doesn't have the same pulling power for foreigners as Mui Ne or Nha Trang, but its a popular place for swimming, sunbathing, beach games and jogging too. With several resorts located here, it's worth considering as a place to rest up, particularly midweek, when it can be very quiet. If you're here at a weekend, be prepared for crowds of families and noisy teenagers.

ARRIVAL AND DEPARTURE   **PHAN RANG AND AROUND**

Note that though fused together with a few stringy roads, the centres of Phan Rang and Thap Cham are around 7km apart. Trains arrive in Thap Cham to the west, and buses in Phan Rang to the east, and you'd be wise to plan accordingly – the train station is right next to the Cham towers, though the bus station is closer to most accommodation and Tuan Tu village.

By train The train station (Ga Thap Cham) sits on the main line, though not all services stop here – you'll find out which ones do when booking your ticket.

Destinations Ho Chi Minh City (2 daily; 6hr 30min); Nha Trang (2 daily; 2hr).

By bus The bus station is 300m north of Phan Rang town centre. Local buses to Ca Na leave from outside the *Ho Phong* hotel.

Destinations Ca Na (1hr); Da Lat (3hr); Ho Chi Minh City (7hr); Nha Trang (2hr); Phan Thiet (3hr).

ACCOMMODATION AND EATING

Accommodation in Phan Rang itself is limited; you're better off avoiding the town completely and heading for **Ninh Chu Beach**, where the options are much more appealing. There are also a few cheap options near the train station in Thap Cham, if you need to stay that way. As for **eating**, there's nothing notable in town, but there are plenty of snack shacks around the train station, and many decent establishments on Ninh Chu Beach itself.

PHAN RANG

Ho Phong 353–363 Ngo Gia Tu ☎ 0683 920333. The best option in the centre, with bare but spacious rooms and (occasionally) an English-speaker at reception. It's at the south end of town, near the bridge. Breakfast not included. 💲25

Thong Nhat 343 Thong Nhat ☎ 0683 827201. A little cheaper than *Ho Phang*, but almost as good. It's at the north end of town, and therefore convenient for the bus station; in addition, there's a restaurant on the ground level. 💲16

NINH CHU

Bau Truc Resort ☎ 0683 874047, ⓦ bautrucresort .com. In the centre of the beach and is itself centred on a wonderful swimming pool, this resort draws heavily on the region's Cham heritage for its design. Rooms are smartly decorated, if rather small; conversely, the size of the

complex as a whole can make it feel deserted outside peak season. 💲75

Hoan Cau ☎ 0683 890077, ⓦ hoancautourist.com.vn. One of the strangest hotels in Vietnam, with rooms made to look like old tree stumps and statues of Snow White characters dotted around the complex. Luridly cheesy, the rooms are ugly and cramped together; nevertheless, they're spacious, clean and good value on the inside. Rooms come in various sizes and prices, so check a few. 💲15

★ **Saigon Ninhchu** ☎ 0683 876000, ⓦ saigonninhchu hotel.com.vn. At the far north end of the bay, this hotel has beautifully furnished, thick-carpeted, spacious rooms, and the executive suites even have beach views from the bath. There's also a big pool, tennis courts, a spa and a classy restaurant that's the best place to eat for miles around and reasonably priced to boot – a bucketful of oysters steamed over lemongrass will set you back 90,000đ. 💲75

Nha Trang

Big enough to bustle, yet small enough to retain its relaxed air, the delightful city of **NHA TRANG** has, despite increasingly stiff competition, earned its place as Vietnam's top beach destination. A grand 6km scythe of soft yellow sand is lapped by rolling waves on one side and fringed on the other by cafés, restaurants, hotels and some unusual modern sculptures. Hawkers are on hand to supply paperbacks, fresh pineapple and massages, while **scuba-diving** classes and all kinds of **watersports** are available. Local companies also offer popular day-trips to Nha Trang's outlying **islands**, combining hiking, **snorkelling** and an onboard feast of seafood. Bear in mind that the rainy season, around November and December, sees the sea get choppy and the beach loses much of its appeal.

Though beach-bumming certainly takes precedence over sightseeing, there's far more to Nha Trang than sea and sand. The city itself sports a handful of attractions – the pick of which are the **Yersin Museum** and a couple of religous buildings – but Nha Trang's **culinary scene** stands out as particularly noteworthy, as does the range of accommodation, set among some stylish boutiques and bars. Then there are a few sights, both in and around the city, with the intriguing **Po Nagar Cham towers** of greatest appeal: by the time Nguyen lords wrested this patch of the country from Champa in the mid-seventeenth century, the towers had already stood here for over seven hundred years. Beyond the centre, you'll find hot springs in which you can wallow in mud, the world's longest cross-sea cable-car ride, and more besides. Last, but not least, is the city's huge and hugely photogenic **fishing fleet**,

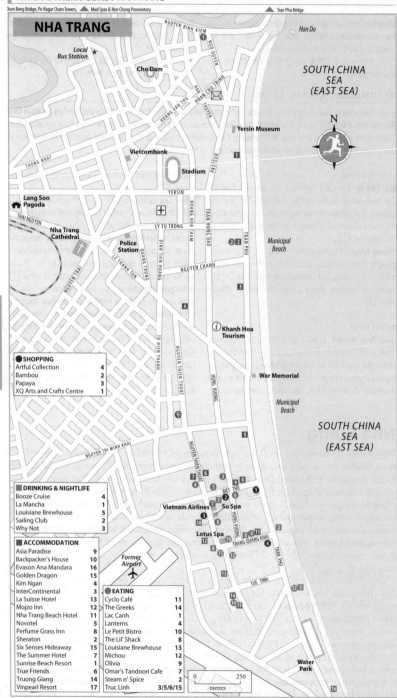

Xom Bong Bridge, Po Nagar Cham Towers, ▲ Mud Spas & Hon Chong Promontory · ▲ Tran Phu Bridge

NHA TRANG

Hon Do

SOUTH CHINA SEA (EAST SEA)

Local Bus Station

Cho Dam

Yersin Museum

Vietcombank

Stadium

Lang Son Pagoda

Nha Trang Cathedral

Police Station

Khanh Hoa Tourism

Municipal Beach

War Memorial

Municipal Beach

SOUTH CHINA SEA (EAST SEA)

● **SHOPPING**
Artful Collection	4
Bambou	2
Papaya	3
XQ Arts and Crafts Centre	1

■ **DRINKING & NIGHTLIFE**
Booze Cruise	4
La Mancha	1
Louisiane Brewhouse	5
Sailing Club	2
Why Not	3

■ **ACCOMMODATION**
Asia Paradise	9
Backpacker's House	10
Evason Ana Mandara	16
Golden Dragon	15
Kim Ngan	4
InterContinental	3
La Suisse Hotel	13
Mojzo Inn	12
Nha Trang Beach Hotel	11
Novotel	5
Perfume Grass Inn	8
Sheraton	2
Six Senses Hideaway	15
The Summer Hotel	7
Sunrise Beach Resort	1
True Friends	6
Truong Giang	14
Vinpearl Resort	17

Vietnam Airlines · Su Spa

Lotus Spa

Former Airport

● **EATING**
Cyclo Café	11
The Greeks	14
Lac Canh	1
Lanterns	4
Le Petit Bistro	10
The Lil' Shack	8
Louisiane Brewhouse	13
Michou	12
Olivia	9
Omar's Tandoori Cafe	7
Steam n' Spice	2
Truc Linh	3/5/6/15

0   250
metres

Water Park

17, 15, Oceanographic Institute, Vinpearl Land Amusement Park, Airport & HCMC ▼

which moors just north of the centre – a place of salty, local appeal in a city that has been embracing change for decades.

Nha Trang Cathedral

Thai Nguyen • Daily 4am–1pm & 2–9pm; weekday mass 4.45am & 5pm, plus five Sunday services • Free

The stolid, grey-brick **Nha Trang Cathedral**, built in the 1930s, rises up over the sloping cobbled track that winds round to its front doors from Nguyen Trai. This is one of Vietnam's most passable impressions of a European cathedral; under the lofty, vaulted ceilings, vivid stained-glass windows depict Christ, Mary, Joseph, Joan of Arc and St Theresa.

Long Son Pagoda

Accessed from Thai Nguyen • Sunrise to sunset • Free

Easily visible from the cathedral is the **Long Son Pagoda**, a 1930s creation whose entrance is marked by stone gateposts topped by lotus buds. An impressive bronze Buddha stands at the head of the altar, and there are the usual capering dragons on the eaves, but it's the huge **White Buddha**, 180-odd steps up the hillside behind, that's the pagoda's greatest asset – and Nha Trang's most recognizable landmark. Crafted in 1963 to symbolize the Buddhist struggle against the repressive Diem regime, around its lotus-shaped pedestal are carved images of the monks and nuns who set fire to themselves in protest, among them Thich Quang Duc (see box, p.82). Note that in recent years, the pagoda has become a popular haunt for beggars.

Yersin Museum

Off Tran Phu • Mon–Fri 7.30–11am & 2–4.30pm • 26,000đ

Another sight worth tracking down in central Nha Trang is the **Yersin Museum**, dedicated to the famed French scientist (see box below). It's stuffed with laboratory equipment, letters, books and other paraphernalia formerly belonging to Yersin, though it shouldn't take you long to navigate the various exhibition rooms.

North of the centre

Just to the north of Nha Trang are a couple of wonderful sights – the evocative Cham towers of **Po Nagar**, and the joyous mud-pools of the **Thap Ba Hot Springs** (see box, p.233). Heading a little further north will bring you to the **Hon Chong Promontory**, a finger of granite boulders dashed by the sea; it's quite possible to clamber down to the rocks. Immediately up the coast is **Hon Chong Beach**, less refined than the city beach but more secluded. Cheap seafood restaurants proliferate at its far end. At night, the views from here across the bay to the central beach zone are very impressive.

ALEXANDRE YERSIN

A Swiss–French scientist who travelled to Southeast Asia in 1889 as a ship's doctor, **Alexandre Yersin** developed a great love for Vietnam and learned to speak Vietnamese fluently. He was responsible for the founding of Da Lat (he recognized the beneficial effects of the climate there for Europeans), and settled in Nha Trang in 1893. By the time of his death in 1943, Yersin had become a local hero, thanks not to his greatest achievement – the discovery of a **plague bacillus** in Hong Kong in 1894 (one named after him; *Yersinia pestis*) – but rather to his educational work in sanitation and agriculture, and to his ability to predict typhoons and thus save the lives of fishermen. Significantly, his name is still given to streets, not only in Nha Trang but around the country, sharing an honour generally only granted to Vietnamese heroes.

Po Nagar Cham towers

1.2km from central Nha Trang • Daily 6am–6pm • 30,000đ • Walk north from the beach and take the first left after the bridge, or hunt down a xe om (20,000–30,000đ)

The glorious **Po Nagar Cham towers** are Nha Trang's most popular sight. Of the estimated ten towers, or *kalan*, constructed here between the seventh and twelfth centuries by the Hindu Cham people (see p.472), only four remain. Their baked red bricks weathered so badly through the centuries that restoration work on the towers has been necessary; nevertheless, the complex manages to produce an age-old atmosphere, despite the gaggles of souvenir sellers.

The northern tower

The complex's largest and most impressive tower is the 25m-high **northern tower**, built in 817 by Harivarman I and dedicated to Yang Ino Po Nagar, tutelary Goddess Mother of the Kingdom and a manifestation of Uma, Shiva's consort. Restored sections stand out for their lighter hue, but the lotus-petal and spearhead motifs that embellish the tower are original, as is the lintel over the outer door, on which a lithe four-armed Shiva dances, flanked by musicians, on the back of an ox. The two sandstone pillars supporting this lintel bear spidery Cham inscriptions.

Inside, a vestibule tapering to a pyramidal ceiling leads to the main chamber, where a fog of incense hangs in the air. The golden statue that originally stood in here was pilfered by the Khmer in the tenth century and replaced by a black stone statue of Uma – minus its head, plundered by the French and now in a Parisian museum. The ten arms of cross-legged Uma are nowadays obscured by a gaudy yellow robe, and a doll-like face has been added. Yang Ino Po Nagar is still worshipped as the protectress of the city and the statue is bathed during the **Merian Festival** each March.

The other towers

Possessing neither the height nor the intricacy of the main *kalan*, the **central tower**, dating back to the seventh century, is dedicated to the god Cri Cambhu, and sees a steady flow of childless couples pass through to pray for fertility at its lingam. The **southern tower** is the smallest of the four, and also features a lingam inside. Beneath its boat-shaped roof, half-formed statues in relief are still visible at the **northwest tower**, and the frontal view of an elephant is just about discernible on the western facade, its serpentine trunk now blackened with age.

Hon Do

Daily 24hr • Free • To get here, hunt down a boat driver from Pham van Dong (30,000–40,000đ return is about right)

Sitting merrily in the bay just north of central Nha Trang, tiny **Hon Do** island makes a highly pleasant diversion. It's home to an eponymous pagoda, and stepping-stones lead from here to a series of altars – try to hunt down one overlooking the sea, and you've some great photo-fodder. One other thing to do before you leave is to pray for love – locals claim it's guaranteed to come true.

South of the centre

Unmissable just south of Nha Trang is **Hon Tre**, the biggest island in the bay by far, and home to one of the country's largest amusement parks. Near the jump-off points of ferry and cable car is the interesting **National Oceanographic Institute**.

Vinpearl Land Amusement Park

Park open daily 8am–9pm; cable car daily 9am–10pm • Entry 550,000đ including round-trip by ferry or cable car; canoe-taxi 150,000đ one-way (4-person minimum) • ☎ 0583 590111, ⓦ vinpearlland.com

Hon Tre is dominated by this massive amusement park, which includes a hotel (see p.231), a waterpark with slides and flumes, a mini-oceanarium, 4-D movies, a shopping mall and some rides – great fun, especially for those travelling with children. You can get here by speedboat or "canoe-taxi", but it's more enjoyable by cable car; the journey, at 3.3km long, is the longest such ride in the world. The mainland station is just south of central Nha Trang.

The National Oceanographic Institute

Beside Cau Da Wharf, 4km south of Nha Trang • Daily 6am–6pm • 30,000đ

Established in 1923 and housed in a colonial mansion, this is a veritable Frankenstein's lab of pickling jars and glass cases yielding crustaceans, fish, seaweed and coral. In one room an 18m-long humpback whale skeleton is displayed, plus a hammerhead shark and bow-mouth guitarfish. If you've been out snorkelling you might spot some recent acquaintances in the aquarium's twenty or so tanks of primary-coloured live fishes and sea horses. There are three large open ponds in the forecourt, home to horseshoe crabs, zebra sharks and various local species of fish; it's all a bit forlorn, though.

ARRIVAL AND DEPARTURE

NHA TRANG

By plane Cam Ranh International Airport (☎0583 989918), 35km south of the city, handles a prodigious number of Russian tourists, though few other international passengers: Vietnam Airlines (91 Nguyen Thien Thuat; daily 7–11.30am & 1.30–5pm; ☎0583 526768) has scheduled flights from Moscow, while in high season charter planes land from all over Russia. From the airport, take a bus (60,000đ) or taxi (around 350,000đ) to Nha Trang; cabs are cheaper heading *to* the airport.

Destinations Da Nang (3 weekly; 1hr 15min); Hanoi (2–4 daily; 1hr 45min); Ho Chi Minh City (3–6 daily; 1hr).

By train Ga Nha Trang (ticket office daily 7.30–11am & 1.30–9pm; ☎0583 822113) is just west of the city centre on Thai Nguyen. Though walkable, it's tempting to take a cab; as always, stepping out of the station and flagging one down on the main road will help you avoid the cowboys. Just about any hotel or travel agency in Nha Trang will get you a ticket, though since commission rates vary widely, it pays to shop around.

Destinations Da Nang (5 daily; 9hr–12hr 30min); Hanoi (5 daily; 24hr–32hr); Ho Chi Minh City (6 daily; 7hr 10min–11hr 15min); Hue (5 daily; 12hr–16hr 10min).

4

ACTIVITIES IN THE SOUTH CHINA SEA

SCUBA DIVING

Nha Trang is the **scuba centre of Vietnam**, as is well evidenced by the number of dive companies that operate here. It's best avoided October to December, when the strong currents stir up the silt and reduce visibility, but during the dry season (Jan–May) there are dive boats kitting out and casting off every day to one of over twenty dive sites in the region. A typical day out, including a couple of dives and lunch, costs around $80, with snorkelling around $25; PADI courses are also available, from basic Discover packs (around $100) to Open Water (4-day; $380).

You may hear grumblings about the size of the fish you'll see in the waters around Nha Trang, and it's true that they're usually pretty small. The Hon Mun area is good for barracuda, but even there they're mostly juvenile. However, one thing the area has in spades is hard coral, with over 350 species found so far – not too far off the Great Barrier Reef, which has around 410.

There are well over a dozen **operators** in Nha Trang and some are downright dangerous – there have been cases of divers left behind, and even a couple of deaths since the turn of the millennium. Many local outfits have licences recognized in Russia, but not anywhere else – stick with proper PADI-certified operators, including the two highly reputable places listed below.

Rainbow Divers 90a Hung Vuong ☎0583 524351, ⌨ divevietnam.com.

Sailing Club Divers 72–74 Tran Pbu ☎0583 521629, ⌨ sailingclubdivers.com.

WATERSPORTS

If you'd rather get your kicks above water, various points on the beach rent out watersports equipment (the section by *Louisiane Brewhouse* is best). Jet-skiing was thankfully recently outlawed in the waters off Nha Trang, though you'll still be able to enjoy **windsurfing** (rental $25, lesson $45) and regular **surfing** (rental $50, lesson $75). These days many operators actually head down south to Long Beach, which is more appropriate for such activities.

BOAT TRIPS TO THE ISLANDS

Several companies in Nha Trang offer day-trips to a selection of islands, including a stop for **snorkelling** and a **seafood lunch** on board – all for around $6–8 per person. However, to fully enjoy the day, you'll need to fork out for several extras if you don't want to sit on the boat and wait till everyone comes back. Some boat rides, particularly those booked through backpacker guesthouses, can be quite wild and alcohol-fuelled, while other operators run gentler tours.

On a typical island day tour, you'll be picked up from your hotel, taken to Cau Da Wharf, 6km south of the town centre, and shuffled on to one of many boats jostling in the harbour. As the boat casts off at around 9.30am, you'll pass beneath the cable car to Hon Tre (see p.228), then chug between islands for about half an hour to **Hon Mun** (Black Island; 10,000đ entry), named after the dark cliffs that rear up from it. There's no beach to speak of on Hon Mun, but the island boasts one of the best places for snorkelling in the area, with some great coral. Boats hang around for an hour or so while people snorkel over the corals or sunbathe on deck, and there are frequently diving groups here too. There's a 40,000đ charge to snorkel in this "protected area", though it's not clear quite how it's being protected.

After a break for lunch in the shelter of Hon Mot, boats head for Hon Tam, where there's a small beach (30,000đ entry), and you get the chance to stretch on the sand or splash about in the sea for an hour before heading for the final destination, the **Tri Nguyen Aquarium** (60,000đ) on **Hon Mieu**. The setting here is wonderfully kitsch: visitors approach the site through giant lobsters and past cement sharks, and the strange building that houses the aquarium looks like a galleon dragged up from the depths and draped in seaweed. Inside, the tanks feature black-tipped sharks, bug-eyed groupers, hawksbill turtles and colourful sea anemones. Finally the boat heads back to the mainland and visitors are whisked back to their hotels.

By bus Most visitors arrive on open-tour buses, which drop off centrally outside affiliated offices or hotels. The long-distance bus station (☎0583 822192) sits 1km west of the city centre, and around 700m west of the train station. **Destinations** Buon Ma Thuot (4hr); Da Lat (4hr); Da Nang (12hr); Ho Chi Minh City (10hr); Hue (15hr).

GETTING AROUND

On foot Nha Trang isn't a very large city, so walking everywhere is perfectly feasible – especially if a daily pilgrimage to the municipal beach marks the extent of your travels.
By bicycle Should you plan to stray a little further afield, bicycle rental is the most efficient and enjoyable way to go.

Bicycles are available for around 40,000đ per day at most of the city's hotels.
By xe om Xe om are everywhere if you need them, and even if you don't; see individual sight details for likely costs.
Car tours Fully fledged car tours of the region (around $50/day) can be arranged by tour operators.

ACCOMMODATION

The fact that Nha Trang is chock-full of hotels doesn't seem to be discouraging developers, and the city's already wide choice of accommodation just keeps on growing; already, beachfront monoliths are gradually blocking out any sea view from the backstreet mini-hotels. Even so, it's worth bearing in mind that the city draws Vietnamese as well as foreign tourists, and that there can be difficulties finding a room over public holidays, when prices rise. **Backpackers** should head straight for "Hostel Alley", opposite the Vietnam Airlines office on Nguyen Thien Thuat.

Asia Paradise 6 Biet Thu ☎0583 524686, ⓦasia paradisehotel.com. Decent mid-ranger, right in the middle of things. Their cheapest rooms are on the small side, but shell out a bit more and you can score yourself a whopper. All are elegant affairs featuring balconies. $40
★**Backpacker's House** 54g Nguyen Thien Thuat ☎0583 524500, ⓦbackpackershouse.net. Good backpacker option, set off the main road in the thick of the bar area. Rooms are comfy, with a/c and complimentary coffee

through the day, and it's a fine place to make new travel buddies. Dorm $7, double $12
Evason Ana Mandara Southern end of Tran Phu ☎0583 522222, ⓦsixsenses.com. Nha Trang's most luxurious resort comes with its own slice of beach and features dreamy bungalows with all mod cons and some traditional touches, including ethnic-minority tapestries. Facilities include two pools, tennis courts, a beach restaurant, and the superb Six Senses spa. $410

Golden Dragon 78/36 Tue Tinh ☎0583 527117, ⓦgoldendragonhotel.com.vn. A cosy and welcoming mini-hotel tucked away down a quiet backstreet in the south of town, just 5min from the beach, with good-value a/c rooms. There's a tiny pool and sundeck on the fourth floor. $20

Kim Ngan 52 Hoang Hoa Tham ☎0583 524411. Set in a relatively tranquil alley, this family-run place offers compact fan or a/c rooms at very competitive prices. On a quiet road and feels far from the action, though in reality it's just a short walk away from all the restaurants and bars. $10

★**InterContinental** 32–34 Tran Phu ☎0583 887777, ⓦintercontinental.com. Newly opened at the time of writing, this is the latest of the big hotel chains to hit town, and it's likely to thrive despite the intense competition. They've lavished attention on the place – check out the artistic metalwork in the lobby, the angular fittings that your breakfast buffet is sitting on, or the Bluetooth-ready speakers in the rooms (which are themselves divine). From some of the shower cubicles you can see the ocean, and there's a glorious pool on site. $145

★**La Suisse Hotel** 34 Tran Quang Khai ☎0583 524353, ⓦlasuissehotel.com. Perhaps the most popular budget hotel in the city, allying great service with cheap but well-appointed rooms. The semi-secluded location is also a bonus, since you're largely off the radar of hawkers and xe om drivers. $27

★**Mojzo Inn** 120/36 Nguyen Thien Thuat ☎0586 255568. Fantastic new place that's essentially a boutique hostel. The friendly staff are full of surprises and helpful advice; rooms and common areas have been artfully decorated along a red-white-black tricolore; and you'll be able to drink in superb views over breakfast from the rooftop. The only sad thing is that they have just fifteen rooms – book early! Dorm $8, private $18

Nha Trang Beach Hotel 4 Tran Quang Khai ☎0583 524468, ⓦnhatrangbeachhotel.com.vn. Smart mini-hotel in the budget district with a/c, hot water, TV and comfortable furnishings in all the rooms. $35

Novotel 50 Tran Phu ☎0583 221027, ⓦnovotel.com. Beautiful beachfront hotel, whose rates occasionally drop below $100 – five-star rooms at three-star prices. There's not too much in the way of facilities bar a small pool and spa, though this adds to the relaxed air. $150

Perfume Grass Inn 4a Biet Thu ☎0583 524286, ⓦperfume-grass.com. This reasonably priced place has

lots of "character" – a double-edged compliment, if ever there was one. Though creaking a bit around the seams, its rooms are worn but cheerful enough, some coming with reclining chairs and bathtubs. Staff are friendly, and there's a relaxing rooftop terrace. $20

★**Sheraton** 26–28 Tran Phu ☎0583 880000, ⓦsheraton.com. A relative newbie and already the flashiest city-centre option by far. Rooms have been decorated with soothing colours and local art, and you'll be able to see the sea from most shower cubicles. You should be able to lop a fair chunk off the rack rates. $250

Six Senses Hideaway Ninh Van Bay ☎0583 728222, ⓦsixsenses.com. Choose from beach villas, rock villas, hill-top villas, over-water villas or spa-suite villas on an idyllic island off the coast, but make sure you can handle the price tag before you come ashore. $500

The Summer Hotel 34 Nguyen Thien Thuat ☎0583 522186, ⓦthesummerhotel.com.vn. A cool 3-star mini-hotel. The rooms are modern and comfortable, if a little on the small side, staff are helpful and there's a swimming pool on the roof. $40

Sunrise Beach Resort 12–14 Tran Phu ☎0583 820999, ⓦsunrisenhatrang.com.vn. Enjoying a superb location towards the northern end of the beach, this elegant, rambling hotel boasts a classical colonial design. Some rooms are a little small, but move up to a suite and you'll be drinking in the sea views from the jacuzzi on your balcony. $210

True Friends 79 Nguyen Thien Thuat ☎0583 523237, ⓔtruefriendsinn@yahoo.com. One of several good new backpacker options, set off the main road in the thick of the bar area (it is, indeed, next door to a beer pong venue). They've only six dorms (and no private ones), but this makes for a snug atmosphere. Dorm $6

Truong Giang 3–8 Tran Quang Khai ☎0583 522125, ⓦtruonggianghotel.hostel.com. With professional service and clean, attractive rooms featuring small TVs, mini bars and colourful bedspreads, this is a great option in the competitive budget price category. It's a good idea to book ahead of time. $14

Vinpearl Resort 7 Tran Phu ☎0583 911 1166, ⓦvinpearlresort-nhatrang.com. This luxurious resort is actually located on Hon Tre out in the bay, and features nearly 500 well-equipped rooms as well as the biggest pool in Southeast Asia (5000sqm). It's accessed by speedboat or cable car from the southern end of Tran Phu. $260

EATING

Finding a decent **place to eat** presents no problem in cosmopolitan Nha Trang, with **seafood** its speciality – it's cheapest, and at its best, in the out-of-town area north of Tran Phu bridge. However, for something local and romantic, track down one of the seafood barbecue folk along the beach: there are no menus to speak of, but it's great fun to sit on the sand or a chair and eat goodies hauled from the sea in front of you. There's also a **night market** south of the water park, and many green-fronted branches of A-Mart, a local minimart chain that's useful for **self-caterers** (or those needing a beer for the beach).

Cyclo Café 130 Nguyen Thien Thuat ☎0582 613322. A friendly ambience along with a solid menu of Vietnamese and Italian food (from 80,000đ per pizza, or 68,000đ for pasta dishes), plus locally brewed beer make this place worth checking out. Daily 7.30am–10pm.

The Greeks 3/12 Tran Quang Khai ☎0945 011863. Greek-owned restaurant that certainly looks the part with its white-painted chairs and ocean blue splashed around the place. Come for a frappe (30,000đ), dips with bread (45,000đ), or a nice big slab of moussaka (100,000đ). Daily 9am–11pm.

Lac Canh 44 Nguyen Binh Kiem ☎0583 821391. Some way north of the centre, this table-side grill restaurant has been here since the 1970s, and remains hugely popular among locals. Not the most salubrious place in town, but the food (around 85,000đ per head) more than compensates – it's also incredibly smoky, so you'll need a good wash afterwards. Daily 9am–9.30pm.

★**Lanterns** 72 Nguyen Thien Thuat ☎0582 471674, ⓦlanternsvietnam.com. This charming restaurant serves delectable Vietnamese food, with burgers, pasta dishes (both from 80,000đ) and local specialities such as *com tam* (60,000đ) and snapper (168,000đ). However, that's not the end of the story – their proceeds, and food, help to support over a dozen local orphanages. They also run cooking classes (daily 9am–2pm; $24). Daily 7am–11pm.

Le Petit Bistro 26b Tran Quang Khai ☎0583 527201. Good-looking French bistro, doling out superb dishes at surprisingly reasonable prices – try the *petits plats* like *moules marinières* (130,000đ), or mains like veal in white wine sauce (165,000đ). The daily special board is usually the best place to start, though ensure you've room for one of their delectable desserts. Good cheese and cold cuts of meat round out the picture. Daily 8am–10.30pm.

The Lil' Shack 97/13 Nguyen Thien Thuat ☎0167 8052168. Tiny shack, as the name may suggest, doling out burritos and similar Mexican wrap options from 48,000đ; there are some great breakfast options, and free delivery within the block. Daily 8.30am–10pm.

★**Louisiane Brewhouse** Tran Phu Beach ☎0583 521948, ⓦlouisianebrewhouse.com.vn. Eat great food with your feet buried in the sand at this large place, which sees tables and chairs spill onto the beach of an evening. The menu features an excellent range of Vietnamese and Western dishes (red snapper for 215,000đ, fish & chips for 130,000đ and eggs benedict for 100,000đ), as well as a sushi corner, a pizza corner, home-made cakes and pastries and a swimming pool that's free for customers. Also a great place to drink (see below). Daily 7am–1am.

Michou 1/39 Tran Quang Khai ☎0120 6270412. It's impossible to walk past this place without being tempted by the cakes sat merrily in the window – lime tart, passion fruit-topped cheesecake, and deliciously gloopy chocolate brownies, all costing around 45,000đ. Daily 7am–11pm.

★**Olivia** 14b Tran Quang Khai ☎0583 522752. The best of the many, many Italian restaurants huddled around this area. The open, alley-like setting is rather nice – slight echoes of *Lady and the Tramp* – and there's good gnocchi, tagliatelle, ravioli, penne and pizza to choose from, costing 75,000–125,000đ. Daily 9.30am–10pm.

Omar's Tandoori Cafe 89b Nguyen Thien Thuat and 96a/8 Tran Phu ☎0582 221625. Not the most attractive restaurant in Nha Trang – or even on this side of the road – but this remains the place to go should you get the urge for an Indian curry. Daily set meals are 150,000đ, including a drink. Daily 7am–10pm.

★**Steam n' Spice** 26–28 Tran Phu ☎0583 880000. Inside the *Sheraton*, this stylish Hong Kong-style restaurant allows you to experience the high life on a moderate budget – you'll be able to eat well for under 150,000đ. *Dim sum*, salads and desserts fill an extensive pick 'n' tick menu; all are lovingly prepared, and absolutely delicious. Daily 11am–2.30pm & 6–10.30pm.

Truc Linh 18 Biet Thu ☎0583 521089. The most atmospheric branch of a successful local chain serving a good range of Western and Vietnamese dishes, with seafood the speciality. Prices are a little above average (most dishes cost over 150,000đ) but the food is still good value – for now, since the chain's popularity has seen standards dropping. Daily 8am–10pm.

DRINKING AND NIGHTLIFE

Nha Trang has a buzzing nightlife scene. There are plenty of chillout and party places around the budget district, and pricier nightspots along the beachfront; many places have generous **happy hours**, sometimes lasting all day. Occasional **crackdowns** have the bars closing at midnight, but left to their own devices, most places will stay open till the wee hours.

Booze Cruise 110 Nguyen Thien Thuat ☎0163 3574522. Super-cheap cocktails and an often raucous atmosphere. There's all-you-can-drink draught beer 2–11pm (149,000đ), with this fact alone convincing a fair proportion of passers-by to pop in. Daily 11am–late.

La Mancha 17 Biet Thu ☎0583 527978. This is an attractive Spanish restaurant with decent food, though it's perhaps even better for evening drinks. For 200,000đ, plus

a little extra per head, you can get a shisha to go with your cocktail – some of the flavours are cocktail-ey themselves, such as rose through apple juice, strawberry through Sambucca, or cappuccino through milk. Daily 7am–1am.

★**Louisiane Brewhouse** Tran Phu Beach ☎0583 521948. Not just an excellent restaurant, but a terrific place to drink. They make a pilsener, a dark lager, a witbier and seasonal ales, all of which can be tried in a cute sampler set (110,000đ). After that, pick a pint of your favourite one, and enjoy it on the beach or over a game of pool. Daily 7am–1am.

Sailing Club 72–74 Tran Phu ☎ 0583 524628. This has been a favourite spot for an eclectic group of party animals for some years. DJs and swing chairs on the beach draw a well-heeled expat crowd and hordes of tourists to its refined beachfront bar, which gets progressively less refined as the night wears on; the night-time cover charge of 120,000đ (150,000đ on weekends) keeps things vaguely respectable. Daily 7am–late.

Why Not 24 Tran Quang Khai ☎ 0583 522652. Big place with inside and outside seating, pool table, dance floor and comfy lounge area. Serves cheap beer and spirits (happy hour 4–10pm; two-for-one cocktails 9–11pm), and there's live music some nights. Daily 9am–late.

MUD SPAS

Besides its status as Vietnam's premier beach resort, Nha Trang's latest attraction is its **mud-bath complexes** – there are now three in town, all essentially following the same pattern. The main event, obviously, is the opportunity to wallow in mineral-enriched mud – allegedly good for the skin, but great fun to boot. After washing off, you're free to have a swim in other pools filled with water rich in sodium silicate chloride, said to have beneficial effects on stress, arthritis and rheumatism. There are a number of other options available at these complexes, including spa treatment, massage and meals. Note that on entry you'll be encouraged to buy a "private" bath (from 250,000đ per person), though in practice foreigners going for the "communal" bath option (usually just over 100,000đ per person) get exactly the same thing.

100 Egg Mud Bath 15 Ngoc Son ☎ 0583 834939, ⓦ 100eggmudbath.com.vn. Everything's egg-shaped at this quirky place – even some of the cocoon-like mud baths themselves. As well as the regular range of mud-bath services, their restaurant serves one hundred different egg-based dishes, and even if you're not a fan of hard-boiled, over-easy or sunny-side up, you can head down to *Egg Café* for some fast food. However, it has to be said that despite such cutesiness, the complex is slightly rough around the edges.

★**iResort** 19 Suan Ngoc ☎ 0583 838838, ⓦ i-resort .vn. Goodness knows how Apple Corp will feel about the name, but this newbie is already the best bathing choice in town – and a little dearer than the other two. Centred around a pool boasting views of distant hills, its mud baths have been stylishly designed – arrive in the hour before sundown for the best visual effects.

Thap Ba Hot Springs 15 Ngoc Son ☎ 0583 834939, ⓦ thapbahotspring.com.vn. A side-road heading west just to the north of the Po Nagar Cham towers takes you through suburbian Nha Trang to this, the oldest bathing complex in town. It's still looking good; its communal pool areas are surrounded by foliage, and the VIP areas are pretty swanky. You can also stay the night here, if you so desire.

SHOPPING

Artful Collection 1 Tran Quang Khai ☎ 0126 376 1020. Part of a small chain selling a number of quirky items, including expert photography on cups (190,000đ), or on iPad cases and bags (350,000đ). Daily 9am–10pm.

Bambou 15 Biet Thu ☎ 0583 523616. Offers original-design T-shirts from 200,000đ each, plus other bright and colourful souvenirs. Daily 9am–9pm.

Papaya 60 Nguyen Thien Thuat. Another good t-shirt shop, with the emphasis on goofy, Vietnam-related puns. Daily 8am–10pm.

XQ Arts and Crafts Centre 64 Tran Phu. Displays and sells embroidered pictures, some of which are stunning works of art, from 350,000đ upwards. Daily 8am–8pm.

DIRECTORY

Bank Vietcombank, 17 Quang Trung, changes cash and has an ATM. There's also a convenient branch of Agribank at 2 Hung Vuong.

Car rental Most tour operators, including Khanh Hoa Tourism at 1 Tran Hung Dao (☎ 0583 528100), can arrange car rental with driver for $40–45 per day; minibuses are

---

PAMPER YOURSELF

Spa, massage and beauty services are now big business in Nha Trang, and there is a host of places to choose from. Some are more proficient than others, but the two below have a great reputation. Both offer a huge range of services, including facials (from $16), body scrubs ($15), hot-stone massages ($25); given the prodigious length of the "menus", it may help to avoid any unnecessary stress by plumping for an all-in package.

Lotus 28 Tran Quang Khai ☎ 0583 526457.   **Su Spa** 93 Nguyen Thien Thuat ☎ 0583 523242.

also available at a slightly higher rate.
Hospital 19 Yersin, below the city stadium ☎ 0583 822168.
Pharmacy 27 Le Thanh Ton.
Police 5 Ly Tu Trong ☎ 0583 822400.

Post office 4 Le Loi (daily 7am–9pm) has IDD facilities, internet access, poste restante and DHL courier desk (closed Sun); there are also several other small post offices scattered around town.

The coast north of Nha Trang

Most tourists leapfrog the 400km-plus of coastline between Nha Trang and Hoi An on a tour bus, but swathes of splendid coastline do exist along this stretch of the country, many of which remain relatively untouched. Visitors to places like **Doc Let**, **Whale Island** and **Bai Dai** will find good accommodation options and uncrowded beaches in front of their resort.

Hon Khoi Peninsula

At Ninh Hoa, about 33km north of Nha Trang, Highway 26 branches off left from Highway 1 to Buon Ma Thuot; about 5km later, a turning on the right leads 12km to the splendid **Hon Khoi Peninsula**, on which you'll find pristine **Doc Let Beach**. You'll probably be keen to linger here awhile: the casuarinas and white sands of the beach are perfect for a day's beach-bumming, although you have to pay a small entrance fee for the privilege unless you are staying at one of the resorts here.

4

ARRIVAL AND DEPARTURE   HON KHOI PENINSULA

The turn-off to Hon Khoi is signed from the highway about 38km north of Nha Trang, just north of the village of Ninh Hoa.

By bus or train Ninh Hoa itself is accessible by bus from Nha Trang (every 30min; 25,000đ), and has a small train station on the main line (served by most trains from north and south); all resorts will be able to arrange pick-up from here, or from Nha Trang (usually $20–30 per vehicle).

ACCOMMODATION

★**Jungle Beach Resort** ☎ 0913 429144, ⓦ junglebeach vietnam.com. On a separate, still-secluded beach, this is a real find – many guests have come for a day and spent a week. There are basic rooms and bungalows for rent, as well as some new a/c "suite" huts; all meals are included in the room price, and the food is excellent. Trails on the hillside behind here are ripe for exploring and the beach is pristine. $25
Paradise Resort ☎ 0583 670480, ⓦ paradiseresort .vn. This cheap, markedly serene resort (no TVs in the rooms or playing over breakfast) has a few huge rooms and some simple bungalows, plus a shady terrace overlooking the beach. Rates include three meals a day, and they provide free rental of kayaks, fishing rods and more. $50
★**Some Days of Silence** ☎ 0583 670952, ⓦ somedays resort.com. Formerly the *Ki-em Art House Resort*, this place in the middle of the beach is in a class of its own. Run by artists, it's a dreamy compound with a handful of individually decorated bungalows, a meditation room, art gallery and huge picnic tables in the garden. $125
White Sand Resort ☎ 0583 670670, ⓦ whitesand resort.com.vn. An attractive low-rise development with beautifully furnished rooms, all with balconies, the resort also has a spa, a pool, tennis courts and free wi-fi. Book online for discounts off their inflated rack rates. $150

Hon Ong

Some 50km or so north from the Hon Khoi Peninsula, a road branches off Highway 1 along the **Hon Gom Peninsula**, accessing the endless beaches on both sides of this swan's neck of land. A short speedboat ride will bring you to **Hon Ong**, also known as "Whale Island". Humpback whales and whale sharks are often seen in the area from May to August, and Rainbow Divers (see box, p.229) runs **scuba diving** here; as well as plenty of fish, off the south coast you can aim for a 7m-deep wreck, or a natural arch and tunnel. Back on dry land, you'll be able to take advantage of some delightful walking

KITESURFING, MUE NE BEACH (SEE BOX, P.218) >

trails – it should only take a couple of hours to perform a full circuit of the island, and if in luck you may get to see muntjac and wading birds on your way around.

ARRIVAL AND DEPARTURE	HON ONG

By boat and bus Hon Ong is accessed by speedboat (5min) from the Dam Mon jetty, about 15km down the Hon Khoi peninsula from Dai Linh, a stop on Highway 1. You can hit Dai Linh on one of the open-tour buses (see p.34) heading up and down the coast, though note that you may have to pay an additional fare; in addition, they're far harder to pick up on your way back out. It's far easier to take a bus-boat transfer from Nha Trang – *Whale Island Resort* (see below) has daily services at 9am and 2pm ($20).

ACCOMMODATION AND EATING

Whale Island Resort ☎ 0583 840501, ⓦ anislandin vietnam.com. On Whale Island itself, this place has a wonderfully relaxing feel, with simple but tasteful bungalows peeking out over dense vegetation at a fabulous view of the bay. The compulsory meals (lunch and dinner both $14 per person) can work out as much as your room, though they're pretty good. For a nominal fee, you'll also be able to rent catamarans, canoes and snorkelling equipment. **$55**

Quy Nhon

A likeable little seaport town, **QUY NHON** is set on a narrow stake of land spearing into the South China Sea. It's a good place to get away from tourists – few come here, thanks in no small part to the fact that the local beach is both less dazzling than others along this coast, and a bit shallow for swimming; it does, however, make a lovely place for a breezy evening stroll. For more adventurous travellers, the lack of foreigners only adds to the town's intrigue, and there are a few places worth checking out in the nearby area, including some superbly restored **Cham towers**. North of Quy Nhon, and within easy day-trip distance, are two more Cham sites: the Banh It towers, and the Cha Ban Citadel – both important remnants of this former civilization.

Brief history

Quy Nhon's origins lie in the Cham migration south, at the start of the eleventh century, under pressure from the Vietnamese to the north. They named the empire they established in the area Vijaya, meaning "Victory"; its epicentre was the citadel of Cha Ban (see p.238), though it was the settlement of Quy Nhon – then known as Sri Bonai – that developed into its thriving commercial centre. Centuries later, the **Tay Son Rebellion** (see p.435) boiled over here; the town became the Tay Son capital after being seized in 1773, and within five years the brothers had control over most of southern Vietnam. During the American War the city served as a US port and supply centre, its population swollen by refugees fleeing from the vicious bombing meted out on the surrounding countryside.

Long Khanh Pagoda

141 Tran Cao Van • Daily sunrise–sunset • Free

Right in the middle of the city, the **Long Khanh Pagoda** is an imposing structure, its nine-tiered roof dominating the skyline. On either side of the main building stands a turret – one containing a drum, the other a giant bell. In the grounds, look out for the tall statue of Buddha, which is currently painted a rather sickly shade of green.

Binh Dinh Museum

28 Nguyen Hue • Mon–Fri 7–11am & 2–5pm • 15,000₫

The **Binh Dinh Museum** contains some superb examples of Cham masonry – exactly what you'd expect, given the prevalence of such sites in the nearby area, although many have been left exposed to the elements in open areas. Other items in the collection

Thap Doi, Highway 1, Banh It, Cha Banh Citadel & Phu Cat Airport

QUY NHON

● EATING AND DRINKING	
Barbara's	4
Café 360	1
Que Huong	3
Thanh Minh	2

■ ACCOMMODATION	
Au Co	3
Avani Quy Nhon	5
Barbara's	4
Quy Nhon Hotel	2
Royal Resort	6
Saigon-Quy Nhon Hotel	1

include ethnic dress worn by minority groups in Binh Dinh Province, and the usual war memorabilia.

Thap Doi

2km west of town on Tran Hung Dao • Daily 6.30–11am & 1.30–6pm • 8,000đ, plus extra for your bike

The most accessible of Quy Nhon's Cham monuments are the **Thap Doi**, or "Double Towers", which have been the subject of an extensive restoration in recent years. Their former shabby backstreet setting has been transformed into a small, green park where the slender towers, framed by palms, command attention. Both taper to an open top like jails that you can only escape from with tremendous difficulty; you'll note that the smaller of the two is both leaning and kinked. The towers date from around the end of the twelfth century, and embellishments such as sandstone pilasters, spearhead-shaped arches and the sandstone statues of winged Garuda – the vehicle of Vishnu – give the buildings a spiritual aura.

Banh It

20km north of Quy Nhon • Daily 7am–5pm • 10,000đ; 90,000đ by xe om, or more like 100,000đ on the way to or from Dieu Tri train station (see p.238)

The superbly restored **Banh It** Cham towers, known locally as Thap Bac, cut a dash on a hilltop over the river from Quy Nhon. Their site is little visited, relative to others in the area, but the short climb from the access road yields tremendous views of the surrounding countryside, enhanced by the giant white statue of a seated Buddha below.

Cha Ban Citadel

2km west of the highway, around 21km north of Quy Nhon; look out for a small lane on the left signposted "Canh Tien"

If you are travelling under your own steam you could search for the last vestiges of **Cha Ban Citadel**, the erstwhile capital of Vijaya; this site constituted the political centre of Champa from the early eleventh century until 1471, when Le Thanh Ton finally seized it, killing fifty thousand Cham people in the process. The Tay Son brothers renamed the site Hoang De and made it their base in the mid-1770s (see p.435). It's undergoing restoration, but you'll be able to see the **Canh Tien Tower**, standing on a slight rise: its distinctive shape is visible from afar, a rectangular brick and sandstone edifice framed by sandstone pilasters.

ARRIVAL AND DEPARTURE

QUY NHON

By plane Phu Cat Airport lies 35km north of Quy Nhon. A Vietnam Airlines minibus shuttles passengers into and out of town (50,000đ), and the company has an office at 55 Le Hong Phong (☎ 0563 825313).
Destinations Hanoi (2 daily; 1hr 40min); Ho Chi Minh City (2 daily; 1hr 10min).
By train Quy Nhon's branch-line train station is beside the Quang Trung statue at the north end of town, though few services use this spur from the main line; you'd be better off taking a taxi or xe om (around 50,000–60,000đ) to the nearby station at Dieu Tri for trains to Ho Chi Minh City or Hanoi.

Destinations (from Dieu Tri) Ho Chi Minh City (5 daily; 14hr); Nha Trang (5 daily; 4hr); Quang Ngai (5 daily; 3hr).
By bus Buses pull up at Quy Nhon's long-distance bus station, a short xe om ride west of the city centre, at the corner of Tay Son and Nguyen Thai Hoc. Almost all open-tour buses bypass the town, though you could get lucky – check when booking your ticket. Services heading to and from the Central Highlands tend to be minibuses, rather than full-sizers.
Destinations Da Nang (8hr); Kon Tum (5hr); Nha Trang (4hr); Pleiku (4hr); Quang Ngai (4hr).

INFORMATION

Tourist information and bike rental The best place for local travel information and bicycle (50,000đ/day) or motorbike (200,000đ/day) rental is *Barbara's* (see below),

at least when the owner's in town. Most hotels will also be able to get you some wheels.

ACCOMMODATION

Au Co 24 An Duong Vuong ☎ 0563 747699. The best of several mini-hotels clustered together opposite the beach to the west of town. The a/c rooms have TVs and are kept spotlessly clean. $15
Avani Quy Nhon around 18km from central Quy Nhon ☎ 0563 840132, ⑩ avanihotels.com. An immaculate resort sitting, with pleasing Cham frills to the design of common areas and rooms alike; the bathrooms in the latter are particularly striking. There are spa facilities and wonderful restaurants, and staff can arrange everything from watersports to tai chi sessions. Reserve online and you can get hefty discounts from the advertised rates. $165
Barbara's 12 An Duong Vuong ☎ 0563 892921, ⓔ kimloan4696@yahoo.com. West of the centre, this cheapie is managed by a Kiwi who knows the local area well. Rooms are super simple and have shared facilities, but they just about do the job; there are also dorm beds

available. It's worth coming here for a meal or drink, even if you're not staying (see opposite). Dorms $5, rooms $9
Quy Nhon Hotel 8 Nguyen Hue ☎ 0563 892402, ⑩ quynhonhotel.com.vn. Not bad for the price – the spacious rooms with bathtubs on the ground floor are good value, though the smaller, cheaper rooms upstairs are less appealing. $25
Royal Resort 1 Han Mac Tu ☎ 0563 747100, ⑩ royal quynhon.com. Luxurious accommodation strung along the seafront at the very western edge of Quy Nhon. Rooms are supremely comfortable, but you'll have to pay $10 extra for a sea view; there's also a pool and a great café. $60
★ Saigon-Quy Nhon Hotel 24 Nguyen Hue ☎ 0563 829922, ⑩ saigonquynhonhotel.com.vn. This high-rise hotel is centrally located, and boasts a pool and health club. The rooms themselves are carpeted and well equipped, and good value for money. $50

EATING AND DRINKING

Barbara's 12 An Duong Vuong ☎0563 892921. This guesthouse turns out cheap and cheerful backpacker staples, such as banana pancakes (25,000đ), Vegemite-and-lettuce or BLT sandwiches (30,000đ and 40,000đ respectively) and fish and chips (30,000đ). Also good for juices, smoothies and lassis, or a cheap evening beer. Daily 7am–9pm.

Café 360 360 Bach Dang ☎0563 821360. What a weird place this café is – in a good way. It just seems to go on forever, stretching a whole block between two parallel roads, and as well as being a good bet for coffee by day, its chic lighting is especially pleasant over an evening beer. Do note that the young staff will likely laugh at you – they don't see foreigners all that often. Daily 6am–11pm.

★**Que Huong** 125 Tang Bat Ho ☎0563 821123. Unassuming two-storey venue with a formidable local reputation; it's regularly full to bursting in the early evenings. Some of the dishes on the huge menu are fancifully named, such as the "fried cracky noodle and roughly fried snake head", but everything tastes great; try the *com ga* (chicken and rice; 45,000đ), pork in clay pot (60,000đ), or one of a range of soups or hotpots. Almost all dishes can be made large or small – great for single travellers who'd like to sample a few things. Daily 8am–9pm.

Thanh Minh 151 Phan Boi Chau ☎0563 821749. This reliable, hole-in-the-wall restaurant continuously doles out dirt-cheap, simple vegetarian fare. Simply point at what you'd like, and try to suppress your surprise when the final bill arrives – eating so much for under 60,000đ just doesn't seem right. Daily 8am–8pm.

Quang Ngai

Slender **QUANG NGAI**, clinging to the south bank of the Tra Khuc River some 130km south of Da Nang, is about as pleasant as you could expect of a town skewered until recently by Vietnam's main highway. The area had a long tradition of resistance against French rule, one that was to find further focus during American involvement. The reward was some of the most extensive bombing meted out during the war: by 1967, American journalist Jonathan Schell was able to report that seventy percent of villages in the town's surrounding area had been destroyed. A year later, the Americans turned their focus on **Son My Village**, site of the **My Lai massacre** (see box, p.240).

Son My Memorial Park

12km east of Quang Ngai • Daily 7am–5pm • 10,000đ • Distance best covered by xe om (130,000đ, including waiting time) or taxi (500,000đ for four people, including waiting time)

In the sub-hamlet of Tu Cung, the site of an infamous massacre of civilians by American soldiers on March 16, 1968, is remembered at the **Son My Memorial Park**. Pacing through this peaceful and dignified place, set within a low perimeter wall, you'll be accompanied by a feeling of blanched horror, and a palpable sense of the dead all around you. Wandering the garden, visitors can see bullet holes in trees, foundations of homes burnt down (each with a tablet recording its family's losses), blown-out bomb shelters, and cement statues of slain animals. One path ends at a large, Soviet-style statue of a woman cradling a dead baby over her left arm while raising her right fist in defiance. Once you've seen the garden, step into the museum to view the grisly display upstairs, though be warned that it's a disturbing place for anyone with a sensitive disposition. Here, beyond a massive marble plaque recording the names of the dead, family by family, and a montage of rusting hardware, a **photograph gallery** documents the event.

My Khe Beach

3km east of Son My • Can usually be added to a xe om or taxi trip to Son My for another 30,000đ

In stark contrast to the chilling Son My site, secluded **My Khe Beach** consists of 7km of powder-soft sand, backed by casuarinas, and is very good for swimming. Hamlets stand along the back of the beach, while fishing boats are sometimes moored off it, and there's a handful of restaurants that only get busy at the weekend. The area is still slowly gearing up for tourism, and could not really be recommended as a place to stay at the time of writing.

THE MY LAI MASSACRE

The massacre of civilians in the hamlets of **Son My Village**, the single most shameful chapter of America's involvement in Vietnam, began at dawn on March 16, 1968. US Intelligence suggested that the 48th Local Forces Battalion of the NVA, which had taken part in the Tet Offensive on Quang Ngai a month earlier, was holed up in Son My. Within the task force assembled to flush them out was **Charlie Company**, whose First Platoon, led by Lieutenant William Calley, was assigned to sweep through My Lai 4 (known to locals as **Tu Cung Hamlet**). Recent arrivals in Vietnam, Charlie Company had suffered casualties and losses in the hunt for the elusive 48th, and always found themselves inflicted by snipers and booby-traps. Unable to contact the enemy face to face in any numbers, or even to distinguish civilians from Viet Cong guerrillas, they had come to feel frustrated and impotent. Son My offered the chance to settle some old scores.

At a briefing on the eve of the offensive, GIs were told that all civilians would be at market by 7am and that anyone remaining was bound to be an active Viet Cong sympathizer. Some GIs later remembered being told not to kill women and children, but most simply registered that there were to be no prisoners. Whatever the truth, a massacre ensued, whose brutal course Neil Sheehan describes with chilling understatement in *A Bright Shining Lie*:

The American soldiers and junior officers shot old men, women, boys, girls, and babies. One soldier missed a baby lying on the ground twice with a .45 pistol as his comrades laughed at his marksmanship. He stood over the child and fired a third time. The soldiers beat women with rifle butts and raped some and sodomised others before shooting them. They shot the water buffalos, the pigs, and the chickens. They threw the dead animals into the wells to poison the water. They tossed satchel charges into the bomb shelters under the houses. A lot of the inhabitants had fled into the shelters. Those who leaped out to escape the explosives were gunned down. All of the houses were put to the torch.

In all, the Son My body count reached 500, 347 of whom fell in Tu Cung alone. Not one shot was fired at a GI in response, and the only US casualty deliberately shot himself in the foot to avoid the carnage. The 48th Battalion never materialized. The military chain of command was able temporarily to suppress reports of the massacre, with the army newspaper, *Stars and Stripes*, and even the *New York Times* branding the mission a success. But the awful truth surfaced in November 1969, through the efforts of former GI Ronald Ridenhour and investigative journalist Seymour Hersh, and the incontrovertible evidence of the grisly colour slides of army photographer Ron Haeberle. When the massacre did finally make the cover of *Newsweek* it was under the headline "An American Tragedy" – which, as John Pilger pointed out, "deflected from the truth that the atrocities were, above all, a *Vietnamese* tragedy".

Of 25 men eventually charged with murder over the massacre, or for its subsequent suppression, only Lieutenant William Calley was found guilty, though he had served just three days of a life sentence of hard labour when Nixon intervened and commuted it to house arrest. Three years later he was paroled.

It's all too easy to dismiss Charlie Company as a freak unit operating beyond the pale. A more realistic view may be that the very nature of the US war effort, with its resort to unselective napalm and rocket attacks, and its use of body counts as barometers of success, created a climate in which Vietnamese life was cheapened to such an extent that an incident of this nature became almost inevitable. If indiscriminate killing from the air was justifiable, then random killing at close quarters was only taking this methodology to its logical conclusion.

Michael Bilton and Kevin Sim, whose *Four Hours in My Lai* remains the most complete account of the massacre, conclude that "My Lai's exposure late in 1969 poisoned the idea that the war was a moral enterprise." The mother of one GI put it more simply: "I gave them a good boy, and they made him a murderer."

ARRIVAL AND DEPARTURE

By train Quang Ngai has a station on the main line about 2km west of town, and most services stop here.
Destinations Da Nang (4 daily; 2hr 40min); Nha Trang (4 daily; 7hr); Quy Nhon (4 daily; 3hr).

By bus The bus station is a little over 500m south of the centre, and 50m east of Quang Trung on Le Thanh Ton.
Destinations Da Nang (4hr); Nha Trang (7hr); Quy Nhon (4hr).

ACCOMMODATION AND EATING

There are few good places to eat in town, but if you're up for a beer, head for the snack-shacks that line the river at night, outside the *Petro Song Tra* – also note that at 5,000đ per bottle, Quang Ngai's own brews are about the cheapest in Vietnam.

Hung Vuong 45 Hung Vuong ☎0553 710477. Slightly shabby mid-ranger with good-value rooms, some with carpets and bathtubs. There are two places with the same name on this road; the other is a fair bit cheaper. **$35**

Petro Song Tra 1 An Duong Vuong ☎0553 714468.

Again, there are two of these in the same part of town, near the river. The one you'll be after is marked "Petrosetco", which is newer and sports delightful rooms, many with a river view. The older one has a pool, but you'll be free to use this even when staying at the newer place. **$70**

DIRECTORY

Bank There's an ATM at the *Hung Vuong Hotel*, and several others along Quang Trung.

Post The post office is about 100m west of the highway, at the junction of Hung Vuong and Phan Dinh Phung.

4

The central coast

CITADEL WALL, HUE

5

The central coast

The narrowest part of the country holds an astonishingly dense collection of sights. From the south, you'll come first to the town of Hoi An, highly traditional and hugely popular on account of its wonderful architecture, laidback air and superb culinary scene. Further north is Da Nang, whose bars, restaurants and sleek new buildings make it enjoyable in a more contemporary sense. Both places are good bases for a visit to the Cham temple complex at My Son, or for a day out at one of the local beaches. Then there's Hue, erstwhile capital of the Nguyen dynasty. A visit to the old Imperial City, with its splendid palace buildings and manicured gardens, is like a taking a step into the past. Lastly are the sights pertaining to the American War in the famed Demilitarized Zone (DMZ). The area marked the divide between North and South Vietnam, which, some would argue, still exists today.

You'll notice great differences in weather, cuisine, language and even local character to the north and south of the **Ben Hai River**, which runs through the DMZ (see box, p.299). However, Vietnam was not always divided along this point – it was previously the Hoanh Son Mountains, north of Dong Hoi (see p.310) that formed the cultural and political line between the Chinese-dominated sphere to the north, and the Indianized Champa kingdom to the south. As independent Vietnam grew in power in the eleventh century, so its armies pushed southwards to the next natural frontier, the Hai Van Pass near Hue. Here again, the Cham resisted further invasion until the fifteenth century, when their great temple complex at **My Son** was seized and their kingdom shattered.

Since then, other contenders have battled back and forth over this same ground, among them the Nguyen and Trinh lords, whose simmering rivalry ended in victory for the southern Nguyen and the emergence of **Hue** as the nation's capital in the nineteenth century. The Nguyen dynasty transformed Hue into a stately Imperial City, whose palaces, temples and grand mausoleums now constitute one of the highlights of a visit to Vietnam, despite the ravages they suffered during successive wars. In 1954, Vietnam was divided at the Seventeenth Parallel, only 100km north of Hue, where the

MY SON

Highlights

❶ **Hoi An** Sip a latte by lantern-light while waiting for your tailor-made clothes to measure up in this laidback city. **See p.247**

❷ **Hoi An cuisine** Tourists agree that central Vietnam does it best – try the assorted specialities of Hoi An and find out why. **See box, p.256**

❸ **My Son** Majestic Cham ruins covered in moss, grass and leaves – rise early to see them before the crowds. **See p.261**

❹ **Da Nang** Wander the riverside promenade, lounge on the beaches and savour gourmet

cuisine in Central Vietnam's newest hotspot. **See p.265**

❺ **Hue's Imperial City** Cross the Perfume River to meander through the intricately decorated buildings that emperors once called home. **See p.279**

❻ **Vinh Moc tunnels** The most interesting sight in the famed DMZ: a warren of dens where tenacious locals sheltered during the war, often for weeks on end. **See p.303**

HIGHLIGHTS ARE MARKED ON THE MAP ON P.246

5

Ben Hai River and the **DMZ** marked the border between North and South Vietnam until reunification in 1975. Though there's little to see on the ground these days, the desolate battlefields of the DMZ are a poignant memorial to those who fought here on both sides, and to the civilians who lost their lives in the bitter conflict.

Da Nang and nearby **China Beach** are other evocative names from the American War, but the region has lots more to offer than war memorabilia. The compact riverside town of **Hoi An**, with its core of traditional, wood-built merchants' houses and jaunty Chinese Assembly Halls, is a particularly captivating place, and for many a highlight of their trip to Vietnam. Inland from Hoi An, the Cham spiritual core, **My Son**, survives as a haunting array of overgrown ruins, some now partially but tastefully restored, while to the east and north of Hoi An you'll find a succession of beaches that are undergoing rapid development.

This region has a particularly complicated **climate** as it forms a transitional zone between the north and south of Vietnam. In general, around Da Nang and Hue the **rainy season** lasts from September to February, with most rain falling between late September and December; during this season it's not unusual for road and rail links to be cut. Hue suffers particularly badly and, even during the "dry season" from March to August, it's possible to have several days of torrential downpours, giving the city an annual rainfall average of three metres. Overall, the best time to visit this region is in spring, from February to late May, before both temperatures and humidity reach their summer maximum (averaging around 30°C), or just at the end of the summer before the rains break in September.

THE CENTRAL COAST

QUANG BINH

THE DMZ **6**

Ben Hai River

QUANG TRI

Dong Ha

Quang Tri

Lao Bao

HWY-9

Khe Sanh

THUA THIEN-HUÉ

HWY-1

Hue **5**

SOUTH CHINA SEA (EAST SEA)

N

Á Luoi

Cau Hai

Lang Co

Hai Van Pass

Hai Van Tunnel

BACH MA NATIONAL PARK

Monkey Mountain

LAOS

Ba Na Hill Station

Da Nang **4**

Marble Mountain

Non Nuoc Beach

Cham Islands

Cua Dai Beach

Thu Bon River

Tra Kieu

Hoi An **2** **1**

My Son **3**

HWY-1

HWY-14

QUANG NAM

HIGHLIGHTS

1. Hoi An
2. Hoi An cuisine
3. My Son
4. Da Nang
5. Hue's Imperial City
6. Vinh Moc tunnels

0 ——— 50
kilometres

Hoi An

5

Wonderfully preserved and full of compelling sights, the small town of **HOI AN** exudes a laidback atmosphere and boasts a rich architectural fusion of Chinese, Japanese, Vietnamese and European influences dating back to the sixteenth century. In its heyday, the now drowsy channel of the Thu Bon River was a jostling crowd of merchant vessels representing the world's great trading nations (see below), and its narrow streets comprising wooden-fronted shophouses topped with moss-covered tiles still emanate a timeless air. A concerted effort has been made to retain the town's old-world charm: by way of example, it's the only place in Vietnam that bans traffic in the town centre, and the only place that forces local businesses, by law, to dangle **lanterns** from their facades. These come to the fore as evening encroaches, and by nightfall you'll see them shining out from narrow alleys and the riverbank in their hundreds, the light reflecting in the waters of the **Thu Bon River**. Also notable are the city's many **tailors**, who will whip up made-to-measure clothes in no time, and a **culinary scene** that ranks among the best in Asia.

The city's most photographed sight is the beautiful **Japanese Covered Bridge**. However, the most noteworthy monuments in town stem from Hoi An's resident Chinese population. These include the **merchant homes**, some of them more than two hundred years old, and still inhabited by the descendants of prosperous Chinese traders. Between their sober wooden facades, riotous confections of glazed roof tiles and writhing dragons mark the entrances to **Chinese Assembly Halls**, which form the focal point of civic and spiritual life for an ethnic Chinese community that, today, constitutes one-quarter of Hoi An's population.

Granted UNESCO World Heritage status in 1999, Hoi An is now firmly on most visitors' agendas. Many who plan to stay for a day become enamoured of the place and stay a week, but be warned that the main sights are prone at times to tourist overload and hassles from souvenir sellers. If you get frustrated by these aspects of the town, it's easy to avoid the crowds, taking day-trips to the atmospheric Cham ruins of **My Son**, biking out into the surrounding country or spending a day or two on the nearby beaches. If possible, try to time your visit to coincide with the **Full-Moon Festival**, on the fourteenth day of the lunar calendar every month, when traditional arts performances take place in the lantern-lit streets. However, it's worth making a point of avoiding the town in October and November, when Hoi An is prone to serious flooding, and the water in the streets can be knee- or waist-high.

Brief history

For centuries, Hoi An played an important role in the **maritime trade** of Southeast Asia. This goes back at least as far as the second century BC, when people of the so-called Sa Huynh culture exchanged goods with China and India, but things really took off in the sixteenth century when Chinese, Japanese and European vessels ran with the trade winds to congregate at a port then called Fai Fo, whose annual **spring fair** brought in traders from far and wide (see box below). Tax collectors arrived to fill

---

FAI FO SPRING FAIR

Hoi An owes its popularity in no small part to the annual spring fair of **Fai Fo** (the former name of the town), which once attracted traders from far and wide, though it ceased to exist long ago. From humble beginnings in the sixteenth century, the event grew into an exotic showcase of world produce. From Southeast Asia came silks and brocades, ivory, fragrant oils, fine porcelain and a cornucopia of medicinal ingredients. The Europeans brought their textiles, weaponry, sulphur and lead – as well as the first Christian missionaries in 1614. During the four-month fair, travelling merchants would rent local lodgings and warehouses; many went on to establish a more permanent presence through marriage to Vietnamese women, who were (and still are) renowned for their business acumen.

5

▲ Red Bridge Cooking School, **4**, **5**, **6** (3km) & Cua Dai Beach (4km)

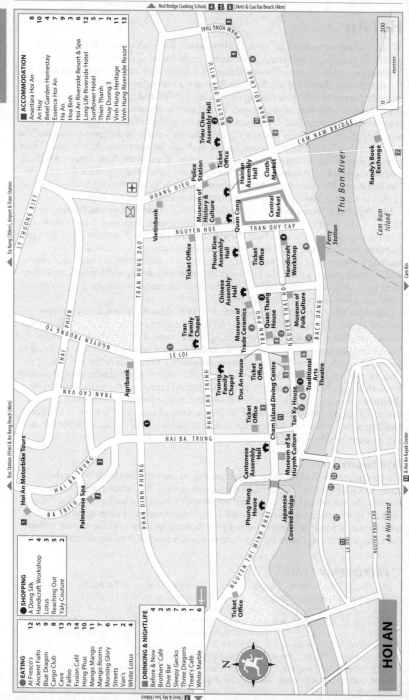

■ ACCOMMODATION

Anantara Hoi An	8
An Huy	10
Betel Garden Homestay	4
Essence Hoi An	7
Ha An	9
Hoa Binh	6
Hoi An Riverside Resort & Spa	12
Long Life Riverside Hotel	5
Sunflower Hotel	1
Thien Thanh	3
Thuy Duong 3	2
Vinh Hung Heritage	11
Vinh Hung Riverside Resort	13

● EATING

Al Fresco's	12
Ancient Faifo	5
Blue Dragon	9
Cargo Club	8
Cava	13
Faifoo	3
Fusion Café	14
Hong Phuc	10
Mango Mango	11
Mango Rooms	6
Morning Glory	7
Streets	1
Van's	2
White Lotus	4

● SHOPPING

A Dong Silk	1
Handicraft Workshop	4
Lotus	3
Reaching Out	5
Yaly Couture	2

■ DRINKING & NIGHTLIFE

Before & Now	4
Brothers' Café	2
Dive Bar	5
Sleepy Gecko	7
Three Dragons	3
Treat's Café	1
White Marble	6

HOI AN

0 — 200 metres

Da Nang (30km), Airport & Train Station

Bus Station (95m) & An Bang Beach (4km)

My Son & My Son (40km)

Randy's Book Exchange

Thu Bon River

Cam Nam Island

Ferry Station

Cam Kin

& Hoi An Kayak Center

An Hoi Island

N

the Imperial coffers, and the town swelled with artisans, moneylenders and bureaucrats as trade reached a peak in the seventeenth century.

Commercial activity was dominated by Japanese and Chinese merchants, many of whom settled in Fai Fo, where each community maintained its own governor, legal code and strong cultural identity. But in 1639 the Japanese shogun prohibited foreign travel and the "Japanese street" dwindled to a handful of families, then to a scattering of monuments and a distinctive architectural style. Unchallenged, the Chinese community prospered, and its numbers grew as every new political upheaval in China prompted another wave of immigrants to join one of the town's self-governing "congregations", organized around a meeting hall and place of worship.

In the late eighteenth century, silt began to clog the Thu Bon River just as markets began to open in China, and from then on the port's days were numbered. Although the French established an administrative centre in Fai Fo, and even built a rail link from Tourane (Da Nang), they failed to resuscitate the economy, and when a storm washed away the tracks in 1916 no one repaired them. The town, renamed Hoi An in 1954, somehow escaped damage during both the French and American wars and retains a distinctly antiquated air.

Phung Hung House

4 Nguyen Thi Minh Khai • Daily 7am–6pm • Under ticket scheme (see box, p.250)

Just west of the covered bridge, this has been home to the same family since around 1780, since they moved from Hue to trade cinnamon and hardwoods from the central highlands, as well as silk and glass. The large two-storey house is Vietnamese in style, although its eighty ironwood columns and small glass skylights denote Japanese influence, and the gallery and window shutters are Chinese in style. From the upstairs windows, there are pretty views across the tiled roofs of neighbouring houses, and before leaving most visitors are invited to buy embroidery souvenirs by the staff.

Japanese Covered Bridge

Linking Nguyen Thi Minh Khai and Tran Phu • 24hr • Free • Temple under ticket scheme (see box, p.250)

The western extremity of Tran Phu is marked by a small arched bridge of red-painted wood, popularly known as the **Japanese Covered Bridge**, which has been adopted as Hoi An's emblem. It was known to exist in the mid-sixteenth century, and has subsequently been reconstructed several times to the same simple design. According to local folklore, the bridge was erected after Japan suffered a series of violent earthquakes which geomancers attributed to a restless monster lying with its head in India, tail in Japan and heart in Hoi An. The only remedy was to build a bridge whose stone piles would drive a metaphorical sword through the beast's heart and fortuitously provide a handy passage across the muddy creek. Inside the bridge's narrow span are a collection of stelae and four statues, two dogs and two monkeys, which suggest that work began in the year of the monkey and ended in that of the dog. The small **temple** suspended above the water is a later addition dedicated to the Taoist god Tran Vo Bac De ("Emperor of the North"), a favourite of sailors as he controls wind, rain and other "evil influences".

Cantonese Assembly Hall

176 Tran Phu • Daily 7am–6pm • Under ticket scheme (see box, p.250)

The westernmost of the Chinese assembly halls sits just east of the Japanese Bridge, and belonged to Hoi An's Cantonese population. You can't miss its gaudy entrance arch, a recent embellishment to the original late eighteenth-century hall built by immigrants from Guangdong. Though there's nothing of particular merit here, it's an appealing place, partly because of its plant-filled courtyard, ornamented with dragon and carp carvings (see box, p.253), and partly because of the fact that it's the least visited Chinese hall in Hoi An.

VISITING HOI AN'S SIGHTS

Hoi An has a **ticket scheme** covering the majority of its most famous sights, the proceeds of which contribute to the preservation of the old centre. A ticket costing 120,000đ (valid for one day), allows access to five places:

- Either Chua Ong or the temple on the Japanese Covered Bridge (the bridge itself is free)
- One of the museums
- One of the three Chinese Assembly Halls requiring tickets
- One of the merchants' houses or family chapels requiring tickets
- The Hoi An Handicraft Workshop at 9 Nguyen Thai Hoc

If you want to visit more sights in the scheme, you have to fork out for another ticket. If, like most, you're only aiming for one round, it's important to choose carefully – particular recommendations are the Phuoc Kien Assembly Hall, the Museum of History and Culture and Tan Ky House. Also note that though "The Heritage Town" appears on your ticket, you walk on any Hoi An street for free. In fact, some wish they hadn't paid to get into crowded buildings only to find that the guides are more interested in selling souvenirs. With careful planning, it's possible to get a good taste of Hoi An architecture without even doing the "heritage tour".

Tickets are on sale at four **outlets**: 78 Le Loi, 5 Hoang Dieu, 10 Nguyen Hue and 30 Tran Phu (see map, p.248). Groups of more than eight people are entitled to a free guide to accompany them on a tour; otherwise, you can hire one for around $15. The ticket outlets are **open** from 7am to 6pm, sometimes later, as are most of the sights included in the scheme. Prices and conditions of the ticket scheme are occasionally subject to change; for the latest information, visit ⓦ hoianworldheritage.org.vn.

Museum of Sa Huynh Culture

149 Tran Phu • Daily 7am–6pm • Under ticket scheme (see box above)

Occupying a two-storey French-era house, this tiny museum focuses on a distinct culture which flourished along the coast of central Vietnam between the second century BC and the second century AD; the name comes from the town 130km south of Hoi An where evidence of the **Sa Huynh** was first discovered in 1902. Little is known about their culture, though they were probably the predecessors of the Cham. The most interesting exhibits are ceramic cremation jars.

Tan Ky House

101 Nguyen Thai Hoc • Daily 8am–noon & 2–5.30pm • Under ticket scheme (see box above)

In the thick of things near the covered bridge, this is a beautifully preserved example of a two-storey, late eighteenth-century shophouse, amalgamating Vietnamese, Japanese and Chinese influences in an architectural style typical of Hoi An. The long, narrow building is constructed of dark hardwoods, including termite-resistant jackfruit for its main columns. Look out for two hanging poem-boards inlaid with mother-of-pearl birds in flight, and for markers showing the height of various Hoi An floods (some above your head). It can get crowded, so come early or late in the day, to appreciate the weight of history here.

Duc An House

129 Tran Phu • Daily 8.30am–noon & 1.30–5.30pm • Under ticket sheme (see box above)

A humble building, erected in the 1850s to house a family that had already been living on this site for more than two centuries. It is beautifully decorated with solid, traditional furnishings and features a plant-strewn courtyard. The owner, Mr Tram, is a direct descendant of the founding family, and is often on hand to show visitors around. In the past, it functioned as a bookshop, a medical dispensary and a meeting place for revolutionary thinkers, of whom there are a few photos on the walls.

Quan Thang House

77 Tran Phu • Daily 7am–6pm • Under ticket scheme (see box opposite)

A modest, single-storey shophouse, this was founded in the early eighteenth century by a captain from Fujian in China, and was home to a medicine-trading business. Frankly speaking, it's a mediocre affair – you'll find far more interesting places to visit under this section of the ticket scheme.

Museum of Trade Ceramics

80 Tran Phu • Daily 7am–6pm • Under ticket scheme (see box opposite)

This small museum is housed in a traditional timber residence-cum-warehouse. It showcases the history of Hoi An's ceramics trade, which peaked in the fifteenth and sixteenth centuries, with most of the exhibits from Vietnam, China and Japan. Unfortunately, most of these exhibits are shards or fragments of bowls and vases, and visitors will find more interest in the building itself, which is well preserved. The rear room on the ground floor houses a small display about the architecture of Hoi An.

Tran Family Chapel

21 Le Loi • Daily 7am–6pm • Under ticket scheme (see box opposite)

The two-hundred-year-old **Tran Family Chapel** stands within a walled compound at the junction of Phan Chu Trinh and Le Loi. On the altar, oblong funerary boxes contain a name-tablet and biographical details of deceased family leaders and their wives – carved lotus blossoms indicate adherents of Buddhism. Each year the entire family – more than eighty people – gather round the altar to venerate their ancestors and discuss family affairs.

Chinese Assembly Hall

64 Tran Phu • Daily 7am–6pm • Free

Historically, Hoi An's ethnic Chinese population organized themselves according to their place of origin – Fujian, Guangdong, Chaozhou or Hainan. Each group maintained its own **assembly hall** as both community centre and house of worship, while a fifth hall also provided assistance to all the local groups and to visiting Chinese merchants.

Plum in the centre of town, the **Chinese Assembly Hall**, or Chua Ba, was built in 1740 as an umbrella organization for all Hoi An's ethnic Chinese population. Thien Hau graces the altar, but the hall is nowadays used mainly as a language school where local ethnic Chinese children and adults come to learn their mother tongue.

Museum of Folk Culture

33 Nguyen Thai Hoc • Daily 7am–6pm • Under ticket sheme (see opposite)

Housed in the largest two-storey building in town, the **Folk Culture Museum** highlights the value of intangible culture through photographs and artefacts such as farming and household implements. If you don't find the displays exactly riveting, at least there are pleasant views of the river from the upstairs windows.

Handicraft Workshop

9 Nguyen Thai Hoc • Daily 9am–5pm • Under ticket sheme (see opposite) • Cultural Show daily at 10.15am, 3.15pm and 7.15pm

Most visitors are keen to experience something of Hoi An's long-held reputation for **traditional crafts**, and this place offers a good introduction to skills such as lantern-making and embroidery. It's worth timing your visit to see one of the half-hour cultural shows, which feature song and dance performances accompanied by traditional instruments.

5

Phuoc Kien Assembly Hall

46 Tran Phu • Daily 7am–6pm • Under ticket scheme (see box, p.250)

The most populous of Hoi An's Chinese groups hailed from Fujian, or **Phuoc Kien**, and their hall is a suitably imposing edifice with an ostentatious, triple-arched gateway added in the early 1970s. The hall started life as a pagoda built in the late seventeenth century when, so it's said, a Buddhist statue containing a lump of gold washed up on the riverbank. Almost a century later, the Chinese took over the decaying structure and rededicated it as a temple to **Thien Hau**, Goddess of the Sea and protector of sailors. She stands, fashioned in two-hundred-year-old papier-mâché, on the principal altar flanked by her two assistants, green-faced Thien Ly Nhan and red-faced Thuan Phong Nhi, who between them can see or hear any boat in distress over a range of a thousand miles. A second sanctuary room behind and to the right of the main altar shelters a deity favoured by couples and pregnant women: the awesome **Van Thien** and her aides, the "twelve heavenly midwives", who decide the fundamentals of a child's life from conception onwards, including the fateful matter of gender.

Central market

Tran Phu

Hoi An's **central market** retains an appealing, traditional atmosphere, and is at its best in the early morning, especially among the fresh-food stalls that line the river. Look out for jars of tiny preserved tangerines, a regional speciality, amid neat stacks of basketware, bowl-shaped lumps of unrefined cane-sugar, liniments, medicinal herbs and every variety of rice.

Around the market

Wandering down through the market square brings you out by the **ferry docks** on Bach Dang, which regularly disappears each autumn under the swollen river. For most of the year it's dry, and the spectacle of sampans bobbing on the water is best captured between 6 and 7am when the fishing boats are unloading their catch.

Quan Cong Temple

24 Tran Phu (opposite the market) • Daily 7am–6pm • Under ticket scheme (see box, p.250)

This colourful temple is dedicated to the Chinese general Quan Cong, the deity of martial virtue who was famed for his loyalty, piety and righteousness. It combines well with a visit to the market and the Museum of History and Culture as it sits between the two. There's a small but attractive courtyard, lots of statues and of course, an image of Quan Cong himself on the main altar, standing nearly 3m tall. The temple dates back to 1653 and is better known to locals as "Chua Ong".

Museum of History and Culture

7 Nguyen Hue • Daily 7am–6pm • Under ticket scheme (see box, p.250)

Located behind Quan Cong temple, this museum is housed in a former pagoda. Apart from the copies of ancient **maps** of Fai Fo, the primary appeal of this small, informative museum is its quiet courtyard and carved, wooden door panels, depicting the four sacred animals: crane, dragon, turtle and the mythical *kylin*.

Hainan Assembly Hall

10 Tran Phu • Daily 7–11.30am & 2–5pm • Free

East of Quan Cong Temple on Tran Phu stands the hall founded by Chinese from the island of **Hainan**, or Hai Nam, and also noted for its ornately carved, gilded altar table.

> ## ARCHITECTURAL MOTIFS OF HOI AN
>
> You can't walk far in Hoi An without confronting a carving of a **mythical beast** with a fish's body and dragon's head on an ancient building; though they're found all over northern Vietnam they seem to have struck a particular chord with Hoi An's architects. One of the most prominent examples tops a weather vane in the Phuoc Kien Assembly Hall, but there are plenty of more traditional representations about, carved into lantern brackets and beam ends, or forming the beams themselves. The **carp** symbolizes prosperity, success and, here, metamorphosing into a **dragon**, serves a reminder that nothing in life comes easily. To become a dragon, and thereby attain immortality, a fish must pass through three gates – just as a scholar has to pass three exams to become a mandarin, requiring much patience and hard work.
>
> Another typical feature of Hoi An's architecture are *mat cua*, "door **eyes**" watching over the entrance to a house or religious building, which are often in the form of a yin and yang symbol. Two thick wooden nails about 20cm in diameter are driven into the lintel as protection against evil forces, following a practice that originated in the pagodas of northern Vietnam. Assembly halls offer the most highly ornamented examples; that of Phuoc Kien consists of yin and yang symbols with two dragons in obeisance to the sun, while the Cantonese version is a fearsome tiger. The **yin and yang** symbol became fashionable in the nineteenth century and is the most commonly used image on houses, sometimes set in a chrysanthemum flower, such as at the Tan Ky House.

Its unusual history is intriguing – in 1851 a Vietnamese general plundered three merchant ships, killing 108 passengers, after which the vessels were painted black to imply they were pirate ships. A lone survivor revealed the crime to King Tu Duc, who promptly condemned the general to death and ordered that the booty be returned to the victims' families. When the hall was built later in the century, it was dedicated to the unlucky passengers.

Trieu Chau Assembly Hall

157 Nguyen Duy Hieu • Daily 7am–6pm • Under ticket scheme (see box, p.250)

This hall is located just east of the market, and it's worth the stroll. Built in the late eighteenth century by Chinese from the city of Chaozhou, or Trieu Chau, it's renowned for its remarkable display of woodcarving. In the altar niche sits the gilded **Ong Bon**, a general in the Chinese navy believed to hold sway over the wind and waves, surrounded by a frieze teeming with bird, animal and insect life so lifelike you can almost hear it buzz. The altar table itself depicts life on land and in the depths of the ocean, while panels on either side show two decorative ladies of the Chinese court modelling the latest Japanese hair fashions.

Phan Boi Chau

East of the market along the river, Hoi An takes on a distinctly European flavour – louvred shutters, balconies and stucco – along **Phan Boi Chau**, in what was the beginnings of a **French quarter**. The interiors of these late nineteenth-century town houses are characterized by vast, high-ceilinged rooms and enormous roof-spaces, markedly different from the Chinese abodes. Several of them now operate as restaurants and bars, such as *Brothers Café* and *White Lotus* (see p.257).

ARRIVAL AND DEPARTURE   HOI AN

By train or plane The nearest train station and airport are both 30km away in Da Nang (see p.268), a distance easily covered by taxi (around 400,000đ) or xe om (200,000đ). Ask to take the new road to the east, which has better views and far less traffic. For a small commission, hotel booking desks and tour agents are able to arrange onward train and plane tickets from Da Nang, and handle visa extensions.

5

ACTIVITIES IN AND AROUND HOI AN

Hoi An isn't just about sightseeing and shopping – there's a whole raft of activities to tempt you to stay here longer.

Bicycle or motorbike hire One of Hoi An's most popular activities is to rent a bicycle or motorbike and head off to explore the gorgeous surrounding countryside with the aid of a map; most hotels can arrange either, or contact Hoi An Motorbike Tours (11 Ba Trieu ☎ 0510 391 1930, ⓦ motorbiketours-hoian.com). If you're more interested in an eco-adventure, sign up for a tour with Scooter Tours Vietnam ($50–75 half- to full-day; ⓦ scootertoursvietnam.com) and ride round on a totally silent electric scooter.

Boat rides along the Thu Bon River Most visitors enjoy spending an hour or two gliding along the (usually) tranquil Thu Bon River. Many hotels can organize this for around $20, or you can haggle with sampan-rowers near the market (around 100,000đ per hour). Sunrise and sunset are the most popular times.

Cooking classes Several riverside restaurants offer cooking classes that vary in quality and price. Hugely popular is the one offered by *Morning Glory* (ⓦ restaurant-hoian.com, see p.256; $32), which lasts about five hours, and includes an all-you-can-eat

breakfast. Another popular school is *Red Bridge* (ⓦ visithoian.com/redbridge), which ferries "students" out to its hide-away location for a similar course at a similar fee.

Diving and snorkelling From April to October is the best time to explore the depths around the offshore Cham Islands. The most reliable tour operator in town is the Cham Island Diving Centre (see p.261).

Kayaking Hoi An's aquatic surroundings just beg to be explored by kayak. You can hire kayaks for one to three people for around $10 an hour at Hoi An Kayak Center (on the south side of An Hoi Island, beside *Vinh Hung Emerald Resort*; ⓦ hoiankayak.com). Not much fun Oct–Feb.

Spas There are some who think that visiting a spa isn't really an activity, as you just lie still and get pampered. Yet after a busy day's sightseeing and shopping, that's just what some visitors want. Recommended places include the *Anantara Hoi An* (see opposite) and Palmarosa Spa (90 Ba Trieu ☎ 0510 393 3999, ⓦ palmarosaspa.com).

By bus Open-tour buses usually drop you at their relevant booking office (also the place to confirm your onward tickets), or affiliated hotel.

Destinations Da Nang (45min); Hue (4hr); Nha Trang (11hr); Quang Ngai (4hr).

GETTING AROUND

By bicycle or motorbike Almost every hotel and many shops and tour agents rent out bicycles (around 40,000đ/day), or can arrange motorbikes (from 100,000đ) – the latter are a popular way to visit My Son (see p.261). Note that motorbikes are prohibited from the centre most of the time.

On foot While bikes are recommended for touring the outlying districts, Hoi An's central sights are all best

approached on foot, especially since traffic restrictions apply in the town centre. The regulations are part of a much-needed effort to save the old town from the worst effects of its fame.

By guided tour Hotel booking desks and tour agents along Tran Hung Dao, Phan Dinh Phung and Hai Ba Trung offer outings to My Son and craft villages around Hoi An.

INFORMATION

Maps Most hotels can provide you with a map of the town centre, and many will encourage you to sign up for this or that tour.

Magazines To glean hot tips from local expats, look out for the free magazine *Live Hoi An* (ⓦ livehoianmagazine .com).

ACCOMMODATION

The **number of hotels** in Hoi An continues to grow at an astonishing rate. The local authorities put a block on developments in the centre – too late to prevent some eyesores in the old streets – but a whole new enclave of pleasant and cheap mini-hotels has sprung up to the north along Ba Trieu; some of these have **swimming pools**, which provide welcome relief in warmer months. There are also several new places on **An Hoi Island**, across the Thu Bon River to the south of the town centre. Competition means that, in general, **prices** have come down and standards have risen; most places will bargain and there's unlikely to be a shortage of beds in peak season, though choices may be limited. If you do have difficulty, just head for the hotels further from the centre. Hotels on the beach are listed under "Around Hoi An".

CENTRAL HOI AN

★**Anantara Hoi An** 1 Pham Hong Thai ☎0510 391 4555, ⓦanantara.com. Luxurious, beach-style resort (though in fact it's beside the river) in central Hoi An, blending minimalist Japanese design with maximum service and facilities; these include a fantastic pool, an excellent spa and restaurants exuding a sophisticated air. They also offer complimentary bikes, as well as free classes in yoga, lantern-making and coconut-leaf art. **$150**

An Huy 30 Phan Boi Chau ☎0510 386 2116, ⓦanhuy hotel.com. This deceptively large place in a great central location opens out behind a tiny entrance, concealing simple but well-equipped rooms. Family rooms, with solid wood floors, are a good deal, and the owner is welcoming and helpful. Doubles **$30**, family rooms **$48**

★**Ha An** 6 Phan Boi Chau ☎0510 386 3126, ⓦhaan hotel.com. Welcoming, family-run hotel set back from the street in a quiet residential area. Its 24 rooms are arranged in an L-shape around a relaxing communal garden; they're highly attractive, with petals strewn across the beds, and superior rooms have delightful stone-floor showers. The breakfast buffet is another big selling point. **$65**

Hoa Binh 696 Hai Ba Trung ☎0510 391 6838. Large, clean rooms with satellite TV at this presentable hotel – rarely will you get a swimming pool at this price, but there it is on the ground floor. Things can get a bit chaotic when it's full, which is often. **$20**

★**Thien Thanh** 16 Ba Trieu ☎0510 391 6545, ⓦhoian thienthanhhotel.com. Comfortable and intimate mini-hotel with exceptionally attentive staff who try to make your stay as restful as possible. It has all mod cons, such as cable TV, a/c and internet access; the more expensive rooms have balconies overlooking water-spinach fields. Many guests return again and again. **$50**

Thuy Duong 3 92–94 Ba Trieu ☎0510 391 6565, ⓦthuyduonghotel-hoian.com. Well placed for open-tour bus drop-offs, the rooms here are comfortable, well maintained and reasonably priced, though those on the ground floor around the courtyard pool can be noisy. **$35**

Vinh Hung Heritage 143 Tran Phu ☎0510 386 1621, ⓦvinhhungresort.com. There are few more atmospheric places to stay in Hoi An than this broodingly dark old Chinese shophouse – come in the evening and it'll feel like you're entering an Oriental period drama. The rooms are also traditional in style; best is the Heritage Suite (#206),

complete with balcony, wood panelling, antique furniture and four-poster beds. **$90**

AN HOI, CAM NAM AND OUTSIDE THE CENTRE

Betel Garden Homestay 161 Tran Nhan Tong ☎0510 392 4165, ⓦbetelgardenhomestay.com. In a small village a 15min walk from central Hoi An, this traditionally styled mini-resort is a remarkably relaxing place to stay – great for those who would like to enjoy Hoi An without the crowds. Call for a pick-up. **$60**

★**Essence Hoi An** 132 Hung Vuong ☎0510 391 5915, ⓦessencehotels.com. This low-key, out-of-town resort is a real find. Set among fields about 2km west of the centre, it features 70 rooms in two buildings, all tastefully furnished and well equipped, plus an appealing pool and cosy spa. If you're too lazy to walk into town, there's a regular shuttle or free bicycles for guests. **$70**

Hoi An Riverside Resort & Spa 175 Cua Dai ☎05120 386 4800, ⓦhoianriverresort.com. This attractive mid-range resort, located between the town and beach, is great value, offering the comforts of more expensive resorts at a reasonable price. Rooms in the two-storey building are comfortably furnished and have great views over rice fields from the balconies. There's a spa, fitness centre, good pool and regular shuttle buses to the town and beach. **$80**

Long Life Riverside Hotel 61 Nguyen Phuc Chu ☎0510 391 1696, ⓦlonglifehotels.com. Located on fast-developing An Hoi Island, this place has a lovely little swimming pool, and staff are attentive. Rooms are clean though a bit dark and have been given pleasant traditional flourishes, but are tuned into the modern day with flat-screen TVs and, in most, computers. **$30**

Sunflower Hotel 397 Cua Dai ☎0510 393 9838, ⓔsunflowerhoian@gmail.com. This budget hotel between the town and beach has become backpacker central with lots of dorm rooms with locker. Family rooms ($40) are not such a good deal. There's a tiny pool that's often crowded when the weather is hot. Dorm bed **$9**, double **$15**

Vinh Hung Riverside Resort 110 Ngo Quyen An Hoi ☎0510 386 4074, ⓦvinhhungresort.com. Part of the *Vinh Hung* chain, this simple resort has moderately attractive rooms, but the location is quite wonderful – quiet, and with a lovely view of the Thu Bon River. **$70**

EATING

Hoi An is perhaps Vietnam's best food city – nowhere else are there so many **wonderful restaurants** within walking distance of each other. The array of **local delicacies** (see box, p.256) has been augmented by places serving Japanese, Italian, Indian, Thai, Turkish and Tex-Mex, as well as delectable French pastries. In the evenings, tables and chairs line Bach Dang, whose restaurants may look more Mediterranean than Vietnamese but largely focus on local produce; there's also a string of trendy new restaurants and cafés across the water on An Hoi Island. In addition to cut-price **set meals** featuring local specialities, many of Hoi An's restaurants also offer **cooking classes** (see box opposite); some establishments will help you select your ingredients at the market.

5

HOI AN SPECIALITIES

Hoi An has a number of tasty specialities to sample. Most famous is *cao lau*, a mouthwatering bowlful of thick rice-flour **noodles**, bean sprouts and pork-rind croutons in a light soup flavoured with mint and star anise, topped with thin slices of pork and served with grilled rice-flour crackers or sprinkled with crispy rice paper. Legend has it that the genuine article is cooked using water drawn from one particular local well. Lovers of **seafood** should try the delicately flavoured steamed manioc-flour parcels of finely diced crab or shrimp called *banh bao*, translated as "white rose", with lemon, sugar and *nuoc mam*, complemented by a crunchy onion-flake topping, adding extra flavour. A local variation of *hoanh thanh chien* (fried wonton), using shrimp and crab meat instead of pork, is also popular. One less heralded dish (and one of the cheapest) is *mi quang*, which sees a simple bowl of meat noodles enlivened with the addition of flavoursome oils, a quail egg and fresh sprigs of leaves. To fill any remaining gaps, try Hoi An **cake**, *banh it*, triangular parcels made by steaming green-bean paste and strands of sweetened coconut in banana leaves.

Al Fresco's 43 Nguyen Phuc Chu ☎0510 392 9707, ⑩alfrescosgroup.com. If you ever tire of the superb Vietnamese cuisine in Hoi An, you can rely on *Al Fresco's*, part of a growing restaurant empire, to come up with generous portions of comfort foods such as BBQ ribs, steaks and pizzas; most mains are 100,000–150,000đ. Part of the newish strip of restaurants on the north side of An Hoi Island. Daily 9am–10pm.

★**Ancient Faifo** 66 Nguyen Thai Hoc ☎0510 391 7444, ⑩ancientfaifo.com.vn. Surrender to an evening of indulgence at this ancient house where artistic and culinary delights await. Perfectly prepared slow-caramelized pork and roasted prawns are two highly recommended dishes; most mains are 160,000–300,000đ, and two-course set menus at 280,000đ are good value. There's often a soft piano playing and sometimes traditional musicians perform. There's also a top-class café, bar and art gallery on site. Daily 7am–10pm.

Blue Dragon 46 Bach Dang ☎0510 391 1227. Offering a similar standard of Vietnamese food and service to many other restaurants on Bach Dang, the *Blue Dragon* donates part of its profits to a charity that helps rural children stay in school. The fact that the tasty five-course meal is just 170,000đ is a bonus. Daily 9am–9.30pm.

Cargo Club 107–109 Nguyen Thai Hoc ☎0510 391 0489, ⑩restaurant-hoian.com. Despite having a good selection of local and international dishes, the real draw is the French bakery downstairs, which offers decadent pastries (from around 40,000đ) and an array of take-to-the-beach bread rolls. The home-made ice cream also has the crowds lining up. Daily 8am–11pm.

★**Cava** 53 Nguyen Phuc ☎090 758 9615. Try not to go here on your first day in Hoi An, or you may not get anywhere else. A winning location on An Hoi Island is further enhanced by the wonderfully prepared Vietnamese dishes on the menu (from 80,000đ), which is itself spiced up with a few Mediterranean choices. Superb. Daily 8am–11pm.

Faifoo 104 Tran Phu ☎0510 386 1548. Locals rate the banh bao (30,000đ) at this well-established and attractive restaurant as the best in town, though many travellers choose the cheap five-course sampler (130,000đ) of Hoi An specialities (see box above). Daily 8am–10.30pm.

Fusion Café 35 Nguyen Phuc Chu ☎0510 393 0333. A classic chill-out bar serving breakfasts, burgers, coffee and cocktails to a laidback bunch of travellers snuggled on the sofas. Daily 9am–10.30pm.

Hong Phuc 86 Bach Dang ☎0510 927 105. A friendly, good-value and popular riverside place run by two multi-lingual female cousins, serving scrumptious local food – if you want to know the secret, you can sign up for an afternoon cookery class, during which you learn how to make four dishes (500,000đ). They offer good-value set menus at 140,000đ. Get here early for a table on the balcony. Daily 7am–11pm.

Mango Rooms 111 Nguyen Thai Hoc ☎0510 391 0839, ⑩mangorooms.com. The menu at this chilled out restaurant is constantly changing but always wonderfully creative – imagine red snapper with coriander and pineapple, or duck in a passion fruit and chocolate sauce (480,000đ) – and there's also an excellent wine list. Its sister restaurant – *Mango Mango* – is directly across the river from the Japanese Bridge at 45 Nguyen Phuc Chu, views from which make this a better choice for sampling maverick owner Duc's signature cocktails. Daily 9am–12am.

★**Morning Glory** 106 Nguyen Thai Hoc ☎0510 224 1555, ⑩restaurant-hoian.com. Probably Hoi An's most popular restaurant, this place can accommodate lots of customers on two floors, but it's still often packed, and for good reason – everything is delicious, beautifully presented and served with a smile. Try the roast duck with banana flower salad (145,000đ); it's a masterful blend of tastes and textures. Owner Ms Vy runs several other restaurants in town, including *Cargo Club*. Daily 8am–10.30pm.

Streets 17 Le Loi ☎0510 391 1948. As you might guess from the name, this place is all about giving street kids a chance to work as kitchen staff or waiting tables, and the enthusiasm of the staff is infectious. The short menu covers items like pork in a clay pot (130,000đ) and filling baguettes. Daily noon–9.30pm.

Van's 329 Nguyen Duy Hieu ☎093 497 1791. Simple, streetside café serving generous portions of yummy *cao lao* or *mi quang* for just 40,000đ. Ideal for when you need a quick and filling meal, but note it's closed in the evening. Daily 7am–5pm.

White Lotus 11 Phan Boi Chau ☎0510 391 5545, ⓦwhitelotushoian.com. Operated by Project Indochina and staffed by disadvantaged kids, this smart venue is a good spot to try a tangy green papaya salad or BBQ beef in vine leaves; most main dishes are around 120,000đ–160,000đ, and there are some Western items too. Daily 9am–10pm.

DRINKING AND NIGHTLIFE

Hoi An is a small town and most inhabitants are tucked up by 9pm. However, there's a growing Western contingent, leading to a gradually expanding range of options for places to spend your evenings.

Before & Now 51 Le Loi ☎0510 391 0599. Double-storey Italian restaurant and bar inside a traditional shophouse. However, forget the food – it's far better as a venue for evening drinks, and about as lively as Hoi An gets. Daily 10am–2am.

Brothers' Café 27 Phan Boi Chau ☎0510 391 4150, ⓦbrothercafehoian.com. The garden setting on the banks of the Thu Bon River is reason enough to visit this Hoi An institution, though the food on the whole is overpriced – better to come for an atmospheric coffee or sundowner. Daily 10am–11pm.

Dive Bar 88 Nguyen Thai Hoc ☎0510 391 0782, ⓦvietnamscubadiving.com. The folks who run the Cham Islands Dive Center also know how to make a mean cocktail. In fact they're so good they offer courses in making them too. Induldge for around 100,000đ and see if you need that skill. Shisha pipes and cool beats too. Daily 10am–2am.

Sleepy Gecko 5 Thon Xuyen Trung, Cam Nam Island ☎0908 426349, ⓦsleepygeckohoian.com. Stride over the bridge to Cam Nam Island to drink in yet another picture-perfect sunset at this chilled, English-owned bar. It can get nice and busy some evenings, but on other nights you'll be more or less on your own. Daily 10am–midnight.

Three Dragons 51 Phan Boi Chau ☎0510 391 4742, ⓦ3dragonshoian.com. This sports bar is the place to head for if you want to catch a live football game, an F1 Grand Prix, or other sporting event. There's a well-stocked bar and meals available too. Daily 10am–1am.

Treat's Café 158 Tran Phu ☎0510 386 1125. Upbeat bar-restaurant with good music, a shady interior courtyard, pool and cheap happy-hour deals (4–9pm). Daily 8am–10pm.

★**White Marble** 98 Le Loi ☎0510 391 1862. This place operates as a restaurant and bar, and it fulfils both functions very well. It has a fine menu of dishes like charcoal-grilled sesame pork (110,000đ), as well as a wide selection of wines (several by the glass; about 130,000đ), tapas-style snacks and a laidback atmosphere, making it a great spot to pass an evening. Daily 11am–11pm.

SHOPPING

While sightseeing may be the most popular activity in Hoi An, shopping comes a close second, and few visitors leave without a few extra kilos to carry in their bags. Workshops are scattered around town where you can see a range of **local crafts**, from embroidery, wood-carving and pottery to silk being made by traditional methods; visits are free, though afterwards you'll be directed to the souvenir shop-cum-showroom, not that there's any obligation to buy.

ARTS AND FESTIVALS

With the influx of tourists, Hoi An is becoming a centre for the **arts**. A delightful hour-long medley of **traditional music and dance** is performed most evenings in a cramped room rather grandly known as the Traditional Theatre, 75 Nguyen Thai Hoc ☎0510 386 1159 (Mon–Sat 9pm; 100,000đ). Folk musicians also play short concerts at the Hoi An Handicraft Workshop, 9 Nguyen Thai Hoc (see p.258).

Once a month, coloured silk lanterns replace electric lights and shopkeepers don traditional costume to celebrate the **Full-Moon Festival** (fourteenth day of the lunar calendar). It's a tourist event, but a great occasion nonetheless: there are traditional music performances, with food stalls selling local specialities by the Japanese Bridge and on the waterfront.

During the **Mid-Autumn Festival**, a much bigger affair celebrated nationwide on the fourteenth day of the eighth lunar month, people also float lanterns on the river. In recent years – usually in spring but dates vary – Quang Nam Province, which includes Hoi An, has also staged a week-long **cultural heritage festival** in Hoi An and My Son, including Cham dances and folk songs.

5

HANDICRAFTS AND SOUVENIRS

Handicraft Workshop 9 Nguyen Thai Hoc. A good place to view a variety of Hoi An handicrafts and included as part of the ticket scheme (see p.250). Daily 9am–9pm.

Lotus 82 Tran Phu ☎0510 391 7889, ⊛lotusjewellery -hoian.com. There's good handmade jewellery at this American-run shop – proof of its popularity lies in the fact that many local copycats are now using the same hardwood display cases. Daily 8am–10pm.

Reaching Out 103 Nguyen Thai Hoc ☎0510 391 0168, ⊛reachingoutvietnam.com. Clothing and accessories, ceramics, toys, lacquerware, silver and embroidery are some of the products made by other-abled people in this fair trade gift shop. The workshop (where you can watch products being made) is closed at lunchtimes and on Sunday. Mon–Fri 8.30am–9pm, Sat & Sun 9.30am–8pm.

SILK AND TAILORING

Hoi An is particularly famous for its silk and tailoring, with prices generally cheaper than in Hanoi or Ho Chi Minh City. You'll find shops all over town but the original outlet was the market, where even now rows of tailors sit at sewing machines next to rainbow-coloured stacks, and for a few dollars will make up beautiful garments in a matter of hours. It's worth shopping around – ask to see some finished articles before placing an order. If you have time, it's a good idea to have one item made first to check the quality and fit. In addition to the two reliable, upmarket places listed below, there are a number of smaller-scale operations.

A Dong Silk 62 Tran Hung Dao ☎0510 391 0579, ⊛adongsilk.com. One of the most renowned tailors in town, and in the country as a whole.

Yaly Couture 358 Nguyen Duy Hieu ☎0510 391 4995, ⊛yalycouture.com. Another revered local tailor, particularly good for suits.

DIRECTORY

Banks and exchange You can exchange cash and get over-the-counter cash advances on credit cards at Vietcombank, 2 Tran Cao Van, and Agribank, 6 Hoang Dieu and 92 Tran Phu. There are also several ATMs around town.

Books Randy's Book Exchange on Cam Nam Island (☎093 608 9483, ⊛bookshoian.com) may well be the best secondhand bookstore in Vietnam; he now deals in e-books too. Daily 8am–7pm.

Hospital 4 Tran Hung Dao ☎0510 386 1365.

Laundry Places along Tran Hung Dao offer laundry services at around 20,000đ per kilo.

Pharmacies In addition to small pharmacies near the hospital, there's a convenient one at 4CTran Hung Dao. Daily 7am–9pm.

Police 8 Hoang Dieu ☎0510 386 1204.

Post office The unusually fancy and well-organized GPO is at 4b Tran Hung Dao (daily 6am–10pm).

Around Hoi An

From Hoi An you can bike out along meandering paths to the white expanse of **Cua Dai** or **An Bang beaches** or hop on a sampan to one of the **islands** of the Thu Bon River. River tours take you to low-lying, estuarine islands and the **craft villages** along their banks, while it's also possible to visit the distant **Cham Islands**, renowned for their sea swallows' nests.

Cui Dai and An Bang beaches

Cua Dai and An Bang Beaches are 4km east and north of Hoi An respectively • Taxi to either around 120,000đ, xe om around 60,000đ

It's a popular bike ride to the clean, white sands of **Cua Dai Beach** or the slightly more distant **An Bang Beach** – you can detour along the way through the beautiful, canal-riddled Cam Thanh area, which lies to the south of the main road; head east on Nguyen Duy Hieu and take a right when the road ends a couple of kilometres east of Hoi An. Though the beaches themselves are not much fun when it's cold and rainy (any time between October and February), they are cool places to hang on sunny days.

Cua Dai

Cua Dai is the busier strip of sand, with hawkers patrolling the area, but you can minimize the hassle by walking away from the main centre, or by taking an umbrella

FROM TOP LANTERN SHOP, HOI AN; CAO LAU, HOI AN (SEE BOX, P.256) >

5

and deck chair for the day at one of the many beachfront café-restaurants; in return you'll be expected to buy at least a drink, though many also serve excellent seafood – just be sure to check the prices before ordering. This beach is also the departure point for trips to the **Cham islands** (see opposite).

An Bang

More popular for foreigners than Cua Dai is **An Bang** – follow Hai Ba Trung north out of town. Its bars, set back from the beach, attract plenty of local expats, and the whole stretch has a pleasantly scruffy vibe – sometimes tinged with marijuana smoke.

ACCOMMODATION AND EATING   CUA DAI AND AN BANG BEACHES

Golden Sand Resort Cua Dai, 300m south from the Hoi An Beach Resort ☎0510 392 7550, ⓦgoldensand resort-spa.com.vn. Aiming for a contemporary-traditional fusion, and largely getting the balance right, this resort has some of the best rooms on the strip, and by far the largest pool; little touches such as wafts of frangipani in the gardens make most stays special, though customer service is not always five-star. $120

Hoi An Beach Resort Cua Dai, at the end of the road from Hoi An, to the south on the right ☎0510 392 7011, ⓦhoianbeachresort.com.vn. Separated from the beach by a quiet road, this is slightly cheaper than nearby resorts. Rooms are elegant in cool, sand colours and bathrooms are generously proportioned; it's worth paying the extra for a room overlooking the river. Other attractions include two pools, a pleasant beach in front and a restaurant recommended for its well-priced local dishes. Free shuttle bus to Hoi An. $90

Nam Hai Hamlet 1, Dien Duong Village, Dien Ban District. ☎0510 394 0000, ⓦghmhotels.com. Thought by many to be the best resort in Vietnam, this luxurious complex of private and pool villas sits on 35 hectares of beach land a few kilometres north of An Bang Beach, and is well positioned for visiting all the area's attractions, such as My Son. Trouble is, you'll feel so comfortable in this paradisiacal setting, with your butler attending your every whim, that you probably won't want to leave the resort. $550

Palm Garden Resort Cua Dai, on the north of the Hoi An road, about 700m from the small bridge ☎0510 392 7927, ⓦpalmgardenresort.com.vn. This resort takes its name from the four-hundred-odd trees dotting the complex; some at beachside have hammocks for lazing or cocktail sipping. The rooms are spacious and well up to standard, while the seafood in the on-site restaurants is superb. $120

Soul Kitchen An Bang Beach ☎090 644 0320, ⓦsoulkitchen.sitew.com. It's worth mentioning this cool spot out on An Bang Beach, as it's hidden to the north of the main beach road by about half a dozen other ordinary places. This one stands out for its attractive thatched bar, its trim garden and pool table, plus its extensive menu that features items like beef fillet with garlic potatoes (220,000đ), salads, snacks, cocktails at around 80,000đ each, and friendly staff. Mon 7am–5pm, Tues–Sun 7am–11pm.

Under the Coconut Tree An Bang Beach, about 250 metres north of the beach road ☎0510 652 9168, ⓦunderthecoconuttreehoian.com. This newish homestay is a dream come true for travellers. Stylish dorm rooms with shared bathrooms set in a well-tended garden and the beach just a couple of minutes' walk away. Dorms $7, doubles $30

Victoria Hoi An Resort Cua Dai, immediately alongside the Hoi An Beach Resort ☎0510 392 7040, ⓦvictoriahotels.asia/en. The ritziest hotel on Cua Dai Beach, right down to the named and signed "streets" within its large compound. Some of the top bungalows open onto a lovely stretch of beach, while the cheapest rooms occupy luxurious two-storey villas. There are also all the amenities you'd expect of an international-class resort, including a restaurant serving good but expensive meals, a free shuttle bus to Hoi An and a range of activities. $160

Cam Kim Island and the craft villages

A ten-minute ferry ride from the pier in Hoi An (10,000đ)

The large island of **Cam Kim** is famed for its **craft villages**, which have been inhabited by skilled artisans since the sixteenth century. Most carpenters have moved out of the village but a handful remain, building fishing boats (you'll find one of the few surviving boatyards right beside the island's jetty) or crafting furniture for export. The work of one famous community of wood-carvers, from Kim Bong Village, can be seen throughout Hoi An. Cam Kim is also a nice escape from Hoi An; it's worth taking a bike over and exploring the rest of the island.

> **NEST HARVESTS ON THE CHAM ISLANDS**
> Cham islanders have been harvesting **sea swallows' nests** since the late sixteenth century.
> Today the government-controlled trade contributes greatly to the local economy, with
> astronomical prices per kilo for the culinary delicacy, to which extraordinary medicinal virtues
> are also attributed. Each spring, when thousands of the tiny, grey-and-black birds nest among
> the islands' caves and crevices, villagers build bamboo scaffolding or climb up ropes to prise
> the diminutive structures, about the size of a hen's egg, off the rock.

The Cham islands

The mountainous **Cham islands**, or Cu Lao Cham, are clearly visible 10km from the
coast off Hoi An. Now inhabited by about three thousand fishermen and collectors of
highly prized birds' nests (see box above), until 1995 even Vietnamese people weren't
allowed to visit because of the naval base here. However, since it was designated a
UNESCO Biosphere Reserve in 2009 for its abundant marine life – 135 species of
coral, 202 species of fish and 84 species of molluscs – visitors have been coming in
droves, causing fears for the fragile environment. The best time to **dive or snorkel** is
between April and August; for the rest of the year, visibility is poor and the sea is
frequently rough.

ARRIVAL AND DEPARTURE   THE CHAM ISLANDS

Boat trips take an hour each way, and depart from Cua Dai beach (see p.258); it's best to arrange them through agencies
in Hoi An (including Cham Island Diving).

DIVING

★**Cham Island Diving Centre** 88 Nguyen Thai Hoc
☎0510 391 0782, ⍟chamislanddiving.com. Excellent
operator offering diving trips to the islands from *Dive Bar*
in Hoi An. Snorkel trips from $42, two dives from $80,
open-water PADI courses from $370.

My Son

Daily 6.30am–5.30pm • 100,000đ • Short performances of Cham music at 9.30am, 10.30am and 2.30pm • Guides are usually available for
hire (around 100,000đ) at the car park

Vietnam's most evocative Cham site, **My Son** (pronounced "mee sern") lies 40km
southwest of Hoi An, in a bowl of lushly wooded hills towered over by the aptly
named Cat's Tooth Mountain. A tangible sense of faded majesty still hangs over the
mouldering ruins, enhanced by the assorted lingam and Sanskrit stelae strewn around
and by the isolated rural setting, and it's possible, with a little stirring of the
imagination, to visualize how the functioning temple complex would have appeared in
My Son's heyday.

Brief history

Excavations at My Son have revealed that Cham kings were buried here as early as
the fourth century, indicating that the site was established by the rulers of the early
Champa capital of **Simhapura**, sited some 30km back towards the highway, at
present-day Tra Kieu. The stone towers and sanctuaries whose remnants you see today
were erected between the seventh and thirteenth centuries, with successive dynasties
adding more temples to this holy place, until in its prime it comprised some seventy
buildings. The area was considered the domain of gods and god-kings, and living on
site would have been an attendant population of priests, dancers and servants.

French archeologists discovered the ruins in the late nineteenth century, when the
Chams' fine **masonry** skills were still evident – instead of mortar, they used a resin
mixed with ground brick and mollusc shells, which left only hairline cracks between
brick courses. After the Viet Cong based themselves here in the 1960s, many unique

5

buildings were pounded to oblivion by American B52s, most notably the once magnificent A1 tower. Craters around the site and masonry pocked with shell and bullet holes testify to this tragic period in My Son's history.

The museum
Your first stop should be the small but well-organized **museum** to get your bearings before approaching the actual site. There are permanent and thematic sections that explain the history and lay-out of My Son, and provide a helpful explanation of mythical beasts like the *hamsa* and the *gajasimha*, useful if you're not accompanied by a guide.

Groups H, C and B
First up is **Group H**, off to the right beside the entrance, though there's little to see here and most people head straight for **Groups C and B**, which were once divided by a wall but are now difficult to tell apart. The most impressive building in Group C is the central *kalan*, **C1**, which is standing and fairly well preserved, while in Group B, it's the **repository room**, or B5, which is of most interest for its statues of deities and bas reliefs of elephants on the outer walls.

Group D
Group D is located behind Group B but appears to be connected to it, and it's here that most visitors get their best insights into Cham culture, as the two *mandapa* (meditation halls), D1 and D2, have both been converted into modest **galleries**. They contain a lingam, the remains of a carving of Shiva, a statue of Nandi (Shiva's bull), a many-armed Shiva dancing, and an impressive statue of Vishnu's vehicle, Garuda. The ground between these two galleries was named the **Court of Stelae** by early archeologists, a reference to the stone tablets, etched with Sanskrit script, that litter it. This area gets packed with tour groups at peak times.

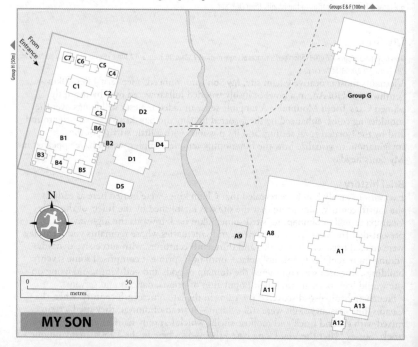

EXPLORING MY SON

After buying a ticket and visiting the museum, cross the bridge and drive about a kilometre to a car park, then walk another 500 metres or so to the site entrance. Though groups of buildings are unimaginatively named with the letters of the alphabet, the route through them does not follow alphabetical order; groups B, C, D and G most warrant your attention. Stick to the route shown on signboards around the site, as there could be **unexploded ordnance** hidden in the tangled vegetation around. Needless to say, a visit is not much fun on a rainy day (February to August are the best months).

Other groups

From Group D, cross a stream to the east and turn right to **Group A**, where the once spectacular *kalan*, **A1**, was reduced to a heap of toppled columns and lintels by US bombs in 1969. A small amount of restoration work has been done here, but the biggest recent changes have taken place at **Group G**, just north of Group A. Originally built in the twelfth century, the small complex has been partially rebuilt to show clearly the location and function of the main buildings (the *kalan*, *mandapa*, *gopura*, tower-house and stele) of a Cham temple. More restoration work is ongoing at **Groups E and F**, a short way north of Group G, and these are the oldest structures at the site, dating to the eighth century. The *mandapa* at Group E has been entirely rebuilt, and it's interesting to see the contrast between month-old and thousand-year-old bricks. Finally, **Group K**, at the end of the route near the car park, holds little of interest.

ARRIVAL AND DEPARTURE

Tours Most people visit on a guided tour from Hoi An. Prices start at $10 per person, depending on the number in the group.

By bike or taxi It's also possible to rent a taxi (around $35 for the round trip) or motorbike in Hoi An and travel to My Son independently; the road to the site strikes west from Highway 1 at Duy Xuyen, from where there are signs for My Son. Almost all tours go at around 8am, so to beat them leave a couple of hours earlier, or visit in the afternoon when most groups have departed.

The Marble Mountains

Daily 6am–5pm • 15,000đ; tickets on sale at the base of either sets of steps

Rising from flat land about 20km north of Hoi An and about 10km south of Da Nang, the fabled **Marble Mountains**, named for the marble of which they are constituted, resemble an image from a Chinese painting and have been revered for centuries by the Vietnamese. More like hills than mountains – the summits are only around 100 metres high – the five peaks are considered auspicious (see box, p.264), though it's only the highest, **Thuy Son**, that tourists visit. At the base of Thuy Son, two sets of steep steps leading up from the village of Non Nuoc provide access to the south side of the mountain; visitors with mobility problems are advised to take the lift (see p.264).

A couple of hours allows time to both climb Thuy Son and visit its caves and pagodas, as well as wander round the marble-cutting workshops in the village at its base. It's not worth visiting when it's raining as there's nothing to see and the steps can be very slippery.

Non Nuoc Village

At the foot of the mountain is the dusty, unkempt village of **NON NUOC**, set behind Non Nuoc Beach (see p.271), which, since the fifteenth century, has echoed to the chink of stone masons chiselling away at religious statues, memorials and imitation Cham figures. The marble used was once quarried from the neighbouring mountains, but as this risked destroying the sacred peaks the stone is now imported from places

5

THE TURTLE GOD

Most distinctive peaks in Vietnam tend to have their creation fixed in folklore, and the Marble Mountains are no different. Local mythology tells of the **Turtle God** hatching a divine egg on the shore; the shell cracked into five pieces, represented by the five small mountains. In Vietnamese these are named Ngu Hanh Son, meaning the five ritual elements: Thuy Son (water mountain), Moc Son (wood), Tho Son (earth), Kim Son (gold or metal) and Hoa Son (fire). Historically, Cham people came here to worship their Hindu gods and then erected Buddhist altars in the caves, which became places of pilgrimage, drawing even the Nguyen kings to the sacred site.

---

like Thanh Hoa Province and as far away as China. It's fascinating to watch the masons at work, and they produce a huge variety of subjects, ranging from mythical beasts to abstract figures. Some of the larger pieces can fetch up to $50,000, and the shopkeepers will do their best to show you round and sell you a small souvenir.

Thuy Son

Though only 107m high, **Thuy Son** is both the highest and most important peak in the Marble Mountains. Two **staircases**, built for the visit of Emperor Minh Mang, lead up its southern flank; a **lift** (15,000đ) beside the eastern staircase offers an easier ascent, but isn't always in operation. The main, westernmost entrance (furthest from Non Nuoc Beach), brings you to the hollow summit, centred on pretty **Tam Thai pagoda**, itself surrounded by jagged rocks and grottoes.

Huyen Khong Cave

Beyond Tam Thai Pagoda, a narrow defile under a natural rock arch leads to **Huyen Khong Cave**, the largest and most impressive cave on the mountain – descending steep, dark steps into the eerie half-light and swirling incense is quite an experience. Locals will point out stalactites resembling wrinkled faces and so on, but the cave's best feature are the holes in its roof through which sunlight streams like spotlights (only on a sunny day of course) – you'll catch it in the hours either side of midday. It was once used as a hospital by the Viet Cong, and some say the holes in the roof were caused by bombs in the war. A wall plaque commemorates a deadly accurate women's Viet Cong guerrilla unit, which during the war destroyed nineteen planes with just 22 rockets.

Tang Chon Cave

The path heading east from Tam Thai Pagoda ducks under a couple of rock arches, passing the missable Van Thong Cave in between, and then climbs slightly before starting to descend towards the eastern exit, affording expansive views over Non Nuoc Beach, the Cham Islands and north to Monkey Mountain. About halfway down you pass Linh Ung Pagoda behind which lurks **Tang Chon Cave**, in this case occupied by tenth-century Cham Hindu altars and two Buddhas, one sitting and one standing. The standing Buddha is also illuminated by shafts of light in the morning. From here you can descend the eastern staircase or climb a few more steps to enjoy the views from the seven-storey Xa Loi Pagoda and then take the lift down (if it's working).

ARRIVAL AND DEPARTURE   THE MARBLE MOUNTAINS

Tours Any hotel in Da Nang or Hoi An can arrange a half-day tour to the Marble Mountains for around $20 each, depending on number in group.

By bike or motorbike The mountains are not difficult to find and the journey makes a pleasant bicycle or motorbike ride from either Hoi An or Da Nang.

By taxi or xe om You could make a deal with a taxi or xe om driver to stop by for an hour or so while travelling between Hoi An and Da Nang.

Da Nang

The largest city in Central Vietnam, **DA NANG** has long been ignored as a destination in its own right, eclipsed until recently by the glories of Hue's Imperial City to the north and the ancient town of Hoi An (see p.247), which lacks its own airport and train station. But things are changing fast, and the city is finally acquiring a character of its own, which, with its cafés and infrastructure of gleaming towers and bridges, is a pleasing blend of modern, cool and laidback. The city also makes a convenient place from which to **head onwards to Laos**, as you can get a visa in town and then catch one of the direct daily buses over the border.

The city itself occupies a small headland protruding into the southern curve of Da Nang Bay, and its elongated oval of a centre harbours a few worthwhile sights, foremost among which is the **Cham Museum** with its unparallelled collection of sculpture from the period. Other attractions include the fire-breathing **Dragon Bridge** and the **riverside promenade** along Bach Dang, where most of the city's bars are located. East of the Han River and protective Son Tra Peninsula, **Da Nang's beaches** form a broad stretch of sand between **Monkey Mountain** to the north and the **Marble Mountains** to the south, and are gradually being lined with top-notch resorts that attract discerning and well-heeled travellers.

DA NANG DURING THE WAR

The city of Da Nang mushroomed after the arrival of the first American combat troops on March 8, 1965. An advance guard of two battalions of Marines waded ashore at Red Beach in Da Nang Bay (to the north of the city), providing the press with a photo opportunity that included amphibious landing craft, helicopters and young Vietnamese women handing out garlands – not quite as the generals had envisaged. The Marines had come to defend Da Nang's massive **US Air Force base**; as the troops flew in so the base sprawled. Eventually Da Nang became "a small American city", as journalist John Pilger remembers it, "with its own generators, water purification plants, hospitals, cinemas, bowling alleys, ball parks, tennis courts, jogging tracks, supermarkets and bars, lots of bars". For most US troops the approach to Da Nang airfield formed their first impression of Vietnam, and it was here they came to take a break from the war at the famous **China Beach**.

At the same time the city swelled with thousands of **refugees**, mostly villagers cleared from "free-fire zones" but also people in search of work – labourers, cooks, laundry staff, pimps, prostitutes and drug pushers, all inhabiting a shantytown called Dogpatch on the base's perimeter. Da Nang's population rose inexorably: twenty thousand in the 1940s, fifty thousand in 1955 and, some estimate, a peak of one million during the American years. North Vietnamese mortar shells periodically fell in and around the base, but the city's most violent scenes occurred when two South Vietnamese generals engaged in a little power struggle. In March 1966 Vice Air Marshal Ky, then prime minister of South Vietnam, ousted a popular Hue overlord, General Thi, following his open support of Buddhist dissidents. Demonstrations spread from Hue to Da Nang where troops loyal to Thi seized the airfield in what amounted to a **mini civil war**. After much posturing Ky crushed the revolt two months later, killing hundreds of rebel troops and many civilians. In the preceding chaos, the beleaguered rebels held forty Western journalists hostage for a brief period in Da Nang's largest pagoda, Chua Tinh Hoi, while streets around filled with Buddhist protesters.

When the North Vietnamese Army finally arrived to **liberate** Da Nang on March 29, 1975, they had less of a struggle. Communist units had already cut the road south, and panic-stricken South Vietnamese soldiers battled for space on any plane or boat leaving the city, firing on unarmed civilians. Many drowned in the struggle to reach fishing boats, while planes and tanks were abandoned to the enemy. Da Nang had been all but deserted by South Vietnamese forces, leaving the mighty base to, according to Pilger, be "taken by a dozen NLF cadres waving white handkerchiefs from the back of a truck".

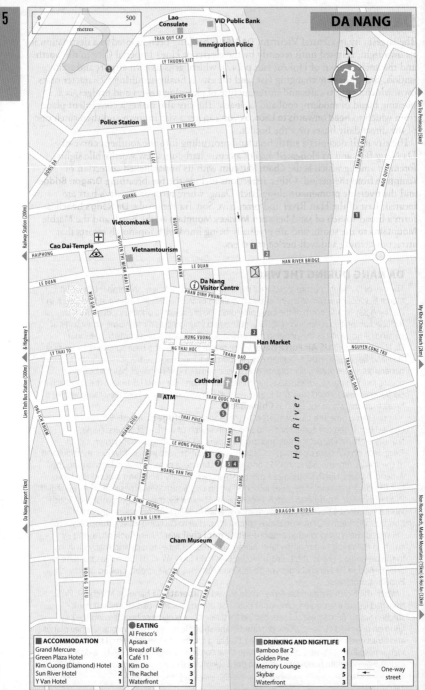

DA NANG

0 — 500
metres

Lao Consulate
VID Public Bank
Immigration Police
TRAN QUY CAP
LY THUONG KIET
NGUYEN DU
Police Station
LY TU TRONG
TRUNG
QUANG
Vietcombank
Cao Dai Temple
Vietnamtourism
HAIPHONG
LE DUAN
Da Nang Visitor Centre
HAN RIVER BRIDGE
PHAN DINH PHUNG
LE DUAN
HUNG VUONG
Han Market
NG THAI HOC
Cathedral
ATM
TRAN QUOC TOAN
THAI PHIEN
Han River
LE HONG PHONG
HOANG VAN THU
LE DINH DUONG
NGUYEN VAN LINH
DRAGON BRIDGE
Cham Museum

San Tra Peninsula (5km)
My Khe (China) Beach (2km)
Non Nuoc Beach, Marble Mountains (15km) & Hoi An (32km)
Railway Station (200m)
& Highway 1
Lien Tinh Bus Station (500m)
Da Nang Airport (1km)

One-way street

ACCOMMODATION
Grand Mercure   5
Green Plaza Hotel   4
Kim Cuong (Diamond) Hotel 3
Sun River Hotel   2
Y Van Hotel   1

EATING
Al Fresco's   4
Apsara   7
Bread of Life   1
Café 11   6
Kim Do   5
The Rachel   3
Waterfront   2

DRINKING AND NIGHTLIFE
Bamboo Bar 2   4
Golden Pine   1
Memory Lounge   2
Skybar   5
Waterfront   3

▼ 5 (200m)

Brief history

During the sixteenth and seventeenth centuries, trading vessels waiting to unload at Fai Fo (Hoi An) often sheltered in nearby Da Nang Bay, until Hoi An's harbour began silting up and Da Nang developed into a major port in its own right. After 1802, when Hue became capital of Vietnam, Da Nang naturally served as the principal point of arrival for foreign delegations to the royal court. However, the real spur to the city's growth came in the American War when the neighbouring air base spawned the greatest concentration of US military personnel in South Vietnam (see box, p.265).

The Cham Museum

24 Tran Phu • Tues–Sun 8.30–11.30am & 1.30–4.30pm • 40,000đ • ☎ 0511 388 6236

Even if you're just passing through Da Nang, try to spare an hour for the small **Cham Museum**, particularly if you plan to visit the Cham ruins at My Son (see p.261). The museum – whose design incorporates Cham motifs – sits in a garden of frangipani trees at the south end of Bach Dang, and its display of graceful, sometimes severe, terracotta and sandstone figures gives a tantalizing glimpse of an artistically inspired culture that ruled most of southern Vietnam for a thousand years. In the late nineteenth century French archeologists started collecting statues, friezes and altars from once magnificent Cham sites dotted around the hinterland of Da Nang, and opened the museum in 1916. Though this is undoubtedly the most comprehensive display of Cham art in the world, it's said that many of the best statues were carried off into European private collections.

The exhibits are grouped according to their place of origin and are positioned in **two main halls**. Be sure to make use of the excellent reading material dotted around the exhibits.

The first hall

In the **first hall**, a massive, square altar pedestal (late seventh century) from the religious centre of My Son is considered a masterpiece of early Cham craftsmanship, particularly its frieze depicting jaunty dancing girls, and a soulful flute player. However, experts and amateurs alike usually nominate two lithe dancers with Mona Lisa smiles, their soft, round bodies seemingly clad in nothing but strings of pearls, as the zenith of Cham artistry. The piece also features two musicians on a fragment of capital produced by Tra Kieu sculptors in the late tenth century, just before the decline of the Champa kingdom.

The second hall

The **second hall** is a new extension at the back; three times larger than the first hall, it includes a further 146 stone sculptures, dating from the seventh to the fourteenth centuries. There's also a small upstairs room; exhibits revolve around earthenware artefacts, though there's a collection of palanquins and other gilded woodwork (though these are from dynastic, rather than Cham, times).

CHAM ART

Recurring images in Cham art are lions, elephants and Hindu **deities**, predominantly Shiva (founder and defender of Champa) expressed either as a vigorous, full-lipped man or as a lingam, but Vishnu, Garuda, Ganesha and Nandi the bull are also portrayed. **Buddhas** feature strongly in the ninth-century art of Indrapura, a period when Khmer and Indonesian influences were gradually assimilated. The most distinctive icon is **Uroja**, a breast and nipple that represents the universal "mother" of Cham kings.

As the Viets pushed south during the eleventh century, so the Cham retreated, and their sculptures evolved a bold, cubic style. Though less refined than earlier works, the chunky **mythical animals** from this period retain pleasing solidity and a playful charm.

5

Dragon Bridge and Bach Dang Promenade

In 2013, two new bridges across the Han River were opened. The Tran Thi Ly Bridge, with cable stays that look like an orange sail, is quite impressive, but the **Dragon Bridge**, which actually breathes fire (weekend evenings at 9pm), has quickly become the city's new icon. Measuring 666 metres long and carrying six lanes of traffic across the river, the steel arches of the bridge form the shape of a writhing dragon with its head facing east, and it makes a striking sight when illuminated by 2500 LED lights after dark.

A good vantage point to view the bridge from is the **Bach Dang promenade** between the Han River Bridge and the Dragon Bridge itself, where it seems half the city's inhabitants congregate after dark, to stroll, munch on snacks and sometimes even practise ballroom dancing. Bach Dang is home to many of the city's best restaurants and bars, so you won't have too far to go when you're in need of refreshment.

ARRIVAL AND DEPARTURE
DA NANG

BY PLANE

Da Nang International Airport is just 2km southwest of the city, and has connections to most major domestic airports as well as international services to Cambodia, China, Korea and Singapore, among others. A taxi to the city centre costs around 50,000đ.

Airlines Vietnam Airlines, 27 Dien Bien Phu (☎0511 382 1130), and VietJet, 157–159 Ham Nghi (☎0511 369 2665). Both also have offices at the airport.

Destinations Buon Ma Thuot (daily; 1hr); Da Lat (daily; 1hr 30min); Hanoi (10 daily; 1hr 30min); Ho Chi Minh City (11 daily; 1hr 30min); Nha Trang (2 daily; 1hr); Pleiku (daily; 50min).

BY TRAIN

Ga Da Nang Station is west of the city centre at 122 Haiphong. There will be plenty of taxis (40,000đ to the centre) and xe om (about 20,000đ) vying for your attention.

Destinations Hanoi (6 daily; 15–20hr); Ho Chi Minh City (6 daily; 16–21hr); Hue (6 daily; 2hr 30min–3hr); Nha Trang (6 daily; 9–12hr).

BY BUS

The intercity bus station is about 3km west of the city centre on Dien Bien Phu.

Destinations Dong Ha (5hr); Hoi An (1hr 30min–2hr); Hue (3hr–4hr); Quang Ngai (5hr); Quy Nhon (11hr); Savannakhet, Laos (21hr); Vientiane, Laos (24hr).

GETTING AROUND

By bike and motorbike Da Nang is big enough and its sights sufficiently spread out to make walking round town fairly time-consuming, though most attractions are concentrated around Bach Dang in the centre. Most hotels either rent bikes or can direct you to somewhere that does (around $2/day); otherwise, there's no shortage of cyclo or xe om. Self-drive motorbikes (around $5–8/day) are available from tour agencies and most hotels.

By taxi Call Mai Linh taxi ☎0511 356 5656.

INFORMATION

Tourist information The Da Nang Visitor Centre at 32a Phan Dinh Phung (☎0511 355 0111; daily 7am–noon & 2–5pm) can provide a useful map of the city and around and, they hope, sell you tours of the area. For listings, try ⓦindanang.com, a useful resource primarily aimed at expats living in the city.

ACCOMMODATION

The majority of Da Nang's hotels are geared to business travellers or tour groups, though these days more and more independent travellers are using it as a base to explore the area. There are few budget options, but plenty of competitively priced, mid-range places. For five star comforts, however, you'll have to head to the big resorts lining My An and Non Nuoc beaches (see p.271).

Grand Mercure Green Island ☎0511 379 7777, ⓦaccorhotels.com. Sitting on a patch of reclaimed land to the south of the city centre, overlooking a grand new sports complex taking shape to the south, the *Grand Mercure* offers a glimpse of a city in transition from the windows of its 272 rooms, and for those on the upper floors it's more than a glimpse. Rooms are very stylish, in fact the whole hotel gives off a super-hip vibe, but note that superior rooms don't include breakfast. **$120**

Green Plaza Hotel 238 Bach Dang ☎0511 322 3399, ⓦgreenplazahotel.vn. It's hard to miss this twenty-floor tower on the riverside; service is excellent and the rooms fresh and immaculate, though you'll pay extra for a river view. Non-guests are also welcome to use the *Skybar* on the top floor (see p.270). **$90**

Kim Cuong (Diamond) Hotel 21 Thai Phien ☎0511 356 5937, ⓦkimcuonghoteldn.com. Tucked back from the riverfront, this welcoming mini-hotel has bright, clean doubles with a/c, wi-fi and cable TV. Ask for a room out back to avoid street noise. **$20**

★Sun River Hotel 132–136 Bach Dang ☎0511 384 9188, ⓦsunriverhoteldn.com.vn. This boutique hotel is the one of the best mid-range options on the Bach Dang strip. Its modern rooms have faux-wood floors, solid furnishings and a cream-through-brown colour scheme. Rooms at the front cost a little more, and have river views from the curved windows. The café/bar also makes a good place to drink, even if you're not staying here. **$45**

Y Van Hotel 21 Tran Hung Dao ☎0511 393 6156, ⓦyvanhotel.com. Situated on the quieter east side of the Han River, this fifteen-room mini-hotel offers good value. Rooms are luxuriously furnished with all amenities including full-size baths. The rooftop bar is a great spot to watch the city at night. **$20**

EATING

Da Nang has no shortage of places to eat, with the majority of foreigner-friendly places clustered around Bach Dang in the centre of the city.

Al Fresco's 178 Tran Phu ☎0511 356 6866, ⓦalfrescos group.com. If you need a break from Vietnamese fare, drop by *Al Fresco's* for BBQ ribs (120,000đ) or good old fish and chips (220,000đ). It's located just a block back from the Bach Dang promenade. Daily 8am–11pm.

★Apsara 222 Tran Phu ☎0511 356 1409, ⓦapsara danang.com. Prices are surprisingly reasonable at this atmospheric restaurant with a small replica Cham tower in the garden. Main dishes on the seafood-centred menu starting at 100,000đ, and soups going for around 60,000đ. A popular starter is the *chao tom* – ground shrimp roasted on sugar cane (70,000đ). Traditional music is performed every night from 7–8pm. Daily 10am–2pm & 5–9pm.

Bread of Life 4 Dong Da ☎0511 356 5185, ⓦbreadof lifedanang.com. A great place to throw down some Western comfort food. Baked goods, pancakes, pizza and a lot more are made and served by an all-deaf staff, and proceeds go towards a related local charity. Mains from 80,000đ. Mon–Sat 8.30am–9.30pm.

Café 11 11 Than Phien ☎0511 389 7901. It can get hot wandering Danang's streets, and the perfect antidote is a fresh fruit juice for just 20,000đ. Choose from coconut, mango, custard apple and many other tropical fruits. Daily 7am–7pm.

Kim Do 180 Tran Phu ☎0511 356 1457, ⓦkimdo danang.com.vn. This local favourite serves a broad range of Chinese cuisine and provides comfortable, a/c dining with attentive service. Their speciality is Peking duck (300,000đ). Portions can be on the small side, but with a bit of care you can eat reasonably well for around 160,000đ per head. Daily 7am–9.30pm.

The Rachel 166–168 Bach Dang ☎0511 352 5585, ⓦtherachel.com.vn. With a prime location on Bach Dang, this smart, newish restaurant is a worthy challenger to nearby *Waterfront* for dining and drinking options. With dishes like pork in clay pot (160,000đ), tuna steak (250,000đ), lamb chop (400,000đ) and daily specials, there's plenty to choose from. Add a well-stocked bar (open till 2am!) and attentive staff, and you get the picture. Daily 7.30am–2am.

★Waterfront 150–152 Bach Dang ☎0511 384 3373, ⓦwaterfrontdanang.com. This two-storey restaurant and bar is probably Da Nang's most popular choice for expat diners, and the upstairs balcony seats with views of the promenade and Dragon Bridge are always first to be occupied. Sharply attired staff float around upstairs delivering burgers, seafood baskets and steaks (160,000–500,000đ). The downstairs bar is also a good place to drink (see p.270). Daily 10am–11pm.

DRINKING AND NIGHTLIFE

There are several decent **bars** in Da Nang, and more are opening all the time to cater to the growing crowd of local and foreign party animals. Also notable is a small selection of local beers to quaff – Da Nang Export and Bière la Rue.

★Bamboo Bar 2 216 Bach Dang ☎0905 544769. One of Da Nang's most popular bars located right on the riverfront. Dim-lit and noisy, it can be tough to find a seat some nights, but it's worth hanging round to get a handle on all things Da Nang. Daily noon–2am.

Golden Pine 52 Bach Dang ☎0935 210113. Located on Bach Dang just north of the Han River Bridge, this place attracts a mixed crowd of locals and foreigners, and gets packed at weekends. You'll need to shout to hold a conversation as the music is cranked up loud. Daily 2pm–2am.

Memory Lounge 7 Bach Dang ☎0511 357 5899, ⓦloungememory.com. This classy restaurant/bar is about the only place in town that sits right by the river so there are great views from its outdoor patio, where you can sip on a passion mojito while soaking up the colourful scene; a bit pricey (cocktails around 130,000–200,000đ) but worth it. Daily 7am–11.30pm.

5

Skybar Green Plaza Hotel, 238 Bach Dang ⓦ greenplaza hotel.vn. Sitting on the 20th floor of *Green Plaza Hotel*, this café and bar offers a diverse, well-stocked bar and wonderful river views, though prices are a bit steeper than elsewhere. The music is generally uninspiring, but it's the views that you come for. Daily 7am–midnight.

Waterfront 150–152 Bach Dang ⓦ waterfrontdanang .com. This swanky place is good for coffee during the day or alcohol by night – there's a choice of 15 different beers and 9 different wines by the glass. Live music on Friday evenings, DJ on other nights. Daily 10am–11pm.

DIRECTORY

Banks and exchange Vietcombank, 140 Le Loi; Incombank, 172 Nguyen Van Linh; VID Public Bank, 2 Tran Phu. ATMs now dot the city and are located in front of most higher-end hotels. There's also a bank and 24hr ATM at the airport.

Consulate The Lao consulate, with its visa-issuing service, is located at 12 Tran Quy Cap (Mon–Fri 8–11.30am & 2–4.30pm; ☏ 0511 382 1208). Visa applications will take around three working days.

Hospital The Family Medical Practice at 50–52 Nguyen Van Linh (☏ 0511 358 2699, ⓦ vietnammedicalpractice .com) has foreign staff and a dental clinic and offers 24hr emergency service.

Immigration police 7 Than Quy Cap ☏ 0511 382 3383. The place to go if you've lost your passport or have similar difficulties.

Post office Main office at 60 Bach Dang, just south of the Han River Bridge.

Around Da Nang

Da Nang is a good base for visiting nearby **beaches**, or even the Marble Mountains (see p.263) and My Son (see p.261) to the south. Other appealing destinations for day-trips are the **Son Tra Peninsula** and **Ba Na Hill Station**, both to the north of the city. Few foreigners visit the Son Tra Peninsula or Ba Na Hill Station; to see everything could take up a week of your time. If you're confident riding a motorbike, this is the cheapest way to get around and offers most flexibility in your itinerary. Alternatively, hire a xe om (negotiate a fee first) or sign up for a tour through your hotel.

Da Nang's beaches

Xe om 20,000–50,000đ, depending on where you are going

Just a couple of kilometres east of Da Nang's city centre lies the beginning of a 30km-long strip of sand that stretches all the way south to Hoi An. Sometimes incorrectly marked "China Beach" on foreign maps (see box opposite), it becomes less busy the further you get from the city, though also more built up with resorts, especially on Non Nuoc Beach. Be warned that there's a powerful **undertow** off this coast and that when the northeasterly winter monsoon blows up, riptides become particularly dangerous. The best time to hit these beaches is from February to May.

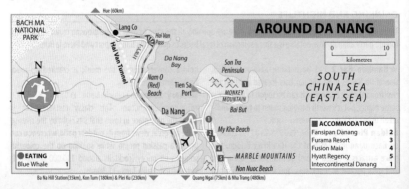

WHERE IS CHINA BEACH?

You won't find it on any Vietnamese maps, and if you ask a local, they'll shake their head and say they've never heard of it. Yet **China Beach** still appears on many maps printed in the West and in many guidebooks, referring to the entire stretch of beach between Da Nang and Hoi An. The name was given to the area by American troops who were sent here for some welcome R&R between bouts of battle with the North Vietnamese and Viet Cong. Today, with the troops long gone, the beach names have reverted to Vietnamese: from north to south, My Khe, My An, Non Nuoc, An Bang and Cau Dai. While there's no official segregation, you'll find Vietnamese predominate at My Khe and Cua Dai, while it's mostly foreigners on My An, Non Nuoc and An Bang.

My Khe Beach

As the most easily accessible of Da Nang's beaches, **My Khe** is often crowded with large groups of locals, especially at weekends. The access road is lined with simple bars and restaurants that do a roaring trade when the weather is good. If you're here with hired transport, it's worth heading on north from the beach to explore the steep trails on the **Son Tra Peninsula** (see p.272), which has a wild feel about it.

My An and Non Nuoc beaches

At the south end of My Khe Beach the road veers inland to follow behind an incredibly long stretch of **luxury resorts** covering several kilometres. The beaches from here are known as **My An** and further south as **Non Nuoc**, though it's difficult to tell where one ends and the other begins. The vibe here makes a marked contrast to My Khe, as security guards stand watch in front of high walls that shield shoulder-to-shoulder international hotel chains. Though the beach here is not technically private, access is very difficult to non-guests, so it gets less crowded. It's worth combining a visit to Non Nuoc Beach with an exploration of the **Marble Mountains** (see p.263), which you'll see to the west of the coast road just 10km south of Da Nang.

ACCOMMODATION	DA NANG'S BEACHES

Fansipan Danang Truong Sa, My Khe Beach ☎0511 391 3555, ⓦfansipandananghotel.com.vn. This high-rise, three-star hotel on My Khe Beach offers a good compromise if you want to stay by the sea without paying top dollar. Rooms are bright and well maintained, and there are big discounts in the low season (Sept–Dec). $50

Furama Resort Vo Nguyen Giap, My An Beach ☎0511 384 7333, ⓦfuramavietnam.com. Set in lush gardens, this enormous development stands out as one of Vietnam's top beach resorts, and it's still growing, with new villas being offered for sale. It offers luxuriously appointed rooms, international cuisine, two swimming pools plus a guarded beach and a range of recreational activities from tennis and golf to scuba-diving, ocean-kayaking and windsurfing. $176

★**Fusion Maia** Son Tra-Dien Ngoc St, Non Nuoc Beach

☎0511 396 7999, ⓦmaiadanang.fusion-resorts.com. This all-inclusive spa resort has been a hit since day one, suggesting that the owners know what they are doing. The rates for these luxurious pool and spa villas, which include all meals and two spa treatments a day, aren't cheap, but with the aid of your personal fusionista (whose job is to enhance your well-being), it's bound to be a memorable stay. $430

Hyatt Regency Truong Sa, Non Nuoc Beach ☎0511 398 1234, ⓦdanang.regency.hyatt.com. Cut off from the outside world and occupying a huge beach frontage within walking distance of the Marble Mountains (see p.263), this stylish resort has spacious rooms with large balconies overlooking an enormous pool. There are several dining and eating options on site and staff, as you'd expect, are efficient and helpful. $250

EATING

Blue Whale Son Tra-Dien Ngoc ☎0511 394 2777, ⓦbluewhale.com.vn. With a location right on My Khe beach and set in a smartly furnished, colonial-style villa, the *Blue Whale* is one of the most reliable places to head for a seafood

feast. Check prices before ordering, as everything depends on the day's market prices, then settle down on the terrace to enjoy the seaside ambiance. Expect to pay 200,000–300,000đ for a meal and drink. Daily 10am–11pm.

5

Son Tra Peninsula

No public transport; hire a motorbike or join a tour from Da Nang

About 5km northeast of Da Nang at the top end of My Khe beach, the mountainous, hammerhead-shaped **Son Tra Peninsula** rises to a shade under 700m high. There's a wild feel to the peninsula, which can be explored by motorbike if you're confident riding round sharp curves and up steep slopes; there are roads round the perimeter and up to the summit. The highest peak, Nui Son Tra, is often referred to as "**Monkey Mountain**", and monkeys still inhabit the promontory, parts of which are restricted to military use, though a viewing tower near the top is open to the public.

Son Tra Nature Reserve

Around 43 square kilometres of the peninsula is set aside as the **Son Tra Nature Reserve**, specifically to protect the rare **red-shanked douc langurs** that live here. These primates are sometimes called "the costumed ape" due to their unusual appearance, with a golden face, white ruff, blue eyelids and red legs that look like stockings. They are rarely seen, however, as they are very shy. Also in the reserve is a banyan tree believed to be a thousand years old, which has several root clusters up to a metre in diameter.

Quan Yin Statue

Erected in 2010 on the south coast of the Son Tra Peninsula at Linh Ung Pagoda, this enormous **statue of Quan Yin** (the Goddess of Mercy) stands nearly 70 metres tall, and is easily visible from My Khe Beach, several kilometres across the water. When it's open, which is not often, visitors can go inside and climb seventeen storeys for a dizzying view of the bay. Not surprisingly, the statue has quickly become one of Da Nang's most memorable icons.

ACCOMMODATION   **SON TRA PENINSULA**

Intercontinental Da Nang Bai Bac, Son Tra Peninsula ☎ 0511 393 8888, ⓦ danang.intercontinental.com. Hidden away on the north of the Son Tra Peninsula, the *Danang Intercontinental* is a superb place to unwind and relax. Finding it is half the fun, at the end of a winding mountain road. From the moment you step across the threshold, it's all about fantasies fulfilled in this Bill Bensley-designed resort, which cascades down the mountain to a private beach. Rooms, accessed by a funicular railway or electric cars, are beautifully laid out in a black and white theme, and facilities include two excellent restaurants – *Citron* and *La Maison 1888* – as well as a spa, a pool and watersports. **$280**

Ba Na Hill Station

48km west of Da Nang • Cable car 400,000đ return • Return trip by taxi from Da Nang, including waiting time, around $60 • Da Nang tour agents offer various organized bus tours, mostly in summer

Perched 1500m up a mountain to the west of Da Nang, **Ba Na Hill Station** provides a cool escape from the coast, though it is much more popular among Vietnamese than foreigners, many of whom find the experience rather tacky. The site was first developed by the French in the 1920s, who came in numbers to escape the summer heat and enjoy some cool, mountain air. After a brief heyday in the 1930s the resort was abandoned and soon fell victim to the ravages of war and the encroaching jungle. Dense forest growth cloaks the mountain, which is home to over five hundred species of plants and 250 types of animal.

Recently, local authorities have poured money into Ba Na, converting some of the old French villas into guesthouses and restaurants, laying forest trails and a new access road and even putting in a **two-stage cable car** – currently the longest (over 11km) and the highest (1369 metres) in the world. The 17-minute ride is a great hit with the locals, who come up here at night to admire the lights of Da Nang twinkling far below. The resort at the top is something of a theme park, though the **views** are indeed spectacular, taking in the Hai Van Pass, Son Tra Peninsula and Marble Mountains (on a clear day), but you may want to avoid summer weekends, when the place can be packed out.

North of Da Nang

Up the coast from Da Nang, Highway 1 zigzags over the **Hai Van Pass** (see box below), a wonderfully scenic ride by road or (especially) rail. These days, most buses and cars travel via the Hai Van Tunnel, leaving a more peaceful journey for those who choose to take on the pass: from the top there are superb views, weather permitting, over the sweeping curve of Da Nang Bay, with glimpses of the rail lines looping and tunnelling along the cliff.

North of the pass, the two routes converge at the small beach town of **Lang Co**, whose beach boasts brilliant white sands – and is still, as yet, comparatively undeveloped. To the west is **Bach Ma National Park**, a gorgeous place where the remains of another French-era hill station are swamped by some of the lushest vegetation in Vietnam.

Lang Co

Forty kilometres north of Da Nang, **LANG CO** village hides among coconut palms on the sandy peninsula, its presence revealed only by a white-spired church. Lang Co's **beach** is particularly attractive on a sunny day, and makes a popular lunch stop on the road between Da Nang and Hue. There's also a large **lagoon** to the west of Highway 1, which looks very pretty with its backdrop of mountains. Lang Co is worth considering as somewhere to enjoy a few days by the beach without hordes of tourists, apart from June to August when it's crowded with domestic visitors. There are a few resorts in operation and a number of seafood restaurants.

ARRIVAL AND DEPARTURE

LANG CO

By train or bus The train station is on the lagoon's western side, or public buses will drop you off anywhere on the highway.

ACCOMMODATION AND EATING

Though not yet over-busy, Lang Co has a growing array of options if you decide to stay. All places listed here serve food as well.

Banyan Tree Cu Du Village, ☏ 054 369 5888, ⊚ banyan tree.com. The opening of this 5-star resort in a small village just north of Lang Co is proof that this beach is a worthwhile destination, and its pool villas offer a tranquil escape that is also near the attractions of Hue and Da Nang. $530

Lang Co Beach Resort Lang Co ☏ 054 387 3555, ⊚ langcobeachresort.com.vn. Government-owned resort complex, with green-roofed, Hue-style villas, a landscaped pool and a replica covered bridge. The rooms are big, light and well equipped and the beach here is kept scrupulously clean. Notable are the few "budget" rooms; these, and all other rooms on site, have their rates halved between Oct and March. Double $85, budget room $45

Thanh Tam Resort Lang Co, Phu Loc ☏ 054 387 4456, ⊚ thanhtamresort.com.vn. Good-value, mid-range option, on the highway about 1500m north of the village. It's a surprisingly large place, with two restaurants to choose from, which are popular with tour groups. The rooms themselves are smart with balconies shaded by casuarinas; all have a/c and free wi-fi; ask for one of the bungalows with a sea view. $45

PASS OF THE OCEAN CLOUDS

Thirty kilometres north of Da Nang, the first and most dramatic of three mountain spurs off the **Truong Son range** cuts across Vietnam's pinched central waist, all the way to the sea. This thousand-metre-high barrier forms a climatic frontier blocking the southward penetration of cold, damp winter airstreams, which often bury the tops under thick cloud banks and earn it the title **Hai Van**, or "Pass of the Ocean Clouds". These mountains once formed a national frontier between Dai Viet and Champa, and Hai Van's continuing strategic importance is marked by a succession of forts, pillboxes and ridge-line defensive walls erected by Nguyen-dynasty Vietnamese, French, Japanese and American forces.

5

HIGHWAY 49B

Highway 1 links Lang Co to Hue, but if you have your own transport and are in the mood for adventure, you could turn north about 6km before Phu Loc (for Bach Ma) and follow **Highway 49B** up a little-trafficked peninsula where much of the road is bordered by elaborate tombstones. The road leads to **Thuan An Beach**, then turns inland for the final 15km to Hue.

Bach Ma National Park

28km west of Lang Co and 40km southeast of Hue • 40,000đ • ⓦ bachmapark.com.vn

Well off the beaten track, **Bach Ma National Park** occupies around 220 square kilometres of mountainous terrain ranging peaking at around 1450m high and stretching from near the coast to the Lao border. It is being developed as an eco-tourism destination, and dedicated ornithologists and botanists may want to make the effort to get here for the chance of seeing some of the region's 330 bird species and more than 1400 species of flora. Bach Ma is also home to some rare mammals, including the Asiatic black bear, leopard, the recently discovered – and seldom seen – **saola** and **giant muntjac** (see p.478), as well as more visible deer and macaque monkeys.

Though it's possible to make a day-trip here to tackle one of the shorter trails, nature lovers should **spend a night** or two in the park since some of the more elusive species like the crested argus (a pheasant-like peafowl) are most active at dawn and dusk. Apart from its flora and fauna, the park's greatest attraction is the cool climate near its upper reaches; in fact it's a good idea to take a jacket if staying overnight.

Bach Ma is one of the **wettest** places in Vietnam, with a staggering eight metres of rainfall a year at the summit. The best time to visit is May to early September, but even then be prepared to get wet.

ARRIVAL AND DEPARTURE   BACH MA NATIONAL PARK

By car or bike By far the easiest way to reach Bach Ma is with your own transport – 26km west of Lang Co, look for a big blue sign to the park pointing south off Highway 1 in Phu Loc town, then drive for another 4km to the park gate. A rented car from Hue will cost around $100 for the return journey.

By bus Both public and open-tour buses will drop you at the turning in Phu Loc, from where you can pick up a xe om for the final 4km stretch to the park gates (about 30,000đ).

GETTING AROUND

By rented transport Note that, while cars are allowed inside the park, motorbikes and bicycles are not. Instead, you'll have to rent one of the park's minibuses (900,000đ for an eight-seater), which will take you to the summit and back again, but can't drop off or pick up passengers en route.

INFORMATION AND TOURS

Visitors' Centre At the entrance to the park, stop first at the Visitors' Centre (daily 7am–5pm; ☎054 387 1330, ⓦ bachmapark.com.vn) to buy your entrance tickets and arrange transport and accommodation. If you are arriving outside these hours, phone in advance. Make sure you pick up a map of the trails.

Guides Although it's not a requirement, it's definitely a good idea to take a guide ($25 for an English-speaker) when you're walking in the park, principally for your own safety – it's easy to get lost. Note that it's normal "forest etiquette" to share drinks, meals and carrying the loads.

ACCOMMODATION AND EATING

The highlands at Bach Ma were previously the location of a French summer resort, where Emperor Bao Dai also kept several luxury villas. The majority of buildings, tennis courts and rose-beds are now in ruins, but a number of villas have been restored to provide tourist accommodation. There's also a **campsite** (bring your own tent) at Km 18, though facilities are limited. There's a small **restaurant** at the park entrance, where you can also buy water and snacks. Meals have to be ordered in advance if you're staying at the summit. Alternatively, you can bring your own food from Phu Loc market.

BACH MA TRAILS

Five short **nature trails** branch off the steep, tarmacked road which leads 16km from the entrance gate almost to the summit of Hai Vong Dai Mountain (1450m). Note that all marker distances refer to the distance from Highway 1 rather than from the park entrance.

Pheasant Trail (2.5km). Starts at the Km 8 marker to reach a series of waterfalls and pools, where you can swim. On the way you may hear the calls of white-cheek gibbons or some of the seven types of pheasant that inhabit the park, or see the fifty-centimetre-long earthworms which the locals cook and eat as a treatment for malaria.

Parashorea Trail (300m). At Km 14, a short but very steep trail named after this area's towering trees.

Rhododendron Trail (1.5km). Leads up 689 steps from Km 16 to a waterfall, with views over primary forest.

Five Lakes Trail (2km). Also starts at Km 16, ends at a series of five pools fed by a waterfall, where you can also swim.

Summit Trail Leads 900m from the end of the road (at Km 19) to the crest of Hai Vong Dai with good views over Cau Hai lagoon and surrounding mountains.

Do Quyen Villa Especially popular for its location near the summit, nestled among the trees. In peak season (June–Aug) it's advisable to book in advance; contact the Visitors' Centre for reservations. $15

Morin Bach Ma ☏ 054 387 1199. Located just below the summit, this restored French villa is a bit classier than the *Do Quyen Villa*, with slightly higher prices too. $20

Hue

Still packed with the accoutrements of its dynastic past, **HUE** is one of Vietnam's most engaging cities. It boasts an unparalleled opportunity for historic and culinary exploration, thanks in no small part to its status as national capital from 1802 to 1945. Though the Nguyen dynasty is no more, Hue still exudes something of a regal, dignified air – its populace, indeed, is considered somewhat highbrow by the rest of the country. The city still nurtures poets, artists, scholars and intellectuals, and you'll notice far more youngsters here than in other cities – largely because, unlike elsewhere in Vietnam, female students still wear the traditional *ao dai*. Unfortunately, it's also a breeding ground for hustlers pushing sexual services and drugs, especially to solo travellers, so be on your guard if travelling alone.

Hue repays exploration at a leisurely pace, and contains enough in the way of historical interest to swallow up a few days with no trouble at all. The city divides into three clearly defined urban areas, each with its own distinct character. The nineteenth-century walled **citadel**, on the north bank of the Perfume River, contains the once magnificent **Imperial City** as well as an extensive grid of attractive residential streets and prolific gardens. Across Dong Ba Canal to the east lies **Phu Cat**, the original merchants' quarter of Hue where ships once pulled in, now a crowded district of shophouses, Chinese Assembly Halls and pagodas. What used to be called the **European city**, a triangle of land caught between the Perfume River's south bank and the Phu Cam Canal, is now Hue's modern administrative centre, where you'll also find most hotels and tourist services.

Pine-covered hills form the city's southern bounds; this is where the Nguyen emperors built their palatial **Royal Mausoleums** (see p.291). And through it all meanders the Perfume River, named somewhat fancifully from the tree resin and blossoms it carries, passing on its way the celebrated, seven-storey tower of **Thien Mu Pagoda** (see p.289). Other nearby sights of interest include **Thuan An Beach** (see p.296) and the **Thanh Toan Covered Bridge** (see p.296). Hue is also the main jumping-off point for day-tours of the **DMZ** (see p.297).

With all this to offer, Hue is inevitably one of Vietnam's pre-eminent tourist destinations. Nevertheless, the majority of people pass through fairly quickly, partly

5

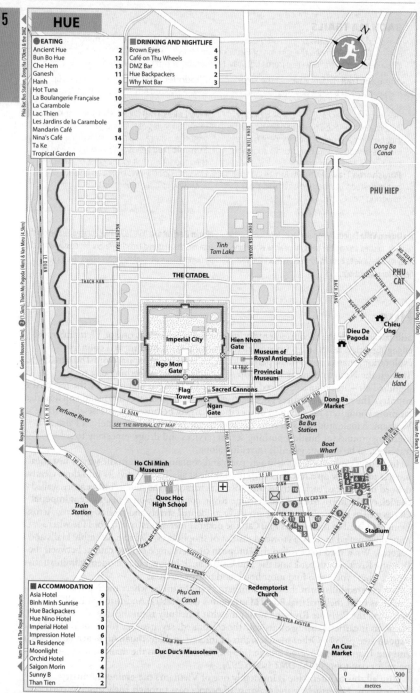

HUE

EATING

Ancient Hue	2
Bun Bo Hue	12
Che Hem	13
Ganesh	11
Hanh	9
Hot Tuna	5
La Boulangerie Française	10
La Carambole	6
Lac Thien	3
Les Jardins de la Carambole	1
Mandarin Café	8
Nina's Café	14
Ta Ke	7
Tropical Garden	4

DRINKING AND NIGHTLIFE

Brown Eyes	4
Café on Thu Wheels	5
DMZ Bar	1
Hue Backpackers	2
Why Not Bar	3

ACCOMMODATION

Asia Hotel	9
Binh Minh Sunrise	11
Hue Backpackers	5
Hue Nino Hotel	3
Imperial Hotel	10
Impression Hotel	6
La Residence	1
Moonlight	8
Orchid Hotel	7
Saigon Morin	4
Sunny B	12
Than Tien	2

Phia Bac Bus Station, Dong Ha (70km) & the DMZ

Garden Houses (1km), Thien Mu Pagoda (4km) & Van Mieu (4.5km) 1.5km,

Royal Arena (2km)

Nam Giao & The Royal Mausoleums

THE CITADEL

Tinh Tam Lake

Imperial City

Hien Nhon Gate

Ngo Mon Gate

Museum of Royal Antiquities

Provincial Museum

Flag Tower

Sacred Cannons

Ngan Gate

Perfume River

SEE 'THE IMPERIAL CITY' MAP

Ho Chi Minh Museum

Quoc Hoc High School

Train Station

Dong Ba Market

Dong Ba Station

Boat Wharf

Dieu De Pagoda

Chieu Ung

Hen Island

PHU HIEP

PHU CAT

Chua Ong (150m)

Thuan An Beach (12km)

Dong Ba Canal

Redemptorist Church

Phu Cam Canal

Duc Duc's Mausoleum

An Cuu Market

Stadium

0   500
metres

Phia Nam Bus Station (2km) & Phu Bai Airport (14km)

Thanh Toan Bridge (5km)

because high entrance fees make visiting more than a couple of the major sights beyond many budgets, and partly because of its troublesome **weather**. Hue suffers from the highest rainfall in the country, mostly falling over just three months from September to December when the city regularly floods for a few days, causing damage to the historic architecture, though heavy downpours are possible at any time of year.

Brief history

The land on which Hue now stands belonged to the Kingdom of Champa until 1306, when territory north of Da Nang was exchanged for the hand of a Vietnamese princess under the terms of a peace treaty. The first Vietnamese to settle in the region established their administrative centre near present-day Hue at a place called Hoa Chan, and then in 1558 Lord Nguyen Hoang arrived from Hanoi as governor of the district, at the same time establishing the rule of the Nguyen lords over southern Vietnam which was to last for the next two hundred years. In the late seventeenth century the lords moved the citadel to its present location where it developed into a major town and cultural centre – **Phu Xuan**, which briefly became the capital under the Tay Son emperor Quang Trung (1788–1801).

The Nguyen dynasty

However, it was the next ruler of Vietnam who literally put Hue on the map. In 1802 Prince Nguyen Anh, one of the southern Nguyen lords, defeated the Tay Son Dynasty with the help of a French bishop, Pigneau de Behaine, assumed the throne under the title **Emperor Gia Long** and founded the **Nguyen Dynasty**. Gia Long sought to unify the country by moving the capital, lock, stock and dynastic altars, from Thang Long (Hanoi) to the renamed city of **Hue**. Though he owed his throne to French military support, Gia Long's Imperial City was very much a Chinese concept, centred on a Forbidden City reserved for the sovereign, with separate administrative and civilian quarters.

The Nguyen emperors were Confucian, conservative rulers, generally suspicious of all Westerners yet unable to withstand the power of France. In 1884 the French were granted land northwest of Hue citadel, and they then seized the city entirely in 1885, leaving the emperors as nominal rulers only. Under the Nguyen, Hue became a famous centre of the arts, scholarship and Buddhist learning, but their extravagant building projects and luxurious lifestyle demanded crippling taxes.

1945–1968

Hue ceased to be the capital of Vietnam when Emperor Bao Dai abdicated in 1945; two years later a huge fire destroyed many of the city's wooden temples and palaces. From the early twentieth century the city had been engulfed in social and political unrest led by an anti-colonial educated elite, which simmered away until the 1960s. Tensions finally boiled over in May 1963 when troops fired on thousands of Buddhist nationalists demonstrating against the strongly Catholic regime of President Ngo Dinh Diem (see p.443). The protests escalated into a wave of self-immolations by monks and nuns until government forces moved against the pagodas at the end of the year, rounding up the Buddhist clergy and supposed activists in the face of massive public demonstrations.

War and reconstruction

During the 1968 **Tet Offensive** Hue was torn apart again when the North Vietnamese Army (NVA) held the city for 25 days. Communist forces entered Hue in the early hours of January 31, hoisted their flag above the citadel and found themselves in control of the whole city bar two small military compounds. Armed with lists of names, they began searching out government personnel, sympathizers of the Southern regime, intellectuals, priests, Americans and foreign aid workers. Nearly three thousand bodies were later discovered in mass graves around the city – the victims were mostly civilians who had been shot, beaten to death or buried alive. But the killing hadn't

5

THE CITADEL

Hue's days of glory kicked off in the early nineteenth century when Emperor Gia Long laid out a vast **citadel**, comprising three concentric enclosures, ranged behind the prominent flag tower. Within the citadel's outer wall lies the **Imperial City**, containing administrative offices, parks and dynastic temples, with the royal palaces of the **Forbidden Purple City** at its centre. Though wars, fires, typhoons, floods and termites have all taken their toll, it's these Imperial edifices, some now restored to their former magnificence, that constitute Hue's prime tourist attraction. Apart from one museum, there are no specific sights in the outer citadel, but it's a pleasant area to cycle round, especially the northern sector where you'll find many lakes and the prolific **gardens** for which Hue is famed.

In accordance with ancient tradition, the citadel was built in an **auspicious location** chosen to preserve the all-important harmony between the emperor and his subjects, heaven and earth, man and nature. Thus the complex is oriented southeast towards the low hummock of Nui Ngu Binh ("Royal Screen Mountain"), which blocks out harmful influences. Just in case that wasn't protection enough, the whole 5.2 square kilometres are enclosed within 7m-high, 20m-thick brick and earth walls built with the help of French engineers, and encircled by a moat and canal. Eight villages had to be relocated when construction began in 1805, and over the next thirty years tens of thousands of workmen laboured to complete more than three hundred palaces, temples, tombs and other royal buildings, some using materials brought down from the former Imperial City in Hanoi.

finished: during the ensuing counter-assault as many as five thousand North Vietnamese and Viet Cong, 384 Southern troops and 142 American soldiers died, plus at least another thousand civilians. Hue was all but levelled in the massive fire power unleashed on NVA forces holed up in the citadel but it took a further ten days of agonizing, house-to-house combat to drive the Communists out, in what Stanley Karnow described as "the most bitter battle" of the entire war. Seven years later, on March 26, 1975, the NVA were back to liberate Hue in its pivotal position as the first major town south of the Seventeenth Parallel.

The mammoth task of **rebuilding** Hue received a boost in 1993 when UNESCO listed the city as a World Heritage Site, which served to mobilize international funding for a whole range of projects, from renovating palaces to the biennial Hue Festival.

The citadel walls, flag tower and sacred cannons

The citadel's massive, 10km-long **perimeter wall** has survived intact, as has its most prominent feature, the **flag tower**, or *Cot Co* (also known as *Ky Dai*, "the King's Knight"), which dominates the southern battlements. The tower is in fact three squat, brick terraces topped with a flagpole first erected in 1807. Ten gates pierce the citadel wall, and just inside the Ngan Gate, to the east of the flag tower, is a parade ground flanked by the nine **sacred cannons**, which were cast in the early nineteenth century. They represent the four seasons and five ritual elements of earth, fire, metal, wood and water.

The Imperial City

Daily 7am–5pm · 105,000đ

A second moat and defensive wall inside the citadel guard the **Imperial City**, which follows the same symmetrical layout as Beijing's Forbidden City – though oriented northwest–southeast, rather than north–south. The Vietnamese version, popularly known as *Dai Noi* ("the Great Enclosure"), has four gates – one in each wall – though by far the most impressive is south-facing **Ngo Mon**, the Imperial City's principal entrance. In its heyday the complex must have been truly awe-inspiring, a place of glazed yellow and green roof tiles, pavilions of rich red and gilded lacquer and lotus-filled ponds – all surveyed by the emperor with his entourage of haughty mandarins. However, many of its buildings were badly neglected even before the battle for Hue raged through the Imperial City during Tet 1968, and by 1975 a mere twenty out of the original 148 were left standing among the vegetable plots. Some are in the midst of extensive restorations, and those which have been completed are stunning – notably **Thai Hoa Palace**, the **The Mieu** complex and **Dien Tho**. The rest of the Imperial City, especially its northern sector, is a grassed-over expanse full of birds and butterflies where you can still make out foundations and find bullet pockmarks in the plasterwork of ruined walls.

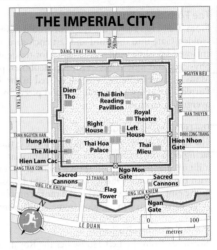

Ngo Mon Gate

In 1833 Emperor Minh Mang replaced an earlier, much less formidable gate with the present dramatic entrance-way to the Imperial City, **Ngo Mon**, considered a masterpiece of Nguyen architecture. Ngo Mon (the "Noon" or "Southwest" Gate) has five entrances: the emperor alone used the central entrance paved with stone; two smaller doorways on either side were for the civil and military mandarins, who only rated brick paving, while another pair of giant openings in the wings allowed access to the royal elephants.

Five Phoenix Watchtower

The bulk of Ngo Mon is constructed of massive stone slabs, but perched on top is an elegant pavilion called the **Five Phoenix Watchtower** as its nine roofs are said to resemble five birds in flight when viewed from above. Note that the central roof, under which the emperor passed, is covered with yellow-glazed tiles, a feature of nearly all Hue's royal roofs. Emperors used the watchtower for two major ceremonies each year: the declaration of the lunar New Year; and the announcement of the civil service exam results, depicted here in a lacquer painting. It was also in this pavilion that the last Nguyen emperor, Bao Dai, abdicated in 1945 when he handed over to the new government his symbols of power – a solid gold seal weighing ten kilos and a sheathed sword encrusted with jade.

Thai Hoa Palace

Walking north from Ngo Mon along the city's symmetrical axis, you pass between two square lakes and a pair of *kylin*, mythical dew-drinking animals that are harbingers of peace, to reach **Thai Hoa Palace** ("the Palace of Supreme Harmony"). Not only is this the most spectacular of Hue's palaces, its interior glowing with sumptuous red and gold lacquers, but it's also the most important since this was the throne palace, where major ceremonies such as coronations or royal birthdays took place and foreign ambassadors were received (see box, p.280).

The palace was first constructed in 1805, though the present building dates from 1833 when the French floor tiles and glass door panels were added. Nevertheless, the throne room's eighty ironwood pillars, swirling with dragons and clouds, had been eaten away by termites and humidity and were on the point of collapse when rescue work began in 1991. During the restoration every column, weighing two tonnes apiece, had to be replaced manually and then painted with twelve coats of lacquer, each coat taking one month to dry.

5

The Forbidden Purple City

From Thai Hoa Palace the emperor would have walked north through the Great Golden Gate into the third and last enclosure, the **Forbidden Purple City**. This area, enclosed by a low wall, was reserved for residential palaces, living quarters of the state physician and nine ranks of royal concubines, plus kitchens and pleasure pavilions. Many of these buildings were destroyed in the 1947 fire, leaving most of the Forbidden Purple City as open ground, a "mood piece", haunted by fragments of wall and overgrown terraces.

The Left House and Right House

The handful of remaining buildings include the restored **Left House** and **Right House** facing each other across a courtyard immediately behind Thai Hoa Palace. Civil and military mandarins would spruce themselves up here before proceeding to an audience with the monarch. Of the two, the Right House (actually to the left – the names refer to the emperor's viewpoint) is the more complete with its ornate murals and gargantuan mirror in a gilded frame, a gift from the French to Emperor Dong Khanh.

Thai Binh Reading Pavilion

Northeast from the Left House lies the Royal Theatre, built in 1826 and restored in 2004, to find the **Thai Binh Reading Pavilion**, an appealing, two-tier structure surrounded by bonsai gardens. The pavilion was built by Thieu Tri and then restored by Khai Dinh, who added the kitsch mosaics. This was where the emperor came to listen to music and commune with nature, and it has once again been restored to its former splendour.

The urns and ancestral altars

The other main cluster of sights lies over in the southwest corner of the Imperial City. Aligned on a southeast–northwest axis, the procession kicks off with **Hien Lam Cac** ("Pavilion of Everlasting Clarity"), a graceful, three-storey structure with some notable woodwork, followed by the **Nine Dynastic Urns**. Considered the zenith of Hue craftsmanship, the bronze urns were cast during the reign of Minh Mang and are ornamented with scenes of mountains, rivers, rain clouds and wildlife, plus one or two stray bullet marks. Each urn is dedicated to an emperor: the middle urn, which is also the largest at 2600kg, honours Gia Long.

The urns stand across the courtyard from the long, low building of **The Mieu**, the Nguyens' dynastic temple erected in 1822 by Minh Mang to worship his father. Since then, **ancestral altars** have been added for each emperor in turn, except Duc Duc and Hiep Hoa, who reigned only briefly, and Bao Dai who died in exile in 1997; the three anti-French sovereigns – Ham Nghi, Thanh Thai and Duy Tan – had to wait until after Independence in 1954 for theirs. Take a look inside to see the line of altar tables, most sporting a portrait or photo of the monarch.

CEREMONIES AT THAI HOA PALACE

On these occasions the emperor sat on the raised dais, wearing a golden tunic and a crown decorated with nine dragons, under a spectacular gilded canopy. He faced south across the **Esplanade of Great Salutations**, a stone-paved courtyard where the mandarins stood, civil mandarins to the left and military on the right, lined up in their appointed places beside eighteen stelae denoting the nine subdivided ranks. A French traveller in the 1920s witnessed the colourful spectacle, with "perfume-bearers in royal-blue, fan-bearers in sky-blue waving enormous yellow feather fans, musicians and guardsmen and ranks of mandarins in their curious hats and gorgeous, purple-embroidered dragons, kow-towing down, down on their noses amid clouds of incense – and all in a setting of blood-red lacquer scrawled with gold".

Hung Mieu

Outside The Mieu's west door, beside a 170-year-old pine tree trained in the shape of a flying dragon, a path leads north into the next compound and **Hung Mieu**. This temple is dedicated to the Nguyen ancestors and specifically to the parents of Gia Long, and is distinguished by its fine carving.

Dien Tho

Over in the northeastern side of the Imperial City, **Dien Tho**, the queen mother's residence, is worth a look. Built in a mix of Vietnamese and French architectural styles, the palace later served as Bao Dai's private residence, and the downstairs reception rooms are now set out with period furniture, echoing the photos of the palace in use in the 1930s.

Museum of Royal Antiquities

3 Le Truc • Tues–Sun 8–11.30am & 1.30–5pm • 50,000đ

From the eastern exit of the Imperial City (via Hien Nhon Gate – the "Gate of Humanity") it's a short walk to the **Museum of Royal Antiquities** (also known as the Imperial Museum or the Royal Fine Arts Museum), which boasts an interesting display of former royal paraphernalia, though there is little information about the exhibits. Objects on display include porcelain, costumes and personal items of the Nguyen emperors, but visitors are more likely to be impressed by the **Long An Palace** in which the museum is housed, with its forest of hardwood pillars, which was restored and re-opened in 2012.

Dong Ba Market

Tran Hung Dao

If crossing the Perfume River on Trang Thien Bridge, you'll pass **Dong Ba Market**, a rambling covered market at the southeast corner of the citadel, and one of the epicentres of Hue's commercial life. Fruit, fish and vegetable vendors overflow into the surrounding spaces, while in the downstairs hall you'll find Hue's contribution to the world of fashion, the *non bai tho*, or **poem hat**. These look just like the normal conical hat but have a stencil, traditionally of a romantic poem, inserted between the palm fronds – and only visible when held up to the light.

Phu Cat district

Hue's civilian and merchant quarter grew up to the east of the citadel on a triangular island now divided into **Phu Cat**, Phu Hiep and Phu Hau districts. This part of town still boasts some single-storey, wood and red-tiled houses as well as more ornate, colonial-era shophouses. The area was once home to Hue's Chinese community, and five **assembly halls** still stand along Chi Lang. Old trees shade the Dong Ba Canal on the island's southwestern side, where Bach Dang was the site of anti-government demonstrations in the 1960s, centred around **Dieu De Pagoda**.

Chua Ong Assembly Hall

Chua Ong 319 Chi Lang • Free

Chinese immigrants to Hue settled in five congregations around their separate **assembly halls**, of which the most interesting is **Chua Ong**. Founded by the Phuoc Kien (Fujian) community in the mid-1800s and rebuilt on several occasions, including after Viet Cong mortars hit a US munitions boat on the river nearby in 1968 and destroyed the pagoda plus surrounding houses. Surprisingly, there's no Buddha on the main altar but instead several doctors of medicine, along with General Quan Cong to the right

5

and Thien Hau to the left, both protectors of sailors. The story goes that Quan Cong sat on the main altar until a devastating cholera epidemic in 1918 when he was displaced by the doctors, and the outbreak ended soon after.

Chieu Ung Assembly Hall
Chieu Ung 223 Chi Lang • Free

Of the other halls, **Chieu Ung** is worth dropping in to. The gilded altar displays some skilled carpentry. This pagoda was also founded in the nineteenth century by ethnic Chinese from Hainan, and has been rebuilt at least twice since.

The European city

Although the French became the de facto rulers of Vietnam after 1884, they left the emperors in the citadel and settled their administration over the water on the south bank of the Perfume River. The main artery of the **European city** was riverside Le Loi where the French Resident's office stood (now *Le Residence* hotel), together with other important buildings such as **Quoc Hoc High School** and the *Frères Morin* hotel (now the *Saigon Morin*). Residential streets spread out south of the river as far as the Phu Cam Canal, and are linked to the citadel by Clemenceau Bridge, renamed Trang Tien Bridge after 1954, and the Bach Ho (White Tiger) Bridge, completed in 2012. Having said all this, the district's only major sight is the **Ho Chi Minh Museum**, not just the obligatory gesture in this case as Ho did spend much of his childhood in Hue.

The Ho Chi Minh Museum
7 Le Loi • Tues–Sun 7.30–11am & 2–4.30pm • Free

Ho Chi Minh spent ten years at school in Hue (1895–1901 and 1906–1909) where his father worked as a civil mandarin. The **Ho Chi Minh Museum** presents these years in the context of the anti-French struggle and then takes the story on to 1960 peace protests in Hue and reunification. The most interesting material consists of family photos and glimpses of early twentieth-century Hue, but if you've visited a Ho Chi Minh Museum elsewhere on your travels, you're unlikely to find anything new here.

Redemptorist Church
Nguyen Hue • Dawn to dusk • Free

The extraordinary, tiered spire of the **Redemptorist Church** dominates the city's southern horizon with its improbable blend of Gothic and Cubism, created by a local architect in the late 1950s. The church caters to some of Hue's twenty thousand Catholics and is interesting to view in passing, though the interior is less striking.

REVOLUTIONARY EDUCATION

Ho Chi Minh was the most famous student to attend **Quoc Hoc High School**, which stands almost opposite his museum on Le Loi. The school was founded in 1896 as the National College, dedicated to the education of royal princes and future administrators who learnt the history of their European "motherland" – all in French until 1945. Ho studied here for at least a year before being expelled for taking part in anti-government demonstrations. Other revolutionary names that appear on the roster are Prime Minister Pham Van Dong, General Giap and Party Secretary Le Duan, while former president of South Vietnam Ngo Dinh Diem was also a student. Even during the 1960s Quoc Hoc had a justly earned reputation for breeding dissident intellectuals, and after reunification in 1975 some staff were sent for "re-education". Quoc Hoc is still a functioning school today – and, in fact, one of the most prestigious in the whole land.

FROM TOP DRAGON BRIDGE, HUE (P.268); IMPERIAL CITY, HUE (P.278) >

5

ARRIVAL AND DEPARTURE

HUE

By plane Phu Bai Airport lies 15km southeast of the city centre. Arriving flights are met by a bus (60,000đ), which takes you to central hotels, and by metered taxis (around $15). The Vietnam Airlines office is at 23 Nguyen Van Cu (☎054 382 4709).

Destinations Hanoi (6 daily; 1hr 10min); Ho Chi Minh City (8 daily; 1hr 20min).

By train The station lies about 1.5km from the centre of town at the far western end of Le Loi. Note that trains out of Hue get booked up, especially sleepers to Ho Chi Minh City and Hanoi, so make onward travel arrangements as early as possible (ticket office open daily 7–11.30am & 1.30–8pm).

Destinations Da Nang (6 daily; 2hr 20min–3hr); Dong Ha (5 daily; 1hr–1hr 20min); Dong Hoi (6 daily; 2hr 40min–3hr 30min); Hanoi (6 daily; 13–16hr); Ho Chi Minh City (6 daily; 19–24hr); Nha Trang (6 daily; 11hr 20min–15hr); Ninh Binh (3 daily; 14hr).

By bus Public buses arrive at one of two stations – Phia Nam, 2km south of the city centre in An Cuu, for links with the south; and Phia Bac, off the citadel's northwest corner, for links with the north. *Hue Backpackers* (see below) also runs a daily minibus to Phong Nha.

Destinations Da Nang (3hr); Dong Ha (2hr 30min); Dong Hoi (5hr); Hoi An (4hr); Savannakhet, Laos (14hr).

GETTING AROUND

By bicycle Hue's wide avenues become crowded during rush hour (7–9am & 4–6pm), but generally the most enjoyable way of getting around the city's scattered sights – and especially of touring the Royal Mausoleums – is by bicycle. Most hotels and guesthouses, plus a few cafés, offer bike rental (from $1/day) and motorbikes (from $5/day).

By motorbike and car tour Hue Riders (38 Tran Cao Van ☎090 574 3858, ⓦhueriders.com) offers guided motorbike tours of Hue and its environs, while *Mandarin Café* (see p.286) can arrange car rental (around $40 per day).

By taxi Two reputable taxi companies are Mai Linh Taxi (☎054 389 8989) and Yellow Taxi (☎054 379 7979).

INFORMATION AND TOURS

Tourist information The best bet for tourist information is either your hotel or one of the tour agents; staff at *Mandarin Café* (see p.286) are particularly helpful. Every hotel and tour agent hands out photocopied maps, but for a

detailed city plan try the big hotels and bookstalls on Le Loi.

Tours Two of the more reliable tour operators are *Mandarin Café* (see p.286) and ABS Travel, 51 Le Loi (☎054 393 2499, ⓦabstravel.asia).

ACCOMMODATION

Most accommodation in Hue is located south of the Perfume River; **top-class establishments** overlook the river, while budget hotels and guesthouses are scattered in the streets behind, particularly the **backpacker enclaves** around Pham Ngu Lao and Nguyen Tri Phuong.

Asia Hotel 17 Pham Ngu Lao ☎054 383 0283, ⓦasia hotel.com.vn; map p.276. Tall boutique-style hotel, with attractive, generously proportioned rooms and breakfasts with a view. There's also a tiny pool, as well as sauna facilities. Book online for some healthy discounts. $75

Binh Minh Sunrise 36 Nguyen Tri Phuong ☎054 382 5526, ⓦbinhminhhue.com; map p.276. Bright, welcoming hotel in a great location with a range of clean, homely rooms, some with balconies looking towards the mountains. A popular and good-value option, though rooms at the front will be noisy; it's worth an extra $5–10 for the better ones. $15

Hue Backpackers 10 Pham Ngu Lao ☎054 382 6567, ⓦvietnambackpackerhostels.com; map p.276. All dorm rooms are en suite, while the ground-floor common area is always buzzing – especially in the evening. Couples may be interested in the "queen-sized dorm beds", which, it has to be said, occasionally result in predictable consequences. Dorm $8, double $12

★**Hue Nino Hotel** 14 Nguyen Cong Tru ☎054 625 2171, ⓦhueninohotel.com; map p.276. Superb value,

friendly staff and mouthwatering breakfasts at this small hotel, which has become a real favourite with budget travellers to the city. Staff have a habit of welcoming you back with a glass of juice – even if you've just popped to the shops. $18

Imperial Hotel 8 Hung Vuong ☎054 388 2222, ⓦimperial-hotel.com.vn; map p.276. The first five-star hotel in Hue dominates the skyline near the Perfume River; plush carpets lead the way to suitably well-appointed rooms, with fabulous views from the upper floors. The complex also includes a fitness centre, swimming pool and classy restaurant. Ask about discounts – the place often feels near-empty. $150

Impression Hotel 7/66 Le Loi ☎054 382 8403, ⓦhueimpressionhotel.com; map p.276. Also known as the *Dong Tam*, this is cheap yet looks rather plush from the outside, especially when the sun is shining on the pool in the front garden. The rooms are sparsely furnished but for these rates it's still a steal. It's on a small alley off Le Loi. $10

★**La Residence** 5 Le Loi ☎054 383 7475, ⓦla-residence-hue.com; map p.276. Formerly the

French governor's residence (hence the name), and overlooking the Perfume River, this *M Gallery* hotel blends early twentieth-century Art Deco design with excellent services. There's a palpable colonial air to the place, one best savoured with a cocktail by the riverside pool. **$135**

Moonlight 20 Pham Ngu Lao ☏ 054 397 9797, ⊚ moonlighthue.com; map p.276. With an ideal location on Pham Ngu Lao, this new place can't go wrong, and its enthusiastic staff seem determined to make it the city's most popular hotel. Rooms are smallish but luxuriously furnished, some have balconies and many enjoy great views. There's a swimming pool and gym on the 5th floor, buffet breakfast is served on the 14th floor, and a hip bar, *Sirius*, is on the 15th floor. **$70**

Orchid Hotel 30a Chu Van An ☏ 054 383 1177, ⊚ orchid hotel.com.vn; map p.276. A strong contender for the friendliest hotel staff in the city – smiling attendants usher their customers to superbly stylish rooms, decorated with orchid petals and other attractive flourishes. Lastly, the breakfasts are astonishingly good – the staff must be tired of guests singing praises morning after morning. **$50**

Saigon Morin 30 Le Loi ☏ 054 382 3526, ⊚ morinhotel .com.vn; map p.276. Hue's most famous French-era hotel has been renovated to four-star standards, but still retains some of its colonial charm, not least in the garden courtyard; swing by for a look, even if you're not staying. The rooms are a good size, if a little bland, and kitted out with all the equipment you'd expect, including mini-bar, bathtub and hairdryer. Facilities include a rooftop bar, two restaurants and a small pool ($5 to non-residents). **$110**

Sunny B 4/34 Nguyen Tri Phuong ☏ 054 383 0145, ⊚ binhduonghotel.com; map p.276. A wonderful place to stay – cheap, friendly and cosy. Rooms are big and bright with bamboo furnishings and the top rooms have two double beds and big balconies. If it's full, *Sunny A* and *Sunny C* are nearby with similar rooms and rates. Doubles **$15**, top rooms **$35**

Than Thien 10 Nguyen Cong Tru ☏ 054 383 4666, ⊚ thanthienhotel.com.vn; map p.276. There are three types of room here – superior, deluxe and VIP – and all offer excellent value, especially the VIP rooms, which are massive. All rooms have comfortable furnishings, but some of the superior rooms don't have windows, so take a look before you decide. Superior rooms **$19**, VIP rooms **$50**

EATING

If you're here for a few nights, it's worth exploring Hue's local cuisine (see box, p.286) by sampling a range of **restaurants**, both Vietnamese and colonial-style. If your visit to Hue is fleeting, you could tick off three essential Hue experiences – cuisine, *ca hue* (folk songs) and cruising on the Perfume River – all at one go. Most hotels offer such a **dinner cruise** each evening, lasting around two hours, with prices ranging around $20–40 a person. As you might expect, the quality of the boat, the food, the service and the entertainment is relative to the cost of the tour.

★**Ancient Hue** 104/47 Kim Long ☏ 054 359 0356, ⊚ ancienthue.com.vn; map p.276. Located to the west of the Citadel, this atmospheric compound consists of five ancient wooden houses, three of which function as restaurants, one as an art gallery and one as a garden house. They serve both royal cuisine and Western fusion dishes, and this is the place to go for the full "Imperial Hue" feeling. There are frequent performances of traditional music and dance, and cooking classes are also offered. Set menus around 400,000đ, mains 120,000–400,000đ. Daily 8am–10pm.

Bun Bo Hue 17 Ly Thuong Kiet ☏ 054 382 6460; map p.276. Of all the places serving *bun bo*, this simple affair has by far the most reknown – any local will confirm this. You should definitely sample it yourself (30,000đ). Daily 6am–7.30pm.

Che Hem 29/31 Hung Vuong; map p.276. For a local speciality, there aren't as many places serving *che* as you'd expect, but this is centrally located and as tasty as you'll get. Around 10,000đ a glass. Daily 8am–9pm.

Ganesh 34 Nguyen Tri Phuong ☏ 054 382 1616; map p.276. Formerly *Omar Khayyam's*, this restaurant is deservedly popular for its authentic Indian fare, which includes a good vegetarian and *thali* selection. You'll pay around 120,000đ per head for a decent meal. Daily 7am–9pm.

Hanh 11 Pho Duc Chinh; map p.276. Here you'll find *banh khoai* freshly prepared throughout the day – 20,000đ will be enough for a plateful, or try a five-course meal for 100,000đ. It's a local favourite, and packed at mealtimes – many of the regulars will wonder what on earth you're doing on their turf. Daily 7am–9.30pm.

Hot Tuna 37 Vo Thi Sau ☏ 054 361 6464; map p.276. A great combination of welcoming atmosphere and top-value food, covering a huge range of Vietnamese and Western dishes. Good for breakfasts, burgers (60,000đ) and hot pots. Daily 8am–11pm.

La Boulangerie Française 46 Nguyen Tri Phuong ☏ 054 383 7437; map p.276. A French charity runs this café and bakery school for local orphans in the hope that they gain employment after graduation. Their shop has an array of light and delicious French pastries (starting at around 20,000đ), perfect for breakfast or packed away for long boat rides. Daily 8am–8pm.

La Carambole 19 Pham Ngu Lao ☏ 054 381 0491; map p.276. The original branch of foreign-owned *Les Jardins de la Carambole* still serves up great food, though service is erratic. Prices are surprisingly reasonable (mains 100,000đ

5

HUE SPECIALITY FOODS

One good argument for staying in Hue an extra couple of days is its many **speciality foods**, best sampled at local stalls and street kitchens.

Banh beo Order this afternoon dish and you get a whole trayful of individual plates, each containing a small amount of steamed rice-flour dough topped with spices, shrimp flakes and a morsel of pork crackling; add a little sweetened *nuoc mam* sauce to each dish and tuck in with a teaspoon. *Banh nam*, or *banh lam*, is a similar idea but spread thinly in an oblong, steamed in a banana leaf and eaten with rich *nuoc mam* sauce. Manioc flour is used instead of rice for *banh loc*, making a translucent parcel of whole shrimps, sliced pork and spices steamed in a banana leaf, but this time the *nuoc mam* is pepped up with a dash of chilli. Finally, *ram it* consists of two small dollops of sticky rice-flour dough, one fried and one steamed, to dip in a spicy sauce. You'll find

good places in which to sample these dishes all over the city.

Banh khoai Probably the most famous Hue dish, a small, crispy yellow pancake made of egg and rice flour, fried up with shrimp, pork and bean sprouts and eaten with a special peanut and sesame sauce (*nuoc leo*), plus a vegetable accompaniment of star fruit, green banana, lettuce and mint. Amazingly, it's even more delicious than it sounds.

Bun bo Spicy rice-noodle beef soup flavoured with citronella, shrimp and basil; also called *bun ga* with chicken, or *bun bo gio heo* with beef and pork.

Che A refreshing drink made from green bean and coconut (*che xanh dua*), fruit (*che trai cay*) or, if you're lucky, lotus seed (*che hat sen*).

and up), and the menu is full of tempting French goodies hard to find in Vietnam – cheese platters, quiche, banana flambé and so on. Daily 7am–11pm.

Lac Thien 6 Dinh Tien Hoang ☎054 352 4674; map p.276. Restaurant run by a deaf-mute family who communicate by sign language. The food is cheap but pretty tasty, especially the Hue staples (see box above); most plump for the *banh khoai* (40,000đ), served with a mountain of leaves and lashings of peanut sauce. Daily 8am–7pm.

Les Jardins de la Carambole 32 Dang Tran Con ☎054 354 8815, ⓦlesjardinsdelacarambole.com; map p.276. This upscale version of *La Carambole* is located in a gorgeous colonial villa on a leafy lane to the west of the citadel, and French owner Christian goes out of his way to please guests. There's a good range of French, Mediterranean and Vietnamese dishes; try the beef bourguignon (240,000đ) and the Nicoise salad (120,000đ). Daily 7am–11pm.

★**Mandarin Café** 24 Tran Cao Van ☎054 382 1281, ⓦmrcumandarin.com; map p.276. A leading light of Hue's backpacker business, this unassuming café off the

main road rustles up cheap but very tasty Vietnamese and Western fare (mains from 40,000đ). Owner-photographer Mr Cu and his staff are also excellent sources of information and can assist with boat trips, bike and car rental and tours. Daily 7am–10pm.

Nina's Cafe 16/134 Nguyen Tri Phuong ☎054 383 8636; map p.276. Simple, cheap and friendly affair tucked away on backpacker alley, with wooden chairs arrayed around a small courtyard. It's great for spring rolls, soups, meat and vegetarian dishes (around 40,000–60,000đ), and set menus at 140,000–200,000đ. Daily 7.30am–10.30pm

Ta Ke 34 Tran Cao Van ☎054 384 8262; map p.276. This unpretentious Japanese restaurant offers fantastic value meals in a central location – the sushi and tempura dishes (around 70,000đ) are particularly recommended. Daily 10am–10pm.

Tropical Garden 27 Chu Van An ☎054 384 7143; map p.276. Choose to dine in the bamboo garden or air-con interior of this upscale restaurant, which lays on performances of traditional music each evening for tour groups. A choice of Hue specialities plus set menus (from 240,000đ) and plenty of seafood. Daily 9am–10.30pm

DRINKING AND NIGHTLIFE

The bars listed here are open through the day, and closing times are essentially based on demand – at least one place will be going until the wee hours.

Brown Eyes 56 Chu Van An ☎054 382 7494; map p.276. "Red Eyes" would be a more appropriate name for this bar – many a sozzled backpacker has stumbled from its doors into the light of early morning. Staff are fun, and there's a pool table to test your focus.

Café on Thu Wheels 3/34 Nguyen Tri Phuong ☎054 383 2241; map p.276. Owner Thu has moved on, but her sister is doing a decent job at this tiny café-bar, which has long been a popular backpacker pit-stop. It also runs good motorbike tours around Hue.

THE HUE FESTIVAL

Since 1992, every two years the city of Hue has held a **nine-day long festival** that features top musicians and artists not only from Vietnam, but also from around the world. For this spectacular event, the city's main attractions and bridges are illuminated and key events include theatrical and street performances, royal banquets and fashion parades. It's extremely photogenic though a bit crowded as all the city's inhabitants come out to join in. The event usually takes place between April and June in even-numbered years (2016, 2018, etc). For more information visit ⓦ huefestival.com.

DMZ Bar 60 Le Loi ☎ 054 382 3414; map p.276. Exactly what you'd expect of a Western bar – pool table, cold beers, Western grub and occasional live music. The downstairs bar can get raucous, while the upstairs dining area offers excellent people-watching from the small balcony.

Hue Backpackers 10 Pham Ngu Lao ☎ 054 382 6567; map p.276. Located on Hue's busiest street for nightlife, this place offers not only cheap dorm beds but also a buzzing ground-floor bar and an extensive list of cocktails.

Why Not Bar? 46 Pham Ngu Lao ☎ 054 382 4793; map p.276. With a bar, restaurant and hotel all along Pham Ngu Lao, it looks as if *Why Not?* is taking over Hue. Big-screen TV for sports events, sexy beer girls, hundreds of cocktails and loud music are its main attractions.

DIRECTORY

Banks and exchange Vietcombank, 78 Hung Vuong, exchanges cash and has a 24hr ATM outside. There's also an exchange bureau outside the *Saigon Morin* hotel, which is open longer hours (Mon–Sat 7am–10pm), with a 24hr ATM.

Hospital Hue Central Hospital, 16 Le Loi ☎ 054 382 2325.

Pharmacies You'll find well-stocked pharmacies on Ngo Quyen and behind the hospital on Le Loi.

Post office The GPO occupies a grand building at 8 Hoang Hoa Tham, and also has internet facilities.

Around Hue

For the most part the Nguyen emperors lived their lives within Hue's citadel walls, but on certain occasions they emerged to participate in important rituals at symbolic locations around the city. Today these places are of interest more for their history than anything much to see on the ground, though the mouldering **Royal Arena** still hints at past spectacles. A visit to at least a couple of the **Royal Mausoleums**, however, is not to be missed – it's in these eclectic architectural confections in the hills to the south of Hue that the spirit of the Nguyen emperors lives on. Taking a boat along the **Perfume River** to get to the best mausoleums also offers the chance to stop off at the **Thien Mu Pagoda** and **Hon Chen Temple** on the way (see box, p.289).

Thuan An Beach is a short distance away from the city, and makes a fun contrast to slogging round historic monuments, especially on a sunny day. Though it's tempting to go by bike, the traffic can be heavy. A better bike ride is east of town to the **Thanh Toan Covered Bridge**, surrounded by paddy fields and rural scenes. Further afield, one of the most popular excursions from Hue is a whirlwind day-trip round the **DMZ** (see p.297). **Bach Ma National Park** (see p.274) is also within striking distance.

West along the Perfume River

Hug the north bank of the Perfume River west of the citadel and you'll stumble across a few interesting sights, including the pagodas of **Thien Mu** and **Van Mieu**, the traditional garden houses of **Kim Long Village**, and the Temple of **Hon Chen**.

These sights are most easily covered on a **boat tour** (see box, p.289), but all bar Hon Chen can be visited on an easy **bike ride** from the centre of Hue (6km; 30min), crossing the river on the new Bach Ho Bridge. If you've got time, note there is a pleasant cycle ride on from Van Mieu (see p.289) along an empty country lane beside the river.

5

The garden houses

Located on the north bank of the river to the southwest of the citadel is **Kim Long** village, a peaceful area of quiet lanes and canals where in the late nineteenth-century mandarins and other Imperial officials built their **houses**, surrounded by lush gardens. Some of these houses are strung along Phu Mong lane, which heads north from the riverbank just before 86 Kim Long. There is a wonderfully tranquil atmosphere along the shady lane and you can glimpse some impressive buildings, though most are closed to the public. One exception is the atmospheric restaurant *Ancient Hue* (see p.285).

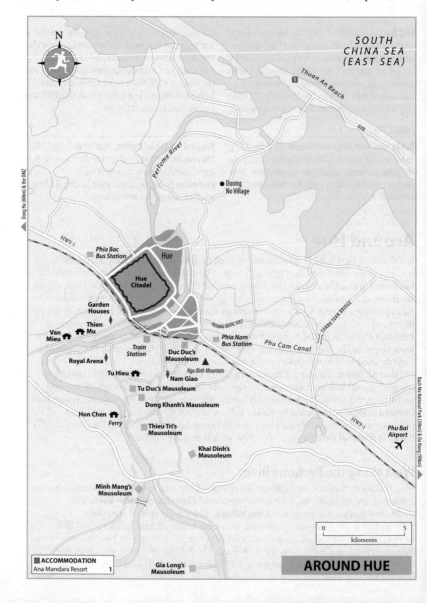

AROUND HUE

■ ACCOMMODATION
Ana Mandara Resort ... 1

BOAT TRIPS ON THE PERFUME RIVER

A number of people still live in boats on the **Perfume River** and the waterways of Hue, such as the Dong Ba and Phu Cam canals, despite government efforts to settle them elsewhere. It's possible to join them, if only temporarily, by taking a **boat trip**, puttering about in front of the citadel on a misty Hue morning, watching the slow bustle of river life.

The standard day-long boat trip takes you to **Thien Mu Pagoda**, **Hon Chen Temple** and the most rewarding mausoleums, usually those of **Tu Duc** and **Minh Mang**, from where you return by bus. However, if you want to visit some of the others or spend more time exploring, it's usually possible to take a bicycle on the boat and cycle back to Hue, though double-check this when you book the trip.

Most tour agents (see p.284) and hotels offer river tours for about $25 per boat for a group of ten. However, all entrance fees are extra, which can work out costly at 80,000đ per mausoleum. If you'd rather do it independently, practise your bargaining skills at the boat wharf beside the Trang Tien Bridge.

An Hien
58 Kim Long • Daily 7am–5pm • 30,000đ

One place worth visiting to get an idea of a **typical garden house** is on Kim Long's main road at **An Hien**, where there's a caretaker on duty to take your money, but no guide to show you round. Built in the late nineteenth century, An Hien has all the classical traits of a garden house – a grand archway at the entrance, a long, shaded approach path, and a brick wall concealing the main entrance, behind which is an ornamental pond. A large orchard of fruit trees surrounds the house, which features a family altar, sturdy wooden columns and beautifully carved doors.

Thien Mu Pagoda
3km west of the citadel • Dawn to dusk • Free • Best reached by bicycle or xe om (around 60,000đ return including waiting time), or as part of a boat tour

The seven-storey **Thien Mu Pagoda** ("Pagoda of the Celestial Lady") is possibly Hue's most photographed structure. In 1601 Lord Nguyen Hoang left Hanoi to govern the southern territories. Upon arriving at the Perfume River he met an elderly woman who told him to walk east along the river carrying a smouldering incense stick and to build his city where the incense stopped burning. Later Lord Hoang erected a pagoda in gratitude to the lady, whom he believed to be a messenger from the gods, on the site where they met. The pagoda was founded in 1601, making it the oldest in Hue.

During the 1930s and 1940s Thien Mu was already renowned as a centre of Buddhist opposition to colonialism, and then in 1963 it became instantly famous when one of its monks, the Venerable **Thich Quang Duc**, burned himself to death in Saigon, in protest at the excesses of President Diem's regime (see box, p.82); the powder-blue Austin car he drove down in is now on display just behind the main building, with a copy of the famous photograph that shocked the world.

Despite its turbulent history, the pagoda is a peaceful place where the breezy, pine-shaded terrace affords wide views over the Perfume River. Approaching by either road or river you can't miss the octagonal, seven-tier brick **stupa**, built by Emperor Thieu Tri in the 1840s; each tier represents one of Buddha's incarnations on earth. Two **pavilions**, one on each side, shelter a huge bell, cast in 1710, weighing over 2000kg and said to be audible in the city, and a large stele erected in 1715 to record the history of Buddhism in Hue.

Van Mieu Pagoda
Van Mieu Pagoda is 1km further on from Thien Mu Pagoda, and 4km from the city centre • Dawn to dusk • Free • Xe om from Hue about 80,000đ return

Confucianism had been the principal state religion in Vietnam since the eleventh century and the Nguyens were a particularly traditional dynasty. Early in his reign,

5

in 1808 Gia Long dedicated a national temple to Confucius, known as **Van Mieu** or Van Thanh (the "Temple of Literature"), to replace that in Hanoi. Nothing much remains of the complex, beyond a collection of 32 stone stelae listing the names of 297 recipients of doctorates from exams held between 1822 and 1919. Two other stelae, under small shelters, record edicts from Minh Mang and Thieu Tri banning the "abuse of eunuchs and royal maternal relatives". You get a fine view of the royal landing stage and temple gate passing by on a Perfume River boat trip (see box, p.289).

Hon Chen Temple

9km downstream from Hue • Daily 8am–5pm • 40,000đ • Only accessible from the river; aside from boat tours, you can cross the river on a sampan from the ferry station directly opposite the temple (see map, p.288)

Beyond Van Mieu boats stop at the rocky promontory of **Hon Chen Temple**, named "Temple of the Jade Bowl" after the concave hill under which it sits. Again it's the scenery of russet temple roofs among towering trees that is memorable, though the site has been sacred since the Cham people came here to worship their divine protectress Po Nagar, whom the Vietnamese adopted as Y A Na, the Mother Goddess. Emperor Minh Mang restored Hon Chen Temple in the 1830s, but it was Dong Khanh who had a particular soft spot for the goddess after she predicted he would be emperor. He enlarged the temple in 1886, declared himself Y A Na's younger brother and is now worshipped alongside his favourite goddess in the main sanctuary, **Hue Nam**, up from the landing stage and to the right. Keep your eyes open for some unusual, smiling figurines with clasped hands in the glass cabinets here.

South of the river

There are a few sights on the way south to the mausoleums (bar that of Duc Duc, which sits immediately south of the city centre). Happily, all are easily accessible by bicycle.

The Royal Arena

4km southwest from central Hue • Dawn to dusk • Free • From Hue, follow Bui Thi Xuan along the Perfume River's south bank through Phuong Duc, a famous metal-casting village; each alley on the left has a sign, and Kiet 373 is the one to look for

Tucked away near the south bank of the Perfume River stands the **Royal Arena**, or Ho Quyen. Unfortunately, the site has not been well looked after and there's little to see here today apart from a decaying brick stadium surrounding a grassy area. If you're lucky, it might be possible to track down a guard with the keys, but this would allow you to see little more than you can glimpse through the metal gates. However, it's possible to climb a brick staircase to get a view not much different from what the emperor would have seen over a century ago. Considering the fact that no preservation work has taken place here, the site has so far deteriorated very little.

Long Chau Dien

After they died, fighting elephants were worshipped nearby in a small temple, **Long Chau Dien**, which stands to the west of the arena, although almost completely hidden by undergrowth and with only a couple of elephant statues to see: follow the path round the arena's south side to find the temple, overlooking a small lake.

THE HON CHEN TEMPLE FESTIVALS

Festivals at Hon Chen were banned between Independence and 1986 but have now resumed, taking place **twice yearly** in the middle of the third and seventh lunar month. The celebrations, harking back to ancient rituals, include trance-dances performed by mediums, usually females dressed in brightly coloured costumes, who are transported by a pulsating musical accompaniment. These events have proven popular with the few foreign tourists lucky enough to be here at the right time, and to hear that they're actually happening.

ELEPHANTS AND TIGERS

In Imperial times, Ho Quyen was where the emperors amused themselves with **fights between elephants and tigers**. Originally the contests were held on open ground in front of the citadel, but after a tiger attacked Minh Mang they were staged in the arena from 1830, until the last fight in 1904. This was not entirely sport: elephants symbolized the unequalled might of the sovereign while tigers represented rebel forces, and the arena was built on the site of an old Cham fort just to underline the message of Imperial power. It was, apparently, a pretty one-sided fight which the elephant was never allowed to lose, and contemporary accounts suggest that in later years the tigers were tied to a stake and had their claws removed first.

Nam Giao Esplanade

At the end of Dien Bien Phu, 3km south of central Hue • Free

First and foremost in the ceremonial and religious life of the nation was **Nam Giao** ("Altar of Heaven"), where the emperor reaffirmed the legitimacy of his rule in sacred rituals, held here roughly every three years from 1807 to 1945. The ceremonies were performed on a series of three terraces, two square-shaped and one round, symbolizing heaven, earth and man in descending order. Before each occasion the monarch purified himself, keeping to a strict regime of vegetarian food and no concubines for several days. He then carried out the sacrifices, with the assistance of some five thousand attendants, to ensure the stability of both the country and the dynasty. Re-enactments of the sacred rituals at Nam Giao take place during the biannual **Hue Festival** (see box, p.287); otherwise, there's not much to see apart from the terraces and walkways shaded by towering pine trees, but it makes a pleasant place to stroll.

Tu Hieu Pagoda

About 1km west of Nam Giao on Le Ngo Cat • Free • xe om from Hue (about 40,000đ) • By bike, take the road towards Tu Duc's Mausoleum from the Nam Giao T-junction, turn right down a dirt road near the top of the hill by two tall columns announcing "Tu Hieu", then fork left to reach the pagoda's triple-arched gate

The splendid **Tu Hieu Pagoda** is buried in the pine forests east of Nam Giao. Though not the most famous pagoda in Hue, it's one of the most attractive, and it does have an Imperial link since this is where royal eunuchs retired to and were worshipped after their deaths. The pagoda was founded in 1843 and still houses an active community of monks who extend a warm welcome to their occasional visitors. The main altar is dedicated to Sakyamuni, with the Buddhist trinity sitting up above, while a secondary shrine room behind contains altars to several famous mandarins and the eunuchs. Between the two buildings is a small courtyard festooned with orchids, and a star-fruit vine that has been here since the reign of Thanh Thai (1889–1907).

The Royal Mausoleums

Unlike previous Vietnamese dynasties, which buried their kings in ancestral villages, the Nguyen built themselves magnificent **Royal Mausoleums** in the valley of the Perfume River among low, forested hills to the south of Hue. For historical reasons only seven mausoleums were built, but each one is a unique expression of the monarch's personality, usually planned in detail during his lifetime to serve as his palace in death. More than anywhere else in Hue, it's here that the Nguyen emperors excelled in achieving a harmony between the works of man and his natural surroundings. Along with the Imperial City, these constitute Hue's most rewarding sights.

The mausoleums are intoxicating places, occasionally grandiose but more often achieving an elegant simplicity, where it's easy to lose yourself wandering in the quiet gardens. However, given the entry fee for each – except on public holidays, when entry is free – you'll want to pick the ones you visit carefully. Of the seven, the contrasting

5

TOURING THE ROYAL MAUSOLEUMS

A **motorbike tour** of the mausoleums normally includes at least three and costs around $8. Another popular option is a **Perfume River boat trip** (see box, p.289), though with one of these you'll face a couple of longish walks.

With your own wheels – either **bicycle or motorbike** – you'll have more time to explore and won't be restricted to the three main mausoleums. A good compromise is to take a bike on board a tour boat and cycle back to Hue from the last stop.

mausoleums of **Tu Duc**, **Khai Dinh** and **Minh Mang** are the most attractive and best preserved, as well as being easily accessible. These are also the three covered by the boat trips, so they can get crowded (especially at weekends); don't let this put you off – but if you do want something more off the beaten track then those of **Gia Long**, **Dong Khanh** and **Thieu Tri** are worth calling in on. Finally, **Duc Duc**'s temple and mausoleum are very modest but they are the closest to Hue and still tended by members of the royal family.

The Mausoleum of Duc Duc

Daily 7am–5pm • 80,000đ • Opposite 74 Tran Phu (see map, p.288), head down Duong Duy Tan; the mausoleum is 100m along on the right • Unoffical guides will show you around for a small donation

Three emperors are buried at the **Mausoleum of Duc Duc**, which, although it's the closest to Hue, is rarely visited. Duc Duc (ruled 1883) and his wife are buried in a walled compound, while emperors Thanh Thai (ruled 1889–1907) and Duy Tan (ruled 1907–16) are interred in a separate row of graves behind the main temple, built in 1899. Duc Duc was forced to resign in 1883 by his senior courtiers after a mere three days as emperor, and died a year later in prison, while his son, **Thanh Thai**, was also removed in 1907 after a suspected anti-French conspiracy. The French then put Thanh Thai's 8-year-old son, **Duy Tan**, on the throne, but he fled the palace nine years later amid another revolutionary plot, and was eventually exiled with his father to the French territory of Réunion in the Indian Ocean. Duy Tan died in a World War II plane crash in 1945, fighting on the side of the Allies, but Thanh Thai was allowed back to Vietnam in 1947 and died in Saigon in the 1950s. Descendants of the Imperial family still live in the temple buildings, and possess a historic collection of family photos, including some of the funeral of Thanh Thai.

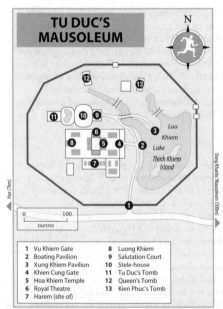

TU DUC'S MAUSOLEUM

N

Luu Khiem Lake

Thinh Khiem Island

Hue (7km)

Dong Khanh's Mausoleum (500m)

0   100
metres

1 Vu Khiem Gate	8 Luong Khiem
2 Boating Pavilion	9 Salutation Court
3 Xung Khiem Pavilion	10 Stele-house
4 Khien Cung Gate	11 Tu Duc's Tomb
5 Hoa Khiem Temple	12 Queen's Tomb
6 Royal Theatre	13 Kien Phuc's Tomb
7 Harem (site of)	

The Mausoleum of Tu Duc

7km from central Hue by road • Daily 7am–5pm • 80,000đ • It's 2km from the boat jetty to the west; walk on the dirt track, or take one of the xe om waiting on the riverbank (about 40,000đ)

With elegant pavilions and pines reflected in serene lakes, this walled, twelve-hectare **park** is the most harmonious of all the Nguyen mausoleums. This may seem quite a claim, considering their careful design, though it's not such a surprise considering the emperor in question – Tu Duc, who ruled from 1847 to 1883, longer than any other Nguyen emperor.

Entering by the southern gate, **Vu Khiem**, brick paths lead beside a lake covered in water lilies and lotus to a small three-tiered **boating pavilion** which looks across to larger **Xung Khiem Pavilion**, where Tu Duc drank wine and wrote poetry; *khiem*, meaning "modest", appears in the name of every building. From the lake, steps head up through **Khiem Cung Gate**, the middle door painted yellow for the emperor, into a second enclosure containing the main temple, **Hoa Khiem**, which Tu Duc used as an office before his death. The royal funerary tablets here are unusual in that Tu Duc's, bearing a dragon, is smaller than the phoenix-decorated tablet of the queen. Beyond is a second temple, **Luong Khiem**, which served as the royal residence, and the elegant **royal theatre**, while behind the storerooms opposite once stood the quarters for Tu Duc's numerous concubines.

The emperor's tomb

The second group of buildings, to the north of the royal theatre, is centred on the **emperor's tomb**, preceded by the salutation court and stele-house. Tu Duc's stele, weighing twenty tonnes, is by far the largest; unusually, Tu Duc wrote his own self-critical eulogy, running to over four thousand characters, to elucidate all his difficulties. Behind the stele is a kidney-shaped pond, representing the crescent moon, and then a bronze door leading into a square enclosure where the unadorned tomb shelters behind a screen adorned with the characters for longevity. Emperor Kien Phuc, one of Tu Duc's adopted sons, is also buried here, just north of the lake.

The Mausoleum of Dong Khanh

500m from Tu Duc's mausoleum • Daily 7am–5pm • 80,000đ

Dong Khanh (ruled 1885–89) was put on the throne by the French as titular head of their protectorate. A pliant ruler with a fondness for French wine, perfume and alarm clocks, he died suddenly at the age of 25 after only three years on the throne; having never got round to planning his final resting place he was buried near the temple he dedicated to his father. As a result this is a modest, countryside **mausoleum** with a rustic charm but is particularly well preserved.

The mausoleum consists of **two parts**: the main temple, and then the tomb and stele in a separate, walled enclosure on a slight rise 100m to the northwest. The complex was built mostly by Dong Khanh's son, Khai Dinh, after 1889, though has been added to since.

The main temple

The **main temple** holds most interest, especially the coloured-glass doors and windows, as well as the murals on each side wall showing scenes of daily life. Twenty-four glass-paintings, illustrated poems of Confucian love, hang on the temple's ironwood columns and, at either end of the first row, there are two engravings of **Napoleon** and

---

MAUSOLEUM DESIGN

It often took years to find a site with the right aesthetic requirements that would also satisfy the court cosmologists charged with interpreting the underlying supernatural forces. Artificial lakes, waterfalls and hills were added to improve the geomantic qualities of the location, at the same time creating picturesque, almost romantic, **garden settings** for the mausoleums, of which the finest examples are those of Tu Duc and Minh Mang.

Though details vary, all the mausoleums consist of three elements: a **temple** dedicated to the worship of the deceased emperor and his queen; a large, stone **stele** recording his biographical details and a history of his reign, usually written by his successor; and the royal **tomb** itself at the highest spot, enclosed within a wall and a heavy, securely fastened door. Traditionally the burial place was kept secret as a measure against grave-robbers and enemies of the state, and in extreme cases all those who had been involved in the burial were killed immediately afterwards.

5

TU DUC

Emperor **Tu Duc** (ruled 1847–83) was a romantic poet trying to rule Vietnam at a time when the Western world was challenging the country's independence. Although he was the longest reigning of the Nguyen monarchs, he was a weak ruler who preferred to hide from the world in the lyrical pleasure gardens he created. The walled, twelve-hectare park took only three years to complete (1864–67), after which Tu Duc spent his time boating and fishing, meditating, drinking tea made from dew collected in lotus blossoms and composing some of the four thousand poems he is said to have written, besides several important philosophical and historical works. Somehow he also found time for fifty-course meals, plus 104 wives and a whole village of concubines living in the park, though – possibly due to a bout of smallpox – he fathered no children. Perhaps it's not surprising that Tu Duc was also a tyrant who pushed the three thousand workmen building his mausoleum so hard that they rebelled in 1866, and were savagely dealt with.

the Battle of Waterloo. The three principal altars honour Dong Khanh with his two queens to either side, while his seven concubines have a separate altar in the back room. Finally, there is an altar to Y A Na in a small side-chamber, off to the right as you enter: Dong Khanh had this built to honour her after she appeared in a dream and foretold that he would be emperor.

The Mausoleum of Thieu Tri

About 6km from central Hue • Daily 7am–5pm • 80,000đ • Head south from either Nam Giao or Tu Duc's mausoleum

Emperor **Thieu Tri** (ruled 1841–47) was the son of Minh Mang (see box, p.296) and shared his father's aversion to foreign influences – it's said he destroyed anything Western he found in the Imperial palaces – and his taste in architecture. His **mausoleum** follows the same basic pattern as Minh Mang's though without the attractive walled gardens, and is split into two sections placed side by side. As it's also smaller it took less than a year to build (1847–48), but its most distinctive feature is that it faces northwest, a traditionally inauspicious direction, and many people believed that this was the reason the country fell under the French yoke a few years later. The mausoleum has been subject to recent restoration work, and the temple is in reasonable shape. It contains numerous poems, in mother-of-pearl or painted on glass, since Thieu Tri was a prolific poet who would pen a stanza or two at a moment's notice.

The Mausoleum of Khai Dinh

10km southeast of Hue by road • Daily 7am–5pm • 80,000đ • Arriving by boat, it's a 1.5km walk, heading eastwards up a valley with a giant Quan Am statue on your right until you see the mausoleum on the opposite hillside

Khai Dinh's mausoleum is most people's favourite, with its monumental confection of European baroque, highly ornamental Sino–Vietnamese style and even elements of Cham architecture. Though it's in a beautiful setting on a wooded hill, you'll need to climb the 130-odd steps to see the most impressive aspects of the sanctuary itself.

Khai Dinh (ruled 1916–25) was the penultimate Nguyen emperor and his mausoleum is a radical departure from its predecessors, with neither gardens nor living quarters and only one main structure. Khai Dinh was also a vain man, a puppet of the French very much taken with French style and architecture, and though he only reigned for nine years it took eleven (1920–31) to complete his mausoleum, and it cost so much he had to levy additional taxes for the project.

The principal temple

The approach is via a series of grandiose, dragon-ornamented **stairways** leading first to the salutation courtyard, where statues of mandarins stand, and on to the stele-house. Climbing up a further four terraces brings you to the **principal temple**, built of reinforced concrete with slate roofing imported from France.

Inside, everything is decorated to the hilt, writhing with dragons and peppered with symbolic references and classic imagery such as the Four Seasons panels in the antechamber. Most of this lavish display, not as garish as it might sound, is worked in glass and porcelain mosaic – even the central canopy, which looks like fabric. A life-size gilded bronze **statue of the emperor** holding his royal sceptre sits under the canopy, while his altar table and funerary tablet are up on the mezzanine floor behind. His portrait stands on the incense table in the antechamber. Khai Dinh was a particularly flamboyant dresser and it's rumoured that he brought back a string of fairy lights from France and proceeded to wear them around the palace, twinkling, until the batteries ran out.

The Mausoleum of Minh Mang

Daily 7am–5pm • 80,000đ • From Khai Dinh's tomb, follow the road to the highway, cross over the river and turn left after 50m

Court officials took fourteen years to decide on the location for the **Mausoleum of Minh Mang** – for which the mandarin responsible was awarded two promotions; it then took only three years to build (1841–43), using ten thousand workmen. It was designed along traditional Chinese lines, with all the principal buildings symmetrical about an east–west axis. The mausoleum's stately grandeur is softened by fifteen hectares of superb landscaped gardens, almost a third of which is taken up by lakes reflecting the handsome, red-roofed pavilions.

Inside the mausoleum a processional way links the series of low mounds bearing all the main buildings. After the salutation courtyard and stele-house comes the **principal temple** (*Sung An*), where Minh Mang and his queen are worshipped. Continuing west you reach **Minh Lau**, the elegant, two-storey "Pavilion of Pure Light" standing among clouds of frangipani trees, symbols of longevity; beyond, two stone gardens trace the Chinese character for long life. From here the ceremonial pathway crosses a crescent lake and ends at the circular burial mound.

The Mausoleum of Gia Long

16km south of Hue • Daily 7am–5pm • 80,000đ • Best reached by sampan from the jetty near Minh Mang's mausoleum or by road via a new bridge from Minh Mang's mausoleum

As the first Nguyen ruler, **Gia Long** (ruled 1802–20) had his pick of the sites, and he chose an immense natural park 16km from Hue on the left bank of the Perfume River. Unfortunately his **mausoleum** – begun in 1814 and completed shortly after his death

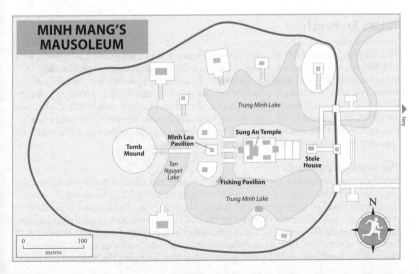

MINH MANG'S MAUSOLEUM

Trung Minh Lake

Sung An Temple

Minh Lau Pavilion

Tomb Mound

Tan Nguyet Lake

Stele House

Fishing Pavilion

Trung Minh Lake

ferry

N

0   100
metres

5

MINH MANG

Minh Mang, the second Nguyen emperor (ruled 1820–41), was a capable, authoritarian monarch who was selected for his serious nature and distrust of Western religious infiltration. This revered emperor was also passionate about architecture – it was he who oversaw the completion of Hue citadel after Gia Long's death. Minh Mang's queen died at the age of 17, but despite this early loss Minh Mang managed to father 142 children with his 33 wives and 107 concubines.

in 1820 – was badly damaged during the American War, but recent restoration work has revealed some fine carving, and it's worth visiting the double tomb with pitched roofs housing Gia Long and his wife. This is the least-visited of Hue's mausoleums and is recommended for the boat trip and the peaceful stroll through sandy pine forest, though some visitors complain of attracting a convoy of persistent soft-drink sellers for the duration of the two-kilometre walk. You approach the complex from the north to find the main temple, tomb and stele-house all aligned on a horizontal axis, looking south across a lake towards Thien Tho Mountain.

Thanh Toan Bridge

6km east of Hue

Thanh Toan Bridge is a beautiful structure that will remind you of the Japanese Covered Bridge in Hoi An if you've been there, though this place is not at all touristy as yet. Built in 1776 to honour a mandarin's wife who came from around here, it is a sturdy structure of wood pillars with ceramic tiles on the roof. It is divided into seven sections and features an altar to **Tran Thi Dao**, the woman in question, in the middle section. The other six sections are fitted with deep wooden seats, shiny with use, where locals dangle their legs over the stream and daydream. It's in a very rural area, so you're likely to see duck herders and rice farmers along the way.

ARRIVAL AND DEPARTURE   THANH TOAN BRIDGE

By bike This makes a pleasant bike ride, though it can be tricky to find. Head east on Truong Chin, which branches east off of Huong Vuong to the south of the city centre. Cross a ring road then continue east for 3km more. Alternatively, hire a guide from somewhere like *Mandarin Café* (see p.286).

Thuan An Beach

15km northeast of Hue

Though Hue is one of the wettest places in Vietnam, it can get pretty hot between May and August, when it's worth calling a halt for a day to sightseeing round historic monuments in order to head for the **beach**. Thuan An is probably not the prettiest you've ever seen, but none too bad either, and good enough for *Ana Mandara* to build a five-star resort on. There's a broad swathe of sand and though there's little shade, there are plenty of thatched beach stalls selling food and drinks. The sea is quite clear as a rule and outside the months of September to April it's good for swimming. It gets crowded with locals at weekends and on public holidays.

The southern peninsula

With your own transport it's worth exploring the **peninsula south of Thuan An**, where Highway 49B snakes down to meet up with Highway 1 about 50km to the south, after crossing the Cua Hai Lagoon on a long bridge. The road is lined with simple houses and shops but also with extremely elaborate **tombs** and family temples; it seems that the locals have inherited the Nguyen lords' lifelong obsession with preparing for death. At times it feels like you're driving through an endless cemetery, and the tombs are mostly decorated in eye-catching combinations of pastel colours such as lilac, primrose, sky blue and soft pink.

ARRIVAL AND DEPARTURE

By bike or motorbike The easiest way to get to Thuan An Beach is by rented motorbike or bicycle, though you need

to watch out for heavy traffic. Follow Le Loi north out of town and keep going.

ACCOMMODATION

Ana Mandara Thuan An Beach ☏ 054 398 3333, ⓦanamandarahue-resort.com; map p.288. *Ana Mandara* runs some of Vietnam's most luxurious hotels, and this is no

exception. Pool villas occupy an enormous 275 square metres and are lavishly furnished. Facilities include several dining and drinking options, a pool and spa, a kids' club and library. $\underline{120}$

The DMZ

During the American War, **Quang Tri** and **Quang Binh**, the two provinces either side of the **DMZ** (see box, p.299), were the most heavily bombed and saw the highest casualties – civilian and military, American and Vietnamese. Names made infamous in 1960s and 1970s America have been perpetuated in countless films and memoirs: Con Thien, the Rockpile, Hamburger Hill and Khe Sanh. For some people the DMZ will be what draws them to Vietnam, the end of a long and difficult pilgrimage; for others it will be a bleak, sometimes beautiful, place where there's nothing particular to see but where it's hard not to respond to the sense of enormous desolation.

North of the DMZ is one of the region's main attractions – **the tunnels of Vinh Moc**, where villages created deep underground during the American War have been preserved.

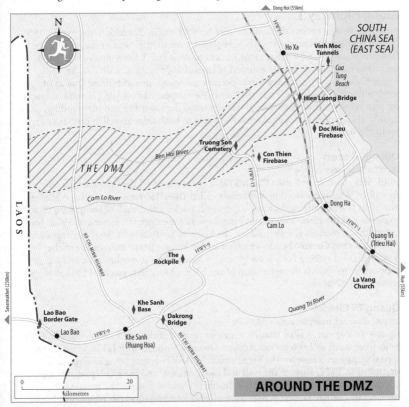

AROUND THE DMZ

5

DMZ TOURS

Considering the paucity of public transport in this area, most people opt to visit the DMZ on a **guided tour** – guides usually do a good job of relaying the essential historical information. Most tours come straight from Hue, which usually cost $15–20 per person and include visits to Doc Mieu Firebase, Hien Luong Bridge, the Vinh Moc tunnels, the Rockpile, Dakrong Bridge and Khe Sanh combat base; it's a long day out starting at 6am and returning to Hue around 6pm. To take things in a more leisurely manner, you could base yourself in Dong Ha, then spend one day seeing the sights near Highway 1 and another heading west along Highway 9, either on a rented motorbike or on tours offered by places like *Tam's Café* (see p.300).

The area's other points of interest lie south of the Ben Hai River, and while it's not possible to cover everything in a day, the most interesting of the places described here are included on **organized tours** from Hue (see p.284). Alternatively, it's possible to use **Dong Ha** as a base or cover a more limited selection of sights on the drive north. If you have limited time then the **Vinh Moc tunnels** should be high on your list, along with a drive up Highway 9 to Khe Sanh, both for the scenery en route and the sobering battleground itself. Note that, although you can now visit the DMZ without a **local guide**, this is not recommended as most sites are unmarked and, more importantly, the guides – arranged in Dong Ha (see opposite) – know which paths are safe; local farmers are still occasionally killed or injured by **unexploded ordnance** in this area.

Along Highway 1

American troops weren't the first to suffer heavy losses in this region: during the 1950s, French soldiers dubbed the stretch of **Highway 1** north of Hue as *la rue sans joie*, or "street without joy", after they came under constant attack from elusive Viet Minh units operating out of heavily fortified villages along the coast. Later, in the 1972 Easter Offensive, Communist forces overran the whole area, capturing **Quang Tri** town, some 60km north of Hue, from the South Vietnamese Army (ARVN) and holding it for four months while American B-52s pounded the township and surrounding countryside, before it was retaken at huge cost to both sides as well as civilians caught up in the battle.

Quang Tri town

East off the highway down Tran Hung Dao

Blink and you may well miss **QUANG TRI**, a town wiped off the map during the American War, and indeed now officially called **Trieu Hai**. Keep your eyes peeled for one of its few identifying features – the small, pockmarked shell of **Long Hung Church** to the east of the road, 55km from Hue, kept as a memorial to victims of 1972. Just before this, a road on the west side of the highway leads 2km to the more impressive ruin of **La Vang Church**, beside which stands an extraordinary monument of the Virgin Mary clutching baby Jesus beneath a forest of giant mushroom trees, which supposedly represents the apparition of the Virgin Mary to persecuted Catholics on this spot in 1798.

Quang Tri Citadel

Just north of town on Tran Hung Dao; entrance on Ly Thai To • Daily 7am–5pm • Free

Quang Tri's square, walled **citadel**, a smaller version of the one in Hue, was originally built from earth in 1806 by the Nguyen Dynasty, fortified with bricks in 1827, and served in turn as a base for the French and the ARVN before being overrun and destroyed in 1972. Parts of the wall and moat remain, and the south gate, through which visitors enter, has been rebuilt. Inside is a war memorial, the remains of a nineteenth-century French prison consisting of fourteen tiny cells measuring 1m by

2m, and a small war **museum** with English captions. The museum houses some excellent photos of the fierce hand-to-hand fighting that took place towards the end of 1972 as ARVN troops eventually retook the city after 81 days.

Dong Ha

As a former US Marine Command Post and then ARVN base, **DONG HA** was also obliterated in 1972, but unlike Quang Tri it has bounced back, thanks largely to its administrative status and location at the eastern end of Highway 9, which leads through **Laos** to Savannakhet on the Mekong River. The future looks rosy as well: a new deep-water port has been built to serve landlocked Laos, a number of special economic zones are under construction along the border, and Highway 9 has been upgraded as part of the massive Trans-Asian Highway project.

As the **closest town to the DMZ**, Dong Ha attracts a lot of tourist traffic, though few people choose to stay here, preferring the comfort and facilities of Hue. It is essentially a two-street town: Highway 1, known here as Le Duan, forms the main artery as it passes through on its route north, while Highway 9 takes off inland at a central T-junction.

Mine Action Visitor Centre

Kids First Village, 185 Ly Thuong Kiet · Mon–Sat 8am–5pm · Free · ☎ 053 356 7338, ⓦ landmines.org.vn

Run by Project Renew, the **Mine Action Visitor Centre** makes the perfect introduction to a tour of the DMZ: you'll learn more about the reality of this region from this small museum's displays than you will at all the other sights in the DMZ. Project Renew's aim is to inform, educate and prevent further accidents caused by unexploded

---

THE HISTORY OF THE DMZ

Under the terms of the 1954 Geneva Accords, Vietnam was split in two along the Seventeenth Parallel, pending elections intended to reunite the country. The demarcation line ran along the Ben Hai River and was sealed by a strip of no-man's-land 5km wide on each side known as the **Demilitarized Zone**, or DMZ. All Communist troops and supporters were supposed to regroup north in the Democratic Republic of Vietnam, leaving the southern Republic of Vietnam to non-Communists and various shades of opposition. When the elections failed to take place, the river became the de facto border until 1975.

In reality both sides of the DMZ were anything but demilitarized after 1965, and anyway the border was easily circumvented – by the Ho Chi Minh Trail to the west (see box, p.388) and sea routes to the east – enabling the North Vietnamese to bypass a string of American fire bases overlooking the river. One of the more fantastical efforts to prevent Communist infiltration southwards was US Secretary of Defense Robert McNamara's proposal for an **electronic fence** from the Vietnamese coast to the Mekong River, made up of seismic and acoustic sensors that would detect troop movements and pinpoint targets for bombing raids. Though trials in 1967 met with some initial success, the "McNamara Line" was soon abandoned: sensors were confused by animals, especially elephants, and could be triggered deliberately by the tape-recorded sound of vehicle engines or troops on the march.

Nor could massive, conventional bombing by artillery and aircraft contain the North Vietnamese, who finally stormed the DMZ in 1972 and pushed the border 20km further south. Exceptionally bitter fighting in the territory south of the **Ben Hai River** (I Corps Military Region) claimed more American lives in the five years leading up to 1972 than any other battle zone in Vietnam. Figures for North Vietnamese losses during that period are not known, though thousands more have died since the end of the war from inadvertently detonating unexploded ordnance. So much fire power was unleashed over this area, including napalm and herbicides, that for years nothing would grow in the impacted, chemical-laden soil, but the region's low, rolling hills are now almost entirely reforested with a green sea of pine, eucalyptus, coffee and acacia.

5

ordnance in the area, and the display at the centre, which is laid out clearly and professionally, gives a stark impression of the enormity of their task. Quang Tri Province alone was bombarded by over 350,000 tons of ordnance, of which thousands of tons failed to go off, resulting in nearly ten thousand civilian casualties here since the end of the war.

Beginning with maps showing the intensity of bombing during the war (the DMZ a glaring blotch of bright red), the display includes some graphic images and statistics of casualties in the area, a collection of home-made prosthetic limbs, as well as examples of the unexploded ordnance (UXO) recovered by the mine-clearing team. From just four staff in 2001, the project now employs over a hundred, and they are constantly receiving calls to send out a bomb disposal team.

ARRIVAL AND DEPARTURE   DONG HA

By train The station lies 1km south of town, just west of the highway.
Destinations Dong Hoi (6 daily; 1hr 20min–2hr 10min); Hanoi (6 daily; 12–15hr); Hue (6 daily; 1hr 20min).
By bus The bus station is at 68 Le Duan, 500m north of the train station and near the junction of Highways 1 and 9.

Unfortunately there's a mafia run by xe om drivers which makes sure foreigners are overcharged, so try to avoid taking a bus here if possible. To get to Laos, it's best to use the direct buses to Savannakhet run by Sepon Travel (see below).
Destinations Dong Hoi (2hr); Hue (2hr); Lao Bao (2hr); Savannakhet (8hr).

INFORMATION

Tourist information *Tam's Café* (see below) is a great source of information, and can help to organize DMZ tours. Other reliable operators include Sepon Travel (☏ 053 355 5289), 189 Le Duan, and Annam Tour, 207b Nguyen Du

(☏ 053 352 2600, ⓦ annamtour.com).
Services There are several ATMs around the town centre, including one at Vietcombank, 51 Tran Hung Dao.

ACCOMMODATION

Huu Nghi 68 Tran Hung Dao ☏ 053 385 2361. Though the place looks a bit drab from the outside, rooms here are much better value than those at the *Saigon Dong Ha* – they're bright and clean and come with a/c and satellite TV. Breakfast is included but there's not much to it. Double $20, VIP room $48
Saigon Dong Ha 11 Bui Thi Xuan ☏ 053 357 7888,

ⓦ saigondonghahotel.com. This flashy, new 4-star place looks the part, and its rooms are certainly modern, with light pine furnishings and carpeted floors. There's also a pool, sun terrace and fitness centre. Yet as in many government-run hotels, it lacks the personal touch that's so important, and service is hit-and-miss. $125

EATING

Dong Que 109 Le Duan ☏ 053 385 2303. This welcoming restaurant on the east side of the main road about a kilometre north of the town centre is a favourite stop for groups touring the DMZ, and for good reason. It has an extensive English menu featuring tasty dishes like fish with tomato sauce (80,000đ) and mixed veg with meat (50,000đ). Daily 7am–9pm.

★**Tam's Café** 79 Hung Vuong ☏ 090 542 5912, ⓦ tamscafe.jimdo.com. Charming café serving a range of coffees, juices, smoothies and ice cream, plus a few main dishes at around 80,000đ. The owners donate much of their profits to charitable causes – most of the staff, in fact, are youths with impaired hearing. Owner Tam is your one-stop Mr Fixit for all things DMZ. Daily 6.30am–9pm.

West of Dong Ha

Heading west from Dong Ha on Highway 9 (also now known as Asian Highway 16, or AH16 for short), you begin to climb into the foothills of the Truong Son range. Where the highway veers south, a sheer-sided isolated stump 230m high dominates the valley: the **Rockpile**. For a while American troops, delivered by helicopter, used the peak for directing artillery to targets across the DMZ and into Laos, but the post was abandoned after 1968. The highway continues over a low pass and then follows a picturesque valley past the **Dakrong Bridge**, which carries a spur of the Ho Chi Minh Highway before climbing among ever-more forested mountains to emerge at **Khe Sanh** (now officially rechristened **Huang Hoa**), 63km from Dong Ha. In this area you'll still see a few stilthouses from the Bru and Co minorities, most of whom have been moved on – ostensibly for reasons of health and hygiene, though cynics would point to the fact that both the Bru and the Co helped the Americans during the war.

Khe Sanh

The bleak settlement of **KHE SANH**, its frontier atmosphere reinforced by the smugglers' trail across the border to Laos only 19km away (see box, p.302), sits on the edge of a windswept plateau that was the site of a pivotal battle in the American War. Because of the high concentration of chemical and explosive contamination, it's only recently that the soil around Khe Sanh has been able to support vegetation again, and the hills are now green with coffee plantations. Nothing else remains: when American troops were ordered to abandon Khe Sanh, everything was blown up or bulldozed.

The Museum

Daily 7am–5pm • 20,000đ

The only memorial is a small **museum**, 2km north of Khe Sanh town, commemorating the siege – made even more poignant by the hauntingly beautiful mountains all around. The small halls are dotted with photos and war paraphernalia, and surrounded by a reconstructed bunker, a helicopter, military vehicles and the contorted shapes of exploded bombs. Be sure to peek over the fence at the red gash of the old airstrip.

THE BATTLE OF KHE SANH

The **battle of Khe Sanh** was important not because of its immediate outcome, but because it attracted worldwide media attention and, along with the simultaneous Tet Offensive, demonstrated the futility of America's efforts to contain their enemy. In 1962 an American Special Forces team arrived in Khe Sanh Town to train local Bru minority people in counter-insurgency, and then four years later the first batch of Marines was sent in to establish a forward base near Laos, to secure Highway 9 and to harass troops on the Ho Chi Minh Trail. Skirmishes around Khe Sanh increased as intelligence reports indicated a massive build-up of North Vietnamese Army (NVA) troops in late 1967, possibly as many as forty thousand, facing six thousand Marines together with a few hundred South Vietnamese and Bru. Both the Western media and American generals were soon presenting the confrontation as a crucial test of America's credibility in South Vietnam and drawing parallels with Dien Bien Phu (see box, p.411). As US President Johnson famously remarked, he didn't want "any damn Dinbinfoo".

The **NVA attack** came in the early hours of January 21, 1968; rockets raining in on the base added to the terror and confusion by striking an ammunition dump, gasoline tanks and stores of tear gas. There followed a seemingly endless, nerve-grinding NVA artillery barrage, when hundreds of shells fell on the base each day, interspersed with costly US infantry assaults into the surrounding hills. In an operation code-named "**Niagara**", General Westmoreland called in the air battalions to silence the enemy guns and break the siege by unleashing the most intense bombing raids of the war: in nine weeks nearly a hundred thousand tonnes of bombs pounded the area round the clock, averaging **one airstrike every five minutes**, backed up by napalm and defoliants. Unbelievably the NVA were so well dug in and camouflaged that they not only withstood the onslaught but continued to return fire, despite horrendous casualties, estimated at ten thousand. On the US side around five hundred troops died at Khe Sanh (although official figures record only 248 American deaths, of which 43 occurred in a single helicopter accident), before a relief column broke through in early April, seventy-odd days after the siege had begun. NVA forces gradually pulled back and by the middle of March had all but gone, having successfully diverted American resources away from southern cities prior to the Tet Offensive. Three months later the Americans also quietly withdrew, leaving a plateau that resembled a lunar landscape, contaminated for years to come with chemicals and explosives; even the trees left standing were worthless because so much shrapnel was lodged in the timber.

LAO BAO BORDER CROSSING

Of all the **border crossings** open to foreigners between Vietnam and Laos, the most popular is still **Lao Bao**, 80km west of Dong Ha along Highway 9. It's an attractive ride, through misty mountains on a reasonable road, and the crossing is hassle-free beyond having to walk 1km between inspection posts. However, since reports of extortion are still common with travellers trying to do this route independently, or even from the bus station in Dong Ha, it's best to book a seat on one of the through-buses to Savannakhet from Dong Ha (see p.299) or Hue.

You can obtain a thirty-day **visa** for Laos at the border ($30–42, depending on nationality; two passport photos required). Otherwise, get your visa in advance at the Lao consulates in Da Nang (see p.270) or in Ho Chi Minh City (see p.106), or at their embassy in Hanoi (see p.384).

North of Dong Ha

There are a few sights in and around the DMZ itself. Northwest of Dong Ha on Highway 15 are **Con Thien Firebase** and the **Truong Son Cemetery**, both notable wartime locations, while directly north of Dong Ha off Highway 1 are another firebase and the **Vinh Moc Tunnels**, the latter being the most worthwhile sight in the whole area.

Con Thien Firebase

Dawn to dusk • Free • Head west along Highway 9 to Cam Lo, then turn north on Highway 15 and go 12km to the site

There's nothing to see at **Con Thien Firebase** today, beyond a view north to what were once NVA positions, chillingly close on the opposite bank of the Ben Hai River. In the lead-up to the 1968 Tet Offensive, as part of the NVA's diversionary attacks, the base became the target of prolonged shelling, followed by an infantry assault during which it was briefly surrounded. The Americans replied with everything in their arsenal, including long-range strafing from gunships in the South China Sea and carpet-bombing by B-52s. The North Vietnamese were forced to withdraw temporarily, but then completely overran the base in the summer of 1972.

Truong Son Cemetery

Dawn to dusk • Free • Head west along Highway 9 to Cam Lo, then turn north on Highway 15 and go 20km to the site

Truong Son War Martyr Cemetery is dedicated to the estimated 25,000 men and women who died on the Truong Son Trail, better known in the West as the Ho Chi Minh Trail (see box, p.388). A total of 10,036 graves lie in the fourteen-hectare cemetery among whispering glades of evergreen trees. Arranged in five geographical regions, the graves are subdivided according to native province, and centred round memorial houses listing every name and grave number in the sector. Each headstone announces *liet si* ("martyr"), together with as many details as are known: name, date and place of birth, date of enrolment, rank and the date they died.

Doc Mieu Firebase

Dawn to dusk • Free • Head north on Highway 1 about 14km and the memorial is on the right, about 2km south of the Hien Luong Bridge

Before the NVA overran Doc Mieu in 1972, this base played a pivotal role in the South's defence. From here American guns shelled seaborne infiltration routes and, for a while, this was the command post for the "**McNamara Line**", calling in airstrikes from Da Nang to pound targets – both real and faked – along the Ho Chi Minh Trail. These days the site is marked by a Soviet-style memorial to fallen Vietnamese.

Hien Luong Bridge and Ben Hai River Museum

Ben Hai River Museum Daily 7am–5pm • 20,000đ

Just north of Doc Mieu, Highway 1 drops down into the DMZ, running between paddy fields to the Ben Hai River, which lies virtually on the Seventeenth Parallel. You will see two bridges, the newly built one, which is open to traffic, and the unused **Hien Luong Bridge** that runs parallel to it. Until it was destroyed in 1967, the original

5

THE HISTORY OF THE VINH MOC TUNNELS

When American bombing raids north of the DMZ intensified in 1966 the inhabitants of Vinh Linh District began digging down into the red laterite soils, excavating more than **fifty tunnels** over the next two years. Although they were also used by North Vietnamese soldiers, the tunnels were primarily built to shelter a largely civilian population who worked the supply route from the Con Co Islands lying 28km offshore. Five tunnels belonged to **Vinh Moc**, a village located right on the coast where for two years 250 people dug more than 2km of tunnel, which housed all six hundred villagers over varying periods from early 1967 until 1969, when half decamped north to the relative safety of Nghe An Province. The tunnels were constructed on three levels at 10, 15 and 20–23m deep (though nowadays you can't visit the lowest level) with good ventilation, freshwater wells and, eventually, a generator and lights. The underground village was also equipped with a school, clinics and a maternity room where seventeen children were born. Each family was allocated a tiny cavern, the four-person space being barely larger than a single bed. They were only able to emerge at night and lack of fresh air and sunlight was a major problem, especially for young children who would sit in the tunnel mouths whenever possible. In 1972, the villagers of Vinh Moc were finally able to abandon their underground existence and rebuild their homes, rejoined by relatives from Nghe An a year later.

Hien Luong Bridge was painted half red and half yellow as a vivid reminder that this was a physical and ideological boundary separating the two Vietnams. The reconstructed iron-girder bridge, now painted blue and yellow, officially re-opened in 1975 as a symbol of reunification. On the north bank of the river, the Ben Hai River Museum features some striking images of the region during wartime, as well as a few remnants such as a US pilot's helmet, some bombs and guns.

The Vinh Moc tunnels

Daily 7am–5pm • 20,000₫ • The tour takes around fifty minutes and although these tunnels are bigger than those of Cu Chi (the ceiling is almost 2m high in places) it's not recommended for the claustrophobic

Vinh Moc comprises an amazing **complex of tunnels** where over a thousand people sheltered, sometimes for weeks on end, during the worst American bombardments (see box above). A section has been restored and opened to visitors as a powerful tribute to the villagers' courage and tenacity, with a small **museum** at the entrance providing background information.

ARRIVAL AND DEPARTURE   THE VINH MOC TUNNELS

By road The tunnels feature on almost all DMZ tours but it's possible to get there independently if you have your own transport. In Ho Xa township, 7km north of the Ben Hai River and 28km from Dong Ha, a signposted right turn takes you 15km to the tunnels.

The northern coast

HA LONG BAY AT SUNSET

The northern coast

Although largely devoid of beaches, Vietnam's northern coast boasts one of the country's foremost attractions, and one of the most vaunted spots in all of Southeast Asia – the mystical scenery of Ha Long Bay, where jagged emerald islands jut out of the sea in their thousands. Heading in by boat, you approach wave after wave of hidden bays, needle-sharp ridges and cliffs of ribbed limestone. The waters here are patrolled by squadrons of tourist junks, on which you'll be able to spend a night at sea. Cat Ba Island also makes a great base from which to explore Ha Long Bay, while Bai Tu Long Bay has the same dramatic views without the fleets of tourist boats. You'll find similar karst scenery inland around the small city of Ninh Binh, while other notable sights in the area are the colonial buildings of Haiphong, the ancient Ho Citadel and the monstrous caves around Phong Nha.

Heading north from the DMZ (see p.297), the first stretch is hemmed in by the jagged Truong Son Mountains, which separate Vietnam from Laos. Here, Vietnam shrinks to a mere 50km wide and is edged with sand dunes up to 80m high, marching inland at a rate of 10m per year despite efforts to stabilize them with screw-pine and cactus. The first place of note on this stretch is **Dong Hoi**, which has a decent beach but little else to slow you down. Better to push on to **Phong Nha** with its spectacular caves, which include **Phong Nha Cave** itself, **Paradise Cave** and **Son Doong Cave**, which is yet to be fully charted but is already considered the largest in the world.

The area north of Dong Hoi is one of the poorest in Vietnam, and has little to detain the traveller; however, the mountains brushing the Lao border are home to a number of unique animal species, including the elusive **saola ox** and the more numerous **giant muntjac deer**. The only place that sees travellers in any number is **Vinh**, a rather dull place, but a logical stopover on this long stretch; you may care to track down **Ho Chi Minh's birthplace** in the nearby village of Kim Lien.

Despite the presence of these attractions, the vast majority of tourists make a bee-line from Hue to **Ninh Binh**. This is a rather unattractive city, but such is the wealth of nearby sights that visitors tend to stay for at least a couple of days; said attractions include more karst scenery, underground rivers that can be paddled through by boat, an ancient capital city and Vietnam's largest temple complex.

From Ninh Binh, most travellers push straight on north to Hanoi, just an hour's drive to the north. However, it's quite possible to head directly from here towards Ha Long Bay, via the buzzing city of **Haiphong** – one of the largest in Vietnam, and more appealing than most northern cities thanks to great colonial-era architecture and a young, friendly populace.

Then, of course, there's **Ha Long Bay** itself. A doyen of local tourist literature, you'll most likely have seen dozens of images of this unbelievably scenic place long before

CATBA SUNRISE RESORT

Highlights

❶ Phong Nha Caves Visit one or more of Phong Nha's mind-blowing caves, which include the world's biggest. **See p.312**

❷ Ho Citadel Marvel at the massive stones used to build this seven-hundred-year-old citadel in the middle of nowhere. **See p.316**

❸ Cycling from Tam Coc to Hoa Lu A fantasy landscape of limestone crags provides the backdrop for a leisurely cycle ride through Ninh Binh's prolific rice lands. See p.321

❹ Haiphong's colonial architecture Hectic Haiphong features a number of striking colonial-era buildings, which give hints as to this port city's importance under French rule. See p.325

❺ Cat Ba With its cluttered harbour, lush interior and easy access to some of Ha Long Bay's most beguiling scenery, this is a cool spot to spend a few days. **See p.329**

❻ Cruising Ha Long Bay Passing through the maze of limestone pinnacles punctuating the turquoise waters is an unmissable experience. **See p.338**

HIGHLIGHTS ARE MARKED ON THE MAP ON PP.308–309

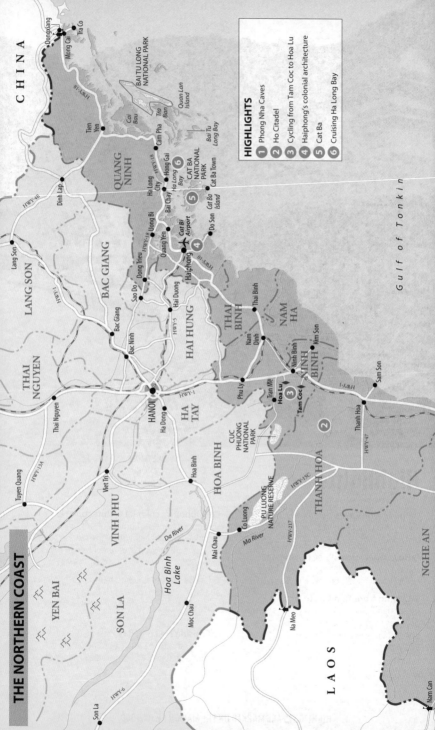

THE NORTHERN COAST

HIGHLIGHTS

1. Phong Nha Caves
2. Ho Citadel
3. Cycling from Tam Coc to Hoa Lu
4. Haiphong's colonial architecture
5. Cat Ba
6. Cruising Ha Long Bay

CHINA

Gulf of Tonkin

LAOS

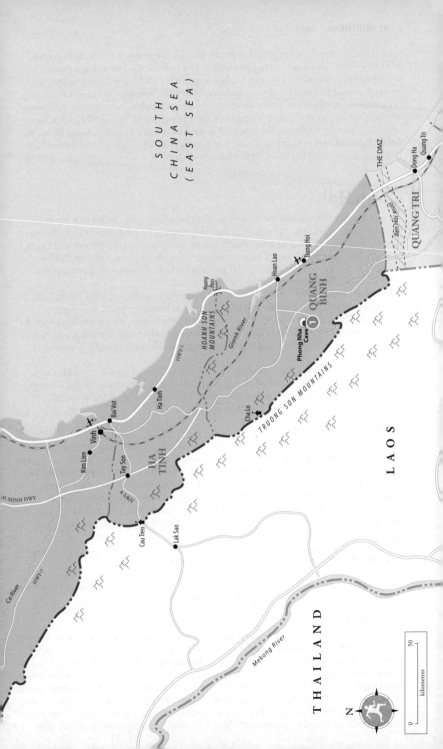

6

your arrival – happily, it really is that pretty, though the weather doesn't always reveal it in its best light. Tourism is taking its toll too, and pollution is becoming a major issue, so an increasing number of visitors are heading further afield to **Bai Tu Long Bay**. Many overnight aboard a traditional wooden junk; their tea-coloured sails are just for show since almost all vessels are motor-driven, but there's a timeless, romantic air to floating among pristine moonlit peaks. By far the largest island in the bay, **Cat Ba** makes an appealing base for exploring the area with some fine scenery as well as being home to **Cat Ba National Park**, a forest and maritime reserve that requires the usual mix of luck and dedication to see anything larger than a mosquito.

Dong Hoi

Almost entirely flattened in the American War's bombing raids, **DONG HOI** has risen from its ashes to become a prosperous, orderly provincial capital of over sixty thousand people. Tourists who pass by here usually use the town as a base for **Phong Nha Caves**, though there are now plenty of accommodation options in Phong Nha itself. However, Dong Hoi also has a decent beach, and the relative lack of tourists makes it a good place to step off the beaten track.

The **Nhat Le River** oozes through town just before hitting the sea, with the bulk of Dong Hoi clustered around its west bank. Here you'll find remnants of a Nguyen dynasty **citadel** – the only notable part is its pretty south gate, which has been restored and now functions as the city's focal point. There's a lively riverside **market** east of the gate and an area of covered stalls where in summer vendors sell ice-cold glasses of sweet-bean *che*.

Crossing the Nhat Le, you'll find yourself on a small spit of land, named **My Canh**. This is also the name of the small beach rifling down the eastern edge of the isthmus. As with sandy stretches up and down the land, it's been developed as a resort area, though it attracts more Vietnamese than foreigners.

ARRIVAL AND DEPARTURE
DONG HOI

By plane Dong Hoi's small but surprisingly swish airport, Dong Hoi Airport, is 6km to the north of town.
Destinations Hanoi (2 daily; 1hr 30min); Ho Chi Minh City (daily; 1hr 30min).
By train The station, Ga Dong Hoi, is 3km out of town west along Tran Hung Dao – you'll easily find a taxi or xe om to take you into town.

Destinations Dong Ha (5 daily; 1hr 40min–2hr 35min); Hanoi (6 daily; 10hr–12hr); Hue (6 daily; 3hr–4hr); Ninh Binh (4 daily; 9hr–11hr); Vinh (6 daily; 3hr 30min–5hr).
By bus The bus station is 1km west of the centre at the junction of Tran Hung Dao and Nguyen Huu Canh.
Destinations Da Nang (5hr); Dong Ha (2hr); Hue (4hr); Phong Nha (2hr; 1 daily at 2pm); Vinh (4hr).

TOURS

Most hotels run tours to Phong Nha, but the following independent outfit is also recommended.

Phongnha Discovery Tours 63 Ly Thuong Kiet ☎ 052 385 1660, ⓦ phongnhadiscovery.com. Small outfit able to book tickets and organize tours around Phong Nha-Ke Bang National Park.

ACCOMMODATION

Luxe 55 Truong Phap ☎ 052 384 5959, ⓦ luxehotel.vn. Newish hotel with English-speaking staff. Rooms are simple but immaculate, and some have a river view. $35
★**Nam Long** 22 Ho Xuan Huong ☎ 052 382 1851 and **Nam Long Plus** 28a Phan Chu Trinh ☎ 052 382 6926, ⓔ sytrang25@yahoo.com. The couple (Nga and Sy) who run these two excellent-value places are incredibly switched on and can help with any travel plans, including visits to Phong

Nha. There's a wide variety of rooms, including clean, bright dorms and comfortable doubles. Dorms $5, doubles $15
Sun Spa Resort My Canh ☎ 052 384 2999, ⓦ sunspa resortvietnam.com. Luxurious five-star on My Canh Beach. It's easily Dong Hoi's top hotel, and worth popping into even if you're not staying – for a small fee non-guests can use the tennis courts, pool and other facilities. Rooms are often discounted, though they are still rather pricey. $210

EATING

QB Bar 3 Le Loi ☎ 052 382 4694. This flashy, air-conditioned restaurant serves an amazing range of dishes such as hotdogs (35,000đ) and grilled lamb ribs (280,000đ). Ice creams, coffee and cocktails (50,000đ) as well. The staff are eager to please. Daily 7am–9pm.

Tu Quy 17 Co Tam ☎ 052 382 1371. On a sidestreet just east of the market, this no-frills place has an English menu and serves tasty Vietnamese staples such as *banh khoai* (a crispy pancake stuffed with prawns and pork) and *banh cuon* (rice noodle rolls with ground pork) for 35,000đ. Cheap beers too. Daily 7am–9pm.

Phong Nha-Ke Bang National Park

Admission free, though there are fees to individual attractions (see below).

There are plenty of opportunities to visit **caves** in Vietnam – especially around Ha Long Bay – but for sheer scale nothing can compare with those at **Phong Nha-Ke Bang National Park**, which was designated a World Heritage Site in 2003. Until recently, most of the national park was actually off-limits to visitors, but now – in addition to **Phong Nha Cave** itself – it's possible to explore other attractions too, including the enormous Paradise Cave and the attractive Nuoc Mooc Eco-Trail. Besides the caves mentioned below, other recently opened attractions include **Dark Cave**, where you can go kayaking, swimming and ziplining, as well as **Tu Lan** and **Hang En Caves**, though these last two involve some serious trekking. And while the caves are the main attraction, the availability of cheap lodging, good food, motorbikes for rent and decent maps of the local area means that increasing numbers of travellers are spending a few days here.

Located on Highway 20, which leads into the national park, little **Phong Nha town** (also known as **Son Trach**) has also seen big changes recently, with a visitors' centre, several recently opened hotels and hostels as well as foreigner-friendly eateries to cater for the growing numbers of visitors, mostly backpackers, who are eager for adventure. Keep in mind that **flooding** frequently occurs in October and November, when most caves are inaccessible; the best months to visit are from March to May.

Brief history

The karst formations of the Phong Nha-Ke Bang National Park constitute the **oldest karst areas** in Asia, dating back some four hundred million years, and the area has been subject to massive tectonic changes in that time. This has resulted in the creation of unique geological formations, which include underground rivers, dry caves, terraced caves, suspended caves and intersecting caves. The best known cave, Phong Nha itself, is around 44km long, though tour boats only go about 1.5km inside. The recent discovery of Son Doong (Mountain River), and Thien Dong (Paradise), thought to be the world's longest dry cave, has attracted a lot of attention, and considering the fact that only ten percent of the area has been fully explored, much more remains to be discovered. The rugged terrain provides an ideal habitat for many **animals**, and the park

---

THE WORLD'S LARGEST CAVE

Rarely can the word "cavernous" have been used with such justification. In 2009, a group of British cavers attempted the first-ever detailed survey of the **Son Doong (Mountain River) Cave** in Phong Nha-Ke Bang National Park, finally giving up 4.5km in. Their records and photographs showed chambers large enough to swallow up whole city blocks – the largest found so far is over 250m high, and 150m wide. Subsequent investigations have added another 2km to the cave's charted length, and shown the presence of 70m-long stalactites, gigantic shards of crystal and grapefruit-sized calcite pearls. The cave is highly remote but is now open to a limited number of visitors (around 300 a year) and despite the whacking $3,000 fee for the week-long trek there and back, there's a long waiting list already. Contact Oxalis (see Tours, p.313) for more information.

is home to over one hundred species of mammal, including bears, elephants and muntjacs, as well as over eighty species of reptiles and amphibians, three hundred birds and seventy types of fish.

Phong Nha Cave

Daily 6.30am–4.30pm • 80,000đ • Dragon boat seating fourteen people 320,000đ; it's theoretically possible to join other groups, but to assemble your own ask at *Easy Tiger Hostel* down the road

The only way to visit **Phong Nha Cave** is by dragon boat, which wend their way 5km (30min) upstream to the cave entrance, after which the pilot cuts the engine and starts to paddle through. Keep your eyes open for scars on the rock in the entrance caused by an American rocket attack. You'll drift awhile between rippling walls of limestone, and see immense stalactites and stalagmites, all tastefully illuminated. The boat eventually draws into a small subterranean beach, from which you follow an easy, 500m-long trail around the cave (flip-flops will be fine) – note that visitors must stick to the path to avoid any risk of rock damage. Your driver will be waiting for you at the end of the path. Late afternoon is a good time to go, when there are few other tourists about.

Tien Son Cave

Daily 6.30am–4.30pm • 40,000đ

Tien Son Cave can be reached from Phong Nha Cave by taking a steep, 330-step climb up steps. From the top you'll have a grand view of the valley, while inside there are Cham inscriptions dating as far back as the ninth century. Fortunately, walkways have now been built making access easier, and the lurid, disco lighting has been replaced with more neutral illumination, as in Phong Nha and Paradise Caves.

Thien Duong (Paradise) Cave

Daily 6.30am–5pm • 120,000đ includes guide • Electric cart 100,000đ • The cave is about 12km southwest of Phong Nha town; follow Highway 20 right through the town, then turn right on the Ho Chi Minh Highway (West).

Even if you're not a "cave person", the sight of **Paradise Cave** will probably leave you spellbound. You can ride to the foot of the hill where the cave is located in an electric cart, though it's a pleasant, 1.6km walk in good weather. Then you climb around 500 steps, or go up a ramp (easier), but when you see the tiny entrance, it's difficult to imagine the enormous cavern inside. You descend a dizzying staircase to the cavern floor, from where a sturdily built walkway takes you for a kilometre through a magical display of **natural sculptures** formed by mineral deposits, which are cleverly illuminated.

Most of these sculptures are in the form of colossal stalagmites (growing up from the floor) and stalactites (growing down from the roof), but no doubt your guide will also impress you with caving terminology by pointing out formations such as draperies (which look like curtains) and soda straws (which look like, er, soda straws). Not surprisingly, word of this cave's wonder has got around and sometimes it can get very busy with tour groups, which somewhat spoils the experience, as tour guides spout forth an amplified commentary in various languages. A smart restaurant by the car park provides welcome refreshment after exploring the cave, though most of its customers are from tour groups.

Nuoc Mooc Eco-trail

Opening times vary • 60,000đ • From Paradise Cave head north on the Ho Chi Minh Highway (West) for a few kilometres and you'll find it on the right

Sprawling along picturesque riverside territory and lassoed together with bamboo bridges, the kilometre-long **Nuoc Mooc Eco-trail** shows the reassuring direction in which local tourism is heading. You're highly unlikely to see any animals, but there are a couple of opportunities to swim. It's a great spot to cool off after sweating through Paradise Cave.

ARRIVAL AND DEPARTURE   PHONG NHA-KE BANG NATIONAL PARK

By bus There's a daily bus which departs from Dong Hoi at 2pm and leaves Phong Nha for Dong Hoi at 8am.

By minibus A daily minibus operated by *Phong Nha Farmstay* departs from the *Why Not?* bar in Hue (see p.287) at 1pm, stopping at the Ben Hai River Museum and the Vinh Moc Tunnels, and leaving from the *Easy Tiger Hostel* (see below) for Hue at 6.30am. Either way costs 500,000đ.

By taxi *Phong Nha Farmstay* (see below) operates shared taxis to and from Dong Hoi according to demand.

By car or motorbike With your own wheels, from Dong Hoi take Highway 15 north for about 50km until you see a Hollywood-type sign on a mountain to the left announcing the Phong Nha-Ka Be National Park. Turn left here on Highway 20 into the town.

TOURS

Oxalis Highway 20, Phong Nha ☎ 052 367 7678, ⓦ oxalis .com.vn. Runs caving tours from one to six days to Tu Lan, Hang En and Son Doong caves with highly professional staff. Contact them to get on the waiting list for Son Doong.

Phong Nha Farmstay Cu Nam Village ☎ 0944 759864, ⓦ phong-nha-cave.com. Offers a day tour of the national park for $60, which includes a visit to Paradise Cave and several other sights, as well as many other, multi-day tours. Owner Ben Mitchell is a mine of local information; see their website for details.

ACCOMMODATION AND EATING

You'll find a fair number of near-identical budget hotels and simple restaurants lining the road around the Visitors' Centre in Phong Nha (Son Trach).

Cavern Bar On the main road a few steps east of the Visitors' Centre ☎ 052 367 7677. Attractive, open-sided bar and restaurant serving a wide range of cheap food (most main dishes around 70,000đ) and cold beer. Cool beats too. Daily 7am–10pm.

Easy Tiger Hostel Phong Nha main road ☎ 052 367 7844, ⓦ easytigerhostel.com. Backpacker central in Phong Nha, just a couple of minutes walk east of the Visitors' Centre. Takes care of all needs, including comfort food, cheap cocktails, tours, bicycle and motorbike rental, transport to Dong Hoi and Hue. Part-owned by the folks at *Phong Nha Farmstay*. Dorms $8

★**Phong Nha Farmstay** Cu Nam Village, about 8km east of Phong Nha town ☎ 0944 759864, ⓦ phong -nha-cave.com. Superb hotel run by affable Aussie Ben and his Vietnamese wife Bich. The setting is gloriously rural

and highly picturesque, and though rooms are quite basic, the on-site swimming pool more than makes up for it. In addition, the kitchen serves up delectable, and fairly priced meals – a good thing, as there are no restaurants for miles around. There's daily transportation to both Dong Hoi and Hue, bicycles and motorbikes for rent, and a whole raft of activities to keep you busy. $35

Saigon Phongnha Hotel ☎ 052 367 7016, ⓦ sgquang binhtourist.com.vn. Small government-run hotel right next to the Visitors' Centre for boats to Phong Nha Cave. Rooms are a bit drab, but there's a pleasant riverside terrace for relaxing. $30

Thanh Tam Hotel On the main road a few steps west of the Visitors' Centre ☎ 052 367 7999. Smart mini-hotel with friendly staff and a decent restaurant on the ground floor. Rooms 203 and 205 have great river views. $15

DIRECTORY

Money There's an ATM opposite the Visitors' Centre on the main road in town (Highway 20).

Vinh

Although a place of pilgrimage for Vietnamese tourists – **Ho Chi Minh** was born in the nearby village of Kim Lien – **VINH** receives very few foreign guests, most of whom use the city as a stop on the long journey between Hue and Hanoi, or a jumping-off point for the Lao border (see box, p.315). Still, the place has its merits – plenty of cheap accommodation around the train and bus stations, and the chance to discover a real Vietnamese city, almost entirely unaffected by international tourism.

Brief history

Vinh fared particularly badly in the twentieth century. As an industrial port-city dominating major land routes, whose population was known for rebellious tendencies, the town became a natural target during both French and American wars. In the 1950s French bombs destroyed large swathes of the city, after which the Viet Minh burnt down what remained rather than let it fall into enemy hands. Vinh was flattened once again during American air raids; many of these were aimed at preventing North Vietnamese troops crossing the nearby border into Laos and heading south on what later became known as the **Ho Chi Minh Trail** (see p.388). Reconstruction of the town proceeded slowly after 1975, mostly financed by East Germany, though fortunately the decrepit hulks of barrack-like apartment blocks, totally unsuited to the Vietnamese climate, have now largely been replaced by sleek high-rises; smart new villas and hotels have also sprung up, and there are even multistorey supermarkets stocked with all manner of goodies.

ARRIVAL AND DEPARTURE
VINH

By plane Vinh Airport is 6km to the north of town (100,000đ by taxi; 50,000đ by xe om).

Destinations Da Lat (3 weekly; 1hr 30min); Da Nang (1hr 15min); Hanoi (daily; 1hr); Ho Chi Minh City (4 daily; 1hr 45min); Vientiane, Laos (3–4 weekly; 1hr 20min).

By train Ga Vinh is in Vinh's northwestern suburbs, and it's an easy walk from a number of hotels.

Destinations Dong Hoi (6 daily; 4–5hr); Hanoi (6 daily; 6hr–6hr 30min); Hue (6 daily; 6–9hr); Ninh Binh (4 daily; 4hr).

By bus The long-distance bus station (Ben Xe Vinh) is in the centre of the city. Buses to Vientiane in Laos, when running, leave early in the morning. Open-tour buses can set down passengers in Vinh en route, but confirm onward travel with the relevant company beforehand.

Destinations Dong Ha (6–7hr); Dong Hoi (4hr); Hanoi (7hr); Hue (8hr); Ninh Binh (5hr); Tay Son (2hr); Vientiane (12–14hr).

INFORMATION AND GETTING AROUND

Tourist information Information is hard to come by, as there's no official tourist office in town and little English is spoken in Vinh. Staff at the *Saigon Kim Lien* hotel can sometimes help out with the basics.

Vehicle rental Car and motorbike rental are available through most hotels, and you can pick up xe om anywhere in town (from 20,000đ for a short ride).

ACCOMMODATION

A transport hub, Vinh has a large number of hotels, which means places are willing to bargain. Many hotels sit right on the highway, so wherever possible go for a room at the back.

Muong Thanh 1 Phan Boi Chau ☎038 353 5666, ⓦmuongthanh.vn. There are several *Muong Thanh* hotels in Vinh, of which this is the friendliest and most convenient as it's near the station. The rooms are smart and well equipped, and there's a swimming pool on the second floor. $25

Saigon Kim Lien 25 Quang Trung ☎038 383 8899, ⓦsaigonkimlien.com.vn. One of Vinh's top hotels, this place opened in 1990 to commemorate the hundredth anniversary of Ho Chi Minh's birth. Prices are surprisingly affordable for comfortable and well-proportioned rooms, and staff are used to dealing with foreigners. Facilities include a

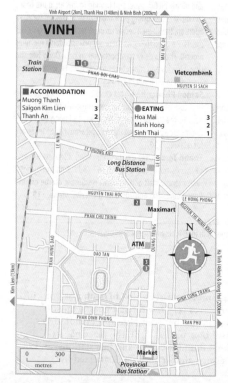

Vinh Airport (2km), Thanh Hoa (140km) & Ninh Binh (200km)

VINH

Train Station

Vietcombank

MAI HAC DE
HA HUY TAP
PHAN BOI CHAU
NGUYEN SI SACH

■ **ACCOMMODATION**
Muong Thanh — 1
Saigon Kim Lien — 3
Thanh An — 2

● **EATING**
Hoa Mai — 3
Minh Hong — 2
Sinh Thai — 1

LE NINH
LY THUONG KIET
LE LOI

Long Distance Bus Station

NGUYEN THAI HOC
LE HONG PHONG
Maximart
NGUYEN THI MINH KHAI
PHAN CHU TRINH

ATM

N

QUANG TRUNG
TRAN HUNG DAO
DAO TAN

Ha Tinh (46km) & Dong Hoi (200km)

Kim Lien (13km)

DINH CONG TRANG
PHAN DINH PHUNG
TRAN PHU
CAO XUAN HUY

Market

0   300
metres

Provincial Bus Station

6

BORDER CROSSINGS INTO LAOS

There are **border crossings into Laos** at Cha Lo, Cau Treo and Nam Can: since all are remote with haphazard bus connections, it's essential to get up-to-date advice from the bus station or local guesthouses before attempting any crossing.

There are direct buses from Vinh to Vientiane via **Cau Treo**, usually leaving at 6am, though the service is erratic and prone to over-charging, so it's worth considering the short and cheap flight (around $30–40) on Vietnam Airlines.

There are direct buses from Vinh to Phonsavan, via the **Nam Can** border crossing – comparatively devoid of complications, but still a rough ride. They leave from Vinh's long-distance bus station daily at 6am and take 12hr to get to Phonsavan; a couple per week continue straight through to Luang Prabang. No major bus routes pass through the Cha Lo–Na Phao border.

You can obtain Lao **visas** at both Cau Treo and Nam Can border posts ($30–42, depending on nationality; two passport photos required), but not at Cha Lo. If using this crossing, get your visa at the Lao consulates in Ho Chi Minh City (see p.106) or Da Nang (see p.270), or at their Hanoi embassy (see p.384).

recommended restaurant, bar, pool, business centre and money exchange. **$70**

Thanh An 158 Nguyen Thai Hoc ☎ 038 358 8366. Just

10 rooms in this centrally located mini-hotel, where all the facilities are well maintained. Pay a few dollars extra and you'll get a more spacious room with a balcony. **$12**

EATING

There's not much choice for places to eat in Vinh, although you'll find a whole host of street kitchens on Le Loi, with a group outside the bus station and another starting just east of the train station.

Hoa Mai 25 Quang Trung ☎ 038 383 8899. The smartest option in town is this restaurant at the *Saigon Kim Lien* hotel, which serves fairly priced Asian and European dishes, starting at around 100,000đ. Daily 6am–9pm.

Minh Hong 3 Phan Boi Chau ☎ 038 384 2706. Popular with the locals (always a good sign), this simple restaurant is worth tracking down if you're based near the train station, and serves standard Vietnamese rice, noodle and

meat dishes for 40,000đ and up. They also have *bia hoi*. Daily 6am–9pm.

Sinh Thai 1 Phan Boi Chau ☎ 038 353 5666. Situated in a garden beside the *Muong Thanh Hotel*, this open-sided bamboo pavilion features an extensive selection of Vietnamese dishes, with main dishes costing anywhere between 65,000đ and 382,000đ. There's also a good breakfast buffet (50,000đ) from 6am to 9am. Daily 6am–10pm.

Kim Lien

Both houses daily 7–11.30am & 1.30–5pm • Free

Ho Chi Minh was born in 1890 in Hoang Tru Village, **KIM LIEN** commune, 14km west of Vinh. The two simple houses made of bamboo wattle and palm-leaf thatch are reconstructions; Ho's birthplace is said to be the hut by itself on the left as you approach, while behind stands the brick-built family altar.

At the age of 6 Ho moved 2km west, to what is now called **Lang Sen** (Lotus Village), to live with his father in very similar surroundings. The two houses here are also replicas, with nothing much to see inside, but the complex is often swarming with Vietnamese on pilgrimage. There's a **shrine** to Ho here too, built with huge wooden pillars, surrounded by bonsai trees and containing an old Russian jeep. You can pick up your Uncle Ho rubber sandals at the kitsch souvenir shops before you leave.

ARRIVAL AND DEPARTURE

KIM LIEN

By car or motorbike Take Phan Dinh Phung west from Vinh market. The road soon becomes Highway 46; follow this until you reach the signed turning south for Kim Lien. The signed route takes you first to Ho's birthplace and then

loops round to Lang Sen.

By xe om or taxi A xe om to both sites from Vinh should set you back around 150,000đ, including waiting time. A taxi would be around double that.

Thanh Hoa Province

Thanh Hoa Province is right off the tourist radar, but there are a couple of destinations that would interest adventurous travellers. The first is the **Ho Citadel**, designated by UNESCO as a World Heritage Site in 2011, and the other is the **Pu Luong Nature Reserve**, an area of cascading rice terraces and minority villages.

Ho Citadel

Daily 7am–5pm • 10,000đ • An informative booklet is available for 120,000đ at the museum

The **Ho Citadel**, built in the late fourteenth century along feng shui principles for an influential and powerful Confucian state, sits in a pretty area between the Truong Son and Don Son mountains and between the Ma and Buoi rivers. The Ho dynasty that built the place was short lived, lasting just seven years (1400–07), but their legacy lives on in this remarkable structure. After six centuries, its **walls** – measuring nearly a kilometre on each side, pierced by giant gateways and made of massive stones, some weighing over 20 tons – still stand virtually intact, though there's nothing within them now but rice paddies, which lend an enigmatic atmosphere to the place. A small **museum** near the south gate displays a few artefacts such as stone cannonballs that were found on the site; another display in a nearby thatched hut explains how the citadel was built with stone cut and transported from nearby quarries.

ARRIVAL AND DEPARTURE   HO CITADEL

By motorbike or rented car The Ho Citadel sits to the south of Cuc Phuong National Park, about 60km northwest of Thanh Hoa and 50km southwest of Ninh Binh, near the junction of Highways 217 and 45 (Vinh Loc is the nearest town). There's no public transport, so one option is to rent a motorbike or car with driver from Ninh Binh or Hanoi, which would cost between $15 and $100 for a day out. Alternatively, you could combine it with a tour of Pu Luong Nature Reserve (see below), organized through Mai Chau Trek (☎04 6293 8797, ⓦmaichautrek.com), based in Hanoi, or the *Xuan Hoa Hotel* (☎030 388 0970, ⓦxuanhoa hotel.com) in Ninh Binh.

Pu Luong Nature Reserve

Free

Pu Luong Nature Reserve (the "pu" is pronounced "fu") is a region of spectacular natural beauty, a pristine environment that has somehow evaded tour operators. Covering an area of around 175 square kilometres in the northwest of Thanh Hoa Province, it consists of two parallel mountain ridges running in a northwest–southeast direction. The valley between these ranges is not considered part of the nature reserve, and the ranges themselves are very different – the southwestern range is formed of igneous and metamorphic rocks, while the higher, northeastern range is part of a range of limestone karst that runs all the way from nearby Cuc Phuong National Park up to Son La.

Pu Luong is home to a rich variety of animals, such as the extremely rare **Delacour's leaf monkey**, of which there an estimated forty or so in the reserve. However, what is likely to stick in the memories of most visitors are the glorious views of rice terraces cascading down the hillside, as well as the simple, thatched and stilted houses of the White Thai and Muong **minority groups**, some of which offer **home-stay accommodation** where you can sleep, eat and join in the family's daily routine. After a few days slowing down to the steady pace of life as lived by the locals, it can be tough to head back to the cacophonous city.

Simply **trekking** though the valley is a joy, with fabulous views opening up at every turn, and in the southern part of the reserve, a string of bamboo waterwheels lines the river to assist in irrigating the flatter part of the valley. None of the **reserve trails** are marked, so you really need to go with a guide (see opposite), and you'll need a minimum of two days to allow for getting there and away.

ARRIVAL AND DEPARTURE

By car or motorbike It's possible to get to Pu Luong by car or motorbike from Hanoi (190km), Mai Chau (50km) or Ninh Binh (about 150km), though local roads can get messy after heavy rain.

Tours Though it's possible to go there independently, you'll get more out of the experience if you travel with a

PU LUONG NATURE RESERVE

guide who knows the locals; Dinh Cong Xuan, who runs *Xuan Hoa Hotel* in Ninh Binh (☎030 388 0970, ⓦxuan hoahotel.com), comes recommended. A Hanoi-based tour operator that offers several-day treks in Pu Luong is Mai Chau Trek (☎04 6293 8797, ⓦmaichautrek.com).

ACCOMMODATION

Home-stays Several hospitable minority families in the area have adapted their houses to operate as home-stays, offering sit-down loos and maybe a hot shower; these

include Mr Binh at Ban Kho Muang village (☎0169 490 4372) and Mr Si at Ban Hieu village (☎0123 818 0616). Daily bed and board costs around $12

Cuc Phuong National Park

55,000đ including entrance and guide to the Primate Center • ☎030 384 8006, ⓦ cucphuongtourism.com

In 1962 Vietnam's **first national park** was established around a narrow valley between forested limestone hills on the borders of Ninh Binh, Thanh Hoa and Hoa Binh provinces, containing over two hundred square kilometres of tropical evergreen rainforest. **Cuc Phuong** is well set up for tourism and sees a steady stream of visitors, attracted principally by the excellent **primate rescue centre**, though other attractions include a 3km, botanical garden loop trail (get there early and listen to the dawn chorus), a turtle conservation center with over 1100 turtles confiscated from illegal wildlife traders, and a carnivore and pangolin conservation center.

Even now Coc Phuong National Park hasn't been fully surveyed but is estimated to contain approximately three hundred **bird species** and ninety **mammal species**, some of which were first discovered here, such as red-bellied squirrels and a fish that lives in underground rivers. Several species of bat and monkey inhabit the park, while bears and leopards roam its upper reaches. Hunting has taken its toll, though, and you're really only likely to see butterflies, birds and perhaps a civet cat or a tree squirrel, rather than the more exotic fauna. What you can't miss, though, is the luxuriant **vegetation** including **one-thousand-year-old trees** (living fossils up to 70m high), tree ferns and kilometre-long corkscrewing lianas, as well as a treasure-trove of medicinal plants.

With more time, you can **hike** into the park interior, **overnight in a Muong village** and experience the multi-layered forest. The most enjoyable time for walking in these hills is October to January, when mosquitoes and leeches take a break and temperatures are relatively cool – but this is also peak season. Flowers are at their best February and March, while April and May are the months when lepidopterists can enjoy the "**butterfly festival**" as thousands of butterflies colour the forest. Apart from walking, you can rent mountain bikes to ride the park's trails and kayaks to paddle round **Mac Lake**.

WALKING IN CUC PHUONG

Of several **walks** in Cuc Phuong, one of the most popular starts at Car Park A, 18km from the park gate. For a steamy 7km (roughly 2hr), a well-trodden path winds through typical rainforest to reach the magnificent **cho xanh tree**, a 45m-high, one-thousand-year-old specimen of *Terminalia myriocarpa* – its dignity only slightly marred by a viewing platform. A more adventurous challenge is a 16km hike through the park to a Muong village, where you spend the night in a traditional stilthouse; for this you'll need a guide, which you can arrange at park headquarters.

Endangered Primate Rescue Center

Daily 9.30–11.30am & 1.30–4.30pm • ☎ 030 384 8002, ⓦ primatecenter.org

Some of the luckier victims of illegal hunting in Vietnam are now to be seen in the **Endangered Primate Rescue Center** located near the park gate. Opened in 1993, the centre not only cares for rescued animals, but also tries to rehabilitate them by releasing them into an adjacent semi-wild area. In addition, the centre runs crucial research, conservation and breeding programmes. At any one time there may be between sixty and a hundred animals here, including **Delacour's langur**, with its distinctive black body and white "shorts", the Cat Ba, or **golden-headed langur**, and the **grey-shanked douc langur**, as well as various lorises and gibbons – a unique opportunity to see these incredibly rare species at close quarters.

ARRIVAL AND DEPARTURE   CUC PHONG

By bus There are regular buses from Ninh Binh to Cuc Phuong, and from Giap Bat in Hanoi to Nho Quan, from where it's a short xe om ride.

By motorbike Cuc Phuong lies 45km north and west of Ninh Binh. Head north on Highway 1 for 10km to find the sign indicating "Cuc Phuong" to the left. From the gate it's

a further 18km to the heart of the forest.

On a tour Day-trips from Hanoi start at $30 per person in a minibus and include lunch and guide. Or, if you are already there, it is easy to organize guided treks, including an overnight stay in a Muong village, through the Visitors' Centre.

INFORMATION

Visitors' Centre You'll find the Primate Center and Visitors' Centre just beyond the Cuc Phuong park gate (daily 7–11.30am & 1.30–4pm). Entry tickets are on sale here,

and you can also arrange accommodation. Be aware that Cuc Phuong is some way above the plains and winter nights can get chilly.

ACCOMMODATION

National Park ⓦ cucphuongtourism.com. Accommodation ranges from unexpectedly comfortable bungalows and bamboo chalets to a basic stilthouse with no hot water and shared bathrooms, located either at the headquarters

or in the wild interior. Booking online is easy, and you can even arrange an airport pickup. Bungalows or chalets $\underline{\$23}$, beds in a stilthouse $\underline{\$7}$

Ninh Binh

The provincial capital of **NINH BINH** is an unattractive, traffic-heavy northern town with no sights of its own worth seeing. However, it makes an ideal base for trips out to several nearby attractions, including caves, pagodas, ancient temples, a cathedral and **Van Long Nature Reserve**. It is also the most convenient jumping off place for a visit to **Cuc Phuong National Park** (see p.317), and because of the steady stream of tourists passing through, the town offers a good range of accommodation options at all levels.

ARRIVAL AND DEPARTURE   NINH BINH

By train Ga Ninh Binh, Ninh Binh's pint-sized station, sits in a convenient location on the east side of town, an easy walk from the centre.
Destinations Dong Hoi (4 daily; 10hr); Hanoi (4 daily; 2hr 30min); Hue (4 daily; 13–14hr); Vinh (4 daily; 4hr).

By bus The refreshingly well-organized bus station is also on the east side of town.
Destinations Haiphong (3hr); Hanoi (2hr); Kim Son, for Phat Diem (1hr); Mai Chau (4–5hr); Vinh (5hr).

GETTING AROUND

Ninh Binh is quite a sprawl, though it's easy to cover the area near the bus and train stations on foot. If you need to go further afield, a xe om should get you anywhere in town for 20,000đ to 30,000đ.

By motorbike and bicycle Almost every hotel can arrange motorbike rental at $5–8 a day, while bicycles cost

$2–5 a day, depending on quality. This is the best way to visit nearby sights independently.

RED-SHANKED DOUC LANGUR, VAN LONG NATURE RESERVE (P.324) >

6

ACCOMMODATION

Ninh Binh Legend Le Thai To ☎030 389 9880, ⓦninhbinhlegendhotel.com. Currently Ninh Binh's most luxurious option, the 11-floor monolith is no beauty from the outside, but the rooms are much more appealing: wood floors, solid furnishings, deep mattresses on the beds and marble counters in the bathroom. There's a pool, fitness centre, spa and tennis courts, and good views of limestone hills from some rooms. It's about 3km north of the town centre, but as there's nothing to see in town, that's not a problem. $95

Queen 19 & 20 Hoang Hoa Tham ☎030 389 3535, ⓦqueenhotel.vn. Right next to the train station, the Queen has been housing budget travellers for years in two locations opposite each other. This relatively new one features flatscreen TVs and excellent en-suite facilities, while rooms in the old wing (at number #19) are a little worn. Breakfast is included in the rates and they also arrange tours and rent out bikes and motorbikes. $20

Thanh Thuy 53 Le Hong Phong ☎030 387 1811, ⓦhotelthanhthuy.com. A popular backpackers' hotel with two distinct sections. Rooms are cheaper in the guesthouse out front, while the hotel out back is shielded from street noise. Breakfast is not included at the cheapest rates. Guesthouse $7, hotel $10

★**Xuan Hoa** 31d Minh Khai ☎030 388 0970, ⓦxuanhoahotel.com. Owner Xuan and his family provide the friendliest welcome in Ninh Binh. They have two hotels, situated almost side by side just off the main drag;

relatively quiet by Ninh Binh standards, they overlook a lake. The rooms are spotless, modern and well equipped, and some have views of the mountains to the west. The owners are particularly knowledgeable about the area, run excellent day-tours of the surrounding sights, and organize trips to Pu Luong Nature Reserve (see p.316). $12

EATING

There are few restaurants of significant appeal in Ninh Binh, though on the plus side hotels provide excellent food at reasonable prices.

Queen 20 Hoang Hoa Tham ☎030 389 3535. The restaurant at *Queen Hotel* serves the local speciality (goat), with dishes 120,000–180,000đ, as well as pizzas and spaghetti in a modern setting. Daily 7am–10pm.

Trung Tuyet 14 Hoang Hoa Tham ☎098 367 7324. This simple family restaurant almost next door to *Queen Hotel* features an extensive menu of Vietnamese food (most dishes 60,000–80,000đ) in four different sizes of serving.

Be warned – the "small" is pretty big already. Try the beef with pineapple – yum. Daily 7am–9.30pm.

★**Xuan Hoa** 31d Minh Khai ☎030 388 0970. As with the hotel, so with the restaurant – it's great value. Simple surroundings but fantastic food served by Hoa, the wife of owner Xuan. They serve goat dishes (120,000đ), as well as rabbit, frog, snail and eels. Most mains around 60,000đ, set menus upwards of 100,000đ. Daily 7am–10pm.

DIRECTORY

Banks There are ATMs all over town, including at Vietinbank on Tran Hung Dao about 50 metres north of the Lim Bridge.

Around Ninh Binh

While the town of Ninh Binh has little to detain you, the surrounding hills shelter several natural, historical and architectural attractions that could keep you busy for several days. A few kilometres southwest of town is **Tam Coc**, where sampans queue up to take tourists on boat trips through the limestone tunnels and between karst outcrops.

West of Ninh Binh, **Trang An** offers a similar experience to Tam Coc, though boats are a bit bigger and it's generally more popular with domestic tourists. A little further north from here is one of Vietnam's ancient capitals, **Hoa Lu**, represented by two darkly atmospheric dynastic temples. Still further on is **Bai Dinh Pagoda** – though decidedly non-ancient, this ranks as the largest Buddhist complex in Vietnam, and is worth a look for its sheer scale alone. All of these places can be tackled in one day by car or motorbike, or by bicycle via the back lanes.

Northwest of Ninh Binh, more boat trips are in store at **Kenh Ga**, to visit a limestone cave, and at **Van Long Nature Reserve**, which are both on the road that leads to Cuc Phuong (see p.317). The only attraction to the southeast of Ninh Binh, the stone mass of **Phat Diem Cathedral** wallows in the rice fields, an extraordinary amalgam of Western and Oriental architecture that still shepherds an active Catholic community.

Hanoi is only a couple of hours away, and the Hoa Lu-Tam Coc-Bich Dong circuit makes a popular and inexpensive day tour out of the capital. However, with more time, it's far better to take advantage of Ninh Binh's **hotels** and services to explore the area at a more leisurely pace.

Tam Coc

Boats 7am–5pm • Entry and boat hire 130,000đ • Take sunscreen and an umbrella, as the boats are not shielded from the elements

It's hard not to be won over by the mystical, watery beauty of **Tam Coc** – the "Three Caves" – which is effectively a miniature landlocked version of Ha Long Bay, just 7km southwest of Ninh Binh. Be aware, however, that the excursion can seem relentlessly commercial, with many travellers having a wonderful day spoiled by hard-sell antics – persistent peddling of embroideries and soft drinks by the rowers.

The two-hour boat trip (each boat seats two people) from Dinh Cac pier in Van Lam village brings some memorable sights, especially of dumpling-shaped karst hills in a flooded landscape where river and rice paddy merge serenely into one. Sometimes the rowers switch from rowing with their arms to rowing with their legs to give their muscles a rest, which is a novel sight if you've never seen this technique before. Keep an eye open for mountain goats high on the cliffs, and bright, darting kingfishers. Journey's end is **Tam Coc** itself, three long, dark tunnel-caves (Hang Ca, Hang Giua and Hang Cuoi) eroded through the limestone hills with barely sufficient clearance for the sampan after heavy rains.

Bich Dong

The cave-pagoda of **Bich Dong**, or "Green Pearl Grotto", is just 2km southwest of Tam Coc. In fact there are three pagodas here; one at the base, one in the middle, and one at the top of Ngu Nhac Mountain. Stone-cut steps, entangled by the thick roots of banyan trees, lead up a cliff face to the middle pagoda. Though originally built in the fifteenth century, several of the buildings you see are quite recent. Inside the cave, three Buddhas sit on lotus thrones beside a head-shaped rock, which purportedly bestows longevity if touched. Walk through the cave to emerge higher up the cliff, from where steps continue to the third and final temple and a viewpoint from where you can gaze over the waterlogged scene.

ARRIVAL AND DEPARTURE   **TAM COC**

To avoid the worst of the crowds at Tam Coc, it's best to set off either very early in the morning or in the late afternoon.

By bicycle or motorbike From Ninh Binh, the easiest and most enjoyable way to reach Tam Coc is to rent a bicycle or motorbike; the signed turning is 4km south on Highway 1. From Tam Coc, it's also possible to take a delightful 10km cycle ride through rice fields and limestone karst scenery to Hoa Lu (see p.322).

Tours Tours from Ninh Binh start at $10 on a bike or $20 per car, including Hoa Lu. Hanoi agencies also run day-trips, starting at $20 per seat in a minibus.

ACCOMMODATION

Tam Coc Garden Hai Nam Hamlet, Ninh Hai Commune, Hoa Lu ☎096 603 2555, ⓦtamcocgarden.com. This rural resort sits among rice fields and limestone mountains just near Tam Coc, and offers stone bungalows that are equipped with a pleasing blend of wood and bamboo furnishings and local pottery. There's a restaurant, pool and free bikes for guests' use. $116

Trang An Grottoes

Boats 7am–5pm • Admission and boat hire 150,000đ; boats here need a minimum of four people, or it's 600,000đ to go alone • From Ninh Binh, head north on Tran Hung Dao, and turn left onto Trang An, a broad new highway, to Trang An itself • Take a hat or umbrella and sunscreen, as the boats are not covered; a torch is useful for seeing stalactites in the caves

The boat trip to the **Trang An Grottoes**, 7km west of Ninh Binh, is basically the same as the one at Tam Coc, so unless you really love the experience, you wouldn't want to do both. Differences are that there are a generous **nine caves** here, the journey takes longer (about three hours), and it's a bit more expensive. Rowers steer their boats along the Sao Khe River, through the various caves and along lush valleys between them, and the trip includes one or more stops at **temples** to stretch your legs.

Mind your head when passing through caves as some have very low clearance; in fact, some caves have been widened or heightened to accommodate boats, which detracts somewhat from their beauty. As at Tam Coc, it's a rather commercial experience, with hundreds of boats lined up at the pier, but there's less hassle from vendors and once you're on the river you can concentrate on the natural beauty around you. It's hugely popular among Vietnamese tourists, but by going early in the morning or late in the afternoon, you can avoid the worst of the crowds. If you're cycling in the area, you can see the pier and boats bobbing along the river from the main road.

Hoa Lu

Admission to temples 10,000đ • From Ninh Binh, head north on Tran Hung Dao, and turn left onto Trang An, a broad new highway, pass Trang An and continue to Hoa Lu

Twelve kilometres northwest of Ninh Binh, **Hoa Lu** makes another rewarding excursion. In the tenth century, this site was the capital of an early, independent Vietnamese kingdom called **Dai Co Viet**. The fortified royal palaces of the Dinh and Le kings are now reduced to rubble, but their dynastic **temples** (seventeenth-century copies of eleventh-century originals) still rest quietly in a narrow valley surrounded by wooded, limestone hills. Though the temple buildings and attractive walled courtyards are unspectacular, the inner sanctuaries are compelling – mysterious, dark caverns where statues of the kings, wrapped in veils of pungent incense, are worshipped by the light of candles.

The temples

The more impressive of the two temples is the one dedicated to **Dinh Tien Hoang**, who seized power in 968 AD and moved the capital south from Co Loa in the Red River Delta to this secure valley, far from the threat of Chinese intervention. Dinh Tien Hoang's gilded effigy can be seen in the temple's second sanctuary room, flanked by his three sons.

The second temple, dedicated to **Le Dai Hanh**, came about as the result of the anarchy that followed the death of King Dinh Tien Hoang. Le Hoan, commander of Dinh's army and supposed lover (and eventual husband) of his queen, wrested power and declared himself King Le Dai Hanh in 980. Le Dai Hanh is enshrined in the temple's rear sanctuary with his eldest son and Queen Duong Van Nga. If you have the energy to climb the steep hill opposite the ticket office, you'll find the tomb of Dinh Tien Hoang as well as some sweeping views of the karst landscape.

Bai Dinh Pagoda

Free • From Ninh Binh, head north on Tran Hung Dao, and turn left onto Trang An, a broad new highway; past Trang An and Hoa Lu, branch left on to Highway 38B to Bai Dinh

Twelve kilometres west of Hoa Lu is the jaw-dropping **Bai Dinh Pagoda**, which only opened up in 2010 and is yet to be fully completed. Bai Dinh's sheer scale makes it unique among Vietnamese Buddhist complexes – its numerous halls and courtyards sprawl up the mountainside for almost a kilometre. The front courtyard is lined with over five hundred arhat statues (each individually designed), while the largest bell and Buddha statue weigh in at 36 and 100 tons respectively. Although the temple is a functioning place of worship, it feels like a tourist trap, but one laid on primarily for locals. It is nonetheless a spectacular thing to behold, particularly the wild extravagance of the three main hall interiors, all of which are filled with gigantic golden statues, and have their walls lined with dozens of smaller versions of the same.

Phat Diem

Strike southeast from Ninh Binh and there's no mistaking that you've stumbled on a **Christian enclave**, where church spires sprout out of the flat paddy land on all sides; it's said that 95 percent of the district's population attend church regularly. These coastal communities of northern Vietnam were among the first to be targeted by Portuguese missionaries in the sixteenth century, and this area owes its particular zeal to the Jesuit Alexandre de Rhodes who preached here in 1627. The greatest monument to all this religious fervour is the stone cathedral, **Phat Diem**, built in 1891 and situated 28km from Ninh Binh in **Kim Son Village**.

If travelling with your own transport, it's worth stopping about 5km before Phat Diem to also take in the imposing **Tran Dao Cathedral** beside the main road, with its amusing gargoyles and a lifelike statue of the Virgin Mary clutching a bloodied Jesus.

The cathedral

Daily 7.30–11.30am & 1.30–5pm, but these times are not always adhered to • Free

The first surprise at Phat Diem cathedral is its monumental **bell pavilion**, whose curved roofs and triple gateway could easily be the entrance to a Vietnamese temple save for a few telltale crosses and a host of angels. The structure is built entirely of dressed stone, as is the equally impressive cathedral facade sheltering in its wake. Behind, the tiled double roof of the **nave** extends for 74m, supported by 52 immense ironwood pillars and sheltering a cool, dark and peaceful sanctuary. The **altar** table is chiselled from a

---

FATHER SIX AND THE QUIET AMERICAN

The idea for Phat Diem cathedral was conceived and carried out by Father Tran Luc (also known as **Father Six**), whose tomb lies behind the bell tower. It was more than ten years in the preparation, as stone and wood were transported from the provinces of Thanh Hoa and Nghe An, though it apparently took a mere three months to build in 1891. During the French War, the Catholic Church formed a powerful political group in Vietnam that stood virtually independent of the French administration but also opposed to the Communists. The then bishop of Phat Diem, Monseigneur Le Huu Tu, was outspokenly anti-French and an avowed nationalist, but, as his diocese lay on the edge of government-held territory, the French supplied him with sufficient arms to maintain a militia of two thousand men in return for containing Viet Minh infiltration. However, in December 1951 the Viet Minh launched a major assault on the village and took it. When paratroopers came in to regain control, the Viet Minh withdrew, taking with them a valuable supply of weapons. The author **Graham Greene** was in Phat Diem at the time, on an assignment for *Life Magazine*, and watched the battle from the bell tower of the cathedral – later using the scene in his novel *The Quiet American*.

single block of marble, decorated with elegant sprays of bamboo, while the altarpiece above glows with red and gold lacquers in an otherwise sober interior. Twelve priests conduct daily services here for the large community of Catholics.

ARRIVAL AND DEPARTURE	PHAT DIEM

By bus Frequent public buses depart from Ninh Binh bus station for the 1hr journey to Kim Son, though note that the last bus back leaves at around 3.30pm.

By bike or xe om Phat Diem is near enough to reach by rented motorbike or bicycle. Take Highway 10 heading straight east from Ninh Binh's Lim Bridge and, when you get to Kim Son Village, 100m after passing an elegant covered bridge, take a right turn to the cathedral.

Tran Me

TRAN ME, a town 23km from Ninh Binh on the road to Cuc Phuong, is the departure point for a couple of very different but worthwhile **boat trips**. It's possible to do them both in a day, or either one can be combined with a visit to Cuc Phuong or Hoa Lu.

Van Long Nature Reserve

90min boat trip 90,000đ

The more beguiling of the two boat trips in the area takes you round the shallow, reed-filled lagoons of **Van Long Nature Reserve**, signed to the right about 2km to the east of Tran Me. From the ticket office you are poled across the wetlands and among the limestone outcrops in a low-slung bamboo sampan. Take binoculars, sunscreen and an umbrella. The crags are home to Vietnam's largest population of the exceptionally rare **Delacour's langur**, and the reed beds provide refuge for migratory waterfowl. **Hawkers** are banned from using boats but they gather round the ticket office whenever a tour bus appears. All things considered, it's a much more peaceful place than Tam Coc, and if you go early or late in the day, you might not see another boat.

Kenh Ga

Boat trips 70,000đ per person for a 90min ride

The village of **Kenh Ga** sits on a canal and is accessible only by water; though the trip may not be as scenic as others in the Ninh Binh area, it's still worth the journey. Take care when hiring a boat however, as many are noisy, motorized vessels and some boat owners ask exorbitant prices. Many village families live on boats and the whole place seems to be engaged in watery pursuits: boatyards turn out concrete-hulled barges to take gravel and quarried stone downstream; there are fish farms and great flocks of ducks, and sampans bustle about, often propelled by people rowing with their feet. Kenh Ga (Chicken Canal) supposedly gets its name from the nearby hot spring where chickens were soaked in the near-boiling water to make them easier to pluck.

ARRIVAL AND DEPARTURE	TRAN ME

By car or bike Van Long and Kenh Ga can be reached independently by car or motorbike, though you'll have to haggle with boat-owners when you get there.

Tours Hotels in Ninh Binh (and a few Hanoi tour agencies) offer organized tours combining both places, usually roping in Hoa Lu and/or Tam Coc; prices start at around $12 per person for a one-day excursion, including all boat trips.

ACCOMMODATION

Emeralda Resort Van Long Reserve, Gia Van Commune, Gia Vien District ☎ 030 365 8333, ⓦ emeraldaresort.com. This rural resort features huge rooms (the smallest are 50 square metres), equipped with natural wood furnishings and enjoying wonderful views of the surrounding countryside. There's also a spa, a large outdoor pool and heated indoor pool, kids' club, movie room and mini golf. $139

Haiphong

Buzzing **HAIPHONG** is a great place to get a handle on urban Vietnam. A city of almost two million souls, it's the third largest in the land, though with just a fraction of Hanoi's and Ho Chi Minh City's tourists and expats, your presence is likely to be greeted with genuine curiosity. Haiphong is well connected to both Hanoi and Cat Ba and can function as a good stopping-off point for those who don't fancy joining a Ha Long Bay tour; hole up here for a while and you'll uncover varied eating and drinking options, and enjoy the pleasant lack of street hustlers. Although a little scruffy around the edges, Haiphong's broad and bustling central avenues are shaded by ranks of flame trees and dotted with well-tended **colonial villas**, most of which lie along the crescent-shaped nineteenth-century core that forms a southern boundary to today's city centre.

Brief history

Haiphong lies 100km east of Hanoi on the Cua Cam River, one of the main channels of the Red River Estuary. Originally a small **fishing village** and military outpost, its development into a major port in the seventeenth century stems more from its proximity to the capital city than from favourable local conditions. In fact it was an astonishingly poor choice for a harbour, 20km from the open sea with shallow, shifting channels, no fresh water and little solid land. The first quay was only built in 1817 and it was not until 1874, when Haiphong was ceded to the French, that a town began to develop. With remarkable determination, the first settlers drained the

HAIPHONG

ACCOMMODATION	
AVANI Haiphong Harbour View	2
Huu Nghi	3
Maxim	1
Monaco	4

EATING AND DRINKING	
Bangkok	4
Hai Quan	8
Indian Kitchen	6
Julie's Bar	5
Maxim's	2
Nam Giao	3
Texas BBQ	7
Van Tue	1

mosquito-ridden marshes, sinking foundations sometimes as deep as 30m into huge earth platforms that passed for building plots. Doubts about the harbour lingered, but then, in 1883, the nine-thousand-strong **French Expeditionary Force**, sent to secure Tonkin, established a supply base in Haiphong and its future as the north's principal port was secured.

The twentieth century

In November 1946 Haiphong reappeared in the history books when rising tensions between French troops and soldiers of the newly declared Democratic Republic of Vietnam erupted in a dispute about customs control. Shots were exchanged over a Chinese junk suspected of smuggling, and the French replied with a **naval bombardment** of Haiphong's Vietnamese quarter, killing many civilians (estimates range from one to six thousand), and only regained control of the streets after several days of rioting. But the two nations were now set for war – a war that ended, appropriately, with the citizens of Haiphong watching the last colonial troops embark in 1955 after the collapse of French Indochina.

Barely a decade later the city was again under siege, this time by American planes targeting a major supply route for Soviet "aid". In May 1972 President Nixon ordered the mining of Haiphong harbour, but less than a year later America was clearing up the mines under the terms of the **Paris ceasefire agreement**. By late 1973 the harbour was deemed safe once more, in time for the exodus of desperate **boat people** as hundreds of refugees escaped in overladen fishing boats (see box, pp.450–451).

Haiphong Museum

66 Dien Bien Phu • Tues & Thurs 8–11am, Wed & Sun 7.30–9.30pm • 5000đ

On the northern side of the city centre, the wine-red **Haiphong Museum** is an attractive example of Haiphong's colonial-era structures, even if the displays themselves lack glamour. The collection spans seventeen rooms and contains around 3000 exhibits, which are divided into three sections – on natural resources, local history before 1955, and from 1955 to the present. These exhibits include ancient jewellery, household implements and colonial-era photos, and many exhibits are labelled in English. In the garden outside are war relics such as an MIC-17 aircraft and a minesweeper of the Vietnamese Navy. Note that opening hours are limited, and even during listed times it isn't always open.

Haiphong Cathedral

46 Hoang Van Thu • Sunrise to sunset

Just to the southwest of the Haiphong Museum is the square tower of **Haiphong Cathedral**, built in the late nineteenth century and renovated in 2010 after years of neglect; it's European in style but with an altar decorated along the same burgundy-and-gold colour scheme as a Vietnamese pagoda. Enter via the east gate.

Haiphong Opera House

27 Tran Hung Dao

South from Haiphong Cathedral is the buttermilk-yellow **opera house**; constructed of materials shipped from France in the early 1900s, it faces onto a wide, open square – a site remembered locally for the deaths of forty revolutionaries during the street battles of November 1946 "after a valiant fight against French invaders". Unfortunately, performances here are very irregular, usually only taking place when huge tour groups are in town. There's a **flower market** just west of the opera house in the city park, and a new flag tower in front of it.

City Park

Haiphong's **City Park** consists of a crescent of public land that slices through the city centre between Tran Hung Dao and Tran Phu. In French times this was the **Bonnal Canal**, which once ran past the theatre, linking the Tam Bac and Cua Cam rivers. Nowadays it consists of parkland, pedestrianized walkways and an amusement park; though cut up regularly by major roads, some sections remain good for a stroll. To its western end is **Tam Bac Lake**, the only surviving remnant of the canal; at the eastern end of the lake you'll see a massive **bronze statue** of the city's heroine, Le Chan (see below), made in a bold Socialist Realist style.

The merchants' quarter

To the north of Tam Bac Lake is Haiphong's **merchants' quarter**, a lively area of street markets, chandlers and ironmongers. At its western end is **Cho Sat (Iron Market)** whose original nineteenth-century halls have been replaced by an ugly, six-storey block. Still, it's an interesting place to spend some time; the lower levels are home to literally hundreds of stalls, selling all sorts of food, clothing, electronic items and household gadgets, while on the fourth level you'll find a few simple restaurants.

Den Nghe Temple

Corner of Le Chan and Me Linh • Daily 7am–noon & 1.30–7pm • Free

Den Nghe Temple, located in a busy shopping district, is an atmospheric religious compound noted for its sculptures; you'll find the entrance on the northern side, which leads into a large courtyard. The finest carvings are on the massive stone table in the first courtyard, but make sure you also look above the perfumed haze of incense for some detailed friezes along the rooftops. **General Le Chan**, who led the Trung Sisters' Rebellion (see p.432), is worshipped at the main altar in the building on the right; on the eighth day of each second lunar month she receives a birthday treat – platefuls of her favourite food, crab with rice noodles.

Du Hang Pagoda

121 Du Hang, 2km south of the city centre • Dawn to dusk • Free

Located across the railway tracks in the south of town, **Du Hang Pagoda** is a rewarding attraction. In its present form, the pagoda dates from the late seventeenth century and is accessed through an imposing triple-roofed bell tower. Interestingly, the architecture reveals a distinct Khmer influence in the form of vase-shaped pinnacles ornamenting the roof and pillars of the inner courtyard – according to Buddhist legend these contain propitious *cam lo*, or sweet dew. Beside it lies a small, walled garden of burial stupas.

Dinh Hang Kenh

Nguyen Cong Tru • Dawn to dusk • Free

It's worth visiting **Dinh Hang Kenh**, 1km east of the Du Hang Pagoda, if you haven't yet seen a *dinh*, or communal house. This one is a low, graceful building with a sweeping expanse of tiled roof facing across a spacious courtyard to an ornamental lake. Despite the surrounding apartment blocks, it's still an impressive sight. Thirty-two monumental ironwood columns hold up the roof and populate the long, dark hall that is also noted for its carvings of 308 dragons sculpted in thirty writhing nests.

ARRIVAL AND DEPARTURE   **HAIPHONG**

By plane The Cat Bi Airport is 7km southeast of the city. Vietnam Airlines (166 Hoang Van Thu ☎031 381 0890, ⓦvietnamairlines.com.vn), Jetstar (36 Hoang Van Thu ☎031 355 9550, ⓦjetstar.com) and VietJet (7 Tran

6

THE BATTLES OF BACH DANG RIVER

The **Vietnamese navy** fought its two most glorious and decisive battles in the Bach Dang Estuary, east of Haiphong. The first, in 938 AD, marked the end of a thousand years of Chinese occupation when General **Ngo Quyen** led his rebels to victory, defeating a vastly superior force by means of a brilliant ruse. Waiting until high tide, General Ngo lured the **Chinese fleet** upriver over hundreds of iron-tipped stakes embedded in the estuary mud, then counter-attacked as the tide turned and drove the enemy boats back downstream to founder on the now-exposed stakes.

History repeated itself some three centuries later during the struggle to repel **Kublai Khan's** Mongol armies. This time it was the great **Tran Hung Dao** who led the Vietnamese in a series of battles culminating in that of the Bach Dang River in 1288. The ingenious strategy worked just as well second time round when over four hundred vessels were lost or captured, finally seeing off the ambitious Khan.

Nguyen Han (031 363 0032, vietjetair.com) all operate services here.
Destinations Da Nang (3–4 daily; 1hr 45min); Ho Chi Minh City (6–8 daily; 2hr).
By train The station, Ga Haiphong, is an easy walk from the centre, and has services to Hanoi only; note that some of these services terminate at Hanoi's lesser-used Long Bien station.
Destinations Hanoi (4 daily; 2hr 15min–3hr).
By bus Lac Long bus station is centrally located on Cu Chinh Lan and receives buses from the northeast. Niem Nghia, out in the southwest, usually receives buses from the south. Tam Bac, on the edge of the merchants' quarter, is the most common arrival point for buses from the capital, Hanoi.
Destinations Bai Chay, Ha Long City (every 30min; 2hr); Hanoi (every 10–20min; 2hr); Ninh Binh (every 30min; 4hr).
By hydrofoil and express boat Ben Binh Ferry Station, on Ben Binh, handles departures to Cat Ba daily, costing around 150,000–220,000đ; it's best to buy tickets through your hotel as there are touts at the terminal who can easily confuse travellers. Quickest is the hydrofoil, the earliest leaving at 9am, while express boats depart at intervals through the day. On arrival at Cat Ba, services dock in the harbour, within walking distance of most hotels.
Destinations Cat Ba by hydrofoil (1–3 daily; 45min); Cat Ba by express boat (6–8 daily; 1hr 10min).

GETTING AROUND

Xe om and cyclo are readily available and a good way of getting around the central district, although it's quite possible to tackle most of it on foot.

By taxi Haiphong Taxi (031 383 8383; Mai Linh Taxi (031 383 3833. The flag fare is around 12,000đ.

INFORMATION

Tourist Information Centre 56 Hoang Van Thu (Mon–Sat 8am–5pm; (031 356 9600, haiphongtourism.gov.vn).

A fairly useful little office, able to organize tours and sell maps of the area. There's usually an English-speaker present.

ACCOMMODATION

Haiphong has a fair number of hotels, but **budget accommodation** is hard to come by – there are no dorms or hostels here. Most hotels cluster on and around Dien Bien Phu, the city's main artery, with others dotted around town.

AVANI Haiphong Harbour View 12 Tran Phu (031 382 7827, avanihotels.com. This mock-colonial, international-class hotel is as plush as Haiphong gets; just don't expect a view of the harbour. It boasts two restaurants, a piano bar and a pocket-sized pool, not to mention very stylish rooms, impeccable service and a superb buffet breakfast. **$135**
Huu Nghi 60 Dien Bien Phu (031 382 3244, huunghihotel@hn.vnn.vn. The largest hotel on the central strip is housed in an unsympathetic eleven-storey block. Some rooms are a bit worn for the price, but facilities include a small pool (heated in winter), tennis court and gym. **$100**
Maxim 3k Ly Tu Trong (031 374 6540, hotelhaiphong .com. Central, attractive and friendly, this has long been a magnet for budget travellers so you'd be wise to book ahead. It's also notable for being on what passes for a quiet road in Haiphong. Rooms come with satellite TV, a/c and fridges; ask to look at one first as some have no windows. There's a decent restaurant downstairs (see opposite), but breakfast isn't included in the room rate. **$21**
Monaco 103 Dien Bien Phu (031 374 6468, haiphongmonacohotel.com. The most attractive of Dien Bien Phu's many hotels, with an art-gallery-like reception hall and rooms, going for up to $60, are designed with more attention than usual. Service can be a little off, but breakfast is included in the rate. **$30**

EATING AND DRINKING

Haiphong is well endowed with a fair **range of places** to eat and drink, serving everything from Indian to Italian as well as traditional Vietnamese cuisine; some (such as *Bangkok*) are quite classy. There's also good-value **seafood** and some increasingly fancy bia hoi outlets, including Haiphong's very own microbrewery. In the evenings, hit the cafés and small restaurants **around the theatre**, or join the throng promenading up and down the gardens, pausing at ice-cream parlours or beneath the flickering lights of popcorn vendors. If you're looking for more action, take a stroll along Minh Khai and Le Dai Hanh, both lined with restaurants and bars.

Bangkok 22a Minh Khai ☎031 382 3994. Authentic Thai food served in an up-market and stylish restaurant; the menu features dishes like *larb* (minced pork salad; 120,000đ), plus a range of spicy stir-fries and curries (most mains around 160,000đ). Good range of wines too. Look for the sign saying "BKK". Daily 10am–10pm.

Hai Quan 41 Le Dai Hanh. Street venue serving delectable plates of *banh beo* (20,000đ) – rice-cake sprinkled with lime and chilli slices, and eaten with a broth. Note the early closing time. Daily 9am–7.30pm.

Indian Kitchen 22d Minh Khai ☎031 384 2558. This newish place is smartly decorated and offers a broad menu of competitively priced dishes such as tandoor kebabs (70,000đ) and fish in banana leaf (150,000đ). Daily 10am–11pm.

Julie's Bar 22c Minh Khai ☎031 352 1198, ⊕juliesbarhaiphong.vn. Classic, dim-lit bar with inebriated wisdom scrawled on the walls. From a glance at the shelves, tequila seems the favourite tipple here. Daily 5pm–2am.

Maxim's 51 Dien Bien Phu ☎031 382 2934. Decorated along contemporary Oriental lines, this restaurant-bar is a great place for a drink when there's a bit of a crowd.

Cosy seating, friendly staff, and an extensive menu too in case you get peckish. There's often live music after 8.30pm. Daily 7am–11pm.

Nam Giao 22 Le Dai Hanh ☎031 381 0600. Looking more like a temple or museum, this atmospheric place has a short menu with dishes like grilled prawns for just 60,000đ, as well as teas, juices and beers. Daily 8am–10.30pm.

Texas BBQ 22h Minh Khai ☎031 382 2689. Hugely popular with locals and tourists alike, this place offers everything from pizzas to Thai curries and Mexican enchiladas; combo platters too, as well as cheap beer. Daily 8am–10.30pm.

Van Tue 1a Hoang Dieu ☎031 374 6338. A curious venue that's part restaurant, part beer-hall, with waiters bustling about with jugs of pilsner and great platters of food. The beer from the microbrewery is excellent, and there's a veritable Noah's Ark of meat on the menu – this features a few European dishes, but the Vietnamese ones are quite superb, and are served quickly despite the customer levels. Daily 9am–2pm & 5–9pm.

DIRECTORY

Banks and exchange There are 24hr ATMs around almost every corner, including one outside Vietcombank at 2 Minh Khai and another in the foyer of the *Huu Nghi Hotel*.

Hospital Haiphong International Hospital, 124 Nguyen Duc Canh, ☎031 395 5888.

Post office The GPO is at the junction of Nguyen Tri Phuong and Hoang Van Thu.

Cat Ba Island

Dragon-back mountain ranges mass on the horizon 20km out of Haiphong as you approach **Cat Ba Island**. The island, the largest member of an archipelago sitting on the west of Ha Long Bay, boasts only one settlement of any size – **Cat Ba town**, a fishing village now redefining itself as a tourist centre. The rest of the island is largely unspoilt and mostly inaccessible, with just a handful of paved roads across a landscape of enclosed valleys and shaggily forested limestone peaks, occasionally descending to lush coastal plains. In 1986 almost half the island and its adjacent waters were declared a **national park** in an effort to protect its diverse ecosystems, which range from offshore coral reefs and coastal mangrove swamps to tropical evergreen forest. Its value was further recognized in 2004, when the Cat Ba Archipelago was approved as an **UNESCO Biosphere Reserve**.

The wild terrain of Cat Ba Island lends itself to **adventure sports**, and many come here for rock climbing, hiking, kayaking and mountain biking, as well as cruising round **Ha Long Bay** or the nearer **Lan Ha Bay** (see p.334). With a string of mini-hotels and tourist restaurants lining the town's harbour, Cat Ba caters mostly for Western visitors to Ha Long Bay, while Ha Long City (see p.334) is the preferred base for

6

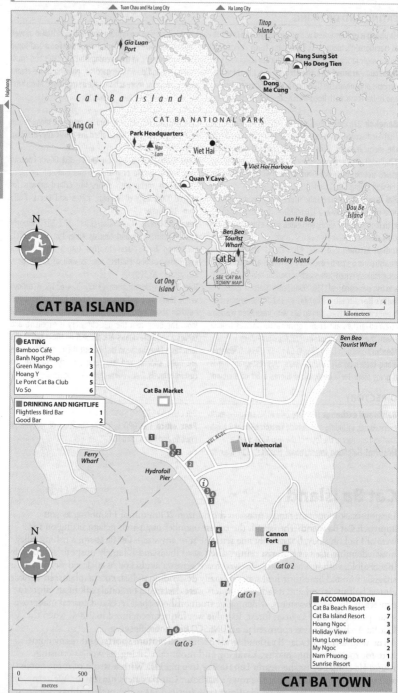

Tuan Chau and Ha Long City

Ha Long City

Titop Island

Haiphong

Gia Luan Port

Cat Ba Island

CAT BA NATIONAL PARK

Ang Coi

Park Headquarters

Ngu Lam

Viet Hai

Hang Sung Sot
Ho Dong Tien

Dong Me Cung

Quan Y Cave

Viet Hai Harbour

Dau Be Island

Lan Ha Bay

Ben Beo Tourist Wharf

Cat Ba

SEE 'CAT BA TOWN' MAP

Monkey Island

Cat Ong Island

N

CAT BA ISLAND

0   4
kilometres

● EATING

Bamboo Café	2
Banh Ngot Phap	1
Green Mango	3
Hoang Y	4
Le Pont Cat Ba Club	5
Vo So	6

■ DRINKING AND NIGHTLIFE

Flightless Bird Bar	1
Good Bar	2

Ben Beo Tourist Wharf

Cat Ba Market

NUI NGOC

War Memorial

Ferry Wharf

Hydrofoil Pier

ⓘ

Cannon Fort

Cat Co 2

Cat Co 1

Cat Co 3

N

■ ACCOMMODATION

Cat Ba Beach Resort	6
Cat Ba Island Resort	7
Hoang Ngoc	3
Holiday View	4
Hung Long Harbour	5
My Ngoc	2
Nam Phuong	1
Sunrise Resort	8

0   500
metres

CAT BA TOWN

Chinese, Korean and other Asian visitors. However, Cat Ba's appeal declines from June to August, when it's packed with domestic tourists and room rates rocket, and between November and March, when it's usually cold and damp.

Brief history

Archeological evidence shows that humans inhabited Cat Ba's many **limestone caves** at least six thousand years ago. Centuries later these same caves provided the perfect wartime hideaway – the military presence on Cat Ba has always been strong, for obvious strategic reasons. When trouble with China flared up in 1979, hundreds of ethnic Chinese islanders felt compelled to flee and the exodus continued into the next decade as "boat people" sailed off in search of a better life, depleting the island's population to fewer than fifteen thousand. Now that prosperity has come in the form of tourism, the population is growing rapidly.

6

Cat Ba town

Caught between green hills and a horseshoe bay alive with multicoloured fishing boats, **CAT BA TOWN**'s west-facing location makes it perfect for sunsets over outlying islands. Outside the summer peak, it retains a pretty laidback ambience despite the recent onslaught of tourism, which has seen a slew of new hotels and restaurants open along the harbour front. The town is divided into two sections: most tourist facilities are grouped around the **hydrofoil pier**, while 800m to the north lies the original, workaday **fishing village** with a bustling market and its accompanying food and bia hoi stalls. Directly behind the pier is a small hill topped by the town's **war memorial**, erected during Ho Chi Minh's visit to the island in 1953; behind this, on a higher hill, is an even better viewpoint at **Cannon Fort** (see p.333).

The beaches

To the south of town, on the far side of the peninsula, are three small, sandy **beaches**, romantically named Cat Co 1, Cat Co 2 and Cat Co 3. Cat Co 1, the middle bay, is the most popular with locals and a cliffside path links it with Cat Co 3, which makes a very pleasant walk. Cat Co 2 is quieter and cleaner, but is dominated by the new *Cat Ba Beach Resort*, which discourages non-guests from using the beach.

ARRIVAL AND DEPARTURE   **CAT BA TOWN**

Tours Many people visit Cat Ba on a tour from Hanoi – several companies offer three-day tours of Ha Long Bay with one night on board and another on Cat Ba (see box, p.339). Most tours of Ha Long Bay from Cat Ba embark at Ben Beo Tourist Wharf, about 3km northeast of Cat Ba town.

By hydrofoil and express ferry Hydrofoils (220,000đ) from Haiphong's Ben Binh ferry pier dock in Cat Ba harbour within walking distance of most hotels. Some express boats also use the harbour, while others use Cai Vieng port in the northwest of the island, and buses run passengers to and from here and the town.

Destinations Haiphong hydrofoil (1–3 daily; 45min);

Haiphong express boat (6–8 daily; 1hr 10min).

By ferry and bus There's a combined bus and ferry service to and from Hanoi run by Hoang Long Tourist Company (☎031 392 0920, ⌨hoanglongasia.com; 240,000đ); buy tickets at Hanoi's Long Yen bus station. Getting back to Hanoi this way is easy: operators in Cat Ba town all sell tickets (with a small mark-up).

Destinations Hanoi (4 daily; 4hr).

By motorbike Take the passenger and vehicle ferry (about 6 daily; 1hr; 50,000đ) from Tuan Chau, just southwest of Bai Chay (Ha Long City), to Gia Luan on the north coast of Cat Ba Island, then ride south across the island to Cat Ba Town.

GETTING AROUND

By motorbike and bicycle To explore the island independently, your best bet is to rent a motorbike with or without a driver. Xe om cruise around town and most hotels rent motorbikes ($7 per day) and mountain bikes ($4 a day, but the steep hills are hard going in the heat). There are

also tandems for rent (15,000đ per hour) for fun evening rides along the harbour promenade.

Electric cars These hang around by the ferry terminal in the middle of the harbour and charge 10,000–20,000đ for short trips around town and to the beaches.

6

ORGANIZED TOURS IN CAT BA

Most hotels and agencies in Cat Ba Town arrange **tours**, with little to choose between them on price; to ensure that you have quality to match, it pays to ask fellow travellers for up-to-date advice on the best choices. Tours include boat trips (around $12 for a half day, $20 for a full day), of which the most pleasant is the short sail north into **Lan Ha Bay**, including a visit to a floating village, and then either walk into the national park (see p.334) or a half-day cruise around the maze of limestone islands, stopping at one of the coral-sand beaches for a spot of swimming or kayaking. You can also explore **Ha Long Bay** (see p.338) from here, either as a one- or two-day trip, with the option of returning to Cat Ba or being dropped off in Bai Chay. If you'd rather spend the day paddling a kayak than sitting on a junk, contact **Blue Swimmer Adventures** (Ben Beo Pier, Cat Ba Island; ☎031 368 8237, ⍵blueswimmersailing.com).

In addition to boat tours, hotels also arrange **trekking** in the national park. Pretty much every agency in Cat Ba will be willing to take you – hunt around on the harbour road. Lastly, one of the most enjoyable activies on Cat Ba – and, indeed, the bay as a whole – is **rock-climbing**. ★ **Asia Outdoors** (222 Harbour Road ☎031 368 8450, ⍵asiaoutdoors.com.vn) pioneered rock-climbing in Vietnam and remain the best operator to go with; going with a copycat outfit may save you a couple of bucks, but none of them are certified. They take climbers on a phenomenal network of routes, including some on a deserted island off Cat Ba, and others which you simply climb until you fall into the sea.

INFORMATION

Tourist information Cat Ba's information office is at 228 Harbour Road (daily 7am–8pm; ☎031 368 8215), though not much English is spoken; staff at your hotel will probably be more helpful. The Harbour Road is also known as 1st April Street (1/4 Street).

ACCOMMODATION

Thanks to a building boom, **accommodation** on Cat Ba represents good value on the whole. The exception is during the peak summer holiday period of June through August, when the place is absolutely packed and prices can more than double. There are few upper-range options in town, while budget hotels are popping up everywhere, especially along Nui Ngoc, where several hostels offer dorm beds at anywhere between $5 and $18. Note also that this street is home to many noisy clubs.

Cat Ba Beach Resort Cat Co 2 Beach ☎031 388 8686, ⍵catbabeachresort.com. Cat Ba's newest resort is also its flashiest, and also happens to occupy the prettiest beach around. Classy thatched family duplexes and attractive seafront bungalows set amid a shady coconut grove (though the seaview bungalows in between are rather cramped), with a smart restaurant and beachside bar. Off-season discounts available. $125

Cat Ba Island Resort Cat Co 1 Beach ☎031 368 8686, ⍵catbaislandresort-spa.com. Located next to the island's busiest beach, this is a large, family-friendly hotel aimed mostly at domestic visitors, with swimming pools, water slides and many other facilities. Rooms are a bit overpriced but stocked with all mod cons, and they have a fresh, modern design scheme. $150

Hoang Ngoc 245 Harbour Rd ☎031 368 8788. Rooms at this family-run guesthouse are fresh and pleasant, and there's a communal balcony on every floor; ask for a room out front to enjoy sea views. Staff are helpful and friendly, not always a given in Cat Ba. $25

Holiday View 251 Harbour Rd ☎031 388 7200, ⍵holidayviewhotel-catba. You can't miss this fourteen-storey monstrosity sticking up to the east of the pier. It does, however, boast three-star comforts, including a restaurant and terrace café, and its rooms are tastefully decorated, if a tad bland. $70

Hung Long Harbour 268 Harbour Rd ☎031 626 9086, ⍵hunglonghotel.vn. At this newish place at the south end of the harbour road, most rooms have fabulous views of the bay, and its rooms provide stiff competition to the nearby (and older) *Holiday View*. However, the staff are often busy checking tour groups in and out. $80

My Ngoc 212 Harbour Rd ☎031 388 8199, ⍵khachsanmyngoc.com. This hotel offers cheap rates for its seafront location, and rooms are well equipped, but it's often bustling with tour groups coming and going. It also arranges reasonable tours. $20

Nam Phuong 288 Harbour Rd ☎031 388 8561. Located towards the northern end of the harbour, this offers just a handful of small but clean rooms with good views. The novelty of this place is that the back wall of the hotel is formed by a cliff, and staff can help arrange any tour or vehicle rental. $10

★ **Sunrise Resort** Cat Co 3 Beach ☎031 388 7360, ⍵catbasunriseresort.com. If you want to feel the sand between your toes, head for this low-rise resort hotel, situated right on Cat Co 3 beach. The burgundy-trimmed rooms all have seaview balconies; best value are the deluxe rooms, whose "Extra King Size" beds are colossal. Hotel facilities include an excellent restaurant (see below), bar, pool and sauna. **$150**

EATING

The number of restaurants on Cat Ba is gradually expanding, with some offering tasty food – especially **seafood** – at reasonable prices. The **floating restaurants** in Cat Ba harbour and off Ben Beo tourist wharf seem a nice idea but are to be avoided owing to the staggeringly poor value for money.

Bamboo Café Harbour Rd ☎031 388 7552. Simple place with bamboo furnishings (as you might guess) that serves tasty and inexpensive Vietnamese dishes, and is particularly good for breakfast (both Western and Vietnamese) – significant in a town where many hotels don't include breakfast in the price. Daily 6.30am–11pm.

Banh Ngot Phap 196 Harbour Rd ☎0397 509 5144. Small, family-run bakery churning out round after round of delectable croissants, brownies and brioche, as well as home-made crème caramel; all for around 20,000đ. Coffee and beer too. Daily 6am–10pm.

Green Mango Harbour Rd ☎031 388 7151. One of Cat Ba's classiest restaurants, *Green Mango* has a menu that ranges from lasagna, pizza and spicy Thai soups to Mexican and Mediterranean. Presentation is excellent, but sometimes the fusion-type dishes, such as wok-tossed lemongrass, marinated chicken and sprouts (120,000đ), just don't work. Daily 6.30am–11.30pm.

Hoang Y towards the south end of Harbour Rd. This is one of the best choices for a seafood meal, with very reasonable prices; for example, shrimp with lemon and garlic for 130,000đ and whole steamed fish with ginger for 100,000đ. Daily 7am–10.30pm.

Le Pont Cat Ba Club Dung Ho Bay ☎031369 6668. Occupying an ideal location on a promontory at the south end of Cat Ba harbour, and with its terrace looking like the prow of a ship, this is a wonderful spot to enjoy a sundowner or indeed a full meal from their tempting menu. Steaks at 300,000đ, pizzas at 140,000đ and noodle dishes for 100,000đ, plus friendly and helpful staff. Daily 7am–10pm.

Vo So Sunrise Resort, Cat Co 3 Beach ☎031 388 7360. The restaurant at the *Sunrise Resort* has surprisingly reasonable prices given the opulent surroundings. Salads, soups and pasta dishes (from 80,000đ) are offered as well as the Vietnamese regulars, and some of the desserts are simply irresistible. Daily 6.30am–10pm.

DRINKING AND NIGHTLIFE

In the evenings, locals and visitors stroll along the harbour front, stopping to enjoy a beer or juice at one of the many drink stalls that set up around sunset. If the moon is out, the path running between Cat Co 1 and Cat Co 3 makes for a spectacular place to drink. Closing time depends on how many tourists are in town – if there's enough of a crowd, things can easily go on to 4am.

Flightless Bird Bar Harbour Road ☎031 388 8517. Kiwi-run establishment known to locals as the "Penguin Bar", there being no word for Kiwi in Vietnamese. In addition to fairly priced drinks, they also offer good pedicures – an odd combination, admittedly. Daily 7am–late.

★**Good Bar** 221 Harbour Road ☎031 388 8363. The most happening bar in town by a country mile; it gets pretty wild whenever there's a crowd. Staff serve strong cocktails, which you can enjoy over a game of pool, and play music suitable for dancing to. Daily 6pm–late.

DIRECTORY

Banks and exchange There's an ATM just 50 metres north of the hydrofoil jetty on the promenade, and another at the *Holiday View Hotel*, where there's also a bank to exchange cash.

Post office is on the harbour front, opposite the hydrofoil pier (daily 7am–noon & 1pm–6pm).

Cannon Fort

2km from Cat Ba Town • Sunrise to sunset • 50,000đ • You can ride a motorbike or take a xe om up the steep road to the top; look out for a sign at the top of Nui Ngoc St

There are amazing vistas from various points at the old hilltop **Cannon Fort**, built in 1942, even though it's only 177 metres high. Several remnants of the fort remain intact, including a helipad, two enormous anti-warship cannons with a 40km range (and statues of Vietnamese soldiers appearing to operate one of them), plus a few **underground tunnels** and bunkers. The best views are out to the east, gazing over limestone islands in the bay; at this viewpoint there's a telescope and a well-appointed café.

Quan Y Cave

8km from Cat Ba Town • 15,000đ

The main cross-island road climbs sharply out of Cat Ba Town, giving views over distant islands and glimpses of secluded coves, and then follows a series of high valleys. After 8km look out on the right for the distinctive **Quan Y Cave**, a gaping mouth embellished with concrete, not far from the road. During the American War the cave became an army hospital big enough to treat 150 patients at a time. You can walk through and look at the empty rooms, a large meeting hall and the site of a pool once used for hydrotherapy; there's another entrance on the other side of the hill.

Cat Ba National Park

16km from Cat Ba Town • 15,000đ • A xe om to the park headquarters should cost around 100,000đ one way

Taking up much of the island is **Cat Ba National Park**, established in 1986 and little changed in decades. Its most famous inhabitant is a sub-species of the critically endangered **golden-headed langur**, a monkey found only on Cat Ba and now probably numbering around sixty individuals. Considerably more visible will be the rich diversity of plant species, including some 350 of medicinal value, as well as birds, snakes and plenty of mosquitoes. Remember to take repellent, good boots, a hat and lots of water if you plan to do any **walks** in the park. A **compass** wouldn't come amiss either, as people have become seriously lost.

The short trek

There are two main **trails** through the park. The "**short trek**" (about 3hrs there and back) takes you to a viewpoint at the top of Ngu Lam peak. The path is easy enough to follow, but it's a steep climb, scrambling over tree roots and rocks in places, and extremely slippery in wet weather. Not everyone agrees that the views merit the effort.

The long trek

If you've got the time and energy, the "**long trek**" (about 6hr) is a rewarding experience. It involves a strenuous eighteen-kilometre hike via **Frog Lake** (Ao Ech), over a steep ridge for a classic view over countless **karst towers**, then dropping down to **Viet Hai village** where groups usually stop for lunch. From there it's about an hour's walk through lush scenery to the jetty, and then it's back to Cat Ba by boat through fjord-like **Lan Ha Bay** with a stop for swimming and snorkelling or kayaking through cave tunnels to find secret lagoons. The easiest way to tackle this walk is on an **organized tour** arranged by agents in Cat Ba.

Lan Ha Bay

Tours through agents in Cat Ba, including Asia Outdoors (see box, p.332)

One of the most rewarding ways to explore the area around Cat Ba Island is by boat, passing into the labyrinth of **Lan Ha Bay**, which is located to the northeast of Cat Ba town en route to Ha Long City. It's a miniature version of neighbouring Ha Long Bay but one which receives fewer visitors. A popular stop here is **Ho Ba Ham** (see p.340), a hidden lagoon only accessible at low tide. There are also fish farms and **oyster farms** in the area, which can be included in tour itineraries. Other options are **kayaking**, **rock-climbing** and visits to isolated **beaches** where the water is noticeably cleaner than elsewhere in the bay.

Ha Long City

Vietnam evidently has grand plans for **HA LONG CITY**. South-facing, and with **Ha Long Bay** raising its limestone fingers just across the sea, this place has great potential, but unfortunately development has been haphazard. The vast majority of Western tourists hitting the bay do so on the express service from Hanoi, seeing the city only on the short walk between bus and junk. However, tourists from Vietnam and China pack the place out during the busy season, and Ha Long City now boasts several huge resort-style hotels. Recent development has focused on **Tuan Chau Island**, just to the southwest, where a new tourist wharf was under construction at the time of writing, along with many new hotels and restaurants.

Ha Long City is an amalgam of easterly **Hong Gai** and westerly **Bai Chay**, two towns merged in 1994, and now lassoed together by a bridge. For the moment, locals still use the old names – as do ferry services, buses and so on – as a useful way to distinguish between the two areas, each with its own distinct character, lying either side of the narrow Cua Luc channel. The hub of tourist activity and accommodation is Bai Chay, a rather unattractive beach resort and the main departure point for boat tours. For those in search of more local colour, or who are put off by Bai Chay's overwhelming devotion to tourism, Hong Gai provides only basic tourist facilities but has a more bustling, workaday atmosphere.

Bai Chay

Neon signs and flashing fairy lights blaze out at night along the **BAI CHAY** waterfront, acting like a magnet to foreign visitors and advertising north Vietnam's most developed resort, with shoulder-to-shoulder hotels and a picturesque backdrop of wooded hills. While Bai Chay is swamped in summer with local holidaymakers and tourists from China, out of season it's a pretty sleepy place and decidedly less sleazy. Apart from strolling the seafront boulevard and taking a quick look at its very indifferent beach, Bai Chay has nothing to distract you from the main business of touring Ha Long Bay. If you're staying here, you can take a turn through the seafront **market**, a somewhat desultory array of stalls selling tourist tat.

Hong Gai

In contrast to Bai Chay, **HONG GAI** has a compelling, raw vitality plus an attractive harbour to the east, crowded with scurrying sampans. It's worth spending an hour or so wandering round the market and **Long Tien Pagoda**, which frequently hosts ceremonies in its small courtyard, offering fascinating glimpses into local rituals. The pagoda sits in the shadow of **Nui Bai Tho**, a limestone outcrop named after a collection of poems (*bai tho*) carved into the rock, that detail Ha Long Bay's beauty. The earliest of these poems was penned by King Le Thanh Tong in 1468.

TO CHINA VIA MONG CAI

Of the five border crossings between Vietnam and China open to foreigners, the one at **Mong Cai**, 130km northeast of Ha Long City along Highway 18, is probably the least used, as those at Lao Cai and Dong Dang have the advantage of rail connections on the Vietnamese side. To get to Mong Cai, take a bus from either My Dinh or Gia Lam bus station in Hanoi or from Ha Long City bus station in Bai Chay.

Those who make it to Mong Cai will find a fun little frontier town, whose streets are lined with signs for karaoke and massage parlours – an interesting start or finish line to a trip through Vietnam. It thrives on cross-border trade: Vietnamese tourists flock here to snap up cheap Chinese clothes, while the Chinese come for gambling and girls. You'll find no shortage of places to stay, though local restaurant menus tend to have Chinese, rather than English, as a second language.

The border (7am–7pm) is 1km from central Mong Cai, and just over the border is the small Chinese city of **Dongxiang**, which has bus connections to Nanning and Guangzhou.

Whichever way you're going, you'll need to have your **visa** organized in advance; the nearest Chinese embassy is in Hanoi and the nearest Vietnamese one in Nanning.

6

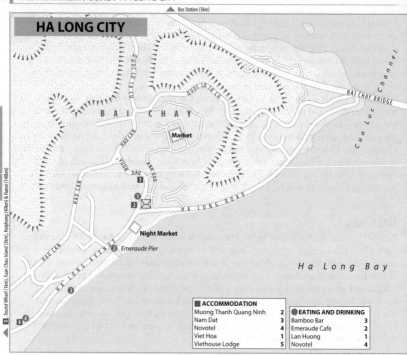

HA LONG CITY

BAI CHAY

Market

Night Market

Emeraude Pier

Ha Long Bay

Tourist Wharf (1km), Tuan Chau Island (3km), Haiphong (40km) & Hanoi (148km)

■ ACCOMMODATION		● EATING AND DRINKING	
Muong Thanh Quang Ninh	2	Bamboo Bar	3
Nam Dat	3	Emeraude Cafe	2
Novotel	4	Lan Huong	1
Viet Hoa	1	Novotel	4
Viethouse Lodge	5		

ARRIVAL AND GETTING AROUND   HA LONG CITY

Several **tourist wharfs** serve as junk-boat launchpads for the bay: one 2km west of Bai Chay, one just southeast of the bridge in Hong Gai, and another on Tuan Chau Island, to the southwest of Bai Chay. Most tourists arrive on tours directly **from Hanoi**, though it's also possible to begin Ha Long Bay cruises from Cat Ba.

By bus The bus station is 6km northwest of Bai Chay on Highway 18. It's around 100,000đ into central Bai Chay by taxi, 50,000đ by xe om; double that for Hong Gai.
Destinations Haiphong (1hr 30min); Hanoi (4hr) and Mong Cai (4hr).
By ferry Ben Tau pier is tucked away down a sidestreet in Hong Gai, from where boats go to Quan Lan Island in Bai Tu Long Bay (Mon–Fri 160,000đ; Sat & Sun 200,000đ).

There's also a passenger and vehicle ferry that crosses between Tuan Chau Island and Gia Luan port on the northern tip of Cat Ba Island (50,000đ).
Destinations Gia Luan, Cat Ba Island (about 6 daily; 1hr); Quan Lan Island (Mon–Fri 1 daily, Sat & Sun 2 daily; 1hr 30min).
Taxis Mai Linh Taxi ☎ 033 362 8628.

ACCOMMODATION

Despite a continuing increase in the number of hotels, especially in Bai Chay, there are still temporary room shortages during the Vietnamese summer season (June to early Sept) and holiday weekends; at other times, you'll be able to get good discounts. You'll find pretty much all of the more expensive places in **Bai Chay**, though there are several budget places on Vung Dao Street, and plenty more in **Hong Gai**. There's also a peaceful resort on **Tuan Chau**, an island just to the west of Ha Long City (linked to the mainland by a causeway). Note that most Westerners who stay here do so when their cruise around Ha Long Bay is cut short due to bad weather, so it's not a bad idea to have somewhere in mind before you get dumped at the tourist wharf.

BAI CHAY
Muong Thanh Quang Ninh Ha Long Rd ☎ 033 364 6618, ⓦ quangninh.muongthanh.vn. This 34-storey,

508-room mega-hotel is yet further proof that Muong Thanh is taking over Vietnam's hospitality industry, with classy hotels in almost every town. Rooms are fitted with

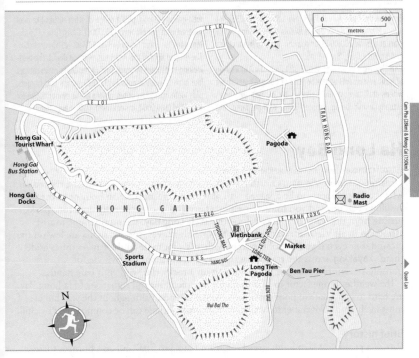

deep-pile carpets and luxurious furnishings, and facilities include a pool, fitness centre and tennis courts. Though they try hard, staff are not always on the ball. $\overline{\$150}$

★**Novotel** 160 Ha Long Rd ☏033 384 8108, ⓦnovotelhalong.com.vn. One of the most immaculately designed hotels in Vietnam – plush carpets lead to subtly lit and delicately scented rooms which are tastefully furnished and have great views from the upper floors. The infinity pool outside is another nice touch and the on-site restaurant serves excellent food. $\overline{\$175}$

Viet Hoa 35 Vuon Dao ☏033 384 6035. One of the better budget hotels on Vuon Dao, just 50 metres up the road from the seafront, this is a clean and welcoming place offering cheerful fan or a/c rooms. They're a decent size and all come with TVs and fridges as standard. $\overline{\$12}$

HONG GAI

Nam Dat 8 Doan Thi Diem ☏033 361 1358. If Bai Chay is too touristy for you, head across the bridge to this newish hotel in the heart of workaday Hong Gai. Carpeted rooms are a good size, with flatscreen TVs and great en-suite facilities. $\overline{\$20}$

TUAN CHAU

Viethouse Lodge Tuan Chau Island ☏033 384 2207, ⓦviethouselodge.com. Owned by a friendly German–Vietnamese couple, this cabin-style hotel is a great place to get away from it all and immerse yourself in a world of bamboo, lanterns, crackling stoves and serene gardens. The stilthouse timbers are over one hundred years old, and were from a Red Dao village in the northern mountains. They whip up tremendous food, too, and run bespoke tours of the area. $\overline{\$50}$

EATING AND DRINKING

Fresh **seafood** is the natural speciality of Ha Long Bay, with excellent lobster, crab and freshly caught fish on offer. However, most dining venues in Bai Chay are remarkably uninspiring, in contrast to cruise boats in the bay, on which dinner is generally a memorable event.

BAI CHAY

Bamboo Bar C 25/1 Royal Park, Ha Long Rd ☏033 364 0899. Good-looking bar that can be hit or miss of an evening, though even when it's a miss in terms of clientele,

you can enjoy beers at 40,0000đ each, cocktails at 80,000–100,000đ as well as a good range of Western and Vietnamese cuisine, and the company of friendly, chatty staff. Daily 7am–3am.

Emeraude Cafe Royal Park, Ha Long Rd ☎ 033 384 9266. Pizzas and pasta dishes in this posh-looking venue start at around 200,000đ, or you can just pop in for coffee and a pastry. Daily 8am–9pm.

Lan Huong 1 Vuon Dao ☎ 033 384 7819. First of a string of basic restaurants at the bottom of budget hotel street where staff almost drag passers-by in, but this one's actually worth being dragged into. Well-prepared and well-priced seafood, plus a range of other dishes like beef sautéed with mushrooms (120,000đ). Daily 7am–10pm.

Novotel Ha Long Rd ☎ 033 384 8108, ⓦ novotel.com. The ground floor of this hotel has, without doubt, the best-looking restaurant in town. Lots of tempting main courses like braised lamb shanks (449,000đ), wraps and burgers, plus Vietnamese favourites, or join in the dinner buffet for 420,000đ (580,000đ at weekends). Daily 6am–10pm.

Ha Long Bay

150,000đ (200,000đ if overnight), usually included in tour prices

Drifting out from Vietnam's north coast in a wooden junk, your eyes will be riveted on what, at first, appears to be a jagged wall of emerald green. After an hour or so the wall swallows you up, and you find yourself in a fairyland of otherworldly limestone peaks, jutting from the water at sheer angles – this is **Ha Long Bay**, the number one tourist attraction in all Vietnam. Bar a clutch of impressive **caves**, specific sights are few on the ground, but even if you tire of the scenery there's a lot to do in the bay – cruises aside, there's **kayaking** across the tranquil waters, **swimming** amid the twinkles of phosphorescent plankton, or even **climbing** up a rocky cliff with your bare hands.

The **weather** is one factor to bear in mind: the splendour and romance of Ha Long Bay are hard to appreciate in poor conditions, which can occur throughout the year but are most likely from November to March – when winter drizzle can be compounded by chill.

Brief history

Part of a geological formation stretching from China to Thailand and Borneo, these limestone karst towers are by no means unique, but nowhere else are they found on such an impressive scale: an estimated 1969 islands pepper Ha Long Bay itself, with a further two thousand punctuating the coast towards China. Local legend tells of a **celestial dragon** and her children, sent by the Jade Emperor to stop an invasion, which spat out great quantities of pearls to form islands and razor-sharp mountain chains in the path of the enemy fleet. After the victory the dragons, enchanted by their creation, decided to stay on, giving rise to the name *Ha Long* ("dragon descending"), and the inevitable claimed sightings of sea monsters.

In 1469, King Le Thanh Tong paid a visit to Ha Long Bay and was so inspired by the scenery that he wrote a poem, likening the islands to pieces on a chessboard; ever since, visitors have struggled to capture the mystery of this fantasy world. Nineteenth-century Europeans compared the islands to Tuscan cathedrals, while a local tourist brochure opts for meditative "grey-haired fairies". With so much hyperbole, some find Ha Long disappointing, especially since this stretch of coast is also one of Vietnam's more **industrialized** regions – a major shipping lane cuts right across the bay. The huge influx of tourism has, of course, added to the problem, not least the litter and pollution from fume-spluttering boats, but a sizeable proportion of tourist income does at least benefit the local communities.

The caves

50,000đ per cave, usually included in tour prices

Organized tours to Ha Long Bay always include visits to one or more **caves**, which constitute the only actual sights in the area. Visually impressive though they are, busy days can see them rammed with tourists, which can detract from their majesty, as can the tour guides' endless comparison of particular rock formations to animals or Buddhist deities.

6

TOURS OF HA LONG BAY

Every Hanoi tour agent offers **Ha Long Bay excursions**, travelling by road to Ha Long City, on the bay's northern shore, then transferring to cruise the bay on a replica wooden junk; these work out far easier – and almost invariably cheaper – than doing the same thing yourself. There are a wide variety of trips available, including **day-tours**, though since the bay is an 8hr round trip from Hanoi these can feel very rushed. Most opt for a **two-day**, **one-night** tour, with the night spent at sea – this can be a delightful experience. However, this still means that you only spend one afternoon and one morning on the bay, so if you can spare the time, opt for a **three-day**, **two-night** trip, which allows you at least one full day in the bay. The **cost** depends on what kind of junk you board, which may be anything from a $500 single-cabin honeymoon cruiser serving gourmet cuisine, to a budget boat with $20 dorm-style beds and basic grub.

TOUR OPERATORS

Competition between tour operators is incredibly fierce, and you can get an overnight trip for as low as $20. However, at this price you're taking risks which may sour your appreciation of the bay: vessels can be dirty, have poor facilities or be horribly overcrowded – it's always best to ask operators if they have a **maximum group size** (sixteen is the usual upper limit), though such promises are often broken. Some junks are also simply unsafe, though regulations have been tightened up since a boat went down in early 2011, killing eleven tourists and their local guide. It is also not unusual for tours to be cut short due to bad weather; note that if your trip is cancelled completely, you are entitled to a **full refund** under Vietnamese law.

Compounding the confusion, few operators have their own vessels – travellers tend to be shunted onto whichever junk has room and you may find yourself sharing a vessel with people who have paid far more or less for the same thing. It's impossible to give concrete recommendations for budget tour operators, but the following make good mid-range and luxury choices.

Buffalo Tours ☎ 04 3828 0702, ✆ buffalotours.com. Impeccable tours of both Ha Long and Bai Tu Long Bay on a range of luxurious junks. In late 2014 the company began combined seaplane and junk tours, offering an aerial perspective of the bay. The seafood is delectable, the wine list none too shabby and kayaking is included in the cost of the trip. Starts at $300 per person for a 2-day, 1-night trip; add $400 for the 25-minute flight over the bay.

Emeraude ☎ 04 3934 0888, ✆ emeraude-cruises .com. A replica of a nineteenth-century paddle-steamer, the five-star *Emeraude* is one of the most luxurious vessels on the bay. Facilities include a restaurant, two bars, beauty salon and massage rooms and spacious sundecks where you can indulge in sunrise tai chi classes. From $200 per person for a 2-day tour.

Ethnic Travel ☎ 04 3926 1951, ✆ ethnictravel.com .vn. This outfit prides itself on low-impact tours, and has a superb reputation. Some tours head to lesser-visited Bai Tu Long Bay; a three-day trip goes from $169 per person (2–9 people).

Hanoi Backpackers (see p.372). This hostel runs 3 day, 2 night trips that involve kayaking and swimming, and a lot of alcohol, for $220 per person.

Indochina Junk ☎ 04 3926 4085, ✆ indochina -junk.com. One of the most reliable outfits offering a variety of tours, with highly capable staff. The 3-day, 2-night tour of Bai Tu Long Bay (around $300 per person) is highly recommended, and features a candle-lit dinner in a cave.

Kangaroo Café ☎ 04 3828 9931, ✆ kangaroocafe .com. This Aussie-owned outfit refuses to cut corners, and deserves its great reputation. In addition, the on-board meals are nothing short of superb. Two-day from $109 per person, three-day from $159.

DIY TOURS FROM HA LONG CITY

Most foreigners visit the bay on tours from Hanoi, but it's just about possible to do the same thing independently, though you won't save much money. First of all you have to get to Ha Long City (see p.334), then head to the Bai Chay tourist wharf, 2km west of town along Ha Long Road. From one booth here it's possible to take one of several **day-trips**, costing $10–20 per person and taking either 4, 6 or 8hrs. However, these boats can get rather crowded and are not really recommended; you'll also need to buy an **entry ticket** for the bay (150,000₫), as well as tickets to the caves (50,000₫).

Better yet, head for the **Ben Tau jetty** in Hong Gai and hop on the boat to Quan Lan Island in Bai Tu Long Bay (see p.340), then after a night or two on the island, take another ferry to Cai Rong on the mainland, which follows a different route. In this way you'll enjoy several hours of superb views (if you're lucky with the weather) and without the big price tag.

6

Hang Dau Go

The bay's most famous cave is also the closest to Bai Chay, and therefore a favourite for day-trippers. **Hang Dau Go** – or the "Grotto of the Wooden Stakes" – is where General Tran Hung Dao amassed hundreds of stakes deep inside the cave's third and largest chamber before the Bach Dang River battle of 1288 (see box, p.328). These are now long gone, but at the entrance to the cave keep an eye out for a stone stele with Chinese inscriptions – this was a paean written about the cave by King Khai Dinh, who visited in 1929.

Hang Thien Cung

On the same island as Hang Dau Go, a steep climb to the "Grotto of the Heavenly Palace" is rewarded by a rectangular chamber 250m long and 20m high, with a textbook display of sparkling stalactites and stalagmites – supposedly petrified characters of the Taoist Heavenly Court.

Hang Sung Sot and around

The most visited of all the caves in the bay, and featuring on almost all one- and two-day itineraries, is **Hang Sung Sot**, or the "Surprise Cave". Inside its three echoing chambers, spotlights pick out the more interesting rock formations, including a "Happy Buddha" and rather surprising pink phallus. At the top you come out onto a belvedere with good views over the flotilla of junks below and sampans hawking souvenirs and soft drinks. Also in this area is **Ho Dong Tien** ("Grotto of the Fairy Lake") and **Dong Me Cung** ("Grotto of the Labyrinth") where, in 1993, ancient fossilized human remains were found; sadly, these only figure on a few tours.

Ho Ba Ham

Dau Be Island, on the southeastern edge of Ha Long Bay, encloses **Ho Ba Ham** ("Three Tunnel Lake"), a shallow lagoon wrapped round with limestone walls and connected to the sea by three low-ceilinged tunnels that are only navigable by sampan or kayak at low tide. This cave is sometimes included in day-trips out of Bai Chay but is most easily visited from Cat Ba and more commonly crops up on trips involving a stay on the island.

Bai Tu Long Bay

East of Ha Long Bay, stretching up towards the Chinese border, lies an attractive area of islands, known as **Bai Tu Long** or "Children of the Dragon". Some of the larger islands feature important forest reserves and are home to a number of rare species, such as the pale-capped pigeon, while dugong (sea cows) inhabit the surrounding waters. In 2001, **Bai Tu Long National Park** was created to protect 15,700 hectares of marine and island habitat. As Ha Long Bay begins to suffer from huge numbers of visitors, more and more tour companies are offering tours to this quieter, but equally impressive, bay. The only downside is that there are few caves to visit and it's more remote, so boats need to use more fuel, but most visitors are happy with this trade-off for a more tranquil experience.

Quan Lan Island

Though there are few specific sights in the area, the odd intrepid tourist heads as far as **Quan Lan Island**, a long skinny strip of land on the outer fringes of the bay. Although there has been much talk of developing the larger islands in Bai Tu Long as eco-tourism destinations, until now Quan Lan retains a welcome "away-from-it-all" vibe.

The island's main attractions are the empty, sandy and relatively clean beaches fringing its east coast; the most attractive is **Minh Chau Beach** on the northeast coast.

A cycle ride makes a pleasant jaunt through rice paddies and over the dunes to the north tip. Otherwise, there's not much to do apart from enjoying simply being off the tourist trail – prepare to find yourself engaging even more closely with locals than you're used to. Take whatever cash you need as there is **no ATM** on the island.

ARRIVAL AND DEPARTURE

QUAN LAN ISLAND

By boat Boats leave from Ben Tau pier on the Hong Gai side of Ha Long City, arriving at Quan Lan pier at the south end of the island (160,000đ). There are also ferries to and from Cai Rong on the mainland (60,000–150,000đ), which can be reached by bus from Ha Long City or Hanoi.
Destinations Cai Rong fast boat (4 daily; 45min); Cai Rong slow boat (1 daily; 2hr); Ha Long City (Mon–Fri 1 daily, Sat & Sun 2 daily; 1hr 30min).
Tours Ethnic Travel in Ha Long City (☎04 3926 1951, ⓦethnictravel.com.vn) offers three-day, two-night cruises that overnight on Quan Lan Island.

GETTING AROUND

Xe om There are plenty of xe om and xe may (three-wheeler motorbike taxis) that wait at Quan Lan pier, on the island's southern tip, to take people 3km north to the main village (about 50,000đ).

ACCOMMODATION

Be warned that **power cuts** are frequent, so take a torch and look for a room where you can open a window and catch the breeze when the air-con shuts down. Rates are higher at weekends when domestic tourists arrive.

Ann Hotel At the junction in town ☎033 387 7889, ⓦannhotel.com.vn. Probably the most switched-on of Quan Lan's few laidback hotels. Staff speak English and can help with onward travel, rooms are big and bright, and some have sea-facing balconies. There's a decent restaurant too, and motorbikes and bikes for rent. **$35**

Ngan Ha Hotel Opposite the post office ☎033 387 7296, ⓦquanlanisland.vn. Cheap and friendly, this is the budget place of choice for most travellers. Rooms are simple but perfectly adequate, while the meals are about as good as you'll get in the village. Bike rental also available. **$15**

Hanoi and around

MORNING EXERCISE, HOAN KIEM LAKE

Hanoi and around

Often dubbed "the most Asian city in Asia", Hanoi provides a full-scale assault on the senses. Its mustard-hued colonial architecture is a feast for the eyes; swarms of buzzing motorbikes invade the ear, while the delicate scents and tastes of delicious street food can be found all across a city that – unlike so many of its regional contemporaries – is managing to modernize with a degree of grace. The city's name means "on a bend in the river", a reference to the Red River that flows through it, and it is the fertility of the Red River Delta that has enabled Hanoi to sustain a large population for over a thousand years. Despite the incessant noise drummed up by a population of around seven million, Hanoi exudes an appeal that is both intimate and urbane. It endears itself to most visitors with its unique attractions, which include the bustling Old Quarter, tranquil Hoan Kiem Lake, atmospheric French Quarter and several museums that bring Vietnam's turbulent history to life.

7

While retaining a sense of importance of its historic heritage, Hanoi has changed almost beyond recognition in the last two decades. It now boasts glitzy megamalls and wine warehouses; spas attract a well-heeled clientele and some seriously expensive cars cruise the streets, though most people zip around on motorbikes (rather than the totally untrendy bicycle). The authorities are trying – with mixed success – to curb traffic anarchy and regulate unsympathetic building projects in the Old Quarter, coupled with an ambitious new metro system that aims to ease traffic congestion. With plenty of money about, wealthy Hanoians are prepared to flaunt it in the sophisticated restaurants, cafés and designer boutiques that have exploded all over the city. Nevertheless, the centre has not completely lost its old-world charm nor its distinctive character.

While Hanoi itself could easily eat up a week of your time, exploring quirky sights like the **Ho Chi Minh Mausoleum** and **Museum of Ethnology**, there are also several **out-of-town destinations** that make for a good day out. Most popular among these is the **Perfume Pagoda**, with its spectacular setting among limestone hills, though other pagodas and crafts villages also offer the chance to glimpse scenes of everyday life in rural Vietnam.

The **best time to visit** Hanoi is during the three months from October to December, when you'll find warm, sunny days and levels of humidity below the norm of eighty percent, though it can be chilly at night. From January to March, cold winds from China combine with high humidity to give a fine mist, which often hangs in the air for

PHO BO

Highlights

❶ The Old Quarter Wander through the intoxicating tangle of streets that make up Hanoi's commercial heart. **See p.352**

❷ The Opera House Check out this stately signature-piece of French colonial architecture, modelled on the one in Paris. **See p.357**

❸ Ho Chi Minh's Mausoleum The ghostly figure of "Uncle Ho", embalmed against his wishes, remains a strangely moving sight. **See p.360**

❹ Temple of Literature Vietnam's foremost Confucian sanctuary and centre of learning provides a haven of green lawns amid the hubbub of Hanoi. **See p.363**

❺ Museum of Ethnology Discover the staggering variety and creativity of Vietnam's ethnic minorities. **See p.367**

❻ Pho bo Join the locals and slurp on Hanoi's traditional beef-and-noodle breakfast soup. **See box, p.377**

❼ Bia hoi bars As night falls parties gather for a few refreshing jars of the local brew. **See box, p.380**

❽ Water puppets Vietnam's quirky but charming art form developed in the floodlands of the Red River Delta. **See p.381**

HIGHLIGHTS ARE MARKED ON THE MAP ON PP.348–349

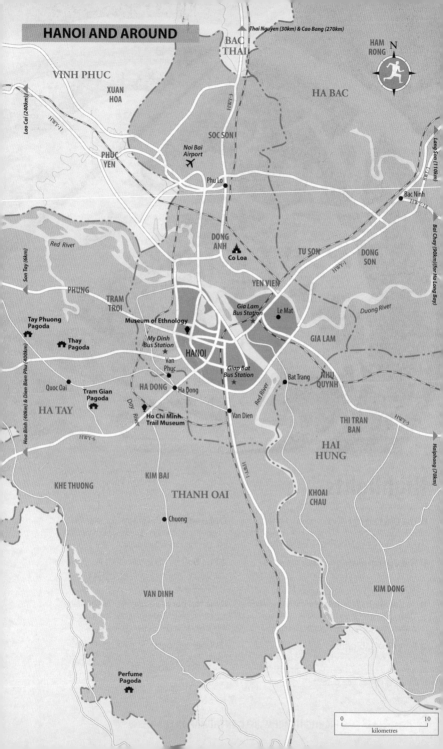

days. March and April usually bring better weather, before the extreme summer heat arrives in late April, accompanied by monsoon storms which peak in August and can last until early October, causing serious flooding throughout the delta.

Brief history

When Tang Chinese armies invaded Vietnam in the seventh century, they chose a small **Red River fort** as capital of their new protectorate, named, optimistically, *Annam*, the "Pacified South". Three centuries later the rebellious Vietnamese ousted the Chinese, in 939 AD. After that, the citadel lay abandoned until 1010 when **King Ly Thai To**, usually credited as Hanoi's founding father, recognized the site's potential and established his own court beside the Red River. It seems the omens were on his side for, according to legend, when the king stepped from his royal barge onto the riverbank a golden dragon flew up towards the heavens. From then on **Thang Long**, "City of the Ascending Dragon", was destined to be the nation's capital, with only minor interruptions, for the next eight hundred years.

Growth of the city

Ly Thai To and his successors set about creating a city fit for "ten thousand generations of kings", choosing auspicious locations for their temples and palaces according to the laws of **geomancy**. They built protective dykes, established a town of artisans and merchants alongside the **Imperial City**'s eastern wall, and set up the nation's first university, in the process laying the foundations of modern Hanoi. From 1407, the country was again under Chinese occupation, but this time only briefly before the great hero **Le Loi** retook the capital in 1428. The Le Dynasty kings drained lakes and marshes to accommodate their new palaces as well as a growing civilian population, and towards the end of the fifteenth century Thang Long was enjoying a **golden era** under the great reformer, King Le Thanh Thong. Shortly after his death in 1497, however, the country dissolved into anarchy, while the city slowly declined until finally Emperor Gia Long moved the royal court to Hue in 1802.

International intervention

By the 1830s Thang Long had been relegated to a provincial capital re-named **Hanoi**, and in 1882 its reduced defences offered little resistance to **attacking French forces**, led by Captain Rivière. Initially capital of the French Protectorate of Tonkin, a name derived from *Dong Kinh*, meaning "Eastern Capital", after 1887 Hanoi became the centre of government for the entire Union of Indochina. Royal palaces and ancient monuments made way for grand residences, administrative offices, tree-lined boulevards and all the trappings of a **colonial city**, more European than Asian. However, the Vietnamese community lived a largely separate, often impoverished existence, creating a seedbed of insurrection.

7

HANOI ORIENTATION

Hanoi city centre comprises an area known as **Hoan Kiem District**, which is neatly bordered by the Red River embankment in the east and the rail line to the north and west, while its southern extent is marked by the roads Nguyen Du, Le Van Huu and Han Thuyen. The district takes its name from its present-day hub and most obvious point of reference, **Hoan Kiem Lake**, and includes the narrow lanes of the endlessly diverting **Old Quarter** in the north, and the tree-lined boulevards of the **French Quarter**, arranged in a rough grid system, to the south. West of this central district, across the rail tracks, some of Hanoi's most impressive monuments occupy the wide open spaces around the **Hanoi Citadel**, including **Ho Chi Minh's Mausoleum** in Ba Dinh Square and the ancient walled gardens of the **Temple of Literature**. A vast body of water called **West Lake** sits to the northwest of the city, harbouring a number of interesting temples and pagodas, but the attractive villages that once surrounded it have now largely given way to upmarket residential areas and luxury hotels.

7

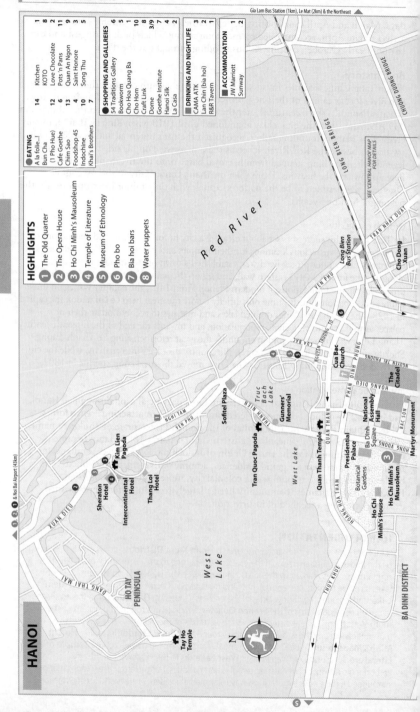

HANOI

HIGHLIGHTS

1. The Old Quarter
2. The Opera House
3. Ho Chi Minh's Mausoleum
4. Temple of Literature
5. Museum of Ethnology
6. Pho bo
7. Bia hoi bars
8. Water puppets

● EATING

A la folie...!	1	Kitchen	1
Bun Cha	8	KOTO	8
(1 Pho Hue)		Love Chocolate	11
Cafe Goethe	12	Pots 'n Pans	6
Chim Sao	6	Quan An Ngon	9
Foodshop 45	13	Saint Honore	3
Indochine	4	Song Thu	5
Khai's Brothers	10		7

■ SHOPPING AND GALLERIES

54 Traditions Gallery	6
Bookworm	5
Cho Hoa Quang Ba	1
Cho Hom	10
Craft Link	8
Dome	3/9
Goethe Institute	7
Hanoi Silk	4
La Casa	2

■ DRINKING AND NIGHTLIFE

CAMA ATK	3
Lan Chin (bia hoi)	2
R&R Tavern	1

■ ACCOMMODATION

| JW Marriott | 1 |
| Sunway | 2 |

Gia Lam Bus Station (1km), Le Mat (2km) & the Northeast

Red River

Long Bien Bus Station

Cho Dong Xuan

LONG BIEN BRIDGE

CHUONG DUONG BRIDGE

SEE CENTRAL HANOI MAP FOR DETAILS

TRAN NHAT DUAT

YEN PHU

CUA BAC

NGUYEN TRUONG TO

Cua Bac Church

PHAN DINH PHUNG

The Citadel

HOANG DIEU

NGUYEN TRI PHUONG

BAC SON

HUNG VUONG

Martyr Monument

National Assembly Hall

Ba Dinh Square

Ho Chi Minh's Mausoleum

Ho Chi Minh's House

Botanical Gardens

Presidential Palace

HOANG HOA THAM

THUY KHUE

BA DINH DISTRICT

Quan Thanh Temple

QUAN THANH

Gunners' Memorial

Truc Bach Lake

Tran Quoc Pagoda

THANH NIEN

NGHI TAM

YEN PHU

Sofitel Plaza

West Lake

Sheraton Hotel

Intercontinental Hotel

Thang Loi Hotel

Kim Lien Pagoda

XUAN DIEU

DANG THAI MAI

HO TAY PENINSULA

Tay Ho Temple

West Lake

◄ ❷ ❶ ① & Noi Bai Airport (43km)

N

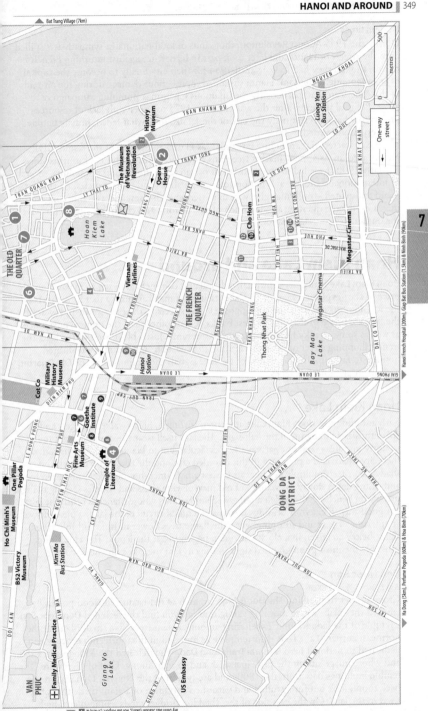

7

▲ Bat Trang Village (7km)

Hanoi French Hospital (200m), Giap Bat Bus Station (1.5km) & Ninh Binh (90km)

Ho Dong (5km), Perfume Pagoda (60km) & Hoa Binh (70km)

My Dinh Bus Station (8km), Noi Bai Airport (37km) & ➊

One-way street

0   500   metres

THE OLD QUARTER

THE FRENCH QUARTER

History Museum

The Museum of Vietnamese Revolution

Opera House

Hoan Kiem Lake

Vietnam Airlines

Hanoi Station

Cho Hom

Megastar Cinema

Megastar Cinema

Thong Nhat Park

Bay Mau Lake

DONG DA DISTRICT

Military History Museum

Cot Co

One Pillar Pagoda

Ho Chi Minh's Museum

B52 Victory Museum

Kim Ma Bus Station

Family Medical Practice

VAN PHUC

Giang Vo Lake

US Embassy

Fine-Arts Museum

Goethe Institute

Temple of Literature

Luong Yen Bus Station

TRAN KHANH DU

TRAN QUANG KHAI

LY THAI TO

LE THANH TONG

TRANG TIEN

HANG BAI

BA TRIEU

PHO HUE

NGO QUYEN

LY THUONG KIET

HAI BA TRUNG

TRAN HUNG DAO

NGUYEN DU

TRAN NHAN TONG

LE DUAN

LE DUAN

GIAI PHONG

DAI CO VIET

NGUYEN KHOAI

LO DUC

TRAN KHAT CHAN

LO DUC

HOA MA

TUE TINH

MAC DINH

NGUYEN CONG TRU

BA TRIEU

TON DUC THANG

KHAM THIEN

DE LA THANH

XA DAN

TON DUC THANG

NGO HAO NAM

DE LA THANH

LE THANH

THAI HA

TAY SON

NGUYEN THAI HOC

TON DUC THANG

CAT LINH

GIANG VO

KIM MA

GIANG VO

DOI CAN

KIM MA

LE HONG PHONG

TRAN PHU

DIEN BIEN PHU

LY NAM DE

TRAN QUY CAP

HOC MON

XA DAN

BAC NGHE THANH

Modern times

During the 1945 **August Revolution**, thousands of local nationalist sympathizers spilled onto the streets of Hanoi and later took part in its defence against returning French troops, though they had to wait until 1954 for their city finally to become the **capital of an independent Vietnam**. Hanoi sustained more serious damage during the air raids of the American War, particularly the infamous Christmas Bombing campaign of 1972. Political isolation after the war ended in 1975 together with lack of resources preserved what was essentially the city of the 1950s, somewhat faded, heavily battered and very overcrowded.

These characteristics are fading fast today, as Hanoi enjoys one of the fastest GDP growth rates in Asia. New market freedoms combined with an influx of tourists since the early 1990s have led to an explosion of privately run hotels and restaurants, several of international standard, and in boutiques, craft shops and tour agencies. As ancient – and antiquated – buildings give way to glittering high-rises, and as traffic congestion increases, the big question is how much of this historic and charming city will survive the onslaught of modernization.

Hoan Kiem Lake and around

Hoan Kiem Lake is the city's spiritual, cultural and commercial heart, so makes a good place to start exploring Hanoi. The lake itself has a magical quality that fully deserves the legend of its naming (see box opposite). The streets to the east, south and west of the lake are home to the city's biggest banks, airline offices and the **general post office**, as well as some swanky hotels and stylish restaurants. Just a block west of the lake, the trendy shopping street of Nha Tho leading to **St Joseph's Cathedral** is a dedicated homage to fashion. The north end of the lake signals the beginning of the **Old Quarter**, with its maze of narrow lanes.

Hoan Kiem Lake

Early morning sees **Hoan Kiem Lake** at its best, stirring to life as walkers, joggers and tai chi enthusiasts limber up in the half-light. The lake itself is small – you can walk round it in thirty minutes – and not particularly spectacular, but to Hanoians this is the soul of their city. Space is at a premium in this crowded city, and the lake's strip of park and shady trees meets multiple needs, at its busiest when lunch-hour hawkers are out in force, and easing down slowly to evenings of old men playing chess and couples seeking twilight privacy on benches half-hidden among weeping willows whose branches brush the lake.

A good way to get your bearings is to make a quick **circuit of the lake**, a pleasant walk at any time of year and stunning when the flame trees flower in June and July. The sights below are given in a clockwise order, beginning at the iconic The Huc Bridge (possibly the most photographed sight in the city), at the lake's northeast corner.

Den Ngoc Son

Daily 7.30am–5.30pm • 20,000đ

Crossing over the striking **The Huc Bridge**, an arch of red-lacquered wood poetically labelled the "place where morning sunlight rests", you find the secluded **Den Ngoc Son**, "Temple of the Jade Mound", sheltering among ancient trees on a small island at the northeast corner of the lake. This temple was founded in the fourteenth century and is dedicated to national hero **General Tran Hung Dao**, who defeated the Mongols in 1288, and whose image sits on the principal altar, and to Van Xuong, God of Literature. The temple buildings date from the 1800s and are typical of the Nguyen Dynasty; in the back room, look out for a stuffed and varnished specimen of a giant turtle that once lived in the lake. On the east side of the The Huc Bridge stands a nine-metre-high

A LEGEND COMES TO LIFE

Hoan Kiem, which means "Lake of the Restored Sword", refers to a **legend** of the great Vietnamese hero, Le Loi, who led a successful uprising against the Chinese in the fifteenth century. The story goes that while out fishing in a sampan on the lake, then known as Luc Thuy, Le Loi netted a gleaming sword, which helped him to defeat the Chinese in battle. When he returned to the lake years later as King Ly Thai To, a **golden turtle** surfaced, took the sword and disappeared with it. The king believed that the turtle had been sent by the gods to reclaim the weapon, and he renamed the lake accordingly.

The legend is not mere fantasy, as the lake is still home to one hardy giant turtle, but it is thought to be the last remaining specimen here. It was captured and examined in early 2011 when wounds on its leg and head were identified, though it still managed to elude captors twice before being netted. Its wounds were thought to be caused by the sharp edges of debris in the lake. It is an extremely rare species of enormous, **soft-shelled turtle** known as *rafetus swinhoei*, of which there are only a few other specimens remaining in Vietnam and China, so it is sadly destined for extinction. This one weighed in at around 170kg and measured about 1.8 metres in length. Scientists estimate its age at around 80–100 years, but of course Hanoians believe it is one and the same creature that took Ly Thai To's sword over five hundred years ago. Though you're unlikely to spot this last turtle, you can get an idea of their enormous size at Den Ngoc Son (see opposite), where a preserved turtle is on display.

obelisk, the **Ink Brush Tower**, on which three outsized Chinese characters proclaim "a pen to write on the blue sky".

Statue of King Ly Thai To

On the eastern side of the lake stands an imperious statue of Hanoi's founding father, **King Ly Thai To**, which was erected in 2004 in anticipation of celebrations to mark the city's millennium in 2010. At dusk, the expanse of polished stone paving around it provides an incongruous venue for Hanoi's small but enthusiastic band of roller bladers.

The Turtle Tower

A squat, three-tiered pavilion known as **Thap Rua**, or the **Turtle Tower**, ornaments a tiny island at the southern end of Ho Hoan Kiem. It's illuminated after dark, and is another of Hanoi's most prevalent icons, with its reflection shimmering in the lake. It was built in the nineteenth century to commemorate the legend of the golden turtle and the restored sword, but is not accessible to the public.

The General Post Office

At the southeast corner of the lake stands the enormous **General Post Office**, which marks the northern fringe of the French Quarter. Opposite the post office, on the shore of the lake, stands a small and ancient brick tower. This is all that remains of an enormous **pagoda complex**, Chua Bao An, after French town planners cleared the site in 1892 to construct the administrative offices and residences of their new possession.

St Joseph's Cathedral

Nha Tho • Daily 5–11.30am & 2–7.30pm • Free • Service times at ⓦ saintjosephcathedral.org

Just a block west of Hoan Kiem Lake stands **St Joseph's Cathedral**, one of Hanoi's most iconic buildings. Its solemn façade makes a stark contrast to the colourful boutiques and cafés that line fashionable Nha Tho ("Big Church") street in front of it. The cathedral was constructed in the early 1880s, partly financed by two lotteries, and though the exterior is badly weathered, its high-vaulted interior is still imposing. Among the first things you notice inside are the ornate altar screen and the stained-glass windows, most of which are French originals. Over the black marble tomb of a former cardinal of Vietnam is one of several statues commemorating martyred

Vietnamese saints, in this case André Dung Lac, who was executed in 1839 on the orders of the fervently anti-Christian emperor Minh Mang.

The cathedral's main door is open during services; at other times walk round to the small door in the southwest corner.

Chua Ba Da
3 Nha Tho

Hidden down a narrow alley at the eastern end of Nha Tho Street, **Chua Ba Da**, or the Stone Lady Pagoda, makes a delightful contrast to the grandeur of St Joseph's Cathedral. A temple has stood on this site for a thousand years but it acquired its current name when a stone statue of a woman was discovered during reconstruction in the fifteenth century. These days it is the headquarters of the Municipal Buddhist Association. A recent restoration has left the pagoda in fine shape, and a wander through its halls lined with Buddha images can be a serene experience. It's not visible from the street; look for a narrow alley and sign beside number 3 Nha Tho.

The Old Quarter

North of Hoan Kiem Lake are the tumultuous streets of the **Old Quarter**, also known as **"the 36 Streets"**, after the guilds which once operated here, though there are many more than 36 streets these days. It occupies a congested square kilometre that was closed behind massive ramparts and heavy wooden gates until well into the nineteenth century. Apart from one **gate**, at the east end of Hang Chieu, the walls have been dismantled, though the crowded enclave still has a distinctive character. To explore it, the best approach is simply to dive into the maze of twisted lanes and wander at will, equipped with a map to find your way out again. Alternatively, you might like to see it first from the seat of a cyclo or one of the electric cars that zigzag through (see box, p.369), to help you pinpoint places you'd like to come back to.

Everything spills out onto pavements which double as workshops for stone-carvers, furniture-makers and tinsmiths, and as display space for merchandise ranging from pungent therapeutic herbs and fluttering prayer flags to ranks of Remy Martin and shiny-wrapped chocolates. With so much to attract your attention at ground level, it's easy to miss the **architecture**, which reveals fascinating glimpses of the quarter's history, starting with the fifteenth-century merchants' houses otherwise found only in Hoi An (see p.247). As you explore the quarter you'll come across some sacred sites – temples, pagodas, *dinh* and venerable banyan trees – tucked away between the houses.

OLD QUARTER ARCHITECTURE

A **dinh** is a kind of communal house that can be found all over Vietnam, but the Old Quarter is peppered with them. They often look like temples, and indeed they operate as places of worship with altars and urns to hold incense. However, they also serve as administrative centres and as training centres for the various guilds, which is why there are so many in the Old Quarter. Another use is as a meeting place for local communities, and some are open to the public, such as **Dinh Kim Ngan** on Hang Bac, while others only open on special occasions.

The most distinctive type of buildings in the Old Quarter, however, are the aptly named **tube-houses**, which evolved from market stalls into narrow single-storey shops, windows no higher than a passing royal palanquin, under gently curving, red-tiled roofs. The moniker comes from their narrow facades (some are just two metres wide), the result of **taxes** levied on street frontages, and deep interiors, which accommodate a succession of storerooms and living quarters up to 60m in length, interspersed with open courtyards to give them light and air. As royal palanquins no longer pass through the Old Quarter, many owners have now added several stories, giving rise to a new architectural term – **rocket houses**.

WHAT'S IN A NAME?

The Old Quarter's **street names** date back five centuries to when the area was divided among 36 artisans' guilds, each gathered around a temple or a *dinh* dedicated to the guild's patron spirit. Even today many streets specialize to some degree, and a few, such as **Hang Bac** ("Silver Street"), are still dedicated to the original craft or its modern equivalent. The most colourful examples are **Hang Quat**, full of bright-red banners and lacquerware for funerals and festivals, and **Hang Ma**, where paper products have been made for at least five hundred years. Nowadays gaudy tinsel dances in the breeze above brightly coloured votive objects, which include model TVs, dollars and cars to be offered to the ancestors. A selection of the more interesting streets with an element of specialization is listed below. Note that *hang* means "merchandise", not "street".

STREET NAME	MEANING	MODERN SPECIALITY
Hang Trong	Drum skin	Bag menders, upholsterers
Hang Bo	Bamboo baskets	Haberdashers
Hang Buom	Sails	Imported foods and alcohol, confectionery
Hang Chieu	Sedge mats	Mats, ropes, bamboo blinds
Hang Dau	Oil	Shoes
Hang Dieu	Pipes	Cushions, mattresses
Hang Duong	Sugar	Clothes, general goods
Hang Gai	Hemp goods	Silks, tailors, souvenirs
Hang Hom	Wooden chests	Glue, paint, varnish
Hang Ma	Paper votive objects	Paper goods
Hang Quat	Ceremonial fans	Religious accessories
Hang Thiec	Tin goods	Tin goods, mirrors
Hang Vai	Fabrics	Bamboo ladders

7

The heart of the Old Quarter

The small area enclosed by **Hang Buom**, **Ma May**, **Hang Bac** and **Hang Ngang** constitutes the heart of the Old Quarter, and it contains a wealth of interesting detail typical of the quarter's patchwork architecture: simple one-storey shophouses, some still sporting traditional red-tiled roofs; elaborate plaster-work and Art Deco styling from colonial days; and Soviet chic of the 1960s and 1970s – each superimposed on the basic tube-house design. Nowadays, the majority of facades bear distinctly European touches – faded wooden shutters, sagging balconies and rain-streaked moulding – dating from the early 1900s when the streets were widened for pavements. Certain occupants were too wealthy or influential to be shifted and you can find their houses still protruding onto the pavements standing out of line.

These streets are also home to some of the city's most popular lodgings and restaurants, especially for those on a budget, though there's no shortage of boutique hotels as well. It's a good area to soak up local culture, whether in the form of a cup of super-strong Vietnamese coffee, a glass of draught beer at bia hoi corner (see box, p.380), watching a local rock band in one of the bars on Ta Hien (see p.380), or a performance of traditional music. Both Heritage House and Dinh Kim Ngan stage evening performances of *ca tru* music (see p.482), which provide a revealing insight into the uses of traditional Vietnamese instruments.

Heritage House

87 Ma May • Daily 8am–noon & 1.30–5pm • 10,000đ

To get a better idea of the layout of tube-houses, pop into the beautifully restored **Heritage House** (sometimes called "Memorial House"). There's usually a volunteer on hand to show you through the various rooms and courtyards, pointing out the fine carving on the doors and balustrades, as well as examples of traditional fine arts and handicrafts such as ceramics and silk paintings on display. You might also see a

7

CENTRAL HANOI

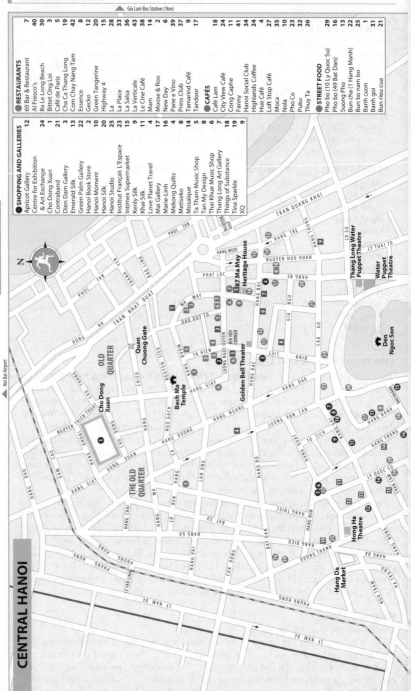

▲ Gia Lam Bus Station (1km)

● SHOPPING AND GALLERIES	
Apricot Gallery	12
Centre for Exhibition & Art Exchange	24
Cho Dong Xuan	1
Contraband	21
Dien Dam Gallery	3
Emerald Silk	13
Green Palm Gallery	22
Hanoi Book Store	2
Hanoi Moment	20
Hanoi Silk	15
Hanoi Studio	25
Institut Français L'Espace	23
Intimex Supermarket	15
Kenly Silk	9
Khai Silk	11
Love Planet Travel	4
Mai Gallery	17
Marie-Linh	16
Mekong Quilts	4
Metiseko	8
Mosaique	14
Ta Tham Music Shop	5
Tan My Design	8
Thai Khue Music Shop	6
Thang Long Art Gallery	7
Things of Substance	18
Tina Sparkle	19
XQ	

● RESTAURANTS	
69 Bar & Restaurant	7
Al Fresco's	40
Ba Le Long Beach	30
Bittet Ong Loi	5
Café de Paris	19
Cha Ca Thang Long	42
Com Chay Nang Tam	8
Essence	12
Gecko	20
Green Tangerine	15
Highway 4	28
La	33
La Place	36
La Salsa	43
La Verticale	38
Le Cine Café	14
Mam	2
Moose & Roo	6
New Day	39
Pane e Vino	37
Press Club	35
Tamarind Café	14
Tandoor	17

● CAFÉS	
Café Lam	18
City View Café	24
Cong Caphe	11
Fanny	41
Hanoi Social Club	34
Highlands Coffee	24
Hue Café	4
Loft Stop Café	27
Moca	35
Nola	10
Pho Co	23
Puku	32
Thuy Ta	26

● STREET FOOD	
Pho bo (10 Ly Quoc Su)	29
Pho bo (49 Bat Dan)	16
Suong Pho	13
Bun cha (1 Hang Manh)	22
Bun bo nam bo	25
Banh cuon	1
Banh goi	31
Bun rieu cua	21

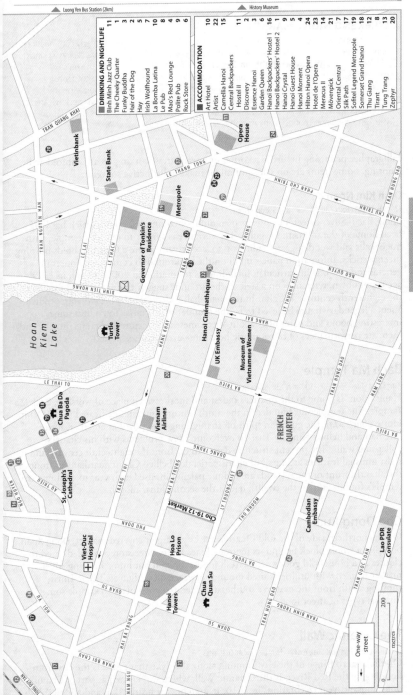

▲ Luong Yen Bus Station (2km)

▲ History Museum

DRINKING AND NIGHTLIFE

Binh Minh Jazz Club	11
The Cheeky Quarter	1
Funky Buddha	3
Hair of the Dog	5
Hay	7
Irish Wolfhound	10
La Bomba Latina	8
Le Pub	4
Mao's Red Lounge	9
Polite Pub	2
Rock Store	6

ACCOMMODATION

Art Hotel	10
Artist	22
Camellia Hanoi	15
Central Backpackers Hostel II	11
Discovery	2
Essence Hanoi	3
Garden Queen	6
Hanoi Backpackers' Hostel 1	16
Hanoi Backpackers' Hostel 2	1
Hanoi Crystal	9
Hanoi Guest House	5
Hanoi Moment	4
Hilton Hanoi Opera	24
Hotel de l'Opera	23
Meracus II	14
Mövenpick	21
Oriental Central	7
Silk Path	17
Sofitel Legend Metropole	19
Somerset Grand Hanoi	18
Thu Giang	12
Tirant	8
Tung Trang	13
Zephyr	20

Opera House

TRAN QUANG KHAI

Vietinbank

State Bank

LE THANH TONG

TRAN NGUYEN HAN

LE LAI

LE THACH

Metropole

Governor of Tonkin's Residence

TRANG TIEN

DINH TIEN HOANG

HAI BA TRUNG

PHAN CHU TRINH

PHAN CHU TRINH

TRAN HUNG DAO

NGO QUYEN

LY THUONG KIET

Hanoi Cinémathèque

HANG KHAY

HANG BAI

UK Embassy

Museum of Vietnamese Women

Hoan Kiem Lake

Turtle Tower

LE THAI TO

BA TRIEU

TRAN HUNG DAO

NAM LONG

FRENCH QUARTER

Chua Ba Da Pagoda

St. Joseph's Cathedral

QUANG TRUNG

Vietnam Airlines

TRANG THI

PHU DOAN

HAI BA TRUNG

LY THUONG KIET

WORH CHI

BA TRIEU

Cho 19-12 Market

Cambodian Embassy

TRAN QUOC TOAN

NGO QUYEN

AU TRIEU

QUAN SU

Viet-Duc Hospital

Hoa Lo Prison

DA TUONG

Lao PDR Consulate

Hanoi Towers

Chua Quan Su

QUAN SU

TRAN HUNG DAO

TRAN BINH TRONG

PHAN BOI CHAU

HAI BA TRUNG

NAM NGU

TRAN NHAN TON

▼ Kim Ma Bus Station (1km), My Dinh Bus Station (10km) & Noi Bai Airport (40km)

One-way street

0   metres   200

7

WEEKEND NIGHT MARKET

From around 7pm every Friday, Saturday and Sunday, Hang Dao and its northerly continuation almost as far as Dong Xuan Market, is closed to traffic and vendors set up stalls selling all kinds of trinkets at the **Weekend Night Market**. Though it's a fun place to touch the pulse of modern Hanoi, there's not much on sale that would interest most Western visitors; most shoppers are Vietnamese youngsters snapping up fashion accessories like mobile phone covers. It can get very crowded at times (so watch out for pickpockets), but winds down after 11pm. Sections of Ha Tien, Hang Buom and Ma May are also technically closed to traffic on weekend evenings, though many motorbikes ignore this.

---

calligrapher practising his art in a corner or a seamstress working on an embroidered painting. Some items are on sale, and might make a distinctive souvenir.

Dinh Kim Ngan

42–44 Hang Bac • Daily 7.30–11.30am & 2–5.30pm • Free

Hang Bac ("Silver Street") retains its own **dinh**, or communal house, which has long been home of the silversmiths' guild. The entrance is similar to that of a temple, with huge walls and wooden gates leading on to a courtyard where a large urn holds burning incense sticks. Infomation panels fill in on the backround to communal houses in general and this one in particular, including its restoration in 2009; though its exact age is unknown, references on a stele in the grounds suggest that it was established in the eighteenth century. The altar in the main hall is dedicated to the worship of Hien Vien, a legendary figure believed to be the founder of all crafts. You'll find some interesting books and pamphlets about Vietnamese architecture and crafts on sale, and there are performances of *ca tru* music here some evenings (see p.482).

Bach Ma Temple

Hang Buom • Tues–Sun 7.30–11.30am & 1.30–6pm • Free

Hang Buom is home to the quarter's oldest and most revered place of worship, **Bach Ma Temple**. The temple was founded in the ninth century and later dedicated to the White Horse (*Bach Ma*), the guardian spirit of Thang Long who posed as an ethereal site foreman and helped King Ly Thai To overcome a few problems with his citadel's collapsing walls. The present structure dates largely from the eighteenth century and its most unusual features are a pair of charismatic, pot-bellied Cham guardians in front of the altar. In front of them stands an antique palanquin, used each year to celebrate the temple's foundation on the twelfth day of the second lunar month.

Cho Dong Xuan

On the northern side of the Old Quarter, the city's largest covered market, **Dong Xuan**, occupies a whole block behind its renovated facade. Its three storeys are dedicated to clothes and household goods, while fresh foodstuffs spill out into a bustling street market stacked with multicoloured mounds of vegetables. Nguyen Thien Thuat, running south from the market's southeast corner, is a great place to sample some unusual types of street food.

The Ceramic Wall

Tran Quang Khai, Tran Nhat Duat, Yen Phu, Nghi Tam and Au Co streets

On the eastern fringe of the city, running along the dyke that protects the city from flooding by the Red River, is the Ceramic Wall, which was created as part of Hanoi's one-thousand-year celebrations in 2010. It stretches for nearly 4km and adds a splash of colour to the traffic-choked streets. It also has a place in the Guinness Book of Records as the **largest ceramic mosaic** in the world. It depicts scenes from Vietnam's history, famous places in the country and the lifestyles of minority groups.

The French Quarter

The first French concession was granted in 1874, an insalubrious plot of land on the banks of the Red River, southeast of where the **Opera House** stands today. Once in full possession of Hanoi, after 1882, the French began to create a city appropriate to their new protectorate, starting with the area between the old concession and the train station, 2km to the west. In the process they destroyed many ancient Vietnamese monuments, which were replaced with Parisian-style buildings and boulevards. Elegant villas gradually filled plots along the grid of tree-lined avenues, then spread south from Hoan Kiem Lake in the 1930s and 1940s towards what is now **Thong Nhat Park**, a peaceful but rather featureless expanse of green marking the French Quarter's southern boundary. The streets south of Le Lai on the east side of Hoan Kiem Lake, which include the *Metropole Hotel* and the State Guest House, are also generally considered part of the French Quarter because of their architectural features.

The Opera House

Near the eastern end of Trang Tien • Open during performances only • ☎ 04 3993 0113, ⓦ hanoioperahouse.org.vn

A grand example of the Parisian-style architecture for which the quarter is famous, the stately **Opera House** (now officially known as the Municipal Theatre) is modelled on the neo-Baroque Paris Opéra, complete with Ionic columns and grey slate tiles imported from France. The theatre was erected on reclaimed land and opened in 1911 after ten years of construction; it was regarded as the jewel in the crown of French Hanoi, the colonial town's physical and cultural focus, until 1945 when the Viet Minh proclaimed the **August Revolution** from its balcony. After Independence, audiences were treated to a diet of Socialist Realism and revolutionary theatre, but now the building has been restored to its former glory after a massive face-lift. Crystal chandeliers, Parisian mirrors and sweeping staircases of polished marble have all been beautifully preserved, although, unfortunately, there's no access to the public unless you go to a performance (see p.381). Otherwise, feast your eyes on the exterior – particularly stunning under evening floodlights or, better still, the soft glow of a full moon.

The History Museum

1 Trang Tien • Daily (closed first Monday of each month) 8am–noon & 1.30–5pm • 40,000đ; with camera 55,000đ • ⓦ baotanglichsu.vn

One block east of the Opera House, the building that houses the **National Museum of History** is a fanciful blend of Vietnamese palace and French villa, which came to be

---

COLONIAL ARCHITECTURE

After the hectic streets of the Old Quarter, the grand boulevards and wide pavements of Hanoi's **French Quarter** are a welcome relief. Again it's the **architecture** that's the highlight, running the gamut of early twentieth-century European styles from elegant Neoclassical through to 1930s Modernism and Art Deco, with an occasional Oriental flourish. One of the most splendid examples is the former residence of the governor of Tonkin, now the State Guest House, at the junction of Ngo Quyen and Le Thach. There are several other elegant colonial mansions along Phan Dinh Phung and Dien Bien Phu in Ba Dinh District, which is sometimes referred to as Hanoi's "other" or "second" French Quarter.

called "**Neo-Vietnamese**" style. The museum was founded in the 1930s by the Ecole Française d'Extrême Orient, but after 1954 changed focus to reflect Vietnam's evolution from Paleolithic times to Independence. Exhibits, including many plaster reproductions, are arranged in chronological order on two floors covering everything from prehistory to 1945, while the building across the street at 216 Tran Quang Khai covers the post-1945 era.

The ground floor

On the ground floor, the museum's prize exhibits are those from the **Dong Son culture**, a sophisticated Bronze Age civilization that flourished in the Red River Delta from 1200 to 200 BC. The display includes a rich variety of implements, from arrowheads to cooking utensils, but the finest examples of Dong Son creativity are several huge, ceremonial **bronze drums**, used to bury the dead, invoke the monsoon or celebrate fertility rites. The remarkably well-preserved **Ngoc Lu Drum** is the highlight, where advanced casting techniques are evident in the delicate figures of deer, birds and musicians ornamenting the drum's surface. Other notable exhibits on this floor include finds from excavations in Hanoi's citadel, a willowy **Amitabha Buddha** of the eleventh century, pale-green celadon ware from the same era and a group of wooden stakes from the glorious thirteenth-century battle of the Bach Dang River (see p.328).

The second floor

Displays on the museum's **second floor** illustrate the great leap in artistic skill that took place in the fifteenth century following a period of Chinese rule. Pride of place goes to a 3m-tall stele inscribed with the life story of Le Loi, who spearheaded the resistance against the Chinese and founded the later Le dynasty, which ruled the country from 1428 to 1788. Also on display is an extensive collection of ceramics and exhibits relating to the nineteenth-century **Nguyen Dynasty** and the period of French rule. A series of ink-washes depicting Hue's Imperial court in the 1890s is particularly eye-catching, as are the embroidered silks and inlaid ivory furniture once used by the emperors cloistered in the citadel.

216 Tran Quang Khai

The former Museum of Vietnamese Revolution is now a part of the History Museum and catalogues the "Vietnamese people's patriotic and revolutionary struggle", from the first anti-French movements of the late nineteenth century to post-1975 reconstruction. Much of the tale is told through documents, including the first clandestine newspapers and revolutionary tracts penned by Ho Chi Minh, and illustrated with portraits of Vietnam's most famous revolutionaries; among them are many photos you won't see elsewhere. There's good coverage of Dien Bien Phu and the War of Independence, and a small but well-presented exhibition on the American War, a subject that is treated in greater depth at the Military History Museum (see p.362).

Trang Tien

Trang Tien, the main artery of the French Quarter, is still a busy shopping street where you'll find bookshops and art galleries, as well as the recently renovated **Trang Tien Plaza** with its flash boutiques and somewhat incongruous supermarket. South of Trang Tien you enter French Hanoi's principal **residential quarter**, consisting of a grid of shaded boulevards whose distinguished villas are much sought after for restoration as embassies and offices or as desirable, expatriate residences. To take a swing through the area, drop down **Hang Bai** onto Ly Thuong Kiet and start heading west.

THE METROPOLE LEGEND

The bright, white Neoclassical facade of the **Metropole** – nowadays *Sofitel Legend Metropole* hotel – opened in 1901 as the *Grand Metropole Palace*, and soon became one of Southeast Asia's great hotels. Even during the French War, Bernard Fall, a journalist killed by a landmine near Hue in 1967, described the hotel as the "last really fashionable place left in Hanoi", where the barman "could produce a reasonable facsimile of almost any civilized drink except water". After Independence it re-emerged as the *Thong Nhat* or *Reunification Hotel*, but otherwise stayed much the same, including en-suite rats and lethal wiring, until 1990 when *Sofitel* transformed it into Hanoi's first international-class accommodation (see p.374). The *Metropole's* illustrious visitors' book includes Charlie Chaplin and Paulette Goddard on honeymoon in 1936; and Graham Greene, who first came here in 1952. Twenty years later Jane Fonda stayed for two weeks while making her famous broadcast to American troops.

Museum of Vietnamese Women

36 Ly Thuong Kiet • Daily 8am–5pm • 30,000đ • ☎ 04 3825 9936, ⓦ womenmuseum.org.vn

This museum has undergone a complete overhaul in recent years and is now one of Hanoi's most interesting attractions, with detailed video presentations on each floor about different aspects of the lives of Vietnamese women. It starts off with a look at **street vendors**, whose presence on the streets of the city with their baskets of goods suspended from bamboo poles is one of the country's most indelible icons. Women's role in the country's wars is the focus of the second floor, while the third floor focuses on family life and the top-floor features an eye-catching display of ethnic **minority costumes**.

Hoa Lo Prison

1 Hoa Lo • Daily 8am–5pm • 20,000đ

The Hanoi Towers complex looms over the sanitized remnants of French-built **Hoa Lo Prison**, nicknamed the "Hanoi Hilton" by American prisoners of war as a wry comment on its harsh conditions and often brutal treatment. The jail became famous in the 1960s when the PoWs, mostly pilots and crew members, were shown worldwide in televised broadcasts. There's a heavy dose of propaganda in the two rooms dedicated to the PoWs, peddling the message that they were well treated, clothed and fed.

The museum mostly concentrates on the pre-1954 colonial period when the French incarcerated many nationalist leaders at Hoa Lo, including no fewer than five future general secretaries of the Vietnamese Communist Party. Some of the cells – which were still in use up to 1994 – have been preserved, along with rusty shackles, a guillotine and instruments of torture. Other rooms display photos and information on the more famous political prisoners.

Chua Quan Su

73 Quan Su, near the junction with Tran Hung Dao • Daily 8–11am and 1–4pm

Chua Quan Su, the Ambassadors' Pagoda, was founded in the fifteenth century as part of a guesthouse for officials from neighbouring Buddhist countries, though the current building dates only from 1942. Nowadays Quan Su is one of Hanoi's most active pagodas: on the first and fifteenth days of the lunar month, worshippers and mendicants throng its forecourt, while inside an iron lamp, ornamented with sinuous dragons, hangs over the crowded prayer-floor and ranks of crimson-lacquered Buddhas glow through a pungent haze of burning incense. The compound, shaded by ancient trees, is headquarters of the officially recognized Central Buddhist Congregation of Vietnam and is a centre of Buddhist learning, hence the well-stocked library and classrooms at the rear.

Ba Dinh District

Hanoi's most important cultural and historical monuments are found in the **Ba Dinh District**, immediately west of the Old Quarter, where the Ly kings established their Imperial City in the eleventh century. The venerable **Temple of Literature** and the picturesque **One Pillar Pagoda** both date from this time, but nothing else remains of the Ly kings' vermilion palaces, whose last vestiges were cleared in the late nineteenth century to accommodate an expanding French administration. Most impressive of the district's colonial buildings is the dignified residence of the governor-general of Indochina, now known as the **Presidential Palace**; part of its former gardens now house two great centres of pilgrimage – **Ho Chi Minh's Mausoleum** and **Museum**.

East of Ba Dinh Square, the recently opened **Hanoi Citadel** was the seat of power for all Vietnamese dynasties apart from the Nguyen dynasty. To the south of the Citadel stands the **Cot Co Flag Tower**, which is accessed via the **Military History Museum**.

There's a lot to see in this area, and though it's possible to cover everything described below in a single day, in order to digest everything it's best to spend one day exploring the sites around Ba Dinh Square and the Citadel, then return another day to see the Temple of Literature, the **Fine Arts Museum** and the Military History Museum.

Ba Dinh Square

Two kilometres west of Hoan Kiem Lake, the wide, open spaces of **Ba Dinh Square** are the nation's ceremonial centre. It was here that Ho Chi Minh read out the Declaration of Independence to half a million people on September 2, 1945, and here that Independence is commemorated each National Day with military parades. You'll see the **National Assembly Hall**, venue for Party congresses, standing on the square's east side.

Ho Chi Minh's Mausoleum

Ba Dinh Square • April–Oct Tues–Thurs 7.30–10.30am, Sat & Sun 7.30–11am; Nov–March Tues–Thurs 8–11am, Sat & Sun 8–11.30am • Free

In the tradition of great Communist leaders, when Ho Chi Minh died in 1969 his body was **embalmed**, though it was not put on public view until after 1975. The mausoleum is probably Hanoi's most popular sight for domestic tourists, attracting hordes of visitors at weekends and on national holidays; from school parties to ageing confederates, all come to pay their respects to "Uncle Ho".

Visitors to the mausoleum (note the very limited opening hours) must leave bags and cameras at a kiosk by the entrance, from where you'll be escorted by soldiers in immaculate uniforms. Respectful behaviour is requested, which means **appropriate dress** (no shorts or sleeveless vests) and removing hats and keeping silence within the sanctum. Note that each autumn the mausoleum usually closes for a few weeks while Ho undergoes maintenance.

Inside the mausoleum

Inside the building's marble entrance hall Ho Chi Minh's most quoted maxim greets you: "Nothing is more important than independence and freedom." Then it's up the stairs and into a cold, dark room where this charismatic hero lies under glass, a small, pale figure glowing in the dim light, his thin hands resting on black covers. Despite the rather macabre overtones, it's hard not to be affected by the solemn atmosphere, though in actual fact Ho's last wish was to be cremated and his ashes divided between the north, centre and south of the country, with each site marked only by a simple shelter. The grandiose building where he now lies seems sadly at odds with this unassuming, egalitarian man.

The Presidential Palace

Just north of Ho's mausoleum lie the grounds of the **Presidential Palace**. The palace was built in 1901 as the home of the governor-general of Indochina – all sweeping stairways, louvred shutters and ornate wrought-iron gates of the Belle Époque – and these days is used to receive visiting heads of state. It's closed to the public but you can admire the outside as you walk through the palace gardens to Ho Chi Minh's house.

Ho Chi Minh's house

Tues–Sun • April–Oct 7.30–11am & 1.30–4pm; Nov–March 8–11am & 2–4pm • 20,000đ

Ho Chi Minh's house, built in 1954 and modelled on an ethnic minority stilthouse, is a simple structure with open sides and split-bamboo screens. Since it stands almost next to the grandiose Presidential Palace where he declined to live, it's tempting to see it as a succinct comment by Ho on the excesses of colonialism; it certainly looks like a cosier place to call home. Ho and his Politburo used to gather in the ground-level meeting area, while his study and bedroom upstairs are said to be as he left them, sparsely furnished, unostentatious and very highly polished. Ho lived here for the last eleven years of his life, even during the American War, tending his garden and fishpond; tradition has it that he died in the small hut next door.

Hanoi Botanical Gardens

3 Hoang Hoa Tham, between West Lake and the mausoleum • Daily 7am–10pm • 2000đ

After the rather solemn sights around Ba Dinh Square, particularly the mausoleum, many visitors feel in need of a breath of fresh air, and the **Botanical Gardens** (signed Vuon Bach Tao at the entrance) is just the place for that. Established by the French in 1890, it's more of a park than a botanical garden, but it does have tall, shady trees, grassy lawns, a couple of small lakes, a network of footpaths, benches to rest on, and some intriguing modern sculptures.

The One Pillar Pagoda

Ong Ich Khiem

Just south of the Ho Chi Minh Mausoleum, the **One Pillar Pagoda** rivals the Turtle Tower as a symbol of Hanoi. It is the most unusual of the hundreds of pagodas sponsored by devoutly Buddhist Ly Dynasty kings in the eleventh century, and represents a flowering of Vietnamese art. The tiny wooden sanctuary, dedicated to **Quan Am** whose statue nestles inside, is only three square metres in size and is supported on a single column rising from the middle of an artificial lake, the whole structure designed to resemble a lotus blossom, the Buddhist symbol of enlightenment. In fact this is by no means the original building – the concrete pillar is a real giveaway – and the last reconstruction took place after departing French troops blew up the earlier structure in 1954.

Ho Chi Minh Museum

19 Ngoc Ha • Tues–Thurs, Sat & Sun 8–4.30pm; Mon & Fri 8am–12pm • 20,000đ • ⓦ baotanghochiminh.vn

The angular, white building housing the **Ho Chi Minh Museum** was built with Soviet aid and inaugurated on May 19, 1990, the hundredth anniversary of Ho's birth. The museum celebrates Ho Chi Minh's life and the pivotal role he played in the nation's history; not surprisingly, this is also a favourite for school outings. Exhibits around the hall's outer wall focus on Ho's life and the "Vietnamese Revolution" in the context of socialism's international development, including documents, photographs and a smattering of personal possessions, among them a suspiciously new-looking disguise

7

Ho supposedly adopted when escaping from Hong Kong. Running parallel on the inner ring are a series of heavily metaphoric "spatial images", six tableaux portraying significant places and events, from Ho's birthplace in Nghe An to Pac Bo cave and ending with a symbolic rendering of Vietnam's reunification. Go in for the surreal nature of the whole experience, but don't expect to come away having learnt much more about the man.

Hanoi Citadel

9 Hoang Dieu • Tues–Sun 8–11.30am & 2–5pm • 30,000đ • ☎ 04 3734 5927, ⊛ hoangthanhthanglong.vn

While not as impressive a sight as the Hue Citadel, **Hanoi's Imperial Citadel** is still of sufficient interest to warrant its World Heritage status (granted in 2010 to coincide with the city's one-thousandth birthday) and to feature on any visitor's itinerary. It comprises **two sections** – the Central Sector of the Citadel to the east of Hoang Dieu, and the archaeological site on the west side of Hoang Dieu. Note that two other surviving fragments of the citadel are accessed separately; the flag tower, or **Cot Co**, through the nearby Military History Museum, and the northern gate, or **Cua Bac** (which still bears huge scars from cannon fire), from Phan Dinh Phung Street.

A citadel was first erected here in the eighth century by the Chinese, though nothing remains from that time, and Ly Thai To is usually credited as the founder of the Imperial Citadel, which was then added to by succeeding dynasties – Tran, Le, Mac and Nguyen – until the capital was moved to Hue in 1802. Though most of its buildings were subsequently razed by the French, enough remains in the twelve-acre complex to keep visitors busy for at least a couple of hours.

The central sector

The central sector of the Citadel is accessed through the **Doan Mon Gate**, where you'll find the ticket desk. This huge wall, topped with a double-roofed pavilion and with five arches leading through it, was once the main entrance to the king's forbidden realm. Inside the gate is an excavated area that reveals an ancient irrigation system.

The next building, **Kinh Thien Palace**, was once the grandest structure in the citadel, but all that remains today are two beautiful stone dragons flowing down a flight of steps that led to the building. Among these ancient remains, it comes as a shock to encounter the **D67 Building**, which dates from 1967 and functioned as command centre for the Northern forces during the American War. The name of military mastermind Vo Nguyen Giap, among others, still sits on the conference table here, and the reinforced underground bunker acts as a reminder of the threat of aerial bombardment in that era.

The final building in this complex is the Hau Lau, or "back pavilion", a mix of Eastern and Western styles. It is sometimes referred to as the "Princess pavilion", as it once housed concubines of the Nguyen kings.

The archeological dig

Once you've seen the central sector, it's worth retracing your steps to the west of Kinh Thien Palace and crossing Hoang Dieu through a side gate to visit the **archaeological dig** on the other side of the road. This huge site was discovered in 2002 when foundations were being dug for a new National Assembly, and it has revealed the remains of more grand palaces and relics from various dynasties, some of which are now on display in the History Museum.

The Military History Museum

28 Dien Bien Phu • Tues–Thurs, Sat & Sun 8–11.30am & 1–4.30pm • 20,000đ

Dien Bien Phu, a road lined with gnarled trees and former colonial offices, interspersed with gingerbread villas, is home to the white, arcaded building of the **Military History**

Museum, opposite a small park with a statue of Lenin. The museum chronicles national history from the 1930s to the present day, a period dominated by the French and American wars, though it's noticeably quiet on China and Cambodia.

The forecourt

The **museum forecourt** is full of weaponry: pride of place goes to a Russian MiG 21 fighter, alongside artillery from the battle of Dien Bien Phu (see box, p.411) and a tank from the American War, while the second courtyard is dominated by the mangled wreckage of assorted American planes piled against a tree.

Inside the museum

The exhibition proper starts on the arcaded building's second floor and runs chronologically from the 1930 Nghe Tinh Uprising, through the August Revolution to the "People's War" against the French, culminating in the decisive **battle of Dien Bien Phu**. If there's sufficient demand, they'll show an English-language video to accompany the battle's diorama; despite the heavy propaganda overlay, the archive footage is fascinating, including Viet Minh hauling artillery up mountain slopes and clouds of French parachutists. Naturally, General Giap and Ho Chi Minh make star appearances – after the ubiquitous still images, it's a shock to see Ho animated. The American War, covered in a separate hall at the rear, receives similar treatment with film of the relentless drive south to "liberate" Saigon in 1975.

Cot Co

In the northwest corner of the museum compound stands the 30m **Cot Co** (Flag Tower), one of the few remnants of Emperor Gia Long's early nineteenth-century citadel, where the national flag now billows in place of the emperor's yellow banner. Built in 1812, it features 36 flower-shaped and six fan-shaped windows. When the French flattened the ramparts in the 1890s they kept Cot Co as a handy lookout post and signalling tower. It is possible to climb a spiral staircase inside for a view of the surrounding area, though the door to the upper part is sometimes locked. There's also a convenient café at its base.

Vietnam Fine Arts Museum

66 Nguyen Thai Hoc • Daily 8.30am–5pm • 30,000đ • Guided tour 150,000đ • ⓦ vnfam.vn

A couple of blocks southwest of the Military History Museum, a three-storey colonial block with chocolate-brown shutters houses the **Vietnam Fine Arts Museum**. It not only boasts the country's most comprehensive collection of fine art, but it is also unusually well presented, with plenty of information in English. Arranged chronologically, the museum illustrates the main themes of Vietnam's artistic development, kicking off with a collection of **Dong Son drums** and statues of graceful Cham dancers. Though many items are reproductions, there are some fine pieces, notably among the seventeenth- and eighteenth-century **Buddhist art**, which spawned such masterpieces as Tay Phuong's superbly lifelike statues. Other highlights include extensive collections of folk art and ethnic minority art, and an interesting exhibition of **twentieth-century artists** charting the evolution from a solidly European style through Socialist Realism to the emergence of a distinct Vietnamese school of art.

The Temple of Literature

Nguyen Thai Hoc, entrance on Quoc Tu Giam • Daily: mid-April to mid-Oct 7.30am–5.30pm; mid-Oct to mid-April 8am–5pm • 20,000đ

Hanoi's most revered temple complex, the **Temple of Literature**, or **Van Mieu**, is both Vietnam's principal Confucian sanctuary and its historical centre of learning. The temple is also one of the few remnants of the Ly kings' original city and retains a strong

7

BECOMING A MANDARIN

Examinations for admission to the **Imperial bureaucracy** were introduced by the Ly kings in the eleventh century as part of a range of reforms that served to underpin the nation's stability for several centuries. Vietnam's exams were based on the Chinese system, though they also included Buddhist and Taoist texts along with the Confucian classics. It took until the fifteenth century, however, for academic success, rather than noble birth or patronage, to become the primary means of entry to the civil service. By this time the system was open to **all males**, excluding "traitors, rebels, immoral people and actors", but in practice very few candidates outside the scholar-gentry class progressed beyond the lowest rung.

First came **regional exams**, *thi huong*, after which successful students (who could be any age from 16 to 61) would head for Hanoi, equipped with their sleeping mat, ink-stone and writing brush, to take part in the second-level *thi hoi*. These **national exams** might last up to six weeks and were as much an evaluation of poetic style and knowledge of the classic texts as they were of administrative ability. Those who passed all stages were granted a doctorate, *tien si*, and were eligible for the third and final test, the *thi dinh*, or **palace exam**, set by the king himself. Some years as few as three *tien si* would be awarded whereas the total number of candidates could be as high as six thousand, and during nearly three hundred exams held between 1076 and 1779, only 2313 *tien si* were recorded. Afterwards the king would give his new mandarins a cap, gown, parasol and a horse on which to return to their home village in triumphal procession.

sense of harmony despite reconstruction and embellishment over the nine hundred years since its dedication in 1070.

Entry is through the two-tiered **Van Mieu Gate**. The temple's ground plan, modelled on that of Confucius's birthplace in Qufu, China, consists of a succession of five walled courtyards. The first two are havens of trim lawns and noble trees separated by a simple pavilion.

The third courtyard

You enter the third courtyard via the imposing **Khue Van Cac**, a double-roofed gateway built in 1805, its wooden upper storey ornamented with four radiating suns. Central to this section of the complex is the **Well of Heavenly Clarity** – a rectangular pond – to either side of which stand the temple's most valuable relics, 82 stone **stelae** mounted on tortoises. Each stele records the results of a state examination held at the National Academy between 1442 and 1779, though the practice only started in 1484, and gives brief biographical details of successful candidates. It's estimated that up to thirty stelae have gone missing or disintegrated over the years, but the two oldest, dating from 1442 and 1448, occupy centre spot on opposite sides of the pond.

The fourth courtyard

Passing through the **Gate of Great Synthesis** brings you to the fourth courtyard, the **Courtyard of Sages**, and the main temple buildings. Two pavilions on either side once contained altars dedicated to the 72 disciples of Confucius, but now house souvenir shops. During Tet this courtyard is the scene of calligraphy competitions and "human chess games", with people instead of wooden pieces on the square paving stones.

The House of Ceremonies

This long, low building whose sweeping tiled roof is crowned by two lithe dragons bracketing a full moon, stands on the courtyard's north side. Here the king and his mandarins would make sacrifices before the altar of Confucius, accompanied by booming drums and bronze bells echoing among the magnificent ironwood pillars. Within the ceremonial hall lies the **temple sanctuary**, at one time prohibited even to the king, where a large and striking statue of Confucius sits with his four principal disciples, resplendent in vivid reds and golds. Between the altar and sanctuary is a

Music Room, where musicians playing traditional instruments sometimes provide a great opportunity for photos.

The fifth courtyard

The fifth and final courtyard once housed the **National Academy**, regarded as Vietnam's first university, which was founded in 1076 to educate princes and high officials in Confucian doctrine. In 1947 French bombs destroyed the academy buildings but they have now been painstakingly reconstructed, including an elegant two-storey pavilion housing a small museum and an altar dedicated to a noted director of the university in the fourteenth century, Chu Van An. Upstairs, three more statues honour King Ly Thanh Tong, the founder of Van Mieu; Ly Nhan Tong, who added the university; and Le Thanh Tong, instigator of the stelae. The pavilion is flanked by an imposing **drum tower** as well as a **bell tower**.

B52 Victory Museum

157 Doi Can, Ba Dinh District • Tues–Sat 8–11.30am & 1–4.30pm • Free

For war buffs, it's worth checking out this intensely patriotic museum that commemorates the **shooting down of 15 B-52 bombers** during the USA's Operation Linebacker II in December 1972. This operation is often referred to in the West as "the Christmas bombings", which were initiated by President Nixon: between December 18 and 29 (with a day off for Christmas), over 15,000 tons of ordnance was dumped on industrial and military targets in and around Hanoi, with a few stray bombs destroying hospitals and schools, causing untold damage and loss of life. However, the event is remembered by Vietnamese as "Dien Bien Phu in the air", since it did not bring about the capitulation of Viet Cong forces so dearly sought by the USA.

The museum is located between Ba Dinh Square and the Ethnology Museum, so can be combined with a visit to either of these attractions to the west of the city centre. It is also just a short distance from Huu Tiep Lake, where one of the bombers came down, and the exhibits, as you'd guess, consist of a bunch of wreckage of B52 bombers.

West Lake and around

As in the days of Vietnam's emperors, **West Lake** (Ho Tay), to the northwest of the city centre, has once again become Hanoi's most fashionable address, complete with exclusive residential developments, lakeside clubs, spas and a clutch of luxury hotels. Don't be surprised if you see lots of foreign faces around here, especially along Xuan Dieu, as it's a popular base for expats working in Hanoi. In the seventeenth century, villagers built a causeway across the lake's southeast corner, creating a small fishing lake now called **Truc Bach** and ringed with little cafés. Attractions around West Lake include several temples and pagodas, and a short distance from its southwest corner stands the **Museum of Ethnology**.

THE WEST LAKE CIRCUIT

A path runs right around the 17km **circumference** of West Lake, making it ideal for a long walk (3–4 hours), a bike ride, or a ride in an electric car. The electric car ride begins at Tran Quoc Pagoda, costs 80,000đ per person (or 560,000đ for the whole car, which holds seven people) and takes an hour and fifteen minutes, making brief stops at around twenty sights along the way, including Quan Thanh and Tay Ho Temples. There's often a fresh breeze coming off the lake, though as it's surrounded by dense human habitation, the lake also suffers badly from pollution. A favourite activity for Vietnamese is to rent a swan-shaped pedal boat (80,000đ per hour) from the southeast corner of the lake, opposite Quan Thanh Temple, and pedal across the waters.

7

THE LEGEND OF WEST LAKE

Back in the mists of time, a gifted monk returned from China, bearing quantities of bronze as a reward for curing the emperor's illness. The monk gave most of the metal to the state but from a small lump he fashioned a bell, whose ring was so pure it resonated throughout the land and beyond the mountains. The sound reached the ears of a golden buffalo calf inside the Chinese Imperial treasury; the creature followed the bell, mistaking it for the call of its mother. Then the bell fell silent and the calf spun round and round, not knowing which way to go. Eventually, it trampled a vast hollow, which filled with water and became **West Lake**. Some say that the golden buffalo is still there, at the bottom of the lake, but can only be retrieved by a man assisted by his ten natural sons.

More prosaically, West Lake is a shallow lagoon left behind as the Red River shifted course eastward to leave a narrow strip of land, reinforced over the centuries with massive embankments, separating the lake and river. The lake was traditionally an area for royal recreation or spiritual pursuits, where monarchs erected summer palaces and sponsored religious foundations, among them Hanoi's most ancient pagoda, **Tran Quoc**.

The causeway and Truc Bach Lake

The name **Truc Bach** derives from an eighteenth-century summer palace built by the ruling Trinh lords which later became a place of detention for disagreeable concubines and other "errant women", who were put to work weaving fine white silk, *truc bach*. The causeway, or Thanh Nien, is an avenue of **flame trees** and a popular picnic spot in summer when a cooling breeze comes off the water and hawkers set up shop along the grass verges.

Quan Thanh Temple

Quan Thanh • Daily 8am–4.30pm • 10,000đ

Although the summer palace no longer exists, the eleventh-century **Quan Thanh Temple** still stands on the lake's southeast bank, erected by King Ly Thai To and dedicated to the Guardian of the North, Tran Vo, who protects the city from malevolent spirits. Quan Thanh has been rebuilt several times, most recently in 1893, along the way losing nearly all its original features.

Tran Vo statue

It's well worth wandering into the shady courtyard to see the 334-year-old black bronze **statue of Tran Vo**, seated on the main altar. The statue, nearly 4m high and weighing four tonnes, portrays the Taoist god accompanied by his two animal emblems, a serpent and turtle; it was the creation of a craftsman called Trum Trong whose own statue, fashioned in stone and sporting a grey headscarf, sits off to one side.

The Shrine Room

The **shrine room** also boasts a valuable collection of seventeenth- and eighteenth-century poems and parallel sentences (boards inscribed with wise maxims and hung in pairs on adjacent columns), most with intricate, mother-of-pearl inlay work.

US Anti-Aircraft Gunners Memorial

North of Quan Thanh Temple, where Thanh Nien bears gently right, on the east side of the road stands a small **memorial**, which is dedicated to teams of **anti-aircraft gunners** stationed here during the American War. In particular the memorial commemorates the downing of Navy Lieutenant Commander John McCain, who parachuted into Truc Bach Lake in October 1967 and survived more than five years in the "Hanoi Hilton". He went on to run for US president in 2008, only to be beaten by Barack Obama.

Tran Quoc Pagoda

Thanh Nien • Daily 7.30–11.30am & 1.30–6.30pm • Free • Visitors are requested not to wear shorts

Tran Quoc Pagoda, Hanoi's oldest religious foundation, occupies a tiny spur of land off Thanh Nien, which separates West Lake from Truc Bach. The pagoda's exact origins are uncertain but it's usually attributed to the sixth-century early Ly Dynasty during a brief interlude in ten centuries of Chinese domination. In the early seventeenth century, when Buddhism was enjoying a revival, the pagoda was moved from beside the Red River to its present, less vulnerable location.

Entry is along a narrow, brick causeway lying just above the water, past a collection of imposing brick stupas, the latest of which – towering over its more modest neighbours – was erected in 2003 on the death of the then master of the pagoda. The sanctuary's restrained interior and general configuration are typical of northern Vietnamese pagodas, though there's nothing inside of particular importance.

Kim Lien Pagoda

7

Sunrise to sunset • Free

About a kilometre north of the causeway, the red-tiled roofs of **Kim Lien Pagoda** provide an incongruous neighbour for the *Intercontinental Hotel*. Though it may appear to be closed, you can usually enter through a small gate to the left of the main building. The pagoda's best attributes are its elaborate carvings and unplastered brick walls dating from an eighteenth-century rebuild. Even if pagodas aren't your thing, you could always come out here to indulge yourself at the nearby Zen Spa (see box, p.368).

Tay Ho Temple

Sunrise to sunset • Free

This temple, located at the end of the Ho Tay Peninsula on the east side of the lake, is dedicated to **Thanh Mau**, the Mother Goddess, who in the seventeenth century appeared as a beautiful girl to a famous scholar out boating on the lake. She refused to reveal her name, just smiled enigmatically, recited some poetry and disappeared. But when the scholar worked out her identity from the poem, local villagers erected a temple where they still worship the goddess, especially on the first and fifteenth day of each lunar month, when the place takes on a carnival atmosphere and vendors line the approach roads. At other times, Tay Ho Temple attracts few tourists and the petitioners here are mostly women and young people asking for favours by burning their fake dollars under the banyan trees.

Museum of Ethnology

Nguyen Van Huyen • Tues–Sun 8.30am–5.30pm • 40,000đ; guide 50,000đ; camera use 50,000đ • Water puppet shows held in a small pond in the grounds Sat & Sun at 10am, 11.30am, 2.30pm and 4pm • ☎ 04 3756 2193, ⓦ vme.org.vn • City bus #14 from Dinh Tieng Hoang, just north of Hoan Kiem Lake, to Nghia Tan, on the main road 500m from the museum; a taxi from the Old Quarter costs around 100,000đ

The **Museum of Ethnology** is 7km west of the city centre and about 1km southwest of West Lake, although it more than repays the effort of getting here, particularly if you'll be visiting any of Vietnam's minority areas. Spread across two floors, the displays are well presented and there's information in English on all the major ethnic groups. Musical instruments, games, traditional dress and other domestic items that fill the displays are brought to life through musical recordings, photos and plenty of life-size models, as well as captivating videos of festivals and shamanistic rites (but don't watch the one on buffalo sacrifice if you're squeamish). This wealth of creativity amply illustrates some of the difficulties ethnologists are up against – the museum also acts as a **research institute** charged with producing ethnologies for Vietnam's 54 main groups plus their confusion of sub-groups. The grounds contain a collection of **minority buildings** relocated from all over Vietnam, dominated by a beautiful example of a Bahnar communal house.

HANOI ACTIVITIES

If you tire of sightseeing in Hanoi, there are plenty of other activities to keep you occupied, ranging from learning how to cook Vietnamese cuisine to pampering yourself in the city's luxurious spas.

COOKING CLASSES

Blue Butterfly 61 Hang Buom ⓦbluebutterfly restaurant.com. This centrally located restaurant in the Old Quarter offers morning and afternoon cookery classes at $35 per person.

Hanoi Cooking Centre 44 Chau Long ⓦhanoi cookingcentre.com. This school offers a range of classes, from Vietnamese Street Food to regional cuisine, at $63 per person.

Hidden Hanoi 147 Nghi Tam, near the Sheraton Hotel ⓦhiddenhanoi.com.vn. Classes are held Mon– Sat at 11am–2pm and cost $45 per person with a minimum of three people.

Highway 4 31 Xuan Dieu ⓦhighway4.com. After a trip to the market, students are shown their own cooking station at the school and then spend two hours learning how to make four dishes. Prices start at $45 per person, depending on number in the group (maximum ten).

LANGUAGE COURSES

Hidden Hanoi ☎0912 254045, ⓦhiddenhanoi .com.vn. Hidden Hanoi runs a range of language classes, from the survival basic course to the advanced course (twenty classes for $200–240). They also offer private tuition.

The Vietnamese Language Centre of Hanoi Foreign Language College 1 Pham Ngu Lao, ☎04 3826 2468. Individual instruction from $10 per hour; the centre also arranges student exchanges and student visas.

SPAS AND SALONS

Salon 15 Ma May ☎04 3926 2036. A handy beauty salon in the Old Quarter where you'll pay from around $10 for a foot massage and $12–14 for a body massage.

SF Spa 30 Cua Dong, Hoan Kiem District ☎04 3747 5301, ⓦsfcompany.net. This highly rated spa on the western fringe of the Old Quarter offers a range of treatments, from their signature 2hr, $50 package to an hour-long foot massage for $17.50, and includes a free taxi ride.

Zen Spa 100 Xuan Dieu ☎04 3719 1266, ⓦzenspa .com.vn. For pure pampering, indulge yourself at Zen Spa near West Lake. The treatments, which include facials, flower baths and foot and body massages, are derived from traditional minority therapies and come complete with wooden tubs and mood music. Prices start at $27.50 for a 1hr foot rejuvenation, up to $200 for a 4hr 30min "Together Forever" session, which includes a foot treatment, a body scrub, a herbal steam bath, herbal therapy and a collagen facial treatment.

SWIMMING

All the five-star hotels have swimming pools and fitness centres that are sometimes open to non-residents for a daily fee ($10–20).

Army Hotel 33c Pham Ngu Lao. Large, open-air saltwater pool which is significantly cheaper than other hotel pools, and popular in summer.

GOLF

Dao Sen Driving Range 125 Nguyen Son, Gia Thuy, Long Bien ☎04 3872 7336, ⓦdaosen.com.vn. This sixty-lane driving range is located about 3km from the city centre.

Hanoi Club 76 Yen Phu ☎04 3823 8115, ⓦhanoi -club.com. One part of the club is the Arena Golf Driving Range, where you can drive floating balls out over West Lake.

The Kings' Island Golf Course 36km west of Hanoi at Dong Mo in Ha Tay Province ☎04 3368 6555, ⓦkingsislandgolf.com. Kings' Island has two eighteen-hole courses open to non-members, though members get priority at weekends. The weekday walk-in fee for eighteen holes is 2,190,000đ.

WALKING

Hidden Hanoi ⓦhiddenhanoi.com.vn. Apart from improvised walks around Hoan Kiem and West Lakes, it's possible to sign up for guided walks of the Old Quarter, the French Quarter or street food outlets with this bunch. Walks last around 2 hours and cost around $20 a person.

Southeast Asia Museum
Entry included in Museum of Ethnology ticket

Right next door to the Museum of Ethnology, the striking, kite-shaped **Southeast Asia Museum** is new and still not fully functional, but displays on the ground floor focus on daily life, social activities, garments, performing arts and religion in eleven countries in the region. Exhibits will be added on the second and third floors later.

ARRIVAL AND DEPARTURE   HANOI

As a major gateway into Vietnam and transit hub for the country, Hanoi is well-served by **long-distance transport**. When it's time to move on, many visitors make a beeline east to the splendours of Ha Long Bay, while more adventurous head either southwest to Mai Chau to begin a tour of the northwest and Sa Pa, or directly north to the stunning landscapes of the Dong Van Karst Plateau Geopark in Ha Giang Province. For those eager to see as much of the country as they can in a single visit, the next step is a plane or train ride south to the Imperial City of Hue, the beaches of Nha Trang, and eventually the sensory pleasures of Vietnam's second city, Ho Chi Minh City. Note that travellers planning on crossing the Lao, Cambodian or Chinese **borders** should first read the information in Basics, p.30.

BY PLANE
Noi Bai airport (☎ 04 3886 5047, ⓦ hanoiairportonline .com) is 45km north of the city. It boasts a brand-new international terminal (opened April 2015) with all the usual facilities.

City buses #7 and #17 (roughly every 20min from 5.30am to 10.30pm; 2hr; 9000đ) depart from outside the arrivals hall; #7 takes you to Kim Ma bus station, to the west of the centre, and #17 to Long Bien station on the northern edge of the Old Quarter. City buses are not a good idea if you have bulky luggage.

Shuttle buses run by Vietnam Airlines (45min–1hr; $2; be prepared to haggle) also leave from outside the terminal and drop you near the airline's main office just south of Hoan Kiem Lake.

Taxis cost around 350,000đ but beware of scams (see box, p.372). The safest option is to get your hotel to send a taxi to meet you.

Airlines Airlines flying from Hanoi include: Aeroflot ☎ 04 3771 8742; Asiana Airlines ☎ 04 3747 4848; British Airways ☎ 04 3934 7239; China Airlines ☎ 04 3936 6364; China Southern Airlines ☎ 04 3771 6611; Japan Airlines ☎ 04 3826 6693; Lao Airlines ☎ 04 3942 5362; Thai Airways ☎ 04 3826 7921; Viet Jet ☎ 04 3584 4494; Vietnam Airlines, 25 Trang Thi ☎ 04 6270 0200.

Destinations Buon Ma Thuot (2 daily; 1hr 40min); Da Lat (3 daily; 1hr 40min); Da Nang (17 daily; 1hr 15min); Dien Bien Phu (2 daily; 1hr); Dong Hoi (1 daily; 1hr 30min); Ho Chi Minh City (41 daily; 2hr); Nha Trang (9 daily; 1hr 40min).

BY TRAIN
Hanoi train station The station is roughly 1km west of centre, at 120 Le Duan. Note there are two gateways: arriving from and departing for Ho Chi Minh City and all points south, or from China, you'll use the main station platforms on Le Duan. However, trains arriving and departing from the east and north (Haiphong, Sa Pa and Lao Cai) pull into platforms at the rear of the main station, bringing you out among market stalls on a narrow street called Tran Quy Cap.

Tickets are available in the main station building (daily 7.30am–12.30pm & 1.30–7.30pm). It's best to make onward travel arrangements well in advance, especially for sleeper berths to Lao Cai, Hue and Ho Chi Minh City. If the station has sold out of tickets for Lao Cai or Hue, try the tour agents as they get their tickets from intermediaries who buy them in bulk. Current timetables and prices can be found at ⓦ vietnam-railway.com.

Destinations Da Nang (6 daily; 14–20hr); Dong Dang (2 daily; 6hr); Dong Ha (4 daily; 12–16hr); Dong Hoi (6 daily; 9–13hr); Haiphong (2 daily; 2–3hr); Ho Chi Minh City (6 daily; 30–40hr); Hue (6 daily; 11–16hr); Lao Cai (5 daily; 7–9hr); Ninh Binh (5 daily; 2hr 20min); Thanh Hoa (5 daily; 3–5hr); Vinh (6 daily; 5–9hr).

7

ECO TRANSPORT – HANOI STYLE

An alternative way to explore the Old Quarter is on **electric cars** that follow a route along its narrow streets and round neighbouring Hoan Kiem Lake. You can hop on board in front of Dong Xuan Market (see p.356) or hire one for a group opposite the Water Puppet theatre on the northeast corner of Hoan Kiem Lake. The cost is 15,000đ per person or 150,000đ for the whole car. While these vehicles themselves are quiet and eco-friendly, and the thirty-minute ride is a fascinating introduction to the Old Quarter, their drivers still hit the horn in a typically relentless Hanoi way.

7

TOUR AGENTS

Hanoi's tourist-service industry has become increasingly diversified over the years, and now comprises a dizzying array of companies – many of which, it has to be said, are dubious, fly-by-night operators who specialize in **ripping off** foreign tourists. There are so many outfits claiming to be affiliated to *Sinh Café*, for example, that the original *Sinh Café* was forced to change its name to *The Sinh Tourist*. To be on the safe side, it's best to go to one of the longer-established and more reliable agents such as those listed below. Most also arrange day city tours, starting at around $20 a person for a half-day tour up to $150 for a luxury option, including meals.

Buffalo Tours 70–72 Ba Trieu ☎ 04 3828 0702, ⓦ buffalotours.com. Long-established experts in organizing tailor-made private tours throughout IndoChina, with a particular focus on adventure and special interest holidays; prices are a little high but the service is extremely professional.

Cuong's Motorbike Adventure 46 Gia Ngu ☎ 0918 763515, ⓦ cuongs-motorbike-adventure.com. Group and custom tours on modern or classic Minsk bikes to all parts of the coutry, including the wild landscapes of Ha Giang Province.

Ethnic Travel 35 Hang Giay ☎ 04 3926 1951, ⓦ ethnictravel.com.vn. Popular operation with a genuine passion for low-impact, environmentally conscious travel; a maximum group size of six also makes for a more personal adventure.

Exotissimo 3rd floor, 66a Tran Hung Dao ☎ 04 3828 2150, ⓦ exotissimo.com. One-stop travel shop offering all travel-related services from visas and ticketing to tours aimed at the middle market and above. It's a highly professional operation, with a strong focus on adventure tours and responsible tourism.

Explorer Tours 85 Hang Bo ☎ 04 3923 1430, ⓦ explorer.com.vn. Specializes in private group tours of Ha Long Bay, but also offers Hanoi day-trips and tours of the northern mountains.

Far East Tours 5 Ly Nam De ☎ 04 3747 5876, ⓦ fareastour.com.vn. Reputable company offering everyuthing from one-day city tours to three-week tours of the whole country.

Handspan Adventure Travel 78 Ma May ☎ 04 3926 2828, ⓦ handspan.com. Environmentally conscious adventure-tour specialist. Options range from sea-kayaking in Ha Long Bay to exploring the north on foot or by mountain bike, staying in minority villages. The tours are well organized, with good equipment and back-up, and are restricted to small groups.

Kangaroo Café 22 Bao Khanh ☎ 04 3828 9931, ⓦ kangaroocafe.com. This Australian-run café is recommended for its innovative, well-organized small-group and adventure tours.

Kim Tours 137 Hang Bac ☎ 04 3993 5766, ⓦ kimtours.net. This long-standing tour company is best known for its open-tour bus services, which operate countrywide.

Queen Travel 65 Hang Bac ☎ 04 3826 0860, ⓦ queen travel.vn. Aims at the middle market and above with tailor-made and small-group tours.

The Sinh Tourist 52 Luong Ngoc Quyen ☎ 04 3926 1568, ⓦ thesinhtourist.vn. Perhaps Vietnam's most famous tour operator, frequently imitated but still reliable, especially for open-tour bus journeys.

Vietnindo Travel 5-239/71 Bo De ☎ 04 3872 7754, ⓦ vietnamholidays.biz. A small but enthusiastic and efficient company offering customized tours countrywide.

BY BUS

Hanoi's four main long-distance bus stations are all located several kilometres from the centre, and you'll need to catch a city bus (see opposite) or hop on a xe om to get to or from the city centre.

From the south Buses from the south generally terminate at Giap Bat station, 6km south of town on Giai Phong, though many sleeper buses from Ho Chi Minh City terminate at Luong Yen, 3km southeast of the centre on Tran Quang Khai.

From the north and northeast Buses from Lang Son, Cao Bang, Ha Long and Haiphong usually arrive at Gia Lam station, 4km away on the east bank of the Red River. However, some Ha Long and Haiphong services, including the through bus from Cat Ba operated by Hoang Long company, drop you at the more central Luong Yen bus station on the eastern edge of the French Quarter.

From the northwest Services from Son La, Mai Chau and Lao Cai arrive at either Giap Bat or My Dinh, about 10km west of centre. Note that some buses from Mai Chau and Hoa Binh terminate in Ha Dong, a suburb of Hanoi also roughly 10km west on Highway 6; jump on one of the waiting city buses for the 40min ride into town.

Open-tour buses The ubiquitous open-tour buses leave from the offices of their respective tour companies every night (see box above) to make the trek down to Hue, Nha Trang and Ho Chi Minh City, but it's a long, uncomfortable and noisy journey: many wish they'd shelled out on a train or plane ticket instead.

Destinations from Gia Lam Bai Chay (Ha Long City; 4hr); Cao Bang (8hr); Haiphong (2hr 30min); Lang Son (3hr); Thai Nguyen (3hr).

Destinations from Giap Bat Hoa Binh (1hr 30min); Hue (12hr); Mai Chau (4hr); Ninh Binh (2hr); Son La (6–7hr); Thanh Hoa (3hr).

GETTING AROUND

Despite the chaotic traffic, getting around **on foot** remains the best way to do justice to Hanoi's central district, taking an occasional **xe om** to scoot between more distant places. Alternatively, enjoy a leisurely tour by **cyclo**. **Bicycle** and **motorbike** hire is not recommended for the city itself, since traffic discipline is an unfamiliar concept in Hanoi: teenagers on their Hondas ride without fear, and everyone drives without signalling, preferring to sound the horn constantly to warn others of their presence. If you prefer something solid between you and the maelstrom, there are numerous **taxi companies** operating in Hanoi and tariffs aren't exorbitant. Finally, the much improved city **buses** are mainly useful for getting out to the long-distance bus stations, and a new metro system is on the horizon.

Metro It's not there yet, but work is well advanced on Hanoi's metro, which will run partly under and partly over ground along several routes connecting key areas of the capital. The first line is scheduled to begin operation in 2016, and the project should be complete by 2020, but don't bet on it.

Xe om These motorbike taxis hover at every intersection and provide the main form of cheap, inner-city transport. An average journey within the city centre should cost around 20,000đ and a trip out to Ho's Mausoleum or West Lake in the region of 40,000đ. Always negotiate a fare before setting off. Drivers are obliged to carry spare helmets for passengers, but it can still be a hair-raising ride.

Metered taxis With a short ride across the city centre averaging 40,000đ, and 80,000đ to the suburbs, taxis are definitely worth considering for hopping around the city. Ask your hotel to call one for you, or call yourself: Hanoi Taxi (☎ 04 3853 5353), CP Taxi (☎ 04 3826 2626), Mai Linh Taxi (☎ 04 3822 2666) and Van Xuan Taxi (☎ 04 3822 2888) all have a decent reputation. Note that prices are metered in dong, though it looks like dollars – for example, 20.00 on the meter means 20,000đ, not $20.

Cyclo Cyclo have been replaced by xe om as the most popular form of public transport, and they now mainly cater to tour groups taking a leisurely amble round the Old Quarter. If you fancy doing the same, the simplest option is to get your hotel to arrange it for you. Otherwise, be prepared to bargain hard, aiming at around $5 per hour. Cyclo are banned from certain roads in central Hanoi, so don't be surprised if you seem to be taking a circuitous route or are dropped off round the corner from your destination.

Motorbike rental Motorbikes are only for the brave in the inner city but are definitely worth considering for exploring sights further afield; some agencies will even arrange for you to pick up a vehicle somewhere like Mai Chau or Ninh Binh. Most rental outlets are located in the Old Quarter – especially along Ta Hien and Hang Bac – offering a standard 110cc Honda Wave for around $5 per day, with the helmet thrown in. Cuong's Motorbike Adventure (see box opposite) buys, sells, rents out and repairs bikes, while Rentabike (6b Tam Thuong ☎ 091 3026878, ⓦ rentabikehanoi.com) offers new machines at reasonable rates (from $45 a month). Staff at the Minsk Club (ⓦ minskclubhanoi.wordpress.com) is an invaluable source of information and occasionally arrange one-off motorbiking excursions and other events. Always use the designated parking areas (gui xe may); the rate for motorbikes should be 5000đ or under.

Car rental Though traffic congestion makes this a cumbersome method of sightseeing in the central districts, for day-trips out of Hanoi, car rental offers greater flexibility than tours. Virtually every tour agency (see box opposite) can arrange an a/c car with driver, starting at around $80 per day for; as few drivers speak English, you may also want to hire a guide for an extra $20–30 a day.

City buses These are mostly only used by travellers as a means to get to or from Noi Bai Airport (see p.369) but other useful routes connect the far-flung long-distance bus stations. Buses run approximately every fifteen to twenty minutes between 5am and 9pm, and are fairly empty except during rush hour (7–9am and after 4pm), when some routes can be hideously overcrowded. The fares are heavily subsidized, with a flat rate of 7000đ within the city centre and 9000đ to the airport and the outer suburbs; pay the ticket collector on board.

Routes #3 runs between Gia Lam and Giap Bat (30min), with stops on Hang Tre (or Tran Quang Khai, heading south), Tran Hung Dao and outside the train station; #34 covers Gia Lam and My Dinh (40min) via Hai Ba Trung and the Opera House.

INFORMATION

Tourist information and tours The big state-run tour agencies, such as Vietnamtourism at 114 Lang Ha, Dong Da District (☎ 04 3943 7072, ⓦ vietnamtourism.com), are more interested in signing you up for a tour than dishing out information. A far better option is to try one of the well-established and reliable private agencies (see box opposite), which can provide information on visas, tours, transport and so forth. For a free guided tour, check out ⓦ hanoifreewalkingtours.com.

Maps of the Old Quarter are given out free by most hotels but for in-depth exploration of the city, you can't beat *Nancy Chandler's Map of Hanoi* (around $15; check ⓦ nancy chandler.net for outlets).

Listings are carried in several publications, but the most useful are *The Word: Hanoi, AsiaLife* and *Citypass Guides*. Look out for free copies of these magazines in tourist-oriented hotels, cafés, restaurants and bars.

ACCOMMODATION

The best place to find **budget accommodation** is in the Old Quarter, and to the west of Hoan Kiem Lake, where you'll find dozens of hotels and hostels ranging from the most basic dormitories to increasingly ritzy places with air-conditioning, wi-fi access and satellite TV. For the cheapest of the cheap, look around Ngo Huyen, just north of the cathedral, where dorm rooms go for $5 a night. The city's most sought-after addresses are in the French Quarter, headed by the venerable *Sofitel Legend Metropole* and its neighbour, the *Hilton Hanoi Opera*. Northwest of the centre, there are also a few **high-end hotels** on the eastern shores of West Lake. Some of the best deals to be found throughout the city are in **mid-range** mini-hotels, where you can often find four-star facilities and service at two-star prices.

THE OLD QUARTER AND WEST OF HOAN KIEM LAKE

Art Hotel 65 Hang Dieu ☎ 04 3923 3868, ⓦ hanoiart hotel.com; map pp.354–355. This newish place is great value; its twenty rooms are kitted out with the latest gadgetry, such as two-way a/c units (hot and cold), and staff fall over each other to help guests. **$45**

Camellia Hanoi 12c Chan Cam ☎ 04 3828 5936, ⓦ camelliahanoihotel.com; map pp.354–355. Friendly staff and spruced-up rooms make this little hotel near the cathedral a decent option; deluxe rooms with balconies are bright and roomy. Rates include free internet access and buffet breakfast. **$15**

Central Backpackers Hostel II 11 Hang Manh ☎ 04 3938 7064 ⓦ centralbackpackershostel.com; map pp.354–355. This place offers a great deal for backpackers – cheap bunk beds with lockers in a good Old Quarter location, plus free wi-fi, free breakfast and even free beer in the evening. The private rooms are not such a good deal but the helpful staff give this place a warm vibe. There's another, older branch at 16 Ly Quoc Su. Dorm **$5**, double **$20**

Discovery 22 Luong Ngoc Quyen ☎ 04 3926 2462, ⓦ discoveryhotel.com.vn; map pp.354–355. This friendly, family-run hotel tucked up an alley off Luong Ngoc Quyen is one of the best budget deals in the Old Quarter. Its six rooms come with fridges, phones, TVs, a/c and minuscule en-suite bathrooms, though some rooms have no windows. **$10**

★**Essence Hanoi** 22 Ta Hien ☎ 04 3935 2485, ⓦ essence hanoihotel.com; map pp.354–355. The comfortable rooms, ideal location and flawless service at *Essence Hanoi* make this one of the best deals in the Old Quarter. Add the fact that on the ground floor you have one of the best restaurants in the whole city (see p.375) and you know you're on to a winner. Reservations highly recommended. **$65**

★**Garden Queen** 65 Hang Bac ☎ 04 3826 0860, ⓦ hotelgardenqueen.com; map pp.354–355. In the heart of the Old Quarter, this homely hotel (only eight rooms) stands out for its eye-catching entrance hall lined with vintage bicycles and mopeds, and for its friendly, family atmosphere. The rooms are decked out in restful creams and beiges offset by the dark wooden floorboards and bamboo furniture, plus there's a wonderful little Zen garden on the roof. **$50**

Hanoi Backpackers' Hostel 48 Ngo Huyen ☎ 04 3828 5372; 9 Ma May ☎ 04 3935 1890, ⓦ vietnam backpackerhostels.com; map pp.354–355. Both locations of this popular hostel, especially the newer one on Ma May, are usually packed to the rafters with fun-seeking backpackers. With friendly staff, free internet access and breakfast, long happy hours, comfort food and dorm rooms, budget travellers have all they need under one roof. There are also regular barbecue nights and staff organize hugely popular – some might say debauched – tours of Ha Long Bay (see p.339). Dorm **$8**, double **$50**

BEWARE THE COPYCAT SCAM

Be warned that **copyright** counts for nothing in Vietnam, so as soon as someone starts a successful business, the copycats jump on the bandwagon. This is especially true of hotels, so for example there are multiple *Queen, Prince* and *Camellia* hotels. However, they are not all under the same management, so you'll need to insist on being taken to the hotel you've specified; check the address with staff when you arrive. Some taxi drivers, especially those at Noi Bai Airport, will try to persuade you that your chosen hotel has closed, moved or changed name, or simply take you to a place with the same name and a different address, in order to get a commission. If this happens, make a note of the vehicle registration number and report it to the hotel you were aiming for so that they can make a complaint.

HO CHI MINH'S MAUSOLEUM (P.360) >

7

Hanoi Crystal 9 Hang Thung ☎04 3934 3608 ⓦhanoicrystalhotel.com; map pp.354–355. Recently renovated place close to Hoan Kiem Lake in the southeast corner of the Old Quarter. Rooms are bright and well equipped, breakfast is included and there's a bar on the 8th floor. It's worth paying a few dollars more for a deluxe room, which is half as big again as the superior rooms. $30

Hanoi Guest House 85 Ma May ☎04 3935 2572, ⓦhanoiguesthouse.com; map pp.354–355. One of the best budget options in the Old Quarter, with friendly staff, smart but compact rooms and an excellent location. Not every place at this price provides an elevator, free breakfast and computers for guests' use. They even have a honeymoon suite. Rooms $20, suite $40

Hanoi Moment 15 Hang Can ☎04 3923 3988, ⓦhanoimomenthotel.com; map pp.354–355. This boutique hotel in the Old Quarter makes good use of limited space, with sixteen tiny but tastefully equipped rooms. All have double glazing (a definite plus), and some even have glassed-in balconies that look like conservatories. $55

JW Marriott 8 Do Duc, Me Tri Ward, South Tu Liem District ☎04 3833 5588, ⓦmarriott.com; map pp.348–349. OK, so it's a long way west of Hoan Kiem Lake and the French Quarter, but this new place is worth a mention for its stunning architecture, its wonderfully appointed and spacious rooms, its comprehensive facilities and its reliable and seamless service. It boasts six dining and drinking options, including the French Grill, which serves divine lobster and steaks. $160

Meracus II 32 Hang Trong ☎04 3938 2526, ⓦmeracushotels.com; map pp.354–355. This is the newer of two branches of Meracus (the older being at 11 Hang Dzau, on the east side of the Old Quarter). Its 13 rooms are beautifully appointed, with deep mattresses and restful decor in a great location between Hoan Kiem Lake and St Joseph's Cathedral. Staff are very friendly and the complimentary breakfast is a good way to start the day. $60

Oriental Central 39 Hang Bac ☎04 3935 1117, ⓦorientalcentralhotel.com; map pp.354–355. This mini-hotel is typical of many mid-range places in the Old Quarter that offer good quality at competitive rates. Rooms are bright and clean with all the facilities you might need, and they'll throw in a free airport transfer if you book for three nights. A generous breakfast is included, and it's in the heart of the action. $50

Silk Path 195–199 Hang Bong ☎04 3266 5555, ⓦsilkpathhotel.com; map pp.354–355. Located in the southwest corner of the Old Quarter, this four-star business hotel offers supreme comfort, with thick-piled carpets, tasteful furnishings and a totally relaxing vibe. $133

Thu Giang 5a Tam Thuong alley ☎04 3828 5734, ⓦthugianggh.com; map pp.354–355. A family-run hotel with inexpensive dorm beds and tiny, no-frills doubles for not much more. Little in the way of facilities

but an interesting location in a quiet alley and the hosts make you very welcome. Dorm $3, doubles $8

Tirant 36–38 Gia Ngu ☎04 6269 8899, ⓦtiranthotel.com; map pp.354–355. Typical of many mid-range places that offer top-end facilities, the Tirant also has a rooftop pool. Staff quickly learn guests' names and enjoy helping out with things like restaurant bookings and calling taxis. Go for a front-facing room on the top floor for views of Hoan Kiem Lake. $65

Tung Trang 13 Tam Thuong alley ☎04 3828 6267, ⓦtungtranghotel.com; map pp.354–355. A step above the rest along this alley, located right opposite Yen Thai Temple, the Tung Trang offers small but clean rooms, all with TVs, a/c and en-suite bathrooms. It's worth paying a couple of dollars extra for a bigger room with a window. $16

THE FRENCH QUARTER

Artist 22a Hai Ba Trung ☎04 3825 3044, ✉artisthotel22A@gmail.com; map pp.354–355. One of the few cheap options in the French Quarter, this quirky hotel was undergoing a long-overdue renovation at the time of this update. It's located by the Hanoi Cinematheque at the end of a long alley. $24

★**Hilton Hanoi Opera** 1 Le Thanh Tong ☎04 3933 0500, ⓦhilton.com; map pp.354–355. Arguably Hanoi's top city-centre address for all-round value, this five-star hotel is carefully designed to blend in with the neighbouring Opera House. Facilities include 269 cheerful and well-proportioned rooms with excellent bathrooms and some local touches in the ceramics, contemporary paintings and chunky furniture. In-house services include three restaurants, a business centre and a fitness room with outdoor swimming pool and spa services. $175

Hotel de l'Opera 29 Trang Tien ☎04 6282 5555, ⓦhoteldelopera.com; map pp.354–355. If the nearby Metropole's room rates seem a bit steep, consider this stylish alternative, a recently opened top-class hotel operated by M Gallery. It has a fantastic location, just down the road from the Opera House, and rooms are beautifully designed with amazingly deep mattresses and a choice of five different pillow styles. There's a gym, a small pool and a sun terrace, as well as two classy restaurants. $150

Mövenpick 83a Ly Thuong Kiet ☎04 3822 2800, ⓦmoevenpick-hotels.com; map pp.354–355. Standard-setting business hotel housed in a colonial-style building near the train station. Rooms are tasteful, but the hotel's most distinctive feature is a female-only floor, which has slightly different rooms with features like a make-up mirror at the work desk for those who like to primp in natural light, padded hangers for silk blouses and ultra-high-powered hairdryers, as well as direct access to the excellent fitness centre. $110

★**Sofitel Legend Metropole** 15 Ngo Quyen ☎04 3826 6919, ⓦsofitel.com; map pp.354–355. Opened in

1901 since when it has hosted numerous illustrious guests, the *Metropole* remains the most sought-after hotel in Hanoi despite increasingly fierce competition. Though rooms in the modern Opera Wing exude international-class luxury, they lack the old-world charm of the original building, with its wooden floorboards and louvred shutters. In-house services include a business centre, a small open-air swimming pool, fitness centre and a choice of bars and restaurants, notably *Spices Garden*, serving upmarket Vietnamese fare. **$300**

Somerset Grand Hanoi 49 Hai Ba Trung ☎ 04 3934 2342, ⓦ somerset.com; map pp.354–355. These serviced apartments, with up to three bedrooms and fully equipped kitchens, can be rented by the night and make a more homely alternative to an upmarket hotel. They also represent surprisingly good value, including access to facilities such as an open-air pool, a gym and a creche. Make sure you book well in advance. **$117**

Sunway 19 Pham Dinh Ho ☎ 04 3971 3888, ⓦ hanoi .sunwayhotels.com; map pp.348–349. An award-winning, four-star boutique hotel where consistently high standards of service and comfortable rooms make up for a slightly inconvenient location to the south of the French Quarter, from where it's quite a trek to the city's major sights. There's an in-house restaurant and a health spa. **$90**

★ **Zephyr** 4–6 Ba Trieu ☎ 04 3934 1256, ⓦ zephyrhotel .com.vn; map pp.354–355. This three-star place offers value for money with its 44 spacious and carpeted rooms in a prime location just a stone's throw from Hoan Kiem Lake. **$70**

EATING

The choice of eating options in Hanoi is staggering and you could easily plan your entire stay in the city around a tour of its restaurants and street food outlets. You'll find everything from humble **food stalls** and street kitchens, the best dishing out top-quality food for next to nothing, to a dizzying range of stylish international **restaurants**: check English-language **listings** magazines such as *The Word: Hanoi* (ⓦ wordhanoi.com) or the *New Hanoian* website (ⓦ tnhvietnam.xemzi.com) for the latest newcomers. There's no shortage, either, of **cafés**, whether one-room coffee houses serving thick, strong cups of the local brew, or fancy Western-style places serving cappuccinos and café lattes. **Juice stalls** are wonderful places to sample Vietnam's wide range of tropical fruits; just look for glass cabinets on the street displaying fruit, then squat on a stool and salivate as they whisk up the juice while you wait.

RESTAURANTS

THE OLD QUARTER AND WEST OF HOAN KIEM LAKE

69 Bar & Restaurant 69 Ma May; ☎ 04 3926 1720; map pp.354–355. Exposed beams and brickwork give a rustic feel to this traditional house which functions as a restaurant. The menu includes several innovative dishes such as caramelized pork claypot with coconut cream, with most main courses priced at around 100,000–140,000đ. Daily 9am–11pm.

Ba Le Long Beach 18 Bao Khanh ☎ 04 3938 0190; map pp.354–355. This simple place offers a good range of comfort food, as well as vegetarian dishes, traditional Vietnamese such as *bun cha* (65,000đ) and *cha ca* (129,000đ), and delicious shakes. It's handy for Hoan Kiem Lake and there's an a/c room upstairs. Daily 7am–10pm.

Bittet Ong Loi 51 Hang Buom ☎ 04 3825 1211; map pp.354–355. Hidden down a long, dark passage, this small and bustling restaurant, with limited opening hours, serves platters of *bittet* – a Vietnamese corruption of French *biftek* – with lashings of garlic and chips for 110,000đ. Or you can opt for roast chicken, roast pigeon, crab or prawn. Daily 5–9pm.

Café de Paris 12 Luong Ngoc Quyen ☎ 04 3926 1327; map pp.354–355. This tiny French bistro, complete with black-and-white tiled floor and brass rail round the bar, serves up a short but excellent range of Western dishes such as beef bourguignon (170,000đ) and fish fillet, as well as good breakfasts for 120,000đ. It's also a/c and right in the heart of the Old Quarter. Daily 7.30am–11pm.

Cha Ca Thang Long 31 Duong Thanh ☎ 04 3824 5115; map pp.354–355. Patronized by locals, this is the best place to sample tasty, inexpensive *cha ca* – fried fish with turmeric, dill and other condiments (120,000đ) – which is one of Hanoi's most famous dishes. Daily 11am–9pm.

★ **Essence** 22 Ta Hien ☎ 04 3935 2485; map pp.354–355. Hotel restaurants can sometimes be rather bland, but *Essence* offers some of the best gourmet food in Hanoi – both Vietnamese and Western – at reasonable prices. Go for one of the set menus (400,000–600,000đ), which include three courses and a glass of wine, or sample the delicious beef in bamboo. Daily 11am–10.30pm.

Gecko 85 Hang Bac ☎ 04 3935 2702; map pp.354–355. There seems to be a branch of this self-styled "cheap and cheerful" eatery on every street in the Old Quarter, and while you shouldn't expect gourmet food, you should expect prompt and friendly service, a cosy, a/c environment and rock-bottom prices. The menu covers everything from spring rolls to pancakes to cocktails. Daily 9am–midnight.

★ **Green Tangerine** 48 Hang Be ☎ 04 3825 1286, ⓦ greentangerinehanoi.com; map pp.354–355. The setting is a 1920s Art Deco villa and its lovely, plant-filled courtyard. It's worth reserving a table to sample the Vietnamese–French fusion cuisine: rich and unusual flavour combinations such as smoked duck breast with goat's cheese and red tuna carpaccio with frozen yoghurt and lime, though the menu changes regularly. The two-course set lunch (218,000đ) is excellent value. Otherwise, this is definitely one for a splurge – a meal for two will set you back 800,000đ or more. Daily 11am–11pm.

Highway 4 5 Hang Tre ☎ 04 3926 4200, ⊚ highway4 .com; map pp.354–355. With several locations scattered round town, *Highway 4* offers moderately priced mainly north Vietnamese dishes – steamboat and earthen-pot dishes, as well as more innovative fare such as their famous catfish spring rolls – to accompany traditional rice wine liquors. These come in more than thirty varieties, the medicinal benefits of which are explained in the English-language menu. Daily 10am–1am; food served to 11pm.

La 25 Ly Quoc Su ☎ 04 3928 8933; map pp.354–355. Standing out among a clutch of restaurants near the cathedral, this mellow dining room is a good place to collect your thoughts and enjoy either a hearty Western dish like an imported steak (260,000đ) or a Vietnamese mild chicken curry (100,000đ). Good range of drinks too. Daily 8am–10.30pm.

La Place 6 Au Trieu ☎ 04 3928 5859, ⊚ laplace hanoi.com; map pp.354–355. Sweet little place with views of the cathedral square from its picture windows. The dishes are small but well prepared, and the coconut chicken curry is a deservedly popular choice (100,000đ). Daily 7.30am–10.30pm.

La Salsa 25 Nha Tho ☎ 04 3828 9052, ⊚ lasalsa-hanoi .com; map pp.354–355. Decently priced tapas (40,000–80,000đ), paella (260,000đ) and French cuisine too in a knockout location near the cathedral. Of an evening, the ground-floor bar is also a popular drinking hole for local expats. Daily 8.30am–10.30pm.

★Mam 11–13 Hang Mam ☎ 04 3935 2888, ⊚ mam restaurant.vn; map pp.354–355. Excellent Vietnamese cuisine, superb service (as long as there's not a tour group in) and a refined ambience combine to making dining at *Mam* a thoroughly enjoyable experience. Go for one of the set menus and wash it down with a reasonably priced bottle of wine. Daily 10am–10pm.

Moose & Roo 42b Ma May ☎ 04 3200 1289, ⊚ moose androo.com; map pp.354–355. This Canadian- and Aussie-run gastropub is a bit pricier than most places in the Old Quarter, but it seems there are plenty of visitors willing to splash out on a steak, burger or home-made pie (most mains 200,000–300,000đ), including backpackers from the hostel opposite. The short menu includes some unusual but tasty items, such as scotch egg with piccalilli (140,000đ) and pulled pork sandwich (180,000đ), so this is a good spot for a break from Vietnamese fare. Daily 9.30am–midnight.

New Day 72 Ma May ☎ 04 3828 0315, ⊚ newday restaurant.com; map pp.354–355. This no-frills diner turns out consistently delicious Vietnamese staples for rock-bottom prices, and customers are welcome to wander in the kitchen to select from pre-prepared dishes. If it's full out front, muscle your way in and they'll find a spot for you somewhere. Daily 8am–10.30pm.

Tamarind Café 80 Ma May ☎ 04 3926 0580; map pp.354–355. A little pricey but worth it for the well-presented contemporary vegetarian food (organic where possible), fresh fruit juices and herbal teas, with a laidback vibe and decor to match: plump sofas and arty Asian-style seating platforms at the rear. Daily 6am–11pm.

Tandoor 24 Hang Be ☎ 04 3824 5359, ⊚ tandoor vietnam.com; map pp.354–355. A perennially popular Indian restaurant with simple decor but cracking curries, Goan fish curry, mutton vindaloo and an extensive range of mouthwatering vegetarian dishes. The *thali* set meals (Mon–Fri only) offer reasonable value at 140,000–180,000đ. Daily 10.30am–10.30pm.

THE FRENCH QUARTER

A la folie...! 63 Ngo Hue ☎ 04 3976 1667; map pp.348–349. This newly opened French restaurant is managed by the folks from neighbouring *Chim Sao*, and adds a welcome option to Hanoi's dining scene. Head upstairs for a/c comfort and choose from dishes like braised shredded duck (150,000đ) and red snapper fillet (170,000đ), or go for the well-priced set menus. Attentive service too. Tues–Sun 11am–2pm & 6–10pm.

Al Fresco's 23l Hai Ba Trung ☎ 04 3826 7782, ⊚ alfrescosgroup.com; map pp.354–355. This is the place to head for when you're really hungry, as portions are huge. Café, bar and grill in one, the menu includes good-quality Aussie and international fare, including great ribs, salads, steaks and a choice of thin- or thick-crust pizzas from 125,000đ upwards. There are several other locations around town, including on Nha Tho near the cathedral; see the website for details. Daily 9am–11pm.

Chim Sao 65 Ngo Hue ☎ 04 3976 0633, ⊚ chimsao.com; map pp.348–349. It's worth hunting down this quirky restaurant for its laidback atmosphere (dining upstairs on floor cushions around low tables) and its menu of unusual items such as buffalo sautéed with morning glory (95,000đ), bamboo shoot salad (50,000đ) and freshwater crab with ginger sauce (85,000đ). Daily 8am–10.30pm.

Com Chay Nang Tam 79a Tran Hung Dao ☎ 04 3942 4140, ⊚ nangtam.com.vn; map pp.354–355. Small, vegetarian restaurant down a quiet alley off Tran Hung Dao and named after Vietnamese Cinderella character. *Goi bo*, a main-course salad of banana flower, star fruit and pineapple, is recommended, or try one of the well-priced set menus all around 60,000–100,000đ a head. The food's all tasty and MSG-free, though purists might not like the way some dishes (mostly made of tofu) emulate meat. Daily 9am–9pm.

Indochine 14 Nam Ngu ☎ 04 3942 4097, ⊚ indochine hanoi.com; map pp.348–349. Food of consistently

STREET FOOD

For sheer value for money and atmosphere your best option is to eat either at the rock-bottom, stove-and-stools **food stalls** or at the slightly more upmarket **street kitchens**, most of which specialize in just one or two types of food. You'll find both these sorts of places scattered across the city, often with no recognizable name and little to choose between individual establishments, but there are a few that stand out from the crowd: we've listed some of the best below.

Pho bo is Vietnam's national dish, a beef noodle soup served with chopped spring onion, usually eaten for breakfast and costing around 30,000–40,000đ. Novels have been written extolling its virtues, and the addresses to head for are 10 Ly Quoc Su, 49 Bat Dan, and our favourite, *Suong Pho* at 24b Ngo Trung Yen (map pp.354–355).

Bun cha, consisting of pork patties served with cold rice noodles and dipping sauce (about 35,000đ), is a popular lunchtime dish and can be found all over the city. The most famed locations are 1 Hang Manh (map pp.354–355) and 1 Pho Hue (map pp.348–349) in the French Quarter.

Bun bo nam bo is a southern dish, and a hot favourite with most Westerners. It consists of lean beef with noodles and beansprouts, topped with roasted peanuts, garlic and basil. Join the lunchtime queue at 67 Hang Dieu (map pp.354–355), throw on a spoonful of chilli sauce, stir it up and fill your belly for 50,000đ.

Banh cuon is a Hanoi snack consisting of almost transparent rice-flour pancakes usually stuffed with minced pork and black mushrooms and sprinkled with fried shallots. Give it a try at 14 Hang Ga (map pp.354–355).

Banh goi, sometimes called "pillow cake", is a fried pastry, somewhat like a samosa, filled with vermicelli, minced pork and mushrooms, and eaten with a thin sweet sauce, parsley and chilli. Sample a serving of two per plate (9,000đ) at 52 Ly Quoc Su (map pp.354–355).

Bun rieu cua, a crab noodle soup laced with tomatoes, tofu, spring onions and fried shallots, is another popular breakfast dish, especially on cold winter mornings. Try it at 34 Cau Go (map pp.354–355).

high quality keeps this well-established restaurant up there with its younger rivals, though prices are a bit expensive. Classic Vietnamese cuisine includes seafood spring rolls, steamboat and the famous prawn on sugar cane at 140,000–300,000đ, or try the set meals from 340,000đ. Evenings are popular with tour groups, so reservations are recommended. Traditional Vietnamese music performed on Thurs (7–9pm). Daily 11am–2pm & 5.30–10pm.

★**La Verticale** 19 Ngo Van So ☎04 3944 6317, ⓦverticale-hanoi.com; map pp.354–355. Spice is the word at this recently refurbished colonial house – the laboratory-like ground floor is pungent with French chef Didier Corlou's cooking. These are possibly the most carefully constructed dishes in the country, such as muscovy duck with lemongrass, ginger, honey and Thai basil (680,000đ). The open top level is perfect for an evening drink. Set lunch 350,000đ, a la carte 540,000– 900,000đ. Daily 11am–2pm, 6–9.30pm.

Le Cine Café 22a Hai Ba Trung ☎04 3433 9362; map pp.354–355. Duck down the alley of the *Hanoi Cinematheque* (see p.381) to find this delightful courtyard café-bar. It serves a great range of ready-made Vietnamese dishes at lunchtime, and there are several Western items like steak and chips (200,000đ) in the evening. It's a good people-watching spot, and sometimes there is live music, at showtime. Daily 9am–11pm.

Pane e Vino 3 Nguyen Khac Can ☎04 3826 9080; map pp.354–355. Popular with the local Italian community for its authentic cuisine and relaxed atmosphere. The menu ranges from *caprese* salad and minestrone soup through *osso buco*, roast lamb and veal *saltimbocca* to zabaglione and the obligatory tiramisu – not to mention the gourmet pasta and pizza dishes. Count on around 600,000đ per head for three courses, 160,000–220,000đ for a pizza. Daily 8am–10pm.

Pots 'n Pans 57 Bui Thi Xuan ☎04 3944 0204, ⓦpotsnpans.vn; map pp.348–349. One of the most exciting new arrivals on Hanoi's culinary scene, this slick venue with minimalist decor is run by graduates of *KOTO* (see p.378). While many chefs tend to make a mess of fusion food, this place produces some innovative twists on classics like duck breast and beef tenderloin. It isn't cheap, but you get what you pay for, and the set lunch is good value at around 200,000đ. Daily 11.30am–9.30pm.

Press Club 59a Ly Thai To ☎04 3934 0888, ⓦhanoi -pressclub.com; map pp.354–355. If you're looking to splurge on a meal in Hanoi, you could do worse than the *Press Club*, which has an exclusive feel about it with plush leather chairs and starched tablecloths. The menu, featuring mostly fusion and international dishes (mains 500,000đ), is constantly changing, though you'll always find steaks and exotics like lobster available. Friday evening is party night, when a live band lets rip on the terrace. Daily 11am–2pm & 6–10.30pm.

★**Quan An Ngon** 18 Phan Boi Chau ☎04 3942 8162, ⓦngonhanoi.com.vn; map pp.348–349. Quite possibly the city's most popular restaurant, *Ngon* (meaning "delicious") is often packed full, especially at peak eating hours. The concept is simple, to provide upmarket street food in pleasant surroundings at easily affordable prices. Choose from the menu or see what takes your fancy at stalls cooking up Hanoi and Hue specialities around the garden seating area – there are more tables in the colonial villa behind. Check out their website for other venues. Daily 6.30am–10pm.

WEST AND NORTH OF THE CENTRE

Foodshop 45 59 Truc Bach ☎04 3716 2959, ⓦfoodshop45.com; map pp.348–349. It's worth going out of your way to eat at this welcoming Indian restaurant in an interesting residential district overlooking Truc Bach Lake. The Indian-trained chef cooks up a tasty tandoor dishes and a cracking Kadhai chicken with big chunks of meat. Excellent value for money, and if you're too lazy to go there they'll deliver to your hotel room. There's also a small branch in the Old Quarter, at 32 Hang Buom. Daily 10am–10.30pm.

Khai's Brothers 26 Nguyen Thai Hoc ☎04 3733 3866; map pp.348–349. Through a traditional entranceway on this busy main road, you'll find a peaceful courtyard restaurant with tables set out under the trees. They only serve buffets, which are well priced at $12.50 for lunch and $18.50 in the evening (weekends $23, with wine thrown in). Daily 11.30am–2pm & 6.30–10pm.

Kitchen 30 To Ngoc Van, Tay Ho District ☎04 3719 2679; map pp.348–349. This place with a shady patio and a/c interior (seating upstairs too) is a handy spot for refreshment if you're exploring the West Lake area. They serve Mexican dishes, sandwiches, salads and pasta (all 140,000–220,000đ), as well as yummy juices and shakes. Mon 7am–3pm, Tues–Sun 7am–10pm.

★**KOTO** 59 Van Mieu ☎04 3747 0337; map pp.348–349. Deservedly popular restaurant staffed by erstwhile street kids, under a charity programme to train them in hospitality skills. Start the day with muesli and fresh fruits or a full buffet breakfast, or stop by later for a gourmet sandwich or a barbecued duck salad (most main courses are around 100,000–140,000đ), but make sure you leave room for dessert. Views from the rooftop terrace overlook the Temple of Literature. All proceeds are ploughed back into the charity, and they offer cooking classes too. Daily 7.30am–10pm.

CAFÉS

Hanoi's French legacy is particularly apparent in the city's adoption of café culture. The city boasts hundreds of local cafés, offering minimum comfort but great coffee – usually small, strong shots of the local brew. Two streets that are lined with atmospheric establishments are Nguyen Huu Haan, on the east side of the Old Quarter, and Hang Hanh, near the northwest corner of Hoan Kiem Lake.

Café Lam 60 Nguyen Huu Huan ☎04 3824 5940; map pp.354–355. This shabby but atmospheric one-room café made its name in Hanoi's lean years as a place for artists and young intellectuals to hang out and subsequently has a bohemian vibe. A few paid their bills with paintings, some of which still adorn the walls. If you're not an artist, a coffee will cost you around 25,000đ. Daily 7am–10pm.

City View Café 7 Dinh Tien Hoang ☎04 3934 7911, ⓦcityviewcafe.com.vn; map pp.354–355. This aptly named café has the best views possible of Hoan Kiem from the fifth floor of the tall building at the northern end of the lake. Look for the entrance in the southwest corner of the building, take the lift up, and bag a seat overlooking

---

HANOI'S UNUSUAL EATS

In addition to the traditional favourite street food, it's not uncommon to find dishes featuring goat, dog, rat, snake and porcupine. Some readers may find this ethically challenging, but the eating of animals is deeply entrenched in Vietnamese culture, and an invitation to share in the feast is to be considered an honour.

If you want to sample **dog meat** (*thit cho*), a northern speciality eaten mostly in winter but never during days one to ten of the lunar calendar month, then head out of Hanoi along the Red River dyke to **Nghi Tam Avenue**. There are dozens of stilthouse restaurants to choose from; your best bet is to head for the busiest. The dog meat comes boiled (*luoc*) or grilled (*cha nuong*) and served with green banana and tofu (*rua man*), and is washed down with rice wine.

Le Mat snake village – 4km over Chuong Duong Bridge in the Gia Lam District – is home to a slew of **snake-meat** restaurants, some of which play to the crowd with elaborate theatrics, including killing the snake in front of you. It's then served up in every possible form, from soup and crispy-fried skin accompanied by rice wine liquors laced with blood and bile. The guest of honour gets to eat the still pumping heart – beware, it's alleged to have amphetamine properties. Though not the cheapest of Le Mat's restaurants, *Quoc Trieu* (74/161 Hoa Lam, ☎04 3827 2988; daily 10am–10pm) has a reliable reputation and leaves out the gory bits.

WATCH OUT FOR THE WEASELS

Since Vietnam is one of the world's foremost producers of **coffee**, a bag of aromatic beans makes an ideal gift for friends back home, or even something for your own kitchen to remind you of sitting in Vietnamese cafés. Most coffee vendors sell something they call **weasel coffee** (caphe chon in Vietnamese), which is produced by passing the beans through the digestive system of **civet cats**. This results in a distinctive taste – slightly smoky with a hint of chocolate – and the beans often fetch up to $100 a kilo. Not surprising, then, that some clever coffee producers have managed to mimic the taste using biotechnology, so it's difficult to know whether you're getting the real thing. Also, some countries like Australia now ban the import of this coffee, so think twice before buying some to take home.

the peaceful waters and frantic traffic below. Fruit shakes and beers at reasonable prices, plus an extensive menu of Vietnamese and Western cuisine. Daily 10am–11pm.

Cong Caphe 35a Nguyen Huu Huan w congcaphe.com; map pp.354–355. One in a café chain whose premises are designed like Viet Cong bunkers, (complete with bullet holes in the walls); staff wear Viet Cong gear, and coffee is served in war-style enamel mugs – all very 1970s. Daily 7am–11.30pm.

Fanny 51 Ly Thuong Kiet ☎ 04 3937 8170, w fanny .com.vn; map pp.354–355. Hanoi's top ice-cream parlour serves up a bewildering array of flavours, such as cinammon, avocado and durian. They have recently moved to a new, bigger location in the French Quarter, where there are two floors and an open-air courtyard. Daily 7am–11pm.

Hanoi Social Club 6 Hoi Vu ☎ 04 3938 2117; map pp.354–355. Set in an atmospheric, 1924 building, this is a great place to hang out while checking your email or browsing the web. Choose from three floors of quirky seating (including a rooftop garden), from old sofas to hard-backed chairs, and order from the equally quirky menu (porridge, pumpkin salad, potato pancakes with chorizo and, of course, coffee). Only problem is that the staff sometimes get too wrapped up in the laidback vibe and forget to work. Daily 8am–11pm.

Highlands Coffee 1-3-5 Dinh Tien Hoang ☎ 04 3936 3228, w highlandscoffee.com.vn; map pp.354–355. A Vietnamese *Starbucks* clone with an increasing number of outlets; the best location is on the third floor of the building overlooking the north end of Hoan Kiem Lake, followed by the one outside the Hanoi Opera House. Prices are higher than elsewhere but the quality coffee and comfy seating make it worthwhile. Daily 7am–9pm.

Hue Café 26 Hang Giay; map pp.354–355. This tiny store sells strong coffee from the Central Highlands. The quality is high, every cup is freshly ground and prices are very low (30,000–50,000đ). Also available is "weasel coffee", though this unusual beverage has its complications (see box above). Daily 8am–10pm.

Loft Stop Café 11b Bao Khanh ☎ 04 3928 9433; map pp.354–355. An ideal spot for refreshment while slogging

round the lake and the Old Quarter, this recently renovated café provides a cheaper alternative to its sister restaurant upstairs (the *Millennium*), serving good juices and coffees and a decent range of Western and Vietnamese dishes. Daily 8am–11pm.

Love Chocolate 26 To Ngoc Van ☎ 04 2243 2120, w lovechocolatecafe.com; map pp.348–349. Located some distance from the centre near the northern side of West Lake, but it's well worth the hike to this faux English living room; think mint paint, pot plants and flowery curtains, with batches of delicious home-made cookies rustled up daily. A bit pricey but worth it for the unique atmosphere. Mon–Sat 10am–10pm.

Moca 14–16 Nha Tho ☎ 04 3825 6334; map pp.354–355. Located in the hip cathedral area, *Moca*'s huge picture windows are ideal for people-watching over a mug of the creamiest, frothiest café latte in town, and prices aren't steep either. In winter hunker down by the open fire. Daily 8am–11pm.

★**Nola** Alley beside 89 Ma May ☎ 04 3926 4669; map pp.354–355. This is another difficult-to-find place, despite being almost next door to Heritage House (see p.353), though well worth the effort. Down the twisting alley and up the stairs, you'll find a variety of cosy, high-ceilinged rooms with retro decor, cool beats (Louis Armstrong, vintage Dylan), interesting snacks and cheap beers. Daily 10am–11pm.

Pho Co 11 Hang Gai ☎ 04 3928 8153; map pp.354–355. Finding this fascinating place is half the fun: go through the souvenir shops at number #11, then along a narrow passage and into a hushed courtyard, where you place your order. Head up the stairs, past the family altar, up a spiral staircase and one more flight of regular steps, and you'll finally reach a roof terrace high above Hoan Kiem Lake, where you can sample coffee with added egg white, if you dare. Prices are very reasonable for such a central location. Daily 8am–11pm.

Puku 16–18 Tong Duy Tan ☎ 04 3938 1745; map pp.354–355. This popular café located a couple of blocks north of the railway station offers round-the-clock service, so it's handy for early arrivals looking for a 4am breakfast. It's one of the main hangout venues for Hanoi expats, and deservedly so, offering

7

"couch-surfing food and wifi-enabled coffee", plus sports on TV. Not cheap but worth it for the ambience. Daily 24hrs.

Saint Honore 5 Xuan Dieu ☎04 3933 2355, ⓦsaint honore.com.vn; map pp.348–349. Excellent patisserie and bistro in the West Lake area, serving delicious cakes and main dishes such as steak tartare. Daily 8am–10pm.

Thuy Ta 1 Le Thai To ☎04 3828 8148; map pp.354–355. A breezy lakeside café that's a great spot for breakfast, afternoon tea, ice cream or an evening beer, though the food is only average quality. Very popular among tourists and a bit pricey, but you pay for the location. Daily 7am–10pm.

DRINKING AND NIGHTLIFE

For a capital city, Hanoi sleeps pretty early: most **bars** outside the big hotels sweep up around midnight and **nightclubs** don't stay open much later. The authorities blow hot and cold over enforcing a midnight **curfew**, but one or two places always seem to keep pouring until the last customer leaves: check the English-language listings magazines (see p.372) for the current situation. The choice of nightspots is constantly increasing, however, particularly on Ta Hien, a street packed with lively, dimly lit bars, and nearby Dau Duy Ta, where more of the clientele is Vietnamese. Nevertheless, the busiest venues are without doubt the **bia hoi** outlets selling pitchers of the local brew (see box below).

Binh Minh Jazz Club 1 Trang Tien ☎04 3933 6555, ⓦminhjazzvietnam.com; map pp.354–355. Hanoi's premier jazz club has moved to a spot right behind the Opera House – look for the dimly lit lane with a small sign on Trang Tien. It's run by Hanoi's living jazz legend, the charismatic and highly accomplished saxophonist Quyen Van Minh. Sit back and enjoy a 2hr set of mainstream classics every night between 9pm and 11pm. No cover fee but pricey drinks. Daily 8pm–midnight.

★CAMA ATK 73a Mai Hac De ☎0915 631120, ⓦcama-atk.com; map pp.348–349. One of the few nightspots in the French Quarter, this intriguing venue frequently hosts visiting musicians as the owners are also concert organizers. Check out the website to see what's coming up. Friendly vibe and well-stocked bar. Wed–Sat 6pm–midnight.

The Cheeky Quarter 1 Ta Hien ☎0169 368 3773; map pp.354–355. Good music, great food and table football are on the cards here, though given the size and layout things can feel decidedly dead on a midweek night. Daily 6pm–2am.

Funky Buddha 2 Ta Hien ☎04 3297 7614, ⓦlinkhanoi .com; map pp.354–355. A focus on fixtures, fittings and pulsating lighting has made this one of Hanoi's most popular lounge bars, with beers costing around $3–4. There's an excellent sound system which plays dance music extremely loud, so don't even think of having a conversation here. It attracts 20-something lounge lizards of every nationality. Daily 6pm–1am.

Hair of the Dog 32 Ma May ☎0938 385382; map pp.354–355. Classic dark night club with flashing lights and dancefloor downstairs and a chill-out area with shisha pipes upstairs. It attracts plenty of young locals as well as backpackers from the hostel across the street. Daily 8pm–2am.

Hay 12 Ta Hien; map pp.354–355. This place seems to change its name every few months, but it stands out from other Ta Hien bars for its live music featuring talented locals playing original compositions. Just look for number #12, about 20m north of bia hoi corner on the left. Daily 7pm–midnight.

Irish Wolfhound 4 Luong Ngoc Quyen ☎04 2212 6821, ⓦirishwolfhoundpub.com; map pp.354–355. Appealing bar on the eastern side of the Old Quarter where you'll find imported beers, sports on TV and a welcoming smile. There's usually a live band on Friday and Saturday nights – check out the events calendar on the website. Daily 11am–2am.

★La Bomba Latina 46 Ngo Huyen ☎0917 245155; map pp.354–355. This music club is a must-visit for lovers of merengue, bachata, zouk, reggaeton, salsa or any other Latin beats. Located along a narrow lane of budget hotels near the cathedral, it attracts a mixed crowd of Vietnamese and foreigners with one thing in common; they all love to dance. Daily 6pm–2am.

Le Pub 25 Hang Be ☎04 3926 2104; map pp.354–355. A good range of drinks at reasonable prices – including genuinely *cold* beers – plus above-average food, decent music and friendly bar staff ensures a real pub atmosphere in an Old Quarter tube-house. There are different drink promotions most days. Daily 8am–1am.

BIA HOI CORNER

During the day it's just like any other corner in the Old Quarter, but if you go to the junction of **Luong Ngoc Quyen and Ta Hien** any time after 5pm, you'll find the crossroads full of Westerners squatting on tiny stools set out by one of a few **bia hoi** bars around here, drinking fresh draught beer poured straight from the barrel. Bia hoi needs to be drunk quickly before it loses its fizz, but there are usually plenty of takers as it's tasty, refreshing and only 5000đ a glass. If you'd rather sup your suds in the company of locals rather than backpackers, head for **Lan Chin**, at 2 Trang Tien, directly opposite the History Museum.

Mao's Red Lounge 7 Ta Hien ☎04 3926 3104; map pp.354–355. Cheap prices and strong cocktails make this two-level bar one of the most popular places on Hanoi's nighttime strip; at weekends, it can achieve rowdiness quite at odds with its loungey setting and mood music. Daily 6pm–2am.

Polite Pub 5b Bao Khanh ☎0904 198086; map pp.354–355. It claims to be the oldest pub in town, and it certainly has a loyal clientele of expats who drop in after work for a beer or a single malt scotch and maybe a cigar. There's a pool table, cool tunes and ice-cold drinks. Daily 5pm–midnight.

R&R Tavern 256 Nghi Tam ☎04 6295 8215, ⊛rockandrolltavern.com; map pp.348–349. One of Hanoi's longest-running live music venues, now relocated to the West Lake area, the *Tavern* is still pumping out Sixties and Seventies classics on Friday nights. There's also an open-mic night on Mondays and quiz night on Tuesdays. Daily 9am–2am.

Rock Store 61 Ma May ☎0987 132586, ⊛linkhanoi.com; map pp.354–355. With a choice location on Ma May, this two-floor bar always has some event going on, whether it's a sexy nurse party, a live band or a visiting DJ. Cocktails around 100,000đ. It's run by Link Hanoi, which now operates around half a dozen bars in the Old Quarter. Daily 10am–1am.

ENTERTAINMENT

Hanoi offers an unusual mix of highbrow entertainment, from traditional Vietnamese **water puppetry** to performances of traditional music, such as *ca tru*, and theatres featuring classical opera. The shows at the Golden Bell and Hong Ha theatres offer a glimpse of traditional Vietnamese folk music and drama, but apart from these and a few tourist-oriented restaurants that feature traditional music in the evenings (such as *Indochine*; see p.376), there are no other venues regularly showcasing Vietnamese traditional culture in Hanoi. However, things are changing fast, so it's worth asking the concierge at your hotel if there's anything interesting happening in your part of town. For movie buffs, there are cinema complexes in shopping malls that screen English-language films, and the unique Cinémathèque showing art-house films.

★ Ca Tru Recognized by UNESCO in 2009 as an intangible heritage in need of safeguarding, *ca tru* music is performed by an ensemble consisting of just three musicians, one of whom is a female singer. The haunting sounds are not everyone's cup of tea, but if you can open your ears and close your eyes for an hour, you might just find it very moving. Currently shows start at 8pm on Tues, Thurs and Sat at 87 Ma May and Wed, Fri and Sun at 42 Hang Bac (see map, pp.354–355), but check ☎0122 3266897, ⊛catruthanglong.com for any changes. Tickets cost $10.

Cinema Megastar, at the top of Vincom Towers (191 Ba Trieu ☎04 3974 3333; map pp.348–349), shows English-language films with tickets priced at $4–5. If you're in Hanoi for a while, it's well worth joining the members-only Hanoi Cinémathèque (22a Hai Ba Trung ☎04 3936 2648; map pp.354–355) for its range of international non-mainstream movies (200,000đ per year, 60,000đ donation for non-members). There's often live music before movie showings at *Le Cine Café* (see p.377) in front of the cinema.

Opera Hanoi's Opera House (1 Trang Tien ☎04 3933 0113, ⊛hanoioperahouse.org.vn; map pp.354–355) makes a grand setting for performances of classical music and opera; this historic building features a truly sumptuous interior of plush red fabrics, mirrors and chandeliers. Tickets are available from the foyer (200,000–700,000; daily 8am–5pm) or can be booked by phone or online. The Hong Ha Theatre (51 Duong Thanh ☎04 3825 2803; map pp.354–355) hosts performances of Vietnamese classical opera (*Hat Tuong*), usually on Thurs from 6pm to 7pm, but call to check. Admission 150,000đ.

Theatre The Golden Bell Theater (72 Hang Bac ☎098 8307 272, ⊛goldenbellshow.vn; map pp.354–355) is housed in a beautiful colonial building in the heart of the Old Quarter. One-hour shows geared to tourists (Sat 8–9pm; 150,000đ) present eight performances of traditional folk styles.

Water puppets The Thang Long Water Puppet Troupe is by far the most popular, and polished, of Hanoi's water-puppeteers; though aimed at tourists, their shows feature modern stage effects to create an engaging spectacle. Catch them at the small, a/c Thang Long Water Puppet Theatre (57b Dinh Tien Hoang ☎04 3936 4335, ⊛thanglongwaterpuppet.org; map pp.354–355), located by the northeast corner of Hoan Kiem Lake. Performances are held daily at 1.45pm, 3pm, 4.10pm, 5.20pm. 6.30pm, 8pm and 9.15pm, with an additional 9.30am show on Sundays; front row tickets cost 100,000đ, rear rows 60,000đ.

SHOPPING AND MARKETS

When it comes to shopping for crafts, silk, accessories and souvenirs, Hanoi offers the best overall choice, quality and value for money in the country. **Specialities** of the region are embroideries, wood- and stone-carvings, inlay work and lacquer; the best areas to browse are the south end of the Old Quarter, such as along Hang Gai and the streets around St Joseph's Cathedral. Though smarter establishments increasingly have fixed prices, at many shops you'll be expected to **bargain** (see box, p.56), and the same goes, naturally, for market stalls. Hanoi has over fifty **markets**, selling predominantly foodstuffs – you'll rarely be far from one.

7

7

FOOD AND FLOWER MARKETS

Cho Dong Xuan Dong Xuan; map pp.354–355. This is Hanoi's largest covered market, covering two enormous floors with numerous sections to explore. It's the most convenient market for the Old Quarter and also the starting point of electric car tours of the area. Daily 8am–5pm.

Cho Hoa Quang Ba 236 Au Co; map pp.348–349. This flower market, sometimes called Quang An market, is located near West Lake at the northern junction of Au Co with Xuan Dieu; it's at its busiest from midnight to early morning, though some stalls open all day. It's where hotels, restaurants and street vendors go to stock up for each day's business, and as you'll imagine, the air is thick with the scent of tropical blooms. It's particularly busy in the weeks before Tet (January/February), when everyone wants flowers to brighten their home. Daily midnight–5pm.

Cho Hom Pho Hue; map pp.348–349. Though it's quite a trek from the Old Quarter, this market is one of the best places to buy fabrics in the city, and it functions as a fresh market as well. Daily 6am–5pm.

ANTIQUES AND INTERIORS

It's illegal to export antiques from Vietnam, but you'll find plenty of fake "antique" jewellery or watches on sale, and beautifully crafted copies of ancient religious statues. The following details supply elegant if pricey home accessories and gifts.

54 Traditions Gallery 30 Hang Bun ☎04 3715 0194, ⓦ54traditions.com.vn; map pp.348–349. This place deals in genuine antiques and artefacts of the ethnic minority groups, and provides full documentation for each item. These items include tribal textiles, tribal tools for living and shamanic arts. It's worth a visit to their gallery even if you're not buying. Daily 8am–6pm.

Dome 10 Yen The ☎04 3843 6036 and 27 Au Co ☎04 3719 0099, ⓦdome.com.vn; map pp.348–349. The tempting displays here show off items of home decor such as lacquerware boxes, candle holders and vases at their best. Daily 9am–5.30pm.

Hanoi Moment 101 Hang Gai ☎04 3928 7170, ⓦhanoimoment.vn; map pp.354–355. Classy souvenirs are laid out in an uncluttered manner, unlike at most souvenir shops, making it easy to view products like tea sets, original jewellery and bags. Daily 9am–6pm.

La Casa 51 Xuan Dieu ☎04 3718 4084, ⓦlacasa vietnam.com.vn; map pp.348–349. An upmarket souvenir and home decor store, this place sells eye-catching items from an Italian designer and made by Vietnamese craftsmen. Daily 9am–5pm.

Mosaïque 6 Ly Quoc Su ☎04 6270 0430, ⓦmosaique decoration.com; map pp.354–355. The new location of Mosaique displays three floors of gorgeous interiors that feature elegant drapes, graceful vases, silk hangings, lamps, ready-to-wear items and silver jewellery. Daily 9am–5pm.

BOOKS AND NEWSPAPERS

There's not a great choice of English-language reading material in Hanoi, though wandering vendors in the Old Quarter and near the lake sell pirated English-language publications, including guides, phrasebooks and novels.

Bookworm 44 Chau Long ☎04 3715 3711, ⓦbookworm hanoi.com; map pp.348–349. Located to the north of the Old Quarter, this is probably Hanoi's best bookshop with a great selection of new and secondhand English-language books for sale or exchange. There's a second branch at Lane 1/28, Nghi Tam Village. Daily 9am–7pm.

Hanoi Book Store 43 Luong Ngoc Quyen ☎016 9566 7777, ⓦhanoibookstore.com; map pp.354–355. Your best bet for books in the Old Quarter, stocking new guide-books and thousands of secondhand books. Exchange accepted as well. Daily 8.30am–9.30pm.

Love Planet Travel 25 Hang Bac ☎091 4846 452; map pp.354–355. This place buys and sells used books, and also stocks a few guidebooks, but it's only open for limited hours. Daily 10.30am–noon and 3–8pm.

CLOTHES AND ACCESSORIES

Although the selection is limited, you'll find no shortage of places to buy embroidered and printed T-shirts, notably along Hang Gai and Hang Dao. To complete your look, head for Hang Dau, near the northeast corner of the lake, and pick up a pair of sneakers or high heels.

Contraband 23 Nha Chung ☎04 3928 9891, ⓦprieure .com.vn; map pp.354–355. Operated by the owners of Things of Substance, this place sells versatile fabrics that are comfortable to wear. Daily 9am–9pm.

Marie-Linh 74 Hang Trong ☎093 9286 309, ⓦmarie -linh.com; map pp.354–355. Beautiful handmade silk clothes are available here, with the emphasis on modernity, glamour and simplicity. Daily 8am–7pm.

Metiseko 71 Hang Gai ☎04 3935 2645, ⓦmetiseko .com; map pp.354–355. Promoting an "eco chic" lifestyle, this store has become hugely popular for its organic and eco-friendly clothing in sensible yet eye-catching styles. Daily 8.30am–9pm.

Things of Substance 5 Nha Tho ☎04 3828 6965, ⓦprieure.com.vn; map pp.354–355. This Aussie-run store features designs for Western sizes, mostly in soft cotton jersey and linens, that look and feel good for both work and leisure. Daily 9am–9pm.

Tina Sparkle 17 Nha Tho ☎04 3928 7616, ⓦipa-nima .com; map pp.354–355. If you're looking for accessories that make heads turn, here's your place. They make outrageous bags – and the decadent decor is worth a look. Daily 8.30am–8.30pm.

EMBROIDERY

Embroideries and drawn threadwork make eminently packable souvenirs. Standard designs range from traditional

Vietnamese to Santa Claus and robins, but you can also take along your own artwork for something different. Many of the silk and accessories shops also sell embroidered items.

Mekong Quilts 13 Hang Bac ☎04 3926 4831, ⓦmekong-quilts.org; map pp.354–355. Mekong Quilts is a non-profit organization that raises funds for a variety of causes through the sale of bright, patterned quilts, oven gloves and other items; all are made by women in rural provinces. Daily 9am–6pm.

Tan My Design 61 Hang Gai ☎04 3938 1154, ⓦtanmy design.com; map pp.354–355. This is the place to go for the very finest, albeit expensive, embroidered bedlinen, tablecloths, cushion covers and so forth. Daily 8am–8pm.

HANDICRAFTS

Silk lanterns, waterpuppets and silver items – both plated and solid silver – make manageable souvenirs, as do hand-painted greetings cards, usually scenes of rural life or famous beauty spots on paper or silk; the best are unbelievably delicate and sell for next to nothing. Most ordinary souvenir shops also stock ethnic minority crafts, particularly the Hmong and Dao bags, coats and jewellery that are so popular in Sa Pa. Though it's virtually impossible to tell, in fact the majority of these are now made by factories in and around Hanoi, partly to meet the huge demand and partly to get a slice of the action. Of course, everyone will insist their goods are genuine, and they are very well made, but it's something to be aware of.

Craft Link 43–51 Van Mieu ☎04 3733 6101, ⓦcraftlink .com.vn; map pp.348–349. One of the more interesting craft outlets, Craft Link is a not-for-profit organization working with small-scale producers of traditional crafts, particularly among the ethnic minorities, helping develop increasingly high-quality modern designs. Daily 9am–6pm.

XQ 110 Hang Gai ☎04 3938 1905, ⓦtranhtheuxq.com; map pp.354–355. This place produces exquisite silk embroidered paintings that make distinctive souvenirs, and it's fascinating to watch the painstaking process by which they are made. Daily 8.30am–6pm.

LACQUERWARE

Lacquerware makes a pretty portable souvenir: chopsticks, boxes, bowls, vases – the variety of items coated in lacquer is endless. Natural lacquer gives a muted finish, usually in black or rusty reds. However, lacquerware in a rainbow array of colours – made from imported synthetic products – is now very popular in Old Quarter souvenir shops, especially on Hang Be and Ma May. Some designs incorporate eggshell to give a crazed finish, and gold leaf on black lacquer for a more dramatic effect.

MUSICAL INSTRUMENTS

For more unusual mementoes, have a look at the traditional Vietnamese musical instruments on sale at a clutch of little workshops on Hang Non and round the corner on Hang Manh.

Ta Tham Music Shop 16a Hang Manh; map pp.354–355. Sells tiny percussion instruments and jew's harps, which make great little gifts, as well as bamboo xylophones and the classic *dan bau*. Daily 9am–6pm.

Thai Khue Music Shop 1a Hang Manh ☎04 3828 9469; map pp.354–355. This tiny but excellent shop sells a range of unusual instruments from packable pipes and flutes to lithophones and bronze gongs from the central highlands. Daily 8am–8pm.

PROPAGANDA

Several small shops on Hang Bong supply Communist Party banners and badges as well as Vietnamese flags. Reproduction posters are another popular souvenir from the Communist days, and you'll find these in shops throughout the Old Quarter.

SILK

Hanoi has so many silk shops concentrated on Hang Gai, at the southern edge of the Old Quarter, that it's now referred to as "Silk Street"; competition is fierce, but take care since you'll find a fair amount of shops selling tat standing alongside more reputable outlets. Classy designer boutiques offering excellent quality at premium prices now also concentrate around the cathedral. Most bigger places have multilingual staff, accept credit cards and also offer less expensive souvenirs, such as ties, purses, mobile-phone holders and sensuous, silk sleeping bags.

Emerald Silk 9 Bao Khanh ☎04 3824 7215, ⓦngocdiepsilk.com; map pp.354–355. This place is filled with a rainbow array of silk items at very reasonable prices. Well worth rooting around. Daily 9am–8pm.

Hanoi Silk Sheraton, 11 Xuan Dieu; Thang Long Opera Hotel, 1 Tong Dan ⓦhanoisilkvn.com; map pp.348–349. Hanoi Silk specializes in design and tailoring of exclusive silk items; prices are high but the quality is top-notch. Daily 9am–5pm.

Kenly Silk 108 Hang Gai ☎04 3826 7236, ⓦkenlysilk .com; map pp.354–355. Kenly specializes in expensive but high-quality Vietnamese silks (raw, taffeta, satin and even knitted) as well as other fabrics. It also stocks ready-made clothes and has a reputation for reliable tailoring. Daily 9am–6pm.

Khai Silk 113 Hang Gai ☎04 3928 9883, ⓦkhaisilkcorp .com; map pp.354–355. Exclusive and expensive silk creations from Vietnam's leading fashion designer. Daily 9.30am–6pm.

SUPERMARKETS

If you are self-catering, there are two well-stocked and easily accessible supermarkets: one is on the top floor of Trang Tien Plaza at the southeast corner of Hoan Kiem Lake, and the other is Intimex, at 22 Le Thai To on the west side of Hoan Kiem Lake.

7

GALLERIES AND EXHIBITIONS

As Vietnamese art continues to attract international recognition, so ever more **art galleries** appear on the streets of Hanoi. Many of these are merely souvenir shops selling reproduction paintings of variable quality but usually at affordable prices, while some of the big galleries, such as Apricot Gallery and Thang Long Art Gallery, deal exclusively with the country's top artists. However, a number of the galleries listed below showcase more **experimental work** and promote promising newcomers; ⓦ hanoigrapevine.com is one of the best sources of up-to-date information. At the cheap end of the spectrum, you can watch artists running up bootleg "masterpieces" at a number of shops at the north end of Hang Trong. A few photographers have also set up shops which double as exhibition space.

Apricot Gallery 40b Hang Bong ☎ 04 3828 8965, ⓦ apricotgallery.com.vn; map pp.354–355. This is a great place to get an idea of where the latest trends in Vietnamese art are going, but if you ask the prices of any, the answer will probably make your hair stand on end, because they are very expensive. Daily 8am–8pm.

Centre for Exhibition & Art Exchange 2f/43 Trang Tien ☎ 04 3824 0038, ⓦ ceae-artgallery.com; map pp.354–355. This government-run gallery combines a small rental space, which changes every month or so with a regular, commercial gallery at the rear. Daily 8am–5pm.

Dien Dam Gallery 4b Dinh Liet ☎ 04 3825 9881, ⓦ diendam-gallery.com; map pp.354–355. Shop-cum-gallery of award-winning photographer Lai Dien Dam. Daily 9am–9pm.

Goethe Institute 56–58 Nguyen Thai Hoc ☎ 04 3734 2251, ⓦ goethe.de/ins/vn/han; map pp.348–349. Puts on an interesting programme of films, concerts and exhibitions. Daily 8am–6pm.

Green Palm Gallery 15 Trang Tien ☎ 04 3936 4757, ⓦ greenpalmgallery.com; map pp.354–355. Big, well-established gallery showcasing the big names alongside lesser-known artists. Daily 8am–8pm.

Hanoi Studio 13 Trang Tien ☎ 04 3934 4433, ⓦ art hanoistudio.com.vn; map pp.354–355. Commercial gallery hosting three or four interesting and well-displayed exhibitions a year promoting young local artists. Daily 10am–8pm.

Institut Français L'Espace 24 Trang Tien ☎ 04 3936 2164, ⓦ ifhanoi-lespace.com; map pp.354–355. Extensive programme of films (subtitled in English), concerts and exhibitions, plus a members-only media centre. Mon–Fri 8am–8.30pm.

Mai Gallery 113 Hang Bong ☎ 04 3938 0568, ⓦ maigallery-vietnam.com; map pp.354–355. This commercial contemporary art gallery, which also fosters new talent, was actually the first private art gallery to be established in Hanoi, back in 1993. Daily 9am–6pm.

Thang Long Art Gallery 41 Hang Gai ☎ 04 3825 0740, ⓦ thanglongartgallery.com; map pp.354–355. Like Apricot Gallery, Thang Long represents both established artists and up-and-coming newcomers, and often displays large canvases with dramatic compositions in its exhibition space. Daily 8am–6pm.

DIRECTORY

Banks and exchange Most travellers use 24hr ATMs which are widespread throughout the city; those operated by Vietcombank and HSBC accept the most overseas cards. The Vietcombank head office, 198 Tran Quang Khai (foreign exchange services Mon–Fri 8–11.30am & 1–3.30pm; all other services Mon–Fri 7.30–11.30am & 1–5pm), handles all services including cash withdrawals on credit cards and telegraphic transfers. It has branches at 32 Quang Trung, 22 Lo Su and 2 Hang Bai, among other locations.

Dentists The Family Medical Practice Dental Clinic in the Van Phuc Diplomatic Compound, 298 Kim Ma (Mon–Fri 8.30am–4.30pm; ☎ 04 33843 0748, ⓦ vietnammedical practice.com), has a 24hr emergency service. The Hanoi French Hospital and International SOS also provide dental care.

Embassies and consulates Australia, 8 Dao Tan, Van Phuc ☎ 04 33774 0100, ⓦ vietnam.embassy.gov.au; Cambodia, 71a Tran Hung Dao ☎ 04 33942 4789, ⓔ camemb.vnm @mfa.gov.kh; Canada, 31 Hung Vuong ☎ 04 3734 5000, ⓦ canadainternational.gc.ca/vietnam; China, 46 Hoang Dieu ☎ 04 3845 3736, ⓦ vn.china-embassy.org; Lao PDR, 22 Tran Binh Trong ☎ 04 3942 4576, ⓦ laoembassyhanoi.org.vn; Malaysia, 43–45 Dien Bien Phu ☎ 04 3734 3836, ⓦ kin.gov .my/web/vnm_hanoi; Myanmar, A3 Van Phuc Compound, Kim Ma ☎ 04 3845 3369, ⓔ mevhan@fpt.vn; New Zealand, 63 Ly Thai To ☎ 04 3824 1481, ⓦ nzembassy.com/viet-nam; Singapore, 41–43 Tran Phu ☎ 04 3848 9168, ⓦ mfa.gov .sg/content/mfa/overseasmission/hanoi; Thailand, 63–65 Hoang Dieu ☎ 04 3823 5092, ⓦ thaiembassy.org/hanoi; UK, 31 Hai Ba Trung ☎ 04 3936 0500, ⓦ gov.uk/government /world/organisations/british-embassy-hanoi; US, Rose Garden Tower, 170 Ngoc Khanh ☎ 04 3850 5000, ⓦ vietnam .usembassy.gov. For information on visas for China and Laos and Cambodia, see p.30.

Emergencies Dial ☎ 113 to call the police, ☎ 114 in case of fire and ☎ 115 for an ambulance; better still, get a Vietnamese-speaker to call on your behalf.

Hospitals and clinics The Hanoi French Hospital, 1 Phuong Mai, offers facilities of an international standard including a 24hr emergency service (☎ 04 3574 1111), an outpatients clinic (Mon–Fri 8.30am–noon & 1.30–5.30pm, Sat 8.30am–noon; ☎ 04 3577 1100, ⓦ hfh.com.vn), dental and optical care, and surgery. Alternatively, the Family Medical Practice, Van Phuc Compound, 298 I Kim Ma, is well known for its reasonable pricing (Mon–Fri 8.30am–5.30pm, Sat 8.30am–12.30pm; ☎ 04 3843 0748, ⓦ vietnammedicalpractice.com). It has an outpatient clinic and a 24hr emergency service. International SOS, at 51 Xuan Dieu, provides routine care (Mon–Fri 8am–7pm, Sat 8am–2pm; ☎ 04 3826 4545, ⓦ internationalsos.com).

Laundry Most hotels have a laundry service, while top hotels also offer dry cleaning, but prices can be steep. Alternatively, try one of the low-priced laundries (*giat la*) in the Old Quarter. Look for laundry signs along Hang Be,

Ma May or Ta Hien; the standard rate is around 20,000đ per kilo for a one-day service.

Pharmacies The Hanoi French Hospital, Family Medical Practice and International SOS (see opposite) all have pharmacies. Of the local retail outlets, those at 37a Ta Hien and 4a Dinh Liet stock a selection of imported medicines. Traditional medicines can be bought on Lan Ong.

Post offices The GPO occupies a whole block at 75 Dinh Tien Hoang (daily 6.30am–9pm). The main entrance leads to general mail and telephone services, while international postal services, including parcel dispatch (Mon–Fri 7.30–11.30am & 1–4.30pm), are located in the southernmost hall.

Around Hanoi

7

When you've taken in Hanoi's main sights, there are plenty more places waiting to be explored in the surrounding area, including the cave-shrine of the **Perfume Pagoda**, which is one of the country's most sacred locations. There are the dozens of other historic buildings, of which the most strongly atmospheric are the **Thay Pagoda** and **Tay Phuong Pagoda**, buried deep in the delta, both of which are fine examples of traditional Vietnamese architecture. You could also spend months exploring the delta's villages – in particular the **craft villages**, which retain their traditions despite a constant stream of tourists passing though. The **Ho Chi Minh Trail Museum**, southwest of the centre, is also well worth a visit, especially if you're heading out of town on Highway 6, for example to Mai Chau. Finally, the ancient citadel of **Co Loa**, just north of the Red River, merits a stop in passing, mostly on account of its historical significance – since there's little to recall its former grandeur.

The Perfume Pagoda

50,000đ • Boats run 8am–4pm

Sixty kilometres southwest of Hanoi, the Red River Delta ends abruptly where steep-sided **limestone hills** rise from the paddy fields. The most easterly of these forested spurs – known as the Mountain of the Perfumed Traces – shelters north Vietnam's most famous pilgrimage site, the **Perfume Pagoda**, Chua Huong, which is named after spring blossoms that scent the air. While the karst scenery is undoubtedly memorable and a visit gives the chance to see the Vietnamese in festive mood, many Western visitors find the trip here a long and tiring day (starting around 8am and returning after dark) with little reward, so consider carefully before signing up for a tour or heading out on your own. If you don't like crowds, then avoid coming here at weekends.

The Perfume Pagoda, one of more than thirty peppering these hills, is in fact an impressive **grotto** over 50m high, with altars in its recesses at which devotees pray and make offerings. The start of the journey is an hour's **row-boat ride** up a silent, flooded valley among karst hills where fishermen and farmers work their inundated fields. The boat drops visitors beside a string of restaurants that hang out deer, weasels and other animals to tempt customers in – which works well with Vietnamese visitors, but horrifies most foreigners. From here a stone-flagged path shaded by gnarled frangipani trees brings you to the foot of the hill from where thousands of steps lead to the principal pagoda, Chua Huong Tich.

Note that **respectful attire** – meaning long trousers, skirts below the knee and no sleeveless tops – should be worn for this trip; nobody will berate you for not doing so, but you might be the subject of unflattering comments. A hat or umbrella is also a help, as the boats have no shelter.

Chua Thien Chu

A magnificent, triple-roofed bell pavilion stands in front of the **Chua Thien Chu**, ("Pagoda Leading to Heaven"), the first of several pagodas at the site. Quan Am, Bodhisattva of Compassion, takes pride of place on the pagoda's main altar; the original bronze effigy was stolen by Tay Son rebels in the 1770s, and some say they melted it down for cannonballs.

Uphill to the pagoda

Cable car 80,000đ one way, 120,000đ return

To the right of Chua Thien Chu as you face it, **steps** lead steeply uphill for two kilometres (about 1hr) to the **Perfume Pagoda** (Chua Huong Tich), also dedicated to Quan Am. Taking the parallel **cable car** might appeal, despite the expense: the hike is not especially interesting and can be hard going, especially in hot or wet weather; you'll need good walking shoes and remember to drink plenty of water (bring your own, or be prepared to pay above the odds at drinks stalls along the route). During festival time, the path is lined all the way with stalls selling tacky souvenirs and refreshments, giving the place more of a commercial than spiritual atmosphere.

The Perfume Pagoda

However you reach it, the grotto that functions as the **Perfume Pagoda** reveals itself as a gaping cavern on the side of a deep depression filled with vines and trees reaching for light beneath the Chinese inscription "supreme cave under the southern sky". Another flight of 120 steps descends into the dragon's-mouth-like entrance where gilded Buddhas emerge from dark recesses wreathed in clouds of incense that is lit as an offering by Vietnamese visitors.

ARRIVAL AND DEPARTURE

THE PERFUME PAGODA

By car or tour The easiest and most popular way to visit the pagoda is on an organized tour out of Hanoi ($25–35, including the boat ride, lunch and entry fee), or with a hired car and driver. One big advantage of this is that your guide will shield you from the persistent hawkers who want to sell you postcards and other souvenirs.

By bike and boat To go it alone, it's a two- to three-hour motorbike ride: follow Highway 6 through Ha Dong,

from where a sign points you left down the QL21B heading due south through Thanh Oai and Van Dinh, to find My Duc Village and the Ben Yen (Yen River boat station). A six-person boat costs 240,000đ (though the rower will expect a tip too), or it's 40,000đ to join a group. Memorize your boat number for the return journey from where you are dropped off, as there are hundreds of identical craft.

Thay Pagoda

Daily 8am–5pm • 10,000đ

Thay Pagoda, or the Master's Pagoda – also known as Thien Phuc Tu ("Pagoda of the Heavenly Blessing") – was founded in the reign of King Ly Nhan Ton (1072–1127) and is an unusually large complex fronting onto a picturesque lake in the lee of a limestone crag.

Despite many restorations over the centuries, the pagoda's dark, subdued interior retains a powerful atmosphere. Nearly a hundred **statues** fill the prayer halls: the oldest dates back to the pagoda's foundation, but the most eyecatching are two seventeenth-century giant **guardians** made of clay and papier-mâché, which weigh a thousand kilos apiece and are said to be the biggest in Vietnam. Beyond, the highest altar holds a Buddha trinity, dating from the 1500s, and a thirteenth-century wooden statue of the Master (see box opposite).

The grounds of the pagoda

In front of the pagoda are two attractive **covered bridges** with arched roofs built in 1602 (though recently renovated) and dedicated to the sun and moon: one leads to

THE MASTER

The Master was the ascetic monk and healer **Tu Dao Hanh** (sometimes also known as Minh Khong) who "burned his finger to bring about rain and cured diseases with holy water", in addition to countless other miracles. He was head monk of the pagoda and an accomplished water-puppeteer – hence the dainty theatre-pavilion in the lake – and, according to legend, he was reincarnated first as a Buddha and then as the future King Ly Than Ton in answer to King Ly Nhan Tong's prayers for an heir. To complicate matters further, Ly Than Ton's life was then saved by the monk Tu Dao Hanh. Anyway, the Thay Pagoda is dedicated to the cult of Tu Dao Hanh in his three incarnations as monk (the Master), Buddha and king.

The highest **altar** in the pagoda holds a thirteenth-century wooden statue of the Master as a bodhisattva, dressed in yellow garb and perched on a lotus throne. On a separate altar to the left he appears again as King Ly Than Ton, also in yellow, accompanied by two dark-skinned, kneeling figures, who are said to be Cambodian slaves, while to the right sits a mysterious, lavishly decorated wooden chamber. The monk's mortal remains and a statue with articulated legs repose in this final, securely locked sanctuary – though a **photo** on the altar shows the statue's beady eyes staring out of a gaunt, unhappy face – to be revealed only once a year: at 1pm on the fifth day of the third lunar month the village's oldest male bathes Tu Dao Hanh with fragrant water and helps him to his feet.

Traditionally, this event was for the monks' eyes only, but nowadays anyone can see, as long as they're prepared to put up with the scrum. The celebrations, attended by thousands, continue for three days and include daily processions as well as a famous **water-puppet festival** held on the lake (fifth to seventh days of the third lunar month).

an islet where spirits of the earth, water and sky are worshipped in a diminutive Taoist temple; the second takes you to a well-worn flight of steps up the limestone hill. In the middle of the lake is an ancient pavilion, which is still occasionally used for performances of water puppets.

ARRIVAL AND DEPARTURE   THAY PAGODA

By car or bike The pagoda lies 30km from Hanoi in Sai Son Village. As this isn't a popular tour destination for Western visitors, you'll probably need to hire a car and driver for the excursion, or rent a motorbike. The easiest route is via the new Thang Long Highway, heading west of Hanoi; after about 25km look out for a right turn to Chua Tay and Sunny Garden City, a new satellite development. Note that this is a popular weekend jaunt for domestic visitors, at its busiest on Sun.

Tay Phuong Pagoda

Daily 8am–5pm • 10,000đ • Though Tay Phuong Pagoda is only about 6km west of the Thay Pagoda, a complex network of lanes between them makes it difficult to find alone. It's best to arrange a customized tour of this pagoda, the Thay Pagoda and Tram Gian Pagoda through one of Hanoi's recommended tour operators (see p.370)

The small "Pagoda of the West", **Tay Phuong Pagoda**, perches atop a 50m-high limestone hillock supposedly shaped like a buffalo. Among the first pagodas built in Vietnam, Tay Phuong's overriding attraction is its invaluable collection of jackfruit-wood **statues**, some of which are on view at Hanoi's Fine Arts Museum (see p.363). The highlights are **eighteen arhats**, disturbingly lifelike representations of Buddhist ascetics as imagined by eighteenth-century sculptors, grouped around the main altar; a torch would help pick out the finer details.

As Tay Phuong is also an important **Confucian sanctuary**, disciples of the sage are included on the altar, each carrying a gift to their master, some precious object, a book or a symbol of longevity, alongside the expected Buddha effigies. Tay Phuong's most notable **architectural features** are its heavy double roofs, whose graceful curves are decorated with phoenixes and dragons, and an inviting approach via 237 time-worn, red-brick steps.

Tram Gian Pagoda

Daily 8am–5pm • Free • Coming from Hanoi, the pagoda's signed to the right of Highway 6 at the 21km marker

With time to spare, you could combine a day's outing to the Thay and Tay Phuong pagodas with a quick detour to the **Tram Gian Pagoda**. Again, the large, peaceful temple sitting on a wooded hill is best known for its rich array of statues. Though not as fine as those of Tay Phuong, they are numerous, including more *arhats* in the side corridors, alongside some toe-curling depictions of the underworld, and an impressive group on the main altar. Among them sits the unmistakable, pot-bellied laughing Maitreya, the carefree Buddha, in stark contrast to the black emaciated figure behind him. According to legend, this is the mummified and lacquered body of **Duc Thanh Boi** (St Boi), who was born nearby in the thirteenth century. He is credited with numerous miracles, including the ability to fly, and with saving the country from a catastrophic drought by summoning rain, though he had to wait for sainthood until a century after his death when devotees disinterred his body to find it in a perfect state of preservation.

7

Ho Chi Minh Trail Museum

Mon–Sat 7.30–11.30am & 1.30–4.30pm • 20,000đ, camera 10,000đ • The museum is set back to the right of Highway 6, just beyond the 14km marker as you leave Hanoi

While this museum is not really worth making a special trip to see, with a bit of forethought it can be combined with visits to the Perfume Pagoda, the Tram Gian or Tay Phuong Pagodas, or on the way to Mai Chau. Once you're here, there's much to

---

THE HO CHI MINH TRAIL

At the end of its "working" life, the Ho Chi Minh Trail had grown from a rough assemblage of animal tracks and **jungle paths** to become a highly effective **logistical network** stretching from near Vinh, north of the Seventeenth Parallel, to Tay Ninh Province on the edge of the Mekong Delta. Initially it took up to six months to walk the trail from north to south. By 1975, however, the trail – comprising at least three main arteries plus several feeder roads leading to various battlefronts and totalling over **15,000km** – was wide enough to take tanks and heavy trucks, and could be driven in just one week. It was protected by sophisticated anti-aircraft emplacements and supported by regular service stations (fuel and maintenance depots, ammunition dumps, food stores and hospitals), often located underground or in caves and all connected by field telephone. Eventually there was even an oil pipeline constructed alongside the trail to take fuel south from Vinh to a depot at Loc Ninh.

The trail was conceived in early 1959 when **General Giap** ordered the newly created Logistical Group 559 to reconnoitre a safe route by which to direct men and equipment down the length of Vietnam in support of Communist groups in the south. Political cadres blazed the trail, followed in 1964 by the first deployment of ten thousand regular troops, and culminating in the trek south of 150,000 men in preparation for the **1968 Tet Offensive**. It was a logistical feat that rivalled Dien Bien Phu (see p.411) in both scale and determination: this time it was sustained over fifteen years and became a symbol to the Vietnamese of their victory and sacrifice. For much of its southerly route the trail ran through **Laos** and **Cambodia**, sometimes on paths forged during the war against the French, sometimes along riverbeds and always through the most difficult, mountainous terrain plagued with leeches, snakes, malaria and dysentery.

On top of all this, people on the trail had to contend with almost constant bombing. By early 1965, **aerial bombardment** had begun in earnest, using napalm and defoliants as well as conventional ordnance, to be joined later by carpet-bombing B-52s. Every day in the spring of 1965 the US Air Force flew an estimated three hundred bombing raids over the trail and in eight years dropped over two million tonnes of explosives, mostly over Laos, in an effort to cut the flow. Later they experimented with seismic and acoustic sensors to eavesdrop on troop movements and pinpoint targets, but the trail was never completely severed and supplies continued to roll south in sufficient quantities to sustain the war.

learn, including the fact that the **Ho Chi Minh Trail** was never a single trail but a complex network of muddy tracks that crisscrossed the border with Laos and Cambodia. Its purpose was to carry men, ammunition and supplies from the north to Communist strongholds in the south. Though the Americans were aware of its presence and frequently bombed it, repairs were almost instant and the supply route was never blocked for long, which is why this trail became one of the key factors in the outcome of the American War (see box opposite).

Visitors are first shown an informative, twenty-minute **video** about the construction of the trail. Exhibits include some of the equipment used in the trail's construction, along with some of the shrapnel-, nail- and cigarette-bombs that were employed to slow down the trail's progress. Outside are a few vehicles that once used the trail, and behind the museum is a forgettable mock-up of an underground operations centre.

The craft villages

Hanoi tour agents (see box, p.370) offer organized day-trips to a selection of craft villages for $20–30, or can include some in a visit to the various pagodas

For centuries, **villages** around Vietnam's major towns have specialized in single-commodity production, initially to supply the local market, and sometimes going on to win national fame for the skill of their artisans. A few communities continue to prosper, of which the best known near Hanoi are **Bat Trang** for pottery and **Van Phuc** for silk. These feature well-run, commercial operations where family units turn out fine, hand-crafted products, and they are used to foreigners coming to watch them at work. Most other villages are far less touristy, and the more isolated may treat visitors with suspicion. Nevertheless, it's worth taking a guide for the day to gain a rare glimpse into a gruelling way of life that continues to follow the ancient rhythms, using craft techniques handed down the generations virtually unchanged.

Bat Trang

BAT TRANG village, across the Red River in Hanoi's Gia Lam District, has been producing **bricks** and **earthenware** since the fifteenth century, and the oldest quarter beside the river has a medieval aura, with its narrow, high-walled alleys spattered with handmade coal-pats (used as fuel in the kilns) drying in the sun. Through tiny doorways, you catch glimpses of courtyards stacked with moulds and hand-painted pots, while all around rise the squat brick chimneys of the traditional coal-fired kilns. Around two thousand families live in Bat Trang, producing time-honoured **blue and white ceramics** alongside more contemporary designs as well as mass-produced floor tiles and balustrades to feed Hanoi's building boom. The village has expanded rapidly in recent years, thanks largely to a healthy export market, and now boasts some 2500 kilns. Most are now gas-fired, but air pollution and respiratory infections remain a problem.

ARRIVAL AND DEPARTURE   **BAT TRANG**

Bat Trang is an easy jaunt by road over Chuong Duong Bridge from Hanoi, then immediately right along the levy. To reach the old quarter of narrow lanes and workshops, continue straight ahead at the end of the main street (Duong Giang Cao) and keep going generally west.

By bicycle Note that pedal cyclists have to use Long Bien Bridge, a short distance further north from the Chuong Duong Bridge. After 10km heading generally south, following signs to Xuan Quan, where a right turn indicates the village entrance.

By xe om A half-day xe om excursion is expensive when waiting time is included – around 400,000đ.
By bus The bus is better value than travelling by xe om. Number #47 (7000đ) departs from Long Bien bus station every fifteen minutes or so and Bat Trang is the last stop.

SHOPPING

Ceramics Showrooms along Bat Trang's main drag offer a bewildering choice of pottery. Prices are not necessarily any cheaper than in Hanoi itself, though the range is superior and it's easier to bargain. At some of the bigger workshops (such as Hoa Lan Ceramics, 81 Duong Giang Cao), you can paint your own design and have the piece delivered to your hotel once it's fired.

Van Phuc

The silk village of **VAN PHUC** is 11km southwest of Hanoi. In the village, the clatter of electric looms from the thirty-odd workshops fills the air. You're welcome to wander into any of them, and will be given a brief explanation, but there's nothing much to detain you unless you're shopping for silk. Material is a shade cheaper than in Hanoi, while finished items such as scarves and clothes can be as little as half the city price.

ARRIVAL AND DEPARTURE   VAN PHUC

By bicycle or motorbike Van Phuc lies to the north of Highway 6, about a kilometre north of Ha Dong post office on the Quoac Hai Road.

By bus Take a #1 bus from Long Bien Station, which costs 7,000đ and takes around half an hour.

Chuong

Conical hats are the staple product of **CHUONG** village (also known as Phuong Trung), which is best visited on market days (held six times each lunar month), when hats are piled high in golden pyramids. At other times it's possible to see artisans deftly assembling the dried leaves on a bamboo frame. Traditionally the designs varied according to the different needs: thick and robust for working in the fields, more delicate for outings to the temple and other special occasions, and flat, ornamented hats for fashion-conscious aristocrats.

ARRIVAL AND DEPARTURE   CHUONG

By bicycle or motorbike Chuong lies just off Highway 21b a couple of kilometres south of Thanh Oai on the road to the Perfume Pagoda.

Co Loa Temple Complex

Daily 7.30am–5.30pm • 10,000đ

The earliest independent Vietnamese states grew up in the Red River flood plain, atop low hills or crouched behind sturdy embankments. First to emerge from the mists of legend was **Van Lang**, presided over by the Hung kings from a knob of high ground

---

THE HISTORY OF THE CITADEL

King An Duong Vuong built his **citadel** inside three concentric ramparts, spiralling like a snail shell, separated by moats large enough for ships to navigate; the outer wall was 8km long, 6–8m wide and at least 4m high, topped off with bamboo fencing. After the Chinese invaded in the second century BC, Co Loa was abandoned until 939 AD, when **Ngo Quyen** established the next period of independent rule from the same heavily symbolic site.

Archeologists have found rich pickings at Co Loa, including thousands of iron arrowheads, displayed in Hanoi's History Museum (see p.357), which lend credence to at least one of the Au Lac legends. The story goes that the sacred **Golden Turtle** gave King An Duong Vuong a magic crossbow made from a claw that fired thousands of arrows at a time. A deceitful Chinese prince married An Duong Vuong's daughter, Princess My Chau, persuaded her to show him the crossbow and then stole the claw before mounting an invasion. The king and his daughter were forced to flee, whereupon My Chau understood her act of betrayal and nobly told her father to kill her. When the king beheaded his daughter and threw her body in a well, she turned into lustrous, pink pearls.

marked today by a few dynastic temples north of Viet Tri (Vinh Phu Province) known as the Hung Kings Temple. Then the action moved closer to Hanoi when King An Duong Vuong defeated the last of the Hung kings and ruled Au Lac (258–207 BC) from an immense **citadel** at **Co Loa** (Old Snail City). At the time it was the first fortified Vietnamese capital, but these days the once massive **earthworks** are barely visible and all that remains are a couple of quiet temples with an interesting history set among the streets of modern Co Loa.

Den An Duong Vuong
The principal temple, **Den An Duong Vuong**, faces a refurbished lake, with a graceful stele-house to one side. Looking across the fields from the stele-house, you can just make out the earthen ramparts of the former citadel. Inside the rebuilt temple, a sixteenth-century black-bronze **statue** of king An Duong Vuong resides on the main altar, resplendent in his double crown, while a subsidiary altar is dedicated to Kim Quy, the Golden Turtle.

Other buildings
About 100m east of Den An Duong Vuong, a **statue** of King An Duong Vuong holding his magic crossbow (see box opposite) stands in a small pond. The lane beside the pond leads to a second group of buildings, where a large, walled courtyard contains the beautifully simple, open-sided **Dinh Da Quy**, furnished with huge, ironwood pillars, and containing ornate palanquins. Next door is a small temple, **Den My Chau**, dedicated to An Duong Vuong's daughter, the Princess My Chau. Inside, she is still honoured in the surprising form of a dumpy, armchair-shaped stone clothed in embroidered finery and covered in jewels but lacking a head.

ARRIVAL AND DEPARTURE   CO LOA TEMPLE COMPLEX

By motorbike Co Loa is about 13km due north of Hanoi, signposted to the right of busy Highway 3.

By bus Take bus #46 from My Dinh bus station, which costs 9,000₫ and takes around 45 minutes.

The far north

FLOWER HMONG PEOPLE

The far north

As Vietnam fans out above Hanoi towards the Chinese and Laos borders, it attains its maximum width of 600km, most of it a mountainous buffer zone wrapped around the Red River Delta. This wild, remote region contains some of Vietnam's most awe-inspiring scenery, sparsely populated by a fascinating mosaic of ethnic minorities. Most visitors gravitate to the northwest, where the country's highest mountain range and its tallest peak, Fan Si Pan, rise abruptly from the Red River Valley. Within its shadow lies Sa Pa, a former French hill station, base for trekking through superb scenery to isolated minority hamlets; while across the Red River, Bac Ha's major draw are the Flower Hmong, whose markets are great fun. These two towns – and the historic battlefield of Dien Bien Phu, site of the Viet Minh's decisive victory over French forces in 1954 – will occupy most of your time, though it's also worth considering the scenic route back to Hanoi, which passes through Son La, Moc Chau and Mai Chau.

8

The little-travelled provinces east of the Red River Valley also deserve attention, especially the stunning scenery and mountain people in the **Dong Van Karst Plateau Geopark**, which occupies over 2000 square kilometres of Ha Giang Province. The northeast region also features **Ba Be National Park**, where Vietnam's largest natural lake hides among forested limestone crags and impenetrable jungle.

Not surprisingly, **infrastructure** throughout the northern mountains is poor: facilities tend to be thin on the ground, and some roads are in terrible condition. However, this area is becoming increasingly popular with tourists as Hanoi's tour agents organize new tours and independent travellers venture into uncharted terrain by jeep or motorbike.

The **best time** to visit the northern mountains is from September to November or from March to May, when the weather is fairly settled with dry sunny days and clear cold nights. **Winters** can be decidedly chilly, especially in the northeast where night frosts are not uncommon from December to February, but the compensation is daybreak mists and breathtaking sunrise views high above valleys filled with early-morning lakes of cloud. The **rainy season** lasts from May to September, peaking in July and August, when heavy downpours wash out bridges, turn unsealed roads into quagmires and throw in the occasional landslide for good measure. Peak season for foreign tourists is from September to November, while the rainy summer months of July and August are when Hanoians head up to the mountains to escape the stifling heat of the delta.

Highlights

❶ Trekking around Sa Pa Exploring the mountainous north is all about stretching your legs, taking in great views of the landscape and spending time with the colourfully dressed montagnards. **See p.403**

❷ Bac Ha Sunday market Bac Ha Sunday market is full of Flower Hmong, perhaps the most dazzling dressers in the country. **See p.405**

❸ Thai minority villages Around Mai Chau visitors can stay in Thai stilthouses and see shows of traditional dancing. **See p.416**

❹ Dong Van Karst Plateau Geopark Vietnam's first geopark, recognized by UNESCO for its unique geological significance, harbours some of the country's most stunning scenery. **See p.421**

❺ Ba Be Lake A laidback spot, where you can either glide around in a boat on its glassy waters, or trek to minority villages near its shore. **See p.425**

❻ Ban Gioc Falls Subject of a tug-of-war between China and Vietnam, these falls are no world-beater in terms of height, but the ride from Cao Bang makes a great day out. **See p.427**

HIGHLIGHTS ARE MARKED ON THE MAP ON P.396

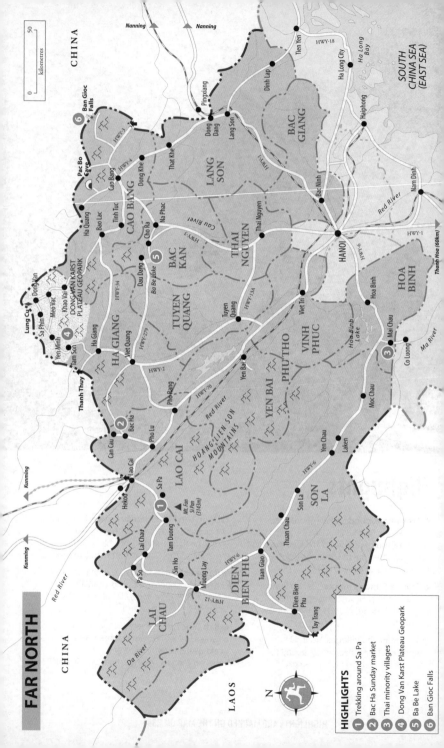

FAR NORTH

CHINA

Nanning · Nanning

Kunming

CHINA

LAOS

Red River

South China Sea (East Sea)

0 — 50 kilometres

HIGHLIGHTS

1 Trekking around Sa Pa
2 Bac Ha Sunday market
3 Thai minority villages
4 Dong Van Karst Plateau Geopark
5 Ba Be Lake
6 Ban Gioc Falls

Ban Gioc Falls

Pac Bo Cave

DONG VAN KARST PLATEAU GEOPARK

Lung Cu
Dong Van
Meo Vac
Khao Vai
Sa Phin
Yen Minh
Tam Son

HA GIANG

Ha Giang
Viet Quang
Pho Rang

Thanh Thuy

HWY-2
HWY-279

Can Cau
Bac Ha
Pho Lu

LAO CAI

Lao Cai
Hekou
Sa Pa
Mt. Fan Si Pan (3143m)

HOANG LIEN SON MOUNTAINS

Red River

LAI CHAU

Lai Chau
Tam Duong
Sin Ho
Pa So
Muong Lay

Da River

DIEN BIEN PHU

Dien Bien Phu
Tuan Giao
Tay Trang

HWY-6
HWY-12

SON LA

Son La
Thuan Chau
Yen Chau
Laken

Moc Chau

Yen Chau

Ha Quang
Bao Lac
Tinh Tuc

CAO BANG

Cao Bang
Dong Khe
That Khe

Gao Bang
Pac Bo Cave
HWY-4
HWY-3

Dong Dang
Lang Son

LANG SON

Na Phac
Na Ri
Cho Ra

BAC KAN

Ba Be Lake
Dau Dang

Bac Kan

TUYEN QUANG

Tuyen Quang

THAI NGUYEN

Thai Nguyen

Cau River

Pingxiang

Dinh Lap

BAC GIANG

Tien Yen
Ha Long City
Ha Long Bay
Haiphong

Bac Ninh

HANOI

HWY-1
HWY-6
HWY-18

Viet Tri

PHU THO

VINH PHUC

Yen Bai

YEN BAI

Hoa Binh Lake
Hoa Binh

HOA BINH

Mai Chau
Co Luong
Ma River

Nam Dinh
Red River
Thanh Hoa (60km)

HWY-70
HWY-3A
HWY-34

GETTING AROUND THE NORTH

Whether you travel by public transport or with your own vehicle, you need to allow around six days' actual **travelling time** to cover the northwestern region. Touring the entire northeast also requires at least six days including Ha Giang Province, but more if you want to spend time on Ba Be Lake, or visit Pac Bo Cave or Ban Gioc Waterfall near Cao Bang. Combining the northwest and northeast loops gives you an unforgettable two weeks of exploration, but bear in mind that travelling these roads is unpredictable, becoming downright hazardous during the rains (see p.13), and it's advisable to allow some **flexibility** in your programme. If you've got only limited time, Sa Pa, Mai Chau and Ba Be National Park make rewarding two- or three-day **excursions out of Hanoi**, either by public transport or hired vehicle. The other alternative is to join an **organized tour** with one of Hanoi's tour agencies.

Travelling through the northern provinces **using local buses** is possible, though it's an uncomfortable experience and it's only the hardiest adventurers who take them. Most visitors **hire a car and driver** or join a **motorbike tour** to travel round the northwest or northeast loop from Hanoi, options that give you more freedom to stop at villages or jaunt off along side tracks. Either a four-wheel-drive vehicle or a motorbike is recommended; the cost of hiring a car and driver (for three to four passengers) in Hanoi averages around $100 per day, while scooters and motorbikes go for between $5 and $8 per day. When planning your route, base your itinerary on an average speed of about 40km per hour.

Brief history

Though Vietnam's far north has been inhabited for thousands of years, as evidenced by the **Ancient Rock Field** in the Sa Pa Valley (see p.404), little of its history was documented until the French and Chinese came to blows over control of northern Vietnam during the 1880s. By the 1920s, the French had established a hill station at Sa Pa, but their tenure was brief. Remote uplands, dense vegetation and rugged terrain suited to guerrilla activities, plus a safe haven across the border, made this region the perfect place from which to orchestrate Vietnam's independence movement. For a short while in 1941, **Ho Chi Minh** hid in the Pac Bo Cave on the Chinese frontier, later moving south to Tuyen Quang Province, from where the Viet Minh launched their August Revolution in 1945. These northern provinces were the first to be **liberated** from French rule, but over in the northwest some minority groups, notably from among the Thai, Hmong and Muong, supported the colonial authorities and it took the Viet Minh until 1952 to gain control of the area. Two years later, they staged their great victory over the French at **Dien Bien Phu**, close to the Laos border.

During the late 1970s **Sino–Vietnamese** relations became increasingly sour for various reasons, not least over Vietnam's invasion of Cambodia, whose genocidal regime was supported by China (see p.449). Things came to a head on February 17, 1979, when the Chinese sent two hundred thousand troops into northern Vietnam, destroying most of the border towns; seventeen days later, however, the invasion force was driven out, some twenty thousand short. Though much of the infrastructural and political damage from the war has been repaired, unmarked minefields along 1000km of frontier pose a more intractable problem: most areas – including all which regularly receive tourists – have been cleared and declared safe, but in the more remote areas it's sensible to stick to well-worn paths.

Sa Pa

The tourist capital of Vietnam's mountainous north, **SA PA** is perched dramatically on the western edge of a high plateau, facing the hazy blue peak of **Fan Si Pan**, Vietnam's highest mountain. Sa Pa's surrounds are a stronghold for **ethnic minorities**, particularly the Red Dao and Black Hmong, and trekking to their villages is the region's major attraction. Its refreshing climate and almost alpine landscape struck a nostalgic chord with European visitors, who travelled up from Lao Cai by sedan chair in the early twentieth century, and by 1930 a flourishing hill station had developed, complete with tennis court, church and over two hundred villas. Nowadays only a handful of the old buildings remain, the rest lost to time and the 1979 Chinese invasion, as well as those involved in the current hotel development spree. Although height restrictions are finally being enforced on new buildings, the damage has already been done and Sa Pa's days as an idyllic haven in the hills have been concreted over.

Sa Pa's invigorating air is a real tonic after the dusty plains, but **cold nights** make warm clothes essential throughout the year: the sun sets early behind Fan Si Pan, and temperatures fall rapidly after dark. During the coldest months (Dec–Feb), night temperatures often drop below freezing and winters bring some snow, but most hotel

THE NORTHERN MINORITIES

Around seven million **minority people** (nearly two-thirds of Vietnam's total minority population) live in the northern uplands, mostly in isolated villages. The largest ethnic groups are Thai and Muong in the northwest, Tay and Nung in the northeast and Hmong and Dao dispersed throughout the region. Historically, all these peoples migrated from southern China at various times throughout history: those who arrived first, notably the Tay and Thai, settled in the fertile valleys where they now lead a relatively prosperous existence, whereas late arrivals, such as the Hmong and Dao, were left to eke out a living on the inhospitable higher slopes. Despite government efforts to integrate them into the Vietnamese community, most continue to follow a way of life little changed over the centuries. For an insight into the minorities' traditional cultures and highly varied styles of dress, visit Hanoi's informative **Museum of Ethnology** (see p.367) before setting off into the mountains.

VISITING MINORITY VILLAGES

The remoteness of Vietnam's minority villages provides much of their appeal, though many are easily accessible from hub towns such as Sa Pa, Bac Ha, Son La, Mai Chau, Ha Giang and Cao Bang. A popular, hassle-free way to visit is to join one of the **organized trips** offered by Hanoi tour agencies (see p.370). The usual destinations are Sa Pa and Bac Ha, coinciding with the Sunday market, or Mai Chau, with the standard package including guided visits to at least two different minorities plus, in the case of Mai Chau, a night in a stilthouse. The four-day Sa Pa tour costs around $200 per person depending on transport and accommodation arrangements, while two days with one night in Mai Chau costs around $70. In Sa Pa and Bac Ha, most **hotels** offer trekking and home-stay trips with their own guides, though note that not all the guides can speak English.

VILLAGE ETIQUETTE

Behaviour that we take for granted may cause offence to some ethnic minority people; remember that you are a guest. Apart from being sensitive to the situation and keeping an open mind, the following rules should be observed when visiting the ethnic minority areas.
• **Dress modestly**, in long trousers or skirt and T-shirt or shirt.
• Be sensitive to people's wishes when taking **photographs**, particularly of older people who are suspicious of the camera; always ask permission first.
• Only go inside a house when invited and **remove your shoes before** entering.
• Small **gifts**, such as fresh fruit from the local market, are always welcome. However, there is a view that even this can foster begging, and that you should only ever give in return for some service or as a sign of appreciation for hospitality. A compromise is to **buy craft work** produced by the villagers – most communities should have some embroidery, textiles or basketry for sale.
• As a mark of respect, learn the local **terms of address**, either in dialect or at least in Vietnamese, such as chao ong, chao ba (see p.499).
• Try to **minimize your impact** on the often fragile local environment; take litter back to the towns and be sensitive to the use of wood and other scarce resources.
• Growing and using **opium** is illegal in Vietnam and is punished with a fine or prison sentence; do not encourage its production by buying or smoking it.

8

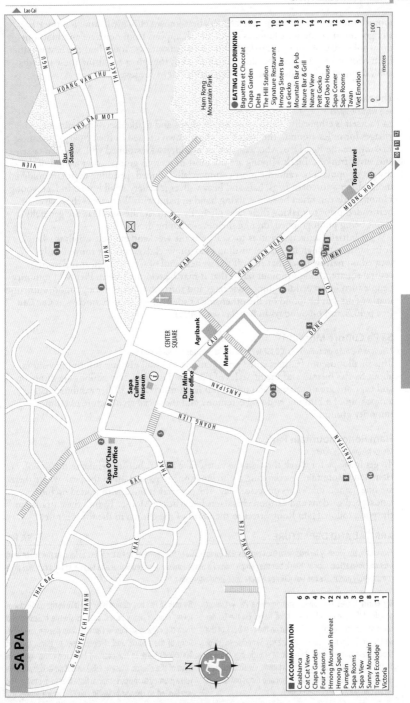

SA PA

Lao Cai

Ham Rong Mountain Park

Bus Station

CENTER SQUARE

Agribank

Market

Sapa Culture Museum

Duc Minh Tour office

Sapa O'Chau Tour Office

Topas Travel

8

● EATING AND DRINKING
Baguettes et Chocolat	5
Chapa Garden	8
Delta	11
The Hill Station	10
Signature Restaurant	15
Hmong Sisters Bar	4
Le Gecko	13
Mountain Bar & Pub	7
Nature Bar & Grill	14
Nature View	3
Petit Gecko	2
Red Dao House	12
Sapa Corner	6
Sapa Rooms	1
Tavan	9

■ ACCOMMODATION
Casablanca	6
Cat Cat View	9
Chapa Garden	4
Four Seasons	7
Hmong Mountain Retreat	12
Hmong Sapa	2
Pumpkin	5
Sapa Rooms	3
Sapa View	10
Sunny Mountain	8
Topas Ecolodge	11
Victoria	1

0 100 metres

rooms now have heating. However, Sa Pa's best-known climatic feature is a thick fog straight out of a Sherlock Holmes novel, which appears from nowhere and blots out the whole town, lending a spooky feel to the town's streets. You'll find the best **weather** from September to November and March to May, though even during these months cold, damp cloud can descend, blotting out the views for several days.

The market
Daily sunrise to sunset

Sa Pa itself is ethnically Vietnamese, but its shops and market serve the minority villages for miles around. The women come to town dressed in their finery – the most striking are the Red Dao, who wear scarlet headdresses festooned with woollen tassels and silver trinkets. Black Hmong are the most numerous group – over a third of the district's population – and the most commercially minded, peddling their embroidered indigo-blue waistcoats, bags, hats and heavy, silver jewellery at all hours. In fact, young Hmong girls can often be seen walking hand in hand with Westerners they have befriended prior to making their sales pitch. By contrast, the Red Dao are generally shy about being photographed, despite their eye-catching dress.

What initially attracted visitors to Sa Pa was the **weekend market**, which is when it's at its busiest, though it's now a bustling place on weekdays too. It's conveniently located on narrow lanes that run off the western end of Cau May, near the town's central square, though rumour has it that it may be relocated soon. Plenty of minority people turn up to peddle ethnic-style bags and shirts to tourists, though more authentic market fairs can be found on the other side of the Red River on Saturdays at **Can Cau** (see p.407) and on Sundays in **Bac Ha** (see p.405).

Sa Pa Culture Museum
2 Fansipan (behind tourist office) • ☎ 020 387 1975 • Daily 7.30–11.30am & 1.30–5pm • Free

This small museum features video presentations and wall displays informing visitors about Sa Pa's history and the lifestyles of the local hilltribes, but exhibits are dimly lit and captions are unclear, so you might not learn much here. Other exhibits include a mock-up of a Hmong wedding ceremony and the social architecture of ethnic minority groups.

Ham Rong Mountain Park
Sunrise to sunset • 70,000đ

To get in shape for a trek through the valley, take a short but steep hike to the top of **Ham Rong Mountain**, overlooking the town. Stone steps lead up to the peak where there are fine, panoramic views on a clear day. The pathway is lined with potted orchids, landscaped gardens and cartoon characters like Mickey Mouse. To find the entrance to the park, follow Ham Rong Street to the north of the church in the town centre.

ARRIVAL AND DEPARTURE   SA PA

Previously, the journey by **bus** from Gia Lam bus station in Hanoi to the centre of Sa Pa took just as long as the **train and bus combination** (about 10hr), but the completion of a new highway between Hanoi and Lao Cai should cut that time considerably and make the bus journey a more appealing alternative.

By train There's no railway station in Sa Pa, yet most people still come here by train from Hanoi via the border town of Lao Cai (see p.405), located on the east bank of the Red River, 38km from Sa Pa and nearly 3km due south of the Chinese border. They then take a shuttle bus (around 50,000đ) from the station up the winding, switchback road to Sa Pa, which takes around an hour and drops passengers off on Cau May, Sa Pa's main street.

By bus Sa Pa's bus station is by the lake in the northeast of town, though many buses, such as shuttle buses to and from the railway station in Lao Cai, drop passengers off in front of the church, and sleeper buses to Hanoi (around 300,000đ) leave in the evening from the main square in front of the church. Most hotels can obtain tickets, to save you a journey to the bus station. Note that to get to Bac Ha, you'll need to change buses in Lao Cai, which makes it a

INTO CHINA FROM LAO CAI

The border crossing from Lao Cai (see p.405) into China, 38km northeast of Sa Pa, is popular with travellers heading to Kunming. The queues at the Hekou Bridge **border gate** (daily 7am–10pm), on the east bank of the Red River, are longest in the early morning, when local traders get their day pass over to Hekou in China. There are no Chinese trains to Kunming, as the line has been out of service for many years due to flooding and landslides. However, it is possible to make your own way to Lao Cai, cross the border on foot, then carry on in China by bus (taking ten hours for the 520km journey to Kunming); you'll need to have arranged your Chinese visa beforehand.

slow journey, though there are tour buses that go directly from Sa Pa on Sundays only for the market; ask at your hotel about these. There's also a daily sleeper bus directly to Bai Chay for Ha Long Bay.

Destinations Bai Chay (1 daily; 12hr); Dien Bien Phu (1–3 daily; 10hr); Hanoi (2–5 daily; 10hr); Lai Chau (1–3 daily; 2hr 30min); Lao Cai (every 30min; 1hr).

GETTING AROUND

By motorbike Motorbikes, with or without driver, can be arranged through hotels in Sa Pa; self-drive is available (from $7 per day) but you need to be an experienced biker to tackle the stony, mountain tracks; make sure you test the bike for faults before leaving town.

By jeep It's also possible to hire your own jeep and driver (around $100 per day) via Sa Pa's tour operators, depending on availability, but if you want to tackle the whole northwestern circuit you'll find cheaper long-term prices in Hanoi.

INFORMATION AND TOURS

Tourist information There's a dedicated and helpful tourist information office facing across the square to the church at 2 Fansipan (daily 7.30am–6.30pm; ☎020 387 1975, ⓦsapa-tourism.com), though their tour prices tend to be inflated. Sa Pa's hotels remain the best source of advice on visiting minority villages.

Maps The tourist office sells a decent map of the town and surrounding area for $1, while most hotels provide guests with a simple sketch map of the town centre.

Tour operators Duc Minh Travel (10 Cau May ☎020 387 1881, ⓦducminhtravel.com) offers tours to hilltribe markets, villages near Sa Pa, as well as car and motorbike rental; owner Minh is in fact Sa Pa's Mr Fixit. Sapa O'Chau (8 Thac Bac ☎020 377 1166, ⓦsapaochau.org) is run (unusually) by a Hmong woman who can organize welcoming home-stays, treks in the Muong Hoa Valley and volunteer experience for visitors.

ACCOMMODATION

SA PA TOWN

Despite the glut of guesthouses and hotels in Sa Pa, rooms can still be in short supply in the summer months, pushing up prices by as much as fifty percent. Most hotels bump up prices over weekends too, when the town is crawling with Vietnamese tourists, so it's worth considering a midweek visit. Most places offer some kind of heating, such as electric blankets, but it's best to check rather than shiver all night. Foreigners can also now stay in many of Sa Pa's surrounding minority villages, though you'll need to arrange this through guesthouses and travel agencies, as independent trekking and village visits are frowned upon.

Casablanca 26 Dong Loi ☎020 387 2667, ⓦcasablanca sapahotel.com. One of Sa Pa's earliest boutique hotels, this place is certainly quirky and all rooms have character. It's just a few steps from the market and all rooms have balconies with mountain views. $25

★**Cat Cat View** 46 Fansipan ☎020 387 1946, ⓦcatcat hotel.com. One of the town's longest-standing mini-hotels, *Cat Cat* has a building on each side of the road and a huge variety of rooms, some with private terraces and fantastic panoramic views across to Mount Fan Si Pan. Popular with budget travellers who socialize on the communal balconies. $35

Chapa Garden 23b Cau May ☎020 387 2907. There are just four rooms here in a colonial villa above a stylish restaurant (see p.402), offering a cosy and intimate stay. Not all rooms have mountain views, so check first, but its location, a few steps away from the town's main street, couldn't be better. $70

Four Seasons 8 Muong Hoa ☎020 365 8668, ⓦfour seasonshotel.vn. One of Sa Pa's newer hotels, this place enjoys a central location and offers well-equipped rooms, some with balconies and great views, at very competitive rates. The suites are a steal. Doubles $25, suites $40

Hmong Sapa 10 Thac Bac ☎020 377 2228, ⓦhmong sapahotel.com. It's worth the uphill, kilometre-long walk from the city centre for the rooms full of character and fabulous views you get from this welcoming hotel in the northwest outskirts of town. Rooms are decorated in vibrant colours and most have canopied beds and balconies with views, and there's also a communal terrace where you can soak up the far-stretching scene. $45

8

Pumpkin 14 Dong Loi ☎ 020 387 2350, ✉ pumpkinsapa @gmail.com. This budget hotel is located down a quiet lane near the town centre, and while it doesn't boast mountain views, its bright rooms with cable TV and free wi-fi are good value. **$15**

Sapa Rooms 18 Fansipan ☎ 020 650 5228, ⊛ sapa rooms.com. There are just half a dozen rooms at this welcoming place, though word has got around so they're often booked out weeks ahead. All rooms are a decent size, with traditional furnishings and stylish bathrooms. **$55**

Sapa View 41 Muong Hoa ☎ 020 387 2388, ⊛ sapa view-hotel.com. This is one of Sa Pa's newest hotels, located to the south of town; most rooms enjoy great views across the valley and the area is fairly quiet. Smallish rooms come with pine furnishings and heaters, and staff are always eager to please. **$70**

Sunny Mountain 10 Muong Hoa ☎ 020 378 7998, ⊛ sunnymountainhotel.com. This efficiently run hotel is one of Sapa's newest and its 75 rooms are well designed, most with mountain views, and all have comfortable beds, cable TV and minibar. There's a decent restaurant on the top floor and a travel desk that can help plan exploration of the local area. **$35**

★**Victoria** Hoang Dieu ☎ 020 387 1522, ⊛ victoria hotels-asia.com. The Victoria's 77 rooms bring a touch of luxury to Sa Pa and find a regular clientele among expat residents of Hanoi looking for an accessible weekend break. Tennis courts, sauna and jacuzzi are on site, as well as an excellent restaurant and a spa with heated pool on a hilltop. **$150**

AROUND SA PA

Hmong Mountain Retreat Ban Ho (6km southeast of of town) ☎ 096 661 1383, ⊛ hmongmountainretreat .com. If you want to get away from it all, then consider this spot where five simple but luxurious (think hand woven raw cotton bedding and duck feather blankets), bamboo and thatch bungalows look out over a dream vista of terraced paddies. **$55**

Topas Ecolodge ☎ 020 387 1331, ⊛ topasecolodge .com; Sapa office 21 Muong Hoa ☎ 020 387 1331. Situated a 45min drive from Sa Pa, the Topas Ecolodge is made up of luxurious yet rustic alpine lodge-style cottages, set on a clifftop with spectacular views looking down over a glorious valley and the ethnic minority village of Ban Ho. The older buildings are eco-friendly, meaning no a/c, TV or wi-fi in rooms, while the refurbished rooms are less so, featuring a/c and even hairdryers. Their office in Sa Pa offers transport to the lodge and a number of tours. **$130**

EATING AND DRINKING

Sa Pa has the widest range of **food** in the north outside Hanoi; one benefit of the building boom is that there is plenty of choice, with many places serving a mixture of local cuisine and foreign dishes. To go where the locals are, try the street **stalls** along Pham Xuan Huan, parallel to Cau May, that serve pho and rice; some stay open late into the night, when the focus shifts to barbecued meat and rice wine. Though there's not much by way of **nightlife**, the Mountain Bar & Pub serves beer and cocktails, or you can shoot some pool at the Three Sisters.

Baguettes et Chocolat 11 Thac Bac ☎ 020 387 1766. Part of a chain that trains disadvantaged children in hospitality, this place offers excellent pastries and, as the name suggests, filling baguettes and chocolate sweets, in a comfortable colonial setting. It also sells custom-made hampers to take on your trekking journey. Mains 80,000– 120,000đ. Daily 7.30am–9.30pm.

★**Chapa Garden** 23b Cau May ☎ 020 387 2907. This secluded restaurant with delectable cuisine (mains 170,000–260,000đ), fine wine and a crackling fireplace has something of an alpine atmosphere. The set menu offers good value but there are always tempting alter- natives on the short à la carte menu. Daily 7am–10pm.

Delta 33 Cau May ☎ 020 387 1799. With a prime location and a good wine list, the Delta is better known for its pizzas than its pasta (120,000–280,000đ), and the soft lighting creates an intimate atmosphere. Daily 7am–10pm.

The Hill Station Signature Restaurant 37 Fansipan ☎ 020 388 7111, ⊛ thehillstation.com. The striking design of this restaurant combines traditional and modern features – think stone walls with mat cushions around low tables. The cuisine is inspired by local ethnic gastronomy and features dishes like rainbow trout and ash-roasted pumpkin. Most dishes 100,000–200,000đ. Daily 7am–10.30pm.

Hmong Sisters Bar 31 Muong Hoa. Currently Sa Pa's most popular late-night bar, with up-to-date music and a pool table. The spacious, dim-lit interior also has a fire- place for cold nights. Daily 4pm–2am.

Le Gecko 4 Ham Rong ☎ 020 387 1504, ⊛ legeckosapa .com. Well-designed, French-run venue serving dishes like venison and mountain goat as well as pizzas at 120,000–160,000đ and some yummy cakes. Opposite, its sister restaurant, the tiny Petit Gecko, is slightly cheaper and styled like a Black Hmong house, but serves similar fare for around 80,000–120,000đ. Daily 7am–10pm.

Mountain Bar & Pub 2 Muong Hoa ☎ 0983 889798. Popular bar serving a good range of beers and cocktails and showing sports on TV. The bar is quite small and can get crowded, but there's an upstairs area too with table football. Daily 10am–midnight.

★**Nature Bar & Grill** 24 Cau May ☎ 020 387 2094. Grilled meat and fish on hot plates is the speciality here, which goes down very well on a cold evening. The set menus are a good deal (around 120,000–140,000đ), the atmosphere is relaxing and service is top-notch. Daily 10am–10pm.

Nature View 51 Fansipan ☎8491 544 9707. You could pay for the views alone and still feel that you'd got value for money; throw in a selection of reasonably priced Vietnamese and Western dishes and it's a really good deal. The *pho bo* is a good choice on a chilly morning. Mains 60,000–100,000đ. Daily 7.30am–10.30pm.

Red Dao House 4b Thac Bac ☎0820 387 2927. Too twee for some but there's a certain kitsch appeal to this large and slightly pricey restaurant, and the food is consistently good; the menu has a good range of Vietnamese and Western dishes, including pastas and pizzas (mains 120,000–220,000đ). Staff are all Red Dao. Daily 7am–10pm.

Sapa Corner 38 Cau May ☎020 387 1238. This is one of Sa Pa's classiest restaurants, featuring starched tablecloths and dishes like *tartiflette de Sapa* (potato, bacon, onion, cheese and wine in a clay pot, 150,000đ) as well as a good range of wines. Daily 7am–9pm.

Sapa Rooms 18 Fansipan ☎020 650 5228. You could spend the whole day here, grazing on home-made muffins and carrot juice for breakfast, delicious fries for lunch and fish fried with coriander and chilli for dinner. Most dishes 80,000–120,000đ. They also serve some of the best coffee in town, and run cookery classes at their out-of-town *Hmong Mountain Retreat*. Daily 7am–10pm.

Tavan Victoria Hotel, Hoang Dieu ☎020 387 1522, ⓦvictoriahotels-asia.com. Specializing in French cuisine with locally grown produce, the meals, service and quality are sumptuous but with a price to match. Also offers an excellent breakfast buffet that is perfect fuel for early morning treks. Mains 200,000–480,000đ. Daily 6.30am–10pm.

Viet Emotion 27 Cau May ☎020 387 2559, ⓦviet emotion.com. Spanish tapas, tempting main courses and a healthy range of cocktails are on the menu at this two-floor gem; try the salmon with sticky rice (240,000đ) or the pork grilled with cardamom, or start the day with a filling set breakfast. Daily 7am–10pm.

DIRECTORY

Banks and money There are several ATMs dotted around Sa Pa, and the Agribank (Mon–Fri 7.30–11am & 1.30–5pm) on Cau May can exchange cash.

Post office Ham Rong (Mon–Fri 8–11.30am & 1–4pm). Service is poor and mail delivery times are exceptionally long.

Around Sa Pa

The main purpose of most visitors to Sa Pa is to **trek to minority villages** in the Muong Hoa Valley, which separates Sa Pa from Mount Fan Si Pan. Until recently, only a few hardy trekkers had stood atop Vietnam's highest peak, but with the completion of a controversial seven-kilometre, three-wire cable car from Sa Pa to the top of Fan Si Pan in late 2014, more visitors will be making the trip. About 12km south of town,

---

VISITING VILLAGES AND TREKKING AROUND SA PA

While it's possible to wander into the Muong Hoa Valley, pass through a couple of minority villages and return to Sa Pa in a day, for the full-on Sa Pa trekking experience you'll want to **overnight in a home-stay** and get to know something about your hosts. The cost to enter most villages is 40,000đ, though this is included in the price of organized treks; expect to pay $20–30 per day per person for these, depending on number in the group. In fact, you are strongly advised to **join a group** to trek in the valley, as the way it is set up means that solo trekkers are not admitted to some villages.

TREKKING PRACTICALITIES

It's important to wear the right **clothing** when walking in these mountains: strong boots with ankle support are the best footwear, though you can get away with training shoes in the dry season. Choose thin, loose clothing – long trousers offer some protection from thorns and leeches; wear a hat and sunblock; take plenty of water; and carry a basic medical kit. If you plan on spending the night in a village you'll need warm clothing as temperatures can drop to around freezing, and you might want to take a **sleeping bag**, mosquito net and food, though these are usually provided on organized tours. Finally, **dogs** can be a problem when entering villages, so it's a good idea to carry a strong stick when trekking, and always be watchful for the **venomous snakes** that are common in this area.

the **Ancient Rock Field** is worth a visit if you are intrigued by unfathomable phenomena. Other possible targets for a half-day outing are the roadside **Silver Falls** (Thac Bac) and view at the **Tram Ton Pass**, both of which are on the way to Lai Chau. Many visitors pass through Lao Cai on the way to or from Sa Pa, and another hugely popular outing is to the Sunday market at Bac Ha.

Cat Cat

The nearest village to Sa Pa is **CAT CAT**, which lies in the valley immediately below. Here chickens and pot-bellied pigs scavenge through trailing pumpkin vines, though the sheer number of visitors makes the experience feel less authentic than it really is. Look out for tubs of **indigo dye**, used to colour the hemp cloth typical of Hmong dress, and for interlocking bamboo pipes that supply the village with both water and power for de-husking rice. Cat Cat **waterfall** is just below the village, a pleasant place to rest before tackling the homeward journey.

Sin Chai and Ta Phin

About 4km north of Cat Cat is **SIN CHAI**, another large Hmong settlement spread out along the path. Some tours include an overnight stop here in a tribal house, and you will also have the chance to watch weavers at work and listen to performances of traditional music. Further north, about 10km from Sa Pa, lies the village of **TA PHIN**, populated by Red Dao and another popular overnight stay.

The Muong Hoa Valley

Heading southeast from Sa Pa along the beautiful **Muong Hoa Valley**, after passing a viewpoint with a fantastic view over rice terraces, the road leads to other **villages** popular for treks such as Ta Van, home to the Dao and Giay minorities, Lao Chai (Hmong), Giang Ta Chai (Dao) and Ban Ho (Tay).

Ancient Rock Field
Follow the Muong Hoa Road southeast of Sa Pa for 12km to the museum

Discovered in the 1920s, the **Ancient Rock Field** is a curious region of inscribed rocks, covering an area of around eight square kilometres between the villages of Ta Van, Hau Thao and Su Pan. It consists or around two hundred large, smooth boulders, buried in the middle of rice paddies or at the roadside, which are clearly carved by human hand; while some pictographs like human or bird forms are easy to decipher, many of the carved patterns are unfathomable. Because of the nature of the motifs, archaeologists estimate these carvings to be around 2500 years old. The small **museum** on site documents the stones' discovery, locations and dimensions, with a few samples of carved rocks beside the road and in the neighbouring field.

Mount Fan Si Pan

Vietnam's highest mountain, **Fan Si Pan** (3143m) lies about 7km west of Sa Pa across the Muong Hoa Valley. At the time of research, a controversial **cable car** project was under construction, with its terminal just south of Sa Pa town centre, capable of transporting two thousand people an hour to the summit of Vietnam's highest peak in just fifteen minutes. Considering that fewer than two thousand people reached the summit during all of 2013, the threat to the environment is evident, not least the prospect of littering; conservationists point out that at other significant mountains in Southeast Asia, such as Mount Kinabalu (4,095m) in Borneo, only around one hundred people a day are allowed on the summit to cause minimum impact.

No doubt the cable car's novelty will attract increased numbers of visitors to Sa Pa, and it is to be hoped that the owners will operate it in a responsible manner. The one group likely to decline on the mountain are trekkers, as the appeal of standing alone on a remote peak will no longer be an option.

Silver Falls

12km from Sa Pa along the westbound road to Lai Chau • Sunrise to sunset • 10,000đ

If you plan to ride the northwest loop back to Hanoi, you'll pass Thac Bach, or **Silver Falls**, along the way. The waterfall itself is very impressive, especially from June to October, but as every passing tour group makes a stop here, and roadside vendors are particularly aggressive, don't expect a quiet time of it. Follow the steep trail beside the falls to escape from the crowds.

Tram Ton Pass

Just 3km beyond the falls, the 2000m-high **Tram Ton Pass** is the highest in Vietnam, and when the weather is clear there are fabulous views west towards Lai Chau, but again you'll have to fend off the pestering vendors.

Lao Cai

For most people, the frontier town of **LAO CAI** is just a staging point between Sa Pa and Kunming in China (see box, p.401), and there's nothing to see unless you get a kick out of watching people crossing a border. There are, however, a couple of useful places to sleep or eat, should you get stuck in transit.

ARRIVAL AND DEPARTURE

By train Most people arrive in Lao Cai by train from Hanoi; taking the night service will land you here in the early morning, saving on both time and accommodation, but a daylight journey gives great views along the Red River Valley and arrives at a convenient 5pm. At Lao Cai, hop on one of the shuttle buses waiting at the station for the hour's winding, uphill run to Sa Pa.
Destination Hanoi (5 daily; 8–9hr).

By bus Lao Cai's bus station is just 200m west of the train station, and operates services to towns throughout Lao Cai Province, though only a few interest most travellers.
Destinations Bac Ha (10 daily; 2hr); Hanoi (about 10 daily; 6–9hr); Sa Pa (every 30min; 1hr).
By foot If you've just walked over the border from China, take a xe om or taxi to the station, where you can catch a train to Hanoi or shuttle bus up to Sa Pa.

ACCOMMODATION AND EATING

Oishi 47 Phan Dinh Phung ☏020 625 2982. Just a few steps west of the *Thien Hai* hotel, between the train and bus stations, *Oishi* is a great restaurant serving dishes like grilled chicken with honey at reasonable prices. The owner, a former Sa Pa tour guide, can also help with bus and train info.
Thien Hai 308 Khanh Yen ☏020 383 3666, ⓦthien haihotel.com. This three-star hotel is an uninspiring but clean and adequate spot to rest your head right beside the train station. $30

Bac Ha

Around 110km northeast of Sa Pa, across the Red River, the small town of **BAC HA** nestles in a high valley, 1200m above sea level. This bustling agricultural community enjoys a scenic backdrop of cone-shaped mountains bobbing up out of the mist; sights revolve around a lively **Sunday market** and **trekking opportunities**, though infrastructure is limited – which in many ways is the key to Bac Ha's charm. One pleasing development has been the clearing of the area around the town's small lake, which backs on to the market and makes for a good, short stroll round its perimeter. Another is the opening of some friendly home-stays in the area.

Bac Ha gets most of its visitors on a Sunday, when convoys of minibuses arrive from Sa Pa for the market, though if you're travelling independently it's worth spending a whole weekend in town in order to take in the rustic and colourful market at **Can Cau** on Saturday as well. Bac Ha also makes a good base for trips out to the surrounding Flower Hmong villages of **Ban Pho** and **Coc Ly**. If you happen to be in town in early June, ask about the **annual horse races** which take place by the stadium to the north of the town centre. Apparently Bac Ha has a formidable reputation for producing war horses, so the local breed should have plenty of stamina.

The Sunday market

Sun 8am–5pm

Bac Ha's Sunday **market**, the town's one big attraction, gradually swells with ethnic minorities arriving from the hills between 8am and 10am, and from then until lunchtime it's a jostling mass of colour, mostly provided by the stunningly dressed **Flower Hmong** women looking for additional adornments to their costume. The scene is filled out with a sizeable livestock market (horses, cows, dogs, ducks and pigs), meat and vegetable sellers, wine sellers and vendors of farming implements. The town returns to a dusty shadow of its former self by 5pm when people head home to their outlying villages.

Hoang A Tuong's Palace

Daily 7.30–11.30am & 1.30–5pm • Free

At the northern end of town, on the left along the main road, you'll find the remarkable folly of **Hoang A Tuong's Palace**, formerly known as **Vua Meo**, or Cat King House, a superbly photogenic structure. Two storeys of pure wedding cake surround a courtyard built in 1921 by the French as a palace for a Hmong leader, Hoang A Toang, whom they had installed as the local "king" (Meo, or "Cat" in Vietnamese, is a disparaging term formerly applied by Vietnamese and French to the Hmong). The building now houses a tourist information office, with a few displays of local ethnic dress and a shop selling hilltribe gear.

ARRIVAL AND DEPARTURE BAC HA

By bus Bac Ha's bus station is beside the southeast corner of the lake. There are nightly sleeper buses to and from Hanoi, along with regular buses to Lao Cai, from where you can catch alternative connections to Hanoi or Sa Pa.
Destinations Hanoi (1 daily; 10hr); Lao Cai (10 daily; 2hr).

Tours Your best bet for a quick visit is to take a tour from one of Sa Pa's guesthouses for around $20, which includes spending the morning at the market, a trek in the afternoon and a ride back to Sa Pa, with the option of being dropped off at Lao Cai station on the way back if you're heading for Hanoi.

SOME BACKROADS FROM BAC HA

If you'd rather embark on the **northeast loop from Bac Ha**, or just head for the wonders of the **Dong Van Karst Plateau Geopark**, there are a few different routes. The most thrilling – and only possible by motorbike in the dry season – is to head north from Bac Ha to Lung Phin, then head east to Viet Quang via Xin Man and Huong Su Phi: the road is awful (though it is being upgraded) but the views are nothing short of spectacular. An easier route is to head back down out from Bac Ha towards Lao Cai, turn left on Highway 70 and follow it about 40km to Pho Rang. Turn left just before the bridge and follow Highway 279 to Viet Quang, then left again on Highway 2, which takes you into **Ha Giang**. The trip takes about six hours in good conditions, but also becomes impassable after heavy rain, in which case you're faced with a long, southward detour on Highway 70 to Yen Binh, then east on Highway 370 and finally north on Highway 2.

INFORMATION

Tourist information There's no tourist office in town, but you can find out anything about the area you want from helpful Dong (☎01277 801988) at the *Ngan*

Nga hotel (see below).

Services Bac Ha has a couple of ATMs on the main street.

ACCOMMODATION

The range of accommodation available in Bac Ha is limited, with few people spending more than one night in town. For an insight into Vietnamese culture, consider the *Bac Ha Homestay*, just a few kilometres from the town centre.

Bac Ha Homestay About 2.5km north of the town centre ☎091 468 3833, ⓦbachahomestay.com. Enjoying an idyllic rural location and overlooking pathways through rice fields that just beg to be explored, this traditional stilthouse of the Tay minority offers simple lodgings (mattress and mosquito net) plus meals with the family included in the price. ‾$15

Cong Fu 152 Ngoc Uyen ☎020 388 0254. The *Cong Fu* has bright rooms, with big windows, some of which directly overlook the lake and market. They are equipped with spartan furnishings and clean tiled floors, plus smart bathrooms, some with bathtubs as well as showers. They also arrange

local tours to places like Can Cau and Coc Ly markets. ‾$15

Ngan Nga 115–117 Ngoc Uyen ☎020 388 0286, ⓦnganngabachahotel.com. There are two *Ngan Ngas* just 100 metres apart on Ngoc Uyen, so check that you've got the right number, or easier, ask for Mr Dong who runs the place and is the best fixer in town for arranging local treks. All rooms have two-way a/c (hot and cold) and some have balconies. ‾$15

Sao Mai ☎020 388 0288, ⓔsaomai@hn.vnn.vn. Probably the biggest place in town, the *Sao Mai*, just west of the junction, has rather soulless rooms, but occasionally hosts minority dancing on Saturday evening. ‾$20

EATING

Bac Ha's **restaurants** are bursting with tourists on Sundays and practically deserted at all other times, but don't expect the same variety that you'd find in Sa Pa.

Cong Fu 152 Ngoc Uyen. The restaurant in the *Cong Fu* hotel produces reasonable Vietnamese dishes for 60,000–120,000đ and has good views of the surrounding countryside. Daily 7am–9pm.

Ngan Nga 115–117 and 133 Ngoc Uyen. When it comes to eating, both versions of the *Ngan Nga* have decent

restaurants. The former features an extensive menu of Vietnamese and Western fare like spaghetti (125,000đ) as well as Dalat wine at 105,000đ a bottle, while the latter often hosts tour groups and serves seasonal specialities such as local mushrooms prepared in a tasty sauce, as well as unusual meat dishes like venison. Daily 7am–10pm.

Villages around Bac Ha

The game of one-upmanship among travellers in North Vietnam is all about which of the dwindling **ethnic minorities** you have spotted that others haven't. In the vicinity of Bac Ha, there's a great opportunity to go a few points ahead on this score by visiting villages such as Can Cau and Coc Ly, with alternative **weekly markets** in many other places, including Sin Cheng and Ta Van Chu.

Ban Pho

It's only a 3km stroll from Bac Ha to the picturesque Flower Hmong hamlet of **BAN PHO**, but the route is not clearly marked so it's best to go with a guide. Along the way you'll pass fields planted with potatoes, artichokes, pumpkins, cabbage, soya, corn and rice. A short way beyond Ban Pho, a country lane leads to the the idyllic Nung village of **Na Hoi**, from where it is possible to follow a different route back to Bac Ha.

Can Cau

The village of **CAN CAU**, 18km north of Bac Ha, hosts a **Saturday market**, which is every bit as colourful as that in Bac Ha, albeit smaller, and is located in a fairy-tale setting among rolling hills. It consists of a disparate mix of livestock on sale – including horses, ponies, buffalo and cattle – with traders trekking in from as far afield as China in search of bargains, plus many vendors selling bright panels of cloth, which attract the Flower Hmong women, already resplendent in their bright outfits. As with Bac Ha, the busy hours are around 10am to lunchtime, and there are some beautiful items of clothing on sale that make great souvenirs. Until now the market retains much of its authenticity, but that is likely to change as more and more visitors arrive every week. Other than the market there's nothing at all to see in Can Cau, but the ride there, across a high, empty range with panoramic views on either side, is glorious.

Coc Ly

One spot rarely visited by foreigners is the Tuesday **flower market** at **COC LY**, about 35km north of Bac Ha on **Highway 154,** where Tay, Flower Hmong and Dao women stand side by side selling carefully selected flowers to neighbouring minority groups. A visit here is usually combined with a **boat ride** downriver to Nam Mon, a Tay village where it's possible to overnight in a home-stay.

GETTING AROUND   **VILLAGES AROUND BAC HA**

Tours The best way to visit villages around Bac Ha is on an organized tour, easily arranged through your accommodation or with Mr Dong (☎01277 801988) at the *Ngan Nga* hotel. Prices are around $10 for a half-day walk or $30 per day depending on number in the group.

By motorbike One journey that could be made by rented motorbike without a guide is to Can Cau, as it's on the road directly north of Bac Ha, but you'll need to be a confident rider to deal with the rugged terrain. You can rent motorbikes at any of the hotels in town for $7–8 per day.

The Northwest Loop

Vietnam's most mountainous provinces lie immediately west of the Red River Valley, dominated by the country's highest range, Hoang Lien Son. From Sa Pa a road loops west across the immense flank of **Fan Si Pan**, the country's tallest peak, to join the Song Da (Black River) Valley running south, through the old French garrison towns of **Muong Lay** (formerly Lai Chau) and **Son La**, via a series of dramatic passes to the industrial town of Hoa Binh on the edge of the northern delta. The only sight as such is the historic battlefield of **Dien Bien Phu**, close to the Laos border, but the scenery makes the diversion worthwhile. Throughout the region, sweeping views and mountain grandeur contrast with ribbons of intensively cultivated valleys, and here more than anywhere else in Vietnam the **ethnic minorities** have retained their traditional dress, architecture and languages. After Sa Pa, the most popular tourist destination in these mountains is **Mai Chau**, an attractive area inhabited by the White Thai minority, within easy reach of Hanoi.

The best way to tackle this **Northwest Loop** is with a rented car (and driver) or motorbike, though it's possible by public transport if you have plenty of patience. You'll need a minimum of three days for this journey, but allowing time for photo stops and exploring places along the way, five to six days is more realistic.

Lai Chau

About two hours' drive west from Sa Pa, the new town of **LAI CHAU** – formerly Tam Duong, not to be confused with the former Lai Chau now called Muong Lay (see box opposite) – is getting uglier by the minute despite being surrounded by immaculate mountain scenery. Huge boulevards without any traffic and characterless office blocks are beginning to give the provincial capital an air of importance, though it is of little interest to travellers except for its lively market in the old town, where various ethnic groups turn up to trade each morning.

ACCOMMODATION AND EATING   LAI CHAU

Muong Thanh 113 Le Duan ☎ 0231 379 0888, ⓦ laichau .muongthanh.vn. One of the few good deals in Lai Chau, the Muong Thanh is situated between the old and new towns, but is quite self-contained, with a good restaurant and even tennis courts. Rooms are big, bright and well equipped, making them good value. It's surrounded by tea fields and affords fantastic views from the upper floors. **$30**
Tuan Anh Restaurant 83 Tran Hung Dao ☎ 0231 387 5217. This is about the only foreigner-friendly restaurant in town, situated on the main road by the market. It has an English menu with dishes like fried beef and potatoes for 170,000đ. Daily 6.30am–10pm.

Sin Ho

From Lai Chau the main route veers north to Pa So (sometimes called Phong Tho), after which it swings south on Highway 12 to Muong Lay. However, there's a more challenging, **less-travelled route** (TL128) that heads southwest out of Lai Chau and climbs up to the market town of **SIN HO** before descending to join up with Highway 12 just north of Muong Lay. Set at an elevation of 1500m, Sin Ho is worth visiting for several reasons: there's a small but bustling and colourful **market** on Saturday and Sunday that attracts diverse ethnic minorities; the climate is cool and fresh; there are superb views on the way up and down; and it's not swarming with tourists. Accommodation is very limited and there are no organized treks, but there's nothing to stop you hiking the steep trails around town.

ACCOMMODATION   SIN HO

Thanh Binh Zone 5 Sinho ☎ 0231 387 0366. This is the best of a mediocre bunch of hotels in Sin Ho, providing all the basics (a/c, TV, hot water), but make sure you lock your room securely as thefts have been known to occur. The rate includes breakfast. **$28**

Muong Lay

MUONG LAY still seems to be shell-shocked, trying to re-invent itself after the old town was inundated a few years ago beneath a **reservoir** behind a new dam built downstream on the Da River. Most of the town's old buildings were submerged, though several wooden stilthouses were taken apart and re-assembled higher up the banks. A huge bridge now connects the two parts of town, and the *Lan Anh Hotel*, once a popular haunt of travellers, has re-appeared in a more luxurious incarnation, offering treks, tours and **boat rides** on the reservoir. However, there's nothing to see in town itself, and it feels as if Muong Lay will revert to being nothing more than a convenient stop-over between Sa Pa and Dien Bien Phu.

ACCOMMODATION AND EATING   MUONG LAY

Lan Anh 9 Song Da ☎ 0231 389 6337, ⓦ lananhhotel .com. Muong Lay's legendary hotel has relocated to the west bank of the reservoir and offers good views from its hilltop perch. Rooms are tastefully designed with stone floors and walls and four-poster beds. There's even a small swimming pool and the restaurant, a cavernous, alpine-style hall, still turns out some of the tastiest food this side of Hanoi. All things considered, it's not a bad spot to rest up. **$30**

WHAT'S IN A NAME?

Only in Vietnam can things become so confusing. A few years ago, the government decided to change the names of certain towns in the northwest region, which is not that uncommon. However, when places began adopting the old names of nearby towns that already had changed their names, travelling became much harder than it needed to be. While some signs have been slow to change on the ground, the **new names** are used throughout this chapter.

In Lai Chau Province, Binh Lu has changed to Tam Doung, and Tam Doung to Lai Chau. In Dien Bien Province, Lai Chau Town has changed to Muong Lay Town, and Moung Lay to Muong Tra.

Dien Bien Phu

South of Muong Lay the road splits: Highway 6 takes off southeast towards Tuan Giao and Son La (see p.413), while Highway 12 ploughs on south for 100km to the small town of **DIEN BIEN PHU**, whose heart-shaped valley was the setting during the 1950s for a key **battle** that signalled the beginning of the end for France's empire in Indochina (see box opposite). The town's trickle of tourists tend to be history buffs, and if you're not interested in sites connected to the war there's little else to attract you, though the valley's population is predominantly White and Black Thai, and the nearby open border provides an alternative **gateway to Laos**.

Dien Bien Phu Victory Museum

Daily 7.30–11am & 1.30–5pm • 15,000đ

To commemorate the sixtieth anniversary of the victory at Dien Bien Phu, this museum exchanged its former premises, which looked like a derelict school surrounded by rusting guns and tanks, for something out of a Star Wars movie – a futuristic, cone-shaped building with three times as much display area. Another subtle change was the addition of the word "victory" to the museum's title, giving a hint at the perspective of events presented within. The thousand or so exhibits focus on the strategic location of Dien Bien Phu, French plans to control the region, Viet Minh preparations for the final siege, the impact of the battle outcome at home and abroad, and the town as it is today. Pride of place goes to an 83-centimetre tall **bronze statue of General Vo Nguyen Giap**, who masterminded the victory and whose death at the age of 102 in 2013 sparked a national outpouring of grief.

8

Viet Minh Cemetery

Sunrise to sunset

Directly opposite the museum, some of the fallen heroes are buried under grey marble headstones marked only with a red and gold star, and the stark simplicity of the scene makes it probably the most moving reminder of the battle. In 1993 an imposing Imperial gateway and white-marble wall of names was added in time for the fortieth anniversary of the battle. The outside of this wall features bas-reliefs in gold-painted concrete of battle scenes.

Hill A1

Daily 7.30–11am & 1.30–5pm • 15,000đ

A small hill overlooking the cemetery, known as **Hill A1** to the Vietnamese and as Eliane 2 to French defenders, was the scene of particularly bitter fighting before it was eventually overrun towards the end of the battle. You can inspect a reconstructed bunker on the summit and various memorials, including the grave of a Viet Minh hero who gave his life while disabling the French tank standing next to him, and you also get a panorama over the now peaceful, agricultural valley.

De Castries' bunker

Daily 7.30–11am & 1.30–5pm • 15,000đ

There's little to see at the last battle site, a reconstruction of **de Castries' bunker**, located on a dusty country

THE BATTLE OF DIEN BIEN PHU

In November 1953 General Navarre, Commander-in-Chief in Indochina, ordered the French Expeditionary Force's parachute battalions to establish a base in Dien Bien Phu. Taunted by Viet Minh incursions into Laos, with which France had a mutual defence treaty, Navarre asserted that this would block enemy lines through the mountains, force the Viet Minh into open battle and end the war in Indochina within eighteen months – which it did, but not quite as Navarre intended. His deputy in Dien Bien Phu was **Colonel de Castries**, an aristocratic cavalry officer and dashing hero of World War II, supposedly irresistible to women, although Graham Greene, visiting the base in January 1954, described him as having the "nervy histrionic features of an old-time actor".

Using bulldozers dropped in beneath seven parachutes apiece, the French cleared two airstrips and then set up nine heavily fortified positions on low hills in the valley floor, reputedly named after de Castries' mistresses – Gabrielle, Isabelle, Béatrice and so on. Less than a quarter of the garrison in Dien Bien Phu were mainland French: the rest were either from France's African colonies or the Foreign Legion (a mix of European nationalities), plus local Vietnamese troops including three battalions drawn from the Thai minority. There were also nineteen women in the thick of things (a stranded French nurse, plus eighteen Vietnamese and Algerian women from the Expeditionary Force's mobile brothel).

Meanwhile, **General Giap**, Commander of the People's Army, quietly moved his own forces into the steep hills around the valley, mobilizing an estimated three hundred thousand porters, road gangs and auxiliary soldiers in support of up to fifty thousand battle troops. Not only did they carry in all food and equipment, often on foot or bicycle over vast distances, but they then hauled even the heaviest guns up the slopes, hacking paths through the dense steamy forest as they went. Ho Chi Minh described the scene to journalist Wilfred Burchett by turning his helmet upside down: "Down here is the valley of Dien Bien Phu. There are the French. They can't get out. It may take a long time, but they can't get out." In early 1954 Giap was ready to edge his troops even closer, using a network of tunnels dug under cover of darkness. By this time the international stakes had been raised: the war in Indochina would be discussed at the Geneva Conference in May, so now both sides needed a major victory to take to the negotiating table.

French commanders continued to believe their position was impregnable until the first shells rained down on March 10. Within five days Béatrice and Gabrielle had fallen, both airstrips were out of action and the siege had begun in earnest; the French artillery commander, declaring himself "completely dishonoured", lay down and took the pin out of a grenade. All French supplies and reinforcements now had to be parachuted in, frequently dropping behind enemy lines, and when de Castries was promoted to general even his stars were delivered by parachute; at the end of the battle, 83,000 parachutes were strewn across the valley floor. The **final assault** began on May 1, by which time the rains had arrived, hindering air support, filling the trenches and spreading disease. Waves of Viet Minh fought for every inch of ground, until their flag flew above de Castries' command bunker on the afternoon of May 7. The following morning, the day talks started in Geneva, the last position **surrendered** and the valley at last fell silent after 59 days. A ceasefire was signed in Geneva on July 21, and ten months later the last French troops left Indochina.

The Vietnamese paid a high price for their victory, with an estimated twenty thousand dead and many thousands more wounded. On the French side, out of a total force of 16,500, some ten thousand were captured and marched hundreds of kilometres to camps in Vietnam's northeastern mountains; less than half survived the rigours of the journey, diseases and horrendous prison conditions.

Over sixty years on, the Battle of Dien Bien Phu remains one of the most significant military conflicts of the twentieth century, with its importance in Vietnam's struggle for independence commemorated in nearly every town by a street named in honour of this famous victory.

8

road across the river a couple of kilometres from central Dien Bien Phu, and now capped by an ugly shelter. Captured tanks, anti-aircraft guns and other weaponry rust away in the surrounding fields. Carry on past the bunker and you'll come to a concrete enclosure with a memorial to "Those who died here for France".

ONWARDS TO LAOS

Dien Bien Phu is only 35km by road from the **border with Laos** at Tay Trang. It's possible to get a visa at the border (prices dependent on nationality), though to be sure, this is best done in advance in Hanoi (see p.384). Buses to **Muang Khoua**, a further 70km over the border in Laos (115,000đ), leave Dien Bien Phu at 5.30am every morning; at other times you can get a xe om to the border (about 200,000đ), though it's a 3km checkpoint-to-checkpoint walk and you may find it hard to get onward transport.

ARRIVAL AND DEPARTURE

DIEN BIEN PHU

By plane Daily flights from Hanoi arrive at the airfield, 1.5km north out of town, with the Vietnam Airlines office next door: it's a ten-minute walk into town from here, or a xe om costs around 30,000đ.

Destinations Hanoi (1–2 daily; 1hr).

By bus The bus station is located at the T-junction a couple of hundred metres from the centre on the western edge of town. This is also where you catch the numerous minibuses for Son La and beyond (first one departs at 6am). The journey to Hanoi is interesting but gruelling.

Destinations Hanoi (12hr); Muong Lay (4hr); Sa Pa (10hr); Son La (5hr).

ACCOMMODATION

Dien Bien Phu–Hanoi 849, 7 Thang 5, south of the roundabout towards the museum ☎ 0230 382 5103, ✉ dienbienphuhotel@gmail.com. This place sees few foreigners, though it has simple but acceptable rooms – the VIP choices are good value – as well as helpful staff. $30

Him Lam Hotel Him Lam ☎ 0230 381 1999, 🖥 himlam hotel.com. Dien Bien Phu's most extravagant accommodation, more like a resort (complete with swan pedal-boats on a lake), lies a few kilometres out of town on Him Lam, in a peaceful setting on a riverbank. The rooms are good and the location superb, though staff are more used to dealing with Vietnamese tour groups than independent foreigners. $35

Muong Thanh 514, 7 Thang 5 ☎ 0230 381 0043, 🖥 dienbienphu.muongthanh.vn. This long-running favourite, located to the northeast of the town centre, represents DBP's top lodgings, with 150 spacious and comfortable rooms, a decent restaurant, tennis courts and a small swimming pool. $25

Viet Hoang 2 69 Phuong Thanh Binh ☎ 0230 382 6300. This is the best of a poor bunch of mini-hotels near the bus station; rooms range from tiny to a reasonable size and some have balconies. Amenities are basic but there's wi-fi and cable TV. Keep earplugs handy when sleeping and lock the door securely when leaving. $15

EATING

Locals tend to patronize the **com pho stalls** around the roundabout and along the main roads – it's worth wandering around and choosing the one with the biggest crowd. Look out for the region's speciality dish, which is the Thai minority's black rice (*com gao cam*).

Muong Thanh 514, 7 Thang 5 ☎ 0230 381 2556, 🖥 dienbienphu.muongthanh.vn. This hotel's restaurant gets the nod simply for its English menu and English-speaking staff, which are difficult to find in this town.

There's a reasonable choice of stir-fries and soups, priced from 65,000đ, though it's not exactly gourmet standard. Daily 6.30am–10pm.

DIRECTORY

Bank Head south from the busy roundabout and market to find an Agribank (Mon–Fri 7.30–11am & 1.30–5pm), which has an ATM and can change US dollars.

Post office Located next to the Agribank.

Highway 6

East of Dien Bien Phu Highway 279 heads through lush countryside, where ancient waterwheels still turn beside rivers and streams, then it climbs into steep mountains to **TUAN GIAO**, where Highway 6 takes off north to Muong Lay or south to Son La. From here, it goes over the Pha Din ("Heaven and Earth") Pass, one of the highest in the north. If you're lucky there are great views from the top, but more often than not it's enveloped in clouds. Highway 6 then drops down to the small town of **Thuan Chau**, where there's a lively market of predominantly Black Thai people each morning until 9 or 10am. The last stretch passes through a valley bordered by massive karst pillars before reaching a softer landscape of paddy and banana plantations, where more waterwheels feed sculpted terraces, to the industrious town of **Son La**.

EATING	HIGHWAY 6

Thanh Thuy Highway 6 ☎ 0230 386 2408. On the south side of the main road about halfway through Tuan Giao, the Thanh Thuy restaurant is located in a large stilted house and features an English menu. It's a good spot for a lunch break when travelling between Dien Bien Phu and Son La, with main dishes costing around 60,000–120,000đ. Daily 7am–10pm.

Son La and around

The welcoming, low-key charm of **SON LA**, the bulk of which straggles for little more than a kilometre along the west bank of the Nam La River, is enhanced by its valley-edge setting, and it merits more than the usual overnight stop. If time allows, there's enough of interest to occupy a few days, taking in the **old French prison** and making forays to nearby **minority villages** on foot or by motorbike.

The French prison

Bao Tang Son La • Daily 7.30–11am & 1.30–5pm • 10,000đ

Son La's principal tourist sight is the **French prison**, which occupies a wooded promontory above To Hieu and offers good views over town. This region was a hotbed of anti-French resistance, and a list of political prisoners interred here reads like a roll call of famous revolutionaries – among them Le Duan and Truong Chinh, veteran Party members who both went on to become general secretary. Local hero **To Hieu** was also imprisoned for seditionary crimes but he died from lung cancer while in captivity in 1944.

The penitentiary

The two turn-offs from the highway are both marked with chunky stylized signs suggesting incarceration; walk uphill to find the prison gates and an arched entrance, still announcing "Pénitencier", leading into the main compound. Most of the buildings lie in ruins, destroyed by a French bombing raid in 1952, but a few were restored in 2007, including a two-storey block beneath which are seven punishment cells. Political prisoners were often incarcerated in brutal conditions: the two larger cells (then windowless) held up to five people shackled by the ankles. Behind this block, don't miss the well-presented **collection of prison memorabilia**. Enter the second arched gate and upstairs in the building on your right you'll find a display about the dozen or so **minorities** who inhabit the area, including costumes, handicrafts, jewellery and photos.

Ban Hin

The Black Thai village of **BAN HIN** is located off to the right of the Son La-Dien Bien Phu highway about 7km north of town. The village consists of traditional, stilthouses and most of the

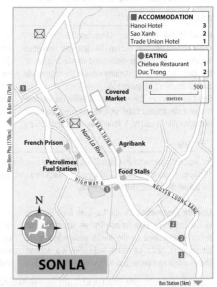

ACCOMMODATION
Hanoi Hotel	3
Sao Xanh	2
Trade Union Hotel	1

EATING
Chelsea Restaurant	1
Duc Trong	2

Covered Market

French Prison

Agribank

Petrolimex Fuel Station

Food Stalls

HIGHWAY 6

Nam La River

TO HIEU

CHU VAN THINH

NGUYEN LUONG BANG

& Ban Hin (7km)

Dien Bien Phu (170km)

N

SON LA

Bus Station (5km)

8

> ## WHITE THAI OR BLACK THAI?
>
> The villages around Mai Chau are predominantly populated by **White Thai**, and those around Son La and Dien Bien by **Black Thai**, but how do you tell the difference? Unfortunately it's not a simple matter that one group wears white and the other black, though the Black Thai definitely have a preference for a black background to tunics and trousers. Here are a few useful pointers:
> **Roofs** Both groups live in stilted houses, but the roofs of White Thai houses are usually thatched, while those of the Black Thai are usually tiled.
> **Dress** The White Thai don't usually wear traditional dress (black dress and pastel-coloured blouse) except for dance performances and special family occasions, while the Black Thai are renowned for the intricately embroidered and colourful head-dresses seen flopping over the heads of their women in everyday scenes, including at the market. Incongruously, many women have a penchant for wearing a crash helmet perched on top of their elaborate head-dresses.
> **Handicrafts** The White Thai sell their handicrafts, usually in the form of colourful textiles, while for the most part the Black Thai don't.

women wear the colourful head-dresses for which they are well known. The hillsides are covered with plum trees, coffee bushes and stands of bamboo. Some minority villages such as Ban Hin occasionally stage events for tour groups, such as **traditional Thai dancing** or supping the local home brew, a sweet wine made of glutinous rice; it's drunk from a communal earthenware container using bamboo straws, and hence named *ruou can*, or stem alcohol.

ARRIVAL AND DEPARTURE   SON LA AND AROUND

By bus Son La's bus station is located 5km southwest of town, so it's necessary to take a xe om into the centre (about 30,000đ).

Destinations Dien Bien Phu (4hr); Hanoi (7hr); Hoa Binh (5hr), via the Mai Chau junction (3hr).

INFORMATION AND TOURS

Tourist information The best place for information is the helpful *Trade Union Hotel*, where you can also hire transport and organize village visits with English-speaking guides ($20–30 a day), or arrange to see Thai dancing and sample rice wine.

ACCOMMODATION

Hanoi Hotel 228 Truong Chinh ☎ 022 375 3299, ⓦ hanoihotel299.com.vn. Son La's most appealing hotel has spacious, comfortable doubles and affordable suites on the upper floors offering cracking views of the countryside around. Doubles $30, suites $55

Sao Xanh 1 Quyen Thang ☎ 022 378 9999. The *Sao Xanh* is a centrally located hotel with decent-sized rooms, all with a/c, cable TV and wi-fi. There's even a lift and staff are very helpful, if limited with their English. $15

Trade Union Hotel 4 Xuan Thuy ☎ 022 385 2244, ⓦ sonlatradeunionhotel.com. After a recent make-over, the rooms here look quite appealing, with canopies over the beds and tubs in bathrooms; plus it's the best place in town to find local information. The restaurant is one of the few in town with an English menu. $25

EATING

For food, both the *Hanoi* and *Trade Union* hotels have passable restaurants, but the latter is open to residents only (closes 10.30pm). If you are yet to try Thai speciality **black rice** (*com gao cam*) then look for it at one of the com pho stalls near the big junction at the south end of town.

Chelsea Restaurant 15 Son La–Dien Bien Highway ☎ 022 385 2915. Even for non-Chelsea supporters, this stylish café, located by the town's main junction and serving pizza, pasta, ice creams and coffee, is a real find. There's a cosy upstairs section with views over a new park in front. Daily 7am–11pm.

Duc Trong 147 Truong Chinh ☎ 0973 806076. Located right in front of the *Hanoi Hotel*, this welcoming place serves a wide range of Vietnamese staples, such as pho for breakfast and plenty of stir-fries and soups. Daily 5.30am–midnight.

DIRECTORY

Banks There are several banks in town, including the Agribank at 8 Chu Van Thinh, which also has an ATM.
Motorbikes Bikes are available for rent through hotels for

around $7 a day.
Post office On the main drag, To Hieu.

Yen Chau

Halfway between Son La and Moc Chau along Highway 6, the town of **YEN CHAU** is famed for its fruit and surrounded by some very pretty Black Thai villages. One such village is **La Ken**, about 15km south of Yen Chau, which can be visited by crossing swaying suspension bridges over the river. With your own transport, you could make a detour about 20km over rolling hills to the **Chi Day Cave**, a popular pilgrimage site for Vietnamese; look for a turning to the west about 20km north of Yen Chau.

Moc Chau

Around 120km southeast of Son La, the sprawling market town of **MOC CHAU** provides a convenient place for a break. The **cool climate** of this thousand-metre-high plateau favours tea and coffee cultivation, mulberry to feed the voracious worms of Vietnam's silk industry and herds of dairy cattle, initially imported from Holland, to quench Hanoi's thirst for milk, yoghurt and ice cream. Just out of town towards Hanoi, the road is dotted with stalls selling local **milk products** such as three kinds of flavoured milk, thick home-made yoghurt and blocks of condensed milk (which they advertise as chocolate when cocoa is added), as well as green tea. The rigid lines of tea bushes that border the road round Moc Chau create curious patterns, and though there are few side roads, this is a region in which some might want to linger.

Mai Chau

The **minority villages** of the Mai Chau Valley, inhabited mainly by White Thai, are close enough to Hanoi (135km) to make this a popular destination, particularly at weekends when it's often swamped with large groups of students. The valley itself, however, is still largely unspoilt, apart from the appearance of a few new resorts that are popping up between the rice paddies. The bucolic scene of pancake-flat rice fields trimmed with jagged mountains is incredibly photogenic, particularly when the rice fields glow an emerald green.

MAI CHAU is the valley's main settlement – a friendly, quiet place that has a bustling morning **market** frequented by minority people who trek in to haggle over buffalo meat, star fruit, sacks of tea or groundnuts. However, most visitors see little of the town, as they are bussed straight into the nearby White Thai villages of Ban Lac and Pom Coong to spend the night in a home-stay.

ARRIVAL AND DEPARTURE   **MAI CHAU**

By bus Buses in Mai Chau pull up and leave from the main road in front of the market. There are several buses a day to Hanoi and Son La.
Destinations Hanoi (4hr); Son La (4hr).
Tours Most people visit Mai Chau on an organized tour out of Hanoi, which usually includes overnighting in a minority

village, or as part of a longer trip into the northwest mountains by jeep or motorbike. Some companies offer day tours from Hanoi but these are not recommended as you'll spend most of the day on the bus. Tour groups tend to stay in the villages of Lac and Pom Coong to the west of Mai Chau and go on organized walks around the valley.

ACCOMMODATION

Mai Chau Lodge On the main road just south of the town centre ☎0218 386 8959, ⓦmaichaulodge.com. The most salubrious accommodation in Mai Chau is at

Mai Chau Lodge, which sits amid bucolic scenery: though somewhat overpriced, its rooms are tastefully decorated with wooden fixtures, and the staff are extremely helpful. **$180**

★**Mai Chau Valley View** Just before the Mai Chau Lodge on the main road ☎0218 386 7080, ⓦmaichau valleyview.com. Enjoying the same idyllic views as the neighbouring *Mai Chau Lodge* but offering rooms at a fraction of the price, this new place seems destined to succeed. Its eight rooms are clean and well furnished and feature knock-out views from small balconies. The staff are also helpful (but not pushy) and the restaurant serves a good range of tasty food. $55

Number 1 Ban Van Guesthouse ☎0218 386 7182. Located on the right as you enter the village of Ban Van, just 1km east of Mai Chau (the opposite side to Ban Lac and Pom Coong), this traditional stilthouse has a nice setting next to the rice fields. Its main appeal is that this village is much less touristy than Ban Lac and Pom Coong. $2.50

EATING

Most people eat a simple set dinner with their hosts in their stilthouse accommodation, with the cost included as part of the tour.

Mai Chau Lodge The lodge's excellent restaurant serves a 4-course set lunch for 320,000đ, or set dinner for 360,000đ. The setting is quite romantic, with views over lotus ponds and rice paddies stretching across the valley. Daily 7am–9.30pm.

Mai Chau Valley View Some of the best food in town is dished up here, including tasty steamed fish in banana leaf. Most mains 80,000–160,000đ. Daily 7am–9pm.

Ban Lac and Pom Coong

Just beyond the *Mai Chau Lodge*, a lane to the right (west) leads across a few paddy fields to **BAN LAC** and **POM COONG**, neighbouring villages that are home to a prosperous community of **White Thai** – though these days their wealth is derived more from tourist dollars than from farming. Most **overnight tours** include a guided trek around the valley, which for many is the highlight of their visit. In the evenings, the traditional dance **performances** staged for tour groups after dinner are also interesting, with coy, long-haired girls acting out agricultural chores in a graceful manner. After the show, the audience is invited to join them in a dance, as well as a sup of local wine from a big bowl through a bamboo straw. While too touristy for some, there is at least the chance to stay in a genuine **stilthouse** – a true taste of rural Vietnam, particularly at dawn if your sleeping quarters happen to be above the henhouse. Avoid a weekend visit if possible, when the village is overrun with students from Hanoi.

During the day the lanes between houses are draped with scarves, bags and dresses, with villagers urging passers-by to stop for a quick look. Though it seems a bit commercial, the vendors are not as pushy as their Black Hmong counterparts in Sa Pa, and if it does get tiring then a few minutes' walk in any direction from the centre leads out to paddies and a view of the ring of purple mountains which make for some of north Vietnam's most classic scenery.

GETTING AROUND   BAN LAC AND POM COONG

By bicycle Many houses in Ban Lac rent out mountain bikes for 50,000–100,000đ per day, which are an ideal way to explore the Mai Chau Valley.

ACCOMMODATION

Most people on a two-day tour from Hanoi overnight in a **home-stay** (though don't expect too much interaction with your hosts), and just about every house in both villages doubles as a guesthouse – all have sit-down toilets fitted below the houses. Some house owners have even changed their roofs from tile back to the original thatch, perhaps to fulfil visitors' expectations.

Mai Chau Nature Place aka Riverside Resort Ban Lac 2 village ☎016 5852 6950, ⓦmaichaunatureplace.com. If the thought of sleeping on a thin mattress in a room with twenty snorers (as can happen in the home-stays) puts you off, here's a good alternative. Individual bamboo bungalows with private balconies overlook a stream; they also serve decent set dinners at around 120,000–140,000đ per person. $30

> ### HOA BINH DURING THE FRENCH WAR
>
> During the French War Hoa Binh was the scene of a disastrous **French raid** into Viet Minh-held territory, which reads like a dress rehearsal for the epic rout of Dien Bien Phu. In November 1951, French paratroop battalions seized Hoa Binh in a daring attempt to hamper enemy supply routes. They met with little resistance and dug in, only to find themselves marooned as Giap's forces cut both road and river access. In February the following year the French fought their way out towards Hanoi in a battle that came to be known as the "hell of Hoa Binh".

Around Mai Chau

One interesting route from Mai Chau is to cycle 12km south on Highway 15 to **Co Luong**, passing timeless rural scenes and reflections of mountains in the flooded paddy fields. At Co Luong, the Ma River joins the road, and huge limestone walls and dense bamboo growth adorn the riverbank. An active **market** on Saturday mornings is worth the trip, to see the array of handicrafts and fish.

Some 25km further south from Cu Luong along Highway 15 lies the **Pu Luong Nature Reserve** (see p.316), over the provincial boundary in Thanh Binh Province, though this journey is better tackled by car or motorbike. It's an hour or two drive to the south, and one that features yet more bucolic scenery, including rice terraces cascading down hillsides and remote home-stays.

Hoa Binh

Northeast of Mai Chau, Highway 6 traverses one final pass before leaving the northwest mountains. It's a steady climb along precipitous hillsides up to a col at 1200m, and then an ear-popping descent through sugar-cane plantations on the east side to **HOA BINH**, on the edge of the Red River plain. The main highway thunders straight past the centre of town on a by-pass, but a hint of quieter days lingers in its shaded main boulevard, Cu Chin Lan, where there are a few simple restaurants. There's little to detain you here, but you could stretch your legs while taking a look at the dam wall southeast of the centre, before pushing on for a couple more hours to either Hanoi or Mai Chau.

Hoa Binh Dam

Less than 2km to the west of the city, the 620m-wide **Hoa Binh Dam** chokes the Da River to create a lake over 200km long, stretching most of the way to Son La. The reservoir is earmarked for tourist development, but its main purpose is to feed Vietnam's largest hydroelectric plant, which came on stream in 1994 and has gone some way to solving Vietnam's chronic power shortage.

You get a worm's-eye view of the dam from the bridge that links Hoa Binh's main street (Cu Chin Lan) with industrial suburbs across the Da River, or you can drive right up to it; follow Cu Chin Lan to its southeastern end and continue round to the right. Staff at Hoa Binh Tourism (see below) can arrange expensive group tours to Muong villages in the vicinity of the reservoir behind the dam.

ARRIVAL AND DEPARTURE
HOA BINH

By bus Hoa Binh's main bus station lies on its eastern edge of town, where you'll find the usual gaggle of xe om waiting to take you 1km into the centre (20,000đ). Buses for Hanoi leave regularly, but note that some terminate at Ha Dong where you have to pick up a Hanoi city bus.

Destinations Hanoi (every 15min; 2hr); Mai Chau (several daily; 2hr).

INFORMATION AND TOURS

Tourist information Hoa Binh Tourism (🌐 hoabinh tourism.com) at the *Hoa Binh Hotel 2* offers boat tours of the dam and hydroelectric plant and of the Muong, Thai, Hmong and Dao minority villages on the shores of the reservoir (around $100), although it is geared primarily to tour groups.

ACCOMMODATION AND EATING

As well as the restaurant at the *Hoa Binh 1* hotel (main dishes such as grilled chicken and pork with tomato sauce around 100,000–120,000đ), there's also a group of local **restaurants**, cafés and ice-cream parlours at the west end of Cu Chin Lan, about 50m before the T-junction.

Hoa Binh 1 and 2 ☎ 0218 385 2051 and ☎ 385 2001. The most popular place to stay for foreigners is the *Hoa Binh 1*, although rooms and facilities are almost identical to the *Hoa Binh 2*. The hotels are located almost opposite each other on a hillside 2km west of the town centre along

Highway 6. Both have about thirty wood-panelled rooms in long, thatched stilthouses. The *Hoa Binh 1* also features folk dancing and music displays and sampling of Thai rice wine from the communal pot. $25

The Northeast Loop

The provinces of northeast Vietnam, looping eastwards from **Ha Giang** to Lang Son, are less frequented than their counterparts west of the Red River Valley, though the region is growing in popularity, especially the fabulous landscapes of the **Dong Van Karst Plateau Geopark** in Ha Giang Province. With the notable exception of the geopark, the peaks in the northeast are lower and the views smaller-scale and of an altogether softer quality; there are also less minority folk wearing traditional dress. Getting to see everything is not as straightforward as in the northwest either, though the upgrading of the road between Meo Vac and Cao Bang means it's now possible to visit Ha Giang Province, as well as **Ba Be Lake** and the region around **Cao Bang**, without backtracking.

Highlights of the northeast are its **rural landscapes**, from traditional scenes of villages engulfed in forest to dramatic limestone country, typified by pockets of cultivation squeezed among rugged outcrops whose lower slopes are wrinkled with terraces. However, population densities are still low, leaving huge forest reserves and high areas of wild, open land inhabited by **ethnic minorities** practising swidden farming. While many have adopted a Vietnamese way of life, in remoter parts the minorities remain culturally distinct – particularly evident when **local markets**, their dates traditionally set by the lunar calendar, are in full swing.

Ha Giang

HA GIANG is the capital of the north's most remote and least-visited province, just over 300km north of Hanoi, where Vietnam's border juts into China and almost reaches the Tropic of Cancer. Until the early 1990s, this region was the scene of fierce fighting between Vietnam and China, and it is still considered a "sensitive area", though its inhabitants nowadays are peaceful and welcoming. Ha Giang itself is a sizeable town, and though its buildings are of no great architectural merit and there's little to see, its setting is very impressive, hemmed in by the imposing Mo Neo and Cam **mountains**. The ochre waters of the **Lo River** carve southward through the centre of town, and traffic is thick on the two bridges that connect the west and east districts. The main reason for a visit is to acquire a **permit** to enter **Dong Van Karst Plateau Geopark** (see p.421).

> **ONWARDS TO CHINA**
>
> In 2014 the border with China at **Thanh Thuy**, just 22km northwest of Ha Giang, opened to foreigners (daily 7.30–11am & 1.30–5pm). This will probably not precipitate long queues of Western visitors, as you must first obtain a **travel permit** at Ha Giang (see box, p.419) and the region of China beyond – the first town is Malipo, en route to larger Weshan – is currently as unexplored as the Dong Van region of Vietnam was until recently. However, adventurous types might like to consider this as a less-travelled route to Kunming.

8

GETTING A TRAVEL PERMIT

One of the reasons that few people visit the Ha Giang region is that foreigners currently must obtain a **permit** ($10; one permit is good for up to five people) from the immigration office or a tour agent or hotel to travel anywhere outside Ha Giang town, including up to the **Chinese border**, which is now open.

Ha Giang's **immigration office** is at 415a Tran Phu, at the northern end of the street opposite the stadium (7.30–11am & 1.30–5pm; ☎0219 387 5210); since there are usually no queues, the process can be completed in a few minutes. If you enter the region from anywhere else – Bao Lac to the south, for instance – you will need to obtain a permit at the first hotel that you stay at inside the geopark, which will probably cost a bit more. You should apply for as many days as possible as you won't be able to extend it and, given the beauty of the area, you may well want to. Previously foreigners were required to **hire a guide**, too, though this is no longer the case; however, as the situation is subject to change, it's best to make enquiries in Hanoi before heading to the area.

The market

Located in a purpose-built hall just northeast of the northern bridge, Ha Giang's **market** is a frenzy of activity in the early morning when members of **minority groups** can often be seen. If you plan to go to Dong Van, however, you're likely to see more authentic markets along the way.

The town museum

Tues–Sun 8–11am & 2–4pm; Sat & Sun also 7.30–9.30pm • Free

The Ha Giang **museum**, located just west of the northern bridge, is well worth a visit to get a preview of the outfits of the many different minority groups (of which there are over twenty) who inhabit the province, as well as to see artefacts such as bronze drums and ancient axe-heads that have been unearthed by digs in the area. Archeological evidence shows that there has been a settlement here for tens of thousands of years, and the region seemingly flourished during the Bronze Age judging by the number of beautifully designed drums that have been found.

ARRIVAL AND DEPARTURE   HA GIANG

By bus The bus station is to the southwest of the town centre on 19 Thang 5 St, just off Nguyen Trai which runs along the west side of the Lo River. Xe om are on hand to run passengers a kilometre or two into the centre.

Destinations Dong Van (2 daily; 8hr); Hanoi (frequent; 8hr); Lao Cai (2 daily; 6hr).
By car or motorbike With a rented car or motorbike, it's possible to approach from Bac Ha (see p.405).

INFORMATION

Tourist information The best source of information for Ha Giang Province is Travel Modest Bees (274 Nguyen Trai

☎091 545 8668), run by Hoang Tuan Anh, who can help organize transport and treks in the region.

ACCOMMODATION AND EATING

There are plenty of **places to stay** in town, though since few foreigners visit, staff speak very little English. This shouldn't be a problem, as rates are usually displayed on the counter, but facilities everywhere are rather basic. There are several **restaurants** along Nguyen Van Linh, which runs beside the west bank of the river just north of the museum, and you can find the usual soup and rice places around the market on the east side of town.

Duc Giang 14 Nguyen Trai ☎0219 387 5648. The *Duc Giang* is typical of most lodgings in town, providing a choice of fan or a/c, tea-making facilities and spartan furnishings, but no lift. $10
Huy Hoan 10 Nguyen Trai ☎0219 386 1288. This place is probably the best hotel in town, which is not saying much.

On the plus side, it has clean rooms with traditional furnishings and wi-fi throughout, but the service is indifferent. $10
★Truong Xuan Resort Km5, Nguyen Van Linh Rd ☎0219 381 1102, ⌨hagiangresort.com. Though it's a few clicks from the centre, this is by far Ha Giang's best

place to rest your head, with rustic, thatched cabins nestled beneath towering trees. Go for a river view room and soak up the wonderful scenery. Rates include a decent breakfast, and staff also provide motorbike and kayak rental and arrange tours of the geopark. $25

DIRECTORY

Bank There are several banks in town, including a branch of Agribank on Nguyen Trai with an ATM just south of the museum.

Post office Located along Nguyen Trai, to the south of the southern bridge.

Dong Van Karst Plateau Geopark

Entry included in obligatory travel permit (see box below) • W dongvangeopark.com

The main reason for a trip to Ha Giang Province is to gaze on the stunning scenery in **Dong Van Karst Plateau Geopark**, to the northeast of Ha Giang town, designated Vietnam's first geopark by UNESCO in 2010. The geopark consists of four districts of Ha Giang Province – Quan Ba, Yen Minh, Dong Van and Meo Vac – covering an area of 2350 square kilometres. The region's newfound status has been accompanied by the erection of **information boards** in places with unique geological formations, and though they employ a lot of "geospeak", these boards help visitors appreciate the special nature of the landscape.

The two biggest towns in the geopark are **Dong Van** and **Meo Vac**, both set in valleys surrounded by forbidding peaks and connected by a hair-raising road with spectacular views. The trip from Ha Giang to Dong Van, then on to Cao Bang via Bao Lac, is about 300km and takes at least two (more often three) full days of driving along narrow, bumpy roads, which may become impassable during the rainy season. This border area is home to several **minority groups**, including the White Hmong and the Lo Lo, the latter having only a few thousand members; most towns along the route, including Dong Van and Meo Vac, have a **Sunday market** attended by villagers from the surrounding valleys, where you'll find few foreigners wandering into your photographic compositions.

There's adequate **accommodation** in the region but note that **eating** is noticeably expensive here, especially in Dong Van, justified, no doubt, by the long haul to get supplies in; be prepared to pay 200,000đ for a chicken dish or 500,000đ for a big hotpot.

Tam Son

Roughly 40km northeast from Ha Giang, after passing a huge, Hollywood-type sign announcing the beginning of the geopark, Highway 4C crosses Quan Ba Pass ("Heaven's Gate"). Just beyond the pass is a pull-off where roadside steps lead up to

8

GETTING AROUND THE GEOPARK

The best way to explore the geopark is to **hire a car and driver** or, if you're an experienced rider, on a rented **motorbike** (something strong to deal with the rugged terrain). Tour operators, such as Truong Xuan Resort in Ha Giang (see opposite) and Cuong's Motorbike Adventure in Hanoi (see p.370) rent out motorbikes and run motorbike tours here. If you're really brave you could take **local buses**, but they're infrequent, cramped and do not stop at the viewpoints. There are between three and six minibuses each day travelling between Ha Giang and Dong Van (115,000đ), leaving early in the morning and passing through Tam Son and Yen Minh. There's a similar service to and from Meo Vac, though at present there is no public bus connecting Dong Van and Meo Vac; a xe om along this hair-raising stretch should cost around 250,000đ.

If you're a patient type, it might be worth hanging around the immigration office in Ha Giang and offering to share fuel costs with a private group heading for the geopark. In this way you'll get to see the sights without the high cost of vehicle rental if you're travelling alone.

a delightful view – when the weather is clear – over the town of **TAM SON** and the patchwork fields and dramatic hills around it. Two perfectly rounded karst hills that stand out are dubbed "Fairy bosom", a typical example of the fanciful terms that Vietnamese, like the Chinese, like to apply to natural phenomena. Unlike most karst outcrops, which weather into contorted and tortured shapes, these perfectly rounded hills have weathered evenly, as a result of their composition – a form of hard-crushed limestone. There's a **market** in Tam Son on Sundays where, apart from the White Hmong, who are the biggest group in this region, you might see Red Dao, Tay, Giay, Co Lao, Pu Peo and Lo Lo people. The valley is great fun to trek or cycle around and there's a surprisingly decent hotel, the *567*.

ACCOMMODATION

TAM SON

Hotel 567 ☎ 0219 384 6129, ✉ phamhuong567@gmail .com. Considering the meagre hotels in the provincial capital, it's a pleasant surprise to find this well maintained place in the middle of Tam Son's high street. Some rooms are a bit dingy, but they're all clean and a good size. Terrific views from the back. **$10**

Yen Minh

Beyond Tam Son, Highway 4C follows a pretty stream for some distance, with steep mountain flanks rising on both sides. After climbing over treeless, terraced hills, which serve to increase the feeling of remoteness, it then descends into **YEN MINH**. This makes a good lunch stop, especially since there is a reasonable restaurant here and a passable hotel located in the centre of town.

ACCOMMODATION AND EATING

YEN MINH

Phuc Cai ☎ 0219 385 2050. This simple eatery serves a good range of soups and stir-fries. It is located in the alley almost opposite the *Thao Nguyen* hotel. Daily 6am–9pm.
Thao Nguyen ☎ 0219 385 2297, ✉ khachsanthao

nguyen2011@gmail.com. This newish, 54-room hotel on the main road in the centre of town is a surprising addition to Yen Minh's facilities. Clean, bright rooms have flat-screen TVs, wi-fi and smart bathrooms. The carpeted VIP rooms are worth the bit extra. **$15**

Yen Minh to Dong Van

Just 4km east of Yen Minh, the road splits and this is where the fun really begins. The northern fork goes to Dong Van and the southern one to Meo Vac; you can follow either as they join up to form a loop, though **the Dong Van stretch** described here has more accommodation options.

There's virtually no traffic on the road, which passes through rugged limestone landscapes, the scenery gradually getting wilder and more dramatic, and there is little evidence of settlements at the roadside. For much of the way, the terrain is pocked with blackened knuckles of rock that must make for difficult farming, though small fields of corn are planted here and there, and cone-shaped bundles of corn stalks, used for fodder and fuel, are scattered among the rock-strewn landscape. The locals, for the most part White Hmong, stoop low under heavy burdens of wood, and it's all too evident that life here is tough.

The Vuong Palace

Sa Phin • Daily 7am–5pm • 20,000đ

At **Sa Phin**, about 15km west of Dong Van, look out for the sturdy building of the People's Committee on the south side of the road. A turning here leads 400m down to Vuong Palace.

The **Vuong Palace** is a large, two-storey residence with three courtyards that was built by the French for the local Hmong king. In 2006 it was subject to sensitive renovation that replaced many collapsing beams but has retained the integrity of the original building. The thick walls show intricate craftsmanship, and have slits set into them that were used to defend the place with rifles in bygone days. In the shade of pine trees beside the gateway to the palace are several impressive tombs of members of the Vuong family. As it's the only real sight for miles around, it's attracted a bunch of souvenir stalls and can sometimes be crowded with visitors.

Dong Van

North from Sa Phin, the scenery is superb – a constant string of cone-shaped peaks standing above fields in the valley below. Your destination in this direction is **DONG VAN**, the northernmost major town in Vietnam, and despite comprising only a single street, arriving here is something of an achievement itself.

Towards its eastern end of Dong Van, the road on the north side named **Pho Co** features some impressive architecture, particularly in the building that houses the *Pho Co Café* (see below). It's also worth hiking up the hill behind, where you'll find the ruins of an **old French fort** and sensational views over town (follow the road heading north from the *Hoa Cuong* hotel). Apart from that, most people visit to witness the cacophonous and colourful **Sunday market**, when hilltribe people dressed in their best come here to buy and sell pigs, farming implements and rice wine. The town is also the jumping-off point to the **flag tower at Lung Cu**, the northernmost point in the country.

Lung Cu

Daily 7am–5pm • 20,000đ

If you have time, head north out of Dong Van along another narrow road with mind-boggling views and continue 22km to **Lung Cu**. There's nothing here except a **flag tower**, built in 2010, that marks the northernmost point of the country. Set on top of a hill, the flag tower is reached by a long flight of steps, and the views into China from the top, of thatched huts and fields being ploughed by buffalo, have probably remained unchanged for centuries. A plaque at the top records the latitude (23°N) and longitude (105°E). Considering its remoteness, this spot has become very popular for Vietnamese visitors.

ACCOMMODATION   DONG VAN

Hoa Cuong ☎ 016 6319 7888. Located at the eastern end of town, this towering, 82-room hotel, under construction at the time of research, is evidence that Dong Van is finally on the map. It will probably be most foreigners' choice in town, providing comfortable rooms. $30

Hoang Ngoc ☎ 0219 385 6020, ✉ hoangngochotel2 @gmail.com. This friendly and clean guesthouse, situated in the middle of Dong Van's main street, is familiar with foreign visitors and offers cable TV and wi-fi. $14

Thai Thinh Motel ☎ 098 524 8741. On the main road between the *Hoang Ngoc* and *Hoa Cuong* hotels, this new place has 10 rooms of varying size, all well equipped and representing good value. $15

EATING

Au Viet next door to the Hoang Ngoc hotel ☎ 094 290 5888. This place has an extensive menu of Vietnamese dishes that are generally very tasty. Though it's foreigner-friendly, it's very popular among Vietnamese visitors too. Main dishes 100,000–500,000đ. Daily 6am–10pm.

Pho Co Café At the north end of Pho Co St. A wonderfully atmospheric café providing delicious coffee and snacks at cheap prices around a courtyard where you'll probably spend your time taking photos of the bare brickwork and carved wooden balconies on the upstairs terrace. Daily 6am–10pm.

Meo Vac

The next stage of the journey, covering just 36km on the way to Meo Vac, is perhaps the most spectacular part of the whole trip. The road clings to the side of a massive canyon and crosses the Ma Pi Leng Pass at around 1500m. The views down to the Nho Que River, a ribbon of turquoise far below, are simply dizzying. There's little to see in **MEO VAC** itself apart from a small statue of Uncle Ho and the town's market that overflows on Sundays, but it's the setting, with a ring of barren mountains forming a bowl around it, which is impressive.

8

ACCOMMODATION AND EATING	MEO VAC

Hoa Cuong ☎ 0219 387 1888. Meo Vac's best hotel by a long shot looks over the central market. Rooms are a good size, though mattresses in some are very hard (check first) and there are plenty of facilities like cable TV and minibar, but be prepared for frequent electricity cuts. **$20**

Mai Dao ☎ 0219 387 1294. On the road into town from Dong Van, this is the best of several mini-hotels in town,

providing decent a/c rooms and wi-fi. English spoken too. **$12.50**

Xuan Hac Almost opposite the Mai Dao Hotel ☎ 091 598 0560. This restaurant is the biggest and fanciest dining venue in town, which isn't saying much. No English menu but the welcoming staff speak English and will help you order. Daily 6am–10pm.

To Bao Lac and beyond

From Meo Vac, Highway 217 descends from the karst plateau, passing Tay villages and the small town of **Khau Vai**, where the annual **love market** – actually more like a wife-swapping ceremony – attracts busloads of domestic tourists in late April or early May. Snaking its way south, the route passes through the large but drab market town of **Bao Lac**, where there are a few basic hotels if you should be delayed by landslides or floods.

Continuing south on Highway 34, the scenery continues to be impressive, particularly near the mining town of **Tinh Tuc**. If you're heading for **Ba Be Lake** in the Ba Be National Park, look for a turn to the south shortly after Tinh Tuc on to Highway 212, which carries you up and over Phia Den Pass at around 1200 metres before dropping down to the valley floor. At the junction with Highway 279, turn west for the last few kilometres to the lake.

8

ARRIVAL AND DEPARTURE	BAO LAC

By bus There is no bus station in Bao Lac, but buses stop on the main road (Highway 34) in front of the market heading for Cao Bang and Bao Lam (for Ha Giang).

Destinations Bao Lam (1 daily at 10.30am; 2hr); Cao Bang (1 daily at 12.30pm; 4hr).

ACCOMMODATION

Song Gam 1km north of the bridge near the centre of town ☎ 026 387 0269. Though this place is nothing to write home about, the rooms are clean and bright, the

owners are friendly and there are good views across the river from the back. **$10**

Ba Be National Park

20,000đ

Designated as Vietnam's eighth national park in 1992 and covering an area of about one hundred square kilometres, **Ba Be** is a region of astounding beauty, from the lush vegetation mirrored in the still waters of **Ba Be Lake**, to the towering **limestone pinnacles** that reach over 1500m high. The main attractions for visitors are **boat trips**

BA BE ITINERARIES

The Ba Be itinerary usually begins with a boat trip along the Nang River to **Hang Puong**, where the waters have tunnelled a 300m-long, bat-filled cave through a mountain. From here they go on to the **Dau Dang Waterfall**, a stretch of beautiful but treacherous rapids. Take care if you walk on the slippery rocks around the falls as there has been at least one tourist fatality here. Next up is a visit to a **Tay** village on the lakeside, and on longer trips an overnight stay in a stilthouse. A road around the south end of the lake has made **Pac Ngoi** less of an isolated Tay community than it used to be; in fact these days its multiple home-stays make it tourist central, but several other less-visited villages in the area, such as **Buoc Luom**, **Ban Vang** and **Bo Lu**, can accommodate visitors too. Few Tay still wear traditional dress, and you're most likely to see it only at a **minority show** at the *National Park Guest House* (see opposite).

on the lake to visit caves, waterfalls and minority villages, with the added bonus of seeing at least some of the park's abundant wildlife. Bears, tigers and one of Vietnam's rarest and most endangered primates, the **Tonkin snub-nosed langur** (*Rhinopithecus avunculus*), live in a few isolated communities on the fringes of the park, but nearer the lake there's a good chance of spotting the more common macaque monkeys, herons and garrulous, colourful flocks of parrots. Few people are around to disturb the wildlife and outside the months of July and August, when Hanoians take their holidays, you'll usually find only a handful of tourists.

Ba Be Lake

Vietnam's largest natural lake, **Ba Be Lake** forms the core of the National Park. Enclosed by steep, densely wooded slopes breaking out here and there into white limestone cliffs, the lake is 7km long, up to 30m deep and 1km wide in parts. A few islands decorate the surface. Kayaks are available to rent to explore the lake – ask at your home-stay or hotel.

ARRIVAL AND DEPARTURE — BA BE NATIONAL PARK

Tours Hanoi tour agencies (see p.370) can arrange three-day tours to Ba Be for around $120 per person. Ba Be is about a five-hour drive from Hanoi.

By rented transport A rented motorbike or car and driver allows maximum flexibility to travel arrangements, and good roads connect Ba Be with Hanoi, Cao Bang and Meo Vac to the north.

By public transport This is just about possible – infrequent buses leave from Gia Lam bus station in Hanoi and pull up in Cho Ra, from where a xe om to Ba Be Lake (16km) will cost around 150,000đ.

INFORMATION AND TOURS

Park information On arrival, first stop for independent travellers should be the park headquarters, which is located a couple of kilometres from the boat jetty on the east side of the lake. Here you can get information about two- to five-day tours, the most popular of which are boat trips to the caves and waterfalls.

Boat trips Most trips are in narrow, covered motorboats, but it's also possible to be rowed around parts of the lake in a narrow dug-out canoe – a more appropriate way to move about in such a tranquil environment. A tour in either costs $20–40.

ACCOMMODATION AND EATING

If your accommodation is a **home-stay**, your hosts will generally provide well-prepared, though not very exciting, set meals. **Snacks and drinks** are available at the boat jetty by Ba Be Lake and the speciality in restaurants in nearby Cho Ra is fish from the lake.

Duc Khuyen's home-stay Pac Ngoi village, 7km from the park headquarters ☎ 0281 389 4140. One of several places within the park to spend a night in a stilthouse at a lakeside Tay village; comes highly recommended, with meals included in the rate. $6

National Park Guest House/Vuon Quoc Gia Ba Be ☎ 0281 389 4026. This place offers smart but pricey rooms, a restaurant and occasional minority shows. In the summer months (June–Aug) it is often booked out by party cadres, who find it a good location for meetings. $35

Thuy Dung 17km away in Cho Ra ☎ 0281 387 6354. The *Thuy Dung* has large, clean rooms and expansive views from the back, plus friendly staff who can help arrange tours on Ba Be Lake. $12.50

Cao Bang

CAO BANG is in Vietnam's northeasternmost corner near the border with China and makes a fine alternative destination for adventurous travellers who want to avoid the crowds in Sa Pa. Though its major attractions are **Pac Bo Cave**, where Ho Chi Minh lived on his return to Vietnam in 1941, and **Ban Gioc Falls**, Vietnam's highest waterfall, right on the border with China, many visitors will be more interested in visiting the markets and home-stays in **ethnic minority villages**, particularly those of the Dao, Nung and Tay, who still maintain their traditional way of life in the more remote uplands.

8

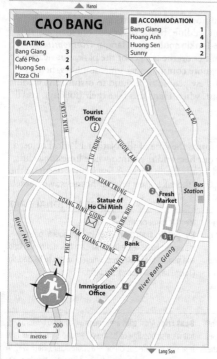

CAO BANG

■ ACCOMMODATION
Bang Giang	1
Hoang Anh	4
Huong Sen	3
Sunny	2

● EATING
Bang Giang	3
Café Pho	2
Huong Sen	4
Pizza Chi	1

The town itself is a likeable place: its centre may be dusty and noisy, but its riverside setting, with dense clumps of bamboo backed by sugar-loaf mountains, helps to blur the edges. The town is built on the southwestern bank of the **Bang Giang River**, on a spur of land formed by the confluence with the Hien River. The narrow, shady park on top of the low hill in the centre of town is worth a wander, and the **statue of Uncle Ho** is a reminder of the fact that this region was vital to the thrust for independence that he led.

The market

Held daily, the enormous **market** to the northwest of the bridge forms the town's focal point, though there are plenty of vendors selling their produce on the narrow road by the river to the south of the bridge too. It's at its liveliest around sunrise when minority women trek into town to buy and sell items like honey, sweet potatoes and fish.

ARRIVAL AND INFORMATION

CAO BANG

By bus Cao Bang's bus station is on Pac Bo, on the east side of the river, near the Bang Giang Bridge.
Destinations Hanoi (7hr); Lang Son (4hr).
Tourist office 47 Ly Tu Trong ☏026 395 4244,

Ⓦ dulichnonnuoccaobang.com.vn; open daily 8–11am & 1–4.30pm. The helpful folks here can provide you with a map of the town and province and provide information about minority markets and home-stays in the region.

ACCOMMODATION

Bang Giang Kim Dong ☏026 385 3431, Ⓔbanggiang .tkv@gmail.com. Located right next to the bridge, this is the largest hotel in town, with helpful, English-speaking staff and a decent restaurant, though the uninspiring rooms are rather overpriced. Ask for a room with a river view to make up for the drab decor. **$24**
★**Hoang Anh** 131 Kim Dong ☏026 385 8969, Ⓔhoanganhhotelcb@yahoo.com.vn. Compared with other options in Cao Bang, the *Hoang Anh* is a stand-out. Its tastefully furnished rooms are spacious, some with picture postcard views, and all amenities are clean and in working order. Considering the reasonable rates, it's your

best choice in town. **$15**
Huong Sen 100 Kim Dong ☏026 385 4654. The *Huong Sen* is good value, with river views from most rooms, cable TV, friendly staff and an excellent restaurant in the lobby: the rooms vary in style and size, so ask to see at least a couple. **$9**
Sunny 40 Kim Dong ☏026 382 8888, Ⓦcaobanghotel .com.vn. This eleven-storey, 52-room hotel was the newest lodgings in Cao Bang at the time of this update. Rooms are well equipped but the place seems more geared to Vietnamese than foreign visitors. **$26**

EATING

Few restaurants cater to foreigners in Cao Bang, so it's time to head for the **market** and track down a steaming bowl of pho. For something a bit more familiar, stop by one of the many bakeries, or look out for stalls selling doner kebab.

Bang Giang Kim Dong ☏026 385 3431. *Bang Giang* has an English menu and serves reasonable food with

most main dishes costing around 120,000–200,000đ. Daily 7am–10pm.

8

Café Pho 140 Vuon Cam ☎026 395 0240. This attractive café has two floors linked by a spiral staircase and serves delicious coffee plus fresh juice and beer. Since there's no nightlife to speak of in Cao Bang, this place is fine to while away an hour or two in the evening. Daily 6.30am–10.30pm.

Huong Sen 100 Kim Dong ☎026 385 4654. *Huong Sen* has no English menu, but since most of the dishes are on display in glass cabinets it's easy to point. Daily 6am–10pm.

Pizza Chi 85 Vuon Cam ☎091 459 3569. The menu is unconventional, with several Vietnamese dishes like pho and baguettes mixed among the pizzas (60,000–100,000đ), but the enthusiastic staff seem determined to make a success of this new venture. Daily 7am–10.30pm.

DIRECTORY

Banks There are a few dotted around town – the easiest to find is outside the *Bang Giang* hotel.

Immigration Office If you're going to Ban Gioc Falls without a guide, stop by the Immigration Office at 54 Kim Dong (☎026 386 9240; Mon–Fri 7.30–11am and 1–4.30pm) to pick up a permit, which costs $10 and is good for up to ten people.

Post office On a hill in the centre of town, the post office is recognizable from its radio mast.

Around Cao Bang

The countryside around Cao Bang is peppered with limestone outcrops and minority villages, several of which provide the opportunity to overnight in a home-stay. While the landscape is not quite as dramatic as that around Dong Van, a trip out to **Ban Gioc Falls** brings ever-changing perspectives of a rural agricultural community. There's an **international border with China** 70km southeast of Cao Bang on Highway 3 at Ta Lung, though it's used predominantly by trucks transporting goods between the two countries.

8

Pac Bo Cave

Museum open daily 7.30–11.30am & 1.30–4.30pm • 10,000đ

Pac Bo Cave is situated right on the border with China, but if you're not a fan of Ho memorabilia then it's hard to justify the 50km excursion from Cao Bang (about an hour each way), though the first stage of the journey, passing minority villages moored in rice-paddy seas and tobacco fields against craggy blue horizons, is a memorable ride.

When Ho Chi Minh walked over from China's Guangxi Province in January 1941, he took his first steps on Vietnamese soil for thirty years. Later that same year he went back to China, to drum up support for his nascent army, and when he next returned to Pac Bo it was after Independence, as a tourist, in 1961. The **cave** today is a strange mixture of shrine and picnic spot, while exhibits in the small **museum** include Ho's Hermes Baby typewriter, bamboo suitcase and Mauser pistol. Next to the museum is a big new memorial dedicated to Ho's memory.

Ban Gioc Falls

Daily sunrise to sunset • 20,000đ • Permits required; see above

The journey from Cao Bang to **Ban Gioc Falls** takes about two hours and is extremely picturesque, passing several minority villages along the way. After 32km, the route passes the forging village of **Phuc Sen**, where you'll see locals hammering new blades into shape on ancient anvils. Just beyond Phuc Sen down a right turn, **Pac Rang** is a Nung village of traditional stilthouses that is well worth exploring. At km38, a turn off to the scruffy town of **Quang Uyen** is worth taking to find a friendly home-stay. A few kilometres before arriving at the falls, there are delightful scenes to the north across the Quay Son River, complete with waterwheels, grazing horses and rugged karst mountains.

At the falls themselves, there are plenty of vendors selling snacks and bamboo rafts offering to take visitors out on the river, and it's a pleasant spot to enjoy a picnic if the weather is good. The falls are not particularly large, but the broad curtain of water spilling over the lip makes a pretty picture in the rainy season. Inevitably, the falls are less than spectacular in the dry season.

Nguom Ngao Cave

Right turn 3km before Ban Gioc Falls • 30,000d

Just a few kilometres back from the falls, the Nguom Ngao Cave requires quite a long trek to reach (up and over a hill, then across fields) and there's nothing unusual inside apart from a "silver tree" – a stalagmite which glitters under the lights.

ACCOMMODATION | AROUND CAO BANG

Quang Uyen Homestay Pho Hong Thai, Quang Uyen ☏ 012 784 5383. This home-stay at Quang Uyen town on the way to the falls offers simple but clean accommodation (mattress and mosquito net with shared hot showers) and provides tasty meals and treks of the area for an all-in price. $10

Lang Son

For most people, **LANG SON** is just a meal stop or overnight rest on the journey through the northeast or en route to China, only 18km away to the north. With a fast highway now linking Lang Son to Hanoi, reasons to linger are even fewer, though the surrounding countryside does have an endearing quality in the form of endless karst outcrops studding the plain. Having acquired the status of a city, Lang Son has a self-important feel, and its booming economy is evident in new construction sites all over town. The **Ky Cung River** splits Long Son in two, leaving the main bulk on the north side of the Ky Lua Bridge and the provincial offices to the south.

The area round **Mau Son Mountain**, just east of town, is good hiking country, and for the intrepid, Lang Son is the start of a little-travelled back road (Highway 4B) cutting across 100km of empty country to Tien Yen on the east coast, offering a route to (or from) Ha Long Bay.

Ky Lua Market

It's along Tran Dang Ninh that you'll find the town's main attraction, bustling **Ky Lua Night Market**. Just east of the highway, this is well worth investigating in the evening when Tay, Nung and Dao women come to trade.

Den Ky Cung

Daily 6am–6.30pm • Free

A kilometre south of the market, and overlooking the river just before the bridge on the north bank, **Den Ky Cung** is a small temple, founded over five hundred years ago. It's dedicated to Tuan Tranh, an army officer of the border guard who is reputed to have slain hundreds of Chinese in battle before he himself fell. There's nothing much to see inside apart from a big bell and a banyan tree, though it is often the scene of colourful ceremonies.

ACROSS THE BORDER TO CHINA

The majority of people taking this route into China travel **by train**, using one of the two weekly services direct from Hanoi to Beijing (see p.30). Note also that you can only board this train in Hanoi (and not at Dong Dang), though on the Chinese side it's possible to disembark up the line; pleasant Nanning is the first major city.

Alternatively, you can use the **road crossing** known as the **Huu Nghi border gate**, which lies 18km north of Lang Son and 4km from Dong Dang at the end of Highway 1 and is open between 7am and 6pm. On the Chinese side, infrequent minibuses head to Pingxiang (15km) for the nearest accommodation. Note that China is **one hour ahead** of Vietnam.

However you cross the border, you must already have a Chinese **visa**, available from the embassy in Hanoi (see p.384).

Dong Kinh Market and around

The three-storey edifice of **Dong Kinh Market** is a temple to Chinese kitsch, where illuminated Buddhas sit in front of posters of Huangguoshu Falls, China's largest waterfall. The broad boulevards south of the bridge are also worth exploring. The atmosphere is less frenetic than in the centre, and there are some interesting colonial buildings in the tree-lined backstreets.

If the weather is good and you have time to spare, take a walk along **Da Tuong** in the southwest of town, which passes remnants of an ancient wall and heads on into a nearby labyrinth of karst hills.

The nearby caves

Daily 7am–6pm · 20,000đ each

Nhi Thanh Cave, located off Tam Thanh, follows the Ngoc Tuyen river underground and is worth a look. **Tam Thanh Cave**, a little further along Tam Thanh, features fake stalactites around a temple altar and chambers linked by illuminated paths and steps. One path on the right leads out to a so-so view over town.

ARRIVAL AND INFORMATION

LANG SON

By bus The bus station in Lang Son is located on Ngo Quyen, which branches off Le Loi just west of the train station.
Destinations Cao Bang (5 daily; 4hr); Hanoi (every 30min; 3hr).

By train The train station in Lang Son is located just a block north of the bus station on Le Loi.
Destinations Hanoi (5 daily; 5hr 30min).
Information There is no official tourist office in Lang Son, but hotel staff at the *Van Xuan* are helpful.

ACCOMMODATION AND EATING

Muong Thanh 68 Ngo Quyen ☎ 025 386 6668, ⓦ langson.muongthanh.vn. Part of the Muong Thanh hotel empire, which now seems to have reached every corner of the country. The four-star facilities are very impressive (spa, pool, gym, etc) but the two-star service is a let-down. **$40**

New Century Phai Loan Lake opposite the Ky Lua Market ☎ 025 389 8000. Surrounded by a lake, this place has an English menu that is a welcome sight, especially if you've been living on noodle soup and sticky rice in the mountains. There's a huge range of standard Vietnamese

fare such as spring rolls, and clay pot dishes, but there are also unusual items such as rabbit and turtle. It's extremely popular with the locals and Chinese visitors and there's a bit of a beer-hall feel to the place. Mains 60,000–160,000đ. Daily 8am–9pm.

★**Van Xuan** 147 Tran Dang Ninh ☎ 025 371 0440, ⓔ lsvanxuanhotel@yahoo.com.vn. The city's best choice by far – just north of the market, overlooking Phai Loan Lake – has attentive staff and a modern feel; the back rooms have good lake views and all rooms have wi-fi. **$18**

DIRECTORY

Bank Next door to the post office, at 51 Le Loi, the Incombank changes US dollars and has an ATM.

Post office Le Loi, next to the Incombank.

STATUE AT THE TAY PHUONG PAGODA

Contexts

History

As a unified state within its present geographical boundaries, Vietnam has only existed since the early nineteenth century. The national history, however, stretches back thousands of years to a legendary kingdom in the Red River Delta. From there the Viet people pushed relentlessly down the peninsula of Indochina on the "March to the South", Nam Tien. The other compelling force, and a constant theme throughout its history, is Vietnam's ultimately successful resistance to all foreign aggressors.

The beginnings

The earliest evidence of human activity in Vietnam can be traced back to a Palaeolithic culture that existed some five hundred thousand years ago. These hunter-gatherers slowly developed agricultural techniques, but the most important step came about four thousand years ago when farmers began to cultivate irrigated rice in the Red River Delta. The communal effort required to build and maintain the system of dykes and canals spawned a stable, highly organized society, held to be the original Vietnamese nation. This embryonic kingdom, **Van Lang**, emerged sometime around 2000 BC and was ruled over by the semi-mythological Hung kings from their capital near today's Viet Tri, northwest of Hanoi. Archeological finds indicate that by the first millennium BC these people, the Lac Viet, had evolved into a sophisticated Bronze Age culture whose influence spread as far as Indonesia. Undoubtedly their greatest creations were the ritualistic **bronze drums**, discovered in the 1920s near Dong Son, and revered by the Vietnamese as the first hard evidence of an indigenous, independent culture.

Early kingdoms

In the mid-third century BC a Chinese warlord conquered Van Lang to create a new kingdom, **Au Lac**, with its capital at Co Loa, near present-day Hanoi. For the first time the lowland Lac Viet and the hill peoples were united. After only fifty years, around 207 BC, Au Lac was itself invaded by a Chinese potentate and became part of **Nam Viet** (Southern Viet), an independent kingdom occupying much of southern China. For a while the Lac Viet were able to maintain their local traditions and an indigenous aristocracy. Then, in 111 BC the Han emperors annexed the whole Red River Delta and so began a thousand years of Chinese domination.

Chinese rule

A millennium under Chinese rule had a profound effect on all aspects of Vietnamese life, notably the social and political spheres. With the introduction of **Confucianism** came the growth of a rigid, feudalistic hierarchy dominated by a mandarin class. This innately conservative elite ensured the long-term stability of an administrative system which continued to dominate Vietnamese society until well into the nineteenth century.

c. 3000 BC	c. 2000 BC	257 BC
First evidence of cultivation in Red River Delta	Birth of Van Lang, first Vietnamese kingdom	Beginning of Au Lac kingdom

FUNAN AND CHAMPA

While China has always exerted a strong influence over north Vietnam, in the south it was initially the Indian civilization that dominated, though as a cultural influence rather than as a ruling power. From the first century AD Indian traders sailing east towards China established **Hindu enclaves** along the southern coast of Indochina. The largest and most important of these city-states was **Funan**, based on a port city called Oc Eo, near present-day Rach Gia in the Mekong Delta (see box, p.142). By the early third century, Funan had developed into a powerful trading nation with links extending as far as Persia and even Rome. But technological developments in the fifth century enabled larger ships to sail round Indochina without calling at any port, and Funan gradually declined.

At around the same time, another Indianized kingdom was developing on the central Vietnamese coast. Little is known about the origins of **Champa**, but in 192 AD, Chinese annals reported that a man named Khu Lien (later to be titled King Sri Mara) had gathered a chain of coastal chiefdoms in the region around Quang Tri in defiance of the expansionism of the Han Chinese to the north, and established an independent state. For most of its existence, Champa was a Hindu kingdom, its economy based on agriculture, wet-rice cultivation, fishing and maritime trade, which it carried out with Indians, Chinese, Japanese and Arabs through **ports** at Hoi An and Quy Nhon. Champa was ruled over by divine kings who worshipped first Shiva and later embraced Buddhism – a fact made apparent in the deities manifest in the extravagant religious edifices that they sponsored, many of which still pepper the Vietnamese coast today (see box, p.222).

Concertinaed between the Khmer to the south and the clans of the Vietnamese (initially under Chinese rule) to the north, Champa's history was characterized by consistent **feuding with the neighbours**. Between the third and fifth centuries, relations with the **Chinese** followed a cyclical pattern of antagonism and tribute, culminating in the 446 AD sacking of Simhapura (near present-day Hoi An) when the Chinese made off with a 50-tonne, solid gold Buddha statue. By the end of the eleventh century Champa had lost its territory north of Hue; wars raged with the **Khmer** in the twelfth and thirteenth centuries, one fateful retaliatory Cham offensive culminating in the **destruction of Angkor**. With the installation on Champa's throne of warmongering Binasuor in 1361, three decades of Cham expansionism ensued; on his death in 1390, though, the Viets regained all lost ground, and soon secured the region around Indrapura (near today's Da Nang). In a decisive push south, the Viets, led by **Le Thanh Tong**, overran Vijaya in 1471. Champa shifted its capital south again, but by now it was becoming profoundly marginalized.

For a few centuries more, the Cham kings still claimed nominal rule of the area around Phan Rang and Phan Thiet, but in 1697 the last independent Cham king died, and what little remained of the kingdom became a Vietnamese vassal state. **Minh Mang** dissolved even this in the 1820s, finally absorbing Champa into Vietnam, and the last Cham king fled to Cambodia. Most of the estimated one hundred thousand **descendants** of the Cham kingdom reside around Phan Rang and Phan Thiet, though there are also tiny pockets in Tay Ninh and Chau Doc.

The Chinese also introduced technological advances, such as writing, silk production and large-scale hydraulic works, while Mahayana Buddhism first entered Vietnam from China during the second century AD.

At the same time, however, the Viet people were forging their national identity in the continuous struggle to break free from their powerful northern neighbour; on at least three occasions the Vietnamese ousted their masters. The first and most celebrated of these short-lived independent kingdoms was established by the **Trung sisters** (Hai Ba Trung) in

111 BC	**40 AD**	**166**
Chinese invade; would rule Vietnam, on and off, for nearly one thousand years	The Trung sisters (Hai Ba Trung) overthrow the Chinese	First envoys arrive from Roman Empire

40 AD. After the Chinese murdered Trung Trac's husband, she and her sister rallied the local lords and peasant farmers in the first popular insurrection against foreign domination. The Chinese fled, leaving Trung Trac ruler of the territory from Hue to southern China until the Han emperor dispatched twenty thousand troops and a fleet of two thousand junks to quell the rebellion three years later. The sisters threw themselves into a river to escape capture, and the Chinese quickly set about removing the local lords. Though subsequent uprisings also failed, the sisters had demonstrated the fallibility of the Chinese and earned their place in Vietnam's pantheon of heroes.

Over the following centuries Vietnam was drawn closer into the political and cultural realm of China. The seventh and eighth centuries were particularly bleak as the powerful Tang Dynasty tightened its grip on the province it called **Annam**, or the "Pacified South". As soon as the dynasty collapsed in the early tenth century a series of major rebellions broke out, culminating in the battle of the **Bach Dang River** in 938 AD (see box, p.328). Ngo Quyen declared himself ruler of **Nam Viet** and set up court at the historic citadel of Co Loa, heralding what was to be nearly ten centuries of Vietnamese independence.

Dynastic rule

The period immediately following **independence from Chinese rule** in 939 AD was marked by factional infighting. Ngo Quyen died after only five years on the throne and Nam Viet dissolved in anarchy while twelve warlords disputed the succession. In 968 one of the rivals, Dinh Bo Linh, finally united the country and secured its future by paying tribute to the Chinese emperor, a system that continued until the nineteenth century. Dinh Bo Linh took the additional precaution of moving his capital south to the well-defended valley of Hoa Lu, where it remained during the two short-lived Dinh and Early Le dynasties.

These early monarchs laid the framework for a centralized state. They reformed the administration and the army, and instigated a programme of road building. But it was the following **Ly Dynasty**, founded by **Ly Thai To** in 1009, that consolidated the independence of **Dai Viet** (Great Viet) and guaranteed the nation's stability for the next four hundred years. One of the first actions of the new dynasty was to move the capital back into the northern rice-lands, founding the city of Thang Long, the precursor of modern Hanoi.

Ly Thai To's successor, **Ly Thai Tong** (1028–54), carried out a major reorganization of the national army, turning it into a professional fighting force, able to secure the northern borders and expand southwards. So confident was this new power that in 1076 the army of Dai Viet, under the revered General Ly Thuong Kiet, launched a pre-emptive strike against the Sung Chinese and then held off their counter-attack.

Mongol and Ming invasions

Having ousted the declining Ly clan in 1225, the following **Tran Dynasty** won spectacular military victories against the **Mongol invasions** of 1257, 1284 and 1288. On the first two occasions, Mongol forces briefly occupied the capital before having to withdraw, while the last battle is remembered for a rerun of Ngo Quyen's ploy in the Bach Dang River. This time it was General Tran Hung Dao, a prince in the royal family, who led Viet forces against the far superior armies of Kublai Khan. While the Mongol navy foundered in the Bach Dang River, its army was also being

544–602	907	938
Early Ly Dynasty; brief respite from Chinese rule	Chinese Tang Dynasty collapses	State of "Nam Viet" declares independence

trounced and the remnants driven back into China; soon after, the khan died, and with him the Mongol threat.

In the confusion that marked the end of the Tran Dynasty, an ambitious court minister, Ho Qui Ly, usurped the throne in 1400. Though the **Ho Dynasty** lasted only seven years, its two progressive monarchs launched a number of important reforms. They tackled the problem of land shortages by restricting the size of holdings and then rented out the excess to landless peasants; the tax system was revised and paper money replaced coinage; ports were opened to foreign trade; and public health care introduced. Even the education system was broadened to include practical subjects along with the classic Confucian texts. Just as the Ho were getting into their stride, so the new **Ming Dynasty** in China were beginning to look south across the border. Under the pretext of restoring the Tran, Ming armies invaded in 1407 and imposed **direct Chinese rule** of Vietnam a few years later. The Chinese tried to undermine Viet culture by outlawing local customs and destroying Vietnamese literature, works of art and historical texts.

Le Loi

This time, however, the Chinese occupation faced a much tougher problem as the Viet people were now a relatively cohesive force. Vietnamese resistance gravitated towards the mountains of Thanh Hoa, south of Hanoi, where a local landlord and mandarin, **Le Loi**, was preparing for a war of national liberation. For ten years Le Loi's well-disciplined guerrilla force harassed the enemy until he was finally able to defeat the Chinese army in open battle in 1427.

Le Loi, as King Le Thai To, founded the third of the great ruling families, the **Later Le Dynasty**, and set in train the reconstruction of Dai Viet, though he died after only five years on the throne. Initially the Le Dynasty reaped the economic rewards of its expanding empire, but eventually their new provinces spawned wealthy semi-autonomous rulers strong enough to challenge the throne. As the Le declined in the sixteenth century, two such powerful clans, the **Nguyen and Trinh**, at first supported the dynasty against rival contenders. Towards the end of the century, however, they became the effective rulers of Vietnam, splitting the country in two. The Trinh lords held sway in Hanoi and the north, while the Nguyen set up court at Hue; the Le, meanwhile, remained monarchs in name only.

The first Westerners

The first Western visitors to the Vietnamese peninsula were probably **traders** from ancient Rome who sailed into the ports of Champa in the second century AD. Marco Polo sailed up the coast in the thirteenth century on his way to China, but more significant was the arrival of a Portuguese merchant, Antonio Da Faria, at the port of Fai Fo (Hoi An) in 1535. The Portuguese established their own trading post at Fai Fo, then one of Southeast Asia's greatest ports, crammed with vessels from China and Japan, and were soon followed by other European maritime powers.

With the traders came **missionaries**, who found a ready audience, especially among peasant farmers and others near the bottom of the established Confucian hierarchy. It didn't take long before the ruling elite felt threatened by subversive Christian ideas; missionary work was banned after the 1630s and many priests were expelled, or even executed. But enforcement was erratic, and by the end of the seventeenth century the Catholic Church claimed several hundred thousand converts. At this time Vietnam was

968	1009	1076
Nam Viet unified by Dinh Dynasty	Ly Thai To inaugurates Ly Dynasty; Vietnam now "Dai Viet"	Major battle with Chinese Sung Dynasty

THE VIETNAMESE DYNASTIES

Ngo	939–65	Ho	1400–07
Dinh	968–80	Ming (Chinese)	1407–28
Early Ly	980–1009	Later Le	1428–1788
Ly	1009–1225	Tay Son	1788–1802
Tran	1225–1400	Nguyen	1802–1945

breaking up into regional factions and the Europeans were quick to exploit growing tensions between the Nguyen and Trinh lords, providing weapons in exchange for trading concessions. However, when the civil war ended in 1674 the merchants lost their advantage. Gradually the English, Dutch and French closed down their trading posts until only the Portuguese remained in Fai Fo.

Towards the end of the eighteenth century, the remaining Catholic missions provided an opening for French merchants wishing to challenge Britain's presence in the Far East. When a large-scale rebellion broke out in Vietnam in the early 1770s, these entrepreneurs saw their chance to establish a firmer footing on the Indochinese peninsula.

The Tay Son rebellion

As the eighteenth century progressed, insurrections flared up throughout the countryside. Most were easily stamped out, but in 1771 three brothers raised their standard in Tay Son village, west of Quy Nhon, and ended up ruling the whole country. The **Tay Son rebellion** gained broad support among dispossessed peasants, ethnic minorities, small merchants and townspeople attracted by the brothers' message of equal rights, justice and liberty. As rebellion spread through the south, the Tay Son army rallied even more converts when they seized land from the wealthy and redistributed it to the poor. By the middle of 1786 the rebels had overthrown both the Trinh and Nguyen lords, again leaving the Le Dynasty intact. When the Le monarch called on the Chinese in 1788 to help remove the Tay Son usurpers, the Chinese happily obliged by occupying Hanoi. At this the middle brother (Nguyen Hue) declared himself **Emperor Quang Trung** and quick-marched his army 600km from Hue to defeat the Chinese at Dong Da, on the outskirts of Hanoi. With Hue as his capital, Quang Trung set about implementing his promised reforms, but when he died prematurely in 1792, aged 39, his 10-year-old son was unable to hold onto power.

One of the few Nguyen lords to have survived the Tay Son rebellion in the south was Prince Nguyen Anh. The prince made several unsuccessful attempts to regain the throne in the mid-1780s. After one such failure he fled to Phu Quoc Island where he met a French bishop, Pigneau de Béhaine. With an eye on future religious and commercial concessions, the bishop offered to make approaches to the French on behalf of the Nguyen. A treaty was eventually signed in 1787, promising military aid in exchange for territorial and trading concessions, though France failed to deliver the assistance due to a financial crisis preceding the French Revolution. The bishop went ahead anyway, raising a motley force of four thousand armed mercenaries and a handful of ships. The expedition was launched in 1789 and Nguyen Anh entered Hanoi in 1802 to claim the throne as **Emperor Gia Long**. Bishop de Béhaine didn't live to see the victory or to enforce the treaty: he died in 1799 and received a stately funeral.

1225	1257	1288
Tran dynasty pushes the Ly out of power; Vietnam now "Dai Ngu"	First Mongol invasion	Third Mongol invasion

ALEXANDRE DE RHODES

Portuguese Dominicans had been the first European missionaries to arrive in Vietnam in the early sixteenth century, but it wasn't until 1615, when Jesuits set up a small mission in Fai Fo, that the Catholic Church gained an established presence. The mission's initial success in the Nguyen territory encouraged the Jesuits to look north. The man they chose for the job was a 28-year-old Frenchman, **Alexandre de Rhodes**, a gifted linguist who, only six months after arriving in Fai Fo, in 1627, was preaching in Vietnamese. His talents soon won over the Trinh lords in Hanoi, where de Rhodes gave six sermons a day and converted nearly seven thousand Vietnamese in just two years. During this time he was also working on a simple **romanized script** for the Vietnamese language, which otherwise used a formidable system based on Chinese characters. De Rhodes merely wanted to make evangelizing easier, but his phonetic system eventually came to be adopted as Vietnam's national language, *quoc ngu*.

The Nguyen Dynasty

For the first time **Vietnam**, as the country was now called, fell under a single authority from the northern border all the way down to the point of Ca Mau. In the hope of promoting unity, Gia Long established his capital in the centre, at Hue, where he built a magnificent citadel in imitation of the Chinese emperor's Forbidden City. The choice of architecture was appropriate: Gia Long and the **Nguyen Dynasty** he founded were resolutely Confucian. The new emperor immediately abolished the Tay Son reforms, reimposing the old feudal order; land confiscated from the rebels was redistributed to loyal mandarins, the bureaucracy was reinstated and the majority of peasants found themselves worse off than before. Gradually the country was closed to the outside world and to modernizing influences that might have helped it withstand the onslaught of French military intervention in the mid-nineteenth century. On the other hand, Gia Long and his successors did much to improve the infrastructure of Vietnam, developing a road network, extending the irrigation systems and rationalizing the provincial administration. Under the Nguyen, the arts, particularly literature and court music, also flourished.

By refusing to grant any trading concessions, Gia Long disappointed the French adventurers who had helped him to the throne. He did, however, permit a certain amount of religious freedom, though his successors were far more suspicious of the missionaries' intentions. After 1825 several edicts were issued forbidding missionary work, accompanied by sporadic, occasionally brutal, persecutions of Christians, both Vietnamese converts and foreign priests. Ultimately, this provided the French with the excuse they needed to annex the country.

French conquest and rule

French governments grew increasingly imperialistic as the nineteenth century wore on. In the Far East, as Britain threatened to dominate trade with China, France began to see Vietnam as a potential route into the resource-rich provinces of Yunnan and southern China. Not that France had any formal policy to colonize Indochina; rather it came about in a piecemeal fashion, driven as often as not by private adventurers or the unilateral actions of French officials. In 1847, two French naval vessels began the process when they bombarded Da Nang on the pretext of rescuing a French priest. Reports of Catholic persecutions were deliberately exaggerated until Napoleon III

1400–07	1407–27	1427
Short-lived Ho Dynasty	Short period under rule of Chinese Ming Dynasty	Le Loi defeats Chinese, inaugurates Later Le Dynasty

was finally persuaded to launch an armada of fourteen ships and 2500 men in 1858. After capturing Da Nang in September, the force moved south to take Saigon, against considerable opposition, and the whole Mekong Delta over the next three years. Faced with serious unrest in the north, Emperor Tu Duc signed a treaty in 1862 granting France the three eastern provinces of the delta plus trading rights in selected ports, and allowing missionaries the freedom to proselytize. Five years later, French forces annexed the remaining southern provinces to create the colony of **Cochinchina**.

France became embroiled in domestic troubles and the French government was divided on whether to continue the enterprise, but their administrators in Cochinchina had their eyes on the north. The first attempt to take Hanoi and open up the Red River into China failed in 1873; a larger force was dispatched in 1882 and within a few months, France was in control of Hanoi and the lower reaches of the Red River Delta. Spurred on by this success, the French parliament financed the first contingents of the **French Expeditionary Force** just as the Nguyen were floundering in a succession crisis following the death of Tu Duc. In August 1883, when the French fleet sailed into the mouth of the Perfume River, near Hue, the new emperor was compelled to meet their demands. **Annam** (central Vietnam) and **Tonkin** (the north) became protectorates of France, to be combined with Cochinchina, Cambodia and, later, Laos to form the **Union of Indochina** after 1887.

The anti-colonial struggle and Ho Chi Minh

For a population brought up on legends of heroic victories over superior forces, the ease with which France had occupied Vietnam was a deep psychological blow. The earliest resistance movements focused on the restoration of the monarchy, such as the "Save the King" (*Can Vuong*) movement of the 1890s, but any emperor showing signs of patriotism was swiftly removed by the French administration. Up until the mid-1920s, Vietnam's fragmented anti-colonial movements were easily controlled by the *Sûreté*, the formidable French secret police. On the whole, the nationalists' aims were political rather than social or economic, and most failed to appeal to the majority of Vietnamese. Gradually, however, the nationalists saw that a more radical approach was called for, and an influential leader named **Phan Boi Chau** finally called for the violent overthrow of the colonial regime.

Meanwhile, over the border in southern China, the **Revolutionary Youth League** was founded in 1925. Vietnam's first Marxist–Leninist organization, its founding father was a certain **Ho Chi Minh**. Born in 1890, the son of a patriotic minor official, Ho was already in trouble with the French authorities in his teens. He left Vietnam in 1911, spending several years wandering the world; he worked in the dockyards of Brooklyn and as pastry chef in London's *Carlton Hotel*, then turned up in Paris after World War I under one of his many pseudonyms, Nguyen Ai Quoc ("Nguyen the Patriot"). In France, Ho became increasingly active among other exiled dissidents exploring ways to bring an end to colonial rule. At this time one of the few political groups actively supporting anti-colonial movements were the Communists; in 1920 Ho became a founding member of the French Communist Party and by 1923 he was in Moscow, training as a Communist agent. A year later he went to southern China, where he set up Vietnam's first Marxist–Leninist organization, the Revolutionary Youth League, which attracted a band of impassioned young Vietnamese.

1535   **1627**

Portuguese create trading post at   French missionary Alexandre de Rhodes arrives in Vietnam – his
Fai Fo (now Hoi An)   romanized version of Vietnamese script remains in use today

LIFE UNDER FRENCH RULE

Despite much talk of the "civilizing mission" of Imperial rule, the French were more interested in the economic potential of their new possession. Governor-general Paul Doumer launched a massive programme of **infrastructural development**, constructing railways, bridges and roads and draining vast areas of the Mekong Delta swamp, all funded by raising punitive taxes, with state monopolies on opium, alcohol and salt accounting for seventy percent of government revenues. During the Great Depression of the 1930s markets collapsed; peasants were forced off the land to work as indentured labour in the new rubber, tea and coffee estates or in the mines, often under brutal conditions. Heavy taxes exacerbated **rural poverty** and any commercial or industrial enterprises were kept firmly in French hands, or were controlled by the small minority of Vietnamese and Chinese who actually benefited under the new regime.

On the positive side, mass vaccination and health programmes did bring the frequent epidemics of cholera, smallpox and plague under control. **Education** was a thornier issue: overall, education levels deteriorated during French rule, particularly among unskilled labourers, but a small elite from the emerging urban middle class received a broader, French-based education and a few went to universities in Europe. Not that it got them very far: Vietnamese were barred from all but the most menial jobs in the colonial administration. Ironically, it was this frustrated and alienated group, imbued with the ideas of Western liberals and Chinese reformers, who began to challenge French rule.

Although many other subsequently famous revolutionaries worked with Ho, it was largely his fierce dedication, single-mindedness and tremendous charisma that held the nationalist movement together and finally propelled the country to independence. The first real test of Ho's leadership came in 1929 when, in his absence, the League split into three separate Communist parties. In Hong Kong a year later, Ho persuaded the rival groups to unite into one **Indochinese Communist Party** whose main goal was an independent Vietnam governed by workers, peasants and soldiers. In preparation for the revolution, cadres were sent into rural areas and among urban workers to set up party cells. The timing couldn't have been better: unemployment and poverty were on the increase as the Great Depression took hold, while France became less willing to commit resources to its colonies. For his efforts, the French authorities placed a death sentence on Ho's head; he was arrested in Hong Kong but escaped with the help of prison hospital staff, who persuaded everyone that he had died of tuberculosis.

Throughout the 1930s Vietnam was plagued with strikes and labour unrest, of which the most important was the **Nghe Tinh uprising** in the summer of 1930. French planes bombed a crowd of twenty thousand demonstrators marching on Vinh; within days, villagers had seized control of much of the surrounding countryside, some setting up revolutionary councils to evict wealthy landlords and redistribute land to the peasants. The uprising demonstrated the power of socialist organization, but proved disastrous in the short term – thousands of peasants were killed or imprisoned, the leaders were executed and the Communist Party structure was badly mauled. Most of the ringleaders ended up in the notorious penal colony of Poulo Condore (see p.205), which came to be known as the "University of the Revolution". It's estimated that the French held some ten thousand activists in prison by the late 1930s.

1771

Beginning of Tay Son rebellion, in a village near Quy Nhon

1802

Proclamation of Nguyen Dynasty, with Hue chosen as the national capital

World War II

The German occupation of France in 1940 suddenly changed the whole political landscape. Not only did it demonstrate to the Vietnamese the vulnerability of their colonial masters, but it also overturned the established order in Vietnam and ultimately provided Ho Chi Minh with the opportunity he had been waiting for. The immediate repercussion was the **Japanese occupation** of Indochina after Vichy France signed a treaty allowing Japan to station troops in the colony, while leaving the French administration in place. By mid-1941 the region's coalmines, rice fields and military installations were all under Japanese control. Some Vietnamese nationalist groups welcomed this turn of events as the Japanese made encouraging noises about autonomy and "Asia for the Asians". Others, mostly Communist groups, declared their opposition to all foreign intervention and continued to operate from secret bases in the mountainous region that flanks the border between China and Vietnam.

By this time, Ho Chi Minh had reappeared in southern China, from where he walked over the border into Vietnam, wearing a Chinese-style tunic and rubber-tyre sandals, and carrying his rattan trunk and trusty Hermes typewriter. The date was February 1941; Ho had been in exile for thirty years. In **Pac Bo Cave**, near Cao Bang, Ho met with other resistance leaders, including Vo Nguyen Giap and Pham Van Dong, to start the next phase in the fight for national liberation; the League for the Independence of Vietnam, better known as the **Viet Minh**, was founded in May 1941.

Over the next few years Viet Minh recruits received military training in southern China; the first regular armed units formed the nucleus of the **Vietnamese Liberation Army** in 1945. Gradually the Viet Minh established liberated zones in the northern mountains to provide bases for future guerrilla operations. With Japanese defeat looking ever more likely, Ho Chi Minh set off once again into China to seek military and financial support from the Chinese and from the Allied forces operating out of Kunming. Ho also made contact with the American Office of Strategic Services (forerunner of the CIA), which promised him limited arms, much to the anger of the Free French who were already planning their return to Indochina. In return for **American aid** the Viet Minh provided information about Japanese forces and rescued Allied pilots shot down over Vietnam. Later, in 1945, an American team arrived in Ho's Cao Bang base where they found him suffering from malaria, dysentery and dengue fever; it's said they saved his life.

Meanwhile, suspecting a belated French counter-attack, Japanese forces seized full control of the country in March 1945. They declared a nominally independent state under the leadership of Bao Dai, the last Nguyen emperor, and imprisoned most of the French army. The Viet Minh quickly moved onto the offensive, helped to some extent by a massive famine that ravaged northern Vietnam that summer. Then, in early August, US forces dropped the first atom bomb on Hiroshima, precipitating the **Japanese surrender** on August 14.

Independence and division

The Japanese surrender left a power vacuum which Ho Chi Minh was quick to exploit. On August 15, Ho called for a national uprising, which later came to be known as the **August Revolution**. Within four days Hanoi was seething with pro-Viet Minh

1858	1867	1887
Napoleon dispatches an armada to Vietnam	Outright French annexation of Cochinchina	Cochinchina becomes part of wider French Union of Indochina

demonstrations, and in two weeks most of Vietnam came under their control. Emperor Bao Dai handed over his Imperial sword to Ho's provisional government at the end of August and on September 2, 1945, Ho Chi Minh proclaimed the establishment of the **Democratic Republic of Vietnam**, cheered by a massive crowd in Hanoi's Ba Dinh Square. For the first time in eighty years Vietnam was an independent country. Famously, Ho's Declaration of Independence quoted from the American Declaration: "All men are created equal. They are endowed by their Creator with certain inalienable rights, among these are life, liberty and the pursuit of happiness." But this, and subsequent appeals for American help against the looming threat of recolonization, fell on deaf ears as America became increasingly concerned at Communist expansion.

The **Potsdam Agreement**, which marked the end of World War II, failed to recognize the new Republic of Vietnam. Instead, Japanese troops south of the Sixteenth Parallel were to surrender to British authority, while those in the north would defer to the Chinese Kuomintang. Nevertheless, by the time these forces arrived, the Viet Minh were already in control, having relieved the Japanese of most of their weapons. In the **south**, rival nationalist groups were battling it out in Saigon, where French troops had also joined in the fray. The situation was so chaotic that the British commander proclaimed martial law and, amazingly, even deployed Japanese soldiers to help restore calm. Against orders, he also rearmed the six thousand liberated French troops and Saigon was soon back in French hands. A few days later, General Leclerc arrived with the first units of the French Expeditionary Force, charged with reimposing colonial rule in Indochina.

THE NORTH–SOUTH DIVIDE

Although Vietnam was reunified in 1975, there still exists a palpable north–south divide, one that many tourists pick up on as they head across the DMZ. Of course, many of the differences stem from the **ideological division** that followed World War II, and the protracted, bloody war between the two sides; however, there have long been other factors at work.

One of these is the relative **fertility of the soil** – parts of the south get three rice harvests per year, while in the north it's usually one. This leads to a difference in character between north and south – northerners are typically more frugal and southerners more laidback, partly because the latter have historically had less work to do for the same reward.

There are also notable differences in **tradition**. Ho Chi Minh City flaunts its Westernization, while Hanoians are just as proud of their city's colonial- and dynastic-era structures.

Then there are **dialectical** differences – ask a traditionally clad Hanoian girl what she's wearing, and she'll say it's "*ao zai*". Ask a woman from Ho Chi Minh City the same thing, and it would be an "*ao yai*". Trained ears will also hear that there's another dialect at work in the centre of Vietnam.

However, for visitors, the most enjoyable aspect of the north–south divide is likely to be the **food**. The quintessential northern food is *pho bo* – this beef noodle soup is found throughout Vietnam, but originated in Hanoi, where it's still at its best. Other northern dishes include hotpots, rice gruels and sweet and sour soups. Southern flavours include curries and spicy dipping sauces, often married with a touch of sugar and coconut milk to balance the heat. However, most renowned nationwide is central cuisine – both Hoi An and Hue boast dishes of astonishing variety.

1890	1925	1940
Birth of Ho Chi Minh	Ho founds anti-colonial Revolutionary Youth League in southern China	Japanese occupy Indochina during World War II

Things were going more smoothly in the north, though the two hundred thousand Chinese soldiers stationed there acted increasingly like an army of occupation. The Viet Minh could muster a mere five thousand ill-equipped troops in reply; forced to choose between the two in order to survive, Ho Chi Minh finally rated French rule the lesser of the two evils, reputedly commenting, "I prefer to smell French shit for five years, rather than Chinese shit for the rest of my life." In March 1946, Ho's government signed a treaty allowing a limited French force to replace Kuomintang soldiers in the north. In return, France recognized the Democratic Republic as a "free state" within the proposed French Union; the terms were left deliberately vague. The treaty also provided for a referendum to determine whether Cochinchina would join the new state or remain separate.

While further negotiations dragged on during the summer of 1946, both sides were busily rearming as it became apparent that the French were not going to abide by the treaty. By late April the Expeditionary Force had already exceeded agreed levels, and there was no sign of the promised referendum; in September 1946 the talks effectively broke down. Skirmishes between Vietnamese and French troops in the northern delta boiled over in a dispute over customs control in Haiphong; to quell the rioting, the French navy bombed the town on November 23, killing thousands of civilians. This was followed by the announcement that French troops would assume responsibility for law and order in the north. By way of reply, Viet Minh units attacked French installations in Hanoi on December 19, and then, while resistance forces held the capital for a few days, Ho Chi Minh and the regular army slipped away into the northern mountains.

The French War

For the first years of the **war against the French** (also known as the First Indochina War, or Franco–Viet Minh War) the Viet Minh kept largely to their mountain bases in northern and central Vietnam. While the Viet Minh were building up and training an army, the Expeditionary Force was consolidating its control over the Red River Delta and establishing a string of highly vulnerable outposts around guerrilla-held territory. In October 1947 the French attempted an ambitious all-out attack against enemy headquarters, but it soon became obvious that this was an unconventional "war without fronts" where Viet Minh troops could simply melt away into the jungle when threatened. In addition, the French suffered from hit-and-run attacks deep within the delta, unprotected by a local population who either actively supported or at least tolerated the Viet Minh. Although the French persuaded Bao Dai to return as head of the Associated State of Vietnam in March 1949, most Vietnamese regarded him as a mere puppet and his government won little support.

The war entered a new phase after the Communist victory in China in 1949. With military aid flowing across the border, Bao Dai's shaky government was seen as the last bastion of the free world; America was drawn in and funded the French military to the tune of at least US$3 billion by 1954. The Viet Minh, under the command of General Giap, recorded their first major victory, forcing the French to abandon their outposts along the Chinese border and gaining unhindered access to sanctuary in China. Early in 1951, equipped with Chinese weapons and confident of success, the Viet Minh launched an assault on Hanoi itself, but in this first pitched battle of the war, suffered a massive defeat, losing over six thousand troops in a battle that saw napalm deployed for

1941	1945
Ho re-enters Vietnam; founds the Viet Minh	Ho proclaims establishment of Democratic Republic of Vietnam

the first time in Vietnam. But Giap (known as "the snow-covered volcano" for his ice-cold exterior concealing a fiery temper) had learnt his lesson, and for the next two years the French sought in vain to repeat their success.

By now France was tiring of the war and in 1953 made contact with Ho Chi Minh to find some way of resolving the conflict. The Americans were growing increasingly impatient with French progress, and at one stage threatened to deploy tactical nuclear weapons against the Viet Minh; the Russians and Chinese were also applying pressure to end the fighting. Eventually, the two sides agreed to discussions at the Geneva Conference, due to take place in May the next year to discuss Korean peace. Meanwhile in Vietnam, a crucial battle was unfolding in an isolated valley on the Lao border, near the town of **Dien Bien Phu**. Early in 1954 French battalions established a massive camp here, deliberately trying to tempt the enemy into the open. Instead the Viet Minh surrounded the valley, cut off reinforcements and slowly closed in. After 59 days of bitter fighting the French were forced to surrender on May 7, 1954, the eve of the Geneva Conference. The eight years of war proved costly to both sides: total losses on the French side stood at 93,000, while an estimated two hundred thousand Viet Minh soldiers had been killed.

The Geneva Conference

On May 8, a day after the French capitulation at Dien Bien Phu, the nine delegations attending the **Geneva Conference** trained their focus upon Indochina. Armed with the knowledge that they now controlled around 65 percent of the country, the Viet Minh delegation arrived in buoyant mood. But the lasting peace they sought wasn't forthcoming: hampered by distrust, the conference succeeded only in reaching a stopgap solution, a necessarily ambiguous compromise which, however, allowed the French to withdraw with some honour and recognized Vietnamese sovereignty at least in part. Keen to have a weak and fractured nation on their southern border, the Chinese delegation spurred the Viet Minh into agreeing to a division of the country; reliant on Chinese arms, the Viet Minh were forced to comply.

Under the terms of July 1954's **Geneva Accords** Vietnam was divided at the Seventeenth Parallel, along the Ben Hai River, pending nationwide free elections to be held by July 1956; a demilitarized buffer zone was established on either side of this military front. France and the Viet Minh, who were still fighting in the central highlands even as delegates machinated, agreed to an immediate ceasefire, and consented to a withdrawal of all troops to their respective territories – Communists to the north, non-Communists plus supporters of the French to the south. China, the USSR, Britain, France and the Viet Minh agreed on the accords, but crucially neither the US nor Bao Dai's government endorsed them, fearing that they heralded a reunited, Communist-ruled Vietnam.

A country divided

In the long term, the Geneva Accords served to cause a deep polarization within the country and to widen the conflict into an ideological battle between the superpowers, fought out on Vietnamese soil. The immediate consequence, however, was a massive exodus from the north during the stipulated three-hundred-day period of "**free movement**". Almost a million (mostly Catholic) refugees headed south, their flight

1946	1949	1951
Beginning of the French War	Bao Dai becomes head of Associated State of Vietnam	Viet Minh launches attack on Hanoi

aided by the US Navy, and to some extent engineered by the CIA, whose distribution of scaremongering, anti-Communist leaflets was designed to create a base of support for the puppet government it was concocting in Saigon. Approaching a hundred thousand **anti-French guerrillas** and sympathizers moved in the opposite direction to regroup, though, as a precautionary measure, between five and ten thousand Viet Minh cadres remained in the south, awaiting orders from Hanoi. These dormant operatives, known to the CIA as "**stay-behinds**" and to the Communists as "winter cadres", were joined by spies who infiltrated the Catholic move south. In line with the terms of the ceasefire, Ho Chi Minh's army marched into Hanoi on October 9, 1954, even as the last French forces were still trooping out.

The Geneva Accords were still being thrashed out as Emperor Bao Dai named himself president and **Ngo Dinh Diem** ("Zee-em") prime minister of South Vietnam, on July 7. A Catholic, and vehemently anti-Communist, Diem knew that Ho Chi Minh would win the lion's share of votes in the proposed elections, and therefore steadfastly refused to countenance them. His mandate "strengthened" by an October 1955 **referendum** (the prime minister's garnering of 98.2 percent of votes cast was more indicative of the blatancy of his vote-rigging than of any popular support), Diem promptly ousted Bao Dai from the chain of command, and declared himself president of the Republic of Vietnam.

Diem's heavy-handed approach to Viet Minh dissidents still in the South was hopelessly misguided: although the subsequent **witch-hunt** decimated Viet Minh numbers, the brutal and indiscriminate nature of the operation caused widespread discontent – all dissenters were targeted, Viet Minh, Communist or otherwise. As the supposed "free world democracy" of the South mutated into a police state, over fifty thousand citizens died in Diem's pogrom.

Back in Hanoi...

In Hanoi, meanwhile, Ho Chi Minh's government was finding it had problems of its own as, aided by droves of Chinese advisers, it set about constructing a socialist society. Years of warring with France had profoundly damaged the country's infrastructure, and now it found itself deprived of the South's plentiful rice stocks. Worse still, the **land reforms** of the mid-1950s, vaunted as a Robin Hood-style redistribution of land, saw thousands of innocents "tried" as landlords by ad hoc **People's Agricultural Reform Tribunals**, tortured and then executed or set to work in labour camps. "Reactionaries" were also denounced and punished, often for such imperialist "crimes" as possessing works of the great French poets and novelists. The **Rectification of Errors Campaign** of 1956 at least released many victims of the reforms from imprisonment, but as Ho Chi Minh himself said, "one cannot wake the dead".

With Hanoi so preoccupied with getting its own house in order, Viet Minh guerrillas south of the Seventeenth Parallel were for several years left to fend for themselves. For the most part, they sat tight in the face of Diem's reprisals, although guerrilla strikes became increasingly common towards the end of the 1950s, often taking the form of assassinations of government officials. Only in 1959 did the erosion of their ranks prompt Hanoi to shift up a gear and endorse a more overtly military stance. Conscription was introduced in April 1960, cadres and hardware began to creep down the **Ho Chi Minh Trail** (see p.388), and at the end of the year Hanoi orchestrated the creation of the **National Liberation Front** (NLF), which drew together all opposition

1953	**1954**
French approach Ho Chi Minh for ceasefire	End of French War – almost three hundred thousand lives had been lost, the majority Vietnamese

forces in the South. Diem dubbed its guerrilla fighters **Viet Cong**, or VC (Vietnamese Communists) – a name which stuck, though in reality the NLF represented a united front of Catholic, Buddhist, Communist and non-Communist nationalists.

The American War

American dollars had been supporting the French war effort in Indochina since 1950. In early 1955 the White House began to bankroll Diem's government and the training of his army, the **ARVN** (Army of the Republic of Vietnam). Behind these policies lay the fear of the chain reaction that could follow in Southeast Asia, were South Vietnam to be overrun by Communism – the so-called **Domino Effect** – and, more cynically, what this would mean for US access to raw materials, trade routes and markets. Though President John F. Kennedy baulked at the prospect of large-scale American intervention, by the summer of 1962 there were twelve thousand American advisers in South Vietnam.

Despite all these injections of money, Diem's incompetent and unpopular government was losing ground to the Viet Cong in the battle for the hearts and minds of the population. Particularly damaging to the government was its **Strategic Hamlets Programme**. Formulated in 1962 and based on British methods used during the Malayan Emergency, the programme forcibly relocated entire villages into fortified stockades, with the aim of keeping the Viet Cong at bay. Ill-conceived, insensitive and open to exploitation by corrupt officials, the programme had the opposite effect, driving many disgruntled villagers into the arms of the resistance. In fact, the majority of strategic hamlets were empty within two years, as villagers drifted back to their ancestral lands.

Militarily, things were little better. If America needed proof that Diem's government was struggling to subdue the guerrillas, it came in January 1963, at the **Battle of Ap Bac**, where incompetent ARVN troops suffered heavy losses against a greatly outnumbered Viet Cong force. Four months later, Buddhists celebrating Buddha's birthday were fired upon by ARVN soldiers in Hue, sparking off riots and demonstrations against religious repression, and provoking **Thich Quang Duc**'s infamous self-immolation in Saigon (see box, p.82). Fearing that the Communists would gain further by Diem's unpopularity, America tacitly sanctioned his ousting in a **coup** on November 1; Diem escaped with his brother to Cho Lon, only to be shot the following day.

The capital staggered from coup to coup, but corruption, nepotism and dependence upon American support remained constant. In the countryside, meanwhile, the Viet Cong were forging a solid base of popular support. Observing Southern instability, Hanoi in early 1964 proceeded to send battalions of **NVA** (North Vietnamese Army) infantrymen down the Ho Chi Minh Trail, with ten thousand Northern troops hitting the trail in the first year. For America, unwilling to see the Communists granted a say in the running of the South, yet unable to envisage Saigon's generals fending them off, the only option seemed to be to "**Americanize**" the conflict.

In August 1964, a chance came to do just that, when the American destroyer the USS *Maddox* allegedly suffered an unprovoked attack from North Vietnamese craft; two days afterwards, the *Maddox* and another ship, the *C Turner Joy*, reported a second attack. Years later it emerged that the *Maddox* had been taking part in a covert mission to monitor coastal installations, and that the second incident almost certainly never happened. Nevertheless, reprisals followed in the form of 64 **bombing** sorties against

1954	1956
Geneva Accords divide Vietnam at the Seventeenth Parallel	Rectification of Errors Campaign begins

THE HUMAN COST OF THE WAR IN VIETNAM

The **toll** of the American War in human terms is staggering. Of the 3.3 million Americans who served in Vietnam between 1965 and 1973, some 58,000 died and more than 150,000 received wounds that required hospital treatment. The ARVN lost 250,000 troops, while perhaps two million **civilians** were killed in the South. Hanoi declared that over two million North Vietnamese civilians and one million troops died during the war. Many more on both sides are still listed as "missing in action" (MIA). Since 1975, an estimated 35,000 people – a third of them children – have been killed by leftover ordnance, while **contamination** from Agent Orange and other chemicals continues to cause health problems (see p.474). In the US, some half a million veterans suffer from post-traumatic stress disorder, while **veteran suicides** have now exceeded the total number of US fatalities during the conflict.

Northern coastal bases. And back in Washington, senators voted through the **Tonkin Gulf Resolution**, empowering Johnson to deploy regular American troops in Vietnam, "to prevent further aggression".

Operation Rolling Thunder

An NVA attack upon the highland town of Pleiku in February 1965 curtailed several months of US procrastination about how best to prosecute the war in Vietnam, and elicited **Operation Flaming Dart**, a concerted bombing raid on NVA camps above the Seventeenth Parallel. **Operation Rolling Thunder**, a sustained carpet-bombing campaign, kicked in a month later; by the time of its suspension three and a half years later its 350,000 sorties had seen twice the tonnage of bombs dropped (around eight hundred daily) as had fallen on all World War II's theatres of war. Despite such impressive statistics, Rolling Thunder failed either to break the North's sources and lines of supply, or to coerce Hanoi into a suspension of activities in the South. Bombing served only to strengthen the resilience of the North, whose population was mobilized to rebuild bridges, roads and railways as quickly as they were damaged. Moreover, NVA troops continued to infiltrate the South in increasing numbers.

As far back as 1954, the American politician William F. Knowland had warned that "using United States ground forces in the Indochina jungle would be like trying to cover an elephant with a handkerchief – you just can't do it". His words fell on deaf ears. The first regular **American troops** from the 3rd US Marine Division landed at Da Nang in March 1965; by the end of the year, two hundred thousand GIs were in Vietnam, and approaching half a million by the winter of 1967. In addition, there were large numbers of Australians and South Koreans, plus smaller units of New Zealanders, Thais and Filipinos. The war these troops fought was a dirty, dispiriting and frustrating one: for the most part, it was a guerrilla conflict against an invisible enemy able to disappear into the nearest village, leaving them unable to trust even civilians.

In the **North**, outrage at the merciless bombing campaign meted out by a remote foreign aggressor engendered a sense of anti-colonial purpose; in the **South**, there was only disorientation. To some, the immensity of the US presence seemed to preclude the possibility of a protracted conflict, and was therefore welcome; to others, it felt so much like an invasion, especially when GIs began to uproot them and destroy their land, that they supported or joined the NLF. The Viet Cong themselves were no angels, though, often

1959	1960	1962
Hanoi adopts tougher military stance against guerrillas	Conscription introduced	12,000 American advisers in Vietnam

WAR TERMINOLOGY

A wholly unconventional conflict at the time, the American War gave birth to a raft of new terms, many of which have been reinforced through movies and other wars. Missions to flush active Viet Cong soldiers out of villages, which were initiated towards the end of 1965, became known as **Search and Destroy** operations; the most infamous of these resulted in the **My Lai massacre** (see p.240). In the highlands, **fire bases** were established, from where howitzers could rain fire upon NVA troop movements; elsewhere, **free fire zones** – areas cleared of villagers to enable bombing of their supposed guerrilla occupants – were declared. In addition, **scorched earth**, the policy of denuding and razing vast swathes of land in order to rob the Viet Cong of cover, was introduced. One such way of doing this was with the use of **Agent Orange**, another term that has gone down in infamy, as have specific missions such as **Operation Rolling Thunder**. And all the while, generals in the field were quick to establish that most symbolic arbiter in this bitter war, the **body count**, according to which missions succeeded or failed.

imposing a reign of terror, augmented by summary executions of alleged traitors. What's more, successive Saigon governments were corrupt and unpopular, but the alternative was the Northern Communists so gruesomely depicted by American propaganda.

To survive, villagers quickly learned to react, and to say the right thing to the right person. Trying to appease the two sets of soldiers they encountered in the space of a day was like treading a tightrope, creating a climate of hatred and distrust that turned neighbours into informants. Since children were conscripted by whichever side reached them first, brothers and sisters often found themselves fighting on opposing sides.

The Tet Offensive

On January 21, 1968, around forty thousand NVA troops laid siege to a remote American military base at **Khe Sanh**, near the Lao border northwest of Hue. Wary that the confrontation might become an American Dien Bien Phu – an analogy that in reality held no water, given the US's superior air power – America responded, to borrow the military jargon of the day, "with extreme prejudice", notching up a Communist body count of over ten thousand in a carpet-bombing campaign graphically labelled "Niagara". However, such losses were seen as a necessary evil by the Communists, for whom Khe Sanh was primarily a decoy to steer US troops and attention away from the **Tet Offensive** that exploded a week later. In the early hours of January 31, a combined force of seventy thousand Communists (most of them Viet Cong) violated a New Year truce to launch offensives on over a hundred urban centres across the South. The campaign failed to achieve its objective of imposing Viet Cong representation in the Southern government; only in Hue did Viet Cong forces manage to hold out for more than a few days.

But success did register across the Pacific, where the offensive caused a sea change in popular perceptions of the war. Thus far, Washington's propaganda machine had largely convinced the public that the war in Vietnam was under control; events in 1968 flew in the face of this charade. Around two thousand American GIs had died during the Tet Offensive; but symbolically more damaging was the audacious assault mounted, on the first day of the offensive, by a crack Viet Cong commando team on the compound of the **US Embassy in Saigon**. The Communists had pierced the underbelly

1963

1965

Buddhists killed in Hue; Thich Quang Duc sets fire to himself in protest

US Army launches massive carpet-bombing campaign known as Operation Rolling Thunder

of the American presence in Vietnam: by the time the compound had been secured over six hours later, five Americans had died – and with them the popular conviction that the war was being won.

This shift in attitude was soon reflected in President Johnson's **vetoing** of requests for a massive troop expansion. On March 31, he announced a virtual cessation of bombing; a month later, the first bout of diplomatic sparring that was to grind on for five years was held in Paris; and, before the year was out, a full end to bombing had been declared.

Nixon's presidency

Richard Nixon's term of office commenced in January 1969, on the back of a campaign in which he promised to "end the war and win the peace". His quest for a solution that would facilitate an American pull-out without tarnishing its image led Nixon to pursue the strategy of "**Vietnamization**", a gradual US withdrawal coupled with a stiffening of ARVN forces and hardware. Though the number of US troops in Vietnam reached an all-time peak of 540,000 early on in 1969, 60,000 of these were home for Christmas, and by the end of 1970 only 280,000 remained. Over the same time period, ARVN numbers almost doubled, from 640,000 to well over a million.

However, the NVA had for several years been stockpiling both men and supplies in **Cambodia**, and in March 1969 US covert bombing of these targets commenced. Code-named **Operation Menu**, it lasted for fourteen months, yet elicited no outcry from Hanoi since they had no right to be in neutral Cambodia in the first place. The following spring, an American-backed coup replaced Prince Sihanouk of Cambodia with Lon Nol and thus eased access for US troops, and a **task force** of twenty thousand soldiers advanced on Communist installations there. The American public was outraged: dismayed that Nixon, far from closing down the war, was in fact widening the conflict, they rallied at mass anti-war demonstrations.

After **Ho Chi Minh's death** on September 2, 1969, the stop-start **peace talks** in Paris dragged along with Le Duc Tho representing the North, and Nixon's national security adviser Henry Kissinger at the American helm. Two stumbling blocks hindered any advancement: the North's insistence on a coalition government in the South with no place for then-president, Thieu, and the US insistence that all NVA troops should move north after a ceasefire. Tit-for-tat military offensives launched early in 1972 saw both sides attempting to strengthen their hand at the bargaining table: Hanoi launched its **Easter Offensive** on the upper provinces of the South; while Nixon countered by resuming the **bombing of the North**. Towards the year's end, negotiations recommenced, this time with Hanoi in a mood to compromise – not least because Nixon let rumours spread of his **Madman Theory**, which involved the use of nuclear weaponry – but the draft agreement produced in October (Nixon was keen to see a resolution before the US elections in November) was delayed by President Thieu in Saigon. By the time it was finalized in January 1973 Nixon had flexed his military muscles one last time, sanctioning the eleven-day **Christmas Bombing** of Hanoi and Haiphong in which 20,000 tonnes of ordnance was dropped.

Under the terms of the **Paris Accords**, signed on January 27 by the United States, the North, the South and the Viet Cong, a ceasefire was established, all remaining American troops were repatriated by April, and Hanoi and Saigon released their PoWs. The Paris talks failed to yield a long-term political settlement, instead providing for the

1969	1973	1976
Death of Ho Chi Minh	Peace treaty ends American War; millions died in the conflict, the vast majority of them Vietnamese	Declaration of the unified Socialist Republic of Vietnam

creation of a **Council of National Conciliation**, comprising Saigon's government and the Communists, to sort matters out at some future date. The agreements allowed the NVA and ARVN troops to retain whatever positions they held. For this fudged deal, Kissinger and Le Duc Tho were awarded the Nobel Prize for peace, though only Kissinger accepted.

The fall of the South

The Paris Accords accomplished little beyond smoothing the US withdrawal from Vietnam: with the NVA allowed to remain in the South, it was only a matter of time before **renewed aggression** erupted. Thieu's ARVN, now numbering a million troops and in robust shape thanks to its new US-financed equipment, soon set about retaking territory lost to the North during the Easter Offensive. The Communists, on the other hand, were still reeling from losses accrued during that campaign. By 1974, things were beginning to sour for the South. An economy already weakened by heavy **inflation** was further drained by the **unemployment** caused by America's withdrawal; corruption in the military was rife, and unpaid wages led to a burgeoning desertion rate. By the end of the year, the South was ripe for the taking.

Received wisdom in Hanoi was that a slow build-up of arms in the South, in preparation for a conventional push in 1976, would be the wisest course of action. Then, over the Christmas period of 1974, an **NVA drive** led by General Tran overran the area north of Saigon now called Song Be Province. Duly encouraged, Hanoi went into action, and towns in the South fell like ninepins under the irresistible momentum of the **Ho Chi Minh Campaign**. Within two months, Communist troops had occupied Buon Ma Thuot, taking a mere 24 hours to finish a job they'd anticipated would require a week. Hue and Da Nang duly followed, and by April 21 Xuan Loc, the last real line of defence before Saigon, had also fallen. ARVN defiance disintegrated in the face of the North's unerring progress: a famous image from these last days shows a highway scattered with the discarded boots of fleeing Southern soldiers. President Thieu fled by helicopter to Taiwan, and leadership of Saigon's government was assumed by **General Duong Van Minh** ("Big Minh"). Minh held the post for just two days before NVA tanks crashed through the gates of the Presidential Palace and Saigon fell to the North on April 30. Only hours before, the last Americans and other Westerners in the city had been **airlifted out** in the frantic helicopter operation known as "Frequent Wind" (see p.83).

Socialist Vietnam

By July 1976, Vietnam was once again a **unified nation** for the first time since the French colonization in the 1850s. At first the new leaders trod softly, in order to impress the international community, but Southerners eyed the future with profound apprehension. Their fears were well founded, as Hanoi was in no mood to grant Saigon autonomy: the Council of National Reconciliation, provided for by the Paris Accords, was never established, and the NLF's **Provisional Revolutionary Government** worked beneath the shadow of the Military Management Committee, and therefore Hanoi, until the **Socialist Republic of Vietnam** was officially born, in July 1976. The impression of a conquering army was exacerbated when Northern cadres – the *can bo* – swarmed south to take up all official posts.

1978	1979
Vietnam invades Cambodia in order to remove Khmer Rouge from power	The "boat people" start to flee Vietnam in large numbers, and would continue to do so until the 1990s

Monumental **problems** faced the nascent republic. For many years, the two halves of Vietnam had lived according to wildly variant political and economic systems. The North had no industry, its agriculture was based on cooperative farms, and much of its land had been ravaged during the war. In stark contrast, American involvement in the South had underwritten what John Pilger describes as "an 'economy' based upon the services of maids, pimps, whores, beggars and black-marketeers", buttressed by American cash that dried up when the last helicopter left the embassy in Saigon.

The changes that swept the country weren't limited to economics. Bitterness on Hanoi's part towards its former enemies was inevitable, yet instead of making moves towards national conciliation – and despite the fact that many families had connections in both camps – recriminations drove further wedges between the peoples of North and South. Anyone with remote connections to America was interned in a **re-education camp**, along with Buddhist monks, priests, intellectuals and anyone else the government wanted to be rid of. Hundreds of thousands of Southerners were sent to these camps, without trial. Some were to remain encarcerated for over a decade. The quagmire Vietnam found itself in after reunification prompted many of its citizens to flee the country in unseaworthy vessels, an exodus of humanity known as the **boat people** (see box, pp.450–451).

While all this was going on, just three weeks before the fall of Saigon in 1975 **Pol Pot**'s genocidal regime seized power in Cambodia: within a year his troops were making **cross-border forays** into regions of Vietnam that had once fallen under Khmer sway, around the Mekong Delta and north of Ho Chi Minh City (as Saigon had been renamed). One such venture led to the massacre at **Ba Chuc** (see p.140), in which almost two thousand people died. Reprisals were slow in coming, but by 1978 Vietnam could stand back no longer; on Christmas Day of that year 120,000 **Vietnamese troops invaded Cambodia** and ousted Pol Pot. Whatever the motives for the invasion, and even though it brought an end to Pol Pot's reign of terror, Vietnam was further ostracized by the international community. In February 1979, Beijing's response came in the form of a punitive **Chinese invasion** of Vietnam's northeastern provinces; Chinese losses were heavy, and after sixteen days they retreated. Meanwhile, Pol Pot had withdrawn across the Thai border, from where he commanded his army in their continued attack on the occupying Vietnamese forces. The Vietnamese remained in Cambodia until September 1989, by which time they had defeated the Khmer Rouge at the expense of fifty thousand soldiers, the majority of them Southern conscripts.

Doi moi

A severe famine in 1985 and the 775 percent inflation that crippled the country in 1986 were just two of the many symptoms of the **economic malaise** threatening to tear Vietnam apart during the late 1970s and early 1980s. An experimental hybrid of planned and market economies tried out in 1979 came to nothing, and by the early 1980s the only thing keeping Vietnam afloat was Soviet aid. Treaties made it illegal for Americans to do business with the Vietnamese, who, largely due to American pressure, were unable to look to the IMF or World Bank for development loans.

The party's conservative old guard resisted change for as long as it could, but the death of General Secretary Le Duan in 1986 finally cleared the way for more reformist politicians to attempt to reverse the country's fortunes: **Nguyen Van Linh** took over as

1979	1986
Chinese launch invasion of northern Vietnam, but retreat after only sixteen days	Nguyen Van Linh becomes General Secretary of Socialist Party; inaugurates *doi moi* policy

THE "BOAT PEOPLE"

In 1979 the attention of the world was caught by images of rickety fishing boats packed with Vietnamese **refugees** seeking sanctuary in Hong Kong and other Southeast Asian harbours. An untold number – some say a third – fell victim to typhoons, starvation and disease or pirates, who often sank the boats after raping the women and seizing the refugees' meagre possessions. Others somehow fetched up on the coast of Australia or were picked up by passing freighters. The prime destination, however, was Hong Kong, where 68,000 asylum-seekers arrived in 1979 alone. The exodus was at its peak in 1979, but it had been going on, largely unnoticed, since reunification four years earlier, and continued up to the early 1990s. Over this period an estimated 840,000 boat people arrived safely in "ports of first asylum", of whom more than 750,000 were eventually resettled overseas.

The first refugees were mostly **Southerners**, people who felt themselves too closely associated with the old regime or their American allies, and feared Communist reprisals. Some were former nationalists and a few were even ex-Viet Cong, disillusioned with the new government's extremism. Then, in early 1978, nationalization of private commerce was instituted in the South, hitting hard at the **Chinese** community, which controlled much Southern business and the all-important rice trade. As anti-Chinese sentiment took hold, thousands made their escape in fishing boats followed in the late 1970s by more Vietnamese, driven by a series of bad harvests, severe hardship and the prospect of prolonged military service in Cambodia.

By 1979 the situation had become so critical that the international community was forced to act, offering asylum to the more than two hundred thousand refugees crowding temporary camps around Southeast Asia. Under the auspices of the UN, the **Orderly Departure Programme** (ODP) also enabled legal emigration of political refugees to the West, resettling over half a million in more than forty Western countries.

In 1987, the South China Sea was once again full of Vietnamese people in overcrowded boats. This **second wave** were mostly Northerners fleeing desperate poverty rather than fear

general secretary, and a raft of market-based economic reforms, known as **doi moi** or "renovation", followed. This encompassed limited moves towards decentralization and privatization; collectivized agriculture was abandoned in favour of individual land-holdings and attempts were made to attract foreign capital by liberalizing foreign investment regulations. Political reforms came a poor second, although the congress did instigate purges on corrupt officialdom and gave the press freer rein to criticize. With the **collapse of Communism** across Europe in 1989, though, the press was again silenced, and in a keynote speech Nguyen Van Linh rejected the concept of a multi-party state; all economic reforms, however, remained in place, and the government set in motion efforts to end Vietnam's isolation.

International rehabilitation, which had already begun with the withdrawal of troops from Cambodia in 1989, gathered momentum in the 1990s, as efforts to aid the US search teams looking for remains of the two-thousand-plus American soldiers still unaccounted for (MIAs, or Missing in Action) were stepped up. In 1993, a year after the reformist **Vo Van Kiet** became prime minister, the Americans duly lifted their veto on aid, and Western cash began to flow. By the year's end, inflation was down to five percent. The rapprochement with the US continued into 1994, as the US trade embargo was lifted by President Clinton, and in February 1995 the two countries opened liaison offices in each other's capitals. Vietnam was admitted into **ASEAN**

1989	1990
Vietnamese soldiers withdraw from Cambodia after more than a decade of occupation	Government relaxes laws governing establishment of private businesses

of persecution, with Hong Kong again bearing the brunt of new arrivals. Governments were less sympathetic this time round and, in an attempt to halt the flow, from early 1989 boat people were denied automatic refugee status. Instead, a screening process was introduced to identify "genuine" refugees; the rest, designated "economic migrants", were encouraged to return under the **Voluntary Repatriation Scheme**, which offered concrete assistance with resettlement.

Then, in early 1996, all parties finally agreed that the only "viable solution" was to send the remaining forty thousand failed asylum-seekers still in Southeast Asian camps back home. In theory deportations were to take place "without threat or use of force", though clashes with security forces became more violent as the programme gained momentum. The situation was worst in Hong Kong, where there was pressure to clear the camps before the handover to China in 1997. The rate of repatriation – both voluntary and, increasingly, forced – was stepped up throughout the region and by mid-1997 nearly all the boat people had been either resettled or returned to Vietnam.

The UN High Commission for Refugees (UNHCR), which monitored returnees in Vietnam up until 2000, said there was little evidence of persecution or discrimination. Others, however, claimed that the monitoring was inadequate and ineffective, and cited examples of returnees being imprisoned. At the same time, various international bodies, such as the European Union, helped returnees reintegrate into the community through job creation schemes, vocational training programmes and low-interest loans. In 1998, a scheme known as ROVR got under way, resettling mostly Southerners who were able to prove some sort of relationship with the Americans during the war.

As the Vietnamese economy improved and as relations between America and Vietnam started to thaw around the turn of the millennium, so the ODP and ROVR programmes were gradually wound up. Their completion marked the end – at least as far as officialdom was concerned – of the whole sorry saga of the boat people.

(the Association of Southeast Asian Nations) in July 1995, and the same month saw full **diplomatic relations restored** with the US.

During the next two years foreign investment continued to flood in, pushing economic growth rates close to ten percent per annum. Revenues from oil, manufacturing and tourism took off and everyone was forecasting Vietnam as the next **Asian tiger**. For all the optimism, however, cracks were beginning to appear: the economic upturn was benefiting city-dwellers (particularly in Ho Chi Minh City) far more than the rural population; top bureaucrats were openly criticized in **corruption** scandals; and an alarmed government launched a campaign against "**social evils**" – videos, advertising, pornography and other Western imports which were seen to be undermining traditional society.

By 1997 the honeymoon period was definitely over. Economic growth flagged as foreign companies scaled back, or pulled out altogether, frustrated by an overblown bureaucracy, miles of red tape and regulations in a constant state of flux. Vietnam's mostly inefficient, state-run industries became increasingly uncompetitive, and smuggling grew at an alarming rate. In May 1997, widespread corruption, growing agricultural unemployment and the ever-widening gulf between urban and rural Vietnam sparked off **demonstrations** by thousands of dissatisfied farmers in Thai Binh Province, part of the traditionally Communist north.

1993	1995	2000
At the Cannes Film Festival, *The Scent of Green Papaya* wins Vietnam's first major movie award	Full diplomatic relations restored with the US	At the Sydney games, Tran Hieu Ngan wins Vietnam's first ever Olympic medal – a silver for taekwondo

Recent events

National **elections** in July 1997 brought a long-awaited change of government, ushering in a band of younger, more world-wise ministers under Prime Minister **Phan Van Khai**. His tenure, however, got off to a shaky start, with Pham The Duyet, a senior member of the Politburo, arrested for corruption in 1998. Compounding this was the Asian Financial Crisis, which hit the same year; Vietnam's economy, on the face of things, handled it fairly well, with GDP growth barely dipping below five percent; such statistics, however, disguised harsh economic realities for the majority of the population, with the burgeoning middle-class feeling most of the benefits. In addition, events in 1999 showed that the government had changed little, despite the accession of younger leaders – Tran Do, previously a high-ranking party member, was expelled after calling for greater democracy and freedom of speech. The following year, in a sign of vastly improved bilateral ties with the USA, Bill Clinton arrived on an official visit. The main upshot of his initial meetings with the government was a pledge to help clear landmines left from the war, while the next year saw a bilateral trade agreement between Vietnam and America, fully normalizing economic relations between the two countries and furthering Vietnam's process of **international reconciliation** and **trade liberalization**.

Phan Van Khai was re-elected in 2002. The same year, Russia had handed back the Cam Ranh Bay naval base, which had, during Soviet times, been the largest such facility outside the Warsaw Pact area. There then followed yet further signs of improved US–Vietnam relations – in 2004, a United jet touched down in Ho Chi Minh City, in the process becoming the first direct American passenger service to Vietnam since the war (at the time of writing, however, this was still the only route in service). Pham Van Khai made a reciprocal visit to the US in 2005, though the following year once again saw his government's reputation take a hit, with senior officials investigated over the embezzlement of millions of dollars of state funds.

2006 saw a second wave of younger leaders elected to top posts. Khai's "chosen one" **Nguyen Tan Dung** took over as Prime Minister, continuing his predecessor's economic reforms – no simple task given the inherent constraints of a "state capitalism" system – and the battle against corruption, resulting in a number of high-profile **anti-corruption trials**. In early 2007, following more than a decade of intense negotiations, Vietnam gained **membership of the World Trade Organization** (WTO). Shortly afterwards, the government announced ambitious plans to build a high-speed rail-line between Hanoi and Ho Chi Minh City (since shelved), a tram system in Hanoi (which has since morphed into a metro plan), and a metro system in Ho Chi Minh City (scheduled to commence operations in 2017).

Human rights issues

While the economy rolled forward, 2008 saw worrying developments running contrary to what the world community expected of a younger and "more enlightened" government. Measures were put in place to prevent bloggers from posting "inappropriate content", while two local **journalists were arrested** and imprisoned after their exposure of a corruption scandal. One of them, Nguyen Van Hai, was freed after pleading guilty, while the other, Nguyen Viet Chien, was one of more than 15,000 released from prison as part of a wide-ranging amnesty early in 2009. Later that year,

2002	2006	2011
Opening of first branch of *Highland Coffee*, Vietnam's first Western-style café chain	Vietnam joins the WTO	Completion of Landmark Tower in Hanoi, the country's tallest building

however, seven **pro-democracy activists** were jailed for anti-government activities, with another following in early 2010. One was Le Cong Dinh, a local lawyer who had been involved with a number of high-profile human rights cases; his detention was roundly criticized by Amnesty International, while Human Rights Watch also chimed in with criticism of the country's suppression of online content. In 2013, a further 22 were arrested for anti-government activities, before a decree was passed banning the online discussion of "current affairs" – a wide-ranging topic, indeed. The arrest of two more prominent bloggers followed in 2014. The suppression of dissent was not just limited to perceived anti-government activities – in 2013 alone at least fifty Christians were arrested, and Open Doors International ranked Vietnam as one of the worst nations worldwide for religious freedom (see p.455).

All the while, the old beast of **corruption** was regularly rearing its ugly head. In 2010 a major scandal almost sank shipbuilder Vinashin, one of the largest state-owned enterprises; its chairman was arrested and jailed. Nguyen Tan Dung was reappointed Prime Minister in 2011, though the following year the Communist Party chief was forced to publicly apologise for a raft of other scandals at state-run companies. In 2014 there was another mammoth fraud trial, this time revolving around state-run Vietinbank – 23 were jailed.

Troubles with China

Ties between Vietnam and China have been fraught for centuries, but in 2011 both sides signed an agreement pertaining to the resolution of the long-running dispute in the South China Sea, whose waters are contested by another four countries in the area. It wasn't long before relations took a turn for the worse – in 2014, Vietnamese state media marked, for the first time, the anniversary of the 1974 clashes with China over the disputed **Paracel Islands**. This may have had something to do with the protests which swept the country later that year, after the repositioning of a Chinese oil rig – Chinese homes and businesses were attacked across Vietnam, leading to twenty deaths, and the evacuation of three thousand ethnic Chinese. Somewhat ridiculously, Korean, Japanese and Taiwanese businesses also found themselves torched during a week of madness. Hundreds of Vietnamese were held as the government tried to put a lid on the protests, though the nation's ire was stoked once more when a Chinese ship hit, and sank, a small Vietnamese fishing boat just a week later.

Reasons to be cheerful

Despite the regular stories of corruption, increasing repression of human rights, dubious religious freedom and a stumbling economy, life is not all bad for the average Vietnamese. Many quality of life indicators seem to be heading the right way, albeit from very low bases: according to World Bank figures, the number of Vietnamese living in poverty has dropped from seventy percent in the 1980s to under fifteen percent today, child mortality has fallen, literacy levels are well over ninety percent, and the average life expectancy is now around 75 years, compared with 65 in 1990. All in all, it's important to remember what a state the country was in at the beginning of independence – divided, damaged and destitute – and how strangely normal life now seems after the atrocities that took place here only a generation ago.

2013	2014	
Vietnam's population passes the ninety million mark, leaving it ranked fourteenth worldwide	Malaysia Airlines flight vanishes near the Ca Mau peninsula	Wave of anti-China protests, in response to Chinese deployment of oil rig in disputed seas

Religion and beliefs

The moral and religious life of most Vietnamese people is governed by a complex mixture of Confucian, Buddhist and Taoist philosophical teachings interwoven with ancestor worship and ancient, animistic practices. Incompatibilities are reconciled on a practical level into a single, functioning belief system whereby a family may maintain an ancestral altar in their home, consult the village guardian spirit, propitiate the God of the Hearth and take offerings to the Buddhist pagoda.

The primary influence on Vietnam's religious life has been Chinese. However, in southern Vietnam, which historically fell within the Indian sphere, small communities of Khmer and Cham still adhere to Hinduism, Islam and Theravada Buddhism brought direct from India. From the fifteenth century on, **Christianity** has also been a feature, represented largely by Roman Catholicism but with a small Protestant following in the south. Vietnam also claims a couple of home-grown religious **sects**, both products of political and social turmoil in the early twentieth century: Cao Dai and Hoa Hao.

The **political dimension** has never been far removed from religious affairs in Vietnam, as the world was made vividly aware by Buddhist opposition to the oppressive regime of President Diem in the 1960s. After 1975, the Marxist–Leninist government of

---

VIETNAMESE DEITIES

BUDDHIST DEITIES

A Di Da or **Amitabha** The Historical Buddha, the most revered member of the Buddhist pantheon in Vietnamese pagodas.

Avalokitesvara A bodhisattva often represented with many arms and eyes, being all-powerful, or as Quan Am (see below).

Di Lac or **Maitreya** The Future Buddha, usually depicted as chubby, with a bare chest and a huge grin, sitting on a lotus throne.

Ong Ac or **Trung Ac** One of the two guardians of the Buddhist religion, popularly known as Mister Wicked, who judges all people. He has a fierce red face and a reputation for severity – of which badly behaved children are frequently reminded.

Ong Thien or **Khuyen Thien** The second guardian of Buddhism is Mister Charitable, a white-faced kindly soul who encourages good behaviour.

Quan Am The Goddess of Mercy, adopted from the Chinese goddess, Kuan Yin. Quan Am is a popular incarnation of Avalokitesvara. She is usually represented as a graceful white statue, with her hand raised in blessing.

Thich Ca Mau Ni or **Sakyamuni** The Present Buddha, born Siddhartha Gautama, who founded Buddhism.

OTHER CHARACTERS

Ngoc Hoang The Jade Emperor, ruler of the Taoist pantheon who presides over heaven.

Ong Tau God of the Hearth, who keeps watch over every family and reports on the household to the Jade Emperor every New Year.

Quan Cong A Chinese general of the Han Dynasty revered for his loyalty, honesty and exemplary behaviour. Usually flanked by his two assistants.

Thanh Mau The Mother Goddess.

Thien Hau Protectress of Sailors.

Tran Vo Properly known as Tran Vo Bac De, Taoist Emperor of the North, who governs storms and generally harmful events.

reunified Vietnam declared the state atheist, while theoretically allowing people the right to practise their religion under the constitution. In reality, churches and pagodas were closed down, religious leaders sent for re-education, and followers discriminated against if not actively persecuted.

In 1992 the situation changed, with the right to **religious freedom** being reaffirmed in a new constitution. A number of high-profile prisoners held on religious grounds were released, while party leaders publicly demonstrated the new freedoms by visiting pagodas and churches. Consequently, an increasing number of Vietnamese are now openly practising their faith again. Indeed, as Vietnam faces the onslaught of new ideas and the "social evils" spawned by the breakdown of its moral codes, people are looking to religion both for personal guidance and as a stabilizing force in society. Despite such moves toward greater freedom of worship, however, the government continues to exercise close control on religious groups through such practices as monitoring appointments, training institutions and publications. It is regularly accused of failing to make real progress on **human rights** issues and came in for particularly severe criticism for its crackdown on ethnic minority Christians following widespread unrest in the central highlands in 2001 and 2004. Later in 2004 the US designated Vietnam a "Country of Particular Concern" because of its violations of religious freedom. The Vietnamese government subsequently released a number of prisoners and passed legislation outlawing forced recantations, among other measures. However, the European Parliament echoed the same concerns as recently as 2009, and international human rights organizations continue to criticize the Vietnamese government for its record on religious freedom and other human rights.

Ancestor worship

One of the oldest cults practised in Vietnam is that of ancestor worship, based on the fundamental principles of filial piety and of obligation to the past, present and future generations. No matter what their religion, virtually every Vietnamese household, even hardline Communist, will maintain an **ancestral altar** in the belief that the dead continue to live in another realm. Ancestors can intercede on behalf of their descendants and bring the family good fortune, but in return the living must pay respect, perform prescribed ceremonies and provide for their ancestors' wellbeing. At funerals and subsequent anniversaries, quantities of paper money and other **votive offerings** (these days including television sets and cars) are burnt, and choice morsels of food are regularly placed on the altar. Traditionally this is financed by the income from a designated plot of land, and it is the responsibility of the oldest, usually male, member of the family to organize the rituals, tend the altar and keep the ancestors abreast of all important family events; failure in any of these duties carries the risk of inciting peeved ancestors to make mischief.

The ancestral altar occupies a central position in the home. On it are placed several wooden tablets, one for each ancestor going back five generations. One hundred days after the funeral, the deceased's spirit returns to reside in the tablet. People without children to honour them by burning incense at the altar are condemned to wander the world in search of a home. Some childless people make provision by paying a temple or pagoda to observe the rituals, while the spirits of others may eventually take up residence in one of the small shrine houses (*cuong*) you see in fields and at roadsides. Important times for remembering the dead are **Tet**, the lunar new year, and **Thanh Minh** ("Festival of Pure Light"), which falls on the fifth day of the third lunar month.

Spirit worship

Residual animism plus a whole host of spirits borrowed from other religions have given Vietnam a complicated mystical world. The universe is divided into **three realms**: the sky, earth and man, under the overall guardianship of Ong Troi, Lord of Heaven, assisted by spirits of the earth, mountains and water. Within the hierarchy are four **sacred animals** who appear everywhere in Vietnamese architecture: the dragon, representing the king, power and intelligence; the phoenix, embodying the queen, beauty and peace; the turtle, symbol of longevity and protector of the kingdom; and the mythical *kylin*, usually translated as unicorn, which represents wisdom.

In addition each village or urban quarter will venerate a **guardian spirit** in either a temple (*den*) or communal house (*dinh*). The deity may be legendary, for example the benevolent horse-spirit Bach Ma of Thang Long (modern Hanoi), and will often come from the Taoist pantheon. Or the guardian may be a historical figure such as a local or national hero, or a man of great virtue. In either case people will propitiate these tutelary spirits – represented on the altar by a gilded throne – with offerings, and will consult them in times of need. The *dinh* also serves as meeting house and school for the community.

Buddhism

The Buddha was born **Siddhartha Gautama** to a wealthy family sometime during the sixth century BC in present-day Nepal. At an early age he renounced his life of luxury to seek the ultimate deliverance from worldly suffering and strive to reach **nirvana**, an indefinable, blissful state. After several years Siddhartha attained enlightenment while sitting under a bodhi tree, and then devoted the rest of his life to teaching the **Middle Way** that leads to nirvana. The Buddha preached that existence is a cycle of perpetual reincarnation in which actions in one life determine one's position in the next, but that it is possible to break free by following certain precepts, central to which are non-violence and compassion. The Buddha's doctrine was based on the **Four Noble Truths**: existence is suffering; suffering is caused by desire; suffering ends with the extinction of desire; the way to end suffering is to follow the eightfold path of right understanding, thought, speech, action, livelihood, effort, mindfulness and concentration.

It's estimated that up to two-thirds of the Vietnamese population consider themselves Buddhist. The vast majority are followers of the Mahayana school which was introduced to northern Vietnam via China in the second century AD. Within this, most Vietnamese Buddhists claim allegiance to the Pure Land sect (*Tinh Do*), which venerates A Di Da or Amitabha Buddha above all others, while the meditational Zen sect (*Thien*) has a moderate following, predominantly in northern Vietnam.

The history of Buddhism in Vietnam

In fact Buddhism first arrived in southern Vietnam nearly one hundred years earlier as **Theravada**, or the "Lesser Vehicle", introduced via the Indian trade routes through Burma and Thailand. Theravada is an ascetical form of the faith based on the individual pursuit of perfection and enlightenment, which failed to find favour beyond the Khmer communities of the Mekong, where it still counts roughly one million followers. One of the salient features of **Mahayana** Buddhism, in contrast, is the belief that intermediaries – **bodhisattvas** – have chosen to forgo nirvana to work for the salvation of all humanity, and it was this that enabled Mahayana to adapt to a Vietnamese context by incorporating local gods and spirits into its array of bodhisattvas. The best-known bodhisattva is Avalokitesvara, usually worshipped in Vietnam as **Quan Am**, the Goddess of Mercy. Mahayana Buddhism spread through northern Vietnam until it became the **official state religion** after the country regained its independence from China in the tenth century. The Ly kings (1009–1225), in particular, were devout Buddhists who sponsored hundreds of pagodas, prompting a flowering of the arts, and established a hierarchy of monk–scholars as advisers to the court. Great landowning monasteries came into being and Buddhist doctrine was incorporated into the civil service examinations along with Confucian and Taoist texts as part of the "triple world-view", *Tam Giao*. At the same time it became apparent that Buddhism was unable to provide the unifying ideology required by a highly centralized state constantly fighting for its survival. Consequently, by the mid-fourteenth century Buddhism had lost its political and economic influence and, when the Later Le Dynasty came to power in 1427, Confucianism finally eclipsed it as the dominant national philosophy.

But by then Buddhism was too deeply rooted, particularly in the folk religion of the countryside, to lose its influence completely. It enjoyed further brief periods of **royal patronage**, notably during the seventeenth and eighteenth centuries when new pagodas were built and old ones repaired. To many people it still offered a spiritual element lacking in Confucian doctrine, and during the colonial era Vietnamese intellectuals turned to Buddhism in search of a national identity. Since then the Buddhist community has been a focus of **dissent**, not least in the 1960s when images of self-immolating Buddhist monks focused world attention on the excesses of South Vietnam's Catholic President Diem. At the time, protesting Buddhists were accused of being pro-Communist, although their standpoint was essentially neutral. In the event they experienced even greater repression after reunification when pagodas were closed, and monks and nuns were sent to re-education camps.

THE BUDDHIST PAGODA

The Vietnamese word *chua*, translated as "pagoda", is an exclusively Buddhist term, whereas a temple (*den*) may be Taoist, Confucian or house a guardian spirit. **Pagoda architecture** reached a pinnacle during the Ly and Tran dynasties, but thanks to Chinese invasions and local, anti-Buddhist movements few examples remain. A majority of those still in existence are eighteenth- or nineteenth-century constructions, though many retain features of earlier designs. Generally, pagoda **layout** is either an inverse T or three parallel lines of single-storeyed pavilions. The first hall is reserved for public worship, while those beyond, on slightly raised platforms, contain the prayer table and principal altar. Other typical elements are a **bell tower**, either integral to the building or standing apart, and a **walled courtyard** containing ponds, stone stelae and, particularly in Mahayana pagodas, the white figure of Quan Am symbolizing charity and compassion.

The most interesting feature inside the pagoda is often the **statuary**. Rows of Buddhas sit or stand on the main altar, where the Buddhist trinity occupies the highest level: A Di Da or Amitabha, the Historical Buddha; Thich Ca Mau Ni or Sakyamuni, born Siddhartha Gautama, the Present Buddha; and Di Lac, or Maitreya, the Future Buddha. Lower ranks comprise the same characters in a variety of forms accompanied by bodhisattvas: look out for pot-bellied Maitreya as the laughing carefree Buddha who grants wishes; the omnipotent Avalokitesvara of a "thousand" arms and eyes; and the Nine Dragon Buddha (Tuong Cuu Long). This latter is a small statue, found more often in northern Vietnam, of Sakyamuni encircled by dragons, standing with one hand pointing to the sky and the other to the earth. According to legend, nine dragons descended from the sky to bathe the newborn Buddha, after which he took seven steps forward and proclaimed, "on earth and in the sky, I alone am the highest".

Two unmistakable figures residing in all pagodas are the giant **guardians of Buddhist law**: white-faced "Mister Charitable" (Ong Thien), holding a pearl, and red-faced "Mister Wicked" (Ong Ac). Ong Thien sees everything, both the good and the bad, while Ong Ac dispenses justice. From an artistic point of view, some of the most fascinating statues are the lifelike representations of *arhats*, ascetic Buddhist saints; the best examples are found in northern pagodas, where each figure is portrayed in a disturbingly realistic style. Finally, Mahayana pagodas will undoubtedly welcome in a few **Taoist spirits**, the favourites being Thien Hau, the Protectress of Sailors, and Thanh Mau, the Mother Goddess. Somewhere in the pagoda halls will be an altar dedicated to deceased monks or nuns, while larger pagodas usually maintain a garden for their burial stupas. Traditionally Buddhists would bury their dead, but increasingly they practise cremation.

The **best times to visit** a pagoda are the first and fifteenth days of the lunar month (new moon and full moon), when they are at their busiest. Note that it's customary to remove your shoes when stepping on the floor mats and sometimes when entering the main sanctuary – watch what the locals do, or ask, to be on the safe side.

The situation has eased considerably in recent years, and pagodas affiliated to the officially recognized Vietnam Buddhist Sangha (VBS) have been allowed to resume their social and educational programmes to a certain extent. Many pagodas, now bustling with life again, have been renovated after years of neglect. Nevertheless, the government continues to exert control over the VBS and Buddhist leaders have persisted in their denunciations of the regime. At a time when the country's leaders are seeking international approval, the monks' campaign for **human rights** is causing them acute embarrassment. In particular, the authorities refuse to recognize the Unified Buddhist Church of Vietnam (UBCV), the main pre-1975 Buddhist organization. According to international human rights bodies, its leaders are regularly placed under "house arrest" without any official charges being made against them.

Confucianism

The teachings of Confucius provide a guiding set of moral and ethical principles, an **ideology** for the state's rulers and subjects onto which ritualistic practices have been grafted.

Confucius is the Latinized name of Kongfuzi (Khong Tu in Vietnamese), who was born into a minor aristocratic family in China in 551 BC. At this time China was in turmoil as the Zhou Dynasty dissolved into rival feudal states battling for supremacy. Confucius worked for many years as a court official, where he observed the nature of power and the function of government at close quarters. At the age of 50, he packed it all in and for the next twenty years wandered the country spreading his ideas on social and political reform in an effort to persuade states and individuals to live peacefully together for their mutual benefit. His central tenet was the importance of **correct behaviour** and **loyal service**, reinforced by ceremonial rites whereby the ruler maintains authority through good example rather than force. Important qualities to strive for are selflessness, respectfulness, sincerity and non-violence; the ideal person should be neither heroic nor extrovert, but instead follow a "golden mean". Confucius remained silent on spiritual matters, though he placed great emphasis on observing ancient rituals such as making offerings to heaven and to ancestors.

Confucian **teachings** were handed down in the *Analects*, but he is also credited with editing the Six Classics, among them the *Book of Changes* (*I Ching*) and the *Book of Ritual* (*Li Chi*). Later these became the basic texts for civil service examinations, ensuring that all state officials had a deeply ingrained respect for tradition and social order. Though Confucianism ultimately led to national inflexibility and the undermining of personal initiative, its positive legacy has been an emphasis on the value of education and a belief that individual merit is of greater consequence than high birth.

After the death of Confucius in 478 BC the doctrine was developed further by his **disciples**, the most famous of whom was Mencius (Mengzi). By the first century AD, Confucianism, which slowly absorbed elements of Taoism, had evolved into a cult and also become the state ideology whereby kings ruled under the Mandate of Heaven. Social stability was maintained through a fixed hierarchy of interdependent relationships encapsulated in the notion of filial piety. Thus children must obey their parents without question, wives their husbands, students their teacher and subjects their ruler. For their part, the recipient, particularly the king, must earn this obedience; if the rules are broken, the harmony of society and nature is disturbed and authority loses its legitimacy. Therefore, by implication, revolution was justified when the king lost his divine right to rule.

The history of Confucianism in Vietnam

Confucian thinking has pervaded Vietnamese society ever since Chinese administrators introduced the concepts during the second century BC. Reinforced by a thousand years of Chinese rule, Confucianism (*Nho Giao*) came to play an essential role in

Vietnam's political, social and educational systems. The philosophy was largely one of an intellectual elite, but Confucian teaching eventually filtered down to the village level where it had a profound influence on the Vietnamese family organization.

The ceremonial **cult of Confucius** was formalized in 1070 when King Ly Thanh Tong founded the Temple of Literature in Hanoi. But it wasn't until the foundation of the Later Le Dynasty in 1427 that Confucian doctrine gained supremacy over Buddhism in the Vietnamese court. The Le kings viewed Confucian ideology, with its emphasis on social order, duty and respect, as an effective means of consolidating their new regime. In 1442, they overhauled the education system and based it on a curriculum of Confucian texts. They also began recruiting top-level mandarins through doctoral examinations, which eventually gave rise to a scholar-gentry class at the expense of the old landed aristocracy. Confucian influence reached its peak during the reign of King Le Thanh Tong (1460–97), which heralded a golden age of bureaucratic reform when public service on behalf of both community and state became a noble ideal. At the same time, however, a strongly centralized administration, presided over by a divine ruler and a mandarin elite, eventually bred corruption, despotism and an increasingly rigid society. The arrival of Western ideas and French rule in the late nineteenth century finally undermined the political dominance of Confucianism, though it managed to survive as the court ideology until well into the twentieth century. The cult of Confucius (*Van Mieu*) continues in a few temples dedicated to the sage, and he also appears on other altars as an honoured ancestor, an exemplary figure remembered for services to the nation.

Many **Confucian ideals** have been completely assimilated into Vietnamese society. After Independence, the Communist Party struggled against inherent conservatism and the supremacy of the family as a political unit; indeed, leaders can still be heard railing against the entrenched "feudal" nature of rural Vietnam. But the party was also able to tap into those elements of the Confucian tradition that suited their new classless, socialist society: conformity, duty and the denial of personal interest for the common good. Today, however, Confucian ideals are being seriously undermined by the invasion of materialism and individual ambition.

Taoism

Taoism is based on the **Tao-te-Ching**, the "Book of the Way", traditionally attributed to **Lao-tzu** (meaning "Old Master"), who is thought to have lived in China in the sixth century BC. The Tao, the Way, emphasizes effortless action, intuition and spontaneity; the Tao is invisible and impartial; it cannot be taught, nor can it be expressed in words. It is the one reality from which everything is born, universal and eternal. However, by virtuous, compassionate and non-violent behaviour, it is possible to achieve ultimate stillness, through a mystical and personal quest. Taoism thus preached non-intervention, passivity and the futility of academic scholarship; Confucians viewed it as suspiciously subversive.

Chinese immigrants brought Taoism (*Dao Giao*) to Vietnam during the long period of Chinese rule (111 BC to 939 AD). Between the eleventh and fourteenth centuries the philosophy enjoyed equal status with Buddhism and Confucianism as one of Vietnam's three "religions", but Taoism gradually declined until it eventually became a strand of folk religion. A few Taoist temples (*quan*) exist in Vietnam but on the whole its deities have been absorbed into other cults. The Jade Emperor, for example, is frequently part of the Buddhist pantheon in Vietnamese pagodas.

Central to the Tao is the **duality** inherent in nature; the whole universe is in temporary balance, a tension of complementary opposites defined as **yin** and **yang**, the male and female principles. Yang is male, the sun, active and orthodox; yin is female, the earth, flexible, passive and instinctive. Harmony is the balance between the two, and experiencing that harmony is the Tao. Accordingly all natural things can be categorized

---

GEOMANCY

The **practice of geomancy** is a pseudo-scientific study, much like astrology or reading horoscopes, which was introduced to Vietnam from China. The underlying idea is that every location has harmful or beneficial properties governed by its physical attributes, planetary influences and the flow of natural energy through the earth. Geomancy is used mainly in **siting buildings**, particularly tombs, palaces, temples and the like, but also ordinary dwellings.

Geomancers analyse the general **topography** of the site, looking at the location of surrounding hills, as well as rivers, streams and other bodies of water, to find the most auspicious situation and orientation. They may suggest improving the area by adding small hills or lakes; if a family suffers bad fortune, a geomancer may be called in to divine the cause of the imbalance and restore the natural harmony.

---

by their property of yin or yang, and human activity should strive not to disrupt that balance. In its pure form Taoism has no gods, only emanations of the Tao, but in the first century AD it corrupted into an organized religion venerating a deified Lao-tzu. The new cult had popular appeal since it offered the goal of immortality through yogic meditation and good deeds. Eventually the practice of Taoism developed highly complex **rituals**, incorporating magic, mysticism, superstition and the use of geomancy (see box above) to ensure harmony between man and nature, while astrology might be used to determine auspicious dates for weddings, funerals, starting a journey or even launching a new business. Ancient spirit worship, the cult of ancestors and the veneration of legendary or historic figures all fused happily with the Taoist idea of a universal essence.

The vast, eclectic pantheon of Taoist **gods and immortals** is presided over by Ngoc Hoang, the Jade Emperor. He is assisted by three ministers: Nam Tao, the southern star who records all births; Bac Dau, the north star who registers deaths; and Ong Tao, God of the Hearth who reports all happenings in the family household to Ngoc Hoang at the end of the year. Then there is a collection of immortals, genies and guardian deities, including legendary and historic figures. In Vietnam among the best known are Tran Vo, God of the North, Bach Ho, the White Tiger of the West, and Tran Hung Dao, who protects the newborn and cures the sick. Confucius is also honoured as a Taoist saint. A distinctive aspect of Taoism is its use of **mediums** to communicate with the gods; the divine message is often in the form of a poem, transmitted by a writing brush onto sand or a bed of rice.

Christianity

Vietnam's **Catholic community** is the second largest in Southeast Asia after the Philippines. Exact figures are hard to come by but estimates vary between six and eight million (seven to ten percent of the population), of which perhaps two-thirds live in the south. The south is also home to the majority of the one million or so adherents to the **Protestant** faith, known as *Tin Lanh*, or the Good News, which was introduced by Canadian and American missionaries in the early twentieth century. Perhaps two-thirds of Protestants belong to ethnic-minority groups in the central highlands and northwest mountains. There's evidence that the number of adherents has been growing rapidly, despite government restrictions on proselytizing.

The first Christian **missionaries** to reach Vietnam were Portuguese and Spanish Dominicans who landed briefly on the north coast in the sixteenth century. They were followed in 1615 by French and Portuguese Jesuits, dispatched by the pope to establish the first permanent missions. Among the early arrivals was the Frenchman Alexandre de Rhodes (see box, p.436), a Jesuit who impressed the northern Trinh lords and won, by his reckoning, nearly seven thousand converts. The inevitable **backlash** against Christianity, which opposed ancestor worship and espoused subversive ideas such as equality, was not long in coming. In 1630 the Trinh lords expelled all Christians, including de Rhodes, who returned to France where he helped create the Society of

Foreign Missions (*Société des Missions Etrangères*). This society soon became the most active proselytizing body in Indochina; by the end of the eighteenth century it had claimed thousands of converts, particularly in the coastal provinces.

Official attitudes towards Christianity fluctuated over the centuries, though the Vietnamese kings were generally suspicious of the Church's increasingly political role. The most violent **persecutions** occurred during the reign of Minh Mang (1820–41), an ardent Confucian, and reached a peak after 1832. Churches were destroyed, the faces of converts were branded with the words *ta dao*, meaning "false religion", and many of those refusing to renounce their faith were killed; 117 martyrs, both European and Asian, were later canonized. Such repression, much exaggerated at the time, provided the French with a pretext for greater involvement in Indochina, culminating in full colonial rule at the end of the nineteenth century.

European influence

Not surprisingly, Catholicism **prospered** under the French regime. Missions re-opened and hundreds of churches, schools and hospitals were built. Vietnamese Catholics formed an educated elite among a population that counted some two million faithful by the 1950s. When partition came in 1954 many Catholics chose to move south, partly because of their opposition to Communism and partly because the new leader of South Vietnam, President Ngo Dinh Diem, was a Catholic. Of the estimated nine hundred thousand Vietnamese who left the North in 1954, it's said that around two-thirds were Catholic; many of these became refugees a second time in the 1970s.

Diem actively discriminated in favour of the Catholic community, which he viewed as a bulwark against Communism. As a result he alienated large sections of the population, most importantly Buddhists whose protests eventually contributed to his downfall. Meanwhile in North Vietnam the authorities trod fairly carefully with those Catholics who had chosen to stay, allowing them freedom to practise their religion, but the Church was severely restricted and reports of persecution persisted.

After reunification, churches were permitted to function but still came under strict **surveillance**, with all appointments controlled by the government, and members of the Church hierarchy frequently received heavy jail sentences for opposition to the regime. Since 1986 the party has been working to reduce the tension by re-opening seminaries, allowing the Church to resume religious educational work and releasing some clergy from prison. Catholics throughout Vietnam now regularly attend Mass, and, when the previous Cardinal of Hanoi died in 1990, thousands attended the funeral in the largest postwar demonstration of Catholic faith. Since the government still insists on vetting all appointments, it took more than seven years to find a new cardinal acceptable to both Vietnam and the Vatican. However, relations between the two continue to improve. All the bishoprics are now filled and there's even talk of re-establishing diplomatic relations in the not too distant future. A senior Vatican emissary visited Hanoi in 2005, though it will undoubtedly be several years before the much hoped-for papal visit occurs.

Protestant problems

The situation is not quite so rosy as regards Vietnam's **Protestant** communities. While the government now officially recognizes the Southern Evangelical Church of Vietnam (SECV) and the smaller Evangelical Church of Vietnam (ECVN), based in the north, it remains deeply suspicious of another evangelical branch known as "Dega Protestantism" practised mainly by the ethnic minorities of the **central highlands**. It's not so much the belief system itself that the authorities are concerned about, but the movement's potential as a political force and, specifically, its alleged association with demands from certain minority groups for greater autonomy. There have been (sometimes violent) clashes between ethnic minorities in the central highlands and the authorities in recent years (see p.465). While the protests were generally sparked by disputes over land and continued poverty, some demonstrators also cited **religious persecution** among their grievances. As a result, the government imposed significant restrictions on all Protestant churches in the region. The government continues to keep a close eye on all Christian activity in the central highlands – as recently as 2010 propaganda campaigns were launched against Catholic sects, and forced renunciation ceremonies took place in Gia Lai province.

Cao Dai

Social upheaval coupled with an injection of Western thinking in the early twentieth century gave birth to Vietnam's two indigenous religious sects, **Cao Dai** and Hoa Hao. Of the two, Cao Dai claims more adherents, with an estimated following of around two million in south Vietnam, plus a few thousand among overseas Vietnamese in America, Canada and Britain. The sect's headquarters, the **Holy See**, resides in a flamboyant cathedral at Tay Ninh (see p.109), where it also maintains a school, agricultural cooperative and hospital. Vietnam's most northerly Cao Dai congregation worships in Hue.

The religion of Cao Dai (meaning "high place") was revealed by the "Supreme Being" to a middle-aged civil servant working in Phu Quoc called **Ngo Van Chieu** during several trances over a period of years from 1919 to 1925 (see p.110). What Chieu preached to his followers was essentially a distillation of Vietnam's religious heritage: elements of Confucian, Taoist and Buddhist thought, intermixed with ancestor worship, Christianity and Islam. According to Cao Dai beliefs, all religions are different manifestations of one **meta-religion**, Cao Dai; in the past, this took on whatever form most suited the prevailing human need, but during the twentieth century could finally be presented in its unity. Thus the **Supreme Being**, who revealed himself in 1925, has had two earlier manifestations, always in human guise: the first in the sixth century BC, appearing as various figures from Buddhism, Taoism and Christianity among many other saints and sages; the second as Sakyamuni, Confucius, Jesus Christ, Mohammed and Lao-tzu. In the third manifestation the Supreme Being has revealed himself through his divine light, symbolized as an all-seeing Eye on a sky-blue, star-spangled globe.

Cao Dai **doctrine** preaches respect for all its constituent religions and holds that individual desires should be subordinate to the common interest. Adherents seek to escape from the cycle of reincarnation by following the five prohibitions: no violence, theft or lying – nor indulgence in alcohol or sexual activity; priests are expected to be completely vegetarian though others need only eschew meat on certain days of the lunar month. The Cao Dai **hierarchy** is modelled on that of the Catholic Church, and divides into nine ranks, of which the pope is the highest. Officials are grouped into three branches, identifiable by the colour of their ceremonial robes: the Confucian branch dresses in red, Buddhist in saffron and Taoist in blue. Otherwise practitioners wear white as a symbol of purity, and because it contains every colour.

Practising Cao Dai

The **rituals** of Cao Dai are a complex mixture of Buddhist and Taoist rites, including meditation and seances. Prayers take place four times a day in the temples (6am, noon, 6pm and midnight) though ordinary members are only required to attend on four days per month and otherwise can pray at home. Note that shoes should always be removed when entering a Cao Dai temple or mansion. At the start of the thirty-minute-long ceremony, worshippers file into the temple in three columns, women on the left, men in the middle and on the right; they then kneel and bow three times – to the Supreme Being, to the earth and to mankind. Cao Dai's most important **ceremony**, a sort of feast day for the Supreme Being, takes place on the ninth day of the first lunar month; other special observances are the day of Taoism (fifteenth day of the second month), Buddha's birthday (fifteenth of the fourth month), the day of Confucius (28th of the eighth lunar month) and Christmas Day.

The religion of Cao Dai is further enlivened with a panoply of **saints**, encompassing the great and the good of many countries and cultures: Victor Hugo, Joan of Arc, William Shakespeare, Napoleon Bonaparte, Lenin, Winston Churchill, Louis Pasteur and Sun Yat Sen, alongside home-grown heroes such as Tran Hung Dao and Le Loi. These characters fulfil a variety of roles from prophet to bodhisattva and even spirit medium, through which followers communicate with the Supreme Being. Contact can occur by means of a ouija board, messages left in sealed envelopes or through human mediums – who enter a trance and write using a planchette (a pencil secured to a wooden board on castors). Apparently, adherents of Cao Dai once appointed an official to take down the further works of Victor Hugo by dictation from his spirit.

The ideology, which had widespread appeal, attracted **converts** in their hundreds of thousands in the Mekong Delta, but only gained official recognition from the French colonial authorities in 1926. Over the next decade the Holy See developed into a **semi-autonomous state** wielding considerable political power and backed by a paramilitary wing which mustered around fifty thousand men in the mid-1950s. Although originally nationalist, Cao Dai followers clashed with Communist troops in a local power struggle, and the sect ended up opposing both the North Vietnamese and President Diem's pro-Catholic regime. Diem moved quickly to dismantle the army when he came to power and exiled its leaders; then after 1975 the Communists purged the religious body, closing down Cao Dai temples and schools, and sending priests for re-education. However, Cao Dai survived as a religion and has gained some **new adherents** since 1990 when its temples and mansions, approximately four hundred in all, were allowed to re-open, albeit under strict control.

Hoa Hao

The second of Vietnam's local sects, **Hoa Hao**, meaning "peace and kindness", emerged in the late 1930s near Chau Doc in the Mekong Delta (see p.136). The movement was founded by a young mystic, **Huynh Phu So**, who disliked mechanical ritual and preached a very pure, simple form of Buddhism that required no clergy or other intermediaries, and could be practised at home by means of meditation, fasting and prayer. Gambling, alcohol and opium were prohibited, while filial piety was once more invoked to promote social order.

As a young man Huynh Phu So was cured of a mysterious illness by the monks of Tra Son Pagoda near his home town of Chau Doc. He continued to live at the pagoda, studying under the monk Xom, but returned to his home village after Xom died. During a storm in 1939, So entered a trance from which he emerged to develop his own Buddhist way. The sect quickly gained followers and, like Cao Dai, was soon caught up in **nationalist politics**. To the French, So was a mad but dangerous subversive; they committed him to a psychiatric hospital (where he promptly converted his doctor to Hoa Hao), and then placed him under house arrest. During **World War II** Hoa Hao followers were armed by the Japanese and later continued to fight against the French while also opposing the Communists. At the end of the war Hoa Hao members formed an anti-Marxist political party, prompting the Viet Minh to assassinate So in 1947.

However, the movement continued to grow, its **private army** equalling the Cao Dai's in size, until Diem came to power and effectively crushed the sect's political and military arm. The sect then splintered, with some members turning to the National Liberation Front, while most sided with the Americans. As a result, when the Communists took over in 1975 many Hoa Hao leaders were arrested and its priesthood was disbanded. Nevertheless some claim that there are now over 1.5 million Hoa Hao practising in the Mekong Delta. The government recognized the principal Hoa Hao sect in 1999, although its more radical offshoots, which are accused of anti-government activities, remain outlawed.

Vietnam's ethnic minorities

The population of Vietnam currently numbers just over ninety million people, of whom around 86 percent are ethnic Vietnamese (known as Viet or Kinh), while almost nine hundred thousand are Chinese, or Hoa, in origin. The remaining eleven million people comprise 53 ethnic minority groups divided into dozens of subgroups, some with a mere hundred or so members, giving Vietnam the richest and most complex ethnic make-up in the whole of Southeast Asia. The vast majority of Vietnam's minorities live in the hilly regions of the north and central highlands – all areas that saw heavy fighting in recent wars – and several groups straddle today's international boundaries.

Little is known about the origins of many of these people, some of whom already inhabited the area before the ancestors of the **Viet** arrived from southern China around four to five thousand years ago. At some point the Viet emerged as a distinct group from among the various indigenous peoples living around the Red River Delta and then gradually absorbed smaller communities until they became the dominant culture. Other groups continued to interact with the Viet people, but either chose to maintain their independence in the highlands or were forced up into the hills, off the ever-more-crowded coastal plains.

Vietnamese legend accounts for this fundamental split between **lowlanders** and **highlanders** as follows: the Dragon King of the south married Au Co, a beautiful northern princess, and at first they lived in the mountains where she gave birth to a hundred strong, handsome boys. After a while, however, the Dragon King missed his watery, lowland home and decamped with half his sons, leaving fifty behind in the mountains – the ancestors of the ethnic minorities.

Vietnam's ethnic groups are normally differentiated according to three main **linguistic families** – Austronesian, Austro–Asian and Sino–Tibetan – which are further subdivided into smaller groups, such as the Viet–Muong and Tay–Thai language groups. Austronesians, related to Indonesians and Pacific Islanders, were probably the earliest inhabitants of the area but are now restricted to the central highlands. Peoples of the two other linguistic families originated in southern China and at different times migrated southwards to settle throughout the Vietnamese uplands.

Despite their different origins, languages, dialects and hugely varied traditional dress, there are a number of similarities among the highland groups that distinguish them from Viet people. Most immediately obvious is the **stilthouse**, which protects against snakes, vermin and larger beasts as well as floods, while also providing safe stabling for domestic animals. The communal imbibing of **rice wine** is popular with most highland groups, as are certain **rituals** such as protecting a child from evil spirits by not naming it

---

VIETNAM'S MINORITY PEOPLE

Below is a list of Vietnam's most colourful minority folk, and where best to come into contact with them:

White Thai Mai Chau (see p.416)	**Red Zao** Sa Pa (see p.397)
Black Thai Son La (see p.413)	**Jarai** Pleiku (see p.191)
Flower Hmong Bac Ha (see p.405)	**Bahnar** Kon Tum (see p.196)
Black Hmong Sa Pa (see p.397)	**Cham** Phan Rang (see p.221)

until after a certain age. Most highlanders traditionally practise **swidden farming**, clearing patches of forest land, farming the burnt-over fields for a few years and then leaving it fallow for a specified period while it recovers its fertility. Where the soils are particularly poor, a semi-nomadic lifestyle is adopted, shifting the village location at intervals as necessary.

Recent history

Traditionally, Viet kings demanded tribute from the often fiercely independent ethnic minorities but otherwise left them to govern their own affairs. This relationship changed with the arrival of Catholic missionaries, who won many converts to Christianity among the peoples of the central highlands – called **montagnards** by the French. Under colonial rule the minorities gained a certain degree of local autonomy in the late nineteenth century, but at the same time the French expropriated their land, exacted forced labour and imposed heavy taxes. As elsewhere in Vietnam, such behaviour sparked off rebellions, notably among the Hmong in the early twentieth century.

The northern mountains

The French were quick to capitalize on ancient antipathies between the highland and lowland peoples. In the northwest mountains, for example, they set up a semi-autonomous Thai federation, complete with armed militias and border guards. When war broke out in 1946, groups of Thai, Hmong and Muong in the northwest sided with the French and against the Vietnamese, even to the extent of providing battalions to fight alongside French troops. But the situation was not clear-cut: some Thai actively supported the Viet Minh, while Ho Chi Minh found a safe base for his guerrilla armies among the Tay and Nung people of the northeast. Recognizing the need to secure the minorities' allegiance, after North Vietnam won independence in 1954 Ho Chi Minh created two **autonomous regions**, allowing limited self-government within a "unified multinational state".

The central highlands

The minorities of the **central highlands** had also been split between supporting the French and Viet Minh after 1946. In the interests of preserving their independence, the ethnic peoples were often simply anti-Vietnamese, of whatever political persuasion. After partition in 1954, anti-Vietnamese sentiment was exacerbated when President Diem started moving Viet settlers into the region, totally ignoring local land rights. Diem wanted to tie the minorities more closely into the South Vietnamese state; the immediate result, however, was that the Bahnar, Jarai and E De joined forces in an organized opposition movement and called a general strike in 1958.

Over the next few years this well-armed coalition developed into the United Front for the Liberation of Oppressed Races, popularly known by its French acronym, **FULRO**. They demanded greater autonomy for the minorities, including elected representation at the National Assembly, more local self-government, school instruction in their own language and access to higher education. While FULRO met with some initial success, the movement was weakened after a number split off to join the Viet Cong. An estimated ten thousand or more remained, fighting first of all against the South Vietnamese and the Americans, and then against the North Vietnamese Army until 1975. After this, FULRO rebels and other anti-Communist minority groups, mainly E De, operated out of bases in Cambodia. The few who survived Pol Pot's killing fields later fled to Thailand and were eventually resettled in America.

During the **American War**, those minorities living around the Seventeenth Parallel soon found themselves on the front line. The worst fighting occurred during the late 1960s and early 1970s, when North Vietnamese troops were based in these remote uplands and American forces sought to rout them. Massive bombing raids were augmented by the use of defoliants and herbicides which, as well as denuding protective forest cover, destroyed crops and animals; this chemical warfare also killed an unknown number of people and caused severe long-term illnesses. In addition, villages were often subject to night raids by Viet Cong and North Vietnamese soldiers keen to "encourage" local support and replenish their food supplies.

It's estimated that over two hundred thousand minority people in the central highlands, both civilian and military, were killed as a result of the American War, out of a population of around one million. By 1975, 85 percent of villages in the highlands had been either destroyed or abandoned, while nothing was left standing in the region closest to the Demilitarized Zone. At the end of the war thousands of minority people were living in temporary camps, along with Viet refugees, unable to practise their traditional way of life.

Post-reunification

After reunification things didn't really get much better. Promises of greater autonomy came to nothing; even the little self-government the minorities had been granted was removed. Those groups who had opposed the North Vietnamese were kept under close observation and their leaders sent for re-education. The new government pursued a policy of **forced assimilation** of the minorities into the Vietnamese culture and glossed over their previous anti-Viet activities: all education was conducted in the Vietnamese language, traditional customs were discouraged or outlawed, and minority people were moved from their dispersed villages into permanent settlements. At the same time the government created **New Economic Zones** in the central highlands and along the Chinese border, often commandeering the best land to resettle thousands of people from the overcrowded lowlands. According to official records, 250,000 settlers were moved into the New Economic Zones each year during the 1980s. The policy resulted in food shortages among minorities unable to support themselves on the marginal lands, and the widespread degradation of over-farmed upland soils.

Doi moi brought a shift in policy in the early 1990s, marked by the establishment of a central office responsible for the ethnic minorities. Minority languages are now officially recognized and can be taught in schools, scholarships enable minority people to attend institutes of higher education, television programmes are broadcast in a number of minority languages, and there is now greater representation of minorities at all levels of government. Indeed, in 2001 Nong Duc Manh, a member of the Tay ethnic group, became the first non-Viet secretary general of the Communist Party (though some rumours, which refuse to go away, suggest that his father was a certain Ho Chi Minh). Cash crops such as timber and fruit are being introduced as an alternative to illegal hunting, logging and opium cultivation. Other income-generating schemes are also being promoted and healthcare programmes upgraded.

All this has been accompanied by moves to preserve Vietnam's **cultural diversity**, driven in part by the realization that ethnic differences have greater appeal to tourists. However, in many areas the minorities' traditional lifestyles are fast being eroded and extreme **poverty** is widespread; while minorities constitute around fourteen percent of Vietnam's population, they account for one-third of those living under the poverty line. This, along with grievances over ancestral land rights and religious freedoms, was one of the issues that sparked widespread **demonstrations** by minority people in the central highlands in 2001 and 2004. While the prime minister ordered more favourable land distribution and promised greater socio-economic development for the region, human rights organizations have criticized the authorities for their harsh treatment of demonstrators, some of whom have received jail sentences of up to twelve years. In 2010, more than seventy Montagnards were arrested in Gia Lai province alone. Human Rights Watch estimates that between 2001 and 2011 more than 350 Montagnards from the central highlands were given long prison sentences for reasons that remain dubious; at least 65 of them were arrested trying to seek asylum in Cambodia.

Minorities in the northern highlands

The mountains of northern Vietnam are home to a large number of ethnic groups, all of them originating from southern China. The dominant minorities are the Tay and Thai, both feudal societies who once held sway over their weaker neighbours. These powerful, well-established groups farm the fertile, valley-bottom land, while Hmong and Dao people, who only arrived in Vietnam at the end of the eighteenth century, occupy the least hospitable land at the highest altitudes. These isolated groups have been better able to lead an independent life and to preserve their traditional customs, though most exist at near-subsistence levels. Local **markets**, usually held at weekly intervals, fulfil an important role in social and economic life in the highlands; the best known are at Sa Pa and Bac Ha, though there are others throughout the area. Most groups maintain a tradition of **call-and-response singing**, which is performed at ceremonies and festivals.

Dao

Population: 500,000 • Based in: Lao Cai, Ha Giang

The **Dao** (pronounced "Zao") ethnic minority is incredibly diverse in all aspects of life: social and religious practices, architecture, agriculture and dress. For several centuries, small, localized groups have settled in the northern border region after crossing over from China; there are related groups in Laos, Thailand and China.

Long ago the Dao adopted the Chinese writing system and they have a substantial literary tradition. One popular legend records the origin of the twelve Dao clans: Ban Ho, a powerful dog of five colours, killed an enemy general and was granted the hand of a princess in marriage, who gave birth to twelve children. Ban Ho is worshipped by the Dao and the five colours of Dao embroidery represent their ancestor. The Dao boast a particularly striking traditional dress, the most eye-catching element of which is a bulky red turban. Dao people live at all altitudes, their house style and agricultural techniques varying accordingly. While groups living at lower levels are relatively prosperous, growing rice and raising livestock, those in the high, rocky mountains live in considerable poverty.

Giay

Population: 50,000 • Based in: Lao Cai, Lai Chau, Ha Giang

The **Giay** (pronounced "Zay") are a relatively small minority group. Traditional society is feudal, with a strict demarcation between the local aristocracy and the peasant classes. All villagers work the communal lands, living in closely knit villages of stilthouses. A few Giay women still wear the traditional style of dress, distinguished by the highly coloured, circular panel sewn around the collar and a shirt-fastening on the right shoulder; the shirt itself is often of bright green, pink or blue. On formal occasions, women may also wear a chequered turban.

Hmong

Population: 800,000 • Based in: the north, villages at high altitude

Since the end of the eighteenth century, groups of Miao people have been fleeing southern China, heading for Laos, Burma, Thailand and Vietnam. Miao meant "barbarian", whereas their adopted name, **Hmong**, means "free people". Poor farming land, geographical isolation and their traditional seclusion from other people have left the Hmong one of the most impoverished groups in Vietnam; standards of health and education are low, while infant mortality is exceptionally high. Hmong farmers grow maize, rice and vegetables on burnt-over land, irrigated fields and terraced hillsides. Traditionally they also grow poppies, though this is now discouraged by the government. Hmong people raise cattle, buffaloes and horses, and have recently started growing fruit trees, such as peach, plum and apple. They are also skilled hunters and gather forest products, including honey, medicinal herbs, roots and bark, either for their own consumption or to trade at weekly markets. Hmong houses are built flat on the ground, rather than raised on stilts.

Until recently there was no written Hmong language, but a strong oral tradition of folk songs, riddles and proverbs. Perhaps the Hmong are best known, however, for their handicrafts, particularly weaving hemp and cotton, cloth which is then coloured with indigo dyes. Many Hmong women, and some men, still wear traditional indigo apparel and chunky silver jewellery. The main subgroups are **White**, **Red**, **Green**, **Black** and **Flower Hmong**; though the origin of the names is unknown, there are marked differences in dialect and social customs as well as dress and hairstyle, especially among the women.

Muong

Population: 1.2 million • Based in: Yen Bai, Son La, Thanh Hoa

The lower hills from the Red River Valley are the domain of the **Muong** ethnic minority, with the majority now living in Hoa Binh Province. The Muong are believed to share common ancestors with the Viet. It's thought that the two groups split around two thousand years ago, after which the Muong developed relatively independently in the highlands. Society is traditionally dominated by aristocratic families, who distribute communal land to the villagers in return for labour and tax contributions; the symbols of their authority are drums and bronze gongs.

Muong stilthouses are similar to those built by the Thai, and the main staple is rice, though fishing, hunting and gathering are all still fairly important. Muong people have a varied cultural tradition, including call-and-response singing and epic tales, and they are famed for their embroidery, typically creating bold geometric designs in black and white. Older Muong women continue to wear the traditional long black skirt and close-fitting shirt; a broad, heavily embroidered belt is the main accessory, and many women also wear a simple white headscarf.

Nung

Population: 750,000 • Based in: Cao Bang, Lang Son

Nung people are closely related to the Tay, sharing the same language and often living in the same villages. Nung farmers terrace the lower slopes to provide extra land, and are noted for the wide variety of crops they grow, including maize, groundnuts and a whole host of vegetables. In fact, the Nung are reckoned to be the best horticulturalists in Vietnam, while their blacksmiths are almost as renowned. Unusually, the traditional Nung house has clay walls and a tiled roof, and is built either flat on the ground or with only one section raised on stilts.

Most Nung are Buddhist, worshipping Quan Am, though they also honour the spirits and their ancestors. They are particularly adept at call-and-response singing, relishing the improvised double entendre. Not surprisingly, Nung traditional dress is similar to that of the Tay, though hemmed with coloured bands. Women often sport a neck scarf with brightly coloured fringes and a shoulder bag embroidered with the sun, stars and flowers, or woven in black and white interspersed with delicately coloured threads.

Tay

Population: 1.5 million • Based in: Cao Bang, Lang Son, Bac Kan

The **Tay** are Vietnam's largest minority group living in the highlands, and are concentrated in the northeast, from the Red River Valley east to the coastal plain, where they settled over two thousand years ago. Through centuries of close contact with lowlanders, Tay society has been strongly influenced by Viet culture, sharing many common rituals and Confucian practices.

Many Tay have now adopted Viet architecture and dress, but it's still possible to find villages of thatched stilthouses, characterized by a railed balcony around the building. Nowadays it's largely the women who still wear the Tay's traditional long, belted dress of indigo-dyed cloth, with a similarly plain, knotted headscarf peaked at the front and set off with lots of silver jewellery. Tay farmers are famous for their animal husbandry, and they also specialize in fish-farming and growing high-value crops, such as anise, tobacco, soya and cinnamon.

The Tay have developed advanced irrigation systems for wet-rice cultivation, including the huge waterwheels found beside rivers in the northeast. They have had a written language – based on Chinese ideograms – since the fifteenth century, fostering a strong literary tradition; call-and-response singing is also popular, as are theatrical performances, kite-flying and a whole variety of other games. Some Tay groups in the more remote regions occasionally erect a funeral house, decorated with fluttering slips of white paper, over a new grave.

Thai
Population: 1.3 million • Based in: Dien Bien Phu, Son La, Mai Chau

The **Thai** minority is the dominant group in the northwest mountains from the Red River south to Nghe An, though most live in Lai Chau and Son La provinces. They are distantly related to the Thai of Thailand and to groups in southern China, their ancestral homeland. However, Thai people have been living in Vietnam for at least two thousand years and show similarities with both Viet and Tay cultures. Traditional Thai society was strongly hierarchical, ruled over by feudal lords who controlled vast land-holdings worked by the villagers. Their written language, which is based on Sanskrit, has furnished a literary legacy dating back five centuries, including epic poems, histories and a wealth of folklore. The Thai are also famous for their unique dance repertoire and finely woven brocades decorated with flowers, birds and dragons, which are on sale in local markets. From their early teens women learn how to weave and embroider, eventually preparing a set of blankets for their dowry. Thai houses are often still constructed on stilts, with wood or bamboo frames, though the architecture varies between regions.

There are two main subgroups: **Black Thai** (around Dien Bien Phu, Tuan Giao and Son La) and **White Thai** (Mai Chau, Muang Lay), whose names are often attributed to the traditional colour of the women's shirts, though this is open to dispute. Both groups wear long, narrow skirts and fitted shirts, topped with an intricately embroidered headdress.

Minorities in the central highlands

Nearly all minority groups living in the central highlands are indigenous peoples; most are matrilineal societies with a strong emphasis on community life and with some particularly complex burial rites. Catholic **missionaries** enjoyed considerable success in the central highlands, establishing a mission at Kon Tum in the mid-nineteenth century; then early in the twentieth century Protestantism was also introduced to the region. Most converts came from among the E De and Bahnar, though other groups have also incorporated Christian practices into their traditional belief systems and the number of converts has been increasing in recent years. Likewise, **Vietnamese influence** has been stronger here than in northern Vietnam, while the **American War** caused severe disruption. Nevertheless, their cultures have been sufficiently strong to resist complete assimilation. For how much longer is a matter of debate, as thousands of lowland Viets, plus significant numbers of northern minorities, are moving into the region, clearing huge swathes of land for coffee plantations on the back of a booming export market.

Bahnar (Ba Na)
Population: 170,000 • Found in: Kon Tum

Now a highland people, the **Bahnar** trace their ancestry back many centuries to communities coexisting on the coastal plains with the Cham and Jarai. The most distinctive aspect of a Bahnar village is its *rong*, or communal house, the roof of which may be up to 20m high. This is the centre of village cultural and ceremonial life, and also the home of adolescent boys, who are taught Bahnar history, the skills of hunting and other manly matters. Village houses grouped around the *rong* are typically stilthouses with a thatched or tiled roof, and are often decorated with geometric motifs.

The Bahnar people are skilled horticulturalists, growing maize, sweet potato or millet, together with indigo, hemp or tobacco as cash crops. Bahnar groups also erect funeral houses decorated with elaborate carvings, although they are less imposing than those of the Jarai. Sometime after the burial, wooden statues, gongs, wine jars and other items of family property are placed in the funeral house.

E De
Population: 270,000 • Found in: Dak Lak

People of the **E De** minority live in stilthouses grouped together in a village, or *buon*. These longhouses, which can be up to 100m in length, are boat-shaped with hardwood frames, bamboo floors and walls, and topped with a high thatched roof. As many as a hundred family members may live in a single house, under the authority of the oldest or most respected woman, who owns all family property, including the house and domestic animals; wealth is indicated by the number of ceremonial gongs. Other much prized heirlooms are the large earthenware jars used for making the rice wine drunk at festivals. Like the Jarai, E De people worship the kings of Fire and Water among a whole host of animist spirits, and also erect a funeral house on their graves. Both the original longhouse and its grave-site replica are often decorated with fine carvings.

The E De homeland lies in a region of red soils on the rolling western plateaux. In the nineteenth and twentieth centuries French settlers introduced coffee and rubber estates to the area, often seizing land from the local people they called Rhadé. Traditional swidden farming has gradually been disappearing, a process accelerated by the American War and the forced relocation of E De into permanent settlements.

Jarai (Gia Rai)
Population: 300,000 • Based in: Gia Lai

The **Jarai** are the largest minority group in the central highlands. It's thought that they left the coastal plains around two thousand years ago, settling on the fertile plateau around Pleiku. Some ethnologists hold that Cham people are in fact a branch of the Jarai, and they certainly share common linguistic traits and a matrilineal social order. Young Jarai women initiate the marriage proposal and afterwards the couple live in the wife's family home, with children taking their mother's name. Houses are traditionally built on stilts, facing north. The focus of village life is the communal house, or *rong*, where the council of elders and their elected chief meet.

Animist beliefs are still strong, and the Jarai world is peopled with spirits, the most famous of which are the kings of Water, Fire and Wind, represented by shamans who are involved in rain-making ceremonies and other rituals. Funeral rites are particularly complex and expensive: each family maintains a funeral house which they ornament with evocative sculptures of people, birds and objects from everyday life. The Jarai also have an extensive musical repertoire, the principal instruments being gongs and the unique *k'long put*, made of bamboo tubes into which the players force air by clapping their hands. During the American War the majority of Jarai villagers moved out of their war-torn homeland, many being resettled in Pleiku; only in recent years are some slowly returning.

Koho (Co Ho) and Lat
Population: 130,000 • Based in: Da Lat

The **Koho** minority is subdivided into six highly varied subgroups, including the **Lat**. The typical Koho house is built on stilts with a thatched roof and bamboo walls and flooring. Although many Koho were converted to Christianity in the early twentieth century, spirit worship is widely practised and each family adopts a guardian spirit from the natural world. Catholic missionaries developed a phonetic script for the Koho language but the oral tradition remains strong. Unlike many minorities in this region, the Koho incorporate dance into their religious rites, and it is an important element of them; a variety of musical instruments, such as gongs, bamboo flutes and buffalo horns, are also involved. Subgroups of the Koho minority are famed for their pottery and ironwork, whereas Lat farmers have a reputation for constructing sophisticated irrigation systems.

Mnong

Population: 90,000 • Based in: Dak Lak, Da Lat

The **Mnong** ethnic minority is probably best known for its skill in hunting elephants and domesticating them for use in war, for transport and for their ivory. Mnong people are also the creators of the lithophone, a kind of stone xylophone thought to be among the world's most ancient musical instruments; an example is on show at the Ethnographic Museum in Buon Ma Thuot (see p.189). Mnong houses are usually built flat on the ground and, though the society is generally matrilineal, village affairs are organized by a male chief. Mnong craftsmen are skilled at basketry and printing textiles, while they also make the copper, tin and silver jewellery worn by both sexes. In traditional burial rituals a buffalo-shaped coffin is placed under a funeral house which is peopled with wooden statues and painted with black, red or white designs.

Sedang (Xo Dang)

Population: 130,000 • Based in: Kon Tum

The **Sedang** were traditionally a warlike people whose villages were surrounded with defensive hedges, barbed with spears and stakes, and with only one entrance. Inter-village wars were frequent, and the Sedang also carried out raids on the peaceable

---

VIETNAM'S REAL-LIFE KURTZ

The Sedang played their part in one of colonial Vietnam's oddest interludes and one which finds echoes in Joseph Conrad's novella *Heart of Darkness*, in which a mysterious voyager named Kurtz proclaims himself king, deep in the Belgian Congo – a story later borrowed by Francis Ford Coppola for his film *Apocalypse Now* (see p.495).

The career of French rogue **Marie-David de Mayréna** was a chequered one to say the least. After a stint with the French army in Cochinchina in the mid-1860s, he made his way back to Paris, only to return to the East after having failed as a banker. Back in Vietnam by the 1880s, he established himself as a planter around Ba Ria, until 1888 when the governor sent him to explore the highlands. Of the hundred or so porters and soldiers who accompanied him, only one, a Frenchman named Alphonse Mercurol, remained by the time he reached Kon Tum. Through the contacts of the French missionaries based there, Mayréna was able to arrange meetings with local tribal chiefs; soon the leaders fell under the spell of his "blue eyes" and "bold, confident stare", and he conspired to proclaim himself **King Marie I of Sedang**, while Mercurol adopted the title "Marquis of Hanoi". For three months, Mayréna ruled from a straw hut flying the national flag (a white cross on a blue background, with a red star in the centre), legislating, creating an army and even declaring war on the neighbouring Jarai people.

But Mayréna was more interested in money than sovereignty, and within months he had decamped, setting off in the hope of getting some mileage from his "title". In his book *Dragon Ascending* Henry Kamm quotes an erstwhile manager of Saigon's *Continental*, where Mayréna boarded on credit with assorted courtiers: "Alas, when, several days later, Mayréna moved out of the hotel, nothing was left to Laval [the then hotel manager] as payment for his services, except for a decoration, that of the National Order of the Kingdom of the Sedangs, which the king gave him before departure." Returning to Europe, Mayréna took to selling fictitious titles and mining concessions to raise cash but, inevitably, cracks began to appear in his story, and he fled back to Southeast Asia in 1890 where he died in penury on Malaya's Tioman Island, supposedly of a snake bite.

Bahnar, mainly to seize prisoners rather than territory. In the past, Sedang religious ritual involved human sacrifices to propitiate the spirits – a practice that was later modified into a profitable business, selling slaves to traders from Laos and Thailand.

In the 1880s, an eccentric French military adventurer called Marie-David de Mayréna established a kingdom in Sedang territory by making treaties with the local chiefs (see box, p.471). A few decades later, the French authorities conscripted Sedang labour to build Highway 14 from Kon Tum to Da Nang; conditions were so harsh that many died, provoking a rebellion in the 1930s. Soon after, the Viet Minh won many recruits among the Sedang in their war against the French. In the American War some Sedang groups fought for the Viet Cong while others were formed into militia units by the American Special Services. But when fighting intensified after 1965, Sedang villagers were forced to flee, and many now live in almost destitute conditions, having lost their ancestral lands.

Each Sedang extended family occupies a longhouse, built on stilts and usually facing east; central to village life is the communal house where young men and boys sleep, and where all the major ceremonies take place. Because villages historically had relatively little contact with each other, there are marked variations between the social customs of the subgroups, and so far seventeen Sedang dialects have been identified. Agricultural techniques are more consistent, mainly swidden farming supplemented by horticulture and hunting. Some Sedang farmers employ a "water harp", a combined bird-scarer, musical instrument and appeaser of the spirits. The harp consists of bamboo tubes linked together and placed in a flowing stream to produce an irregular, haunting sound.

Minorities in the southern lowlands

As the Viet people pushed down the coastal plain and into the Mekong Delta they displaced two main ethnic groups, the Cham and Khmer, whose descendants remain today.

Cham

Population: 130,000 • Based in: Ninh Thuan, Binh Thuan, Cambodian border area

Up until the tenth century powerful **Cham** kings had ruled over most of southern Vietnam (see p.432). Today's surviving coastal communities are still largely Hindu worshippers of Shiva and follow the matrilineal practices of their Cham ancestors; they earn a living from farming, silk-weaving and crafting jewellery of gold or silver. Groups along the Cambodian border are Islamic and, in general, patrilineal. They engage in river fishing, weaving and cross-border trade, with little agricultural activity. On the whole, Cham people have adopted the Vietnamese way of life and dress, though their traditional arts, principally dance and music, have experienced a revival in recent years.

Hoa

Population: 800,000 • Based in: Mekong Delta

Ethnic Chinese people, known in Vietnamese as **Hoa**, form one of Vietnam's largest minority groups. Throughout the country's history, Chinese people, mostly from China's southern provinces, have been emigrating to Vietnam as administrators and merchants or as refugees from persecution. In the mid-seventeenth century the collapse of the Ming Dynasty sent a human deluge southwards, and there were other large-scale migrations in the nineteenth century and then the 1940s. Until the early nineteenth century all Hoa, even those of mixed blood, were considered by the Viets to be Chinese. After that date, however, they were admitted to public office and gradually became integrated into Vietnamese society. Nevertheless, the Hoa remain slightly apart, living in close communities according to their ancestral province in China and preserving elements of their own culture, notably their language and traditional lion dances.

THE VIET KIEU

Overseas Vietnamese are known in their homeland as **Viet Kieu**. There are over two million worldwide, the figure rocketing up in the 1980s as 750,000 fled Vietnam by boat (see box, pp.450–451). Many settled in America, Australia and France, but in recent years the Vietnamese government has gradually made it easier for Viet Kieu to return; procedures for sending money back to family members from overseas were also simplified, providing an important source of extra income for individuals and becoming increasingly valuable in the wider economy, especially in the south. Not surprisingly, however, the attitudes of those who stuck it out in Vietnam towards Viet Kieu are ambivalent, and the government itself is unsure about how to handle relations with the Viet Kieu; in general their money and expertise are welcomed but not necessarily their politics, nor their Western ways.

The Hoa have tended to settle in urban areas, typically becoming successful merchants, artisans and business people, and playing an important role in the economy. Viet people have tended to distrust the Hoa, mainly because of their dominant commercial position and their close links with China. After 1975 the Hoa were badly hit when socialist policies were enforced, in what amounted to an anti-Chinese persecution. Tensions rose even further when China invaded Vietnam in 1979 and thousands of Hoa left the country to escape reprisals, forming a large majority of the "boat people" (see box, pp.450–451). It's estimated that up to one third of the Hoa population eventually left Vietnam.

Khmer
Population: 1,000,000 • Based in: Mekong Delta

Ethnic **Khmer** (known in Vietnam as *Kho Me Khrom*) are the indigenous people of the Mekong Delta, including Cambodia; some arrived in Vietnam in the late 1970s as refugees from Pol Pot's brutal regime in Cambodia. Khmer farmers are noted for their skill at irrigation and wet-rice cultivation; it's said that they farm nearly 150 varieties of rice, each suited to specific local conditions. Traditionally, the Khmer live in villages of stilthouses erected on raised mounds above the flood waters, but these days are more likely to build flat on the earth, along canals and roadways. The pagoda, however, is still a distinctive feature of Khmer villages, its brightly patterned roofs decorated with images of the sacred ancestral dragon, the *neak*. Although ancient beliefs persist, since the late thirteenth century the Khmer have been devout followers of Theravada Buddhism, as practised in Cambodia, Laos and Thailand. They produce fine silk and basketry and wear distinctive red and white scarves.

Environmental issues

Vietnam is endowed with a wide variety of fauna and flora, including an unusually high number of bird species and a rich diversity of primates. Current estimates suggest there are over 12,000 plant species, around three hundred mammals and 850 birds, though remote areas are still being explored. Over recent years, particularly in the forest reserves bordering Laos, the identification of several species of plants, butterflies, snakes, birds and even mammals that were previously unknown has caused a sensation in the scientific community.

Such diversity is largely attributable to Vietnam's **range of habitats**, from the north's subalpine limestone mountains to the Mekong Delta's mangrove swamps and the country's 3400km of coastline. However, the list of endangered and **critically endangered species** is also long – over 880 types of animals and plants – as their domains are threatened by population pressure, widespread logging and pollution, particularly along the coastal zone. One of the biggest environmental challenges facing Vietnam is to preserve its rapidly diminishing forest areas by establishing methods of sustainable use.

Happily, the government does at least seem to recognize the value of Vietnam's biodiversity and the need to act quickly. It has now put in place a number of **laws** dealing with environmental issues, the most important being the Environmental Protection Law, revised in 2005, which sets out national policy covering the prevention and control of pollution, the protection, conservation and sustainable use of natural resources and improving environmental quality. The promulgation of a new law on tourism also came about in 2005, which for the first time contains provisions on sustainable tourism from an environmental and social perspective, aiming to encourage greater community participation and spreading the benefits more widely. The law also includes tougher regulations on tourism-related pollution, though ensuring these laws are effectively implemented is a problem.

Ecological warfare

The word "**ecocide**" was coined during the American War, in reference to the quantity of herbicides dropped from the air to deprive the Viet Cong of their safe areas, deep under the triple-canopy forest, and their food crops. The most notorious defoliant used was **Agent Orange**, along with agents Blue and White, all named after the colour of the respective storage containers. Their active ingredient was **dioxin**, a slowly dissolving poison that has a half-life of seven to eleven years in human tissue. It's estimated that over eighty million litres of chemical defoliants were sprayed from American planes crisscrossing the forests and mangrove swamps of South Vietnam and the Demilitarized Zone between 1961 and 1971. Figures vary, but somewhere between twenty and forty percent of the South's land area was sprayed at least once and in some cases more frequently, destroying up to a quarter of the forest cover.

The environmental impact was perhaps greatest on the **mangrove forests**, which are particularly susceptible to defoliants. Spraying destroyed about a half of all Vietnam's mangrove forests, and since they don't regenerate naturally, they have to be replanted by hand, a slow operation with a low success rate. The herbicides also had a severe impact on **soldiers**, both Vietnamese and American, and **villagers** who were caught in the spraying or absorbed dioxins from the food chain and from drinking water.

Children and the elderly were the worst affected: some died immediately from the poisons, while others suffered respiratory diseases, skin rashes and other ailments. Soon it became apparent that the dioxins were also causing abnormally high levels of miscarriage, birth defects, neurological disease and cancers. Surveys suggest that over three million Vietnamese may be affected, many of whom now receive a tiny monthly allowance from the government.

For years, doctors in Ho Chi Minh City's Tu Do Hospital, supported by international experts, have been trying to convince the American government of the link between the use of defoliants and these medical conditions, in the hope of claiming **compensation** for the victims. In 2004, a group of Vietnamese took their case to a New York court, claiming compensation from 37 American chemical companies on behalf of all victims. The case was dismissed in March 2005 on the grounds that the use of defoliants was not prohibited under international law at the time.

Apart from using herbicides, American and South Vietnamese troops cut down swathes of forest land with specially adapted bulldozers, called **Rome Ploughs**. These vehicles were capable of slicing through a three-metre-thick tree trunk, and were used to clear roadsides and riverbanks against ambushes, or to remove vestiges of undergrowth and trees left after the spraying. Finally, there were the **bombs** themselves: an estimated thirteen million tonnes of explosives were dropped during the course of the war, leaving a staggering 25 million bomb craters, the vast majority in the South. In addition to their general destructive power, explosions compact the soil to the point where nothing will grow, and napalm bombs sparked off forest fires. The worst single incident occurred in 1968 when U Minh forest, at the southern tip of Vietnam, burned for seven weeks; 85 percent of its trees were destroyed. It's estimated that overall more than 20,000 square kilometres of Vietnam's forests were destroyed during the American War as a result of defoliation, napalm fires and bombing.

Since the war, Vietnamese environmentalists led by Professor Vo Quy, founder of the Center for Natural Resources and Environmental Studies at Hanoi University, have instigated **reforestation programmes**, slowly coaxing life back into even the worst-affected regions. This has involved pioneering work in regenerating tropical forest, planting native species under a protective umbrella of acacia and eucalyptus.

A symbolically significant success of local environmentalists has been the **return of the Sarus crane** to the Mekong Delta, near the Cambodian border, though the success promises to be short-lived. The crane, a stately bird with an elaborate courtship dance, abandoned its nesting grounds when the Americans drained the wetlands and dropped herbicides and then napalm in their attempts to rout Viet Cong soldiers from the marshes. After the war thousands of landless farmers were settled in the area, but the acid soils proved difficult to farm so the provincial governor re-established a portion of the wetlands, thus restoring the cranes' natural habitat. The first Sarus cranes reappeared in 1986, after which Tam Nong Bird Sanctuary, now the Tram Chim National Park (see p.133), was set up to protect the crane and other returning species. Though the population increased initially, in recent years no more than a few dozen have returned to spend the dry season in the delta's wetlands.

Postwar deforestation

Originally, perhaps 75 percent of Vietnam's land area would have been covered by forest. By 1945 it had dwindled to 43 percent and was down to just 24 percent (roughly 80,000 square kilometres) in 1975. Since then, at least another 30,000 square kilometres of forest have been lost to commercial **logging**, agricultural **clearance**, forest **fires**, firewood collection and **population pressure**. Cover has now edged back up to 40 percent, however, thanks to one of the world's most ambitious reforestation programmes, launched in 1998, to replant 50,000 square kilometres. Although an impressive 1300 square kilometres are planted each year, this only just exceeds the area

CONSERVATION AND THE NATIONAL PARKS

Vietnam recognized the need for conservation relatively early, establishing its first national park (Cuc Phuong) in 1962 and adopting a **National Conservation Strategy** in 1985. The more accessible or interesting of Vietnam's thirty **national parks** are listed below, but unless you're prepared to spend a lot of time in them, it's unlikely that you'll see many animals. Birds, insects and butterflies are more readily visible and often the dense tropical vegetation or mountain scenery are in themselves worth the journey. To learn more about Vietnam's protected areas, and how to access them, Fauna and Flora International's *Ecotourism Map of Vietnam* is quite useful, though it hasn't been updated since 2005; all proceeds go to support Vietnamese primate conservation. For further information about biodiversity in Vietnam, search the World Conservation Monitoring Centre's comprehensive website, ⓦunep-wcmc.org.

Ba Be (see p.424). A park of 80 square kilometres, containing Vietnam's largest natural lake, over 350 butterfly species and a few extremely rare Tonkin snub-nosed langurs. The park has limited tourist facilities, but boat trips, jungle walks and home-stays in minority villages are possible.

Bach Ma (see p.274). This park of 220 square kilometres sits on the climatological divide between the tropical forests of the south and the northern sub-tropical zone, and contains Vietnam's lushest tropical rainforests. It is also home to a wide variety of bird species, including several rare pheasants, and over 1400 recorded plants. Bach Ma is well set up for tourism, with a network of marked trails, campsites and guesthouses.

Cat Ba (see p.334). The park covers only 152 square kilometres, but 5400 of these are important marine reserves, including areas of coral reef. The limestone island supports a broad range of habitats, a wealth of medicinal plants and a critically endangered population of golden-headed langurs. The park is accessible to tourists either on foot or by boat from Cat Ba Town.

Cat Tien (see p.174). This 740 square-kilometre park was famous for its tiny population of Java rhino, though the last one was shot by a poacher for its horn in 2011. Otherwise the park's wetlands are a haven for water birds, including the critically endangered white-winged duck and white-shouldered ibis, as well as the equally rare Siamese crocodile. Although it's relatively close to Ho Chi Minh City, Cat Tien is not easy to reach by public transport and tourist facilities are fairly limited.

Cuc Phuong (see p.317). Vietnam's first national park, Cuc Phuong was established in 1962 in an area of limestone hills relatively close to Hanoi. The park covers 220 square kilometres and contains a number of unique, ancient trees and provides excellent birdwatching, as well as an opportunity to see some of the world's rarest monkeys in its Endangered Primate Rescue Center. Cuc Phuong is one of the most accessible parks, where it's possible to hike and stay overnight.

Phong Nha-Ke Bang (see p.311). Established in 2002, this 860 square-kilometre park along the mountain chain bordering Laos is best known for its extensive underground river system. The park itself is home to more than sixty endangered animal species, including several types of langur. Access has recently been expanded to include Thien Duong (Paradise) Cave as well as Phong Nha Cave.

Tram Chim (see p.133). One of Vietnam's most important wetlands ecosystems, comprising 75 square kilometres in the Mekong Delta and providing haven to thousands of overwintering water birds. Its most famous visitors are the critically vulnurable sarus crane, though fewer of these are arriving each year.

Yok Don (see p.191). Lying on the border with Cambodia, Yok Don constitutes 1115 square kilometres carved out of Vietnam's most extensive forests. The area is also one of the most biologically diverse in the whole of Indochina, supporting rare Indochinese tigers and Asian elephants. Visitors can overnight in minority villages and camp; elephant-back rides are also on offer.

To support environmental programmes already taking place in Vietnam, contact the following organizations:

BirdLife International UK ⓣ01223 277318, ⓦbirdlife.org. Trip reports are welcomed by their Hanoi office (ⓔbirdlife@birdlife.org.vn).
Fauna and Flora International UK ⓣ01223 571000, ⓦfauna-flora.org.
International Crane Foundation US ⓣ608 356 9462, ⓦsavingcranes.org.
WWF International Switzerland ⓣ22 364 9111, ⓦwwf.panda.org.

being lost to clearance, and the new growth is largely acacia and eucalyptus rather than native species. The area under "high-quality" native forest continues to shrink, and primary forest constitutes less than one percent of the total.

The **worst-affected areas** are Vietnam's northern mountains, the central province of Nghe An and around Pleiku in the central highlands. In these areas soil erosion is a major problem, and countrywide floods are getting worse as a result of deforestation along the watersheds. Many rare hardwoods are fast disappearing and the fragile ecosystems are no longer able to support a wildlife population forced into ever-smaller pockets of undisturbed jungle. Much of the blame for this rapid reduction in the forest cover is often laid on the **ethnic minorities** who traditionally clear land for farming and rely on the forests for building timber and firewood. However, lowland Vietnamese settling in the mountains have also put pressure on scant resources.

Both lowland Vietnamese and minority people have cleared huge swathes of the central highlands for **coffee plantations**, while the carefully replanted coastal mangrove forest is threatened by uncontrolled development of intensive **prawn farming**. Another significant threat to the forests is the highly lucrative **timber trade**, both legal and illegal. By **replanting**, it's hoped to create sustainable forests for commercial logging and to protect the tiny remaining areas of primary forests, but **enforcement** is hampered by lack of resources. The authorities have devolved the management and protection of the forest reserves to local communities, with some success.

Wildlife

Forest clearance, warfare, pollution and economic necessity have all contributed to the loss of natural habitat and reduced Vietnam's broad species base. In 1994, when Vietnam signed the **Convention on International Trade in Endangered Species** (CITES), which bans the traffic in animals or plants facing extinction, the species list identified 365 animal species in need of urgent protection. Among these, the Java rhino, the world's rarest large mammal, has already become extinct in the country, while no fewer than five of the world's most endangered primate species, including the golden-headed (or Cat Ba) langur and the Tonkin snub-nosed langur, survive in small isolated communities in the northern forests. Other severely endangered species include the Indochina tiger and Asian elephant. Vietnam is also home to around 850 species of **birds**, with the highest number of endemic species in mainland Southeast Asia. Again, many of these are under threat of extinction, including the Vietnamese pheasant, small numbers of which have been recorded in Ha Tinh and Quang Binh provinces.

Hunting continues to be a vital source of local income, as a walk round Vietnamese markets soon reveals. Wild animals and birds are sought after for their meat or to satisfy the demand for **medicinal products** and live specimens, an often illegal (but extremely lucrative) business. Since the border with China was re-opened in the early 1990s, smuggling of rare species has increased, among them the Asiatic black bear, whose gall bladder is prized as a cure for fevers and liver problems; relentless hunting has decimated the population to small numbers in the north. Similarly, Vietnam's population of wild Asian elephants is now reduced to fewer than one hundred individuals, down from two thousand in the 1970s. Not only has their habitat along the Cambodian border declined, but since 1975 poachers have been hunting elephants for their tusks. At least ten elephants were killed in Dak Lak and Dong Nai provinces during 2010 and 2011, and wildlife experts are warning that the Asian elephant could be extinct in Vietnam within a decade.

Fortunately, quite large areas of the Vietnamese interior remain amazingly untouched, especially the Truong Son Mountains north of the Hai Van Pass, the southern central highlands and lowland forests of the Mekong Delta. These isolated areas are rich in **biodiversity** and have yielded spectacular discoveries in recent years. In 1992, Dr John MacKinnon and a team of Vietnamese biologists working in the Vu Quang Nature

Reserve, an area of steamy, impenetrable jungle on the Lao border, identified a species of ox new to science, now known as the **saola**. Two years later the **giant muntjac**, a previously unknown species of **deer**, and a new **carp** were found in the same region, followed in 1997 by a smaller type of muntjac deer and the **grey-shanked douc langur**, and in 1999 by a striped **rabbit** thought to be related to the now extinct Sumatran striped rabbit. Three **new bird species** were also discovered in the late 1990s in the mountains of Kon Tum province: two types of laughing thrush and the black-crowned barwing.

An all-out effort is being made to protect this "biological gold mine" and other similar areas both within Vietnam and over the border in Laos. After the saola was discovered, the reserve was put strictly off limits and the total **protected area** enlarged to almost 1600 square kilometres, with buffer zones and corridors linking the reserve to conservation areas in Laos. The task is fraught with difficulties, such as achieving cross-border cooperation and establishing effective policing of the reserve – especially against poaching and illegal logging – with inadequate personnel and financial resources. At the same time, the authorities have been working to find alternative sources of income and food for people living in or near the reserve, and carrying out educational work on the importance of conservation and its relevance to their daily lives.

In a related scheme, special protection areas have also been established around Yok Don and Ba Be national parks as part of a project to establish models of stable biodiversity conservation. The government has also been adding to the number of national parks and nature reserves over recent years. Among the more recent are U Minh Ha National Park, near the southernmost tip of the Mekong Delta, and Xuan Nha Nature Reserve, in Son La Province in the country's northwest. As a further boost to conservation efforts, in 2000 UNESCO recognized an area of mangrove forest at Can Gio in the Mekong Delta and Cat Tien National Park as Vietnam's first "Man and Biosphere" reserves. Since then another half dozen sites have been added.

Sustainable tourism

There's a growing awareness among tourists and travel companies of the negative impact tourism can have on the environment and local culture – the very things most people come to see. All too often the terms **eco-tourism** and **sustainable tourism** are reduced to mere marketing gimmicks, but behind them lies a serious desire, albeit ambitious, to find a new model of small-scale tourism that contributes to the long-term development of the local community without destroying its traditional social and economic structures or the often fragile environment.

Mass tourism didn't really get going in Vietnam until the mid-1990s. From just over one million in 1995, the number of foreign visitors (including business trips) is projected to top nine million in 2015, while the number of domestic holidaymakers currently stands at around 35 million, and is growing even faster. Not surprisingly, the Vietnamese government is eager to promote tourism as a **key revenue-earner** and has significantly eased visa regulations, among other things, in the hope of attracting more foreign visitors. This sudden influx of sightseers, coupled with a lack of effective planning or control, is putting pressure on some of the country's most famous beauty spots.

In response, the government has gradually introduced a number of laws and initiatives placing greater emphasis on the conservation of the nation's natural – and cultural – heritage. Local authorities in **Hoi An** have banned cars from the centre and put a block on further hotel construction in addition to introducing restrictive pricing to control the flow of tourists. Some of this revenue is being ploughed back into improving the townscape – for example, renovating the old houses, hiding television aerials and burying cables. In **Ha Long Bay**, the problems of notoriously haphazard hotel development are exacerbated by **pollution** from tourist boats

RESPONSIBLE TOURISM

Though domestic tourism has the greatest impact through sheer weight of numbers, international travellers can play a positive role by setting examples of **responsible behaviour**. Various NGOs and groups involved in the travel industry have developed **guidelines** for tourists and travel companies. Some of the most important points are: to avoid buying souvenirs made from endangered species or which damage the environment – notably tortoiseshell, ivory and coral in Vietnam; as far as possible, to eat in local restaurants, buy local produce, employ local guides and stay in home-stays or locally owned hotels – not only is it usually a lot more fun, but also your money is more likely to benefit smaller communities; to be sensitive to the local culture, including appropriate standards of dress; and to adopt a responsible attitude towards drugs, alcohol and prostitution. Finally, when booking tours, ask how much – if anything – the tour company contributes to conservation and community development at its chosen destinations. Tour agents in Vietnam with a reputation for their conscientious approach include Handspan, Buffalo Tours, Sinhbalo, Footprint and Ethnic Travel. Intrepid also has a long track record of engaging in sustainable tourism.

(plastic bags and bottles floating on the water tend to spoil otherwise idyllic views), fish farms and nearby coalfields, and by the presence of a major port. Concern over the future of this World Heritage Site, however, means that the issues are at least being discussed, and various measures, such as more effective management of the caves, have been put in place. One or two more remote islands are also being developed as eco-tourism destinations.

Perhaps the key areas, however, are the **uplands** of north and central Vietnam. These are increasingly popular destinations, both for their outstanding natural beauty and their communities of **ethnic minority people**. In the honey-pot market town of **Sa Pa**, for example, the number of hotels and guesthouses has mushroomed – from none before 1991 to around 180 in 2013 – and the town's famous market attracts more tourists than minority people. Some of these people, disturbed by the unwanted attention and intrusive cameras, now shy away from Sa Pa completely, in favour of more inaccessible markets. Most of the "minority crafts" on sale are actually shipped up from Hanoi and, though they are the major attraction, the minority people themselves receive very little economic benefit from tourism; most goes to Kinh Vietnamese or foreign travel companies.

Sa Pa's superb setting and trekking opportunities will continue to make it a popular destination, and it's likely that nearby towns such as Sin Ho and Bac Ha will be developed further. The challenge is how to achieve this in a way that contributes to the **long-term development** of the local community while also preserving cultural and biological diversity. Among other initiatives, the Netherlands Development Organization (SNV; Ⓦsnvworld.org), an NGO active in developing **community-based tourism** in many countries, including Vietnam, is working with local authorities to draw up tourism development plans and to raise awareness of sustainable development issues. It has established a tourism information centre in Sa Pa and has provided training for local guides and hotel and restaurant owners. In Sa Pa and Son La, SNV has also helped devise trekking routes and supported local communities in managing visitor numbers, ensuring revenue is equitably distributed and establishing a code of conduct expected of tourists and tour agents.

The international conservation body Flora and Fauna International (FFI; Ⓦfauna-flora.org) is also active in Vietnam, helping develop **community-based eco-tourism**. In Pu Luong Nature Reserve (see p.316), for example, FFI helped install toilets and washing facilities and supplied bedding and mosquito nets in minority villages wishing to set up home-stays. At the same time, it also provided training in home-stay management and service provision and helped promote the reserve as an eco-tourism destination.

Music and theatre

The binding element in all Vietnam's traditional performing arts is music, and particularly singing (*hat*), which is a natural extension to an already musical language. The origins of Vietnamese music can be traced back as far as the bronze drums and flutes of Dong Son, and further again to the lithophone (stone xylophone) called the *dan da*, the world's oldest known instrument. The Chinese influence is evident in operatic theatre and stringed instruments, while India bestowed rhythms, modal improvisations and several types of drum. Much later, especially during the nineteenth century, elements of European theatre and music were coopted, while during the twentieth century most Vietnamese musicians received a classical, Western training based on the works of Eastern bloc composers such as Prokofiev and Tchaikovsky.

From this multicultural melting pot Vietnamese artists have generated a variety of musical and theatrical forms over the centuries, though, surprisingly, **dance** is less developed than in neighbouring Thailand, Cambodia and Laos. The folk tradition is particularly rich, with its improvised courtship songs and the strident, sacred music of trance dances, to which the more than fifty ethnic minorities add their own repertoire of songs and instruments.

Traditionally, the professions of artists or performers were hereditary, but the wars and political upheavals of the twentieth century have contributed to the loss of much of this largely oral tradition. While certain art forms continue to attract new talent, the younger generation is, on the whole, more interested in higher-paid professions and Vietnamese pop. As revolutionary ("red") music has waned since 1986, so pre-1975 music from the South, previously outlawed as "decadent and reactionary", is back with a vengeance, mixed with a sprinkling of artists from other Asian countries and the West.

Traditional theatre

Vietnam's **traditional theatre**, with its strong Chinese influence, is more akin to opera than pure spoken drama. A musical accompaniment and well-known repertoire of songs form an integral part of the performance, where the plots and characters are equally familiar to the audience. Nowadays, however, the two oldest forms, **Cheo** and **Tuong**, are struggling to survive, while even the more contemporary **Cai Luong** is losing out to television and video. However, other traditional arts have seen something of a revival, most notably **water puppetry** and folk-song performances. The stimulus for this came largely from tourism, but renewed interest in the trance music of **Chau Van** and the complexities of **Tai Tu** chamber music has been very much home-grown.

Hat Cheo

Vietnam's oldest surviving stage art, **Hat Cheo**, or "Popular Opera", has its roots in the Red River Delta where it's believed to have existed since at least the eleventh century. Performances consist of popular legends and everyday events, often with a biting satirical edge, accompanied by a selection of tunes drawn as appropriate from a common fund. Though the movements have become highly stylized over the centuries, Cheo's free form allows the actors considerable room for interpretation; the audience demonstrates its approval, or otherwise, by beating a drum.

Cheo has the reputation of being anti-establishment, with its buffoon character who comments freely on the action, the audience and current events. So incensed were the kings of the fifteenth-century Le Dynasty that Cheo was banned from the court, while artists and their descendants were excluded from public office. Nevertheless, Cheo survived and received official recognition in 1964 with the establishment of the Vietnam Cheo Theatre, charged with reviving the ancient art form. It is now promoted as the country's national theatre, although its local popularity continues to decline despite a body of new work dealing with contemporary issues.

Hat Tuong

Hat Tuong (also known as *Hat Boi* or *Hat Bo*), probably introduced from China around the thirteenth century, evolved from classical Chinese opera, and was originally for royal entertainment before being adopted by travelling troupes. Its story lines are mostly historic events and epic tales dealing with such Confucian principles as filial piety and relations between the monarch and his subjects. Tuong, like Cheo, is governed by rigorous rules in which the characters are rendered instantly recognizable by their make-up and costume. Setting and atmosphere are conjured not by props and scenery but through nuances of gesture and musical conventions with which the audience is completely familiar – and which they won't hesitate to criticize if badly executed. Of the clutch of Tuong troupes still in existence, Hanoi's Vietnam Tuong Theatre is one of the most active.

Hat Cai Luong

While performances of Tuong are comparatively rare events these days, it's still possible to catch an occasional performance of **Hat Cai Luong**, or "Reformed Theatre". Cai Luong originated in southern Vietnam in the early twentieth century, showing a French theatrical influence in its spoken parts, with short scenes and relatively elaborate sets. The action is a tangle of historical drama (such as *The Tale of Kieu*) and racy themes from the street (murder, drug deals, incest, theft and revenge). Its music is a similar hodgepodge: eighteenth-century chamber music played on amplified traditional instruments for the set pieces; electric guitar, keyboards and drums during the scene changes. Cai Luong's constant borrowing from contemporary culture – from language and plots to the incorporation of hit songs – has enabled it to keep pace with Vietnam's social changes. Around thirty professional Cai Luong troupes are currently performing, of which the best known are the Golden Bell Theatre in Hanoi (see p.381) and Ho Chi Minh City's Tran Huu Trang Cai Luong Theatre.

Water puppetry

The origin of **water puppetry** (*mua roi nuoc*) is obscure, beyond that it developed in the flooded rice paddies of the Red River Delta and usually took place in spring when there was less farm work to be done. The earliest record is a stele in Ha Nam Province dated 1121 AD, suggesting that by this date water puppetry was already a regular feature at the royal court.

The art of water puppetry was traditionally a jealously guarded secret handed down from father to son; women were not permitted to learn the techniques in case they revealed them to their husbands' families. This contributed to its decline until the art seemed in danger of dying out altogether. Happily, a French organization, the *Maison des Cultures du Monde*, intervened and, since 1984, with newly carved puppets, a revamped programme and more elaborate staging, Vietnam's water-puppet troupes have played various international capitals to great acclaim – and can be seen daily in Hanoi (see p.381) and Ho Chi Minh City (see p.103). Where before gongs and drums alone were used for scene-setting and building atmosphere, today's national troupes often maintain a larger ensemble, similar to Hat Cheo, including zithers and flutes. The songs are also borrowed from the Cheo repertoire, particularly declamatory styles and popular folk tunes, and the show often includes a short recital of traditional music before the puppets emerge to create their own unique illusion.

Music, dance and song

Quan Ho

One of Vietnam's oldest song traditions is that of **Quan Ho**, or "call-and-response singing", a form which thrives in the Red River Delta, particularly Bac Giang Province, and has parallels among the north's ethnic minorities. These unaccompanied songs are usually heard in spring, performed by young men and women bandying improvised lyrics back and forth. Quan Ho traditionally played a part in the courtship ritual and performers are applauded for their skill in complimenting or teasing their partner, earning delighted approval as the exchange becomes increasingly bawdy.

Hat Chau Van

Found in north and central Vietnam, **Hat Chau Van** is a form of ancient, sacred ritual music used to invoke the spirits during **trance possession ceremonies**. Statues of a pantheon of goddesses are placed in shrines to the Mother Goddess, Thanh Mau, found in Buddhist pagodas and village temples. Throughout the performance of hypnotically rhythmic music (the performers may be one or many, male or female) a medium enters a trance state and is possessed by a chosen deity. Because of the anti-religious stance of the Vietnamese government until 1986, the style was practised in secret, though some pieces were adapted for inclusion in state-sponsored Cheo theatre. Chau Van is currently being revived by older practitioners in its original religious setting, promoted by a class of nouveaux riches keen for the goddesses to intercede and protect their business interests.

Ca Tru

Although the song tradition known as **Ca Tru**, or *Hat A Dao*, dates back centuries, it became all the rage in the fifteenth century when the Vietnamese regained their independence from China. According to legend, a beautiful young songstress, A Dao, charmed the enemy with her songs of the verdant countryside and the way of life in the villages. Fascinated by her voice, the soldiers were encouraged to drink until they became incapacitated and could be pushed into the river and drowned.

The **lyrics** of Ca Tru are often taken from famous poems and are traditionally sung by a woman. The singer also plays a bamboo percussion instrument, and is accompanied by a three-string lute (*dan day*) and drum. She has to master a whole range of singing styles, each differentiated by its particular rhythm, such as *Hat noi* (similar to speech) and *Gui thu* (a more formal style, akin to a written letter). This beguiling genre has undergone a strong revival in Hanoi in recent years, and was recognized by UNESCO as a form of Intangible World Heritage in 2009. It's well worth catching the performances at the Heritage House or the Dinh Kim Ngan in Hanoi (see p.355). In Hue excerpts from the closely related **Ca Hue** song tradition are performed for tourists on sampans on the Perfume River (see p.289).

Nhac Tai Tu

The traditional music accompanying Cai Luong theatre originated in eighteenth-century Hue. Played as pure chamber music, without the voice, it is known as **Nhac Tai Tu**, or "skilled chamber music of amateurs". This is one of the most delightful and challenging of all Vietnamese genres. The players have a great degree of improvisational latitude over a fundamental melodic skeleton; they must think and respond quickly, as in a game, and the resulting independently funky rhythms can be wild. Although modern conservatory training fails to prepare students for this most satisfying of all styles, there is now a resurgence of interest among young players in learning the demands of Tai Tu.

Nha Nhac

It was also in Hue under the Nguyen emperors that the specialized body of **royal music and dance** reached its peak of sophistication. These solemn ceremonial dances again owed their origins to the Chinese courtly tradition and were categorized into a highly complex system according to the occasion on which they would be performed: ritual dances to be held in temples or pagodas, during feasts or at various civil and military functions, and dances to mark particular anniversaries were just some of the distinctions.

As the Imperial court fell under European sway in the twentieth century, so the taste – and opportunity – for such music waned, until the late 1980s when it was revived by the provincial authorities with assistance from UNESCO. Hue's former Royal Theatre has now been renovated and is the venue for occasional performances of courtly music and dance by students of Hue University of Fine Arts. In 2003 UNESCO recognized Nha Nhac ("refined music") as a Masterpiece of Oral and Intangible Heritage.

Traditional instruments

A visiting US general once stepped off a plane with the intention of smoothing relations by attempting a little Vietnamese. This being a tonal language, instead of "I am honoured to be here", listeners heard "the sunburnt duck lies sleeping". The voice and its inherent melodic information are behind all Vietnamese music, and most instruments are, to some extent, made to do what voices do: delicate pitch bends, ornaments and subtle slides. According to classical Confucian theory, instruments fall into eight **categories of sound**: silk, stone, skin, clay, metal, air, wood and bamboo. Although few people play by the rules these days, classical theory also relates five occasions when it is forbidden to perform: at sunset, during a storm, when the preparations have not been made seriously, with improper costumes and when the audience is not paying attention.

String instruments

Many instruments whose strings are now made of steel, gut or nylon originally had **silk** strings; silk is now out of fashion, more for acoustic than ecological reasons. The most famous of these, and unique to Vietnam, is the monochord **dan bau** (or *dan doc huyen*), an ingenious invention perfectly suited to its job of mimicking vocal inflections. It is made from one string (originally silk obtained by yanking apart the live worm), stretched over a long amplified sounding box, fixed at one end. The other end is attached to a buffalo-horn "whammy bar" stalk which can be flexed to stretch or relax the string's tension. Meanwhile the string is plucked with a plectrum at its harmonic nodes to produce overtones that swoop and glide and quiver over a range of three octaves. Other "silk-stringed" instruments include the *dan nguyet* (moon-shaped lute), the *dan tranh* (sixteen-string zither), *dan nhi* (two-string fiddle with the bow running between the strings), *dan day* (a three-stringed lute with a long fingerboard used in Ca Tru and also unique to Vietnam) and *dan luc huyen cam* (a regular guitar with a fingerboard scalloped to allow for wider pitch bends).

Percussion instruments

The *dan da* **stone** lithophone is the world's oldest instrument, consisting of six or more rocks (most commonly eleven) struck with heavy wooden mallets. Several sets have been found originating from one slate quarry in the central highlands where the stones sing like nowhere else. The oldest *dan da* is now in Paris, but other sets exist in museums throughout Vietnam, such as the Ethnographic Museum in Buon Ma Thuot (see p.189).

Various kinds of **drums** (*trong*) are used, played with acrobatic use of the sticks in the air and on the sides. Some originated in China, while others were introduced from

India via the Cham people, such as the double-headed "rice drum" (*trong com*), which was developed from the Indian *mridangam*; the name derives from thin patches of cooked rice paste stuck on each membrane.

Representing **clay**, four thimble-size teacups are held in the fingers and often played as percussion instruments for Hue chamber music. Representing **metal**, the *sinh tien*, **coin clappers**, are another invention unique to Vietnam, combining in one unit a rasping scraper, wooden clapper and a sistrum rattle made from old coins. Bronze **gongs** are occasionally found in minority music, but Vietnam is the only country in Southeast Asia where tuned gamelan-type gong-chimes are not used.

Wind instruments

Air, **wood** and **bamboo** furnish a whole range of wind instruments, such as the many side- and end-blown flutes used for folk songs and to accompany poetry recitals; or the *ken*, a double-reed oboe common across Asia and played, appropriately, in funeral processions and other outdoor ceremonies. Five thin bones often dangle from the *ken* player's mouthpiece to suggest the delicate fingers of a young woman, while disguising the hideous grin necessary to play the instrument. The *song lang* is a slit drum, played by the foot, used to count the measures in Tai Tu skilled chamber music, while the *k'long put*, consisting of racks of bamboo pipes, is the only percussion instrument you don't actually touch but clap in front of. Another instrument from the same folk tradition is the *t'rung*, a type of xylophone made of ladders of tuned bamboo. Some of these instruments can be seen and heard in musical recitals at the Temple of Literature in Hanoi (see p.363).

New folk

Turn on the TV during the Tet Lunar New Year festivities and you can't miss the public face of Vietnamese traditional music: ethnic-costumed dancers, musicians and singers smilingly portraying the happy life of the worker. Fancy arrangements of well-known tunes from all over the country, including some token minorities' music, are spiced up with fancy hats and bamboo pianos. This choreographed entertainment known as **Modernized Folk Music** (*Nhac Dan Toc Cai Bien*) has only been "traditional" since 1956, when the Hanoi Conservatory of Music was founded and the teaching of folk music was deliberately "improved".

For the first time, music was learned from written Western notation (leading to the neglect of improvisational skills while opening the way for huge orchestras), and conductors were employed. Tunings of the traditional eight modes were tempered to accommodate Western-style harmonies, while bizarre new instruments were invented to play bass and to fill out chords in the enlarged bands. Schools, with the mandate of preserving traditional music through "inheritance development", took over from the families and professional apprenticeships, which had formerly been passed on via the oral tradition.

Not surprisingly, a new creature was born out of all this. Trained conservatoire graduates have spread throughout the country and been promoted through competitions and state-sponsored ensembles on TV, radio and even in the lobbies of classier hotels. The new corpus of music and song arrangements has become an emblem of national pride and scientific improvement. Folk songs, melodies from the ethnic minorities, Mozart and Chinese tunes are all ripe fodder for the arranger's pen. Much to the chagrin of the few remaining traditional musicians outside this system, this is now the predominant folk-based music generally heard in public. A visitor to the central highlands asked the local tribal musicians how they felt about their music being "improved". At first they replied what an honour it was for their music to be considered by city people, but after the official interview they privately confessed their horror.

Music for new folk is entertaining and accessible, albeit risking tawdriness; at its best, though, it can be an astonishing display of a lively new art form. One family of six brothers (and one sister-in-law), led by Duc Dau, formed a percussion group in Ho Chi Minh City under the name **Phu Dong**, whose members spent time in the highlands learning the instruments of several minorities. Since 1981 they have played together and developed an infectious musical personality; they still give occasional performances at places like the *Rex Hotel* in Ho Chi Minh City. Circular breathing and lightning-speed virtuosity are just some of the dazzling features of a performance. Most striking, though, is their use of the *dan da* lithophone, a replica of the original, six-thousand-year-old stone *marimba*. The effect of awakening this ancient voice, whatever changes in performance practice there may have been over the last six millennia, is shattering.

V-pop

Though not as popular throughout East Asia as J-pop (from Japan), K-pop (from Korea) and C-pop (from China), **V-pop** has a huge following among young Vietnamese, and the top artists often perform sell-out shows in the country's biggest stadia. Many composers have tried their hand at writing a pop hit but only about three are acknowledged masters: **Van Cao** (who also wrote the national anthem), **Pham Duy** (who died in 2013 after many years writing pointed political songs from the safe distance of California) and **Trinh Cong Son** (whose life of wine, women and song ended in 2001). Joan Baez summed him up well when she dubbed him "the Vietnamese Bob Dylan": the tunes are catchy and the lyrics are thought-provoking. His first songs were written while in hiding from the military draft, and in 1969, when his album *Lullaby* sold over two million copies in Japan, Son's works were banned by the South Vietnamese government, which considered the lyrics too demoralizing. Even the new government sent him to work as a peasant in the fields, but after 1979 he lived in Ho Chi Minh City, painting, writing apolitical-but-catchy love songs and celebrating Vietnam's natural wonders, with over six hundred songs to his credit.

Though many of the top names these days are home grown, from 1975 to 1995 pop music was suppressed by the government, and during that period the most successful singers and songwriters were those who had fled to the US during or after the war. The main Vietnamese community there is based in Orange County, California, which has produced a string of successful pop artists, including Khanh Ha, Don Ho, Lam Nhat Tien, Nhu Quynh, Y Lan, Khanh Ly, Tuan Ngoc, Jimmi Nguyen, Trizzie Phuong Trinh and Thanh Ha. Though many of these are now ageing, they maintain a strong following in their homeland. For example, Khanh Ly performed sell-out concerts in 2014 in Hanoi and Da Nang at the age of 69, though she has still not been given permission to sing in Saigon, perhaps because many of her greatest hits were composed by Trinh Cong Son.

Among Vietnam-based performers, some singers of note are My Linh, Phuong Thanh, Bang Kieu, Hong Nhung, Lam Truong, Thanh Lam, Dam Vinh Hung, Thu Minh and My Tam. Among these, My Tam is currently the country's foremost diva, having won a string of awards, including Best-selling Vietnamese artist at the 2014 World Music Awards.

The ubiquitous **pop-rock band** comprises a singer, bass guitar and one or two electronic keyboards, hailed throughout the country as the greatest labour-saving device, despite their cheesy sound. All the rhythm buttons on these portable keyboards that are so rarely used elsewhere – rumba, tango, bossa nova and surf-rock – are here employed liberally. The slap-echo on the singer's microphone is intentional; without it, they say, it sounds "unprofessional". Each evening, when the traffic noise dies down, you can hear the mournful laments of neighbouring karaoke bars mingling together, the ghostly echoes of lonely pop singers reverberating from another dimension.

Discography

TRADITIONAL

SAMPLERS

Hò! Roady Music from Vietnam Trikont, Germany. Crass, crazy, funky street music taken from pop cassettes and recorded *in situ* with mopeds and car horns in the soundscape. It opens in cracking style with a plucked *dan bau* doing "Riders in the Sky" with what sounds like fireworks as well. There's a wild funeral brass band and all sorts of surprises. Highly recommended.

Music from Vietnam Vol 1 Caprice, Sweden. An introduction (in conservatoire style) featuring songs, instrumental tracks and theatrical forms. Featured instruments include the *dan bau*, *dan nguyet* and *k'long put*. Music includes Quan Ho folk songs, Cai Luong and Hat Cheo theatre, Hat Chau Van possession ritual and Nhac Dan Toc Cai Bien new folk.

Stilling Time: Traditional Musics of Vietnam Innova, US. A sampler of field recordings from all over Vietnam, including songs and gong music of the ethnic minorities. An introduction to the many surprises in store for the musical traveller. Recorded and compiled by Philip Blackburn.

THEATRE

The Art of Kim Sinh King, Japan. Blind singer/guitarist Kim Sinh has something of a cult following and knows how to wrench the emotions from those old Cai Luong opera songs. His venerable musical personality is more affecting than many of the commercial Cai Luong releases available, and it's tempting to make comparisons to the blues. This recording has influenced a whole generation of California guitarists.

Vietnam: Traditions of the South Audivis and UNESCO, France. Southern ritual music from the eclectic Cao Dai, Buddhist and indigenous spirit-possession religions, as well as a good helping of Cai Luong theatre music. The liner notes and recording quality are on the dry side but the music is very lively.

Vietnamese Folk Theatre: Hat Cheo King, Japan. Cheo theatre, expertly played by the Quy Bon family and recorded in Hanoi. Features a Chau Van possession ritual and the famous story of the cross-dressing Thi Mau going to a temple.

SONG AND CLASSICAL MUSIC

Anthology of World Music: The Music of Viet Nam Rounder, US. This is the Vietnamese equivalent of the Rosetta Stone, the earliest published recordings of some of the standards of the repertoire, performed by the masters of their day: Music and Theatre of the Court, Ritual Music and Entertainment Music and the Music of South Vietnam. The presentation may seem a little dusty by modern flashy conservatoire standards, but it's still revelatory.

Ca Tru: The Music of North Viet Nam Inedit, France and Ca Tru Singing House Ho Guom Audio, Hanoi. Performed by the Hanoi Ca Tru Thai Ha Ensemble and Ca Tru Thang Long respectively. Solo voice (with "bouncing seeds" vibrato), lute and chopsticks titillate male visitors for hours on end.

Music from Vietnam Vol 2: The City of Hue Caprice, Sweden. Ceremonial music with *shawms*, drums and a big gong, a military ensemble and a great court orchestra, as well as more intimate chamber groups of singers with *dan bau*, *dan nguyet*, *dan nhi* and *dan tranh*. Three local instrumental and vocal groups give the enticing flavour of this city, the disc features the sprightly aged Nguyen Manh Cam, former drummer to the emperor.

Vietnam: Buddhist Music from Hue Inedit, France. An atmospheric recording, full of ceremonial presence. It begins with sonorous drums and bells before two oboes enter for music marking the ascent to the "Esplanade of Heaven". The complete ceremony of *Khai Kinh*, "Opening the Sacred Texts", is recorded in one of Hue's best pagodas, the Kim Thien. Not easy listening, but the music is nevertheless impressive.

Vietnam: Poésies et Chants Ocora, France. Master musician Tran Van Khe and friends chant poetry (*ngam tho*) and ravish the *dan tranh* and *dan nguyet* (in the Nhac Tai Tu skilled chamber music repertory). Specialized and intimate performances with excellent notes and translations.

ETHNIC MINORITY MUSIC

Gongs: Vietnam, Laos Playasound, France. Before there were skipping records or Steve Reich patterns there were these delicious mellifluously clangorous loops filling the jungle nights.

Music from Vietnam Vol 3: Ethnic Minorities Caprice, Sweden. The mosaic of cultures residing in the central and northern mountains has some astonishing musical traditions. This excellent and accessible selection kicks off with a piece from the E De: a beautiful "free-reed" cow-horn solo followed up by clattering poly-rhythmic gong patterns. There's also music from the Nung, Muong and Hmong. Wonderful pipes, flutes, mouth organs and songs. Good notes.

Musiques des Montagnards Chant du Monde, France. Two CDs of extraordinary recordings (1958–97) from the central and northern highlands. Fourteen ethnic groups are covered and excellently described in the copious 119-page booklet.

Northern Vietnam: Music and Songs of the Minorities Buda Musique/Musique du Monde, France. A selection of recordings from the Giay, Nung, Tay, Dao, Thai and Hmong ethnic groups. A love song, courting melodies, wedding music, funeral music and the extraordinary Hmong *ken*.

NEW FOLK

Echoes of Ancestral Voices: Traditional Music of Vietnam Move, Australia. Music performed by husband and wife duo Dang Kim Hien and Le Tuan Hung. No fireworks, just a fragile, uncompromising intensity.

Moonlight in Vietnam Henry Street/Rounder, US. New music expertly played on Vietnam's most extraordinary musical instruments, including the *dan bau*, *k'long put* and a stick-fiddle with a resonating disc held in the player's mouth. The players are a Vancouver-based ensemble led by *dan bau* virtuoso Ho Khac Chi.

The Music of Vietnam Vols 1.1 & 1.2 Celestial Harmonies, US. Accessible, virtuoso and expertly recorded, these recordings document an array of Vietnam's best conservatoire-mediated styles. Through a compelling series of pieces, this is an entertaining overview of the full range of Vietnamese instruments. Full documentation.

POP

Don Ho *Ru Em/Lullaby* Thuy Nga, US. Heart-throb lullabies from one of California's hottest singers.

Khanh Ha *Doi Da Vang/Vacant Rock-strewn Hill* Khanh Ha Productions, US. Bilingual singing legend compared (favourably) to Barbra Streisand and Celine Dion.

My Linh *Toc Ngan/Short Hair* My Linh Productions, Vietnam. Hot arrangements of pieces all written for her sultry, crackly voice.

My Tam *Melodies of Time* Narimaru, South Korea. A compilation of some of her greatest hits.

Nguyen Thanh Van *Ho Khoan Le Thuy/River Song* Van Nguyen Productions, US. Passion, pathos and folk references from this San Francisco-based artist.

Pham Duy *Voyage Through the Motherland* Co Loa, US. The first Vietnamese CD-ROM, featuring patriotic songs, karaoke options, video and fine photos. A real "coffee table" disc.

Y Lan *Muon Hoi Tai Sao/I Want to Ask Why* Y Lan Productions, US. From a well-known artistic family, she became a café owner before becoming a regular at the *Ritz* and *Paris By Night* circuit.

With contributions by Philip Blackburn (from *The Rough Guide to World Music*).

Books

Of the vast canon of books written on the subject of Vietnam, the overwhelming majority concern themselves, inevitably, with the American War. Some indigenous attempts to come to terms with the conflicts that have caused Vietnam such pain have also filtered through the country's overcautious censorship. Some of the few novels that have reached the West are also reviewed below. Particularly recommended titles are marked with a ★ symbol.

For a decent copy of a book on Vietnam, your best bet is to scour bookshops before you set off from home – only Hanoi and Ho Chi Minh City have ranges of literature of any breadth, and then often only in photocopied offprint form. The exceptions to this are books produced by local presses, notably The Gioi Publishers, which you'll have difficulty finding outside Vietnam.

TRAVEL WRITING

Maria Coffey *Three Moons in Vietnam*. Delightfully jolly jaunt around Vietnam by boat, bus and bicycle. Coffey conspires to meet more locals in one day than most travellers do in a month, making this a valuable snapshot of modern Vietnam.

Sue Downie *Down Highway One*. In 1988 Sue Downie was one of the first Westerners since the American War to travel the length of Highway 1. Returning in the early 1990s, she witnesses the changes – not all good – transforming the country and people's daily lives.

Graham Greene *Ways of Escape*. Greene's global travels in the 1950s took him to Vietnam for four consecutive winters; the coverage of Vietnam in this slim autobiographical volume is intriguing, but tantalizingly short, its memories of dice-playing with French agents over vermouths and opium-smoking in Cho Lon are evidently templates for scenes in *The Quiet American* (see p.490).

Christopher Hunt *Sparring with Charlie*. Hunt can be a maddening travelling companion, but this account of his jaunt down the Ho Chi Minh Trail on a Russian-made motorbike is undeniably a page-turner.

★**Norman Lewis** *A Dragon Apparent*. When in 1950 Lewis made the journey that would inspire his seminal Indochina travelogue, the Vietnam he saw was still a land of longhouses and Imperial hunts, though poised for renewed conflict; the erudite prose of this doyen of travel writers reveals a Vietnam now long gone.

W. Somerset Maugham *The Gentleman in the Parlour*. The fruit of Maugham's grand tour from Rangoon to Haiphong to recharge his creative batteries, *The Gentleman in the Parlour* finds him less than enamoured with Vietnam, his last stop. Nevertheless, his accounts of the Hue court teetering on the brink of extinction, and of a run-in with an old acquaintance in a Haiphong café, are vintage Maugham.

Karin Muller *Hitchhiking Vietnam*. A feisty American, Karin Muller went searching for the "real Vietnam", a Vietnam untouched by commercialism and Western culture. On the way she gets deported, is arrested on numerous occasions and meets some motley characters, but eventually finds what she's looking for among the minorities of the northwest mountains. Beautifully told, with great compassion and a never-failing sense of humour.

Andrew X. Pham *Catfish and Mandala*. After twenty years in America, Pham takes a gruelling bike ride through Vietnam to rediscover the country, his family and – in the process – himself. A compelling insight into the frustrations and fascinations of Vietnam.

Gontran de Poncins *From a Chinese City*. Believing that "the ancient customs of a national culture endure longer in remote colonies than in the motherland", de Poncins opted for a sojourn in Cho Lon as a means to a better understanding of the foibles of the Chinese; the resulting document of life in 1955 Cho Lon is a lively period piece, backed up by fluid illustrations.

Pam Scott *Hanoi Stories* and *Life in Hanoi*. Hanoi and its inhabitants – both local and expat, from its celebrities to its cyclo drivers – viewed through the lens of an Australian who came on business and stayed ten years.

James Sullivan *Over the Moat*. Cultures collide as Sullivan courts a Hue shop-girl he met while cycling through Vietnam in 1992. Part love story, part travelogue.

Paul Theroux *The Great Railway Bazaar*. His elaborate circumnavigation of Europe and Asia by train took Theroux, in 1973, to a South Vietnam still bewildered by the recent American withdrawal. In bleak sound-bite accounts of rides from Saigon to Bien Hoa and Hue to Da Nang, he describes the war's awful legacy of poverty, suffering and infrastructural breakdown, but marvels at the country's unbowed, and unexpected, beauty.

Gabrielle M. Vassal *On and Off Duty in Annam*. An enchanting wander through early twentieth century southern Vietnam, penned by the intrepid wife of a French army doctor. A stint in Saigon is followed by a boat trip to Nha Trang (where she was carried ashore "on the backs of natives through the breakers") and a gutsy foray into the central highlands; amazing prints of the Vietnamese and *montagnards* she encountered further enhance the account. **Justin Wintle** *Romancing Vietnam*. Wintle's genial but lightweight yomp upcountry was one of the first of its kind, post-*doi moi*, and remains a pleasing aperitif to travels in Vietnam.

VIETNAMESE ABROAD

Donald Anderson (ed) *Aftermath: An Anthology of Post-Vietnam Fiction*. As the war's tendrils crept across the Pacific to America, they touched not only the people who fought, but also those who stayed at home. In their depictions of Americans, Amerasians and Asians regathering the strands of their lives, these short stories run the gamut of emotions provoked by war.

★**Robert Olen Butler** *A Good Scent from a Strange Mountain*. Pulitzer Prize-winning collection of short stories that ponder the struggles of Vietnamese in America to maintain the cultural ley lines linking them with their mother country, and the gulf between them and their Americanized offspring. War veteran Olen Butler's assured prose ensures the voices of his Vietnamese characters find perfect pitch.

★**Le Ly Hayslip** *Child of War, Woman of Peace*. In this follow-up to *When Heaven and Earth Changed Places* (see p.491), Hayslip's narrative shifts to America, where the cultural disorientation of a new arrival is examined.

VIETNAMESE LITERATURE

John Balaban and Nguyen Qui Duc (eds) *Vietnam: A Traveller's Literary Companion*. The editors of this entertaining volume of short stories, written by Vietnamese writers based both at home and abroad, chose to avoid tales of war and politics during their selection process, though both themes inevitably make their presence felt.

★**Bao Ninh** *The Sorrow of War*. This is a ground-breaking novel, largely due to its portrayal of Communist soldiers suffering the same traumas, fear and lost innocence as their American counterparts.

Steven Bradbury *Poems from the Prison Diary of Ho Chi Minh*. This beautifully rendered selection of the poems Ho penned while behind bars in 1942, in which he looks to birdsong and moonlight to ease the loneliness of prison life, provide a touching glimpse of the man behind the myth.

Alastair Dingwall (ed) *Traveller's Literary Companion to South-East Asia*. Among the bite-sized essays inside this gem of a book is an enlightening thirty-page segment on Vietnam, into which are crammed biopics, a recommended reading list, historical, linguistic and literary backgrounds. Excerpts range from classical literature to the writings of foreign journalists in the 1960s.

★**Duong Thu Huong** *Novel Without a Name*. A tale of young Vietnamese men seeking glory but finding only loneliness, disillusionment and death, as war abridges youth and curtails loves. A depiction of dwindling idealism, and a radical questioning of the political motives behind the war. Other highly acclaimed works by the same author include *Paradise of the Blind* and *Memories of a Pure Spring*.

★**Duong Van Mai Elliot** *The Sacred Willow*. Mai Elliot brings Vietnamese history to life in this compelling account of her family through four generations.

Wayne Karlin, Le Minh Khue and Truong Vu (eds) *The Other Side of Heaven*. A unique anthology of postwar fiction by Vietnamese and American authors. Though written by former enemies from all sides of the conflict, these stories echo back and forth the unifying themes of sorrow, pain and survival.

Le Minh Khue *The Stars, The Earth, The River*. Fourteen short stories by one of Vietnam's leading contemporary writers, an ex-sapper who gently details the seesaw of "tragedy and hope" which defines her war-torn generation.

Nguyen Du *The Tale of Kieu*. Epic poem of the ill-starred love between Kim and Kieu, a beautiful and educated girl who is forced to become a prostitute in order to free her parents from jail. She eventually escapes and marries Kim, but is now unable to return his affections. Seen as an allegory of Vietnamese history – or simply of the timeless conflict between duty and desire – the poem is widely held to represent the zenith of Vietnamese literature.

★**Nguyen Huy Thiep** *The General Retires and Other Stories*. Perhaps Vietnam's pre-eminent writer, Nguyen Huy Thiep articulates the lives of ordinary Vietnamese in these short stories – instead of following the prevailing trend of re-imagining the lives of past heroes.

NOVELS SET IN VIETNAM

Marguerite Duras *The Lover*. Young French girl meets wealthy Chinese man on a Mekong Delta ferry; the ensuing affair initiates her into adulthood, with all its joys and responsibilities. The novel's depiction of a dysfunctional, hard-up French family in Vietnam provides an interesting slant on colonial life, showing it wasn't all vermouths and tennis.

★**Camilla Gibb** *The Beauty of Humanity Movement*. Gibb's deft characterization creates an endearing and poignant, contemporary tale that revolves around Hung, an old man whose life is dedicated to making pho even when there are no ingredients to be had in post-reunification Hanoi.

★**Graham Greene** *The Quiet American*. Greene's prescient and cautionary tale of the dangers of innocence in uncertain times, which anticipated America's boorish manhandling of Vietnam's political situation by several years, is still the best single account of wartime Vietnam. Its regular name-drops of familiar locales – Tay Ninh, the *Continental*, Dong Khoi – make it doubly enjoyable.

★**Anthony Grey** *Saigon*. Vietnamese history given a blockbuster makeover: a rip-roaring narrative, whose Vietnamese, French and American protagonists conspire to be present at all defining moments in recent Vietnamese history, from French plantation riots to the fall of Saigon.

Nguyen Kien *Tapestries*. This rich and beautifully woven novel is based on the extraordinary real-life story of the author's grandfather, who eventually became an embroiderer in the royal court of Hue. The context is a country on the cusp of change as French influence gains the upper hand.

★**Tim O'Brien** *Going After Cacciato*. A highly acclaimed, lyrical tale of an American soldier who simply walks out of the war and sets off for Paris, pursued by his company on a fantastical mission that takes them across Asia. The savage reality of war stands out vividly against a dream world of peace and freedom.

HISTORY

William J. Duiker *The Communist Road to Power in Vietnam*. One of America's leading analysts of the political context in Vietnam takes a long close look at why Communist Vietnam won its wars – as opposed to why France and America lost.

William J. Duiker *Ho Chi Minh: A Life*. Duiker turns his spotlight on the patriot and revolutionary who led Vietnam to independence. It's a thoroughly researched and exhaustive tome, particularly good on Ho's political evolution, though fails to get under the skin of this enigmatic man.

Bernard Fall *Hell in a Very Small Place*. The classic account of the siege of Dien Bien Phu, capturing the claustrophobia and the fear, written by a French-born American journalist.

★**Bernard Fall** *Street Without Joy*. Another masterpiece by Fall, charting the French debacle in Indochina, which became required reading for American generals and GIs – though it didn't prevent them committing exactly the same mistakes just a few years later.

David Halberstam *Ho*. Diminutive, sympathetic and highly readable biography of Vietnam's foremost icon, though no attempt is made to apportion blame for the disastrous land reforms of the 1950s.

★**Stanley Karnow** *Vietnam: A History*. Weighty, august tome that elucidates the entire span of Vietnamese history.

Michael Maclear *Vietnam: The Ten Thousand Day War*. A solid introductory account of the French and American wars, from Ho's alliance with Archimedes Patti, to the fall of Saigon.

Nguyen Khac Vien *Vietnam: A Long History*. Published by Hanoi's The Gioi Publishers, and therefore heavily weighted in favour of the Communists, but easier to get hold of in Vietnam than most histories.

Keith Weller Taylor *The Birth of Vietnam*. As a GI, Taylor was struck by the "intelligence and resolve" of his enemy. This meticulous account of the dawn of Vietnamese history, trawling the past from the nation's first recorded history up to the tenth century, is the result of his attempt to uncover its roots.

★**Martin Windrow** *The Last Valley: Dien Bien Phu and the French Defeat in Vietnam*. This meticulously researched and detailed account of the battle of Dien Bien Phu gives a brutally realistic picture of what it was like for the French soldiers (many actually Vietnamese, Thai and North African) trapped in what came to be known as the "toilet bowl". Windrow's sympathy and admiration for the soldiers – on both sides – comes across loud and clear.

THE AMERICAN WAR

Mark Baker *Nam*. Unflinching firsthand accounts of the GI's descent from boot camp into the morass of death, paranoia, exhaustion and tedium. Gut-wrenchingly frank at times, the book depicts war as a rite of passage, and moral deterioration as a prerequisite to survival.

Tad Bartimus (ed) *War Torn: Stories of War from the Women Reporters Who Covered Vietnam*. Nine pioneering women journalists who covered the American War tell their tales, from the struggle to get there in the first place and be recognized in what was then an almost exclusively male profession to their reactions to the war itself and coming to terms with the aftermath.

★**Michael Bilton and Kevin Sim** *Four Hours in My Lai*. Brutally candid and immaculately researched reconstruction of the events surrounding the My Lai massacre of 1968; as harrowing a portrayal of the depths plumbed in war as you'll ever read.

★**Philip Caputo** *A Rumour of War*. One of the classics of the American War, Caputo's straightforward narrative is a powerful account of the numbing daily routine of the ordinary US soldier's life, the strange exhilaration of combat and the brutalization that accompanies war.

★**Denise Chong** *The Girl in the Picture*. Kim Phuc was the little girl running naked away from her napalm-bombed village in what is arguably the most famous – and most harrowing – photo taken during the American War. Not only did she survive the burns, just, but her resilience and capacity for forgiveness are remarkable. Denise Chong tells Kim's story simply, letting the horrific events speak for themselves.

Michael Clodfelter *Mad Minutes and Vietnam Months.* Combat reminiscences from a man who found war's false promise of "courage, sacrifice, glory and adventure" displaced by monotony and, occasionally, atrocity.

★**Horst Faas and Tim Page** (eds) *Requiem.* Turning through this compendium of shots by photographers who subsequently lost their lives in Vietnam, Laos or Cambodia will haunt you for weeks. Never was a book more aptly named.

James Fenton *All the Wrong Places.* In Vietnam at the moment of Saigon's liberation, Fenton somehow managed to hitch a lift on the tank that rammed through the palace gates; his easy prose and poet's eye for detail make his account an engrossing one.

★**Frances Fitzgerald** *Fire in the Lake.* Pulitzer Prize-winning analysis of the historical, political and cultural context of the war, this time told from the Vietnamese perspective.

Albert French *Patches of Fire.* Examining his experiences of the infantryman's life in Vietnam and his attempts to exorcise his war-conjured demons back in the US, French's autobiography is at once moving and engrossing.

★**Le Ly Hayslip** *When Heaven and Earth Changed Places.* For giving a human face to the slopes, dinks and gooks of American writing on Vietnam, this heart-rending tale of villagers trying to survive in a climate of hatred and distrust is perhaps more valuable than any history book.

★**Michael Herr** *Dispatches.* Infuriatingly narcissistic at times, Herr's spaced-out narrative still conveys the mud, blood and guts of the American war effort in Vietnam. Herr's distinctive tone is also evident in the classic war movie *Apocalypse Now* (see p.495), for which he wrote the screenplay.

John Laurence *The Cat from Hue.* Highly acclaimed for his coverage of the Vietnam conflict for CBS News from 1965 to 1970, Laurence has written not only an evocative memoir but also a moving testimony to the courage of the American troops who, like him, came of age in the battlefields of Vietnam.

Tom Mangold and John Penycate *The Tunnels of Cu Chi.* The most thorough and captivating account yet written of the guerrilla resistance mounted in the tunnels around Cu Chi.

★**Karl Marlantes** *Matterhorn.* It took Marlantes 35 years to complete this novel about young marines dropped into the jungle and their subsequent battles with the enemy, disease and each other, but it was worth the wait for its mature perspective of the conflict.

★**Robert Mason** *Chickenhawk.* Few people can be better qualified than Mason to deliver an account of the American War: a helicopter pilot with over a thousand missions under his belt, his blood-and-guts, bird's-eye account of the war is harrowing but compelling.

Harold G. Moore and Joseph Galloway *We Were Soldiers Once...and Young.* This blow-by-blow account of the ferocious battle of the Ia Drang valley, among the earliest encounters of the American War, makes compelling reading as the authors recapture the chaos and fear alongside moments of incredible courage and the sheer determination to survive.

★**Tim O'Brien** *The Things They Carried* and *If I Die in a Combat Zone.* Through a mix of autobiography and fiction O'Brien lays to rest the ghosts of the past in a brutally honest reappraisal of the war, his own actions and the events he witnessed (see also O'Brien's novel *Going After Cacciato*; opposite).

★**John Pilger** *Heroes.* Journalist Pilger's systematic dismantling of the myth that America's role was in any way a justifiable "crusade" makes his Vietnam reportage required reading.

William Prochnau *Once Upon a Distant War.* Now that all the journos ever to set foot in Vietnam have published memoirs, Prochnau presents a new twist – the intriguing story of the people (among them Neil Sheehan, David Halberstam and Peter Arnett) who wrote the stories of Vietnam.

★**Neil Sheehan** *A Bright Shining Lie.* This monumental and fluently rendered account of the war, hung around the life of the soldier John Paul Vann, won the Pulitzer Prize for Sheehan; one of the true classics of Vietnam-inspired literature.

Justin Wintle *The Vietnam War.* Written in reaction to the shelves of long-winded texts available on the subject, Wintle's succinct overview manages to condense this mad conflict into fewer than two hundred pages.

Tobias Wolff *In Pharaoh's Army.* A former adviser based in My Tho, Wolff's honest, gentle autobiographical tale takes a wry look at life away from the "front line".

POSTWAR VIETNAM

Bui Tin *Following Ho Chi Minh.* An erstwhile colonel in the North Vietnamese Army, Bui Tin effectively defected to the West in 1990, since when he has been an outspoken critic of Vietnam's state apparatus. These memoirs don't flinch from addressing the underside – corruption, prejudice, naivety and insensitivity – of the party.

Adam Fforde and Stefan de Vylder *From Plan to Market.* Highbrow, laudably researched book plotting the route Vietnam has taken from Stalinist central planning to market economy. Fforde and de Vylder hold the fabric of *doi moi* up to the light for examination in the mid-1990s.

David Lamb *Vietnam, Now: A Reporter Returns.* War journalist David Lamb returned to Vietnam for a four-year stint in 1997. While the war is a constant presence, this is primarily a commentary on contemporary Vietnam and its prospects for the future. Lamb is ultimately optimistic, though his criticisms of the government – notably its failure to reconcile the still-deep divisions between North and South – were sufficient to get the book banned.

Tim Page *Derailed in Uncle Ho's Victory Garden*. The war photographer with a legendary ability to defy death, returns to Vietnam in the 1980s. Buried among the flashbacks and meandering discourse, Page's eye for detail and his delight in the bizarre give a flavour of postwar Vietnam.

Neil Sheehan *Two Cities: Hanoi and Saigon*. Sheehan returned to Vietnam in 1989 to witness first-hand the legacy of the war. Down south, the memories really begin to flow as encounters and travels trigger wartime flashbacks, interspersed with commentary on re-education camps and other deprivations of the dark, pre-*doi moi* years.

★ **Robert Templer** *Shadows and Wind*. This hard-hitting book casts a critical eye over Vietnam's decades of reform, from corruption and censorship to the emergence of a consumer-oriented youth culture. Though written in the late 1980s, the informative and balanced analysis still holds true today.

CULTURE AND SOCIETY

James Goodman *Uniquely Vietnamese*. Asia-based author Goodman has produced an informative catalogue of Vietnamese ingenuity, ranging from conical hats to Cheo theatre, from local festivals to water puppets and the haunting, one-stringed *dan bau*.

Gerald Cannon Hickey *Shattered World*. Detailed but readable account of ethnic minorities living in Vietnam's central highlands by one of the region's leading ethnologists. A fascinating analysis of the minorities' tragic struggle to survive both war and peace.

Henry Kamm *Dragon Ascending*. Pulitzer Prize-winning correspondent Kamm lets the Vietnamese – art dealers, ex-colonels, academics, doctors, authors – speak for themselves. This they do eloquently, resulting in a convincing portrait of contemporary Vietnam.

Norma J. Livo and Dia Cha *Folk Stories of the Hmong*. The Hmong's fading oral tradition is captured in this unique collection, gleaned from US immigrants, while its scene-setting introduction offers a valuable overview of Hmong culture, accompanied by illustrations of traditional costume and embroidered "storycloths".

William S. Logan *Hanoi: Biography of a City*. A heritage adviser, Logan peels back the layers of history revealed in Hanoi's architecture and streetscapes to provide an academic but engaging account of the city. In doing so, he also examines the challenges facing Hanoi at the start of the new millennium as it strives to preserve its unique heritage while also meeting the needs of its citizens.

Robert S. McKelvey *The Dust of Life*. Moving oral histories by Vietnamese Amerasians abandoned by their American fathers and discriminated against by the Vietnamese.

Mai Pham *Pleasures of the Vietnamese Table*. Saigon-born chef and restaurateur rediscovers her Vietnamese culinary roots and puts together one of the best Vietnamese cookbooks.

Nguyen Van Huy and Laurel Kendall (eds) *Vietnam: Journeys of Mind, Body and Spirit*. A broad range of contemporary commentators present an evocative snapshot of Vietnamese society and culture at the start of the new millennium.

★ **Christina Noble** *Bridge Across My Sorrows*. Life-affirming autobiography by a Dublin woman spurred by a dream to channel her considerable strengths into helping Ho Chi Minh City's *bui doi*, or street children. In her sequel, *Mama Tina*, Noble continues the story of her work in Vietnam, and describes her more recent campaign for children's rights in Mongolia.

VIETNAM ON FILM

Gilbert Adair *Hollywood's Vietnam: From the Green Berets to Full Metal Jacket*. Adair's excitable prose guides you past the fire-fights, f-words and R&R hijinks, to a real appreciation of how Hollywood reflected shifting American attitudes to the war.

Jeremy Devine *Vietnam at 24 Frames a Second*. The most wide-ranging analysis of Vietnam movies, covering more than four hundred films.

Linda Dittmar and Gene Michaud (eds) *From Hanoi to Hollywood*. Collected essays on the way the American War encroached on Hollywood.

Vietnam in the movies

The embroilment of France and the US in Vietnam has spawned hundreds of movies, ranging from soft-focused, fond colonial reminiscences to blood-and-guts depictions of the horrors of war. As a means of brushing up on your Indochinese history, their value is questionable: for the most part, they're hardly objective. Yet, through the reflections they cast of the climates in which they were created, these films amplify the West's efforts to come to terms with what went on there, and for this reason they demand attention.

Early depictions

Hollywood was setting movies in Indochina long before the first American troops splashed ashore at Da Nang. As early as 1932, Jean Harlow played a sassy Saigon prostitute to smouldering Clark Gable's rubber-plantation manager, in the steamy pot-boiler **Red Dust**. At this early stage, however, Vietnam was no more than an exotic backdrop.

Even by the mid-1950s, as the modest beginnings of American involvement elicited from Hollywood its first real moves to acquaint itself with Vietnam, the country was often treated less as a nation with its own discernible identity and unique set of political issues, and more as a generic Asian theatre of war, in which the righteous **battle against Communism** could be played out. In its portrayal of noble and libertarian French forces, aided by American military specialists, confronting the evil of Communism, **China Gate** (1957) is an early example of this trend. Dedicated to the French *colons* who "advanced this backward society to its place as the rice bowl of Asia", its laboured plot, concerning an attempt to destroy a Viet Minh arms cache, is of much less interest than its heavy-handed politics.

Vietnam provided Hollywood with a golden opportunity to project its militaristic fantasies, and a chance to tap into the prejudices brought to the surface by more than a decade of anti-Japanese World War II movies – prejudices that painted American involvement as a reprise of past battles with the inscrutable **Asian hordes**. Rather more depth of thought went into the making of **The Quiet American** (1958), in which Michael Redgrave played the British journalist and cynic, Fowler, while Audie Murphy (America's most decorated soldier in World War II) played Pyle, the eponymous "hero" of Graham Greene's novel. To Greene's chagrin, Pyle was depicted not as a representative of the American government, but of a private aid organization – something which the author felt blunted his anti-American message; nevertheless, the movie retained its source's sense of the futility of attempting to rationalize of Vietnam's political quagmire.

Gung ho!

The military mandarins who led America into war failed to get the message, though: with American troops duly deployed in a far-flung corner of the globe by 1965, it was only a matter of time before **John Wayne** produced a patriotic movie to match. This came in the form of the monumentally bad **The Green Berets** (1968), in which a paunchy Wayne starred as "Big" Bill Kirby, a loveable colonel leading an adoring team of American soldiers into the central highlands. That Wayne, while on a promotional trip out to Vietnam, handed out cigarette cases inscribed with his signature and the message "Fuck Communism" speaks volumes about the film's subtlety. Kicking off with a stirring marching song ("Fighting soldiers from the sky, Fearless men who jump and die..."), the movie depicts American soldiers in spotless uniforms and perma-grins fighting against no less a threat than total "Communist domination of the world", yet still abiding, as the critic Gilbert Adair has it, "by Queensberry rules". In stark contrast to the squeaky-clean GIs are the barbaric Viet Cong, depicted as child-abusing rapists who whoop and holler like madmen as they overrun a US camp, all to the strains of suitably eerie Oriental music.

Sweeping Vietnam under the carpet

The war in Vietnam was a much dirtier affair than *The Green Berets* made it seem, its politics far less cut and dried. As the struggle turned into tragedy and popular support for it soured, movie moguls sensed that the war had become **taboo**. "Vietnam is awkward", said the journalist Michael Herr, "and if people don't even want to hear about it, you know they're not going to pay money to sit there in the dark and have it brought up." It was to be a full decade before another major combat movie was released. Instead, film-makers trained their gaze upon returning Vietnam veterans' doomed attempts to ease back into society. The resulting pictures were low in compassion: America's national pride had been collectively compromised by the failure to bring home a victory, and sympathy and forgiveness were at a premium.

A raft of **exploitation movies** was churned out, boasting names such as *Born Losers* (1967), *Angels from Hell* (1968) and *The Ravager* (1970), in which the mental scars of Vietnam provided topical window-dressing to improbable tales of martial arts, motorbikes and mayhem. At best, vets were treated as dysfunctional vigilantes acting beyond the pale of society – most famously in **Taxi Driver** (1976), which has Robert De Niro's disturbed insomniac returnee, Travis Bickle, embarking on a one-man moral crusade to purge the streets of a hellish New York. At worst, they were wacko misfits posing a threat to small-town America. With veterans being portrayed as anything but heroes, it was left to the stars of the **campus riot movies** and films lionizing **draft-dodgers** to provide role models.

Coming to terms with the war

Only in 1978 did Hollywood finally pluck up enough courage to confront the war head-on, and so aid the nation's healing process – **movies-as-therapy**. In the years since John Wayne's *Green Berets* had battened down the hatches against Communism, America had first lost sight of justification for the war, and then effectively lost the war itself. Movies no longer sought to make sense of past events, but to highlight their futility; for the generation of young Americans unfortunate enough to live through Vietnam, mere survival was seen as triumph enough. As audiences were exposed to their first dramatized glimpses of the war's unpalatable realities, they were confronted by disaffected troops seeking comfort in prostitution and drug abuse, along with far more shocking examples of soldiers' fraying moral fibre.

Such themes were woven through the first of the four movies of note released in 1978, **The Boys in Company C**, which follows a band of young draftees through their basic training stateside, and then into action. In one particularly telling scene, American lives are lost transporting what turns out to be whisky and cigarettes to the front. A similar futility underpins **Go Tell the Spartans**, in which Burt Lancaster's drug- and alcohol-hazed troops take, and then abandon, a camp – an idea reused nine years later in *Hamburger Hill*.

Coming Home (1978), which cast Jane Fonda as a military career-man's wife who falls in love with a wheelchair-bound veteran (Jon Voight), was significant for its sensitive consideration of the emotional and physical tolls exacted by the war, and initiated the trend for more measured and intelligent vet movies.

Similarly concerned with the ramifications of the war, both home and away, was **The Deer Hunter** (1978), in which the conscription of three friends fractures their Russian Orthodox community in Pennsylvania. The friends' "one-shot" code of honour, espoused on a last pre-Vietnam hunting trip, contrasts wildly with the moral vacuum of the war, whose random brutality is embodied in the movie's central scenes of Russian roulette.

The picture's ending, with its melancholy rendition of *God Bless America* by the central characters, is only semi-ironic, and alludes to the country's regenerative process. For all its power, *The Deer Hunter* is marred by overt racist stereotyping of the Vietnamese who, according to John Pilger, are dismissed as "sub-human Oriental barbarians and idiots". The Vietnamese we see are grotesque caricatures interested only in getting their kicks from gambling and death, and there's a strong sense that American youths ought never to have been exposed to such primordial evil as existed across the Pacific.

Francis Ford Coppola's hugely indulgent but visually magnificent **Apocalypse Now** (1979) rounded off the vanguard of postwar Vietnam combat movies. Described by one critic as "Film as opera…it turns Vietnam into a vast trip, into a War of the Imagination", the picture's Dantean snapshots of the war rob Vietnam of all identity other than as a "heart of darkness". Fuelled by his desire to convey the "horror, the madness, the sensuousness, and the moral dilemma of the Vietnam war", Coppola totally mythologizes the conflict, rendering it not so much futile as insane. The usual elements of needless death, casual atrocity, moral decline and spaced-out soldiers leaning heavily on substance abuse are all here, played out against a raunchy soundtrack. However, with its stylized representation of montagnards as generic savages deifying Westerners, and its depiction of the Viet Cong as butchers who happily lop the arms off children who have had "American" inoculations, *Apocalypse Now* is little more enlightened than *The Deer Hunter*. Coppola subsequently compared the creation of the film itself to a war: "We were in the jungle, there were too many of us. We had access to too much money and too much equipment and little by little we went insane" – a process graphically depicted in **Hearts of Darkness: A Filmmaker's Apocalypse** (1991).

Returning home

The precedent set by *Coming Home* of sympathetic consideration for **returning veterans**' mindsets spurred many movies along similar lines in subsequent years. These focused on the disillusionment and disorientation felt by soldiers coming back not to heroes' welcomes, but to indifference and even disdain.

One of the first of these movies was **First Blood** (1982), which introduced audiences to Sly Stallone's muscle-bound super-vet John Rambo. As we witness Rambo's torment in small-town America, the picture is more "shoot 'em up" than cerebral. Yet its climax, in which Rambo's former colonel becomes a surrogate father figure to him, underscores the tender ages of the troops who fought the war. Other movies of the genre – among them Alan Parker's **Birdy** (1984) and Oliver Stone's **Born on the 4th of July** (1989) – reiterated the message of stolen youth and innocence by screening idyllic, elegiac scenes of childhood. Stone has his hero (played by Tom Cruise) swallowing the anti-Communist line, and returning to an indifference symbolized by the squalor of the army hospital in which he recuperates and by the breakdown of his relationship with his mother. In *Birdy*, doctors at a loss as to how to treat a catatonic patient turn to a fellow vet for help – this sense of America's inability to relate to returnees subsequently resurfaces in **Jacknife** (1989).

Rewriting history

Not content with squaring up to the war in Vietnam, Hollywood during the 1980s attempted, bizarrely, to rewrite its script in a series of **revisionist movies**. Richard Gere had made the armed forces hip again in 1982's weepie **An Officer and a Gentleman**; a year later the first of an intriguing sub-genre of films hit cinemas, in which Americans returned to Vietnam, invariably to rescue MIAs, and "won".

Uncommon Valor (1983), a rather silly piece about an MIA rescue starring Gene Hackman, kicked things off, closely followed by **Missing in Action** (1983), in which Chuck Norris, the poor man's Stallone, karate-kicks his way towards the same resolution with sufficient panache to justify a speedy follow-up. The mother of them all, though, was **Rambo: First Blood, Part II**

(1985), in which the hero of *First Blood* gets to settle some old scores. "Do we get to win this time?" asks Rambo, at the top of the movie. As he riots through the Vietnamese countryside in order to extricate a band of American PoWs, he answers his own question by slaying Vietnamese foes at an approximate rate of one every two minutes.

"It don't mean nothing"

The backlash to the patent nonsense of the revisionist films came in the form of a series of shockingly realistic movies which attempted, in the words of the director Oliver Stone, to "peel the onion" and reveal the **real Vietnam**, routine atrocities, indiscipline and all. There are no heroes in these GI's-view movies, only fragile, confused-looking young men in fatigues, emphasizing that this was a war that affected a whole generation – not just its most photogenic individuals.

In **Platoon** (1986), Oliver Stone, himself a foot soldier in Vietnam, created the most realistic cinematographic interpretation of the American involvement yet. Filmed on location in the Philippines, this movie reminded audiences that killing gooks wasn't as straightforward as Rambo made it seem. As well as portraying the depths to which humankind can sink, Stone shows the circumstances under which it was feasible for young American boys to become murderers of civilians. Its oppressive sensory overload powerfully conjures the paranoiac near-hysteria spawned by fear, confusion, loss of motivation and inability to discriminate between friend and foe. Inherent in its shadowy, half-seen portrayal of the enemy is a grudging respect for their expertise in jungle warfare.

If *Platoon* portrays a dirty war, in **Hamburger Hill** (1987), which dramatizes the taking of Ap Bia hill during May 1969's battle for the A Shau valley, it has degenerated into a positive mud bath. As troops slither and slide on the flanks of the hill in the highland mists, they become indistinguishable, and the image of an entire generation stumbling towards the maws of death is strengthened by the fact that the cast includes no big-name actors – the men who fall on the hill are neighbours, sons or brothers, not film stars. American losses are taken in order to secure a useless hill, a potent symbol of the futility of America's involvement in the war; as one soldier says, time after time, in a weary mantra, "it don't mean nothing, not a thing."

Stanley Kubrick's **Full Metal Jacket** (1987) picks up *Hamburger Hill*'s theme of the war's theft of American youth in its opening scene, as the camp barber strips conscripts of their hair and, by implication, their individuality. A brutal drill-sergeant completes the alienation process by replacing the soldiers' names with nicknames of his choosing, and then sets about expunging their humanity – on the grounds that it will only hamper them when they experience first-hand the insanity of the war. However, as US troops plod wearily through a smouldering Hue in the movie's final scene, the usual macho marching tunes are replaced with a plaintive echo of youth: "Who's the leader of the club that's made for you and me, M-I-C, K-E-Y, M-O-U-S-E."

Hollywood offerings since the 1990s

In the majority of Hollywood movies about Vietnam, Vietnamese people have mostly been noticeable by their absence, or through the filter of blatant stereotyping. **Heaven and Earth** (1993), the final part of Oliver Stone's Vietnam trilogy, went some way towards rectifying this imbalance. Its depiction of a Vietnamese girl's odyssey (based on the life of Le Ly Hayslip), from idyllic early childhood to the traumas of life as a wife in San Diego, symbolizes the trials and tribulations of the country as a whole, and acts as a timely reminder that not only Americans suffered during the struggle.

Only in the late 1990s were American movie-makers allowed to shoot on location in Vietnam again. Filmed in Ho Chi Minh City, **Three Seasons** (1999) was directed by Vietnamese–Californian Tony Bui, and features Harvey Keitel at the head of a predominantly local cast. It provides a lyrical and graceful portrayal of a city trying to come to terms with the return of the West – personified by an ex-marine (Keitel) looking for the Amerasian daughter he abandoned decades before.

Perhaps the best-known Vietnam-based movie of the new millennium is Philip Noyce's atmospheric remake of **The Quiet American** (2002), which sticks much closer than the original to Graham Greene's novel in its indictment of American involvement in Vietnam. This, coupled with its portrayal of the Vietnamese struggle as a patriotic fight against colonial oppression, earned the film official approval, allowing it to be screened widely within Vietnam – a first for a major Hollywood production.

Hollywood was still not done with the war. In the same year (2002), Randall Wallace made **We Were Soldiers**, his adaptation of Lt Col Hall Moore and Joe Galloway's blow-by-blow account of the catastrophic battle of Ia Drang, with Mel Gibson as the caring commander. Though the movie made some effort to be impartial, it did not meet with Vietnamese approval: the government banned the film, saying it distorted Vietnamese history, and branded actor Don Duong a "traitor" for his portrayal of the NVA leader pitting his wits – and his men – against the Americans.

More recently, the lauded director Werner Herzog turned his attention to the American War with **Rescue Dawn** (2007), based on the true story of Dieter Dengler, a pilot who was shot down over Laos in 1966, then captured and tortured by villagers sympathetic to the Pathet Lao (Lao communists). Though ostensibly a straightforward tale of escape from a nightmarish situation, Herzog's unique spin on the situation makes it appear that there is little to choose between the lives of the captives and the captors.

French and Vietnamese movies

French cinema only began to tackle the subject of Vietnam in the 1990s. If in **Dien Bien Phu** (1992) it confronted its own ghosts, on the whole its output has been limited to visually captivating colonial whimsies, to which the Vietnamese setting merely adds an exotic tang. For example, **The Lover** (1992) works not because it does justice to Marguerite Duras' poignant rites-of-passage novella, but because its extended interludes of heaving flesh are cloaked with a veneer of Oriental mystique created by location filming in Ho Chi Minh City, Sa Dec and Can Tho.

Among **Vietnamese film-makers**, probably the best known is Tran Anh Hung, whose **The Scent of Green Papaya** (1993), filmed entirely in Paris, is a fondly nostalgic period piece in which the East's languorous elegance and beauty are shown, minus its squalor, which won two awards at the Cannes Film Festival. His second film, Cyclo (1996), is an altogether different matter, a grimy tale of murder and prostitution set in a bleak rendition of Ho Chi Minh City – so bleak that the film is banned in Vietnam. Nevertheless, Tran Anh Hung obtained permission to shoot **At the Height of Summer** (aka *The Vertical Ray of the Sun*, 2000) on location in Hanoi. It's a gentler film with the same languid, dream-like quality of *Cyclo*, in which three sisters prepare to commemorate their parents' deaths. Hung's latest offering is *Norwegian Wood* (2010), based on the novel by Haruki Murakami.

Vietnamese censors are infamously strict concerning topics broached in Vietnam-based movies, but they lightened up a little in allowing Vietnamese director Dang Nhat Minh to make his ground-breaking **The Season of Guavas** (2001), which deals with the extremely sensitive issue of 1950s Communist land reforms; however, the film has yet to be released in Vietnam. Other **Vietnamese directors** beginning to attract an international audience include Tran Van Thuy (*Sand Life*, 2000), Bui Thac Chuyen (*Course de Nuit*, 2000) and **Le Hoang**, whose stark portrayal of prostitutes in **Bar Girls** (2003) caused a major stir. That the film was made at all is thanks to a radical change of policy at Vietnam's Ministry of Culture, which in 2002 stopped vetting scripts and allowed private film studios to start making films. A sign of growing confidence in the Vietnamese film industry was the release in 2007 of **The White Silk Dress**, directed by **Luu Huynh** with a record budget of $2 million, about the struggles of an impoverished couple in the 1950s to provide their daughters with *ao dai* to wear to school.

Vietnamese

Linguists are uncertain as to the exact roots of Vietnamese, though the language betrays Thai, Khmer and Chinese influences. A tonal language, it's extremely tricky for Westerners to master, though the phrases below should help you get by. English superseded Russian as *the* language to learn following the sweeping changes of *doi moi*, and as a visitor you'll generally find that being able to speak Vietnamese isn't called for. Then again, nothing will endear you to locals as much as showing conversational ability – or even willingness.

Vietnamese was set down using Chinese characters until the fourteenth century, when an indigenous **script** called *chu nom* was created. This, in turn, was dropped in favour of *quoc ngu*, a Romanized script developed by a French missionary in the seventeenth century, and it's this form that's universally used today – though you'll still occasionally spot lavish *chu nom* characters daubed on the walls of more venerable pagodas and temples.

Three main **dialects** – northern, central and southern – are used in Vietnam today, and although for the most part they are pretty similar, pronunciation can be so wildly variant that some locals have trouble understanding each other; in the words and phrases listed below, we indicate important differences between variants used in the north and south. Bear in mind, too, that Vietnam's minority peoples have their own languages, and may look blankly at you as you gamely try out your Vietnamese on them.

If you want more scope than the expressions below allow and are determined to master the basics of spoken Vietnamese, try one of the **self-teaching packs** on the market, such as those produced by Audio-Forum (ⓦaudioforum.com).

Pronunciation

The Vietnamese language is a **tonal** one, that is, one in which a word's meaning is determined by the pitch at which you deliver it. Six tones are used – the mid-level tone (syllables with no marker), the low falling tone (syllables marked à), the low rising tone (syllables marked ả), the high broken tone (syllables marked ã), the high rising tone (syllables marked á) and the low broken tone (syllables marked ạ) – though you'll probably remain in the dark until you ask a Vietnamese person to give you spoken examples of each of them. Depending on its tone, the word *ba*, for instance, can mean three, grandmother, poisoned food, waste, aunt or any – leaving ample scope for misunderstandings and diplomatic faux pas.

With tones accomplished, or at least comprehended, there are the many vowel and consonant sounds to take on board. These we've listed below, along with phonetic renderings of how they should be pronounced.

VOWELS

a "a" as in f**a**ther	**o** "o" as in h**o**t
ă "u" as in h**u**t (slight "u" as in unstressed English "a")	**ô** "aw" as in **aw**e
â "uh" sound as above only longer	**ơ** "ur" as in f**ur**
e "e" as in b**e**d	**u** "oo" as in b**oo**
ê "ay" as in p**ay**	**ư** "oo" closest to French "u"
i "i" as in -**i**ng	**y** "i" as in -**i**ng

VOWEL COMBINATIONS

ai	"ai" as in Th**ai**	oe		"weh"
ao	"ao" as in M**ao**	ôi		"oy"
au	"a-oo"	ơi		"uh-i"
âu	"oh" as in **oh**!	ua		"waw"
ay	"ay" as in h**ay**	uê		"weh"
ây	"ay-i" (as in "ay" above but longer)	uô		"waw"
eo	"eh-ao"	uy		"wee"
êu	"ay-oo"	ưa		"oo-a"
iu	"ew" as in f**ew**	ưu		"er-oo"
iêu	"i-yoh"	ươi		"oo-uh-i"
oa	"wa"			

CONSONANTS

c	"g"	ng/ngh	"ng" as in si**ng**
ch	"j" as in **j**ar	nh	"n-y" as in ca**ny**on
d	"y" as in **y**oung	ph	"f"
đ	"d" as in **d**ay	q	"g" as in **g**oat
g	"g" as in **g**oat	t	"d" as in **d**ay
gh	"g" as in **g**oat	th	"t"
gi	"y" as in **y**oung	tr	"j" as in **j**ar
k	"g" as in **g**oat	x	"s"
kh	"k" as in **k**eep		

Useful words and phrases

How you greet and then speak to somebody in Vietnam depends very much on their sex, and on their age and social standing relative to your own. As a general rule of thumb, if you address a man as *ông*, and a woman as *bà*, you can be sure you aren't being impolite. If you find yourself in conversation, either formally or informally, with someone of your approximate age, you can use *anh* (for a man) and *chi* (for a woman). You can also use the same formula to address someone when you know their name. Vietnamese names are traditionally written with the family name first (Nguyen, Tran, Le and Pham are among the most common) and the given name last and between them a qualifying name, which often indicates a person's sex or the particular branch of the family to which they belong. People are usually referred to by their given name so, for example, you would address an older man called Nguyen Van Hai as Ong Hai.

GREETINGS AND SMALL TALK

Hello	chào ông/bà	**My name is...**	tên tôi là...
How are you?	ông/bà có khỏe không?	**Where do you come from?**	ông/bà ở đâu đến?
Fine, thanks	toẻ, cảm ơn.	**I come from...**	tôi ở . . .
Pleased to meet you	hân hạnh gặp bạn ông/bà	**...England**	. . . nước Anh
Goodbye	chào, tạm biệt	**...America**	. . . nước Mỹ
Good night	chúc ngủ ngon	**...Australia**	. . . nước Úc
Excuse me (to say sorry)	xin lỗi	**What do you do?**	ông/bà làm gì?
Excuse me (to get past)	xin ông/bà thứ lỗi	**Do you speak English?**	ông/bà biết nói tiếng
Please	làm ơn		Anh không?
Thank you	cảm ơn ông/bà	**I don't understand**	tôi không hiểu
Thank you very much	cảm ơn bạn rất nhiều	**Could you repeat that?**	xin ông/bà lặp lại?
Don't mention it	không có chi	**Yes**	vâng (north); dạ (south)
What's your name?	ông/bà tên gì?	**No**	không

EMERGENCIES

Can you help me?	ông/bà có thể giúp tôi không?	hospital	bệnh viện
There's been an accident	có một vụ tai nạn	police station	đồn công an
Please call a doctor	làm ơn gọi bác sĩ		

GETTING AROUND

Where is the...?	ở đâu...?	train station	bến xe lửa
How many kilometres is it to...?	bao nhiêu cây số thì đến...?	taxi	tắc xi
		car	xe hơi
How do I get to...?	tôi phải đi...bằng cách nào?	filling station	trạm xăng
We'd like to go to...	chúng tôi muốn đi...	bicycle	xe đạp
To the airport, please	làm ơn đưa tôi đi sân bay	baggage	hành lý
Can you take me to the...?	ông/bà có thể đưa tôi đi...?	bank	nhà băng
Where do we catch the bus to...?	ở đâu đón xe đi...?	post office	sở bưu điện
		passport	hộ chiếu
When does the bus for Hoi An leave?	khi nào xe Hội An chạy?	hotel	khách sạn
		restaurant	nhà hàng
Can I book a seat?	tôi có thể đặt ghế trước không?	Please stop here	xin dừng lại đây
How long does it take?	phải tốn bao lâu?	over there	bên kia
ticket	vé	here	đây
aeroplane	máy bay	left/right	bên trái/bên phải
airport	sân bay	north	phía bắc
boat	tàu bè	south	phía nam
bus	xe buýt	east	phía đông
bus station	bến xe buýt	west	phía tây

ACCOMMODATION AND SHOPPING

Do you have any rooms?	ông/bà có phòng không?	room with a private bathroom	một phòng tắm riêng
How much is it per night?	mỗi đêm bao nhiêu?	cheap/expensive	rẻ/đắt
How much is it?	bao nhiêu tiền?	single room	phòng một người
How much does it cost?	cái này giá bao nhiêu?	double room	phòng hai người
Can I have a look?	xem có được không?	single bed	giường một người
Do you have...?	ông/bà có không...?	double bed	giường đôi
I want a...	tôi muốn một...	air-conditioner	máy lạnh
I'd like...	cho tôi xin một...	fan (electric)	quạt máy
How much is this?	cái này bao nhiêu?	mosquito net	cái màn
That's too expensive	đắt quá	toilet paper	giấy vệ sinh
Do you have anything cheaper?	ông/bà còn gì rẻ hơn không?	telephone	điện thoại
		laundry	quần áo dơ
Could I have the bill please?	làm ơn tính tiền?	blanket	chăn (north); mền (south)
room with a balcony	một phòng có ban công	open/closed	mở cửa/đóng cửa

TIME

What's the time?	mấy giờ rồi?	tomorrow	mai
noon	buổi trưa	yesterday	hôm qua
midnight	nửa đêm	now	bây giờ
minute	phút	next week	tuần tới
hour	giờ	last week	tuần vừa qua
day	ngày	morning	buổi sáng
week	tuần	afternoon	buổi chiều
month	tháng	evening	buổi tối
year	năm	night	ban đêm
today	hôm nay		

NUMBERS

Note that for numbers ending in 5, from 15 onwards, **nhăm** is used in northern Vietnam and **lăm** in the south, rather than the written form of **năm**. Also, bear in mind that an alternative for numbers that are multiples of ten is **chục** – so, for example ten would be **một chục**, twenty would be **hai chục**, etc.

zero	không	**fifteen**	mười lăm/nhăm
one	một	**sixteen**	mười sáu
two	hai	**seventeen**	mười bảy
three	ba	**eighteen**	mười tám
four	bốn	**nineteen**	mười chín
five	năm	**twenty**	hai mươi
six	sáu	**twenty-one**	hai mươi một
seven	bảy	**twenty-two**	hai mươi hai
eight	tám	**thirty**	ba mươi
nine	chín	**forty**	bốn mươi
ten	mười	**fifty**	năm mươi
eleven	mười một	**one hundred**	một trăm
twelve	mười hai	**two hundred**	hai trăm
thirteen	mười ba	**one thousand**	một ngàn
fourteen	mười bốn	**ten thousand**	mười ngàn

EATING AND DRINKING

USEFUL PHRASES

bát (north); **chén** (south)	bowl
bao nhiêu?	how much is it?
cạn chén (north); **cạn ly** (south)	cheers!
chúc sức khỏe	to your good health
cúp	cup
đá	ice
không có đá cảm ơn	no ice, thanks
đũa	chopsticks
ít đường	a little sugar
lạnh	cold
chay	vegetarian
tôi không ăn thịt	I don't eat meat
nóng	hot
rất ngon	delicious

RICE AND NOODLES

bún	round rice noodles
bún bò	beef with bun noodles
bún chả	vermicelli noodles with pork and vegetables
bún gà	chicken with bun noodles
cơm	cooked rice
cơm rang (north); **cơm chiên** (south)	fried rice
cơm trắng	boiled rice
cháo	rice porridge
mì xào	fried noodles
phở	flat rice noodle soup
phở bò	noodle soup with beef
phở với trứng	noodle soup with eggs

FISH, MEAT AND VEGETABLES

cá	fish
cá rán (north); **cá chiên** (south)	fried fish
cua	crab
con lươn	eel
mực	squid
tôm	shrimp or prawn
tôm hùm	lobster
thịt	meat
bít tết	beefsteak
bò	beef
gà	chicken
lợn (north); **heo** (south)	pork
vịt	duck
rau cỏ or rau các loại	vegetables
bắp cải	cabbage
cà chua	tomato
cà tím	aubergine
đậu	beans
giá	beansprouts
khoai tây	potato
khoai lang	sweet potato
măng	bamboo shoots
ngô (north); **bắp** (south)	sweet corn
rau xào các loại	stir-fried vegetables
xà lách	salad
xà lách cà chua	tomato salad
xà lách rau xanh các loại	green salad

DESSERTS AND FRUIT

bánh ngọt	cakes and pastries
đường	sugar

kem	ice cream or cream	**mứt**	jam
mật ong	honey	**ớt**	chilli
sữa chua	yoghurt	**tàu hũ** (north); **đậu phụ** (south)	tofu
trái cây	fruit	**tiêu**	pepper
bưởi	pomelo/grapefruit	**trứng**	egg
cam	orange	**trứng tráng** or **trứng ốp lếp**	omelette
chanh	lemon/lime	**trứng rán** (north) or	fried eggs
chôm chôm	rambutan	**trứng chiên** (south)	
chuối	banana		
dâu tây	strawberry	**DRINKS**	
dừa	coconut	**bia**	beer
dứa (north); **thơm** (south)	pineapple	**cà phê**	coffee
dưa hấu	watermelon	**cà phê đá**	iced coffee
đu đủ	papaya	**cà phê đen**	black coffee
khế	star fruit	**cà phê đen không đường**	black coffee without sugar
măng cầu (north);	custard apple	**cà phê nóng**	hot coffee
quả na (south)		**cà phê sữa**	coffee with milk
măng cụt	mangosteen	**cà phê sữa nóng**	hot milk coffee
mít	jackfruit	**trà**	tea
nhãn	longan	**trà với chanh**	tea with lemon
quả bơ	avocado	**trà với sữa**	tea with milk
sầu riêng	durian	**không đá**	no ice
xoài	mango	**nước**	water
táo tây	apple	**nước khoáng**	mineral water
thanh long	dragon fruit	**nước xô-đa**	soda water
vải	lychee	**nước cam**	orange juice
		nước chanh	lime juice
MISCELLANEOUS		**nước dừa**	coconut milk
bánh	cake (sweet or savoury)	**rượu rắn**	snake wine
bánh mì	bread	**rượu cơm**	rice alcohol
bơ	butter	**xô-đa cam**	orange soda
pho mát	cheese	**xô-đa chanh**	lime soda
lạc (north); **đậu phộng** (south)	peanuts (groundnuts)	**sữa**	condensed milk
muối	salt	**sữa tươi**	fresh milk

Glossary

Agent Orange Defoliant herbicide used by the Americans during the American War to deprive guerrillas of forest cover

Annam ("Pacified South") A term coined by the Chinese to refer to their protectorate in northern Vietnam before 939 AD; the French later applied the name to the middle reaches of their protectorate, from the southern central highlands to the edge of the Red River Delta

ao dai Traditional Vietnamese dress for women, comprising baggy pants and a long, slit tunic

arhat Ascetic Buddhist saint, whose statues are found in northern pagodas

ARVN (Army of the Republic of Vietnam) The army of South Vietnam

ben xe Bus station

bo doi Northern soldiers

boat people Ethnic Chinese who fled Vietnam by boat in the late 1970s to escape persecution at the hands of the Communists and, later, Vietnamese escaping poverty (see box, pp.450–451)

bodhisattva An intermediary who has chosen to forgo Buddhist nirvana to work for the salvation of all humanity

body count Term coined by the Americans to measure the success of a military operation, determined by the number of dead bodies after a battle

bonze Buddhist monk

buu dien Post office

Cao Dai Indigenous religion, essentially a hybrid of Buddhism, Taoism and Confucianism, but hinged around an attempt at unification of all earthly codes of belief (see box, p.110)

Champa Indianized Hindu empire that held sway in much of the southern half of Vietnam until the late seventeenth century (see box, p.432)

Charlie Nickname for the VC ("Vietnamese Communists") used by American soldiers

cheo Form of classical theatre (see p.480)

cho Market

chu nom Classic Vietnamese script, based on Chinese

chua pagoda Buddhist place of worship

Cochinchina A Portuguese term adopted by the French colonial government for its southern administrative region

colon French colonial expatriate

com pho Literally, "rice noodles", often used to indicate restaurant serving basic dishes

cyclo Three-wheeled bicycle with a carriage on the front

dao Island

den Temple (Taoist or other non-Buddhist place of worship)

dinh Communal meeting hall

DMZ ("dee-em-zee") The Demilitarized Zone along the Seventeenth Parallel, marking the border between North and South Vietnam from 1954 to 1975

doi moi Vietnam's economic restructuring programme, begun in 1986

DRV (Democratic Republic of Vietnam) The North Vietnamese state established by Ho Chi Minh following the August Revolution in 1945

duong Avenue

FULRO (United Front for the Liberation of Oppressed Races) An opposition movement formed by the ethnic minorities of the central highlands, demanding greater autonomy

Funan Indianized empire, a forerunner of the great Khmer empires

GI (General Infantryman) Soldier in the US Army

gopuram Bank of sculpted deities over the entrance to a Hindu temple

"grunt" American infantryman

gui xe Bicycle compound

hang Cave

ho Lake

Ho Chi Minh Trail Trail used first by the Viet Minh and later by the North Vietnamese Army to transport supplies to the South, via Laos and Cambodia

Hoa Ethnic Chinese people living in Vietnam

Honda om Literally "Honda embrace" – a motorbike taxi

"Huey" Nickname given to American helicopter, the HU-1

Indochina The region of Asia comprising Vietnam, Laos and Cambodia

kalan Sanctuary in a Cham tower

khach san Hotel

Khmer Ethnic Cambodian

kylin Mythical, dew-drinking animal (often translated as unicorn); a harbinger of peace

Lien Xo Translating as "Soviet Union", this is also used as a term of abuse – and may very occasionally be hurled at foreigners in more remote regions

lingam A phallic statue representing Shiva, often seen in Cham towers

mandapa Meditation hall in Cham temple complex

MIAs (Missing in Action) Soldiers who fought – on both sides – in the American War, but have still not been accounted for

monkey bridge basic log bridge over a stream or small river

STREET NAMES

In travelling around Vietnam, it doesn't take long before you can recite the **street names**, a litany of the principal characters in Vietnamese history. Just a few from this cast list of famous revolutionaries, party leaders, legendary kings and peasant heroes are given below. Other favoured names commemorate the glorious victories of Bach Dang and Dien Bien Phu, and the momentous date when Saigon was "liberated" in 1975: 30 Thang 4 (30 April).

Hai Ba Trung The two Trung sisters led a popular uprising against the Chinese occupying army in 40 AD and established a short-lived kingdom (see p.432).

Hoang Hoa Tham (or De Tham) Famous pirate with a Robin Hood reputation and anti-French tendencies, assassinated in 1913.

Hung Vuong The semi-mythological Hung kings ruled an embryonic kingdom, Van Lang, around 2000 BC.

Le Duan General Secretary of the Communist Party, 1960–86.

Le Hong Phong Leading Communist and patriot who died from torture in Poulo Condore prison (Con Son Island) in 1942.

Le Loi One of the most revered Vietnamese heroes, Le Loi defeated the Ming Chinese in 1427, and then ruled as King Le Thai To.

Ngo Quyen First ruler of an independent Vietnam following his defeat of the Chinese armies in 938 AD (see p.433).

Nguyen Hue Middle member of the three Nguyen brothers who led the Tay Son rebellion in the 1770s (see p.435), and then ruled briefly as Emperor Quang Trung.

Nguyen Thai Hoc Founding member of the Vietnam Nationalist Party (VNQDD), executed in 1930 following the disastrous Yen Bai uprising.

Nguyen Thi Minh Khai Prominent anti-colonialist revolutionary of the 1930s, the wife of Le Hong Phong and sister-in-law of General Giap.

Nguyen Trai Brilliant strategist who helped mastermind Le Loi's victories over the Chinese. His ideas on the popular struggle ("it is better to conquer hearts than citadels") were used to good effect by Northern leaders in the French and American wars.

Pham Ngu Lao General in the army of Tran Hung Dao.

Phan Boi Chau Influential leader of the anti-colonial movement in the early twentieth century (see p.437).

Tran Hung Dao Thirteenth-century general who beat the Mongols twice in the space of four years, and reached the ripe old age of 87.

Tran Phu Founding member and first General Secretary of the Indochinese Communist Party (see p.438), he died in prison in 1931 at the age of 27.

---

montagnards French term for Vietnam's ethnic minority peoples

mua roi nuoc Water-puppet show

mui Cape

mukha lingam Lingam fashioned into the likeness of a deity

napalm Jellied fuel dropped by US forces during the American War, and capable of causing terrible burns

ngo Alley

NGO Non-governmental organization

nha hang Restaurant

nha khach Hotel or guesthouse

nha nghi Guesthouse

nha tro Basic dormitory accommodation, usually found near stations

NLF (National Liberation Front) Popular movement formed in South Vietnam in 1960 by opponents of the American-backed Southern regime

nui Mountain

nuoc mam Fish sauce

NVA (North Vietnamese Army) The army of the Democratic Republic of Vietnam

Oc Eo Ancient seaport of the Funan empire, east of modern-day Rach Gia in the Mekong Delta

ODP (Orderly Departure Programme) A United Nations-backed scheme enabling legal emigration of Vietnamese refugees

paddy Unharvested rice

pagoda not just a tower, but an entire Buddhist temple complex

PoW Prisoner of war

quan District

R&R ("Rest and Recreation") Term coined during the American War to describe a soldier's temporary leave of duty

roi nuoc see *mua roi nuoc*

rong Communal house of ethnic minorities in the central highlands

RVN (Republic of Vietnam) The official name for South Vietnam from 1954 to 1976

sampan Small, flat-bottomed boat

song River

SRVN (Socialist Republic of Vietnam) The post-liberation amalgamation of the DRV and RVN, and the official name of modern Vietnam

tai chi Chinese martial art, commonly performed as early-morning exercise

Tet Vietnam's lunar New Year

thung chai Coracle

Tonkin One of the three administrative regions of French colonial Vietnam, from Ninh Binh northwards

tunnel rats American soldiers trained for warfare in tunnels such as those at Cu Chi

VC (Viet Cong) Literally "Vietnamese Communists"; term used by the Americans to describe the guerrilla forces of the NLF

Viet Kieu Overseas Vietnamese

Viet Minh Shortened version of Viet Nam Doc Lap Dong Minh, the League for the Independence of Vietnam, established by Ho Chi Minh in 1941

VNQDD Abbreviation for Viet Nam Quoc Dan Dang, the Vietnam Nationalist Party, founded in 1927

xe lam Motorized three-wheeler buggy carrying numerous passengers

xe om Northern equivalent of the Honda om, a motorbike taxi

Small print and index

A ROUGH GUIDE TO ROUGH GUIDES

Published in 1982, the first Rough Guide – to Greece – was a student scheme that became a publishing phenomenon. Mark Ellingham, a recent graduate in English from Bristol University, had been travelling in Greece the previous summer and couldn't find the right guidebook. With a small group of friends he wrote his own guide, combining a highly contemporary, journalistic style with a thoroughly practical approach to travellers' needs.

The immediate success of the book spawned a series that rapidly covered dozens of destinations. And, in addition to impecunious backpackers, Rough Guides soon acquired a much broader readership that relished the guides' wit and inquisitiveness as much as their enthusiastic, critical approach and value-for-money ethos.

These days, Rough Guides include recommendations from budget to luxury and cover more than 120 destinations around the globe, as well as producing an ever-growing range of ebooks.

Visit **roughguides.com** to find all our latest books, read articles, get inspired and share travel tips with the Rough Guides community.

Rough Guide credits

Editor: David Leffman
Senior editor: Edward Aves
Layout: Nikhil Agarwal
Cartography: Rajesh Chhibber
Picture editor: Raffaella Morini
Proofreader: Susannah Wight
Managing editor: Keith Drew
Assistant editor: Payal Sharotri
Production: Janis Griffith

Cover design: Nicole Newman, Raffaella Morini, Nikhil Agarwal
Photographer: Tim Draper
Editorial assistant: Rebecca Hallett
Senior pre-press designer: Dan May
Programme manager: Gareth Lowe
Publisher: Joanna Kirby
Publishing director: Georgina Dee

Publishing information

This eighth edition published April 2015 by
Rough Guides Ltd,
80 Strand, London WC2R 0RL
11, Community Centre, Panchsheel Park,
New Delhi 110017, India
Distributed by Penguin Random House
Penguin Books Ltd,
80 Strand, London WC2R 0RL
Penguin Group (USA)
345 Hudson Street, NY 10014, USA
Penguin Group (Australia)
250 Camberwell Road, Camberwell,
Victoria 3124, Australia
Penguin Group (NZ)
67 Apollo Drive, Mairangi Bay, Auckland 1310,
New Zealand
Penguin Group (South Africa)
Block D, Rosebank Office Park, 181 Jan Smuts Avenue,
Parktown North, Gauteng, South Africa 2193
Rough Guides is represented in Canada by Tourmaline
Editions Inc. 662 King Street West, Suite 304, Toronto,
Ontario M5V 1M7
Printed in Singapore

© Rough Guides, 2015
Maps © Rough Guides
No part of this book may be reproduced in any form
without permission from the publisher except for the
quotation of brief passages in reviews.
520pp includes index
A catalogue record for this book is available from the
British Library
ISBN: 978-1-40937-186-1
The publishers and authors have done their best to
ensure the accuracy and currency of all the information in
The Rough Guide to Vietnam, however, they can accept
no responsibility for any loss, injury, or inconvenience
sustained by any traveller as a result of information or
advice contained in the guide.
1 3 5 7 9 8 6 4 2

MIX
Paper from responsible sources
FSC™ C018179

Help us update

We've gone to a lot of effort to ensure that the eighth edition of **The Rough Guide to Vietnam** is accurate and up-to-date. However, things change – places get "discovered", opening hours are notoriously fickle, restaurants and rooms raise prices or lower standards. If you feel we've got it wrong or left something out, we'd like to know, and if you can remember the address, the price, the hours, the phone number, so much the better.

Please send your comments with the subject line "**Rough Guide Vietnam Update**" to mail@uk.roughguides.com. We'll credit all contributions and send a copy of the next edition (or any other Rough Guide if you prefer) for the very best emails.

Find more travel information, connect with fellow travellers and plan your trip on roughguides.com.

ABOUT THE AUTHORS

Ron Emmons (⊕ronemmons.com) lived and worked in Africa and the Americas before moving to northern Thailand, where he is now based. He is the author and photographer of *Portrait of Thailand*, and *Walks along the Thames Path* and author of DK Eyewitness's *Top 10 Bangkok*. He has contributed to several other guidebooks and his travel articles and images appear regularly in international publications.

Martin Zatko has been trying to cover every square inch of Asia since first arriving on its shores in 2002. In that time he has written or contributed to the Rough Guides to Korea, Seoul, China, Beijing, Japan, Tokyo, Myanmar, Turkey and Europe, as well as Vietnam – a country he continues to hold dear on account of its food, scenery, people and super-cheap passion fruit juice.

Acknowledgements

Ron Emmons would like to thank all those people who shared their knowledge of this rapidly changing country. These include Phan Cu in Hue; Tam Nguyen in Dong Ha; Ben Mitchell in Phong Nha; Dinh Cong Xuan in and around Ninh Binh; Pham Ngoc Minh on the north coast; Francoise Bricout for hints on good home-stays; Dang Duc Thuc, Nguyen Le Thuy and Nguyen Duc Tuyen in Hanoi; and Thai Hoang Ngoc, Le Cong Hoang, Hoa Le and Hoang Tuan Anh in the far north.

Martin Zatko I would like to thank the staff at Amica Travel, InsideVietnam Tours and SinhBalo Adventure Travel for their kind assistance on my research trip; David Leffman for his kind, thoughtful editing work; Jee Young Lee and Eivind Hestetun Thomassen for joining me in the Mekong Delta and Mui Ne respectively; Doan Tram for the drink on the rooftop and all the bee stings we endured on the way back down; and the various restaurants, bars, juice stands and (especially) swimming pools I had the pleasure to experience on the long trip around Vietnam.

Readers' updates

Thanks to all the readers who have taken the time to write in with comments and suggestions (and apologies if we've inadvertently omitted or misspelt anyone's name):

Guy Burton, Felipe Castro, Nancy Corley, Thierry Corp, Teal Francis, Rob ter Heine, Jim Jonas, Summer Lewis, Rui Rodriguez, Tricia Score, Inge Stamm

Photo credits

All photos © Rough Guides except the following:
(Key: t-top; c-centre; b-bottom; l-left; r-right)

p.1 Jamie Marshall/Tribaleye Images/Getty Images
p.2 Bruno De Hogues/Getty Images
p.4 Jordan Banks/4Corners
p.5 Bruno De Hogues/Getty Images
p.9 Paul Panayiotou/4Corners (t); Gavriel Jecan/Getty Images (b)
p.11 Henry Westheim Photography/Alamy (t); Fergus Mackay/Alamy (b)
p.12 Günter Gräfenhain/4Corners
p.15 Aldo Pavan/4Corners
p.17 David R. Frazier/Alamy (b)
p.18 Paul Thompson Images/Alamy (tl); Ron Emmons (tr); Andrew Woodley/Alamy (c)
p.19 Thomas David Pinzer/Alamy (t); Joan Gravell/Alamy (b)
p.20 Bruno De Hogues/Getty Images (b)
p.21 David Noton Photography/Alamy (t)
p.22 Bruno De Hogues/Getty Images (t); Hemis/Alamy (c)
p.23 JTB Photo Communications/Alamy (t); Gonzalo Azumendi/SuperStock (b)
p.24 LOOK Die Bildagentur der Fotografen GmbH/Alamy (tl); Bruno De Hogues/Getty Images (br)
p.25 Kristjan Porm/Alamy (b)
p.26 Mark Phillips/Alamy
p.43 Peter Adams/AWL Images

pp.66–67 Stuart Fox/Getty Images
p.115 Tim Hall/Getty Images
p.171 Imagebroker/SuperStock
p.183 Pham Le Huong Son/Getty Images
p.195 Hemis/Alamy (t)
pp.200–201 Imagebroker/Alamy
p.235 Rosita So Image/Getty Images
pp.242–243 Robert Francis/Getty Images
p.245 Zoonar GmbH/Alamy
p.259 Stefano Paterna/Alamy (t)
p.283 Aliaksandr Mazurkevich/Dreamstime.com (t)
pp.304–305 Jose Fuste Raga/SuperStock
p.307 Andrew Woodley/Alamy
p.319 Terry Whittaker/FLPA
p.373 Gareth Jones/Getty Images
p.415 Gerhard Zwerger Schon/SuperStock (t); Bjorn Svensson/Alamy (b)

Front cover & spine Cyclo © Stuart Pearce/Corbis
Back cover Lak Lake © Zoonar GmbH/Alamy (t); Paddy field, Sa Pa © Cultura Travel/Ben Pipe Photography/Getty Images (bl); Local tribal dress in Bac Ha © Ahmad Faizal Yahya/Getty Images (br)

Index

Maps are marked in grey

Map symbols

The symbols below are used on maps throughout the book

International boundary	Hospital	Mosque	★ Transport stop
Province boundary	Lighthouse	Hindu temple	Airport
Chapter division boundary	Border crossing	Cao dai temple	Golf course
Major road	Point of interest	Waterfall	Steps
Minor road	@ Internet access	Cave	Church
Motorway road	Gardens	Viewpoint	Building
Pedestrian road	⊙ Statue	Swimming area	Stadium
Railway	Bridge	Dive site	Park
Ferry route	⊠ Gate	Spring	Beach
River	Tower	Wall	Cemetery
⊠ Post office	Museum	Mountain range	
ⓘ Tourist office	Buddhist temple/Pagoda	Mountain peak	

Listings key

- ■ Accommodation
- ● Eating
- ■ Drinking and nightlife
- ● Shopping

Celebrating **ANN TOURS** *25 Years*

COME WITH US DISCOVER VIETNAM

Services:

✓ Customized package tours East Asia
✓ Hotel discounts
✓ Airticketing throughout Southeast Asia
✓ Visa assistance throughout Southeast Asia
✓ Providing leisure and corporate travel

Website: www.anntours.com - Email: info@anntours.com
www.facebook.com/anntourstravel

SAIGON OFFICE: 58 Ton That Tung St., District 1. HCMC, Vietnam
TEL: (84.8) 38332584 - 39253636 FAX: (84.8) 38323866
HANOI OFFICE: TEL: (84.4) 37150950 FAX: (84.8) 38323866

"THE REAL VOYAGE OF DISCOVERY CONSISTS NOT IN SEEKING NEW LANDSCAPES, BUT IN HAVING NEW EYES."
— MARCEL PROUST —

AMICA TRAVEL

Journeys Across Indochina
Vietnam - Laos - Cambodia

CONTACT US

⊕ www.en.amica-travel.com
✉ info@amicatravel.com
☎ 84(0)4 62 73 44 55

Sinh Balo
Adventure Travel

- Specializing in cycling trips
- Cruise up the Mekong river
  to Angkor temples / Cambodia
- Family & study tours throughout Vietnam
- Customized / special interest journeys

Sinhbalo Adventure Travel
283/20 Pham Ngu Lao St.
District 1. HCM City. Vietnam.
Tel: (++84 8) 38376766 (3 lines)
Fax: (++84 8) 38367682

off the beaten track!

www.sinhbalo.com | www.cyclingvietnam.net

VietindoTravel

Incredible Indochina
Vietnam ☆ Laos ☆ Cambodia ☆ Myanmar
www.vietindotravel.com

QueenTravel
Your Family in Vietnam

Queen Travel
specialists in customized tours in Vietnam.
Just tell us where you want to go !

Hotel Garden Queen
your home-from-home in Hanoi's Old Quarter.

E-mail: info@queentravel.vn
Tel: (84-4) 3 8260 860
Fax: (84-4) 3 8260 300
Adress: 65 Hang Bac Street - Hanoi - Vietnam
www.queentravel.vn   www.azqueentravel.com

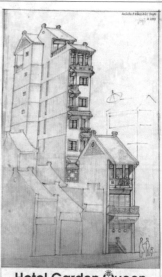

Hotel Garden Queen

Buffalo tours
Discover Your Asia

Discover **Your** Vietnam
through Extraordinary Travel Experiences

ABTA
The Travel Association
ABTA number Y2723

Call 84.4.3926.3425
or scan the QR code
to start planning your
trip to Vietnam

www.buffalotours.com

info@buffalotours.com

INSIDE
Vietnam
Cambodia • Laos

Small Group Tours

Fully Tailored Journeys

Experiences & Inspiration

Designed by the
Vietnam
travel experts

Tel: 0117 244 3370
www.insidevietnamtours.com
info@insidevietnamtours.com

Get beneath the surface

Part of **InsideAsia Tours Ltd,** an award-winning travel company
offering group tours, tailored travel and cultural experiences
across Japan, Vietnam, Cambodia, Laos and Burma.